I J K L M N O

TO OHIO UNIVERSITY AIRPORT AT ALBANY VIA U.S. 50 WEST 747 COLUMBIA RD.

RIVER

RESEARCH & ENTERPRISE PARK

LIBRARY ANNEX

PARKING GARAGE

INFORMATION

PARK PLACE

HOCKIN

Numerical Index to Buildings

1 Cutler Hall
2 McGuffey Hall
3 Wilson (administrative)
4 Alden Library
5 Ellis Hall
6 Galbreath Chapel
7 Galbreath Chapel
8 Templeton-Blackburn Alumni Memorial Auditorium
9 Chubb Hall
10 Scripps Hall
11 Class Gateway
12 Copeland Hall
13 Computer Service Center
14 President Street Academic Center
15 Pilcher House
16 Bentley Hall
17 Lindley Hall
18 Crewson House
19 Research and Technology Center
20 Haning Hall
21 Lasher Hall
22 Voigt Hall
23 Heating Substation
24 Central Classroom Building
27 Athens County Courthouse
28 Parking Garage, Athens City
29 Athens City Building
30 Kantner Hall
31 Radio-Television Building
32 Former Baker Center
33 Yamada International House
34 Voigt Hall
35 Hudson Health Center
36 Trisolini House
37 Jennings House
38 Sculpture Studio
39 Seigfred Hall
40A Glidden Hall
40B Music Rehearsal Hall
41 Putnam Hall
42 McCracken Hall
43 Brown Hall
44 Lincoln Hall
45 Jefferson Hall
46 Johnson Hall

48 Read Hall
49 Washington Hall
50 Bush Hall
51 Biddle Hall
52 Perkins Hall
53 Gamertsfelder Hall
54 Shively Hall
55 Tiffin Hall
56 Guest/Visitor Parking
57 Bryan Hall
58 Tupper Hall
59 McKee House
60 Konneker Alumni Center
61 Upper Grounds Maintenance Building
63 Edgehill Maintenance Building
64 Claire Oates Ping Cottage
68 Pickering Hall
69 Brown Hall
70 Mackinnon Hall
71 Crawford Hall
72 Nelson Commons
73 Golf Course
74 Zoology Building
75 Botanical Research
76 Scott Quadrangle
78 Morton Hall
80 District Water Cooling
79 Wolfe Street Apartments
81 Clippinger Laboratories
82 Edwards Accelerator Lab
83 35 Park Place
84 Gordy Hall
85 President's Residence
86 Porter Hall
87 Baker University Center
88 Grounds Maintenance
89 Grover Center
90 Bird Arena
91 Tennis Courts
92 Aquatic Center
93 Wren Stadium
94 Peden Stadium
95 Convocation Center

96 Grosvenor Hall
97 James Hall
98 Sargent Hall
99 Treudley Hall
100 Boyd Hall
101 Ryors Hall
102 Irvine Hall
103 Stocker Center
104 Wilson Hall (residence hall)
105 University Medical Associates, Parks Hall
106 Pruitt Field - Multipurpose Athletic Facility
107 Ohio University Inn
108 Lausche Heating Plant
109 University Garage
110 Facilities Management Shops
111 Food Services, Central Foods Facilities
112 Facilities Management Shops
113 Electric & Life Safety Shops
114 Airport, Directions to
115 Recreation Areas
116 Intramural Field
117 Credit Union
118 Bingham House
119 Grosvenor, West
122 Fenzel House
123 O'Bleness Inn
124 Cady House
125 Foster House
126 Brough House
127 Martzolff House
128 Weld House
129 Armbruster House
130 Atkinson House
131 Smith House
132 True House

133 Dougan House
134 Wray House
135 Ewing House
136 Hoover House
137 Chessa Field - Soccer Facility
138 Softball Complex
139 Bentley Annex
140 Ping Recreation Center
141 Sing Tao Center
142 HDL Center
143 Howard Park
144 Golf and Tennis Facility
145 Carin Strength Training Center
146 Emeriti Park
147 Athena Cinema
148 Bromley Hall
149 Life Science Research Facility
150 Human Resources and Training Center
151 Football Practice Field
152 Biochemistry Research Facility
153 Corrosion and Multi-Phase Technology Center
154 Innovation Center
155 Walter International Education Center
156 Walter Hall (Margaret M. Walter Hall)
157 Adams Hall
158 South Green Field House
159 Library Annex
167 West Green Practice Facility
175 Surface Science Lab
176 AFSCME 1699
177 Tunnel and Sheetmetal Shops
178 9 Factory Street
179 Tunnel and Sheetmetal Shops
180 Facilities and Auxiliaries Administration Building

NOT TO SCALE

N

OHIO
UNIVERSITY
1804

©2011 Ohio University Printing and Graphic Services. Map art by staff Illustrator Tad Gallaugher.

A Customized Version of
Thriving in College and Beyond

Research-Based Strategies for Academic Success and Personal Development

Joseph B. Cuseo
Emeritus, Marymount College

Michele Campagna
Montclair State University

Aaron Thompson
Eastern Kentucky University

Viki Sox Fecas
University of South Carolina–Columbia

With Foreword by Mary Stuart Hunter

Designed Specifically for Kris Kumfer and Lisa Kamody at Ohio University

Kendall Hunt
publishing company

Cover image © Ohio University

publishing company

www.kendallhunt.com
Send all inquiries to:
4050 Westmark Drive
Dubuque, IA 52004-1840

Printed in the United States of America
10 9 8 7 6 5 4 3 2 1

Brief Contents

Contents

Chapter 1: Touching All the Bases
Using Powerful Student Success Principles and Key Campus Resources   1

Chapter 2: Liberal Arts and General Education
What It Means to Be a Well-Educated Person in the 21st Century   35

Chapter 3: Goal Setting, Motivation, and Character
Moving from Dreams to Plans to Action   65

Chapter 4: Time Management
Preventing Procrastination and Promoting Self-Discipline   87

Chapter 5: Strategic Learning and Studying
Learning Deeply and Remembering Longer   109

Chapter 6: Test-Taking Skills and Strategies
What to Do before, during, and after Exams   139

Chapter 11: Educational Planning and Academic Decision Making
Making Wise Choices about College Courses and a College Major   275

Chapter 12: Finding a Path to Your Future Profession
Career Exploration, Preparation, and Development   305

Chapter 13: Fiscal Literacy
Managing Money and Minimizing Debt   331

Chapter 14: Health and Wellness
Body, Mind, and Spirit   353

Foreword

The very fact that you have this book in your hands and are reading tese words is evidence that you are well on your way to becoming a successful student—congratulations. You join hundreds of thousands of other undergraduate students who each year take important steps toward ensuring their success through enrolling in a first-year seminar, participating in a learning community, or engaging in other special programs on college and university campuses. College can be an exciting experience with challenges and opportunities that you've never faced before. It is a time for personal growth and development far beyond simply the learning of facts and figures. How you choose to spend your time in college will impact your life for years to come. You will discover new ideas about the world and your place in it both in the classroom and beyond as you accept the challenges before you and take responsibility for your own educational experience. And along the way, you will certainly learn more about yourself as an individual.

My own work with college students over the past 25 years tells me that students of all types, ages, and abilities can succeed. But I have also, unfortunately, seen far too many very bright and capable students fail. The fact that your college accepted you for admission is evidence enough that you have the capacity to succeed. But, making the transition from a high school learning culture to that of college is not automatic. Simply being a college student doesn't mean that you will be as successful as you were in high school or in the world of your pre-college experience. What worked for you before may not work for you in this new environment. Understanding the difference in teaching and learning cultures is key to student success.

This book is one of the many resources available to you as a college student. The title itself, *Thriving in College and Beyond*, should tell you that college is just the beginning of a life full of learning. The pages of this book address the critical and multifaceted opportunities in front of you as a college student. Throughout the book you will find information that will assist you as you navigate the complex and often mysterious collegiate experience. The authors have masterfully constructed a book that contains a wide variety of elements, including exercises, checklists, cartoons, "take action now" suggestions, quotes, reflection guides, and thought questions, all carefully chosen to engage and inform you while at the same time providing meaningful material to help you find success in college.

As individuals, the authors have a wealth of experience in assisting college students and they are sharing their best information, ideas, and strategies with you. Joe Cuseo is a well-respected first-year educator and professor of psychology who has many years of experience helping new students successfully transition from high school to college. He is an award-winning faculty member at Marymount College, and his passion for student success and creativity in teaching are hallmarks of his teaching and can be easily witnessed in the pages of this book. Viki Sox Fecas has helped countless students at the University of South Carolina transition to college and her campus through teaching sections of the first-year seminar and through her good work as a career counselor. Her positive attitude and enthusiasm for the collegiate experience have made her a sought-after and valuable resource for students at all levels. Aaron Thompson has many years of experience helping students attain educational success as well; he has teaching and administrative experience at several public institutions, and his contributions to this book are important and noteworthy. The partnership formed by these authors has resulted in a rich and practical book that will help countless students. You, too, can be one of these students.

So, read this book intentionally, and apply what you read to yourself. Approach the exercises with vigor. Ask questions. Challenge the ideas. Discuss what you have read with your classmates and friends. Make the most of the generous resources in the book. But, most of all, use what you learn from the book to help you be the very best student you can be. You'll be better for having done so. And then, you will be able to look back and appreciate all that this book has taught you!

Mary Stuart Hunter
Director
National Resource Center for the First-Year
Experience and Students in Transition
University of South Carolina

Preface

Welcome to Our Book

ACTIVATE YOUR THINKING | *Reflection* **P.1**

What do you think are the key characteristics or features of a textbook that:

1. Make you *want* to read it?

2. Enable you to *learn the most* from it?

Plan and Purpose of This Book

This book is designed to help you make a smooth transition to college and equip you with strategies for success in college and beyond. It's intended to promote the academic excellence and personal development of all students—whether you are a student transitioning directly from high school or from a full-time or part-time job, living on or off campus, or attending college on a full-time or part-time basis. Whatever your previous educational record may have been, college is a new ballgame played on a different field with different rules and expectations. If you haven't been a successful student in the past, this book will help you become a successful student in the future; if you have been a strong student, it will make you an even stronger student.

The book's major goal is to help you put into practice one of the most powerful principles of human learning and personal success: *mindfulness.* When you're mindful, you're aware of what you're doing and whether you're doing it effectively and to the best of your ability. Self-awareness is the critical first step toward self-improvement and success in any aspect of your life. If you develop the habit of remaining aware of how you're doing college and if you're doing it effectively (e.g., using the key strategies identified in this book), you will have taken a huge step toward college success.

"More than 30 years of research has shown that mindfulness is figuratively and literally enlivening. It's the way you feel when you're feeling passionate."

—Dr. Ellen Langer, Harvard University, mindfulness researcher and author of *The Power of Mindful Learning*

Rather than leaving you on your own to figure out how to do college by trial and error and hoping you'll eventually discover what works best, this book gives you a game plan for getting it right from the start. It provides a plan that's built on a solid foundation of research and equips you with well-documented strategies for doing college strategically and successfully.

Specific, action-oriented strategies make up the heart of this book. You'll find that these practical strategies aren't presented to you in the form of a laundry list of isolated and disconnected tips. Instead, they are accompanied by a research-based rationale for *why* they're effective and by specific practices organized into broader *principles* that tie the strategies together into a meaningful plan. It's not only important to know *what* you should do in college, but also *why* you should do it. If you understand the reason behind a suggested strategy, you're more motivated to take the strategy seriously and implement it effectively. Also, when specific strategies are organized into general principles, they become more powerful because you're able to see how the same principle may be generalized and applied across different subjects and situations. You're empowered with the ability to create specific strategies of your own that flow or follow from the same general principle.

Learning about the research and reasons why strategies work promotes deeper learning than simply acquiring tips about what you should or shouldn't do in college. We believe that you're ready and able to meet this challenge of deeper learning.

Since the strategies we recommend are research-based, you'll find references cited regularly throughout all the chapters and a sizable reference section at the end of the book. You'll also find that the references cited represent a balanced blend of older "classic" studies and more recent "cutting-edge" research from a wide variety of fields. This highlights the wide-ranging relevance of the ideas being discussed and their power to withstand the test of time. It also underscores the fact that the subject of success in college and beyond, like any other subject in the college curriculum, rests on a solid body of research and scholarship that spans multiple decades.

Preview of Content

Introduction: Welcome to College

In the introduction to this book, you'll learn why your college experience has the potential to be the most enriching experience of your life and provide you with multiple ongoing benefits throughout life. The first year of college, in particular, is a critical stage of educational development, during which students undergo the greatest amount of learning and personal growth. It's also the time when students experience the greatest challenges, the most stress, the most academic difficulties, and the highest dropout rate. This highlights the power of the first-year experience, the importance of first-year courses designed to promote college success, and the importance of this book.

In the introduction, you will find convincing evidence that new students who participate in first-year experience courses (first-year seminars) are more likely to continue their college education, complete their college degree, and get the most out of their college experience.

"The man who also knows why will be his own boss. As to methods there may be a million and then some, but principles are few. The man who grasps principles can successfully select his own methods. The man who tries methods, ignoring principles, is sure to have trouble."

—Ralph Waldo Emerson, 19th-century author, poet, and philosopher

Student

Perspective

"I could really relate to everything we talked about. It is a great class because you can use it in your other classes."

—First-year student comment made when evaluating a first-year seminar (college success course)

Student
Perspective

"Everything we learned we will apply in our lives."

—First-year student comment made when evaluating a first-year seminar (college success course)

Student
Perspective

"This is the only course I've ever taken that was about me."

—First-year student comment made when evaluating a first-year seminar (college success course)

Chapter 1. Touching All the Bases: Using Powerful Student Success Principles and Key Campus Resources

This chapter provides an overview and preview of the most powerful principles of college success. Its major goals are to equip you with "big picture" principles you can use on your own to promote success in college and raise your awareness of the wide range of campus resources you can use to support your quest for success. The chapter describes the services provided by various campus resources, explains why they're worth using, and shows how you can most effectively capitalize on them during your college experience.

Chapter 2. Liberal Arts and General Education: What It Means to Be a Well-Educated Person in the 21st Century

The liberal arts represent the core of your college experience; they provide you with foundational, versatile skills that promote success in all college majors, careers, and life roles. In this chapter, you will gain a deeper understanding and appreciation of the liberal arts and acquire strategies for making the most of general education. You will also acquire strategies for gaining a perspective on the whole world, developing yourself as a whole person, and enriching the overall quality (and marketability) of your college experience.

Chapter 3. Goal Setting, Motivation, and Character: Moving from Dreams to Plans to Action

The journey to success begins with identifying a desired outcome (an end goal), and then continues with finding the means (succession of steps) to reach that goal. Studies show that setting specific goals is a more likely to lead to success than simply telling ourselves that we're going to try hard or do your best. This chapter identifies the key steps involved in setting and reaching personal goals, identifies self-motivational strategies for staying on track and moving toward your goals, and describes the inner qualities (virtues) associated with personal success and personal character.

> "Watch your thoughts. They become words. Watch your words. They become deeds. Watch your deeds. They become habits. Watch your habits. They become character. Character is everything."
>
> —Ralph Waldo Emerson, American philosopher, public speaker, and advocate for the abolition of slavery

Chapter 4. Time Management: Preventing Procrastination and Promoting Self-Discipline

In college, you will encounter an academic calendar and class schedule that differ radically from those of your previous years of schooling. You may be surprised by how much "free time" you seem to have because you'll be spending less time sitting in class; however, you'll be expected to spend much more time outside of class on work related to class. Learning to use your out-of-class work time strategically and productively is critical to ensuring academic success in college; you will learn ways to do so in this chapter. Furthermore, time is a valuable personal resource—if you gain greater control of it, you can gain greater control of your life. Time management not only enables you to get your work done in a timely manner, but also enables you to attain and maintain balance in your life. This chapter offers a comprehensive set of strategies for managing time, combating procrastination, and ensuring that your time-spending habits are aligned with your educational goals and values.

Student *Perspective*

> "In high school, a lot of the work was done while in school, but in college all of your work is done on your time. You really have to organize yourself in order to get everything done."
>
> —First-year student's response to a question about what was most surprising about college life

Chapter 5. Strategic Learning and Studying: Learning Deeply and Remembering Longer

This chapter will help you apply research on human learning and the human brain to become a more effective and efficient learner. It takes you through three key stages of the learning process—from the first stage of acquiring information through lectures and readings, through the second stage of studying and retaining the information you acquire, to the final stage of retrieving (recalling) the information that you studied. The ultimate goal of this chapter is to supply you with a set of powerful strategies that can be used to promote learning that's *deep* (not surface-level memorizing), *durable* (long-lasting), and *retrievable* (accessible to you when you need it).

Chapter 6. Test-Taking Skills and Strategies: What to Do before, during, and after Exams

This chapter is designed to prepare you for the three key tasks that are most commonly used to evaluate your academic performance in college: tests, papers, and presentations. The chapter supplies you with a systematic set of test-taking strategies that can be used before, during, and after exams to improve your test performance to help you become more "test wise" and less "test anxious."

Chapter 7. Three Keys to Academic Success and Lifelong Learning Skills: Information Literacy, Writing, and Speaking

Strategies for researching and evaluating information, writing papers and reports, and using writing as a learning and thinking tool will be provided in this chapter. Strategies will also be shared for making effective oral presentations, overcoming speech anxiety, and gaining social self-confidence as a speaker. Research, writing, and speaking effectively are transferable skills that are applicable in all majors and all careers, and will be used throughout life. This chapter is designed to "jump start" your development of these powerful lifelong learning skills, enabling you to use them immediately to achieve early success in your first year of college.

Chapter 8. Higher-Level Thinking: Moving Beyond Basic Knowledge to Critical and Creative Thinking

Surveys indicate that teaching students how to think is the primary goal of college faculty. This chapter was written to help you understand the type of thinking that professors expect from you and empower you to think in this way, taking you beyond learning to acquire and retain information to higher levels of critical and creative thinking. Specific forms of higher-level thinking are identified, self-questioning strategies that prompt your mind to use these forms of thinking are suggested, and practical strategies for demonstrating higher-level thinking on exams and assignments are provided.

Chapter 9. Social and Emotional Intelligence: Relating to Others and Regulating Our Emotions

Communicating and relating effectively with others is an important life skill and an important form of human intelligence. Similarly, emotional intelligence—the ability to identify and manage our emotions when dealing with others and to be aware of how our emotions are influencing our thoughts and actions—is an important life skill that has been found to improve academic performance and promote career success. This chapter identifies effective ways to communicate, relate, and form meaningful relationships with others, as well as ways to understand and regulate key emotions such as stress, anxiety, anger, and depression. The information included in this chapter should improve not only the quality of your performance in college, but the overall quality of your life.

Chapter 10. Diversity: Learning about and from Human Differences

This chapter clarifies what "diversity" really means, demonstrates how experiencing diversity can deepen learning, promotes critical and creative thinking, and contributes to your personal and professional development. Included are ideas for overcoming cultural barriers and biases that interfere with developing rewarding relationships with diverse people and strategies for learning from people whose personal and cultural backgrounds are different than our own. Simply stated, we learn more from people who differ from us than we do from people similar to us. There is more diversity among college students today than at any other time in history. This chapter will help you capitalize on this learning opportunity.

Chapter 11. Educational Planning and Academic Decision Making: Making Wise Choices about College Courses and a College Major

Making wise choices about your courses and your major is essential to your achieving success in college. Whether you are undecided about a college major or think you have already reached a final decision, you need to be sure that your choice is truly compatible with your personal interests, talents, and values. You should have a strategic plan in mind (and in hand) that enables you to strike a healthy balance between continuing to explore your options and making a final commitment. This chapter will help you strike this balance and reach educational decisions that put you in the best position to reach your long-term goals.

Reflection **P.2**

What percentage of beginning college students do you think have already made up their minds about a major?

What percentage of these "decided" students do you think eventually change their minds and end up graduating with a different major?

(See Chapter 11, p. 275 for answers to these questions.)

Chapter 12. Finding a Path to Your Future Profession: Career Exploration, Preparation, and Development

It may seem unusual or premature to find a chapter on career success in a book for beginning college students. However, career exploration and planning should begin in the first term of college because it gives you a practical, long-range goal to strive for. It also enables you to become aware of how the skills you're using and developing in college align with the skills that are sought by employers and that promote your career success after college. Since career planning is really a form of *life* planning, the sooner you start this process, the sooner you gain control of your future and start to build a life for yourself that allows you to do what most interests you, what you do best, and what matters most to you.

> "It is hard to know how any student could truly understand whom [he or she] wants to be without thinking carefully about what career to pursue."
>
> —Derek Bok, former president of Harvard University

Chapter 13. Fiscal Literacy: Managing Money and Minimizing Debt

Research shows that accumulating high levels of debt while in college is associated with higher stress, lower academic performance, and greater risk of withdrawing from college. The good news is that research also shows that students who learn to use effective money-management strategies are able to minimize unnecessary spending, reduce accumulation of debt and stress, and improve the quality of their academic performance. This chapter identifies effective strategies and personal habits for tracking your income and expenses, minimizing and avoiding debt, balancing time spent on school and work, and making wise decisions about how to spend and save money while you're in college.

Reflection P.3

What does being a "well-rounded" person and leading a "well-balanced" life mean to you?

Chapter 14. Health and Wellness: Body, Mind, and Spirit

Humans cannot reach their full potential and achieve peak levels of performance without attending to our physical selves. Sustaining health and attaining optimal levels of performance depend on how well we treat our *bodies*—what we put into them (healthy food), what we keep out of them (unhealthy substances), what we do with them (exercise), and how well we rejuvenate them (sleep). This chapter examines strategies for maintaining nutritional balance, attaining quality sleep, promoting total fitness, and avoiding risky behaviors that jeopardize our health and impair our performance in college and beyond.

Sequence of Chapter Topics

The chapters in this book have been arranged in an order that allows you to ask and answer the following sequence of questions:

1. Why am I here?
2. Where do I want to go?
3. What must I do to get there?
4. How do I know when I've arrived?

The early chapters are intended to help you get immediately situated and oriented to your college environment, reinforce your decision for being in college, and help you decide where you want college to take you. These chapters supply you with a mental map for your trip through college, helping you to set educational goals and become fully aware of the wide array of campus resources available to you. Once you get a clear sense of why college is worth doing and where it will take you, you should become more enthused and motivated to take action on the strategies suggested throughout the remainder of the book.

The middle chapters of the text are devoted to helping you handle the more practical, day-to-day academic work responsibilities you encounter in college and how to get the job done. They focus on the core academic tasks of dealing with lectures, reading, writing, learning, thinking, and test taking.

The final chapters shift beyond academics to planning for your future and developing yourself as a whole person.

Process and Style of Presentation

How information is delivered is as important as *what* information is delivered. When writing this text, we made an intentional attempt to deliver our message in a way that would:

- Stimulate your motivation to learn;
- Deepen your learning; and
- Strengthen your retention (memory) for what you have learned.

We attempted to do this by incorporating the following principles of motivation, learning, and memory throughout the text.

- Each chapter begins with an **Activate Your Thinking** exercise that is designed to stimulate your thoughts and feelings about the upcoming topic. This pre-reading exercise is designed to "warm up" or "tune up" your brain, preparing it to relate the ideas you're about to encounter in the chapter with the ideas you already have in your head. It's an instructional strategy that implements one of the most powerful principles of learning: humans learn most effectively by connecting what they're going to learn with what they have already learned and what is already stored in their brains.
- Within each chapter, we periodically interrupt your reading with opportunities for **Reflection** that ask you to pause, reflect, and think deeply about the material you've just read. These timely pauses for reflection and journal entries keep you mentally alert and active throughout the reading process. They serve to interrupt and intercept "attention drift" that normally takes place when the brain continually receives and processes information for an extended period—such as it does

when it's engaged in reading. Furthermore, reflecting and journaling deepen your understanding of the material you read because you are *writing* in response to what you read. Writing encourages more thoughtful reflection, deeper learning, and a higher level of thinking than simply underlining or highlighting sentences.

- **Exercises** at the *end* of each chapter ask you to reflect further on the knowledge you've acquired by reading the chapter and transform that knowledge into informed action. As discussed in Chapter 3, wisdom isn't achieved by simply acquiring knowledge, but by *applying* the knowledge you have acquired—i.e., using your knowledge by putting it into practice.

- The strategic positioning of the **Activate Your Thinking** exercises at the beginning of each chapter, the reflections interspersed during the chapter, and the application exercises at the end of the chapter creates an effective learning sequence that should keep you actively involved in the reading process from start to middle to end.

- The information in each chapter is delivered through a variety of formats that include diagrams, pictures, cartoons, advice from current and former college students, words of wisdom from famous and successful people, and stories drawn from the authors' personal experiences. Delivering information through these multiple delivery formats allows you to process it through multiple sensory modalities (input channels), which deepens learning by enabling your brain to lay down multiple memory tracks (traces) of the information in different storage areas.

> "One must learn by doing. For though you think you know, you have no certainty until you try."
>
> —Sophocles, ancient Greek philosopher

What follows is a complete list of the book's key instructional features. As you read about these features, make a quick note in the side margin on how effectively you think each feature will motivate you to read the book and promote your learning from the book.

Snapshot Summary Boxes

At different points in the text, you'll find boxes containing summaries of key concepts and strategies. These boxed summaries are designed to connect major ideas related to the same concept and get them in the same place (physically), which, in turn, should help you get them in the same place (mentally).

Do It Now! Boxes

These attention getters are designed to give you a signal to immediately put these suggested strategies and suggestions into action to enhance your learning experience at a deeper level.

Remember Cues

Periodically, you'll encounter a "Remember" box. This is a clue indicating it's a high-priority recommendation that deserves special attention and long-term retention.

Quotes

Throughout the book, quotes from famous and influential people appear in the side margins that relate to and reinforce the ideas being discussed at that point in the chapter. You'll find quotes from accomplished individuals who have lived in different historical periods and who have specialized in fields including politics, philosophy, religion, science, business, music, art, and athletics. The wide-ranging time frames, cultures, and fields of study represented by the people quoted demonstrate that the wisdom of their words is timeless and universal. It is our hope that the words of these highly successful and respected individuals will inspire you to aspire to similar levels of achievement.

Student Perspectives

You can learn a lot from the firsthand experiences and actual words of "real people." Throughout the book, you'll find comments and advice from students at different stages of the college experience, including college graduates (alumni). Studies show that students can learn a great deal from other students—especially from students who've been there and experienced what you are about to experience. You can bene- fit from their experiences by hearing about their success stories and stumbling blocks.

Author's Experience

In each chapter, you'll find author's experiences related to the topic. We have learned from our own experiences as college students, from our professional experiences working with students as instructors and advisors, and from our life experiences. Studies show that sharing personal stories promotes understanding and memory for the concepts contained in the story. We share our experiences with you to personal- ize the book and with the hope that you'll learn from our experiences—even if it's learning not to make the same mistakes we made!

Reflection **P.4**

Have you received any tips or advice from friends or family about what to do or what not to do in college?

If yes, what was this advice? Do you think the advice is accurate and worth following?

If you haven't received any advice from anyone, why do you think no one has offered it?

Concept Maps: Verbal-Visual Aids

Appearing throughout the book are concept (idea) maps that visually organize ideas into diagrams, charts, and figures. When key concepts are presented in a visual-spa- tial format, you're more likely to retain them because two different memory traces are recorded in your brain: verbal (words) and visual (images).

Cartoons: Emotional-Visual Aids

You'll find cartoons sprinkled throughout the text. These intended attempts at humor are included to provide you with a little entertainment, but more importantly, they are intended to strengthen your retention of the concept depicted in the cartoon by reinforcing it with a visual image (drawing) and an emotional experience (humor). If the cartoon triggers at least a snicker, your body will release adrenalin—a hormone that facilitates memory formation. If the cartoon generates actual laughter, it's likely to stimulate release of endorphins—the brain's natural, morphine-like chemicals that lower stress (and elevate mood!).

Learning More through the World Wide Web

Web-based resources for information relating to each chapter's major ideas are included at the end of the chapter. One of the major goals of a college education is to prepare you to become an independent, self-directed learner. Our hope is that the material presented for each chapter topic will stimulate your interest and motivation to learn more about the topic. If it does, you can use these online resources to access additional information.

Reflection **P.5**

Quickly review the features of this book described on pp. xiii–xxii. Which of these features do you think will be most effective for stimulating your interest in reading and learning from the book?

Summary and Conclusion

It is our hope that the content of this book, and the manner in which the content is presented, will motivate and empower you to make the most of your college experience. Don't forget that the skills and strategies discussed are relevant to life beyond college. Effective planning and decision making, learning deeply and remembering longer, thinking critically and creatively, speaking and writing persuasively, managing time and money responsibly, communicating and relating effectively with others, and maintaining health and wellness are more than just college skills; they are life skills.

Learning doesn't stop after college: it's a lifelong process. If you strive to apply the ideas in this book, you should thrive in college and beyond.

Author's Experience

I've learned a lot from teaching the first-year seminar (college success course) and from writing this book. Before teaching this course, I didn't have a clear idea about what the liberal arts were or how general education was so important for achieving personal and professional success. I also learned new strategies for managing my time, my money, and my health. The strategies and skills that I've learned from teaching the course and writing this book have convinced me that this course and this book go beyond developing skills for success in college: they develop skills for success in life.

— *Joe Cuseo*

Remember

This is more than just a textbook for first-term students. It's a college success and life success book; it contains principles and strategies that can promote your success in college and improve the quality of your life.

Sincerely,
Joe Cuseo, Aaron Thompson, Michele Campagna, & Viki Sox Fecas

Acknowledgments

I'd like to take this opportunity to thank several people who have played important roles in my life and whose positive influence made this book possible. My parents, Mildred (née Carmela) and Blase (né Biaggio) Cuseo, for the many sacrifices they made to support my education. My wife, Mary, and my son, Tony, for their kindness, courage and love. James Vigilis, my uncle, for being a second father and life coach to me during my formative years. Jim Cooper, my best friend, for being a mentor to me in graduate school. My students, who taught me a lot and contributed their insightful perspectives, poignant poems, and humorous cartoons to this book.

—*Joe Cuseo*

I would like to thank my wife Holly and my children, Sonya, Sara, Michael, Maya, Isaiah, and Olivia for being my continual inspiration and source of unconditional love. I would also like to thank my father and mother (Big "A" and Margaret) for instilling in me that education is the key to most all that is valuable in our society. In addition, I would like to acknowledge the support that Eastern Kentucky University gave me a great undergraduate education and wonderful employment. Thanks Rhonda for your always continued friendship and support. In addition, I want to thank Bob King at the Kentucky Council on Postsecondary Education who is a good friend and good boss and believes deeply that high quality education of all is the ultimate path to a truly civilized nation. I would also like to thank my co-authors and Kendall Hunt (Paul, Lynne, and Charmayne) for the opportunity to be part of a great team. Lastly, I would like to thank my mentors and students who gave me the encouragement and motivation.

—*Aaron Thompson*

I would like to express my deepest gratitude to my family, Dominic, Nicolas, and Brianna, for their continuous support. Special thanks go out to my parents, Sal and Yolanda, who despite having only an elementary school education taught me that I needed to have both *educación y ganas* (education and desire/drive) to achieve my dreams. These lessons have always stayed with me, influencing the work that I do and inspiring my contributions to this book. I also thank the colleagues and students who have motivated me, particularly those at Montclair State University who supported me throughout these efforts. I am also especially grateful to my co-authors and to Paul at Kendall Hunt for their creativity and collaboration.

—*Michele Campagna*

If not for the love and support of my parents, Wyman and Fae Sox, and son, Matt Fecas, my involvement in this project would never have happened. Thanks also to Kendall Hunt Publishing's director of the National Book Program, Paul Carty, whose wisdom in assembling the writing team and assignment of a crackerjack editor, Tina Bower, made this idea a fun reality. I also tremendously value my colleagues for their encouragement and feedback through the writing and review process.

—*Viki Sox Fecas*

We gratefully acknowledge the constructive criticism of the colleagues who provided reviews for individual chapters of this text and who participated in the focus groups. They include:

Peg Adams
Northern Kentucky University

Stephanie Adams
William Woods University

Anita Adkins
Northern Kentucky University

Treva Barham
Le Tourneau University

Andrea Berta
University of Texas—El Paso

Paula Bradberry
Arkansas State University

Cynthia Burnley
Eastern Tennessee State University

Norma Campbell
Fayetteville State University

Jay Chaskes
Rowan University

Regina Clark
Tennessee State University

Karen Clay
Miami-Dade College

Geoff Cohen
University of California—Riverside

Amy D'Olivo
Centenary College of New Jersey

Donna Dahlgren
Indiana University Southeast

Rachelle Darabi
Indiana Purdue University—Fort Wayne

Michael Denton
University of North Carolina—Charlotte

Louise Ericson
University of South Carolina Upstate

Betsy Eudey
California State University—Stanislaus

Linda Alvarez
University of Wisconsin—River Falls

Scott Amundsen
Eastern Kentucky University

Suzanne Ash
Cerritos College

Jennifer Gay
Fort Lewis College

Latty Goodwin
Rochester Institute of Technology

Tracy Gottlieb
Seton Hall University

Virginia Granda
University of Texas—El Paso

Laurie Grimes
Lorain County Community College

Allen Grove
Alfred University

Robert Guell
Indiana State University

Laurie Hazard
Bryant College

Marge Jaasma
California State University—Stanislaus

Andrew Koch
Purdue University

Lora Lavery-Broda
St. Leo University

Deborah Lotsof
Mount Union College

Jane Owen
Waynesburg College

Denise Roade
Northern Illinois University

Chris Rubic
Grayslake North High School

Carlisa Finney
Anne Arundel Community College

Janet Florez
Cuesta College

Stephanie Foote
University of South Carolina—Aiken

Paula Fuhst
Yavapai College

Stephanie Fujii
Estrella Mountain Community College

Jane Snyder
Fontbonne University

Mary Taugher
University of Wisconsin—
Milwaukee

Judy Termini
Gallaudet University

Kathie Wentworth
Tri-State University

Carol Williams
Arizona State University

About the Authors

Joe Cuseo holds a doctoral degree in educational psychology and assessment from the University of Iowa. He is a professor emeritus of psychology at Marymount College (California) where for more than 25 years he directed the first-year seminar, a college success course required of all new students. He was also a 14-time recipient of the "Faculty Member of the Year" award, a student-driven award based on effective teaching and academic advising. He's been a recent recipient of the "Outstanding First-Year Student Advocate" Award from the National Resource Center for the First-Year Experience and Students in Transition, as well as the American College Personnel Association (ACPA) Diamond Honoree Award for contributions made to student development and the student affairs profession. Joe has delivered numerous campus workshops and conference presentations across the United States, as well as Canada, Europe, China, and Australia. He's authored multiple articles, monographs, and books on student learning, student retention, and student success. Currently, Joe serves as an educational advisor and consultant for AVID, a nonprofit organization whose mission is to promote the college readiness and success of underserved student populations.

Aaron Thompson, Ph.D., is the senior vice president for academic affairs at the Kentucky Council on Postsecondary Education and a professor of sociology in the Department of Educational Leadership and Policy Studies at Eastern Kentucky University. Thompson has a Ph.D. in sociology in the areas of organizational behavior and race and gender relations. Thompson has researched, taught, and/or consulted in the areas of assessment, diversity, leadership, ethics, research methodology and social statistics, multicultural families, race and ethnic relations, student success, first-year students, retention, and organizational design. He is nationally recognized in the areas of educational attainment, academic success, and cultural competence.

Dr. Thompson has worked in a variety of capacities within two-year and four-year institutions. He got his start in college teaching at a community college. His latest co-authored books are *Infusing Diversity and Cultural Competence Into Teacher Education*; *Diversity and the College Experience*; *Thriving in the Community College and Beyond: Research-Based Strategies for Academic Success and Personal Development*; *Humanity, Diversity, & the Liberal Arts: The Foundation of a College Education*; *Focus on Success*; and *Black Men and Divorce*. His upcoming book is entitled *The Sociological Outlook*. He has more than 30 publications and numerous research and peer-reviewed presentations. Thompson has traveled over the U.S. and internationally, giving more than 700 workshops, seminars, and invited lectures in the areas of race and gender diversity, living an unbiased life, overcoming obstacles to gain success, creating a school environment for academic success, cultural competence, workplace interaction, organizational goal setting, building relationships, the first-year seminar, and a variety of other topics. He has been or is a consultant to educational institutions, corporations, nonprofit organizations, police departments, and other governmental agencies.

Michele Campagna, Ed.D., is the executive director of the Center for Advising and Student Transitions at Montclair State University in New Jersey. Dr. Campagna provides leadership for a comprehensive and holistic program designed to retain and engage first-year, freshman, sophomore, and transfer students. The center supports undergraduate advising, New Student and Family Orientation, Learning Communities, a peer leadership and advising program, the New Student Seminar, the Adult Success Seminar, and sophomore success initiatives. Dr. Campagna has 20 years of experience teaching various types of first-year seminar courses and directing services for students in transition at both two-year and four-year institutions.

Dr. Campagna holds an Ed.D. in higher education. She is the author of "New Student Experience: A Holistic and Collaborative Approach to First-Year Retention" in *Exploring the Evidence: Campus-Wide Initiatives in the First College Year*, published by the National Resource Center for the First-Year Experience and Students in Transition. Dr. Campagna has presented at many statewide and national conferences on designing and implementing engagement and retention initiatives, strategic planning, assessment, and diversity.

Viki Sox Fecas has a Ph.D. in educational administration from the University of South Carolina (USC). In her current role as program manager for freshman and pre-freshman programs, she coordinates the career component for all 150+ sections of the number-one-ranked University 101 program in the country. She serves as a career resource for international scholars visiting the National Resource Center (NRC). She also is an adjunct professor in the Higher Education and Student Affairs graduate program at USC. She was recognized as the *Outstanding Freshman Advocate* in 1996.

She took University 101 as a freshman at USC, and has been teaching for the past 18 years. Since 1995, she has taught the sole section dedicated to transfer students. Her research interests center around the transition of college students, with a special interest in transfer students. She has written career chapters for the U101 *Transitions* book and *Your College Experience*. She regularly presents at both the National First-Year Experience and Students in Transition Conferences sponsored by the NRC.

Introduction

Congratulations and welcome! We applaud your decision to continue your education. Your previous enrollment in school was required; however, you're decision to continue your education in college is entirely *your choice*. You've chosen to enter "higher education," where you will be learning and thinking at a higher level than you did in high school. You are about to begin a new and exciting journey. Your time in college has the potential to be the most enriching experience of your life; it's probably safe to say that after your experience in college, you'll never again be a member of an organization or community with as many resources and services that are intentionally designed to promote your learning, development, and success. If you capitalize on the campus resources available to you, and if you utilize effective college-going strategies (such as those suggested in this book), you can create a life-changing experience for yourself that will enrich the quality of your life for the remainder of your life. (See Snapshot Summary I.1 for a list of the multiple lifelong benefits of a college education and college degree.)

Snapshot Summary

I.1 Why College Is Worth It: The Economic and Personal Benefits of a College Education

Less than 30 percent of Americans have earned a four-year college degree (**College Board, 2008**). When individuals who attend college are compared with people from similar social and economic backgrounds who did not continue their education beyond high school, research reveals that college is well worth the investment. College graduates experience numerous long-lasting benefits, such as those summarized in the following list:

1. **Career Benefits**
   * Career Security and Stability—lower rates of unemployment
   * Career Versatility and Mobility—more flexibility to move out of a position and into other positions
   * Career Advancement—more opportunity to move up to higher professional positions
   * Career Interest—more likely to find their work stimulating and challenging
   * Career Autonomy—greater independence and opportunity to be their own boss
   * Career Satisfaction—enjoy their work more and feel that it allows them to use their special talents
   * Career Prestige—hold higher-status positions (i.e., careers that are more socially desirable and respected)

2. **Economic Advantages**
   * Make better consumer choices and decisions
   * Make wiser long-term investments
   * Receive greater pension benefits
   * Earn higher income: The gap between the earnings of high school and college graduates is *growing*. Individuals with a bachelor's degree now earn an average annual salary of about $50,000 per year, 40 percent higher than that of high school graduates, whose average salary is less than $30,000 per year. When these differences are calculated over a lifetime, families headed by people with bachelor's degrees will take in about $1.6 million more than families headed by people with high school diplomas. **That adds up to double the amount earned by those who complete only a high school diploma.**

3. **Advanced Intellectual Skills**
   * Greater knowledge
   * More effective problem-solving skills
   * Better ability to deal with complex and ambiguous (uncertain) problems
   * Greater openness to new ideas
   * More advanced levels of moral reasoning

- Clearer sense of self-identity—greater awareness and knowledge of personal talents, interests, values, and needs
- Greater likelihood to continue learning throughout life

4. **Better Physical Health**
   - Better health insurance—more comprehensive coverage and more likely to be covered
   - Better dietary habits
   - Exercise more regularly
   - Lower rates of obesity
   - Live longer and healthier lives

5. **Social Benefits**
   - Higher social self-confidence
   - Understand and communicate more effectively with others
   - Greater popularity
   - More effective leadership skills
   - Greater marital satisfaction

6. **Emotional Benefits**
   - Lower levels of anxiety
   - Higher levels of self-esteem
   - Greater sense of self-efficacy—believe they have more influence and control over their life
   - Higher levels of psychological well-being
   - Higher levels of personal happiness

7. **Effective Citizenship**
   - Greater interest in national issues—both social and political
   - Greater knowledge of current affairs
   - Higher voting participation rates
   - Higher rates of participation in civic affairs and community service

8. **Higher Quality of Life for Their Children**
   - Less likely to smoke during pregnancy
   - Provide better health care for their children
   - Spend more time with their children
   - More likely to involve their children in educational activities that stimulate their mental development
   - More likely to save money for their children to go to college
   - More likely that their children will graduate from college
   - More likely that their children will attain high-status and higher-paying careers

"For the individual, having access to and successfully graduating from an institution of higher education has proved to be the path to a better job, to better health and to a better life" (College Board, 2008, p. 41).

References

Andres, L., & Wyn, J. (2010). *The making of a generation: The children of the 1970s in adulthood.* Buffalo, NY: University of Toronto Press.

Astin, A. W. (1993). *What matters in college?* San Francisco, CA: Jossey-Bass.

Bowen, H. R. (1977, 1997). *Investment in learning: The individual & social value of American higher education.* Baltimore, MD: The Johns Hopkins University Press.

College Board. (2008). *Coming to our senses: Education and the American future.* Report of the Commission on Access, Admissions and Success in Higher Education. Retrieved August 5, 2009, from http://advocacy.collegeboard.org/college-admission-completion/access-admissions-success-education-and-american-future/publications/co

College Board. (2011). *Education pays 2010.* Washington, DC: Author.

Dee, T. (2004). Are there civic returns to education? *Journal of Public Economics, 88,* 1697–1720.

Feldman, K. A., & Newcomb, T. M. (1969, 1994). The impact of college on students. San Francisco, CA: Jossey-Bass.

Hamilton, W. (2011, December 29). College still worth it, study says. *Los Angeles Times,* p. B2.

Pascarella, E. T., & Terenzini, P. T. (2005). *How college affects students: A third decade of research* (vol. 2). San Francisco, CA: Jossey-Bass.

Tomasho, R. (2009, April 22). Study tallies education gap's effect on GDP. *Wall Street Journal.*

U.S. Census Bureau. (2008). *Bureau of Labor Statistics.* Washington, DC: Author.

The Importance of the First Year of College

Your movement into higher education represents an important life transition. Somewhat like an immigrant moving to a new country, you're moving into a new culture with different expectations, regulations, customs, and language (Chaskes, 1996). (See the Glossary and Learning the Language of Higher Education: A Dictionary of College Vocabulary at the end of this book for "translations" of the new language that is used in the college culture.)

The *first* year of college is undoubtedly the most important year of the college experience because it's a stage of *transition*. During the first year of college, students report the most change, the most learning, and the most development (Flowers et al., 2001; Doyle, Edison, & Pascarella, 1998; Light, 2001). Other research suggests that the academic habits students establish in their first year of college are likely to persist throughout their remaining years of college (Schilling, 2001). When graduating seniors look back at their college experience, many of them say that the first year was the time of greatest change and the time during which they made the most significant improvements in their approach to learning. Here is how one senior put it during a personal interview:

Interviewer: What have you learned about your approach to learning [in college]?

Student: I had to learn how to study. I went through high school with a 4.0 average. I didn't have to study. It was a breeze. I got to the university and there was no structure. No one took attendance to make sure I was in class. No one checked my homework. No one told me I had to do something. There were no quizzes on the readings. I did not work well with this lack of structure. It took my first year and a half to learn to deal with it. But I had to teach myself to manage my time. I had to teach myself how to study. I had to teach myself how to learn in a different environment. (Chickering & Schlossberg, 1998, p. 47)

Reflection I.1

Why have you decided to attend college?

Why did you decide to attend the college or university you're enrolled in now?

In many ways, the first-year experience in college is similar to ocean surfing or downhill skiing; it can be filled with many exciting thrills, but there's also a risk of taking some dangerous spills. The first year is also the stage of the college experience during which students experience the most stress, the most academic difficulties, and the highest withdrawal rate (American College Testing, 2012; Bartlett, 2002; Sax, Bryant, & Gilmartin, 2004). The ultimate goal of downhill skiing and surfing is to experience the thrills, avoid the spills, and finish the run while you're still standing. The same is true for the first year of college; studies show that if you can complete your first-year experience in good standing, your chances for successfully completing college improve dramatically (American College Testing, 2009).

In a nutshell, your college success will depend on what you do for yourself and how you take advantage of what your college can do for you. You'll find that the research cited and the advice provided in this book point to one major conclusion: Success in college depends on you—you make it happen by what you do and how well you capitalize on the resources available to you.

Student Perspective

"I noticed before when I wasn't going to college, they [my family] didn't look at me as highly as a person. But now since I have started college, everybody is lifting me up and saying how proud they [are] of me."

—First-year student, quoted in Franklin et al. (2002)

Student Perspective

"Being a first-generation college student, seeing how hard my parents worked these past 18 years to give all that they can to get me to where I am now, I feel I cannot let them down. It is my responsibility to succeed in school and life and to take care of them in their old age."

—First-year college student, quoted in Nuñez (2005)

Student Perspective

"My three-month-old boy is very important to me, and it is important that I graduate from college so my son, as well as I, live a better life."

—First-year student response to the question "What is most important to you?"

Student Perspective

"What I would change is what I did after high school. I would have continued with my education so I could have pursued my dreams earlier in life. That way I would have been able to offer more to myself, my wife, and my kids."

—28-year-old sophomore response to the question "What, if anything, would you change about your life if you could start all over again?"

Student Perspective

"Getting the [college] degree meant more to me than an NCAA title, being named All-American or winning an Olympic gold medal."

—Patrick Ewing, Hall of Fame basketball player and college graduate (Georgetown University)

After reviewing 40 years of research on how college affects students, two distinguished researchers reached the following conclusion:

> *The impact of college is largely determined by individual effort and involvement in the academic, interpersonal, and extracurricular [co-curricular] offerings on a campus. Students are not passive recipients of institutional efforts to "educate" or "change" them, but rather bear major responsibility for any gains they derive from their postsecondary [college] experience. (Pascarella & Terenzini, 2005, p. 602)*

Compared to your previous schooling, college will provide you with a broader range of courses, more resources to capitalize on, more freedom of choice, and more decision-making opportunities. Your own college experience will differ from that of any other college student because you have the freedom to actively shape or create it in a way that is uniquely your own. Don't let college happen to you; make it happen *for* you—take charge of your college experience and take advantage of the college resources that are at your command.

Reflection 1.2

In order to succeed in college, what do you think you'll have to do differently than you've done in the past?

Importance of a First-Year Experience Course (a.k.a. First-Year Seminar)

If you're reading this book, you are already beginning to take charge of your college experience because you're enrolled in a course that's designed to promote your college success. Research strongly indicates that new students who participate in first-year experience courses are more likely to stay continue in college until they complete their degree and perform at a higher level. These positive effects have been found for:

- All types of students (underprepared and well-prepared, minority and majority, residential and commuter, male and female),
- Students at all types of colleges (two-year and four-year, public and private),
- Students attending colleges of different sizes (small, mid-sized, and large), and
- Students attending college in different locations (urban, suburban, and rural).

(References: Barefoot et al., 1998; Boudreau & Kromrey, 1994; Cuseo, 2011; Cuseo & Barefoot, 1996; Fidler & Godwin, 1994; Glass & Garrett, 1995; Grunder & Hellmich, 1996; Hunter & Linder, 2005; Porter & Swing, 2006; Shanley & Witten, 1990; Sidle & McReynolds, 1999; Starke, Harth, & Sirianni, 2001; Thomson, 1998; Tobolowsky, 2005).

There has been more carefully conducted research on first-year experience courses, and more evidence supporting their effectiveness for promoting success, than there is for any other course in the college curriculum. You're fortunate to be enrolled in this course, so give it your best effort and take full advantage of what it has to offer. If you do, you'll be taking an important first step toward thriving in college and beyond.

Enjoy the trip!

CONTENT DESIGNED SPECIFICALLY FOR

Welcome from the Dean

Dear UC 1000/UC 1900 students,

As the Dean of University College, I want to welcome you to UC 1000/UC 1900, a class that I believe will benefit you the rest of your time at Ohio University and, for that matter, throughout your lives after graduation. I know this sounds like a grand claim, but I have witnessed the lasting impact it has on students who tell me every year how critically important the lessons they learned in UC 1000/UC 19000 were to their success at Ohio University.

Among the essential lessons that you will learn are how to manage your time, how to study more effectively, and how to select the right major. I know when I arrived at Slippery Rock State College in the fall of 1970, I had no idea how to manage my time, little clue about how to study, and was even less confident about how to choose a major. I struggled mightily my first year and did not do well academically. I ended my first year without understanding why my grades were poor, why I did not do well on exams even though I thought I had studied hard, and still uncertain about a major. I eventually turned around my performance thanks to a great academic advisor who showed me how to manage my time and responsibilities, helped me acquire study skills, and guided me to select the perfect major.

If I had the opportunity to take UC 1000/UC 1900, I would have avoided many of these problems and would have had a solid first year and been ready to start my second year with the right major. UC 1000/UC 1900 will equip you with the knowledge and skills necessary to fulfill your academic promise, to become a self-reliant learner, and to find the ideal major. It is a lively, creatively taught class where activities, group projects, and study groups make it easy to form friendships that may even last the rest of your lives. I look forward to teaching it every year because I know it will make a difference in the lives of my students, and I know will make a difference in your lives as well.

Wishing you all the best in your first year at Ohio University!

David Descutner
Dean of University College,
Executive Vice Provost for Undergraduate Education

• **Academic Advancement Center** (AAC)

The Academic Advancement Center, a department of University College, offers programs and services to help students meet the academic demands of university work. The AAC provides many services: including peer tutoring, a math center, Supplemental Instruction (SI), a computer learning lab, and a writing center, a science center as well as instruction in college reading skills, computing skills, and study skills. Hours 8:00am-5:00pm & evening labs Sun-Thurs.

Email: aac@ohio.edu   Phone: 740-593-2644
Location: 101 Alden Library
http://www.ohio.edu/aac

• **Allen Student Help Center**

Have a problem and don't know where to begin to find help to solve it? The Allen Student Help Center can help you. This friendly office has staff who offer: guidance for students who are academically lost, or who are struggling with multiple concerns and aren't sure where to go; walk-in or appointment assistance; walk-in study skills assistance; academic coaching; free computer loans for eligible students; re-entry/exit interviews; Academic Success Workshops; and Gaining Academic Progress Workshops.

Email: helpcenter@ohio.edu   Phone: 740-566-8888
Location: 419 Baker University Center
http://www.ohio.edu/helpcenter

• **Campus Involvement Center**

The Campus Involvement Center's mission is to provide meaningful, high-quality out-of-class opportunities through programs and experiences that foster: student leadership and leadership development; practical application of classroom learning; the development of healthy lifestyles, including low-risk choices; participation in student organizations; and involvement and service in Athens and the greater community; all guided to reflect the five core values of Ohio University: character, community, citizenship, civility, and commitment.

Email: involvement@ohio.edu   Phone: 740-593-4025
Location: Baker University Center Rooms 339 and 355
www.ohio.edu/involvement

• **Career and Leadership Development Center**

The Career & Leadership Development Center provides support services, resources, and development opportunities throughout your time at OHIO and even after you graduate. We encourage all students to connect with our staff early in their Bobcat career to maximize our development and planning resources. Our leadership programs also develop key skills that you need during college and in the world of work. Whether you're exploring majors, enhancing your leadership skills, seeking job search guidance, or building your résumé, this is your one-stop shop.

Email: careerandleadership@ohio.edu   Phone: 740-593-2909
Location: 503 Baker University Center
http://www.ohio.edu/careerandleadership

• Commuter Student Services (CSS)

CSS provides academic and social support and services for commuter and adult students, as well as academic and social activities. The Commuter Lounge is located in Bromley Hall (requires separate registration).

Email: commuter@ohio.edu   Phone: 740-593-1935
Location: 140 Chubb Hall
http://www.ohio.edu/univcollege/cass/

• Computer Learning Lab

The AAC Computer Learning Lab, located on the first floor of Alden Library, is a modern multimedia facility equipped with Macintosh and Windows computers, scanners, digital cameras, CD and DVD burners, and various supporting software from Adobe, Apple, and Microsoft. Skilled computer assistants are available for one-on-one personalized help with simple and advanced computer use questions. The Computer Learning Lab is a place to experiment with technology, to invent, to create, and to learn with the comfort of knowing that if you need guidance in using technology or run into technical snag, individualized assistance is just a few steps away. For open hours and available software/hardware, go to www.ohio.edu/aac/lab.

Email: aac@ohio.edu   Phone: 740-593-2644
Location: 101 Alden Library
http://www.ohio.edu/aac/lab

• Counseling and Psychological Services (CPS)

CPS provides mental health and adjustment services to students and also consultation to faculty, administrators, and parents of students. Our services are designed to help students understand themselves and their difficulties and ultimately make healthy choices for their lives. We offer developmental, preventive, and remedial services. We also provide programs that promote the intellectual, emotional, cultural, and social development of Ohio University students.

Email: Counseling.Services@ohio.edu   Phone: 740-593-1616
                                              (24/7 Crisis Intervention Service)
Location: Hudson Health Center, 3rd Floor
http://www.ohio.edu/counseling/

• Education Abroad (Study Abroad)

The Office of Education Abroad is the place to begin your search for an appropriate education abroad experience, whether you want to study, teach, work, volunteer, or intern. You may fulfill foreign language or General Education requirements, take courses in English in another country, conduct undergraduate research, or gain practical experience through international internships. Study abroad is an option for any major. Programs range from ten days in length to an entire academic year. The best time to begin planning for your educational experience abroad is during your first year at OHIO. For more information, come to the Office of Education Abroad during walk-in advising hours Monday-Friday, 1:00-4:00 p.m., in Walter International Education Center, 15 Park Place (next to Baker Center). OHIO students can participate in accredited study abroad programs sponsored by other universities in Ohio and throughout the U.S. If you decide to participate in a non-OHIO program, you must register with the Office of Education Abroad and complete necessary forms for credit transfer.

Email: education.abroad@ohio.edu   Phone: 740-593-4583
Location: Walter International Education Center, 15 Park Place
http://www.ohio.edu/educationabroad

• International Student and Faculty Services (ISFS)

ISFS provides support services for international students and their dependents, which includes: Experienced advisors to help international students meet their academic goals, advising and assistance on immigration matters, arrival information and new student orientation programming to welcome new students and provide information on campus and community services

Coordination of the annual International Week and International Street Fair celebrations and support for the International Student Union and other internationally oriented student organizations

Email: isfs@ohio.edu   Phone: 740-593-4330
Location: Walter International Education Center, 15 Park Place
http://www.ohio.edu/isfs

• Lesbian, Gay, Bisexual, Transgender (LGBT) Center

The LGBT Center advances the diversity mission of Ohio University by creating a campus environment that is inclusive and supportive of sexual orientation and gender identity or expression. We focus on the unique academic, cultural, and social needs of LGBT students, and strive to enhance these students' learning and engagement as well as increase their retention. Our broader influence emerges from providing resources, educational opportunities, and social justice initiatives to all students, faculty, staff, alumni, and community members at Ohio University and beyond.

Email: lgbt@ohio.edu   Phone: 740-593-0239
Location: 354 Baker University Center
http://www.ohio.edu/lgbt/

• Math Center

The AAC Math Center offers free tutorial help to undergraduate students enrolled in any math-related course (e.g., math, statistics, accounting, and economics). Students with math-related questions can meet with a tutor by attending the drop-in Math Lab

Sunday-Thursday, 7:00-9:00 p.m., or arranging for a one-on-one 30-minute session. Information on current hours of operation is available at: www.ohio.edu/tutoring/mathCenter.cfm

Email: aac@ohio.edu   Phone: 740-593-2644
Location: 101 Alden Library
www.ohio.edu/tutoring/mathCenter.cfm

• Office of Military and Veterans Resources
The mission of Ohio University's Office of Military and Veterans Resources is to provide, facilitate, and coordinate programs and services for student veterans, military personnel, and their family members. We strive to assist military personnel and veterans in making a successful transition to the Ohio University community and support them through their academic careers.

Email: military@ohio.edu   Phone: 740-593-1935
Location: 140 Chubb Hall
http://www.ohio.edu/military/index.cfm

• Office of Multicultural Student Access and Retention (OMSAR)
OMSAR assists in providing access to a quality academic and enriching social experience at Ohio University for diverse students, while leading the institution's efforts to successfully retain and graduate them. The services provided to students by the OMSAR staff include: oversight of scholarship programs to actively involve students in meaningful educational experiences; access to appropriate campus resources and staff to best meet immediate and/or long-term needs of students; one-on-one meetings with a staff member to develop students' plans for academic and social success; collaborations with academic colleges and departments to assess individual students' academic preparedness, learning styles, and evaluate predictors of academic success; conducting large group informational meetings regarding scholarship requirements and support; providing academic advising in conjunction with assigned faculty advisors for optimal academic success; leadership development education; advocating for students to pursue academic and leadership awards and recognition; the development of research skills and opportunities to share findings with the campus community; and opportunities to grow socially and personally through community service projects.

Email: waltersc@ohio.edu   Phone: 740-593-9387
Location: 052 Lindley Hall
http://www.ohio.edu/omsar/

• Office of Student Financial Aid and Scholarships
The Office of Student Financial Aid and Scholarships normally is open to the public between 8:00 a.m. and 5:00 p.m. Monday through Friday. Our client services area has a very knowledgeable staff that can assist students with a variety of questions.

Email: financial.aid@ohio.edu   Phone: 740-593-4141
Location: 020 Chubb Hall
http://www.ohio.edu/financialaid/

• Office of the Ombudsman

This office is a neutral, informal and confidential service open to all students, faculty, and staff, with the goal of creating a fair and supportive learning and working environment. Contact the office if you need help navigating processes within OHIO or feel you have an issue related to fair treatment or due process. The office works with you to resolve issues related to academic concerns (i.e., grade appeals, classroom treatment, distance learning) and nonacademic concerns (i.e., parking, financial aid, registration, work study). For information on grade appeals and class-related issues, go to the website above and click on FAQs, and then Students, and then Grades, Class-Related Issues.

Email: ombuds@ohio.edu   Phone: 740-593-2627
Location: 501 Baker Center
http://www.ohio.edu/ombuds/

• Ohio University Survivor Advocacy Program (OUSAP)

OUSAP's mission is to create a safe campus for ALL through advocacy, education, and resources. OUSAP provides 24/7 confidential support services for victims and survivors of sexual assault, dating/domestic violence, and/or stalking. Use the entrance on the right hand side of the McKee House for convenience and privacy. You can also call 24/7 to speak with a trained advocate. Services: 24/7 confidential Helpline/Hotline: 740-597-SAFE (7233); a safe space on campus: Office hours are 8:00 a.m.-8:00 p.m. Monday-Friday; walk-ins welcomed; trained advocates, both peer and professional, to assist you in making informed choices; personal support during any medical, law enforcement, legal and/or judicial processes; information and resources for students, faculty/staff, friends, and family. Advocates provide: empathy, support, non-judgment to those experiencing sexual assault, dating/domestic violence, and/or stalking. We listen, help identify concerns, discuss potential paths, and support survivors in their choices.

Email: survivor.advocacy@ohio.edu   Phone: 740-597-SAFE (7233)
Location: 44 University Terrace (lower level of McKee House)
http://www.ohio.edu/womenscenter/advocacy/About.cfm

• Private Peer Tutoring

Individual peer tutoring is available for skill development and for mastery of course content for undergraduate courses. To make an appointment, please use Tutor Trac. Go to http://www.ohio.edu/tutoring/findatutor.cfm and click on Tutor Trac. When working with a Peer Tutor, you will be expected to pay directly. We offer tutoring in over 200 courses. In most areas, particularly 1000-2000 level courses, tutors are readily available. If you cannot find a tutor on Tutor Trac, please stop by the Academic Advancement Center to complete a Tutor Request Form. We will do our best to connect you with a qualified tutor.

Email: aac@ohio.edu   Phone: 740-593-2644
Location: 101 Alden Library
http://www.ohio.edu/tutoring/

• Residential Housing

OHIO's beautiful residential campus is a center for academic, social, cultural, and recreational activities. Residential Housing strives to engage, motivate, and challenge students using our mission, values, and goals for guidance. The department is responsible for the administration and programming within a housing system of 42 residence halls across three residential greens that house nearly 8,000 students. We take pride in creating community and cultivating leaders across Ohio University by providing students with not only a safe and comfortable place to live, but also a thriving and vibrant educational community.

Email: housing@ohio.edu   Phone: 740-593-4090
Location: 060 Chubb Hall
http://www.ohio.edu/housing/

• Safe T Patrol (Safe Arrival for Everyone Tonight)

Studying at Alden Library or meeting with a study group or taking a class in the evening? This is a free walking escort of two trained students in constant radio contact with the Ohio University Police Department who will escort you to any location on campus or in close proximity to the campus. Call and say where you are and where you want to go. A team will arrive in minutes. Call ahead and a team will be waiting for you after a class or meeting. Personal Safety Reminders: walk with others, or make use of the Safe T Patrol escort service by calling (740) 593-4040; stay on well-traveled paths; report suspicious people to police by calling 911; and let friends know where you are going and when you expect to arrive.

Email: police@ohio.edu   Phone: 740-493-4040
Location: 135 Scott Quad
http://www.ohio.edu/police/escort.cfm

• Science Center

Free science help is available to undergraduates enrolled in science courses, (e.g. chemistry, biological sciences and physics). Students can meet with a science tutor by attending the drop-in science center that meets Sunday-Thursday from 7:00 p.m. – 9:00 p.m. or by making a one-on-one 30 minute appointment on Tutor Trac. For more information go to http://www.ohio.edu/tutoring/scienceCenter.cfm

Email: aac@ohio.edu   Phone: 740-593-2644
Location: 101 Alden Library
http://www.ohio.edu/tutoring/sciencecenter.cfm

• Student Accessibility Services

If you have a documented disability or suspect that you have a disability that interferes with your academic performance, getting the support that you need can be crucial to your academic success. Student Accessibility Services provides services and accommodations for students with a disability, which may include (but are not limited to): Learning Disabilities, ADD/ADHD, Psychological Conditions, Chronic Illnesses, Hard of Hearing/Deafness, Mobility Impairments, and Low Vision/Blindness

In order to request accommodations students must present documentation from a qualified health, medical, or educational professional that verifies a condition and the impact on the student in an academic setting. The necessary documentation will vary depending on the disability, so additional information is available on our website at: www.ohio.edu/disabilities/current/guidelines.cfm. It is recommended that students contact the office early to discuss specific needs or questions and before school begins, if possible.

Email: disabilities@ohio.edu   Phone: 740-593-2620
Location: 348 Baker University Center
http://www.ohio.edu/disabilities/

• Student Writing Center

The Student Writing Center, located in the Alden Library (2nd floor), provides free scheduled and walk-in face-to-face appointments, study tables and workshops about academic writing, daily tips about writing on their Facebook page, as well as online appointments for commuting and graduate students. See www.ohio.edu/writing for hours, tutor profiles, and additional information about scheduling appointments.

Assistance is available at any stage of the writing process, from brainstorming to looking over a final draft. You can get help with things like developing a thesis, organizing your ideas, building a bibliography, and identifying/improving ongoing grammar issues in your writing.

Location: 2nd Floor Alden Library   Phone: 740-593-2646
http://www.ohio.edu/writing

• Supplemental Instruction (SI)

SI provides free out of class review sessions for traditionally difficult courses. These sessions are facilitated by undergraduate students (SI Leaders) who have successfully completed the course. SI leaders attend the class and work with the professor to help students share and master the course information. The sessions are open to anyone enrolled in the selected course. Students who regularly attend SI often earn better grades in the course. If a course is selected for SI, the leader is introduced during the class and will announce the SI schedule. Courses with SI and session schedules are at www.ohio.edu/aac/si/.

Email: aac@ohio.edu   Phone: 740-593-2644
Location: 101 Alden Library
http:// www.ohio.edu/aac/si/

• The Office of Community Standards and Student Responsibility

The Ohio University Student Code of Conduct is rooted in the philosophy of educational discipline. The judicial process is a learning experience that spans a continuum--beginning with understanding community expectations to being confronted for behaviors not in keeping with these expectations through the formal adjudication of alleged violations, and, finally, through delivery and completion of sanctions as warranted. The university makes an effort to educate students and student organizations found in violation of the Student Code of Conduct through a sanction while remaining at the university. However, when a student or student organization is assessed to be a danger to the university community or reputation of the university, or when a repetition of misconduct is likely to occur, the student or student organization will be treated the same as one who has failed academically and may be separated from the university. Throughout Ohio University's judicial process, due process protections are provided. Ohio University not only meets but exceeds due process protections required by law. Ohio University provides: an established code of conduct that details Ohio University's expectations for student conduct; written notice of charges when students are accused of violating Ohio University's policies; a procedural interview during which charges, evidence, rights, and options are discussed with students or student organizations accused of misconduct; a hearing for a further exploration of the facts and circumstances of the case in the event that the accused denies the charge; an established standard of proof: preponderance of evidence; and two levels of appeal.

Email: communitystandards@ohio.edu   Phone: 740-593-2629
Location: 349 Baker University Center
http://www.ohio.edu/communitystandards/

• Women's Center

The mission of the Ohio University Women's Center is to act as a catalyst to promote awareness, education, and advocacy about women, gender, and diversity among faculty, staff, and students at Ohio University and its surrounding communities. Founded in 2007, the center is dedicated to creating an inclusive and welcoming campus climate for all members of the community through programs, resources, referrals, advocacy, and education. Through a commitment to educate and advocate, the Women's Center provides opportunities for campus involvement while attending to the specific needs and concerns of women at Ohio University.

Email: womenscenter@ohio.edu   Phone: 740-593-9625
Location: 403 Baker University Center
http://www.ohio.edu/womenscenter/

Academic Advising Planning Worksheet

Academic Advisor: _____ Advisor Phone #:_____

Advisor Email: _____ Advisor's Office: _____

Your Spring Enrollment Appointment- date : _____ time:_____
(Can be found on My OHIO Student Center)

Your Academic Advising Appointment- date:_____ time: _____ location:_____
(Advising hold will not be lifted until AFTER advising appointment)

Are there other registration holds on your account that will prevent you from registering?   Yes or No
(Also found on My OHIO Student Center)

If yes, what office(s) created the hold(s)? _____

_____

Current Grades: (List each course & your current grade in the course):

1)_____ 2)_____

3)_____ 4)_____

5)_____ 6)_____

How are things going outside of class (i.e., living situation, involvement on campus, job, homesickness, and finances)?

_____

_____

_____

_____

Majors that interest me:

1)_____ 2)_____

3)_____ 4)_____

Minors/Certificates that interest me:

1)_____   2)_____

3)_____   4)_____

Classes that interest you for spring semester (List at least ten classes to account for your back-ups):

COURSE	CR. HRS	REQUISITE	WHY? (TIER I, TIER II, Exploration)

1)_____

2)_____

3)_____

4)_____

5)_____

6)_____

7)_____

8)_____

9)_____

10)_____

Which classes listed above are required or recommended for the major(s) in which you are interested?

_____

_____

_____

Other questions or concerns that you want to make sure to ask during your advising session:

_____

_____

_____

Touching All the Bases

Using Powerful Student Success Principles and Key Campus Resources

LEARNING GOAL

To equip you with a set of powerful success strategies that you can use immediately to get off to a fast start in college and that you can use continually throughout your college experience to achieve success.

1. How do you think college will be different from high school?

2. What do you think it will take to be successful in college? (What personal characteristics, qualities, or strategies do you feel are most important for college success?)

The Most Powerful Research-Based Principles of College Success

Research on human learning and student development indicates four powerful principles of college success:

1. Active involvement
2. Use of campus resources
3. Interpersonal interaction and collaboration
4. Personal reflection and self-awareness (Astin, 1993; Kuh et al., 2005; Light, 2001; Pascarella & Terenzini, 1991; 2005; Tinto, 1993).

These principles are introduced and examined carefully in this opening chapter for two reasons:

1. You can put them into practice to establish good habits for early success in college.
2. They represent the foundational bases for the success strategies recommended throughout this book.

The four principles of success can be remembered by visualizing them as the four bases of a baseball diamond—as depicted in Figure 1.1.

FIGURE 1.1

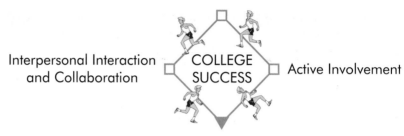

Utilizing Campus Resources

COLLEGE SUCCESS

Interpersonal Interaction and Collaboration

Active Involvement

Personal Reflection and Self-Awareness

□ =Supporting Bases for College Success
▼ =Primary ("Home") Base for College Success

© Kendall Hunt

The Diamond of College Success

Touching the First Base of College Success: Active Involvement

Research indicates that active involvement may be the most powerful principle of human learning and college success (Astin, 1993; Kuh et al., 2005). The bottom line is this: To maximize your success in college, you cannot be a passive spectator; you need to be an active player.

The principle of active involvement includes the following key components:

- The amount of personal time devoted to learning in college.
- The degree of personal effort or energy (mental and physical) put into the learning process.

Think of something you do with intensity, passion, and commitment. If you were to approach academic work in the same way, you would be faithfully implementing the principle of active involvement.

One way to ensure that you're actively involved in the learning process and putting forth high levels of energy or effort is to take action on what you're learning. You can engage in any of the following actions to ensure that you are investing a high level of effort and energy:

- **Writing.** Write in response to what you're trying to learn. Example: Write notes when reading rather than passively underlining sentences.
- **Speaking.** Say aloud what you're trying to learn. Example: Explain course concepts to a study-group partner rather than studying them silently.
- **Organizing.** Connect or integrate the ideas you're trying to learn.
  Example: Create an outline, diagram, or concept map to visually connect ideas, as illustrated in Figure 1.1.

"Tell me and I'll listen. Show me and I'll understand. Involve me and I'll learn."

—Teton Lakota Indian saying

Student *Perspective*

"You don't have to be smart to work hard."

—24-year-old first-year student who has returned to college

The following section explains how you can apply both key components of active involvement—spending time and expending energy—to the major learning challenges that you will encounter in college.

Time Spent in Class

The total amount of time you spend on learning is associated with how much you learn and how successfully you learn. This association leads to a straightforward recommendation: Attend all class sessions in all your courses. It may be tempting to skip or cut classes because college professors are less likely to monitor your attendance or take roll than your high school teachers. However, don't let this new freedom fool you into thinking that missing classes has no impact on your college grades. Over the past 75 years, many research studies in many types of courses have shown a direct relationship between class attendance and course grades—as one goes up or down, so does the other (Anderson & Gates, 2002; Credé, Roch, & Kieszczynka, 2010; Grandpre, 2000; Kowalewski, Holstein, & Schneider, 1989; Launius, 1997; Shimoff & Catania, 2001). Figure 1.2 represents the results of a study conducted at the City Colleges of Chicago, which shows the relationship between students' class attendance during the first five weeks of the term and their final course grades.

© Lisa F. Young, 2013. Under license from Shutterstock, Inc.

Time Spent on Coursework outside the Classroom

In college, you will spend fewer hours per week sitting in class than you did in high school; however, you will be expected to spend more of your own time on academic work outside of class. Studies clearly show that when college students spend more time on academic work outside of class, it results in better learning and higher grades (National Survey of Student Engagement, 2009). For example, one study of more than 25,000 college students found that the percentage of students receiving mostly "A" grades was almost three times higher for students who spent 40 or more hours per week on academic work than it was for students who spent between 20 and 40

Student Perspective

"My biggest recommendation: GO TO CLASS. I learned this the hard way my first semester. You'll be surprised what you pick up just by being there. I wish someone would have informed me of this before I started school."

—Advice to new students from a college sophomore (Walsh, 2005)

Student Perspective

"In high school, you were a dork if you got good grades and cared about what was going on in your class. In college, you're a dork if you don't."

—College sophomore (Appleby, 2008)

FIGURE 1.2

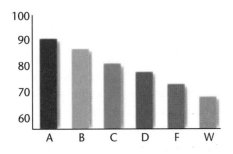

Relationship between Class Attendance Rate and Course Final Grades

hours. Among students who spent 20 or fewer hours per week on academic work, the percentage receiving grades of mostly "C" or below was almost twice as high as it was for students who spent 40 or more hours on academic work (Pace, 1990; 1995).

Unfortunately, less than 40 percent of beginning college students report having studied for six or more hours per week during their final year in high school (Pryor, De Angelo, Palucki-Blake, Hurtado, & Tran, 2012), and only one-third expect to spend more than 20 hours per week preparing for class in college (National Survey of Student Engagement, 2009). Also, less than 10 percent say they will study for at least two hours out of class for every hour spent in class, which is what most college faculty believe is necessary to do well in college (Kuh, 2005). This has to change if new college students are to earn good grades. Just as successful athletes need to put in time and often work hard to improve their physical performance, successful students need to do the same to improve their academic performance.

If you need further motivation to achieve good grades, keep in mind that higher grades earned in college are related to higher prospects for career success after college. Research on college graduates indicates that the higher their grades were in college, the higher: (1) their annual salary, (2) the status (prestige) of their first job, (3) their career mobility (ability to change jobs or move into different positions). This relationship between college grades and career advantages exists for students at all types of colleges and universities, regardless of the reputation or prestige of the institution that the students are attending (Pascarella & Terenzini, 1991; 2005). In other words, how well you do academically in college matters more to your career success than where you went to college.

Student *Perspective*

"I thought I would get a better education if the school had a really good reputation. Now, I think one's education depends on how much effort you put into it."

—First-year college student

Reflection **1.2**

During your senior year of high school, how many hours per week did you spend on schoolwork outside of class?

Active Listening and Note Taking

You'll find that college professors rely heavily on the lecture method—they profess their knowledge by speaking for long stretches of time, and the students' job is to listen and take notes on the knowledge they dispense. This method of instruction places great demands on your ability to listen carefully and take notes that are both accurate and complete.

Student *Perspective*

"I never had a class before where the teacher just stands up and talks to you. He says something and you're writing it down, but then he says something else."

—First-year college student (Erickson & Strommer, 2006)

"All genuine learning is active, not passive. It is a process in which the student is the main agent, not the teacher."

—Mortimer Adler, American professor of philosophy and educational theorist

> **Remember**
>
> *Research shows that, in all subject areas, most test questions on college exams come from the professor's lectures, and that students who take better class notes get better course grades (Brown, 1988; Cuseo, Fecas, & Thompson, 2007; Kiewra, 2000).*

The best way to apply the principle of active involvement during a class lecture is to engage in the physical action of writing notes. Writing down what your instructor is saying in class "forces" you to pay closer attention to what is being said and reinforces your retention of what was said. By taking notes, you not only hear the information (auditory memory), you also see it on paper (visual memory) and feel it in the muscles of your hand as you write it (motor memory).

Remember

Your role in the college classroom is not to be a passive spectator or an absorbent sponge that sits back and simply soaks up information through osmosis. Instead, your role is more like that of an aggressive detective or investigative reporter who's on a search-and-record mission. You need to actively search for information by picking your instructor's brain, picking out your instructor's key points, and recording your "pickings" in your notebook.

See **Do It Now! 1.1** for top strategies on classroom listening and note taking that you can put into action right now.

1.1 DO IT NOW !

Listening and Note Taking

One task that you'll be expected to perform at the start of your first term in college is taking notes in class. Studies show that professors' lecture notes are the number one source of test questions (and test answers) on college exams. Get off to a fast start by using the following strategies to improve the quality of your note taking:

© Joanne Harris and Daniel Bubnich, 2013. Under license from Shutterstock, Inc.

1. **Get to every class.** Whether or not your instructors take roll, you're responsible for all material covered in class. Remember that a full load of college courses (15 units) only requires that you be in class about 13 hours per week. If you consider your class work to be a full-time job, any job that requires you to show up for about 13 hours a week is a pretty sweet deal. It's a deal that supplies you with much more educational freedom than you had in high school. To miss a class session in college when you're required to spend so little time in class per week is an abuse of this educational freedom. It's also an abuse of the money you, your family, or taxpaying American citizens pay to support your college education.

2. **Get to every class on time.** During the first few minutes of a class session, instructors often share valuable information, such as reminders, reviews, and previews.

3. **Get organized.** Bring the right equipment to class. Get a separate notebook for each class, write your name on it, date each class session, and store all class handouts in it.

4. **Get in the right position.**
   - The ideal place to sit is in the front and center of the room, where you're in the best position to hear and see what's going on.
   - The ideal posture is upright and leaning forward, because your body influences your mind. If your body is in an alert and ready position, your mind is likely to follow.
   - The ideal social position is to be near people who will not distract you or detract from the quality of your note taking.

   Remember

   These attention-focusing strategies are particularly important during the first year of college, when class sizes tend to be larger. In a large class, students tend to feel more anonymous, which can reduce their sense of personal responsibility and their drive to stay focused and actively involved. Thus, in large class settings, it's especially important to use effective strategies that eliminate distractions and attention drift (such as those described in Chapter 5).

5. **Get in the right frame of mind.** Get psyched up; come to class with attitude—an attitude that you're going to pick your instructor's brain, pick up answers to test questions, and build up your course grade.

6. **Get it down (in writing).** Actively look, listen, and record important points at all times in class. Pay special attention to whatever information instructors put in writing, whether it is on the board, on a slide, or in a handout.

7. **Don't let go of your pen.** When in doubt, write it out; it's better to have it and not need it than to need it and not have it.

(continued)

8. **Finish strong.** During the last few minutes of class, instructors often share valuable information, such as reminders, reviews, and previews.

Remember
Most college professors do not write all important information on the board for you; instead, they expect you to listen carefully to what they're saying and write it down for yourself.

9. **Stick around.** When class ends, don't immediately bolt; instead, hang out for a few moments and quickly review your notes (by yourself or with a classmate). If you find any gaps, check them out with your instructor before the instructor leaves the classroom. This quick end-of-class review will help your brain retain the information it just received.

Note: For more detailed information on listening and note taking, see Chapter 5.

Finish class with a rush of attention, not a rush out the door!

Active Class Participation

You can become actively involved in the college classroom by arriving at class prepared (e.g., having done the assigned reading), by asking relevant questions, and by contributing thoughtful comments during class discussions. When you communicate orally, you elevate your level of active involvement in the learning process because speaking requires you to exert both mental energy (thinking about what you are going to say) and physical energy (moving your lips to say it). Thus, class participation will increase your ability to stay alert and attentive in class. It also sends a clear message to the instructor that you are a motivated student who takes the course seriously and wants to learn. Since class participation accounts for a portion of your final grade in many courses, your attentiveness and involvement in class can have a direct, positive effect on your final grade.

Reflection **1.3**

When you enter a classroom, where do you usually sit?

Why do you sit there? Is it a conscious choice or more like an automatic habit?

Do you think that your usual seat places you in the best possible position for listening and learning in the classroom?

Active Reading

Writing not only promotes active listening in class but also can promote active reading out of class. Taking notes on information that you're reading (or on information you've highlighted while reading) keeps you actively involved in the reading process because it requires more mental and physical energy than merely reading the material or passively highlighting sentences. (See Do It Now! 1.2 for top tips on reading college textbooks that you can put into practice immediately.)

1.2   DO IT **NOW** !

Top Strategies: Improving Textbook Reading Comprehension and Retention

If you haven't already acquired textbooks for your courses, get them immediately and get ahead on your reading assignments. Information from reading assignments ranks right behind lecture notes as a source of test questions on college exams. Your professors are likely to deliver class lectures with the expectation that you have done the assigned reading and can build on that knowledge when they're lecturing. If you haven't done the reading, you'll have more difficulty following and taking notes on what your instructor is saying in class. Thus, by not doing the reading you pay a double penalty: You miss information that will appear directly on course exams, and you miss information delivered by your instructor in class because you don't have the background knowledge to make sense of it. College professors also expect you to relate or connect what they talk about in class to the

reading they have assigned. Thus, it's important to start developing good reading habits now. You can do so by using the following strategies to improve your reading comprehension and retention.

Student *Perspective*

"I recommend that you read the first chapters right away because college professors get started promptly with assigning certain readings. Classes in college move very fast because, unlike high school, you do not attend class five times a week but two or three times a week."

—Advice to new college students from a first-year student

(continued)

1. **Read with the right equipment.**
   - Bring tools to record and store information. Always bring a writing tool (pen or pencil) to record important information and a storage space (notebook or laptop) in which you can save and retrieve information acquired from your reading for later use on tests and assignments.
   - Have a dictionary nearby to quickly find the meaning of unfamiliar words that may interfere with your ability to comprehend what you're reading. Looking up definitions of unfamiliar words does more than help you understand what you're reading: it's also an effective way to build your vocabulary. A strong vocabulary will improve your reading comprehension in all college courses, as well as your performance on standardized tests, such as those required for admission to graduate and professional schools.
   - Check the back of your textbook for a list of key terms included in the book. Each academic subject or discipline has its own vocabulary, and knowing the meaning of these terms is often the key to understanding the concepts covered in the text. Don't ignore the glossary; it's more than an ancillary or afterthought to the textbook. Use it regularly to increase your comprehension of course concepts. Consider making a photocopy of the glossary of terms at the back of your textbook so that you can have a copy of it in front of you while you're reading, rather than having to repeatedly stop, hold your place, and go to the back of the text to find the glossary.

2. **Get in the right position.** Sit upright and have light coming from behind you, over the side of your body opposite your writing hand. This will reduce the distracting and fatiguing effects of glare and shadows.

3. **Get a sneak preview.** Approach the chapter by first reading its boldface headings and any chapter outline, summary, or end-of-chapter questions that may be provided. This will supply you with a mental map of the chapter's important ideas before you start your reading trip and provide an overview that will help you keep track of the chapter's major ideas (the "big picture"), reducing the risk that you'll get lost among the smaller details you encounter along the way.

4. **Use boldface headings and subheadings.** Headings are cues for important information. Turn them into questions, and then read to find their answers. This will launch you on an answer-finding mission that will keep you mentally active while reading and enable you to read with a purpose. Turning headings into questions is also a good way to prepare for tests because you're practicing exactly what you'll be expected to do on tests—answer questions.

5. **Pay attention to the first and last sentences.** Absorb opening and closing sentences in sections beneath the chapter's major headings and subheadings. These sentences often contain an important introduction and conclusion to the material covered in that section of the text.

6. **Finish each of your reading sessions with a short review.** Recall what you have highlighted or noted as important information (rather than trying to cover a few more pages). It's best to use the last few minutes of reading time to "lock in" the most important information you've just read because most forgetting takes place immediately after you stop processing (taking in) information and start doing something else.

> **Remember**
>
> *Your goal while reading should be to discover or uncover the most important information, and the final step in the reading process is to review (and lock in) the most important information you discovered.*

Note: More detailed information on reading comprehension and retention is provided in Chapter 5.

> **Remember**
>
> *Involvement with campus services is not just valuable, it's also "free"—the cost of these services has already been covered by your college tuition. By investing time and energy in campus resources, you not only increase your prospects for personal success but also maximize the return on your financial investment in college—you get a bigger bang for your buck.*

Touching the Second Base of College Success: Use of Campus Resources

Your campus environment contains multiple resources designed to support your quest for educational and personal success. Studies show that students who take advantage of campus resources report higher levels of satisfaction with college and get more out of the college experience (Pascarella & Terenzini, 1991, 2005).

Using your campus resources is an important, research-backed principle of college success, and it is a natural extension of the principle of active involvement. Successful students are active learners not only inside the classroom, but outside of class as well. Active involvement outside of class includes making use of campus resources.

An essential first step in making effective use of campus resources is to become aware of what they are and what they're designed to do.

The following sections describe what key campus services are offered on most college campuses and why they should be utilized.

Learning Center (a.k.a. Academic Support or Academic Success Center)

This is your campus resource for strengthening your academic performance. The individual and group tutoring provided by this campus service can help you master difficult course concepts and assignments, and the people working here are professionally trained to help you learn how to learn. While your professors may have expert knowledge of the subject matter they teach, learning resource specialists are experts on the process of learning. These specialists can equip you with effective learning strategies and show you how you can adjust or modify your learning strategies to meet the unique demands of different courses and teaching styles you encounter in college.

Studies show that college students who become actively involved with academic support services outside the classroom are more likely to attain higher grades and complete their college degree, particularly if they begin their involvement with these support services during the first year of college (Cuseo, 2003). Also, students who seek and receive assistance from the Learning Center show significant improvement in academic self-efficacy—that is, they develop a stronger sense of personal control over their academic performance and higher expectations for academic success (Smith, Walter, & Hoey, 1992).

Despite the powerful advantages of using academic support services, these services are typically underused by college students, especially by those students who need them the most (Cuseo, 2003; Knapp & Karabenick, 1988; Walter & Smith, 1990). Some students believe that seeking academic help is admitting they are not smart, self-sufficient, or unable to succeed on their own. Do not buy into this belief system. Using academic support services doesn't mean you're helpless or clueless; instead, it indicates that you're a motivated and resourceful student who is striving to achieve academic excellence.

> **Remember**
> *The Learning Center or Academic Support Center is a place where all learners benefit!*

Writing Center

Many college campuses offer specialized support for students who would like to improve their writing skills. Typically referred to as the Writing Center, this is the place where you can receive assistance at any stage of the writing process, whether it be collecting and organizing your ideas, composing your first draft, or proofreading your final draft. Since writing is an academic skill that you will use in many of your courses, if you improve your writing, you're likely to improve your overall academic performance. Thus, we strongly encourage you to capitalize on this campus resource.

"Do not be a PCP (Parking Lot→ Classroom→ Parking Lot) student. The time you spend on campus will be a sound investment in your academic and professional success."
—Drew Appleby, professor of psychology

"The impact of college is not simply the result of what a college does for or to a student. Rather, the impact is a result of the extent to which an individual student exploits the people, programs, facilities, opportunities, and experiences that the college makes available."
—Ernest Pascarella and Patrick Terenzini, *How College Affects Students*

Student Perspective

"Where I learn the material best is tutoring because they go over it and if you have questions, you can ask, you can stop, they have time for you. They make time."
—First-year college student

"At colleges where I've taught, it's always been found that the grade point average of students who use the Learning Center is higher than the college average and honors students are more likely to use the center than other students."
—Joe Cuseo, professor of psychology and lead author of this text

Disability Services (a.k.a. Office for Students with Special Needs)

If you have a physical or learning disability that is interfering with your performance in college, or think you may have such a disability, Disability Services is the campus resource to consult for assistance and support. Programs and services typically provided by this office include:

- Assessment for learning disabilities;
- Verification of eligibility for disability support services;
- Authorization of academic accommodations for students with disabilities; and
- Specialized counseling, advising, and tutoring.

College Library

"The next best thing to knowing something is knowing where to find it."

—Dr. Samuel Johnson, English literary figure and original author of the *Dictionary of the English Language* (1747)

The library is your campus resource for finding information and completing research assignments (e.g., term papers and group projects). Librarians are professional educators who provide instruction outside the classroom. You can learn from them just as you can learn from faculty inside the classroom. Furthermore, the library is a place where you can acquire skills for locating, retrieving, and evaluating information that you may apply to any course you are taking or will ever take.

Your college library is your campus resource for developing research skills that let you access, retrieve, and evaluate information, which are skills for achieving both educational and occupational success.

Academic Advising Center

Whether or not you have an assigned academic advisor, the Academic Advising Center is a campus resource for help with course selection, educational planning, and choosing or changing a major. Studies show that college students who have developed clear educational and career goals are more likely to persist in college until they complete their college degree (Willingham, 1985; Wyckoff, 1999). Research indicates that beginning college students need help clarifying their educational goals, selecting an academic major, and exploring careers (Cuseo, 2005; Frost, 1991). As a first-year college student, being undecided or uncertain about your educational and career goals is nothing to be embarrassed about. However, you should start thinking about your future now. Connect early and often with an academic advisor to help you clarify your educational goals and find a field of study that best complements your interests, talents, and values.

Office of Student Life

The Office of Student Life is your campus resource for student development opportunities outside the classroom, including student clubs and organizations, recreational programs, leadership activities, and volunteer experiences. Research consistently shows that experiential learning that takes place outside the classroom is as important to your personal development and future success as learning from course work (Kuh, 1995; Kuh, Douglas, Lund, & Ramin-Gyurnek, 1994; Pascarella & Terenzini, 2005). (This is why they are referred to as "co-curricular experiences" rather than "extracurricular activities.") More specifically, studies show students who become actively involved in campus life are more likely to:

- Enjoy their college experience;
- Graduate from college; and
- Develop leadership skills that enhance career performance beyond college (Astin, 1993).

Devoting some out-of-class time to these co-curricular experiences should not interfere with your academic performance. Keep in mind that in college you'll be spending much less time in the classroom than you did in high school. As mentioned previously, a full load of college courses (15 units) only requires that you be in class about 13 hours per week. This should leave you with enough time to become involved in learning experiences on campus. Evidence indicates that college students who become involved in co-curricular, volunteer, and part-time work experiences that total *no more than 15 hours per week* earn higher grades than students who do not get involved in any out-of-class activities (Pascarella, 2001; Pascarella & Terenzini, 2005).

Although it is important to get involved in co-curricular experiences on your campus, limit your involvement to no more than two or three major campus organizations at any one time. Restricting the number of your out-of-class activities should enable you to keep up with your studies; it will be more impressive to future schools or employers because a long list of involvement in numerous activities may suggest you're padding your resume with things you did superficially (or never really did at all).

"Just a [long] list of club memberships is meaningless; it's a fake front. Remember that quality, not quantity, is what counts."

—Lauren Pope, director of the National Bureau for College Placement

Financial Aid Office

This campus resource is designed to help you finance your college education. If you have questions concerning how to obtain assistance in paying for college, the staff of this office is there to guide you through the application process. The paperwork needed to apply for and secure financial aid can sometimes be confusing or overwhelming. Don't let this intimidate you enough to prevent you from seeking financial aid; assistance is available to you from the knowledgeable staff in the Financial Aid Office. You can also seek help from this office to find:

- Part-time employment on campus through a work-study program;
- Low-interest student loans;
- Grants; and
- Scholarships.

If you have any doubt about whether you are using the most effective plan for financing your college education, make an appointment to see a professional in your Financial Aid Office.

Remember

Co-curricular experiences are also resume-building experiences, and campus professionals with whom you interact regularly while participating in co-curricular activities (e.g., the director of student activities or dean of students) are valuable resources for personal references and letters of recommendation to future schools or employers.

Counseling Center

Counseling services can provide you with a valuable source of support in college, not only for helping you cope with the stress associated with the transition to college, but also by helping you gain self-awareness and reach your full potential. Personal counseling can promote your self-awareness and self-development in social and emotional areas of your life that are important for mental health, wellness, and personal growth.

Health Center

Making the transition from high school to college often involves adjustments and decisions affecting your health and wellness. Good health habits help you cope with stress and reach peak levels of performance. The Health Center on your campus is the resource for information on how to manage your physical health and maintain wellness. It is also the place to go for help with illnesses, sexually transmitted infections or diseases, and eating or nutritional disorders.

Career Development Center (a.k.a. Career Center)

Research on college students indicates that they are more likely to stay in school and graduate when they have some sense of how their present academic experience relates to their future career goals (Levitz & Noel, 1989; Tinto, 1993; Wyckoff, 1999). Studies also show that most new students are uncertain about what career they would like to pursue (Gordon & Steele, 2003). So, if you are uncertain about your future career, welcome to the club that includes a very large number of other first-year students. This uncertainty is normal because you haven't had the opportunity for hands-on work experience in the real world of careers.

The Career Development Center is the place to go for help in finding a meaningful answer to the important question of how to connect your current college experience with your future career goals. This campus resource typically provides such services as personal career counseling, workshops on career exploration and development, and career fairs where you are able to meet professionals working in different fields. Although it may seem like the beginning of your career is light-years away because you're just beginning college, the process of exploring, planning, and preparing for career success starts in the first year of college.

> "The college years are an important growing period in which new social and intellectual experiences are sought as a means of coming to grips with the issue of adult careers. Students enter college with the hope that they will be able to formulate for themselves a meaningful answer to that important question."
>
> —Vincent Tinto, nationally known scholar on student success

Touching the Third Base of College Success: Interpersonal Interaction and Collaboration

Learning is strengthened when it takes place in a social context that involves interpersonal interaction. As some scholars put it, human knowledge is "socially constructed" or built up through interpersonal interaction and dialogue. According to these scholars, your conversations with others become internalized as ideas in your mind and influence your way of thinking (Bruffee, 1993; Johnson, Johnson, & Smith, 1998). Thus, by having frequent, intelligent conversations with others, you broaden your knowledge and deepen your thinking.

Reflection **1.4**

Look back at the major campus resources that have been mentioned in this section. Which two or three of them do you think you should use *immediately*?

Why have you identified these resources as your top priorities right now?

Ask your course instructor for recommendations about what campus resources you should consult during your first term on campus. Compare their recommendations with your selections.

Four particular forms of interpersonal interaction have been found to be strongly associated with student learning and motivation in college:

1. Student-faculty interaction
2. Student-advisor interaction
3. Student-mentor interaction
4. Student-student (peer) interaction

Interacting with Faculty Members

Studies repeatedly show that college success is strongly influenced by the quality and quantity of student-faculty interaction *outside the classroom.* Such contact is associated with the following positive outcomes for college students:

- Improved academic performance;
- Increased critical thinking skills;
- Greater satisfaction with the college experience;
- Increased likelihood of completing a college degree; and
- Stronger desire to seek education beyond college (Astin, 1993; Pascarella & Terenzini, 1991; 2005).

These positive outcomes are so strong and widespread that we encourage you to immediately begin seeking interaction with college faculty outside of class time. Here are some of the easiest ways to do so.

1. **Seek contact with your instructors immediately after class.** If you are interested in talking about something that was discussed in class, approach your instructor as soon as the class session ends. Interaction with instructors immediately after class can help them get to know you as an individual, which should increase your confidence and willingness to seek subsequent contact in other settings.

2. **Seek interaction with your course instructors during their office hours.** One of the most important pieces of information on a course syllabus is your instructor's office hours. Make note of them and make an earnest attempt to capitalize on them. College professors specifically reserve out-of-class time for office hours during which they are expected to be available to students. Try to make at least one visit to the office of each of your instructors, preferably early in the term, when quality time is easier to find, rather than at midterm, when major exams and assignments begin to pile up. Even if your early contact with instructors is only for a few minutes, it can be a valuable icebreaker that helps your instructors get to know you as a person and helps you feel more comfortable interacting with them in the future.

3. **Connect with your instructors through e-mail.** Electronic communication is another effective way to interact with an instructor, particularly if that professor's office hours conflict with your class schedule, work responsibilities, or family commitments. If you are a commuter student who does not live on campus, or if you are an adult student juggling family and work commitments along with your

Student *Perspective*

"I wish that I would have taken advantage of professors' open-door policies when I had questions, because actually understanding what I was doing, instead of guessing, would have saved me a lot of stress and re-doing what I did wrong the first time."

—College sophomore (Walsh, 2005)

academic schedule, e-mail communication may be an especially effective and efficient mode of student-faculty interaction. In one national survey, almost half of college students reported that e-mail has allowed them to communicate their ideas with professors on subjects that they would not have discussed in person (Pew Internet & American Life Project, 2002). If you're shy or hesitant about "invading" your professor's office space, e-mail can provide a less threatening way to interact and may give you the self-confidence to eventually seek face-to-face contact with an instructor.

However, you should never e-mail faculty with the following questions after missing class:

- Did I miss anything in class today?
- Could you send me your teaching notes or PowerPoint from the class I missed?

Also, when you are with faculty in the classroom, use the following guidelines with respect to use of personal technology.

Snapshot Summary

1.1

Guidelines for Civil and Responsible Use of Personal Technology in the College Classroom

- Turn your cell phone completely off, or leave it out of the classroom. In the rare case of an emergency when you think you need to leave it on, inform your instructor.
- Don't check your cell phone during the class period by turning it off and on.
- Don't text message during class.
- Don't surf the Web during class.
- Don't touch your cell phone during any exam because this may be viewed by the instructor as a form of cheating.

Interaction with Academic Advisors

An academic advisor may serve as a very effective referral agent who can direct you to, and connect you with, campus support services that can promote your success. An advisor can also help you understand college procedures and navigate the bureaucratic maze of college policies and politics.

Your academic advisor should be someone whom you feel comfortable speaking with, someone who knows your name, and someone who's familiar with your personal interests and abilities. Give your advisor the opportunity to get to know you personally, and seek your advisor's input on courses, majors, and personal issues that may be affecting your academic performance.

Reflection **1.5**

Do you have a personally assigned advisor?

If yes, do you know who this person is and where he or she can be found?

If no, do you know where to go if you have questions about your class schedule or academic plans?

If you have been assigned an advisor and cannot develop a good relationship with this person, ask the director of advising or academic dean if you could be assigned to someone else. Ask other students about their advising experience and whether they know an advisor they can recommend to you.

If your college does not assign you a personal advisor, but offers advising services in an Advising Center on a drop-by or drop-in basis, you may see a different advisor each time you visit the center. If you are not satisfied with this system of multiple advisors, find one advisor with whom you feel most comfortable and make that person your personal advisor by scheduling your appointments in advance. This will enable you to consistently connect with the same advisor and help you develop a close, ongoing relationship with that person.

> **Remember**
>
> *An academic advisor is not someone you see just once per term when you need to get a signature for class scheduling and course registration. Advisors can be much more than course schedulers: they can be mentors. Unlike your course instructors, who will change from term to term, your academic advisor may be the one professional on campus with whom you have regular contact and a stable, ongoing relationship throughout your college experience.*

Interaction with a Mentor

A mentor may be described as an experienced guide who takes personal interest in you and the progress you're making toward your goals. (For example, in the movie *Star Wars*, Yoda served as a mentor for Luke Skywalker.) Research in higher education demonstrates that a mentor can make first-year students feel significant and enable them to stay on track until they complete their college degree (Campbell & Campbell, 1997; Knox, 2004). A mentor can assist you in troubleshooting difficult or complicated issues that you may not be able to resolve on your own and is someone with whom you can share good news, such as your success stories and personal accomplishments. Look for someone on campus with whom you can develop this type of trusting relationship. Many people on campus have the potential to be outstanding mentors, including the following:

- Your academic advisor
- Your instructor in a first-year seminar or experience course
- Faculty in your intended major
- Juniors, seniors, or graduate students in your intended field of study
- Working professionals in careers that interest you
- Academic support professionals (e.g., professional tutors in the Learning Center)
- Career counselors
- Personal counselors
- Learning assistance professionals (e.g., from the Learning Center)
- Student development professionals (e.g., the director of student life or residential life)
- Campus minister or chaplain
- Financial aid counselors

Interaction with Peers (Student-Student Interaction)

Studies repeatedly point to the power of the peer group as a source of social and academic support during the college years (Pascarella, 2005). One study of more than 25,000 college students revealed that when peers interact with one another while learning they achieve higher levels of academic performance and are more likely to persist to degree completion (Astin, 1993). In another study that involved in-depth interviews with more than 1,600 college students, it was discovered that almost all students who struggled academically had one particular study habit in common: They always studied alone (Light, 2001).

Peer interaction is especially important during the first term of college. At this stage of the college experience, new students have a strong need for belonging and social acceptance because many of them have just left the lifelong security of family and hometown friends. As a new student, it may be useful to view the early stage of your college experience through the lens of psychologist Abraham Maslow's hierarchy of human needs (see Figure 1.3). According to Maslow's hierarchy of needs, humans cannot reach their full potential and achieve peak performance until their more basic emotional and social needs have been met (e.g., their needs for personal safety, social acceptance, and self-esteem). Making early connections with your peers helps you meet these basic human needs, provides you with a base of social support to ease your integration into the college community, and prepares you to move up to higher levels of the need hierarchy (e.g., achieving educational excellence and fulfilling your potential).

FIGURE 1.3

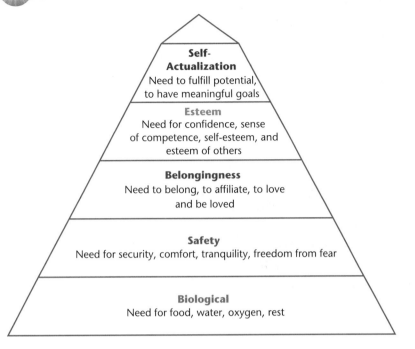

Abraham Maslow's Hierarchy of Needs

Getting involved with campus organizations or activities is one way to connect you with other students. Also, try to interact with students who have spent more time at college than you. Sophomores, juniors, and seniors can be valuable social resources for a new student. You're likely to find that they are willing to share their experiences with you because you have shown an interest in hearing what they have to say. You may be the first person who has ever asked them what their experiences have been like on your campus. You can learn from their experiences by asking them which courses and instructors they would recommend or what advisors they found to be most well informed and personable.

Reflection **1.6**

Think about the students in your classes this term. (1) Are there any students who might be good members to connect with and form learning teams? (2) Do you have any classmates who are currently in more than one class with you and who might be good peer partners to team up with and work together on the courses you have in common?

Remember

Your peers can be more than competitors or a source of negative peer pressure: they can also be collaborators, a source of positive social influence, and a resource for college success. Be on the lookout for classmates who are motivated to learn and willing to learn with you, and keep an eye out for advanced students who are willing to assist you. Start building your social support network by surrounding yourself with success-seeking and success-achieving students. They can be a stimulating source of positive peer power that can drive you to higher levels of academic performance and heighten your drive to complete college.

Collaboration with Peers

Simply defined, collaboration is the process of two or more people working interdependently toward a common goal, rather than working independently or competitively. Collaboration involves true teamwork, in which teammates support each other's success and take equal responsibility for helping the team move toward its shared goal. Research shows that when students collaborate in teams, from kindergarten through college, their academic performance and interpersonal skills improve significantly (Cross, Barkley, & Major, 2005; Cuseo, 1996; Gilles & Adrian, 2003; Johnson et al., 1998).

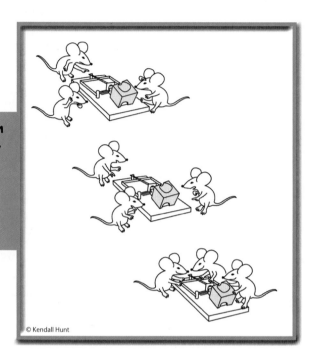

Research shows that when peers work collaboratively to reach a common goal, they learn more effectively and achieve "higher levels" of thinking.

© Kendall Hunt

To maximize the power of collaboration, use the following guidelines to make wise choices about teammates who will contribute positively to the quality and productivity of your learning team:

1. Observe your classmates with an eye toward identifying potentially good teammates. Look for fellow students who are motivated and who will likely contribute to your team's success, rather than those whom you suspect may just be hitchhikers looking for a free ride.
2. Don't team up exclusively with peers who are similar to you in terms of their personal characteristics, backgrounds, and experiences. Instead, include teammates who differ from you in age; gender; ethnic, racial, cultural, or geographical background; learning style; and personality characteristics. Such variety brings different life experiences, styles of thinking, and learning strategies to your team, which enrich not only its diversity but its quality as well. If your team consists only of friends or classmates whose interests and lifestyles are similar to your own, this familiarity can interfere with your team's focus and performance because your common experiences can get you off track and on to topics that have nothing to do with the learning task (e.g., what you did last weekend or what you are planning to do next weekend).

Keep in mind that learning teams are not simply study groups formed the night before an exam. Effective learning teams collaborate more regularly and work on more varied academic tasks than late-night study groups. Following are various types of learning teams that you may join or form to improve your performance on key academic tasks in college.

Note-Taking Teams

Immediately after a class session ends, take a couple of minutes to team up with other students to compare and share notes. Since listening and note taking are demanding tasks, it's likely that a student may pick up an important point that the others overlooked and vice versa. Also, by teaming up immediately after class to review your notes together, your team has the opportunity to consult with the instructor about any missing or confusing information before your instructor leaves the room.

Author's Experience During my first term in college, I was having difficulty taking complete notes in my biology course because the instructor spoke rapidly and with an unfamiliar accent. I noticed another student (Alex) sitting in the front row who was trying to take notes as best he could, but he was experiencing the same difficulty. Following one particularly fast and complex lecture, we looked at each other and noticed that we were both shaking our heads in frustration and began talking about it. We decided to team up immediately after every class and compare our notes to identify points we missed or found confusing. First, we helped each other by comparing and sharing our notes in case one of us got something that the other missed. If there were points that we both missed or couldn't figure out, we went to the front of class together to consult with the instructor before he left the classroom. At the end of the course, Alex and I finished with the highest grades in the course.

Joe Cuseo

Reading Teams

After completing your reading assignments, team up with classmates to compare your highlighting and margin notes. Compare notes on what you identified as the most important points in the reading that should be studied for upcoming exams.

Writing Teams

Students can provide each other with feedback that they can use to revise and improve the quality of their own writing. Studies show that when peers assess each other's writing, the quality of their writing and their attitudes toward writing improve (Topping, 1998). You can form peer writing teams to help at any or all of the following stages in the writing process:

1. **Topic selection and refinement.** To help each other come up with a list of possible topics and subtopics to write about;
2. **Pre-writing.** To clarify your writing purpose and audience;
3. **First draft.** To improve your general writing style and tone; and
4. **Final draft.** To proofread and correct mechanical errors before submitting your written work.

Library Research Teams

Many first-year students are unfamiliar with the process of conducting academic research at a college or university library. Some students experience "library anxiety" and will try to avoid even setting foot in the library, particularly if it's large and intimidating (Malvasi, Rudowsky, & Valencia, 2009). Forming library research teams is an effective way for you to develop a social support group that can make trips to the

"Two heads are better than one, not because either is infallible, but because they are unlikely to go wrong in the same direction."

—C.S. Lewis, English novelist and essayist

library less intimidating and transform library research from a solitary experience into a collaborative venture that's done as a team.

Team-Instructor Conferences

Visiting instructors in their office with other classmates is an effective way to get additional assistance in preparing for exams and completing assignments for the following reasons:

- You're likely to feel more comfortable about venturing onto your instructors' "turf" in the company of peers, rather than entering this unfamiliar territory on your own. As the old expression goes, "There's safety in numbers."
- When you make an office visit as a team, the information shared by the instructor is heard by more than one person, so your teammates may pick up some useful information that you may have missed, misinterpreted, or forgotten to write down (and vice versa).
- You save your instructors time by allowing them to help multiple students at the same time, which reduces the likelihood that they'll have to engage in "repeat performances" for individual students making separate visits at different times.
- You send a message to instructors that you're serious about the course and are a motivated student because you've taken the time—ahead of time—to connect with your peers and prepare for the office visit.

Study Teams

Research clearly demonstrates that college students learn as much from peers as they do from instructors and textbooks (Astin, 1993; Pascarella, 2005). When seniors at Harvard University were interviewed, nearly every one of them who had participated in study groups considered the experience to be crucial to their academic progress and success (Light, 1990, 1992; 2001).

Additional research on study groups indicates that they are effective only if each member has done required course work in advance of the team meeting—for example, if each group member has done the required readings and other course assignments (Light, 2001). Thus, to fully capitalize and maximize the power of study teams, each team member should study individually *before* studying with the group. Each member should come prepared with specific information or answers to share with teammates and specific questions or points of confusion about which they hope to receive help from the team. This ensures that all team members are individually accountable and equally responsible for doing their own learning and contributing to the learning of their teammates.

Test Results-Review and Assignment-Review Teams

After receiving the results of course examinations and assignments, you can collaborate with peers to review your results as a team. When you compare your answers to the answers of other students, you're better able to identify the sources of your mistakes; by seeing the answers of teammates who received maximum credit on certain questions, you get a clearer picture of where you went wrong and what you should do to get it right next time.

Teaming up after tests and assignments early in the term is especially effective because it enables you to get a better idea of what the instructor expects from students throughout the remainder of the course. You can use this information as early feedback to diagnose your mistakes, improve your next performance, and raise your course grade while there's still plenty of time left in the term to do so.

Learning Communities

Your college may offer you the opportunity to participate in a learning community program, in which the same group of students registers for the same block of courses during the same term. If this opportunity is available to you, try to take advantage of it because research suggests that students who participate in learning community programs are more likely to:

- Become actively involved in classroom learning,
- Form their own learning groups outside of class,
- Report greater intellectual gains, and
- Continue their college education (Tinto, 1997; 2000).

If learning community programs are not offered on your campus, consider creating smaller, more informal learning communities on your own by finding other first-year students who are likely to be taking the same courses as you (e.g., the same general education or pre-major courses). Team up with these students during registration to see if you can enroll in the same two or three courses together. This will allow you to reap the benefits of a learning community, even though your college may not offer a formal learning-community program.

Studies repeatedly show that students who become socially integrated or connected with other members of the college community are more likely to complete their first year of college and continue on to complete their college degree (Tinto, 1993; Pascarella & Terenzini, 2005). (For effective ways to make these interpersonal connections, see Do It Now! 1.3.)

1.3   **DO IT NOW!**

Making Connections with Members of Your College Community

Consider these top 10 tips for making important interpersonal connections in college. Start making these connections now so that you can begin constructing a base of social support that will strengthen your performance during your first term and, perhaps, throughout your college experience.

1. Connect with a peer or student development professional whom you may have met during orientation.
2. Connect with peers who live near you or who commute to school from the same community in which you live. If your schedules are similar, consider carpooling together.
3. Join a college club, student organization, campus committee, intramural team, or volunteer service group whose members may share the same personal or career interests as you. If you can't find a club or organization you were hoping to join, consider starting it on your own. For example, if you're an English major, consider starting a writing club or a book club.
4. Connect with a peer leader who has been trained to assist new students (e.g., peer tutor, peer mentor, or peer counselor) or with a peer who has more college experience than you (e.g., sophomore, junior, or senior).
5. Connect with classmates and team up with them to take notes, complete reading assignments, and study for exams. (Look especially to team up with a peer who may be in more than one class with you.)

(continued)

6. Connect with faculty members, particularly in a field that you're considering as a major, by visiting them during office hours, conversing briefly with them after class, or communicating with them via e-mail.

7. Connect with an academic support professional in your college's Learning Center for personalized academic assistance or tutoring related to any course in which you'd like to improve your performance.

8. Connect with an academic advisor to discuss and develop your educational plans.

9. Connect with a college librarian to get early assistance and a head start on any research project that you've been assigned.

10. Connect with a personal counselor or campus minister to discuss any college adjustment or personal life issues that you may be experiencing.

Note: For more information on meeting people and forming friendships, see Chapter 9.

Reflection **1.7**

Four categories of people have the potential to serve as mentors for you in college:

1. Experienced peers

2. Faculty (instructors)

3. Administrators (e.g., office and program directors)

4. Staff (e.g., student support professionals and administrative assistants)

Think about your first interactions with faculty, staff, and administrators on campus. Do you recall anyone who impressed you as being approachable, personable, and helpful? If you did, make a note of the person's name in case you'd like to seek out that person again. (If you haven't met such a person yet, when you do, be sure you remember who it is, because that person may be someone who can serve as a mentor for you.)

Touching the Fourth (Home) Base of College Success: Personal Reflection and Self-Awareness

The final step in the learning process, whether it be learning in the classroom or learning from experience, is to step back from the process, thoughtfully review it, and connect it to what you already know. Reflection may be defined as the flip side of active involvement; both processes are necessary for learning to be complete. Learning requires not only effortful action but also thoughtful reflection. Active involvement gets and holds your focus of *attention*, which enables information to reach your brain, and personal reflection promotes *consolidation*, which locks that information into your brain's long-term memory (Bligh, 2000; Roediger, Dudai, & Fitzpatrick, 2007).

Brain research reveals that different brain wave patterns are associated with the mental states of involvement and reflection (Bradshaw, 1995). In Figure 1.4, the pattern on the left shows the brain waves of someone who is actively involved in the learning task and attending to it. The pattern on the right shows the brain waves of someone who is thinking deeply about information that has been attended to and taken in, which will help consolidate or lock that information into the person's long-term memory. Thus, effective learning combines active mental involvement (characterized by high-amplitude "beta" brain waves) with thoughtful reflection (characterized by high-frequency "alpha" brain waves—similar to someone in a meditative state).

Reflection 1.8

Think about the students in your classes this term. Are there any students whom you might want to join with to form learning teams?

Do you have any classmates who are in more than one class with you and who might be good peer partners for the courses you have in common?

Personal reflection also involves introspection—turning inward and inspecting yourself to gain deeper *self-awareness* of what you've done, what you're doing, or what you intend to do. Two forms of self-awareness are particularly important for success in college:

1. Self-assessment
2. Self-monitoring

Self-Assessment

Simply defined, self-assessment is the process of reflecting on and evaluating characteristics of your "self," such as your personality traits, learning habits, personal strengths, and personal weaknesses that need improvement. Self-assessment is the critical first step in the process of self-improvement, personal planning, and effective decision making. The following are important target areas for self-assessment because they reflect personal characteristics that play a pivotal role in promoting success in college and beyond:

- **Personal interests.** What you like to do or enjoy doing.
- **Personal values.** What is important to you and what you care about doing.

"We learn to do neither by thinking nor by doing; we learn to do by thinking about what we are doing."

—George Stoddard, professor emeritus, University of Iowa

FIGURE 1.4

High-Amplitude Brain Waves Associated with a Mental State of *Active Involvement.*

High-Frequency Brain Waves Associated with a Mental State of *Reflective Thinking.*

- **Personal abilities or aptitudes.** What you do well or have the potential to do well.
- **Learning habits.** How you go about learning and the usual approaches, methods, or techniques you use to learn.
- **Learning styles.** How you prefer to learn—the way you like to:
  - Receive information—the learning format you prefer (e.g., learning by reading, listening, or experiencing);
  - Perceive information—what sensory modality you prefer to use (e.g., vision, sound, or touch);
  - Process information—how you prefer to deal with or think about information you've taken in (e.g., whether you like to think about it on your own or discuss it with others).
- **Personality traits.** Your temperament, emotional characteristics, and social tendencies (e.g., whether you lean toward being outgoing or reserved);
- **Academic self-concept.** What kind of student you think you are and how you perceive yourself as a learner (e.g., your level of self-confidence and whether you believe academic success is within your control or depends on factors beyond your control).

Reflection **1.9**

How would you rate your academic self-confidence at this point in your college experience? (Circle one.)

very confident   somewhat confident
somewhat unconfident   very unconfident

Why did you make this choice?

"Successful students know a lot about themselves."

—Claire Weinstein and Debra Meyer, professors of educational psychology at the University of Texas

Student *Perspectives*

"I wasn't sure what this class was about. Now I understand this class and I really like it. I learned a lot about myself."

"In the start of the semester I thought this class would be a waste of time and busy work. But I realized it is an important way of learning who and what you are . . . I underestimated this class."

—Comments made by first-year students when evaluating their first-year experience course

Self-Monitoring

Research indicates that one characteristic of successful learners is that they monitor or watch themselves and maintain self-awareness of:

- Whether they're using effective learning strategies (e.g., they are aware of their level of attention or concentration in class);
- Whether they're comprehending what they are attempting to learn (e.g., if they're understanding it at a deep level or merely memorizing it at a surface level); and
- How to regulate or adjust their learning strategies to meet the demands of different academic tasks and subjects (e.g., they read technical material in a science textbook more slowly and stop to test their understanding more often than when they're reading a novel; Pintrich, 1995; Pintrich & Schunk, 2002; Weinstein, 1994; Weinstein & Meyer, 1991).

Remember

Successful students are self-aware learners who know their learning strategies, styles, strengths, and shortcomings.

You can begin to establish good self-monitoring habits by creating a routine of periodically pausing to reflect on the strategies you're using to learn and "do" college. For instance, you can ask yourself the following questions:

- Am I listening attentively to what my instructor is saying in class?
- Do I comprehend what I am reading outside of class?
- Am I effectively using campus resources that are designed to support my success?
- Am I interacting with campus professionals who can contribute to my current success and future development?
- Am I interacting and collaborating with peers who can contribute to my learning and increase my level of involvement in the college experience?
- Am I effectively implementing the success strategies identified in this book?

> **Remember**
> *Successful students and successful people are mindful—they watch what they're doing and remain aware of whether they're doing it effectively and to the best of their ability.*

Reflection 1.10

How would you rate your academic self-confidence at this point in your college experience? (Circle one.)

very confident   somewhat confident
somewhat unconfident   very unconfident

Why?

© Robert Kneschke, 2013. Under license from Shutterstock, Inc.

Summary and Conclusion

Research reviewed in this chapter points to the conclusion that successful students are:

1. **Involved.** They invest time and effort in the college experience;
2. **Resourceful.** They capitalize on their surrounding resources;
3. **Interactive.** They interact and collaborate with others; and
4. **Reflective.** They are self-aware learners who assess and monitor their own performance.

Successful students are students who could honestly check almost every box in the following self-assessment checklist of success-promoting principles and practices.

A Checklist of Success-Promoting Principles and Practices

1. **Active Involvement**
   Inside the classroom, I:

   ☑ **Get to class.** Treat it like a job; if you cut, your pay (grade) will be cut.
   ☑ **Get involved in class.** Come prepared, listen actively, take notes, and participate.

   Outside the classroom, I:

   ☑ **Read actively.** Take notes while you read to increase attention and retention.

☑ **Double up.** Spend twice as much time on academic work outside the classroom than you spend in class—if you're a full-time student, that makes it a 40-hour academic workweek (with occasional "overtime").

2. **Use of Campus Resources**
   I capitalize on academic and student support services, such as the following:
   ☑ Learning Center
   ☑ Writing Center
   ☑ Disability Services
   ☑ College library
   ☑ Academic Advising Center
   ☑ Office of Student Life
   ☑ Financial Aid Office
   ☑ Counseling Center
   ☑ Health Center
   ☑ Career Development Center
   ☑ Experiential Learning Resources

3. **Interpersonal Interaction and Collaboration**
   I interact with the following people:
   ☑ **Peers.** I join student clubs and participate in campus organizations.
   ☑ **Faculty members.** I connect with professors and other faculty members immediately after class, in their offices, or via e-mail.
   ☑ **Academic advisors.** I see an advisor for more than just course registration. I've found an advisor with whom I can relate and develop an ongoing relationship.
   ☑ **Mentors.** I try to find experienced people on campus who can serve as trusted guides and role models.
   I collaborate by doing the following:
   ☑ **Forming learning teams.** I join not only last-minute study groups but also teams that collaborate more regularly to work on such tasks as taking lecture notes, completing reading and writing assignments, conducting library research, and reviewing results of exams or course assignments.
   ☑ **Participating in learning communities.** I enroll in two or more classes with the same students during the same term.

4. **Personal Reflection and Self-Awareness**
   I engage in:
   ☑ **Self-Assessment.** I reflect on and evaluate my personal traits, habits, strengths, and weaknesses.
   ☑ **Self-Monitoring.** I maintain self-awareness of how I'm learning in college and whether I'm using effective strategies that will enable me to do college well.

Reflection 1.11

Before exiting this chapter, look back at the Checklist of Success-Promoting Principles and Practices and see how these ideas compare with those you recorded at the start of this chapter, when we asked you how you thought college would be different from high school and what it would take to be successful in college.

What ideas from your list and our checklist tend to match?

Were there any ideas on your list that were not on ours, or vice versa?

Learning More through the World Wide Web

Internet-Based Resources for Further Information on Liberal Arts Education

For additional information related to promoting your success in college, we recommend the following Web sites:

www.cgcc.cc.or.us/StudentServices/TipsCollegeSuccess.cfm

www.dartmouth.edu/~acskills/success/

www.studygs.net

1.1 Birds of a Different Feather: High School versus College

Read the following list of differences between high school and college and rate each difference on a scale from 1 to 4 in terms of how aware you were of this difference when you began college (1 = totally unaware; 2 = not fully aware; 3 = somewhat aware, 4 = totally aware)

Class schedules are typically made for high school students.

College students make their own class schedules, either on their own or in consultation with an academic advisor.

Awareness Rating _____

High school classes are scheduled back-to-back at the same time every day with short breaks in between.

Larger time gaps can occur between college classes, and they are scheduled at various times throughout the day (and night).

Awareness Rating _____

Class attendance in high school is mandatory and checked daily.

Class attendance in college is not mandatory; in many classes, attendance is not even taken.

Awareness Rating _____

> "In college, if you don't go to class, that's you. Your professor doesn't care really if you pass or fail."
> —First-year student (Engle, Bermeo, & O'Brien, 2006).

High school teachers often write all important information they cover in class on the board.

College professors frequently expect students to write down important information contained in their lectures without explicitly writing it on the board or including it on PowerPoint slides.

Awareness Rating _____

High school teachers often re-teach material in class that students were assigned to read.

College professors often do not teach the same material covered in assigned reading and information from the assigned reading still appears on exams.

Awareness Rating _____

High school teachers often take class time to remind students of assignments and their due dates.

College professors list their assignments and due dates on the course syllabus and expect students to keep track of them on their own.

Awareness Rating _____

> "College teachers don't tell you what you're supposed to do. They just expect you to do it. High school teachers tell you about five times what you're supposed to do."
> —College sophomore (Appleby, 2008)

Homework assignments (e.g., math problems) in high school are typically turned in to the teacher, who checks and grades the students' work.

Assigned work in college often is not turned in to be checked or graded; students are expected to have the self-discipline to do the work on their own.

Awareness Rating _____

High school students spend most of their learning time in class; they spend much less time studying outside of class than they spend in class.

College students typically spend no more than 15 hours per week in class and are expected to spend at least two hours studying out of class for every hour they spend in class.

Awareness Rating _____

Tests in high school often take place frequently and cover limited amounts of material. College exams are given less frequently (e.g., midterm and final) and tend to cover large amounts of material.

Awareness Rating _____

Make-up tests and extra-credit opportunities are often available to students in high school.

In college, if an exam or assignment is missed, rarely do students have a chance to make it up or to recapture lost points through extra-credit work.

Awareness Rating _____

A grade of "D" in high school is still passing.

In college, a grade point average below "C" puts a student on academic probation, and if it doesn't improve to C or higher, the student may be academically dismissed.

Awareness Rating _____

> "In high school, they're like, 'Okay, well, I'll give you another day to do it.' In college, you have to do it that day . . . and the teachers are like, 'If you don't do it, that's your problem.'"
>
> —First-year student (Engle, Bermeo, & O'Brien, 2006)

In high school, students go to offices of campuses only if they have to or are required to (e.g., if they forgot to do something or did something wrong).

In college, students go to campus offices to enhance their success by taking advantage of the services and support they provide.

Awareness Rating _____

(Adapted from the following source: Altshuler Learning Enhancement Center, Southern Methodist University: www. smu.edu/alec/transition.asp)

1.2 Constructing a Master List of Campus Resources

Construct a master list of all support services that are available to you on your campus. Your final product should be a list that includes the following:

- The names of different support services your campus offers
- The types of support each service provides
- A short statement indicating whether you think you would benefit from each particular type of support
- The name of a person whom you could contact for support from each service

Use each of the following sources to gain more in-depth knowledge about the support services available on your campus:

- Information published in your college catalog and student handbook
- Information posted on your college's Web site
- Information gathered by speaking with professionals in different offices or centers on your campus

Use the form on the following page to help you construct your master lists of campus resources.

Notes

- You can team up with other classmates to work collaboratively on this assignment. For instance, different team members could identify different campus resources to research and each member could bring information about one resource to share with other members of the team. Working together with a peer on any research task can reduce your anxiety, increase your energy, and generate synergy, which results in a final product that is superior to what could have been produced by one person working alone (independently).
- After you complete this assignment, save your master list of support services for future use. You might not have an immediate need for some of these services during your first term in college, but all of them are likely to be useful to you at some point in your college experience.

1.3 Support Services

Learning Center

How will I benefit?   Whom should I contact?

_____

Writing Center

How will I benefit?   Whom should I contact?

_____

Disability Services

How will I benefit?   Whom should I contact?

_____

College Library

How will I benefit?   Whom should I contact?

_____

Academic Advising Center

How will I benefit?   Whom should I contact?

_____

Office of Student Life

How will I benefit?   Whom should I contact?

_____

Financial Aid Office

How will I benefit?   Whom should I contact?

_____

Counseling Center

How will I benefit?   Whom should I contact?

_____

Health Center

How will I benefit?   Whom should I contact?

Career Development Center

How will I benefit?   Whom should I contact?

Experiential Learning Resources

How will I benefit?   Whom should I contact?

Other Types of Support Available on Campus

How will I benefit?   Whom should I contact?

Alone and Disconnected: Feeling Like Calling It Quits

Josephine is a first-year student in her second week of college. She doesn't feel like she's fitting in with other students on her campus. She also feels guilty about the time she's taking time away from her family and her old high school friends who are not attending college, and she fears that her ties with them will be weakened or broken if she continues spending so much time at school and on schoolwork. Josephine is feeling so torn between college and her family and former friends that she's beginning to have second thoughts about whether she should have gone to college.

Reflection and Discussion Questions

1. What would you say to Josephine that might persuade her to stay in college?

2. What could Josephine's college have done more during her first two weeks on campus to make her (and other students) feel more connected with college and less disconnected from family?

3. What could Josephine do for herself right now to minimize the conflict she's experiencing between her commitment to college and her commitment to family and high school friends?

Liberal Arts and General Education

2

What It Means to Be a Well-Educated Person in the 21st Century

ACTIVATE YOUR THINKING | *Reflection* **2.1**

LEARNING GOAL

To appreciate the meaning, purpose, and benefits of the liberal arts and develop a strategic plan for making the most out of general education.

Before you launch into this chapter, do your best to answer the following question:

Which one of the following statements represents the most accurate meaning of the term *liberal arts*?

1. Learning to be less politically conservative

2. Learning to be more artistic

3. Learning ideas rather than practical skills

4. Learning to spend money more freely

5. Learning skills for freedom

I was once advising a first-year student (Laura) who intended to major in business. While helping her plan the courses she needed to complete her degree, I pointed out to her that she still needed to take a course in philosophy. Here's how our conversation went after I made this point.

Laura (in a somewhat irritated tone): Why do I have to take philosophy? I'm a business major.

Dr. Cuseo: Because philosophy is an important component of a liberal arts education.

Laura (in a very agitated tone): I'm not liberal and I don't want to be a liberal. I'm conservative and so are my parents; we all voted for Ronald Reagan in the last election!

— Joe Cuseo

The Meaning and Purpose of a Liberal Arts Education

If you're uncertain about what the term *liberal arts* means, you're not alone. Most first-year students don't have the foggiest idea what a liberal arts education represents (Hersh, 1997; American Association of Colleges & Universities [AAC&U], 2007). If they were to guess, like Laura, many of them might mistakenly say that it's something impractical or related to liberal politics.

Laura probably would have picked option 1 as her answer to the multiple-choice question posed at the start of this chapter. She would have been wrong; the correct choice is option 5. Literally translated, the term *liberal arts* derives from the Latin words *liberales*, meaning "to liberate or free," and *artes*, meaning "skills." Thus, "skills for freedom" is the most accurate meaning of liberal arts.

The roots of the term *liberal arts* date back to the origin of modern civilization—to the ancient Greeks and Romans, who argued that political power in a democracy rests with the people because they choose (elect) their own leaders. In a democracy, people are liberated from uncritical dependence on a dictator or autocrat. In order to preserve their political freedom, citizens in a democracy must be well-educated critical thinkers so that they can make wise choices about whom they elect as their leaders and lawmakers (Bishop, 1986; Bok, 2006)

> "Knowledge will forever govern ignorance; and a people who mean to be their own governors must arm themselves with the power which knowledge gives."
>
> —James Madison, fourth president of the United States, cosigner of the American Constitution, and first author of the Bill of Rights

The political ideals of the ancient Greeks and Romans were shared by the founding fathers of the United States, who also emphasized the importance of an educated citizenry for preserving America's new democracy. As Thomas Jefferson, third president of the United States, wrote in 1801, "I know of no safe depository of the ultimate powers of a society but the people themselves; and if we think them not enlightened enough to exercise control with a wholesome discretion [responsible decision-making], the remedy is not to take power from them, but to inform their discretion by education" (Ford, 1903, p. 278).

Thus, the liberal arts are rooted in the belief that education is the essential ingredient for preserving democratic freedom. When citizens are educated in the liberal arts, they gain the breadth of knowledge and depth of thinking to vote wisely, preserve democracy, and avoid autocracy (dictatorship).

> **Remember**
>
> *The original purpose of higher education in America was not just to prepare students for a future profession, but to prepare them for citizenship in a democratic nation.*

The importance of a knowledgeable, critically thinking citizenry for making wise political choices is still relevant today. Contemporary political campaigns are using more manipulative media advertisements. These ads rely on short sound bites, one-sided arguments, and powerful visual images that are intentionally designed to appeal to emotions and discourage critical thinking (Goleman, 1992; Boren, 2008).

Over time, the term *liberal arts* has acquired the more general meaning of liberating or freeing people to be self-directed individuals who make personal choices and decisions that are determined by their own well-reasoned ideas and values, rather than blind conformity to the ideas and values of others (Gamson, 1984; Katz, 2008). Self-directed critical thinkers are empowered to resist manipulation by politicians and other societal influences, including:

- Authority figures (e.g., they question excessive use or abuse of authority by parents, teachers, or law enforcers);
- Peers (e.g., they resist peer pressure that's unreasonable or unethical); and
- Media (e.g., they detect and reject forms of advertisement designed to manipulate their self-image and dictate their material needs).

In short, a liberal arts education encourages you to be your own person and to ask, "Why?" It's the component of your college education that supplies you with the mental tools needed to be an independent thinker with an inquiring mind who questions authority and resists conformity.

> "It is such good fortune for people in power that people do not think."
>
> —Adolf Hitler, German dictator

> "If a nation expects to be ignorant and free, it expects what never was and never will be."
>
> —Thomas Jefferson, principal author of the United States Declaration of Independence and third president of the United States

Student Perspective

> "I want knowledge so I don't get taken advantage of in life."
>
> —First-year college student

Author's Experience

I must admit that I graduated from college without ever truly understanding the purpose and value of liberal education. After I became a college professor, two colleagues of mine approached me to help them create a first-year experience course. I agreed and proceeded to teach the course, which included a unit on the meaning and value of a liberal arts education. It was only after preparing to teach this unit that I began to realize that a college education is first and foremost a process of developing enduring (lifelong) learning skills and "habits of mind" that can empower all college graduates to succeed in any career they may pursue. If I hadn't taught a first-year experience course, I don't think I ever would have truly understood the process that was essential to the purpose of a college education and to my role as a college professor.

Joe Cuseo

The Liberal Arts Curriculum

The first liberal arts curriculum (collection of courses) was designed to equip students with (1) a broad base of knowledge that would ensure they would be well informed in various subjects and (2) a range of mental skills that would enable them to think deeply and critically. Based on this educational philosophy of the ancient Greeks and Romans, the first liberal arts curriculum was developed during the Middle Ages and consisted of the following subjects: logic, language, rhetoric (the art of argumentation and persuasion), music, mathematics, and astronomy (Ratcliff, 1997; AAC&U, 2002, 2007).

The original purpose of the liberal arts curriculum has withstood the test of time. Today's colleges and universities continue to offer a liberal arts curriculum designed to provide students with a broad base of knowledge in multiple subject areas and equip them with critical thinking skills. The liberal arts curriculum today is often referred to as *general education*—representing general knowledge and skills that are applicable to a wide variety of situations. General education is what all college students learn, no matter what their major or specialized field of study may be (AAC&U, 2002).

On some campuses, the liberal arts are also referred to as (1) the *core curriculum*, with "core" standing for what is central and essential for all students to know and do because it contributes to successful performance in any field, or (2) *breadth requirements*, meaning that they are broad in scope, spanning a wide range of subject areas.

> **● Remember**
>
> *Whatever term is used to describe the liberal arts on your campus, the bottom line is that they are the foundation of a college education upon which all academic specializations (majors) are built; they are what all college graduates should be able to know and do for whatever occupational path they choose to pursue; they are what distinguishes college education from vocational preparation; they define what it means to*
> **●** *be a well-educated person.*

Major Divisions of Knowledge and Subject Areas in the Liberal Arts Curriculum

The divisions of knowledge in today's liberal arts curriculum have expanded to include more subject areas than those included in the original curriculum devised by the ancient Greeks and Romans. These divisions and the courses that make up each division vary somewhat from campus to campus. Campuses also vary in terms of the nature of courses required within each of these divisions of knowledge and the variety of courses from which students can choose to fulfill their liberal arts requirements. On average, about one-third of a college graduate's course credits are required general education courses selected from the liberal arts curriculum (Conley, 2005).

Reflection 2.2

For someone to be successful in any major and career, what do you think that person should:

1. Know; and

2. Be able to do?

Despite campus-to-campus variation in the number and nature of courses required, the liberal arts curriculum on every college campus represents the areas of knowledge and the types of skills that all students should possess, no matter what their particular major may be. The breadth of this curriculum allows you to stand on the shoulders of intellectual giants from a range of fields and capitalize on their collective wisdom.

On most campuses today, the liberal arts curriculum typically consists of general divisions of knowledge and related subject areas similar to those listed in the sections that follow. As you read through these divisions of knowledge, highlight any subjects in which you've never taken a course.

Humanities

Courses in the humanities division of the liberal arts curriculum focus on the human experience and human culture, asking the important "big picture" questions that arise in the life of humans, such as "Why are we here?" "What is the meaning or purpose of our existence?" "How should we live?" "What is the good life?" and "Is there life after death?"

The following are the primary subject areas in the humanities:

- **English Composition.** Writing clearly, critically, and persuasively;
- **Speech.** Speaking eloquently and convincingly;
- **Literature.** Reading critically and appreciating the artistic merit of various literary genres (forms of writing), such as novels, short stories, poems, plays, and essays;
- **Languages.** Listening to, speaking, reading, and writing languages other than the student's native tongue;
- **Philosophy.** Thinking rationally, developing wisdom (the ability to use knowledge prudently), and living an ethically principled life; and
- **Theology.** Understanding how humans conceive of and express their faith in a transcendent (supreme) being.

> "Never mistake knowledge for wisdom. One helps you make a living; the other helps you make a life."
>
> —Sandra Carey, lobbyist to the California State Assembly

> "Dancing is silent poetry."
>
> —Simonides, ancient Greek poet

Fine Arts

Courses in the fine arts division focus largely on the art of human expression, asking such questions as "How do humans express, create, and appreciate what is beautiful?" and "How do we express ourselves aesthetically (through the senses) with imagination, creativity, style, and elegance?"

The primary subject areas of the fine arts are as follows:

- **Visual Arts.** Creating and appreciating human expression through visual representation (drawing, painting, sculpture, photography, and graphic design);
- **Musical Arts.** Appreciating and creating rhythmical arrangements of sounds; and
- **Performing Arts.** Appreciating and expressing creativity through drama and dance.

© Ekaterina Pokrovskaya, 2013. Under license from Shutterstock, Inc.

Mathematics

Courses in this division of the liberal arts are designed to promote skills in numerical calculation, quantitative reasoning, and problem solving.

The primary subject areas comprising mathematics for general education include:

- **Algebra.** Mathematical reasoning involving symbolic representation of numbers in a language of letters that vary in size or quantity;
- **Statistics.** Mathematical methods for summarizing quantitative data, estimating probabilities, representing and understanding numerical information depicted in graphs, charts, and tables, and drawing accurate conclusions from statistical data; and
- **Calculus.** Higher mathematical methods for calculating the rate at which the quantity of one entity changes in relation to another and calculating the areas enclosed by curves.

> "The universe is a grand book which cannot be read until one learns to comprehend the language and become familiar with the characters of which it is composed. It is written in the language of mathematics."
>
> —Galileo Galilei, 17th-century Italian physicist, mathematician, astronomer, and philosopher

Natural Sciences

Courses in this division of the liberal arts curriculum are devoted to systematic observation of the physical world and the explanation of natural phenomena, asking such questions as "What causes physical events that take place in the natural world?" "How can we predict and control these events?" and "How do we promote mutually productive interaction between humans and the natural environment that contributes to the survival and development of both?"

The following are the primary subject areas of the natural sciences division:

© Yuri Arcurs, 2013. Under license from Shutterstock, Inc.

The natural sciences division of the liberal arts curriculum focuses on the observation of the physical world and the explanation of natural phenomena.

- **Biology.** Understanding the structure and underlying processes of all living things;
- **Chemistry.** Understanding the composition of natural and synthetic (manmade) substances and how these substances may be changed or developed;
- **Physics.** Understanding the properties of physical matter and the principles of energy, motion, electrical, and magnetic forces;
- **Geology.** Understanding the composition of the earth and the natural processes that have shaped its development; and
- **Astronomy.** Understanding the makeup and motion of celestial bodies that comprise the universe.

Social and Behavioral Sciences

"We cannot defend these [democratic] ideals or protect the vitality of our institutions, including our institutional government, unless we understand their origins and how they evolved over time."

—David Boren, president of the University of Oklahoma and longest-serving chairman of the U.S. Senate Intelligence Committee

"Science is an imaginative adventure of the mind seeking truth in a world of mystery."

—Cyril Herman Hinshelwood, Nobel Prize-winning English chemist

"Man, the molecule of society, is the subject of social science."

—Henry Charles Carey, 19th-century American economist

Courses in the division of social and behavioral sciences focus on the observation of human behavior, individually and in groups, asking such questions as "What causes humans to behave the way they do?" and "How can we predict, control, or improve human behavior and human interaction?"

This division of the liberal arts curriculum is composed primarily of the following subject areas:

- **History.** Understanding past events, their causes, and their influence on current events;
- **Political Science.** Understanding how societal authority is organized and how this authority is exerted to govern people, make collective decisions, and maintain social order;
- **Psychology.** Understanding the human mind, its conscious and subconscious processes, and the underlying causes of human behavior;
- **Sociology.** Understanding the structure, interaction, and collective behavior of organized social groups, institutions, and systems that comprise human society (e.g., families, schools, and social services);
- **Anthropology.** Understanding the cultural and physical origin, development, and distribution of the human species;

- **Geography.** Understanding how the places (physical locations) where humans live influence their cultural and societal development and how humans have shaped (and been shaped) by their surrounding physical environment; and
- **Economics.** Understanding how the monetary needs of humans are met through allocation of limited resources and how material wealth is produced and distributed.

Physical Education and Wellness

Courses in the physical education and wellness division of the liberal arts curriculum focus on the human body, how to best maintain health, and how to attain peak levels of human performance. They ask such questions as "How does the body function most effectively?" and "What can we do to prevent illness, promote wellness, and improve the physical quality of our lives?"

These primary subject areas fall under this division:

"To eat is a necessity, but to eat intelligently is an art."

—La Rochefoucauld, 17th-century French author

- **Physical Education.** Understanding the role of human exercise for promoting health and performance;
- **Nutrition.** Understanding how the body uses food as nourishment to promote health and generate energy;
- **Sexuality.** Understanding the biological, psychological, and social aspects of sexual relations; and
- **Drug Education.** Understanding how substances that alter the body and mind affect physical health, mental health, and human behavior.

Most of your liberal arts requirements will be fulfilled during your first two years of college. Don't be disappointed if some of these required courses seem similar to courses you recently had in high school, and don't think you'll be bored because these are subjects you've already studied. College courses are not videotape replays of high school courses; you will examine these subjects in greater depth and breadth and at a higher level of thinking (Conley, 2005). Research shows that most of the thinking gains that students make in college take place during their first two years—the years when they're taking most of their liberal arts courses (Pascarella & Terenzini, 2005). Although you will specialize in a particular field of study in college (your major), "real-life" issues and challenges are not neatly divided and conveniently packaged into specialized majors. Important and enduring issues, such as effective leadership, improving race relations, and preventing international warfare, can neither be fully understood nor effectively solved by using the thinking tools of a single academic discipline. Approaching such important, multidimensional issues from the perspective of a single, specialized field of study would be to use a single-minded and oversimplified strategy to tackle complex and multifaceted problems.

Reflection **2.3**

Look back at the liberal arts subject areas in which you've never taken a course. Which of these courses strike you as particularly interesting or useful?

Why?

Acquiring Transferable Skills That Last a Lifetime

A liberal arts education promotes success in your major, career, and life by equipping you with a set of lifelong learning skills with two powerful qualities:

- **Transferability.** Skills that can be transferred and applied to a range of subjects, careers, and life situations.
- **Durability.** Skills that are enduring and can be continually used throughout life.

To use an athletic analogy, what the liberal arts do for the mind is similar to what cross-training does for the body. Cross-training engages the body in a wide range of different exercises to promote total physical fitness and a broad set of physical skills (e.g., strength, endurance, flexibility, and agility), which can be applied to improve performance in any sport or athletic endeavor. Similarly, the liberal arts and diversity engage the mind in a wide range of subject areas (e.g., arts, sciences and humanities) and multiple cultural perspectives, which develop a wide range of mental skills that can be used to improve performance in any major or career.

There's a big difference between learning factual knowledge and learning transferable skills. A transferable skill can be applied to different situations or contexts. The mental skills developed by the liberal arts are transportable across academic subjects you'll encounter in college and work positions you'll assume after college. It could be said that these lifelong learning skills are mental gifts that keep on giving throughout life.

Remember

The liberal arts not only provide you with academic skills needed to succeed in your chosen major, they also equip you with skills to succeed in whatever career or careers you decide to pursue. Don't underestimate the importance of these transferable and durable skills. Work hard at developing them, and take seriously the liberal arts courses designed to promote their development. The broad-based knowledge and general, flexible skills developed by the liberal arts will multiply your career options, opening up more career doors for you after college graduation and providing you with greater career mobility throughout your professional life.

The transferable skills developed by the liberal arts are summarized in Snapshot Summary 2.1. As you read each of them, rate yourself on each of the skills using the following scale:

4 = very strong, 3 = strong, 2 = needs some improvement,
1 = needs much improvement

Snapshot Summary

2.1 Transferable Lifelong Learning Skills Developed by the Liberal Arts

One way the liberal arts "liberate" you is by equipping you with skills that are not tied to any particular subject area or career field, but which can be transferred freely to different learning situations and contexts throughout life. Some key forms of these versatile, durable skills are listed below.

1. **Communication skills.** Accurate comprehension and articulate expression of ideas. Five particular types of communication skills are essential for success in any specialized field of study or work:

   - **Written communication skills.** Writing in a clear, creative, and persuasive manner;
   - **Oral communication skills.** Speaking concisely, confidently, and eloquently;

Student Perspective

"I intend on becoming a corporate lawyer. I am an English major. The reason I chose this major is because while I was researching the educational backgrounds of some corporate attorneys, I found that a lot were English majors. It helps with writing and delivering cases."

—College sophomore

   - **Reading skills.** Comprehending, interpreting, and evaluating the literal meaning and connotations of words written in various styles and subject areas;
   - **Listening skills.** Comprehending spoken language accurately and sensitively; and
   - **Technological communication skills.** Using computer technology to communicate effectively.

2. **Information literacy skills.** Accessing, retrieving, and evaluating information from various sources, including in-print and online (technology-based) systems.

3. **Computation skills.** Accurately calculating, analyzing, summarizing, interpreting, and evaluating quantitative information or statistical data.

4. **Higher-level thinking skills.** Thinking at a more advanced level than simply acquisition and memorization of factual information.

"Ability to recognize when information is needed and have the ability to locate, evaluate, and use it effectively."

—Definition of *information literacy*, American Library Association Presidential Committee on Information Literacy

Remember

You may forget the facts you learn in college, but you will remember the ways of thinking, the habits of mind, and the communication skills for the rest of your life.

Students often see general education as something to "get out of the way" or "get behind them" so they can get into their major and career (AAC&U, 2007). Don't buy into the belief that general education represents a series of obstacles along the way to a degree. Instead, "get into" general education and take away from it a set of powerful skills that are *portable*— "travel" well across different work situations and life roles— and *stable*—will remain relevant across changing times and stages of life.

Reflection 2.4

Reflect on the four skill areas developed by a liberal arts education (communication, information literacy, computation, and higher-level thinking). Which one do you think is most important or most relevant to your future success?

Write a one-paragraph explanation of why you chose this skill.

Remember

When you acquire lifelong learning skills, you're also acquiring lifelong learning skills.

Remember

The earning potential you acquire after college will depend on the learning potential you develop in college.

Student
Perspective

"They asked me during my interview why I was right for the job and I told them because I can read well, write well and I can think. They really liked that because those were the skills they were looking for."

—English major hired by a public relations firm

"At State Farm, our [employment] exam does not test applicants on their knowledge of finance or the insurance business, but it does require them to demonstrate critical thinking skills and the ability to calculate and think logically. These skills plus the ability to read for information, to communicate and write effectively need to be demonstrated."

—Edward B. Rust Jr., chairman and chief executive officer of State Farm Insurance Companies (AAC&U, 2007)

The skills developed by a liberal arts education are strikingly similar to the types of skills that employers seek in new employees. In numerous national surveys and in-depth interviews, employers and executives in both industry and government consistently report that they seek employees with skills that fall into the following three categories:

1. **Communication skills.** Listening, speaking, writing, and reading (Business-Higher Education Forum, 1999; National Association of Colleges & Employers, 2007; Peter D. Hart Research Associates, 2006). "There is such a heavy emphasis on effective communication in the workplace that college students who master these skills can set themselves apart from the pack when searching for employment." —Marilyn Mackes, executive director of the National Association of Colleges and Employers (Mackes, 2003, p. 1).

2. **Thinking skills.** Problem solving and critical thinking (Business-Higher Education Forum, 1999; Peter D. Hart Research Associates, 2006; Education Commission of the States, 1995). "We look for people who can think critically and analytically. If you can do those things, we can teach you our business." —Paul Dominski, store recruiter for the Robinson-May Department Stores Company.

3. **Lifelong learning skills.** Learning how to learn and how to continue learning throughout life (Conference Board of Canada, 2000). "Employers are virtually unanimous that the most important knowledge and skills the new employee can bring to the job are problem solving, communication, and 'learning to learn' skills (SECFHE, 2006). The workers of the future need to know how to think and how to continue to learn." —David Kearns, former chief executive officer for the Xerox Corporation.

The remarkable resemblance between the work skills sought by employers and the academic skills developed by a liberal arts education isn't surprising when you think about the typical duties or responsibilities of working professionals. They need good communication skills because they must listen, speak, describe, and explain ideas to co-workers and customers. They are required to read and critically interpret written and statistical reports and write letters, memos, and reports. They also need highly developed thinking skills to analyze problems, construct well-organized plans, generate innovative ideas and solutions to problems (creative thinking), and evaluate whether their plans and strategies are effective (critical thinking).

The Liberal Arts Promote Employability

The transferable skills developed by the liberal arts have become more and more sought out by employers. In fact, colleges and universities are hearing from employers that these transferable skills are the very abilities their new staff members need to be successful in today's workplace and to effectively take on "real-life" issues. Given the complexity of today's world, this isn't surprising. The 21st century has increased our interconnectedness with many different countries and cultures. At the same time, the 21st century also has brought with it many new global challenges that were not present even 20 years ago. These changes necessitate that college graduates bring with them the knowledge, experience, and abilities to step into the world they will encounter upon graduating. In fact, according to a recent survey of employers (Peter

D. Hart Research Associates, 2010, p. 5), new employees are expected to do the following to a much greater degree today than in the past:

- Take on more responsibilities and use a broader set of skills
- Work harder to coordinate with other departments
- Address challenges that are more complex
- Use higher levels of thinking and a wider range of knowledge

Clearly, as the world itself has changed in the 21st century, so has the world of work. Given these changes, it makes sense that employers are seeking new hires with a distinct set of knowledge, values, and skills.

So what are employers looking for in the people they hire? They are seeking workers who that can problem-solve and manage projects. They want employees with effective interpersonal skills who can work well with groups. They also want their new hires to be able to adapt to a variety of environments and be skilled communicators. Students develop these qualities while in college through a well-rounded education that balances the curriculum of the liberal arts and their major. In a study conducted by the American Association of State Colleges and Universities (2007, p. 2) employers stated that this curricular balance is ideal since it produces the following highly valued outcomes in students and prepares them for the world of work:

- Integrative learning
  - The ability to apply knowledge and skills to real-world settings
- Knowledge of human cultures and the physical and natural world
  - Concepts and new developments in science and technology
  - Global issues and developments and their implications for the future*
  - The role of the United States in the world
  - Cultural values and traditions in America and other countries*
- Intellectual and practical skills
  - Teamwork skills and the ability to collaborate with others in diverse group settings*
  - The ability to effectively communicate orally and in writing
  - Critical thinking and analytical reasoning skills
  - The ability to locate, organize, and evaluate information from multiple sources
  - The ability to be innovative and think creatively
  - The ability to solve complex problems
  - The ability to work with numbers and understand statistics
- Personal and social responsibility
  - Teamwork skills and the ability to collaborate with others in diverse group settings*
  - Global issues and developments and their implications for the future
  - A sense of integrity and ethics
  - Cultural values and traditions in America and other countries*

*Three items are shown in two learning outcome categories because they apply to both.

Author's Experience   I graduated from college with a BA in political science and sociology. Many of my friends asked me, "What are you going to do with such majors? What kind of job will you get offered?" As it turned out, I received a position in corporate management training after I graduated and spent the next many years working in corporate America. I quickly became aware of the knowledge these liberal arts degrees and my general education bestowed on me. I understood how organizations worked. I could communicate well, orally and written. I understood people and their uniqueness. I could problem solve. I got these degrees in the 20th century and these are the skills still in most demand in the 21st century.

Aaron Thompson

"As times goes on, the technical and practical skills vocational majors learn in college become less important to continued success. Such abilities as communication skills, human relations, creativity, and 'big picture thinking' matter more."

—Derek Bok, president emeritus, Harvard University

This study's results further demonstrate the important contributions made by the liberal arts toward your college success and your marketability upon graduation. When you work with your advisor on your academic plan and map out the courses you'll take to complete your degree, think of your liberal arts requirements as courses that will complement the learning you'll do in your major courses. Delve into both! By doing so, you be will be investing in your academic success and future employability.

A Liberal Arts Education Is Preparation for Your Major

For most college students, choosing a major and choosing a career are not decisions made at the same time because their major doesn't turn into their career. It is this belief that leads some students to procrastinate about choosing a major; they think they're making a lifelong decision and are afraid they'll make the "wrong" choice and get stuck doing something they hate for the rest of their life.

The truth is that the trip from your college major to your eventual career(s) is less like climbing a pole and more like climbing up a tree. As illustrated in **Figure 2.1**, you begin with the tree's trunk (the foundation provided by the liberal arts), which leads to separate limbs (choices for college majors), which, in turn, leads to different branches (different career paths or options).

FIGURE 2.1

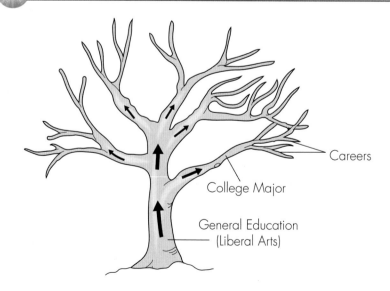

Careers

College Major

General Education
(Liberal Arts)

The Relationship between General Education (Liberal Arts), College Majors, and Careers

Note that the different sets of branches (careers) grow from the same major limb. So, too, do different sets of careers or "career families" grow from each major. For example, an English major will often lead to careers that involve use of the written language (e.g., editing, journalism, or publishing), while a major in art will often lead to careers that involve use of visual media (e.g., illustration, graphic design, or art therapy).

Don't assume that liberal arts courses you're taking as general education requirements have nothing to do with your specialized field of interest. Liberal arts courses provide a relevant foundation for success in your major. Recall our story at the start of the chapter about Laura, the first-year student with a business major who questioned why she had to take a course in philosophy. Laura needed to take philosophy because she would encounter topics in her business major that related either directly or indirectly to philosophy. In her business courses, she would likely encounter philosophical issues relating to (1) the logical assumptions and underlying values of capitalism, (2) business ethics (e.g., hiring and firing practices), and (3) business justice (e.g., how profits should be fairly or justly distributed to workers and shareholders). Philosophy would equip her with the fundamental logical thinking and ethical reasoning skills to understand these issues deeply and respond to them humanely.

The same is true for careers other than business. For example, historical and ethical perspectives are needed for all fields because all of them have a history and none of them are value-free.

Keep in mind that the career path of most college graduates does not run like a straight line directly from their major to their career. For instance, most physics majors do not become physicists, most philosophy majors do not become philosophers, and most history majors do not become historians. It is this mistaken belief that may account for the fact that business continues to be the most popular major among college students (Zernike, 2009). Students (and their parents) see that most college graduates are employed in business settings and think that if you want to get a job in business after graduation, you'd better major in business.

> "Virtually all occupational endeavors require a working appreciation of the historical, cultural, ethical, and global environments that surround the application of skilled work."
>
> —Robert Jones, "Liberal Education for the Twenty-First Century: Business Expectations"

Reflection 2.5

During your college experience, you might hear students say that they need to get their general education (liberal arts) courses out of the way so that they can get into courses that relate to their major and career. Would you agree or disagree with this argument?

Why?

> "The unexamined life is not worth living."
>
> —Socrates, classic Greek philosopher and one of the founding fathers of Western philosophy

The academic skills developed by a liberal arts education are also practical skills that contribute to successful performance in any career.

The Liberal Arts Promote Self-Awareness and Development of the Whole Person

One of the most emphasized goals of a liberal arts education is to "know thyself" (Cross, 1982; Tubbs, 2011). Fully educated people look inward to learn about themselves just as they look outward to learn about the world around them. The ability to turn inward and become aware of ourselves has been referred to as intrapersonal in-

FIGURE 2.2

© Kendall Hunt

Key Elements of Holistic (Whole-Person) Development

telligence (Gardner, 1999, 2006). Self-knowledge represents the key first step in any quest toward personal growth and fulfillment.

To become self-aware requires awareness of all elements that comprise the self. As illustrated in Figure 2.2, the human self is composed of multiple dimensions that join together to form the whole person.

Key Dimensions of the Self

Each of the following elements of self plays an influential role in promoting human health, success, and happiness:

1. **Intellectual.** Knowledge, multiple perspectives, and different ways of thinking;
2. **Emotional.** Awareness of feelings, self-esteem, emotional intelligence, and mental health;
3. **Social.** Interpersonal relationships;
4. **Ethical.** Values, character, and moral convictions;
5. **Physical.** Bodily health and wellness;
6. **Spiritual.** Beliefs about the meaning or purpose of life and the hereafter;
7. **Vocational.** Economic well-being and career success; and
8. **Personal.** Identity, self-concept, and self-management.

Research strongly suggests that quality of life depends on attention to and development of all elements of the self. It's been found that people who are healthy (physically and mentally) and successful (personally and professionally) are those who attend to and integrate dimensions of the self, enabling them to lead well-rounded and well-balanced lives (Covey, 1990; Goleman, 1995; Heath, 1977).

In Figure 2.2, these diverse dimensions of the self are joined or linked to represent how they are interrelated, working together to promote personal development and well-being (Love & Love, 1995). The dimensions of self are discussed separately in this chapter to keep them clear in your mind. In reality, they do not operate independent of one another; instead, they interconnect and influence each other. (This is why the elements of the self in Figure 2.2 are depicted as links in an interconnected chain.) Thus, the self is a diverse, multidimensional entity that has the capacity to develop along various interdependent dimensions.

One of the primary goals of the liberal arts is to provide a well-rounded education that promotes development and integration of the whole person (Kuh, Shedd, & Whitt, 1987). Research on college students confirms that their college experience affects them in multiple ways and promotes the development of multiple dimensions of self (Bowen, 1997; Feldman & Newcomb, 1994; Pascarella & Terenzini, 1991; 2005).

Since wholeness is essential for wellness, success, and happiness, read carefully the following descriptions and skills associated with each of the eight elements of holistic development. As you read the skills and qualities listed beneath each of the eight elements, place a checkmark in the space next to any skill that is particularly important to you. You may check more than one skill within each area.

Skills and Qualities Associated with Each Element of Holistic (Whole-Person) Development

1. **Intellectual development.** Acquiring knowledge and learning how to learn deeply and think at a higher level.
   Goals and skills:
   - ☑ Becoming aware of your intellectual abilities, interests, and learning styles
   - ☑ Maintaining attention and concentration
   - ☑ Improving your ability to retain and apply knowledge
   - ☑ Moving beyond memorization to higher levels of thinking
   - ☑ Acquiring effective research skills for accessing information from various sources and systems
   - ☑ Viewing issues from multiple angles or viewpoints (psychological, social, political, economic, etc.) to attain a balanced, comprehensive perspective
   - ☑ Evaluating ideas critically in terms of their truth and value
   - ☑ Thinking creatively or imaginatively
   - ☑ Responding constructively to differing viewpoints or opposing arguments
   - ☑ Detecting and rejecting persuasion tactics that appeal to emotions rather than reason

2. **Emotional development.** Strengthening skills for understanding, controlling, and expressing emotions.
   Goals and skills:
   - ☑ Dealing with personal emotions in an honest, non-defensive manner
   - ☑ Maintaining a healthy balance between emotional control and emotional expression
   - ☑ Responding with empathy and sensitivity to emotions experienced by others
   - ☑ Dealing effectively with depression
   - ☑ Dealing effectively with anger
   - ☑ Using effective stress-management strategies to control anxiety and tension
   - ☑ Responding effectively to frustrations and setbacks
   - ☑ Overcoming fear of failure and lack of self-confidence
   - ☑ Accepting feedback in a constructive, non-defensive manner
   - ☑ Maintaining optimism and enthusiasm

3. **Social development.** Enhancing the quality and depth of interpersonal relationships.
   Goals and skills:
   - ☑ Developing effective conversational skills
   - ☑ Becoming an effective listener
   - ☑ Relating effectively to others in one-to-one, small-group, and large-group situations

Student Perspective

"Being successful is being balanced in every aspect of your life."

—First-year college student

"The research portrays the college student as changing in an integrated way, with change in any one area appearing to be part of a mutually reinforcing network or pattern of change in other areas."

—Ernest Pascarella and Pat Terenzini, *How College Affects Students*

"It's not stress that kills us, it is our reaction to it."

—Hans Selye, Canadian endocrinologist and author of *Stress Without Distress*

- ☑ Collaborating effectively with others when working in groups or teams
- ☑ Overcoming shyness
- ☑ Establishing meaningful and intimate relationships
- ☑ Resolving interpersonal conflicts assertively, rather than aggressively or passively
- ☑ Providing feedback to others in a constructive and considerate manner
- ☑ Relating effectively with others from different cultural backgrounds and lifestyles
- ☑ Developing leadership skills

4. **Ethical development.** Developing a clear value system for guiding life choices and decisions, building moral character, making ethical judgments, and demonstrating consistency between convictions (beliefs) and commitments (actions). Goals and skills:
   - ☑ Gaining deeper self-awareness of personal values and ethical assumptions
   - ☑ Making personal choices and life decisions based on a meaningful value system
   - ☑ Developing the capacity to think and act with personal integrity and authenticity
   - ☑ Using technology in an ethical and civil manner
   - ☑ Resisting social pressure to act in ways that are inconsistent with personal values
   - ☑ Treating others in an ethical manner
   - ☑ Knowing how to exercise individual freedom without infringing on the rights of others
   - ☑ Demonstrating concern and commitment for human rights and social justice
   - ☑ Developing the courage to confront those who violate the rights of others
   - ☑ Becoming a responsible citizen

5. **Physical development.** Applying knowledge about how the human body functions to prevent disease, preserve wellness, and promote peak performance. Goals and skills:
   - ☑ Maintaining awareness of your physical condition and state of health
   - ☑ Applying knowledge about exercise and fitness training to promote physical and mental health
   - ☑ Understanding how sleep patterns affect health and performance
   - ☑ Maintaining a healthy balance of work, recreation, and relaxation
   - ☑ Applying knowledge of nutrition to reduce the risk of illness and promote optimal performance
   - ☑ Becoming knowledgeable about nutritional imbalances and eating disorders
   - ☑ Developing a positive physical self-image
   - ☑ Becoming knowledgeable about the effects of drugs and their impact on physical and mental well-being
   - ☑ Being knowledgeable about human sexuality and sexually transmitted diseases
   - ☑ Understanding how biological differences between the sexes affect male-female relationships and gender orientation

6. **Spiritual development.** Searching for answers to the big questions, such as the meaning or purpose of life and death, and exploring nonmaterial issues that transcend human life and the physical world.

"Chi rispetta sara rippetato." ("Respect others and you will be respected.")

—Italian proverb

"The moral challenge is simply to abide by the knowledge we already have."

–Søren Kierkegaard, 19th-century Danish philosopher and theologian

"If you don't stand for something you will fall for anything."

—Malcolm X, African American Muslim minister, public speaker, and human rights activist

"A man too busy to take care of his health is like a mechanic too busy to take care of his tools."

—Spanish proverb

Student
Perspective

"You may think I'm here, living for the 'now' . . . but I'm not. Half of my life revolves around the invisible and immaterial. At some point, every one of us has asked the Big Questions surrounding our existence: What is the meaning of life? Is my life inherently purposeful and valuable?"

—College student (Dalton, Eberhardt, Bracken, & Echols, 2006)

Goals and skills:

☑ Developing a personal philosophy or worldview about the meaning and purpose of human existence

☑ Appreciating what cannot be completely understood

☑ Appreciating the mysteries associated with the origin of the universe

☑ Searching for the connection between the self and the larger world or cosmos

☑ Searching for the mystical or supernatural—that which transcends the boundaries of the natural world

☑ Being open to examining questions relating to death and life after death

☑ Being open to examining questions about the possible existence of a supreme being or higher power

☑ Being knowledgeable about different approaches to spirituality and their underlying beliefs or assumptions

☑ Understanding the difference and relationship between faith and reason

☑ Becoming aware and tolerant of religious beliefs and practices

7. **Vocational development.** Exploring career options, making career choices wisely, and developing skills needed for lifelong career success.

Goals and skills:

☑ Understanding the relationship between college majors and careers

☑ Using effective strategies for exploring and identifying potential careers

☑ Selecting career options that are consistent with your personal values, interests, and talents

☑ Acquiring work experience in career fields that relate to your occupational interests

☑ Developing an effective resume and portfolio

☑ Using effective strategies for identifying personal references and acquiring letters of recommendation

☑ Acquiring effective job-search strategies

☑ Using effective strategies for writing letters of inquiry and applications to potential employers

☑ Developing strategies for performing well in personal interviews

☑ Acquiring effective networking skills for connecting with potential employers

8. **Personal development.** Developing positive self-beliefs, personal attitudes, and personal habits.

Goals and skills:

☑ Developing a strong sense of personal identity and a coherent self-concept (e.g., "Who am I?")

☑ Finding a sense of purpose or direction in life (e.g., "Who will I become?")

☑ Developing self-respect and self-esteem

☑ Increasing self-confidence

☑ Developing self-efficacy, or the belief that events and outcomes in life are influenced or controlled by personal initiative and effort

☑ Setting realistic personal goals and priorities

☑ Developing self-motivation and self-discipline

☑ Developing personal resiliency and perseverance to persist to completion of long-range goals

☑ Acquiring practical skills for managing personal affairs effectively and efficiently

☑ Becoming independent and self-reliant

"Everyone is a house with four rooms: a physical, a mental, an emotional, and a spiritual. Most of us tend to live in one room most of the time but unless we go into every room every day, even if only to keep it aired, we are not complete."
—Native American proverb

"Your work is to discover your work and then with all your heart to give yourself to it."
—Hindu Prince Gautama Siddhartha, a.k.a. Buddha, founder of the philosophy and religion of Buddhism

"Remember, no one can make you feel inferior without your consent."
—Eleanor Roosevelt, UN diplomat and humanitarian

"I'm a great believer in luck and I find the harder I work, the more I have of it."
—Thomas Jefferson

The Co-Curriculum: Using the Whole Campus to Develop the Whole Person

The power of a liberal arts education is magnified when you take advantage of the total college environment. This includes not only taking advantage of the courses in the college curriculum; it also includes learning experiences that are available to you outside the classroom—referred to as the *co-curriculum*. Co-curricular experiences include all educational discussions you have with your peers and professors outside the classroom, as well as your participation in the various events and programs offered on your campus. As mentioned in Chapter 1, research clearly indicates that out-of-class learning experiences are equally important to your personal development and professional success as the course curriculum (Kuh, 2005; Kuh et al., 1994; 1995; Pascarella & Terenzini, 2005); hence, these experiences are referred to as the *co-curriculum*.

Reflection **2.6**

Look back and count the number of checkmarks you've placed by each of the eight areas of self-development. Did you find that you placed roughly the same number of checkmarks in all eight areas, or were there large discrepancies across the different areas?

Based on the checkmarks that you placed in each area, would you say that your interests in self-development are balanced across elements of the self, or do they suggest a strong interest in certain dimensions of yourself, with little interest in others?

Do you think you will eventually develop a more balanced set of interests across these different dimensions of self-development? Why?

> "To educate liberally, learning experiences must be offered which facilitate maturity of the whole person. These are goals of student development and clearly they are consistent with the mission and goals of liberal education."
>
> —Theodore Berg, "Student Development and Liberal Education"

Learning that takes place in college courses is primarily vicarious—that is, you learn from or through somebody else, by listening to professors in class and by reading outside of class. This type of academic learning is valuable, but it needs to be complemented by experiential learning (i.e., learning directly through firsthand experiences). For example, you don't learn to be a leader solely by listening to lectures and reading books about leadership. To fully develop your leadership skills, you need to have leadership experiences, such as experiences involving "leading a [discussion] group in class, holding office in student government or by being captain of a sports team" (AAC&U, 2002, p. 30). Capitalizing on experiential learning opportunities enables you to take advantage of your whole college to develop yourself as a whole person.

Listed in Snapshot Summary 2.2 are some programs and services included in a co-curriculum, accompanied by the primary dimensions of the self that they are designed to develop.

Snapshot Summary

2.2

Dimensions of Holistic (Whole-Person) Development Promoted by Different Co-Curricular Programs and Services

Intellectual Development
- Academic advising
- Learning center services
- College library
- Tutoring services
- Information technology services
- Campus speakers
- Academic workshops
- Concerts, theater productions, and art shows

Social and Emotional Development
- Student activities
- Student clubs and organizations
- Multicultural Center
- International student programs
- Counseling services
- Peer counseling
- Peer mentoring
- Residential life programs
- Commuter programs

Ethical Development
- Judicial Review Board
- Student government
- Integrity committees and task forces

Physical Development
- Student health services
- Wellness programs
- Campus athletic activities and intramural sports

Spiritual Development
- Campus ministry
- Peer ministry
- Religious services

Vocational Development
- Career development services
- Internships programs
- Service learning experiences
- Work-study programs
- Major and career fairs

Personal Development
- Financial aid services
- Campus workshops on self-management (e.g., managing time or money)
- Student development workshops and retreats

Note: This list represents just a sample of the total number of programs and services that may be available on your campus. As you can see from the list's length, colleges and universities are organized to promote your development in multiple ways. The power of the liberal arts is magnified when you combine coursework and co-curricular experiences to create a college experience that contributes to your development as a whole person.

> **Remember**
>
> *A liberal arts education includes both the curriculum and the co-curriculum; it involves strategic use of the total college environment, both inside and outside the classroom.*

Broadening Your Perspective of the World around You

Learn about things that go beyond yourself—learn about the world around you. A liberal arts education helps you move beyond yourself and expands your perspective to include the wider world around you (Braskamp, 2008). The components of this larger perspective are organized and illustrated in Figure 2.3.

In Figure 2.3, the center circle represents the self. Fanning out to the right of the self is a series of arches that encompasses the *social–spatial perspective*; this perspective includes increasingly larger social groups and more distant places, ranging from the narrowest perspective (the individual) to the widest perspective (the universe). The liberal arts liberate you from the narrow tunnel vision of a self-centered (egocentric) perspective, providing a panoramic perspective of the world that enables you to move outside yourself and see yourself in relation to other people and other places.

To the left of the self in Figure 2.3 are three arches labeled the *chronological perspective*. This perspective includes the three dimensions of time: past (historical), present (contemporary), and future (futuristic). The liberal arts not only widen your perspective, but also lengthen it by stretching your vision beyond the present, en-

Student
Perspective

"College was not something I deemed important in order to be really rich later on in life. It was something I considered fundamental to learning about myself and the world around me."

—First-year college student (Watts, 2005)

FIGURE 2.3

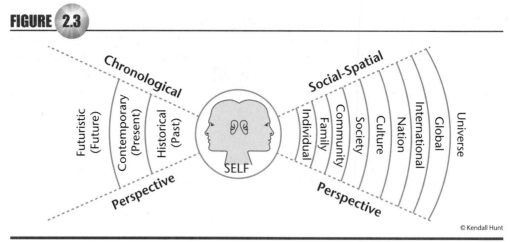

© Kendall Hunt

Multiple Perspectives Developed by the Liberal Arts

abling you to see yourself in relation to humans who've lived before you and will live after you. The chronological perspective gives you hindsight to see where the world has been, insight into the world's current condition, and foresight to see where the world may be going.

It could be said that the chronological perspective provides you with a mental time machine for flashing back to the past and fast-forwarding to the future, while the social-spatial perspective provides you with a conceptual telescope for viewing people and places that are far away. Together, these two broadening perspectives of the liberal arts enable you to appreciate the experiences of humans living in different places and different times.

The specific elements comprising each of these broadening perspectives are discussed next.

Elements of the Social-Spatial Perspective

The Family Perspective

Moving beyond the perspective of yourself as individual, you are part of a larger social unit—a family. The people with whom you were raised have almost certainly influenced the person you are today and how you got to be that way. Moreover, you influence your family. For example, your decision to go to college may make your parents and grandparents proud and may influence the decision of other members of your family to attend college. In addition, if you have children, graduating from college will have a positive influence on their future welfare; as mentioned in the introduction to this book, children of college graduates experience improved intellectual development, better physical health, and greater economic security (Bowen, 1977, 1997; Pascarella & Terenzini, 1991; 2005).

The Community Perspective

Moving beyond the family, you are also a member of a larger social unit—your community. This wider social circle includes friends and neighbors at home, at school, and at work. These are communities where you can begin to take action to improve the world around you. If you want to make the world a better place, this is the place to start—through civic engagement in your local communities.

Civically engaged people demonstrate civic commitment by stepping beyond their narrow self-interests to selflessly volunteer time and energy to help members of their community, particularly those in need. They demonstrate their humanity by being humane—they show genuine compassion for others who are less fortunate than themselves—and by being humanitarian—they work to promote the welfare of other human beings.

The Societal Perspective

Moving beyond your local communities, you are also a member of a larger *society*—a group of people organized under the same social system. Societies include subgroups divided into different regions (e.g., north, south, east, west), different population densities (e.g., urban, suburban, rural), and different socioeconomic classes (e.g., level of income, education, and job status). Within a society, there are typically subgroups that are stratified (layered) into different social classes with unequal levels of economic resources.

In human societies, groups of people are typically stratified into social classes with unequal levels of resources, such as monetary wealth.

> "[Liberal arts education] shows you how to accommodate yourself to others, how to throw yourself into their state of mind, how to come to an understanding of them. You are at home in any society; you have common ground with every class."
>
> —John Henry Newman

The Cultural Perspective

Culture can be broadly defined as a distinctive pattern of beliefs and values that are learned by a group of people who share the same social heritage and traditions. In short, culture is the whole way in which a group of people has learned to live (Peoples & Bailey, 2008); it includes their customary style of speaking (language), fashion, food, art, music, values, and beliefs.

Reflection **2.7**

What would you say is the factor that is most responsible for poverty in human societies?

Intercultural awareness is one of the outcomes of a liberal arts education (Center of Inquiry, 2011). Being able to step outside of your own culture and see issues from a broader worldview enables you to perceive reality and evaluate truth from the vantage points of different cultural groups. This makes your thinking more comprehensive and less ethnocentric (centered on your own culture).

> "It is difficult to see the picture when you are inside the frame."
>
> —Author unknown

The National Perspective

Besides being a member of society, you're also a citizen of a nation. The privilege of being a citizen in a free nation brings with it the responsibility of participating in your country's governance through the process of voting. As a democracy, the United States is a nation that has been built on the foundation of equal rights and freedom of opportunity guaranteed by its constitution.

Exercise your right to vote, and when you do vote, be mindful of political leaders who are committed to ensuring equal rights, social justice, and political freedom. When the personal rights and freedom of any of our fellow citizens are threatened, the political stability and survival of our democratic nation is threatened.

The International Perspective

Moving beyond your particular country of citizenship, you are also a member of an international world that includes close to 200 nations (Rosenberg, 2009). Communication and interaction among citizens of different nations is greater today than at any other time in world history, largely because of rapid advances in electronic technology (Dryden & Vos, 1999; Friedman, 2005). The World Wide Web is making today's world a small world after all, and success in this smaller world requires an international perspective. Our lives are increasingly affected by events beyond our national borders; boundaries between nations are breaking down as a result of international travel, international trading, and multinational corporations. By learning from and about different nations, you become more than a citizen of your own country: you become cosmopolitan—a citizen of the world. Moreover, employers of today's college graduates value employees with international knowledge and foreign language skills (Bok, 2006; Fixman, 1990; Office of Research, 1994).

"A liberal [arts] education frees a person from the prison-house of class, race, time, place, background, family, and nation."

—Robert Hutchins, former dean of Yale Law School and president of the University of Chicago

The Global Perspective

Even broader than the international perspective is the global perspective. It extends beyond the relations among citizens of different nations to include all life forms that inhabit planet earth and the relationships between these diverse life forms and the earth's natural resources (minerals, air, and water). Humans share the earth and its natural resources with approximately 10 million animal species (Myers, 1997) and more than 300,000 forms of vegetative life (Knoll, 2003). As inhabitants of this planet and global citizens, we have a responsibility to address environmental issues that require balancing our industrial-technological progress with the need to sustain the earth's natural resources and preserve the life of our planet's cohabitants.

"Treat the Earth well. It was not given to you by your parents. It was loaned to you by your children."

—Kenyan proverb

The Universal Perspective

Beyond the global perspective is the broadest of all perspectives—the universal. The earth is just one planet that shares a solar system with seven other planets and is just one celestial body that shares a galaxy with millions of other celestial bodies, including stars, moons, meteorites, and asteroids (Encrenaz et al., 2004).

Just as we should guard against being ethnocentric (thinking that our culture is the center of humanity), we should guard against being geocentric (thinking that our planet is at the center of the universe). All heavenly bodies do not revolve around the earth; our planet revolves around them. The sun doesn't rise in the east and set in the west; our planet rotates around the sun to produce our earthly experiences of day and night.

"In astronomy, you must get used to viewing the earth as just one planet in the larger context of the universe."

—Physics professor (Donald, 2002)

"The sun, with all those planets revolving around it and dependent on it, can still ripen a bunch of grapes as if it had nothing else in the universe to do."

—Galileo Galilei

Elements of the Chronological Perspective

The Historical Perspective

A historical perspective is critical for understanding the root causes of our current human condition and world situation. Humans are products of both their social and natural history. Don't forget that the earth is estimated to be more than 4.5 billion years old and our human ancestors date back more than 250,000 years (Knoll, 2003). Thus, our current lives represent one very short time frame in a very long chronological reel. Every modern convenience we now enjoy reflects the collective efforts and cumulative knowledge of diverse human groups that have accumulated over thousands of years of history. By studying the past, we can build on our ancestors' achievements and avoid making their mistakes. For instance, by understanding the causes and consequences of the Holocaust, we can reduce the risk that an atrocity of that size and scope will ever happen again.

Reflection 2.8

Look back at the broadening perspectives developed by a liberal arts education. What college course would develop each perspective? If you're unsure or cannot remember whether a course is designed to develop any of these perspectives, look at the course's goals described in your college catalog (in print or online).

The Contemporary Perspective

The contemporary perspective focuses on understanding the current world situation and the events that comprise today's news. One major goal of a liberal arts education is to increase your understanding the contemporary human condition so that you may have the wisdom to improve it (Miller, 1988; Harris, 2010). For example, despite historical progress in the nation's acceptance and appreciation of different ethnic and racial groups, the United States today remains a nation that is deeply divided with respect to culture, religion, and social class (Brookings Institution, 2008).

The current technological revolution is generating new information and new knowledge at a faster rate than at any other time in human history (Dryden & Vos, 1999). When there is rapid creation and communication of new information, knowledge quickly becomes obsolete (Naisbitt, 1982). Workers in the today's complex, fast-changing world need to continually update their skills to perform their jobs and advance in their careers (Niles & Harris-Bowlsbey, 2002). This creates a demand for workers who have learned how to learn—a hallmark of the liberal arts.

The Futuristic Perspective

The futuristic perspective allows us to flash forward and envision what our world will be like years from now. This perspective focuses on such questions as "Will we leave the world a better or worse place for humans who will inhabit after our departure, including our children and grandchildren?" and "How can humans living today avoid short-term, shortsighted thinking and adopt a long-range vision that anticipates the consequences of their current actions on future generations of humans?"

To sum up, a comprehensive chronological perspective brings the past, present, and future into focus on a single screen. It enables us to see how the current world is a single segment of a temporal sequence that has been shaped by events that preceded it and how it will shape the events of the future.

> **Remember**
>
> *By embracing the perspectives of different times, places, and people, you're embracing the diversity promoted by a liberal arts education. These diverse perspectives liberate or emancipate you from the here and now and empower you to see things long ago and far away.*

"Those who cannot remember the past are damned to repeat it."

—George Santayana, Spanish-born American philosopher

"Yesterday is gone. Tomorrow has not yet come. We have only today. Let us begin."

—Mother Teresa of Calcutta, Albanian Catholic nun and winner of the Nobel Peace Prize

"The only person who is educated is the one who has learned how to learn and change."

—Carl Rogers, humanistic psychologist and Nobel Peace Prize nominee

"In times of change, learners inherit the Earth . . . [they] find themselves beautifully equipped to deal with a world that no longer exists."

—Eric Hoffer, author of *The Ordeal of Change* and recipient of the Presidential Medal of Freedom

"The future is literally in our hands to mold as we like. But we cannot wait until tomorrow. Tomorrow is now."

—Eleanor Roosevelt

"We all inherit the past. We all confront the challenges of the present. We all participate in the making of the future."

—Ernest Boyer and Martin Kaplan, *Educating for Survival*

The Synoptic Perspective: Integrating Diverse Perspectives into a Unified Whole

A liberal arts education helps you not only appreciate multiple perspectives but also how to integrate them into a meaningful whole (King, Brown, Lindsay, & VanHencke, 2007). Understanding of how the perspectives of time, place, and person interrelate to form a unified whole is referred to as a *synoptic* perspective (Cronon, 1998; Heath, 1977). The word derives from a combination of two roots: *syn*, meaning "together" (as in the word *synthesize*), and *optic*, meaning "to see." Thus, a synoptic perspective literally means to "see things together" or "see the whole." Said in another way, it enables you to see how all the trees come together to form the forest.

> "A truly great intellect is one which takes a connected view of old and new, past and present, far and near, and which has an insight into the influence of all these on one another, without which there is no whole, and no center."
>
> —John Henry Newman, *The Idea of a University* (1852)

Reflection 2.9

In light of the information you've read how would you interpret the following statement: "We can't know where we're going until we know where we've been"?

A liberal arts education helps you step beyond yourself to see the wider world and connects you with it. By seeing yourself as an integral part of humankind, you become integrated with the whole of humanity; you're able to see how you, as an individual, fit into the big picture—the larger scheme of things (Cuseo & Thompson, 2010). When we view ourselves as nested within a web of interconnections with other places, cultures, and times, we become aware of the common humanity we all share. This increased sense of connection with humankind decreases our feelings of personal isolation or alienation (Bellah, Madsen, Sullivan, Swidler, & Tipton, 1985). In his book, *The Perfect Education*, Kenneth Eble (1966) skillfully describes this benefit of a liberal arts education:

> "Without exception, the observed changes [during college] involve greater breadth, expansion, and appreciation for the new and different. These changes are eminently consistent with values of a liberal [arts] education, and the evidence for their presence is compelling."
>
> —Ernest Pascarella and Pat Terenzini, How College Affects Students

> *It can provide that overarching life of a people, a community, a world that was going on before the individual came onto the scene and that will continue on after [s]he departs. By such means we come to see the world not alone. Our joys are more intense for being shared. Our sorrows are less destructive for our knowing universal sorrow. Our fears of death fade before the commonness of the occurrence. (pp. 214–215)*

Remember

A liberal arts education launches you on a quest for two forms of wholeness: (1) an inner wholeness in which elements of your "self" become connected to form a whole person, and (2) an outer wholeness in which you become connected to the whole world. This inner and outer quest will enable you to lead a richer, more fulfilling life that's filled with greater breadth, balance, and wholeness.

Educating You for Life

Research shows that the primary reasons students go to college are to prepare for a career and get a better job (Pryor et al., 2012). While these are important reasons and your career is an important element of your life, a person's vocation or occupation represents just one element of the self. It also represents just one of many roles or responsibilities that you are likely to have in life.

Reflection **2.10**

In light of the knowledge you've acquired thus far in this chapter, what points or arguments would you make to counter the claim that the liberal arts are impractical?

"The finest art, the most difficult art, is the art of living."

—John Albert Macy, American author, poet, and editor of Helen Keller's autobiography

Similar to global issues, personal issues and challenges you face as an individual in your everyday life are multidimensional, requiring perspectives and skills that go well beyond the boundaries of a single academic field or career specialization. Your occupational role represents just one of many roles you will assume in life, which in-

Author's Experience

One life role that a liberal arts education helped prepare me for was the role of parent. Courses that I took in psychology and sociology proved to be useful in helping me understand how children develop and how a parent can best support them at different stages of their development. Surprisingly, however, there was one course I had in college that I never expected would ever help me as a parent. That course was statistics, which I took to fulfill a general education requirement in mathematics. It was not a particularly enjoyable course; some of my classmates sarcastically referred to it as "sadistics" because they felt it was a somewhat painful or torturous experience. However, what I learned in that course became valuable to me many years later when my 14-year-old son (Tony) developed a life-threatening disease, leukemia, which is a form of cancer that attacks blood cells. Tony's form of leukemia was a particularly perilous one because it had only a 35 percent average cure rate; in other words, 65 percent of those who develop the disease don't recover and eventually die from it. This statistic was based on patients that received the traditional treatment of chemotherapy, which was the type of treatment that my son began receiving when his cancer was first detected.

Another option for treating Tony's cancer was a bone-marrow transplant, which involved using radiation to destroy all of his own bone marrow (that was making the abnormal blood cells) and replace it with bone marrow donated to him by another person. My wife and I got opinions from doctors at two major cancer centers—one from a center that specialized in chemotherapy, and one from a center that specialized in bone-marrow transplants. The chemotherapy doctors felt strongly that drug treatment would be the better way to treat and cure Tony, and the bone-marrow transplant doctors felt strongly that his chances of survival would be much better if he had a transplant. So, my wife and I had to decide between two opposing recommendations, each made by a respected group of doctors.

To help us reach a decision, I asked both teams of doctors for research studies that had been done on the effectiveness of chemotherapy and bone-marrow transplants for treating my son's particular type of cancer. I read all of these studies and carefully analyzed their statistical findings. I remembered from my statistics course that when an average is calculated for a general group of people (e.g., average cure rate for people with leukemia), it tends to lump together individuals from different subgroups (e.g., males and females or young children and teenagers). Sometimes, when separate statistics are calculated for different subgroups, the results may be different from the average statistic for the whole group. So, when I read the research reports, I looked for any subgroup statistics that might have been calculated. I found two subgroups of patients with my son's particular type of cancer that had a higher rate of cure with chemotherapy than the general (whole-group) average of 35 percent. One subgroup included people with a low number of abnormal cells at the time when the cancer was first diagnosed, and the other subgroup consisted of people whose cancer cells dropped rapidly after their first week of chemotherapy. My son belonged to both of these subgroups, which meant that his chance for cure with chemotherapy was higher than the overall 35 percent average. Furthermore, I found that the statistics showing higher success rate for bone-marrow transplants were based only on patients whose body accepted the donor's bone marrow and did not include those who died because their body rejected the donor's bone marrow. So, the success rates for bone-marrow patients were not actually as high as they appeared to be, because the overall average did not include the subgroup of patients who died because of transplant rejection. Based on these statistics, my wife and I decided to go with chemotherapy and not the transplant operation.

Our son has now been cancer-free for more than five years, so we think we made the right decision. However, I never imagined that a statistics course, which I took many years ago to fulfill a general education requirement, would help me fulfill my role as a parent and help me make a life-or-death decision about my own son.

Joe Cuseo

clude the roles of family member, friend, co-worker, community member, citizen, and possibly mother or father. A liberal arts education provides you with the breadth of knowledge and the variety of skills needed to successfully accommodate the multiple roles and responsibilities you will encounter throughout life.

Summary and Conclusion

The liberal arts represent the foundation of a college education, upon which all academic majors are built. They promote success in any major and career by supplying students with a set of lifelong learning skills that can be applied in multiple settings and that can be continually used throughout life.

The liberal arts also promote your development as a whole person (intellectual, emotional, social, physical, spiritual, etc.) and broadens your perspective on the world by expanding (1) your social-spatial perspective to include increasingly larger social groups and more distant places, ranging from micro (the individual) to macro (the universe), and (2) your chronological perspective, ranging from the past to the present to the future.

Despite popular beliefs to the contrary, the liberal arts have many practical benefits, including promoting career mobility and career advancement. Most importantly, a liberal arts education prepares you for life roles other than an occupation, including roles such as family member, community member, and citizen. In short, a liberal arts education prepares you for more than a career: it prepares you for life.

Learning More through the World Wide Web

Internet-Based Resources for Further Information on Liberal Arts Education

For additional information related to the ideas discussed in this chapter, we recommend the following Web sites:

Liberal Arts Education:

www.aacu.org/resources/liberaleducation/index.cfm

Liberal Arts Resources:

www.iseek.org/education/liberalarts.html

2.1 Planning Your Liberal Arts Education

Since general education is an essential component of your college experience, it should be intentionally planned. This exercise will leave you with a flexible plan that capitalizes on your educational interests while ensuring that your college experience has both breadth and balance.

1. Use your course catalog (bulletin) to identify the general education requirements at your college. The requirements should be organized into general divisions of knowledge similar to those discussed in this chapter (humanities, fine arts, natural sciences, etc.). Within each of these liberal arts divisions, there will be specific courses listed that fulfill the general education requirements for that particular division. (Catalogs can sometimes be difficult to navigate; if you encounter difficulty or doubt about general education requirements, seek clarification from an academic advisor on campus.)

2. You'll probably have some freedom to choose courses from a larger group of courses that fulfill general education requirements within each division. Use your freedom of choice to select courses whose descriptions capture your curiosity or pique your interest. You can take liberal arts courses not only to fulfill general education requirements, but also to test your interest and talent in fields that you may end up choosing as a college major or minor.

3. Highlight the courses in the catalog that you plan to take to fulfill your general education requirements in each division of the liberal arts, and use the form on the following page to pencil in the courses you've chosen. (Use pencil because you will likely make some adjustments to your plan.) Remember that the courses you're taking this term may be fulfilling certain general education requirements, so be sure to list them on your planning form.

2.2 General Education Planning Form

Division of the Liberal Arts Curriculum: _____

General education courses you're planning to take to fulfill requirements in this division (record the course number and course title):

_____   _____

_____   _____

_____   _____

Division of the Liberal Arts Curriculum: _____

General education courses you're planning to take to fulfill requirements in this division (record the course number and course title):

_____   _____

_____   _____

_____   _____

Division of the Liberal Arts Curriculum: _____

General education courses you're planning to take to fulfill requirements in this division (record the course number and course title):

_____   _____

_____   _____

_____   _____

Division of the Liberal Arts Curriculum: _____

General education courses you're planning to take to fulfill requirements in this division (record the course number and course title):

_____   _____

_____   _____

_____   _____

Division of the Liberal Arts Curriculum: _____

General education courses you're planning to take to fulfill requirements in this division (record the course number and course title):

_____   _____

_____   _____

_____   _____

4. Look back at the general education courses you've listed and identify the broadening perspectives developed by the liberal arts that each course appears to be developing. (See p. 54 for a description of these perspectives.) Use the form that follows to ensure that your overall perspective is comprehensive and that you have no blind spots in your liberal arts education. For any perspective that's not covered in your plan, find a course in the catalog that will enable you to address the missing perspective.

Broadening Social-Spatial Perspectives

Perspective   Course Developing This Perspective
(See p. 55 for further descriptions of these perspectives.)

Self   _____

Family   _____

Community   _____

Society   _____

Culture   _____

Nation   _____

International   _____

Global   _____

Universe   _____

Broadening Chronological Perspectives

Perspective   Course Developing This Perspective
(See p. 56 for detailed descriptions of these perspectives.)

Historical   _____

Contemporary _____

Futuristic   _____

5. Look back at the general education courses you've listed and identify what element of holistic (whole-person) development each course appears to be developing. (See p. 49 for a description of each of these elements.) Use the form that follows to ensure that your course selection didn't overlook any element of the self. For any element that's not covered in your plan, find a course in the catalog or a co-curricular experience program that will enable you to address the missing area. For co-curricular learning experiences (e.g., leadership and volunteer experiences), consult your student handbook or contact someone in the Office of Student Life.

Dimensions of Self   Course or Co-Curricular Experience
    Developing This Dimension of Self

(See p. 48 for further descriptions of these dimensions.)
(Consult your student handbook for co-curricular experiences.)

Intellectual   _____

Emotional   _____

Social   _____

Ethical   _____

Physical   _____

Spiritual   _____

Vocational   _____

Personal   _____

Remember

This general education plan is not set in stone; it may be modified as you gain more experience with the college curriculum and campus life. Its purpose is not to restrict your educational exploration or experimentation, but to give you some educational direction, breadth, and balance.

Dazed and Confused: General Education versus Career Specialization

Joe Tech was really looking forward to college because he thought he would have freedom to select the courses he wanted and the opportunity to get into the major of his choice (computer science). However, he's shocked and disappointed with his first-term schedule of classes because it consists mostly of required general education courses that do not seem to relate in any way to his major. He's frustrated further because some of these courses are about subjects that he already took in high school (English, history, and biology). He's beginning to think he would be better off quitting college and going to a technical school where he could get right into computer science and immediately begin to acquire the knowledge and skills he'll need to prepare him for his intended career.

Reflection and Discussion Questions

1. Can you relate to Joe, or do you know of students who feel the same way Joe does?

2. If Joe decides to leave college for a technical school, how do you see it affecting his future (1) in the short run and (2) in the long run?

3. Do you see any way Joe might strike a balance between pursuing his career interest and obtaining his college degree so that he could work toward achieving both goals at the same time?

Goal Setting, Motivation, and Character

3

Moving from Dreams to Plans to Action

How would you define the word "successful"?

LEARNING GOAL

To help you set and strive for meaningful goals and maintain your motivation to reach those goals.

What Does Being "Successful" Mean to You?

"Achieving a desired outcome" is how *success* is commonly defined. The word *success* derives from the Latin root *successus*, meaning "to follow or come after" (as in the word *succession*). Thus, by definition, success involves an order or sequence of actions that lead to a desired outcome. The process starts with identifying an end (goal) and then finding a means (sequence of steps) to reach that goal (achieving success). Goal setting is the first step in the process of becoming successful because it gives you something specific to strive for and ensures that you start off in the right direction. Studies consistently show that setting goals is a more effective self-motivational strategy than simply telling yourself that you should try hard and do your best (Boekaerts, Pintrich, & Zeidner, 2000; Locke & Latham, 1990).

By setting goals, you show initiative—you initiate the process of gaining control of your future and taking charge of your life. When you take initiative, you demonstrate what psychologists call an *internal* locus of control: you believe that the locus (location or source) of control for events in your life is inside of you, rather than being *external*, or outside of you and beyond your control—for instance, determined by such factors as innate ability, luck, chance, or fate (Rotter, 1966; Carlson, Buskist, Heth, & Schmaltz, 2007). They believe that success is influenced more by attitude, effort, commitment, and preparation than by natural ability or inborn intelligence (Jernigan, 2004).

Research has revealed that individuals with a strong internal locus of control display the following characteristics:

1. Greater independence and self-direction (Van Overwalle, Mervielde, & De Schuyer, 1995);
2. More accurate self-assessment (Hashaw, Hammond, & Rogers, 1990);
3. Higher levels of learning and achievement (Wilhite, 1990); and
4. Better physical health (Maddi, 2002; Seligman, 1991).

Student Perspective

"Stopping a long pattern of bad decision-making and setting positive, productive priorities and goals."

—College sophomore's answer to the question "What does being successful mean to you?"

"I'm a great believer in luck, and I find the harder I work the more I have of it."

—Thomas Jefferson, third president of the United States

65

An internal locus of control also contributes to the development of another positive trait that psychologists call *self-efficacy*—the belief that you have power to produce a positive effect on the outcomes of your life (Bandura, 1994). People with low self-efficacy tend to feel helpless, powerless, and passive; they allow things to happen to them rather than taking charge and making things happen for them. College students with a strong sense of self-efficacy believe they're in control of their educational success and can take control of their future, regardless of their past or current circumstances.

People with a strong sense of self-efficacy initiate action, exert effort, and sustain that effort until they reach their goals. If they encounter setbacks or bad breaks along the way, they don't give up or give in; they persevere or push on (Bandura, 1986; 1997). They don't have a false sense of entitlement—that they're entitled to or owed anything; they believe success is something that's earned and the harder they work at it, the more likely they'll get it.

Students with a strong sense of *academic* self-efficacy have been found to:

1. Put considerable effort into their studies;
2. Use active-learning strategies;
3. Capitalize on campus resources; and
4. Persist in the face of obstacles (Multon, Brown, & Lent, 1991; Zimmerman, 1995; 2000).

Reflection 3.2

You are not required by law or by others to attend college; you've made the decision to continue your education. Do you believe you are in charge of your educational destiny?

Why or why not?

Students with a stronger sense of self-efficacy also possess a strong sense of personal responsibility. As the breakdown of the word *responsible* implies, they are "response" "able"—that is, they believe they are able to respond effectively to personal challenges, including academic challenges.

For example, studies show that students who convert their college degrees into successful careers have two common characteristics: personal initiative and a positive attitude (Pope, 1990). They don't take a passive approach and assume good positions will fall into their laps; nor do they believe they are owed a position simply because they have a college degree or credential. Instead, they become actively involved in the job-hunting process and use various job-search strategies (Brown & Krane, 2000).

Strategies for Effective Goal Setting

Motivation begins with goal setting. Studies show that people who neglect to set and pursue life goals are prone to feelings of "life boredom" and a belief that their lives are meaningless (Bargdill, 2000). Goals may be classified into three general categories: long-range, mid-range, and short-range, depending on the length of time it takes to reach them and the order in which they are to be achieved. Short-range goals need to be completed before a mid-range goal can be reached, and mid-range goals must be reached before a long-range goal can be achieved. For example, if your long-range goal is a successful career, you must complete the courses required for a degree (mid-range goal) that will allow you entry into a career; to reach your mid-range goal of a college degree, you need to successfully complete the courses you're taking this term (short-range goal).

This process is called means-end analysis, which involves working backward from your long-range goal (the end) and identifying the order and timing of the mid-range and short-range subgoals (the means) that need to be taken to reach your long-range goal (Brooks, 2009; Newell & Simon, 1959).

Setting Long-Range Goals

Setting effective long-range goals involves a process that has two components: (1) self-awareness, or self-insight into who you are now, and (2) self-projection, or a vision of what you want to become. When you engage in both of these processes, you're able to see a connection between your short-range and long-range goals.

Long-range goal setting enables you to take an approach to your future that is proactive—acting beforehand to anticipate and control your future life rather than putting it off and being forced to react to it without a plan. Research shows that people who neglect to set goals for themselves are more likely to experience boredom with life (Bargdill, 2000). Setting long-range goals and planning ahead also helps reduce feelings of anxiety about the future because when you give forethought to your future, you gain greater power to control it—i.e., you develop a stronger sense of self-efficacy. As the old saying goes, "To be forewarned is to be forearmed."

Reflection **3.3**

In what area or areas of your life do you feel that you've been able to exert the most control and achieve the most positive results?

In what area or areas do you wish you had more control and were achieving better results?

What strategies have you used in those areas of your life where you've taken charge and gained control? Could you apply the same strategies to those areas in which you need to gain more control?

Remember that setting long-range goals and developing long-range plans doesn't mean you can't adjust or modify them. Your goals can undergo change as you change, develop skills, acquire knowledge, and discover new interests or talents. Finding yourself and discovering your path in life are among the primary purposes of a college education. Don't think that the process of setting long-range goals means you are locking yourself into a premature plan and reducing your options. Instead, long-range goal setting just gives you a map that provides you with some sense of direction about where you're going, which can also provide you with the ignition and motivation to get going.

"What keeps me going is goals."

—Muhammad Ali, philanthropist, social activist, and Hall of Fame boxer crowned "Sportsman of the 20th Century" by *Sports Illustrated*

"To fail to plan is to plan to fail."

—Robert Wubbolding, internationally known author, psychologist, and teacher

"You've got to be careful if you don't know where you're going because you might not get there."

—Yogi Berra, Hall of Fame baseball player

"There is perhaps nothing worse than reaching the top of the ladder and discovering that you're on the wrong wall."

—Joseph Campbell, American professor and writer

Steps in the Goal-Setting Process

Effective goal setting involves a four-step sequence:

1. **Awareness of yourself.** Your personal interests, abilities and talents, and values;

↓

2. **Awareness of your options.** The range of choices available to you;

↓

3. **Awareness of the options that best fit you.** The goals that are most compatible with your personal abilities, interests, values, and needs;

↓

4. **Awareness of the process.** The steps you need to take to reach your chosen goal.

Discussed in the next sections are strategies for taking each of these steps in the goal-setting process.

Step 1. Self-Awareness

The goals you choose to pursue say a lot about who you are and what you want from life. Thus, self-awareness is a critical first step in the process of goal setting. You must know yourself before you can choose the goals you want to achieve. While this may seem obvious, self-awareness and self-discovery are often overlooked aspects of the goal-setting process. Deepening your self-awareness puts you in a better position to select and choose goals and to pursue a personal path that's true to who you are and what you want to become.

> **Remember**
>
> *Self-awareness is the first and most important step in the process of making any important life choice or decision. Good decisions are built on a deep understanding of one's self.*

No one is in a better position to know who you are, and what you want to be, than *you*. One effective way to get to know yourself more deeply is through self-questioning. You can increase self-awareness by asking yourself questions that can stimulate your thinking about your inner qualities and priorities. Effective self-questioning launches you on an inward quest or journey to self-insight and self-discovery, which is the essential first step to effective goal setting. For example, if your long-range goal is career success, you can launch your voyage toward achieving this goal by asking yourself thought-provoking questions related to your personal:

- **Interests.** What you like to do;
- **Abilities and talents.** What you're good at doing; and
- **Values.** What you believe is worth doing.

The following questions are designed to sharpen your self-awareness with respect to your interests, abilities, and values. As you read each question, briefly note what thought or thoughts come to mind about yourself.

"You have brains in your head. You have feet in your shoes. You can steer yourself any direction you choose."

—Theodore Seuss Giesel, a.k.a. Dr. Seuss, author of children's books including *Oh, the Places You'll Go!*

"Know thyself, and to thine own self be true."

—Plato, ancient Greek philosopher

"In order to succeed, you must know what you are doing, like what you are doing, and believe in what you are doing."

—Will Rogers, Native American humorist and actor

Your Personal Interests

1. What tends to grab your attention and hold it for long periods of time?
2. What sorts of things are you naturally curious about and tend to intrigue you?
3. What do you enjoy and do as often as you possibly can?
4. What do you look forward to or get excited about?
5. What are your favorite hobbies or pastimes?
6. When you're with friends, what do you tend to talk most about or spend most of your time doing?
7. What has been your most stimulating or enjoyable learning experience?
8. If you've had previous work or volunteer experience, what jobs or tasks did you find most enjoyable or stimulating?
9. When time seems to fly by for you, what are you usually doing?
10. When you choose to read, what topics do you read about?
11. When you open a newspaper or log on to the Internet, where do you tend to go first?
12. When you find yourself daydreaming or fantasizing about your future life, what's going on or what are you doing?

Reflection **3.4**

From your responses to the preceding questions, identify one long-range goal you could pursue that's compatible with your personal interests. In the space that follows, write down the goal and your interests that are compatible with it.

Your Personal Abilities and Talents

1. What seems to come easily or naturally to you?
2. What would you say is your greatest personal strength or talent?
3. What do you excel at when you apply yourself and put forth your best effort?
4. What are your most advanced or well-developed skills?
5. What would you say has been the greatest accomplishment or achievement in your life thus far?
6. What about yourself are you most proud of, or what do you take the most pride in doing?
7. When others come to you for advice or assistance, what is it usually for?
8. What would your best friend or friends say is your best quality, trait, or characteristic?
9. When you had a strong feeling of being successful after you had done something, what was it that you did?
10. If you've received awards or other forms of recognition, what did you do to earn them?
11. In what types of learning tasks or activities have you experienced the most success?
12. In what types of courses do you tend to earn the highest grades?

> "Never desert your line of talent. Be what nature intended you for and you will succeed."
>
> —Sydney Smith, 18th-century English writer and defender of the oppressed

Reflection **3.5**

From your responses to the preceding questions, identify a long-range goal you could pursue that's compatible with your personal abilities and talents. In the space that follows, write down the goal and your abilities and talents that are compatible with it.

Your Personal Values

1. What matters most to you?
2. If you were to single out one thing you stand for or believe in, what would it be?
3. What would you say are your highest priorities in life?
4. What makes you feel good about what you're doing when you're doing it?
5. If there were one thing in the world you could change, improve, or make a difference in, what would it be?
6. When you have extra spending money, what do you usually spend it on?
7. When you have free time, what do you usually spend it on?
8. What does "making it big in life" mean to you?
9. How would you define success? (What would it take for you to feel that you were successful?)
10. How would you define happiness? (What would it take for you to feel happy?)
11. Do you have any heroes or anyone you admire, look up to, or believe has set an example worth following? If yes, who and why?
12. Which of the following four personal qualities would you want to be known for? Rank them in order of priority to you (1 = highest, 4 = lowest).

   _____ Smart

   _____ Wealthy

   _____ Creative

   _____ Caring

Reflection **3.6**

From your responses to the preceding questions, identify a long-range goal you could pursue that's compatible with your personal values. In the space that follows, write down the goal and your values that are compatible with it.

Step 2. Awareness of Your Options

The second critical step in the goal-setting process is to become aware of your options for long-range goals. For example, to effectively choose a career goal, you need to be aware of the career options available to you and have a realistic understanding of the types of work performance required by these careers. To gain this knowledge, you'll need to capitalize on available resources by doing the following:

1. Reading books about different careers
2. Taking career development courses
3. Interviewing people in different career fields
4. Observing (shadowing) people working in different careers

Step 3. Awareness of Options That Best "Fit" You

A third key step in the goal-setting process is becoming aware of the full range of options available to you as potential goals. For instance, in college you have multiple courses and majors from which to choose. To deepen your awareness of whether a field may be a good fit for you, take a course in that field to test out how well it matches your interests, values, talents, and learning style. Ideally, you want to select a field that closely taps into, or builds on, your strongest skills and talents. Choosing a field that's compatible with your strongest abilities will enable you to master the skills required by that field more deeply and efficiently. You are also more likely to succeed or excel in a field that draws on your talents, and the success you experience will, in turn, strengthen your self-esteem, self-confidence, and drive to continue with it. You've probably heard of the proverb "If there's a will, there's a way"—when you're motivated, you're more likely to succeed. It's also true that "If there's a way, there's a will"—when you know how to do something well, you're more motivated to do it.

Step 4. Awareness of the Key Steps Needed to Reach Your Goal

This is the fourth and final step in an effective goal-setting process. For example, if you've set the goal of achieving a college degree in a particular major, you need to be aware of the courses you need to complete to reach that major. Similarly, with a career goal, you need to know what major or majors lead to that career; some careers may require a specific major, but many careers may be reached through a variety of different majors. (See Chapter 11 for more details.)

Reflection 3.7

Think about a major you've chosen or are considering and answer the following questions:

1. Why are you considering this major? What led or caused you to become interested in this choice? Why or why not?

2. Would you say that your interest in this major is motivated primarily by intrinsic factors—i.e., factors "inside" of you, such as your personal abilities, interests, needs, and values? Or is your interest in the career motivated more heavily by extrinsic factors—i.e., factors "outside" of you, such as starting salary or meeting the expectations of parents?

The word motivation derives from the Latin movere, meaning "to move." Success comes to those who overcome inertia—they first initiate momentum to start moving them toward their goal; then they maintain motivation until their goal is reached. Goal setting only creates the potential for success; it takes motivation to turn this potential into reality by converting intention into action. You can have the best-planned goals and all the knowledge, strategies, and skills to be successful, but if you don't have the will to succeed, there's no way you will succeed. Studies show that without a strong personal commitment to achieve a goal, that goal will be not be achieved, no matter how well designed the plan is to reach it (Locke, 2000; Locke & Latham, 1990).

"Mere knowledge is not power; it is only possibility. Action is power; and its highest manifestation is when it is directed by knowledge."
—Francis Bacon, English philosopher, lawyer, and champion of modern science

"You can lead a horse to water, but you can't make him drink."
—Author unknown

Remember
The process of effective goal setting applies to more than just educational goals. It's a strategic process that can and should be applied to any goal you set for yourself in life, at any stage of your life.

Snapshot Summary

3.1 **The SMART Method of Goal Setting**

A popular mnemonic device for remembering the key components of a well-designed goal is the acronym "SMART" (Doran, 1981; Meyer, 2003).

A **SMART** goal is one that is:

Specific: States exactly what the goal is and what will be done to achieve it.

Example: I'll achieve at least a "B" average this term by spending 25 hours per week on my course work outside of class and by using the effective learning strategies described in this book. (As opposed to the non-specific goal, "I'm really going to work hard.")

Meaningful (and Measurable): A goal that really matters to the individual, for which progress can be steadily measured or tracked.

Example: I will achieve at least a "B" average this term because it will enable me to get into a field that I really want to pursue as a career, and I will measure my progress toward this goal by keeping track of the grades I'm earning in all my courses throughout the term.

Actionable: Identifies the concrete actions or behaviors that will be engaged in to reach the goal.

Example: I will achieve at least a "B" average this term by (1) attending all classes, (2) taking detailed notes in all my classes, (3) completing all reading assignments before their due dates, and (4) avoiding cramming by studying in advance of all my major exams.

Realistic: A goal capable of being achieved or attained.

Example: Achieving a "B" average this term will be a realistic goal for me because my course load is manageable and I will not be working at my part-time job for more than 15 hours per week.

Timed: A goal that is broken down into a timeline that includes short-range, mid-range, and long-range steps.

Example: To achieve at least a "B" average this term, first I'll acquire the information I need to learn by taking complete notes in class and on my assigned readings (short-range step). Second, I'll study the information I've acquired from my notes and readings in short study sessions held in advance of major exams (mid-range step). Third, I'll hold a final review session for all information previously studied on the day before my exams, and after exams I'll review my test results as feedback to determine what I did well and what I need to do better in order to maintain at least a "B" average (long-range step).

Note: The strategy for setting **SMART** goals is a transferable process that can be applied to reaching goals in any aspect or dimension of your life, including health-related goals such as losing weight, social goals such as meeting new people, and fiscal goals such as saving money. The **SMART** goal-setting strategy can help you achieve goals for any and all elements of holistic (whole-person) development described in Chapter 2 (p. 49).

Strategies for Maintaining Motivation and Progress toward Your Goals

Reaching your goals requires will and energy; it also requires skill and strategy. Listed here are strategies for maintaining your motivation and commitment to reaching your goals.

Visualize reaching your long-range goal. Create mental images of being successful. For example, if your goal is to achieve a college degree, imagine a crowd of cheering family, friends, and faculty at your graduation. Visualize how you'll be able to cherish and carry this proud memory with you for the rest of your life, and how the benefits of a college degree will last your entire lifetime. Imagine yourself in the career that your college degree enabled you to enter. Visualize your typical workday going something like this: You wake up in the morning and hop out of bed enthusiastically, looking forward to your day at work. When you're at work, time flies by, and before you know it, the day's over. When you return to bed that night and look back on your day, you feel good about what you did and how well you did it.

Put your goals in writing. When you put your goals in writing, you remain aware of them and remember them. This can stimulate your motivation to pursue your plan into action by serving almost like a written contract that holds you accountable to following through on your commitment. Place your written goals where you see them regularly. Consider writing them on sticky notes and posting them in multiple places that you encounter on a daily basis (e.g., your laptop, refrigerator, and bathroom mirror). If you keep them constantly in sight, you'll keep them constantly in mind.

Map out your goals. Lay out your goals in the form of a flowchart to show the steps you'll be taking to move from your short-range to mid-range to long-range goals. Visual diagrams can help you "see" where you want to go, enabling you to connect where you are now and where you want to be. Diagramming can also be energizing because it gives you a sneak preview of the finish line and a map-like overview of how to get there.

Keep a record of your progress. Research indicates that the act of monitoring and recording progress toward goals can increase motivation to continue pursuing them (Locke & Latham, 2005; Matsui, Okada, & Inoshita, 1983). The act of keeping records of your progress probably increases your motivation by giving you frequent feedback on your progress and positive reinforcement for staying on track and moving toward your target (long-range goal) (Bandura & Cervone, 1983; Schunk, 1995). For example, mark your accomplishments in red on your calendar, or keep a journal of the goals you've reached; your entries will keep you motivated by supplying you with concrete evidence of your progress and commitment. You can also chart or graph your progress, which provides a powerful visual display of your upward trends and patterns. Keep the chart where you can see it on a daily basis so you can use it as an ongoing source of inspiration and motivation. You can add musical inspiration by playing a motivational song in your head to keep you going (e.g., "We Are the Champions" by Queen).

Develop a skeletal resume of your career goals. Include your goals as separate sections or categories that will be fleshed out as you complete them. Your to-be-completed resume can provide a framework or blueprint for organizing, building, and tracking progress toward your goals. It can also serve as a visual reminder of the things you plan to accomplish and eventually showcase to potential employers. Furthermore, every time you look at your growing resume, you'll be reminded of your past accomplishments, which can energize and motivate you to reach your goals. As you fill in and build up your resume, you will see (literally) how much you have achieved, which boosts your self-confidence and motivation to continue achieving. (For a sample skeletal resume, see Chapter 12, p. 324.)

Reward yourself for making steady progress toward your long-range goal. Reward is already built into reaching your long-range goal because it represents the end of your trip: it lands you at your desired destination. However, short- and mid-range goals may not be desirable ends in themselves; often, they are merely the means to a desirable end (your long-range goal). Consequently, you need to intentionally reward yourself for landing on these smaller stepping stones up the path to your long-range goal. When you complete these short- and mid-range goals, record and reward your accomplishments (e.g., celebrate your successful completion of midterms or finals by treating yourself to something you enjoy).

Like any other habit, the habit of perseverance and persistence through all intermediate steps needed to reach a long-range goal is more likely to continue if it's followed by a reward (positive reinforcement). The process of setting small goals, mov-

> **Remember**
>
> *The next best thing to accomplishing something immediately is immediately writing down your intention to do it!*

ing steadily toward them, and rewarding yourself for reaching them is a simple but powerful strategy. It helps you maintain motivation over the extended period needed to reach your long-range goal.

Capitalize on available campus resources that can help you stay on track and moving toward your goal. Research indicates that college success results from a combination of what students do for themselves (personal responsibility) and what students do to capitalize on resources available to them—i.e., their resourcefulness (Pascarella & Terenzini, 1991, 2005). Successful college students are resourceful students; they seek out and take advantage of college resources to help them reach their goals.

For example, a resourceful student who is having trouble deciding what field of study to pursue for a degree will seek assistance from an academic advisor on campus. A resourceful student who is interested in a particular career but is unclear about the best educational path to take toward that career will use the Career Development Center as a resource.

Use your social resources. Ask yourself, "Who can help me stick to my plan and complete the steps needed to reach my goal?" The power of social support groups for helping people achieve personal goals is well documented by research in various fields (Brissette, Cohen, & Seeman, 2000; Ewell, 1997). You can use the power of people by surrounding yourself with peers who are committed to successfully achieving their educational goals and by avoiding "toxic" people who are likely to poison your plans or dampen your dreams.

Find supportive, motivated friends and make a mutual pact to help each other reach your respective goals. This step could be taken to a more formal level by drawing up a "social contract" whereby you and your partner are "co-witnesses" or designated social-support agents whose role is to help each other stay on track and moving toward long-range goals. Studies show that making a public commitment to a goal increases your commitment to it, probably because it becomes a matter of personal pride and integrity that's seen not only through your own eyes but also through the eyes of others (Hollenbeck, Williams, & Klein, 1989; Locke, 2000).

Convert setbacks into comebacks. The type of thoughts you have after experiencing a setback can affect your emotional reaction to the setback and the action you take in response to it. What you think about a poor performance (e.g., a poor test grade) can affect your emotional reaction to that grade and what action, or lack of action, you take to improve it. You can react to the poor grade by knocking yourself down with a putdown ("I'm a loser") or by building yourself back up with a positive pep talk ("I'm going to learn from my mistakes on this test and rebound with a stronger performance on the next one").

It's noteworthy that the root of the word *failure* is *fallere*, which means to "trip or fall," while the root word for *success* is *successus*, which means "to follow or come after." Thus, when we fail at something, it doesn't mean we've been defeated: it just means we've stumbled and fallen. Success can still be achieved after the fall by getting up, not giving up, and continuing to take the succession of steps need to successfully reach our goal.

Reflection **3.8**

What would you say is the biggest setback or obstacle you've overcome in your life thus far?

How did you overcome it? (What enabled you to get past it or prevented you from being blocked by it?)

If a poor past performance is seen not as a personal failure but as a learning opportunity, the setback may be turned into a comeback. Here are some notable people who turned early setbacks into successful comebacks:

- Louis Pasteur, famous bacteriologist, who failed his admission test to the University of Paris;
- Albert Einstein, Nobel Prize–winning physicist, who failed math in elementary school;
- Thomas Edison, prolific inventor, who was once expelled from school as "uneducable";
- Johnny Unitas, Hall of Fame football player, who was cut twice from professional football teams early in his career.

In response to their early setbacks, these successful professionals didn't get discouraged. Getting mad or sad about a setback is likely to make you stressed or depressed and leave you focused on a past event that you can no longer control. By reacting optimistically to a poor performance and using the results as feedback to improve your future performance, you gain control of it. You put yourself in the position to bounce back from the setback and turn a liability into an opportunity.

> **Remember**
> *Don't let past mistakes bring you down emotionally or motivationally, but don't ignore or neglect them. Instead, inspect them, reflect on them, and correct them so that they don't happen again.*

Maintain positive expectations. Just as your thoughts in reaction to something that's already taken place can affect your motivation, thoughts about what you expect to happen next can affect what will occur. Your expectations of things to come can be either positive or negative. For example, before a test you could think, "I'm poised, confident, and ready to do it." Or you could think, "I know I'm going to fail this test; I just know it."

Expectations can lead to what sociologists and psychologists have called a self-fulfilling prophecy—a positive or negative expectation leads you to act in a way that is consistent with your expectation, which, in turn, makes your expectation come true. For instance, if you expect you're going to fail an exam ("What's the use? I'm going to fail anyway."), you're less likely to put as much effort into studying for the test. During the test, your negative expectation is likely to reduce your test confidence and elevate you test anxiety; for example, if you experience difficulty with the first item on a test, you may get anxious and begin to think you're going to have difficulty with all remaining items and flunk the entire exam. All of this negative thinking is likely to increase the probability that your expectation of doing poorly on the exam will become a reality.

Reflection **3.9**

Would you consider yourself to be an optimist or a pessimist?

In what situations are you more likely to think optimistically and pessimistically?

Why?

"What happens is not as important as how you react to what happens."
—Thaddeus Golas, *Lazy Man's Guide to Enlightenment*

"When written in Chinese, the word 'crisis' is composed of two characters. One represents danger, and the other represents opportunity."
—John F. Kennedy, 35th president of the United States

"Whether you think you can or you can't, you're right."
—Henry Ford, founder of Ford Motor Company

"A pessimist sees the difficulty in every opportunity; an optimist sees the opportunity in every difficulty."

—Winston Churchill

In contrast, positive expectations can lead to a positive self-fulfilling prophecy: If you expect to do well on an exam, you're more likely to demonstrate higher levels of effort, confidence, and concentration, all of which combine to increase the likelihood that you'll earn a higher test grade. Research shows that learning and practicing positive self-talk serves to promote hope—belief in one's ability to reach goals and the ability to actually reach them (Snyder, 1994).

Keep your eye on the prize. Don't lose sight of the long-term consequences of your short-term choices and decisions. Long-range thinking is the key to reaching long-range goals. Unfortunately, however, humans are often more motivated by short-range thinking because it produces quicker results and more immediate gratification. It's more convenient and tempting to think in the short term ("I like it. I want it. I want it now."). Many years of research reveal that the later consequences follow a decision, the less likely people are to consider those consequences of their decisions (Ainslie, 1975; Elster & Lowenstein, 1992; Goldstein & Hogarth, 1997). For example, choosing to do what you feel like doing instead of doing work that needs to be done is why so many people procrastinate, and choosing to use a credit card to get something now instead of saving money to buy it later is why so many people pile up credit-card debt.

"You've got to think about 'big things' while you're doing small things, so that all the small things go in the right direction."

—Alvin Toffler, American futurologist and author who predicted the future effects of technology on our society

To be successful in the long run, you need to keep your focus on the big picture—your dream. At the same time, you need to focus on the details—the due dates, to-do lists, and day-to-day duties that require perspiration but keep you on track and going in the right direction.

Setting meaningful life goals and steadily progressing toward them require two focus points. One involves a narrow-focus lens that allows you to focus in on the details immediately in front of you. The other is a wide-angle lens that gives you a big-picture view of what's further ahead of you (your long-range goal). Success involves your ability to see and make connections between small, short-term chores and challenges (e.g., completing an assignment that's due next week) and the large, long-range picture (e.g., college graduation and a successful future). Thus, you need to switch back and forth from the wide-angle lens that gives you a vision of the bigger, more distant picture (your dream) to a narrow-focus lens that shifts your attention to completing the smaller tasks immediately ahead of you and keeping on the path to your dream.

"Whoever wants to reach a distant goal must take many small steps."

—Helmut Schmidt, former chancellor of West Germany

Author's Experience

When I was coaching a youth soccer team, I noticed that many of the less successful players tended to make one of two mistakes when they were trying to move with the ball. Some spent too much time looking down, focusing on the ball at their feet, and trying to be sure that they did not lose control of it. By not lifting their heads and looking ahead periodically, they often missed open territory, open teammates, or an open goal. Other unsuccessful players made the opposite mistake: They spent too much time with their heads up, trying to see where they were headed. By not looking down at the ball immediately in front of them, they often lost control of the ball, moved ahead without it, or sometimes stumbled over it and fell flat on their faces. The successful soccer players on the team developed the habit of shifting their focus between looking down to maintain control of the ball immediately in front of them and lifting their eyes to see where they were headed.

The more I thought about how the successful players alternated between handling the ball in front of them and viewing the goal farther ahead, it struck me that this was a metaphor for success in life. Successful people alternate between both of these perspectives so that they don't lose sight of how the short-range tasks immediately in front of them connect with the long-range goal that's far ahead of them.

Joe Cuseo

Remember

Keep your future dreams and current tasks in clear focus. Integrating these two perspectives will produce an image that provides you with the inspiration to complete your college education and the determination to complete your day-to-day tasks.

The Importance of Personal Character

Reaching your goals depends on acquiring and using effective strategies, but it takes something more. Ultimately, success emerges from the inside out; it flows from positive qualities or attributes found within you, which, collectively, form your personal character.

We become effective and successful human beings when our actions and deeds become a natural extension of who we are and how we live. At first, developing the habits associated with achieving success and leading a productive life may require substantial effort and intense concentration because these behaviors may be new to us. However, if these actions occur consistently enough, they're transformed into natural habits.

When you engage in effective habits regularly, they become virtues. A virtue may be defined as a characteristic or trait that is valued as good or admirable, and someone who possesses a collection of important virtues is said to be a person of character (Peterson & Seligman, 2004). There are three key character traits or virtues that typify highly motivated people:

1. Drive
2. Discipline
3. Determination

Drive

Drive is the force within you that supplies you with the energy needed to initiate action. Much like shifting into the drive gear is necessary to move your car forward, it takes personal drive to move forward and toward your goals. People with drive are not just dreamers: they are also doers. They take the action needed to convert their dreams into reality; they hustle—they go all out and give it their all, all of the time, to achieve their goals. College students with drive approach college with passion and enthusiasm. They don't hold back and work halfheartedly; they give 100 percent by putting their whole heart and soul into it. Studies show that individuals with dedication—who are deeply committed to what they do—are more likely to report that they are healthy and happy (Csikszentmihalyi, 1990; Maddi, 2002; Myers, 1993).

Discipline

Discipline includes such positive qualities as commitment, devotion, and dedication. These personal qualities enable us to keep going and moving toward our long-range goals over an extended period of time. Successful people think big but start small; they take all the small steps and diligently do all the little things that need to be done, which, in the long run, add up to a big accomplishment—achievement of their long-range goal.

People who are self-disciplined accept the day-to-day sweat, toil, and perspiration needed to attain their long-term aspirations. They're willing to tolerate short-term strain or pain for long-term gain. They have the self-control and self-restraint

"If you do not find it within yourself, where will you go to get it?"

—Zen saying (Zen is a branch of Buddhism that emphasizes seeing deeply into the nature of things and ongoing self-awareness)

"We are what we repeatedly do. Excellence, then, is not an act, but a habit."

—Aristotle, ancient Greek philosopher

"Sow an act and you reap a habit; sow a habit and you reap a character; sow a character and you reap a destiny."

—Frances E. Willard, 19th-century American educator and women's rights activist

Student
Perspective

"Why is it so hard when I *have* to do something and so easy when I *want* to do something?"

—First-year college student

"Self-discipline is the ability to make yourself do the thing you have to do, when it ought be done, whether you like it or not."

—Thomas Henry Huxley, 19th-century English biologist

needed to resist the impulse for instant gratification or the temptation to do what they feel like doing instead of what they need to do. They're willing to sacrifice their immediate needs and desires in the short run to do what is necessary to put them where they want to be in the long run.

Reflection **3.10**

Think about something that you do with drive, effort, and intensity. What thoughts, attitudes, and behaviors do you display when you do it?

Do you see ways in which you could apply the same approach to achieving your goals in college?

The ability to delay short-term (and shortsighted) gratification is a distinctively human characteristic that differentiates people from other animals. As you can see in Figure 3.1, the upper frontal part of the brain that's responsible for long-range planning and controlling emotions and impulses is much larger in humans than it is in one of the most intelligent and humanlike animals, the chimpanzee.

FIGURE 3.1

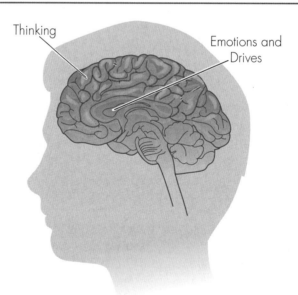

© Kendall Hunt

The part of the brain responsible for long-range planning and controlling emotions and impulses is much larger in humans than in other animals, including the highly intelligent chimpanzee.

Where Thoughts, Emotions, and Drives Are Experienced in the Brain

Author's Experience When I entered college in the mid-1970s, I was a first-generation student from an extremely impoverished background. Not only did I have to work to pay for part of my education, but I also needed to assist my family financially. I stocked grocery store shelves at night during the week and waited tables at a local country club on the weekends. Managing my life, time, school, and work required full-time effort. However, I always understood that my purpose was to graduate from college and all of my other efforts supported that goal. Thus, I went to class and arrived on time even when I did not feel like going to class. One of my greatest successes in life was to keep my mind and body focused on the ultimate prize of getting a college education. That success has paid off many times over.

Aaron Thompson

> **Remember**
> *Sacrifices made for a short time can bring benefits that last a lifetime.*

The ability to postpone immediate wants or needs is a key characteristic of self-discipline.

Determination

People who are determined pursue their goals with a relentless tenacity. They have the fortitude to persist in the face of frustration and the resiliency to bounce back after setbacks. If they encounter something on the road to their goal that's hard to do, they work harder and longer to do it. When they encounter a major bump or barrier, they don't let it stand in their way by giving up or giving in; instead, they dig deeper and keep going.

People with determination are also more likely to seek out challenges. Research indicates that people who continue to pursue opportunities for personal growth and self-development throughout life are more likely to report feeling happy and healthy (Maddi, 2002; Myers, 1993). Rather than remaining stagnant and simply doing what's safe, secure, or easy, they stay hungry and display an ongoing commitment to personal growth and development; they keep striving and driving to be the best they can possibly be in all aspects of life.

"SUCCESS is peace of mind which is a direct result of self-satisfaction in knowing you made the effort to become the best that you are capable of becoming."
—John Wooden, college basketball coach and creator of the "Pyramid of Success"

Studies of highly successful people, whether they are scientists, musicians, writers, chess masters, or basketball stars, consistently show that achieving high levels of skill and success requires dedicated practice (Levitin, 2006). This is true even of people whose success is thought to be due to natural gifts or talents. For example, during the Beatles' first four years as a band and before they burst into musical stardom, they performed live an estimated 1,200 times, and many of these performances lasted five or more hours a night. They performed (practiced) for more hours during those first four years than most bands perform during their entire careers. Similarly, before Bill Gates became a computer software giant and creator of Microsoft, he logged almost 1,600 hours of computer time during one seven-month period alone, averaging eight hours a day, seven days a week (Gladwell, 2008). What these extraordinary success stories show is that success takes dedication to putting in the time and practice to be successful. Reaching long-range goals means making small steps; they aren't achieved in one quick, quantum leap; it requires patience, persistence, and practice.

In addition to drive, discipline, and determination, three other character traits or virtues typify successful people:

1. Wisdom
2. Integrity
3. Civility

> "As gold which he cannot spend will make no man rich, so knowledge which he cannot apply will make no man wise."
>
> —Dr. Samuel Johnson, famous English literary figure and original author of the *Dictionary of the English Language* (1747)

> "Be as smart as you can, but remember that it is always better to be wise than smart."
>
> —Alan Alda, visiting professor at the State University of New York at Stony Brook and six-time Emmy Award and Golden Globe Award winner, best known for his role as Hawkeye Pierce in the TV series *M*A*S*H*

Wisdom

You demonstrate wisdom when you use the knowledge you acquire to guide you toward becoming an effective and successful human being (Staudinger & Baltes, 1994). For instance, if you apply the knowledge you've acquired in this chapter about goal setting and motivation to guide your behavior in college and beyond, you are exhibiting wisdom.

Reflection 3.11

Thus far in your college experience, which of the following four principles of success have you put into practice most effectively? (Circle one.)

active involvement   resourcefulness   collaboration   reflection

Which of the four principles do you think will be the most difficult for you to put into practice? (Circle one.)

active involvement   resourcefulness   collaboration   reflection

Why?

Integrity

The word *integrity* comes from the same root as the word integrate, which captures a key characteristic of people with integrity: their outer selves are integrated or in harmony with their inner selves. "Outer-directed" people decide on their personal standards of conduct by looking outward to see what others are doing (Riesman, Glazer,

& Denney, 2001). In contrast, individuals with integrity are "inner-directed"—their actions reflect their inner qualities and are guided by their consciences.

People of character are not only wise, they're ethical. They don't pursue success at any ethical cost. They have a strong set of personal values that steer them in the right moral direction. Besides doing things effectively and successfully, they do what's good and right. For instance, college students with integrity don't cheat and then rationalize that their cheating is acceptable because "others are doing it." They don't look to other people to determine their goals and values, and they don't conform to the norm if the norm is wrong; instead, they look inward, use their consciences as their guides, and self-determine their goals.

Civility

People of character are personally and socially responsible. They model what it means to live in a civilized community by demonstrating civility—they respect the rights of other members of their community, including members of their college community. In exercising their own rights and freedoms, they don't step (or stomp) on the rights and freedoms of others. They treat other members of their community in a sensitive and courteous manner and are willing to confront others who violate the rights of their fellow citizens. They are model citizens whose actions visibly demonstrate to others that they oppose any attempt to disrespect or interfere with the rights of fellow members of their community.

Snapshot Summary

3.2

Violating Civility: Insensitive Use of Personal Technology in the Classroom

Behavior that interferes with the rights of others to learn or teach in the college classroom represents a violation of civility. Listed below are behaviors illustrating classroom incivility that involve student use of personal technology. These behaviors are becoming more common in college, as is the anger of college instructors and college students who witness them. Be sure to avoid them.

Using Cell Phones

Keeping a cell phone on in class is a clear example of classroom incivility, because if it rings, it will interfere with the right of others to learn. In a study of college students who were exposed to a cell phone ringing during a class session and were later tested for their recall of information presented in class, they scored approximately 25 percent worse when attempting to recall information that was presented at the time a cell phone rang. This attention loss occurred even if the material was covered by the professor prior to the cell phone ringing and if it was projected on a slide during the call. The study also showed that classmates are further distracted when classmates

frantically search through handbags or pockets to find and silence a ringing (or vibrating) phone (Shelton, Elliot, Eaves, & Exner, 2009). These findings clearly suggest that the civil thing to do is turn your cell phone off before entering the classroom, or keep it out of the classroom altogether.

"The right to do something does not mean that doing it is right."

—William Safire, American author, journalist, and presidential speechwriter

Text Messaging

Answering a cell phone during class represents a violation of civility because it interferes with the learning of other members of the classroom community, and so does text messaging. It can distract or disturb classmates who see you messaging instead of listening and learning. It's also discourteous or disrespectful to instructors when you put your head down and turn your attention away from them while they're trying to speak to the class.

Reflection 3.12

Have you observed an example of incivility that you thought was exceptionally admirable or particularly despicable? What was the situation and what uncivil behavior was displayed?

Summary and Conclusion

Goal setting is the key to igniting motivation; maintaining motivation after it has been ignited requires use of effective self-motivational strategies, such as:

- Visualizing reaching your long-range goals;
- Putting goals in writing;
- Creating a visual map of your goals;
- Keeping a record of your progress;
- Rewarding yourself for progress toward long-range goals;
- Converting setbacks into comebacks by using positive self-talk and maintaining positive expectations; and
- Keeping your eye on the long-term consequences of your short-term choices and decisions.

Successfully setting and reaching goals also depends on personal character. The following character traits or virtues typify highly motivated and successful people:

- **Drive.** The internal force that provides energy to overcome inertia and initiate action.
- **Discipline.** Commitment, devotion, and dedication that enable you to sustain your effort over time.
- **Determination.** The capacity to relentlessly pursue your goals, persist in the face of frustration, and bounce back after any setback.
- **Wisdom.** Using knowledge to guide effective behavior and action.
- **Integrity.** Doing what's right, good, or ethical.
- **Civility.** Respecting the rights of other members of the community.

Remember

Success isn't a short-range goal: it's not a sprint but a long-distance run that takes patience and perseverance to complete. What matters most is not how fast you start but where you finish. Goal setting will get you going and motivation will keep you going until you cross the finish line.

Learning More through the World Wide Web

Internet-Based Resources for Further Information on Liberal Arts Education

For additional information related to the ideas discussed in this chapter, we recommend the following Web sites:

Goal Setting:
www.siue.edu/SPIN/activity.html

Self-Motivational Strategies:
www.selfmotivationstrategies.com

Developing Personal Character: Who's Watching? Character and Integrity in the 21st Century:
www.calea.org/calea-update-magazine/issue-100who-s-watching-character-and-integrity-21st-century

3.1 Prioritizing Important Life Goals

Consider the following life goals. Rank them in the order of their priority for you (1 = highest, 5 = lowest).

___ Emotional well-being

___ Spiritual growth

___ Physical health

___ Social relationships

___ Rewarding career

Self-Assessment Questions

1. What were the primary reasons behind your first- and last-ranked choices?
2. Have you established any short- or mid-range goals for reaching your highest-ranked choice? If yes, what are they? If no, what could they be?

3.2 Setting Goals for Reducing the Gap between Your Ideal Future and Your Current Reality

Think of an aspect of your life where there is a gap between what you hoped it would be (the ideal) and what it is (the reality). On the lines that follow, identify goals you could pursue to reduce this gap.

Long-range goal: _____

Mid-range goal: _____

Short-range goal: _____

Use the form that follows to identify strategies for reaching each of these three goals. Consider the following areas for each goal:

*   Actions to be taken:
*   Available resources:
*   Possible roadblocks:
*   Potential solutions to roadblocks:

Long-range goal: _____

*   Actions to be taken:
*   Available resources:
*   Possible roadblocks:
*   Potential solutions to roadblocks:

Mid-range goal: _____

*   Actions to be taken:
*   Available resources:
*   Possible roadblocks:
*   Potential solutions to roadblocks:

Short-range goal: _____

- Actions to be taken:
- Available resources:
- Possible roadblocks:
- Potential solutions to roadblocks:

3.3 Converting Setbacks into Comebacks: Transforming Pessimism into Optimism through Positive Self-Talk

In *Hamlet*, Shakespeare wrote, "There is nothing good or bad, but thinking makes it so." His point was that experiences have the potential to be positive or negative, depending on how people interpret them and react to them.

Listed here is a series of statements representing negative, motivation-destroying interpretations and reactions to a situation or experience:

1. "I'm just not good at this."
2. "There's nothing I can do about it."
3. "Nothing is going to change."
4. "This always happens to me."
5. "Everybody is going to think I'm a loser."

For each of the preceding statements, replace the negative statement with a statement that represents a more positive, self-motivating interpretation or reaction.

No Goals, No Direction

Amy Aimless decided to go to college because it seemed like that was what she was expected to do. All of her closest friends were going and her parents had talked to her about going to college as long as she could remember.

Now that she's in her first term, Amy isn't sure she made the right decision. She has no educational or career goals, nor does she have any idea about what her major might be. None of the subjects she took in high school and none of the courses she's taking in her first term of college have really sparked her interest. Since she has no goals or sense of purpose, she's beginning to think that being in college is a waste of time and money, so she's considering withdrawing at the end of her first term.

Reflection and Discussion Questions

1. What advice would you give Amy about whether she should remain in college or withdraw?

2. What suggestion would you have for Amy that might help her find some sense of educational purpose or direction?

3. How could you counter Amy's claim that no subjects interest her as possible college majors?

4. Would you agree that Amy is currently wasting her time and her parents' money? Why?

5. Would you agree that Amy shouldn't have begun college in the first place? Why?

Time Management

Preventing Procrastination and Promoting Self-Discipline

ACTIVATE YOUR THINKING | *Reflection* **4.1**

Complete the following sentence with the first thought that comes to your mind:

For me, time is . . .

LEARNING GOAL

To help you appreciate the significance of managing time and supply you with a powerful set of time-management strategies that can be used to promote your success in college and beyond.

The Importance of Time Management

Reaching goals requires managing time because it takes time to successfully complete the series of steps that lead to those goals. For first-year college students, time management is especially essential for achieving their goals because the beginning of college brings with it the challenge of independent living and managing their new-found freedom. Even for first-year students who have lived on their own for some time, managing time remains a crucial skill because they will be juggling multiple responsibilities, including school, family, and work.

In addition, the academic calendar and class scheduling patterns in college differ radically from high school. There's less "seat time" in class each week and more "free time" outside of class, which leaves you with a lot more personal time to manage. Your time is not as closely monitored by school authorities or family members, and you are expected to do more academic work on your own outside of class. Personal time-management skills grow in importance when one's time is less structured and controlled by others, leaving the individual with more decision-making power about how to spend personal time. Thus, it's not surprising that research shows the ability to manage time effectively plays a crucial role in college success (Erickson, Peters, & Strommer, 2006).

Simply stated, college students who have difficulty managing their time have difficulty managing college. In one study, college sophomores who had an outstanding first year (both academically and personally) were compared to another group of sophomores who struggled during the prior year. Interviews conducted with these students revealed one key difference between the two groups: The sophomores who experienced a successful first year repeatedly brought up the topic of time during the interviews. The successful students said they had to think carefully about how they spent their time and that they needed to budget their time because it was a scarce resource. In contrast, the sophomores who experienced difficulty in their first year of college hardly talked about the topic of time during their interviews, even when they were specifically asked about it (Light, 2001).

Student
Perspective

"The major difference [between high school and college] is time. You have so much free time on your hands that you don't know what to do for most of the time."

—First-year college student (Erickson & Strommer, 1991)

Studies also indicate that managing time plays a pivotal role in the lives of working adults. Setting priorities and balancing multiple responsibilities (e.g., work and family) that compete for limited time and energy can be a stressful juggling act for people of all ages (Harriott & Ferrari, 1996). Thus, good time management serves as good stress management.

For these reasons, time management should be viewed not only as a college-success strategy but also as a life-management and life-success skill. Studies show that people who manage their time well report they are more in control of their lives and are happier (Myers, 1993; 2000). In short, when you gain greater control of your time, you become more satisfied with your life.

Author's Experience

I started the process of earning my doctorate a little later in life than other students. I was a married father with a preschool daughter (Sara). Since my wife left for work early in the morning, it was always my duty to get up and get Sara's day going in the right direction. In addition, I had to do the same for me—which was often harder than doing it for my daughter. Three days of my week were spent on campus, in class or in the library. (We did not have quick access to research on home computers then as you do now.) The other two days of the workweek and the weekend were spent on household chores, family time, and studying.

I knew that if I was going to have any chance of finishing my Ph.D. in a reasonable amount of time and have a decent family life, I had to adopt an effective schedule for managing my time. Each day of the week, I held to a strict routine. I got up in the morning, drank coffee while reading the paper, took a shower, got Sara ready for school, and took her to school. Once I returned home, I put a load of laundry in the washer, studied, wrote, and spent time concentrating on what I needed to do to be successful from 8:30 a.m. to 12:00 p.m. every day. At lunch, I had a pastrami and cheese sandwich and a soft drink while rewarding myself by watching *Perry Mason* reruns until 1:00 p.m. I then continued to study until it was time to pick up Sara from school. Each night, I spent time with my wife and daughter and prepared for the next day. I lived a life that had a preset schedule. By following that schedule, I was able to successfully complete my doctorate in a decent amount of time while giving my family the time they needed. (By the way, I still watch *Perry Mason* reruns.)

Aaron Thompson

Strategies for Managing Time

Effective time management involves three key mental processes:

1. **Analysis.** Breaking down time into specific segments and work into smaller tasks;
2. **Itemizing.** Identifying all key tasks that need to be done and by what dates;
3. **Prioritizing.** Organizing and attacking tasks in order of their importance.

The following steps can help you apply these skills to find more time in your schedule and use this time more productively.

1. **Break time down into smaller units to become more aware about your time is being spent.** Have you ever asked yourself, "Where did all the time go?" or told yourself, "I just can't seem to find the time"? One way to find out where your time went is by taking a time inventory. Conduct a time analysis by tracking your time and recording what you do and when you do it. By mapping out how you spend time, you become more aware of how much total time you actually have and where it goes, including patches of wasted time during which you get little or nothing accomplished. You just need to do this time analysis for more than a week or two to see where your time is going and to get started on strategies for using your time more productively.

Reflection **4.2**

Do you have time gaps between your classes this term? If you do, what have you been doing during those "free" periods between classes?

What would you say is your greatest time waster?

Do you see a need to stop or eliminate it?

If you don't, why not? If yes, what could you do to convert your wasted time into productive time?

2. **Identify the key tasks you need to accomplish and when you need to accomplish them.** People make lists to be sure they don't forget items they need from the grocery store or people they want to be sure are invited to a party. You can use the same list-making strategy for work tasks so that you don't forget to do them or forget to do them on time. Studies of effective people show that they are list makers; they write out lists not only for grocery items and wedding invitations, but also for things they want to accomplish each day (Covey, 2004).

   You can itemize the tasks on your lists by using the following time-management tools:

   - **Personal digital assistant (PDA) or cell phone.** You can use these to do a lot more than check social networking sites and send and receive text messages. Use the calendar tools in these devices to record due dates and set up the alert functions to remind you of these deadlines. Many PDAs and smartphones will also allow you to set up task or "to-do" lists and to set priorities for each item you enter.

© Gary Woodward, 2013. Under license from Shutterstock, Inc.

   - **Small, portable planner.** List all your major assignments and exams for the term, along with their due dates. Putting all work tasks from different courses into one place makes it easier to keep track of what you have to do and when you have to do it.
   - **Large, stable calendar.** In the calendar's date boxes, record your major assignments for the academic term and when they are due. Place the calendar in a position or location where it's in full view and you can't help but see it every day (e.g., on your bedroom or refrigerator door). If you regularly and literally "look" at the things you have to do, you're less likely to "overlook" them, forget about them, or subconsciously push them out of your mind because you don't really want to do them.

Using a personal planner is an effective way to itemize your academic commitments.

3. **Rank your tasks in order of their importance.** Once you've itemized your work by listing all tasks you need to do, prioritize them—determine the order in which you will do them. Prioritizing basically involves ranking your tasks in terms of their importance, with the highest-ranked tasks appearing at the top of your list to ensure that they are tackled first. How do you determine which tasks are most important and should be ranked highest? Two criteria or standards of judgment can be used to help determine which tasks should be your highest priorities:

   - **Urgency.** Tasks that are closest to their deadlines or due dates should receive high priority. For example, finishing an assignment that's due tomorrow should receive higher priority than starting an assignment that's due next month.

- **Gravity.** Tasks that carry the heaviest weight (count the most) should receive highest priority. For example, if an assignment worth 100 points and another worth 10 points are due at the same time, the 100-point task should receive higher priority. Just like investing money, you want to invest your time in tasks that yield the greatest dividends or payoff.

Author's Experience

My mom was the person who ensured I got up for school on time. Once I got to school, the bell would ring to let me know to move on to the next class. When I returned home, I had to do my homework and chores. My daily and weekly schedules were dictated by others.

When I entered college, I quickly realized that I needed to develop my own system for being organized, focused, and productive without the assistance of my mother. Since I came from a modest background, I had to work my way through college. Juggling schedules became an art and science for me. I knew the things that I could not miss, such as work and school, and the things I could miss—TV and girls. (OK, TV, but not girls.)

After college, I spent 10 years in business—a world where I was measured by being on time and a productive "bottom line." It was during this time that I discovered a scheduling book. When I became a professor, I had other mechanisms to make sure I did what I needed to do when I needed to do it. This was largely based on when my classes were offered. Other time was dedicated to working out and spending time with my family. Now, as an administrator, I have an assistant who keeps my schedule for me. She tells me where I am going, how long I should be there, and what I need to accomplish while I am there. Unless you take your parents with you or have the luxury of a personal assistant, it's important to determine which activities are required and to allow time in your schedule for fun. Use a planner!

Aaron Thompson

Reflection 4.3

Do you have a calendar for the current academic term that you carry with you? What about an up-to-date to-do list?

If yes to either, why? If no to either, why not?

If you carry neither a calendar nor a to-do list, why do you think you don't?

One strategy for prioritizing your tasks is to divide them into A, B, and C lists (Lakein, 1973; Morgenstern, 2004). The A list is for *essential* tasks—what you *must* do now. The B list is for *important* tasks—what you *should* do soon. Finally, the C list is for *optional* tasks—what you *could* or *might* do if there is time remaining after you've completed the tasks on the A and B lists. Organizing your tasks in this fashion can help you decide how to divide your labor in a way that ensures you put first things first. Don't waste time doing unimportant things to deceive yourself into thinking that you're keeping busy and getting things done; in reality, all you're doing is taking time (and your mind) away from the more important things you should be doing.

At first glance, itemizing and prioritizing may appear to be rather boring chores. However, if you look at these mental tasks carefully, they require higher-level thinking skills, such as:

1. **Analysis.** Dividing time into component elements or segments and breaking down work into specific tasks;

2. **Evaluation.** Critically evaluating the relative importance or value of tasks; and
3. **Synthesis.** Organizing individual tasks into classes or categories based on their level of priority.

> **Remember**
>
> *Developing self-awareness about how your time is spent is more than a brainless, clerical activity. When it's done with thoughtful reflection, it becomes an exercise in higher-level thinking. It's also a good values-clarification exercise because it makes us aware of whether we're actually spending our time on those things that we say we really value.*

Develop a Time-Management Plan

Humans are creatures of habit. Routines help you organize and gain control of your lives. Doing things by design, rather than leaving them to chance or accident, is the first step toward making things happen for you rather than allowing them to happen. By developing an intentional plan for how you're going to spend your time, you're developing a plan to gain greater control of your life.

Don't buy into the myth that you don't have time to plan because it takes too much time that could be spent getting started and getting things done. Time-management experts estimate that the amount of time you spend planning your work reduces your total work time by a factor of three (Goldsmith, 2010; Lakein, 1973). In other words, for every one unit of time you spend planning, you save three units of work time. Thus, five minutes of planning time will typically save you 15 minutes of total work time, and 10 minutes of planning time will save you 30 minutes of work time. You save work time by engaging in planning time because you end up with a clearer understanding of what needs to be done and the order of steps you need to take to get it done. This clearer sense of direction reduces the likelihood of losing time to "false starts"—having to restart your work because you started off in the wrong direction. If you have no plan of attack, you're more likely to go off track; when you discover this at some point after you've started, you're then forced to retreat and start all over again.

As the proverb goes, "A stitch in time saves nine." Planning your time represents the "stitch" (unit of time) that saves you nine additional stitches (units of time). Similar to successful chess players, successful time managers plan ahead and anticipate their next moves.

"Time = Life. Therefore waste your time and waste your life, or master your time and master your life."
—Alan Lakein, international expert on time management and author of the bestselling book *How to Get Control of Your Time and Your Life*

"Failing to plan is planning to fail."
—Alan Lakein, author of *How to Get Control of Your Time and Your Life*

Elements of a Comprehensive Time-Management Plan

Once you've accepted the notion that taking the time to plan your time saves you time in the long run, you're ready to design a time-management plan. The following are elements of a comprehensive, well-designed plan for managing time.

1. **A good time-management plan includes short, mid- and long-range time frames.** For instance, a good academic time-management plan for the term should include:
    -   A *long-range* plan for the entire term that identifies deadline dates for reports and papers that are due toward the end of the term;
    -   A *mid-range* plan for the upcoming month and week; and
    -   A *short-range* plan for the following day.

Here's how you can put this three-stage plan into action this term:

- Review the *course syllabus (course outline)* for each class you are enrolled in this term, and highlight all major exams, tests, quizzes, assignments, and papers and the dates on which they are due.

> **Remember**
>
> *College professors are more likely than high school teachers to expect you to rely on your course syllabus to keep track of what you have to do and when you have to do it.*

- Obtain a *large calendar* for the academic term (available at your campus bookstore or learning center) and record all your exams, assignments, and so on, for all your courses in the calendar boxes that represent their due dates. To fit this information within the calendar boxes, use creative abbreviations to represent different tasks, such as E for exam and TP for term paper (not toilet paper). When you're done, you'll have a centralized chart or map of deadline dates and a potential master plan for the entire term. Get in the habit of not only doing short-range academic planning and calendaring for the upcoming day or week, but long-range planning for the academic semester or term.
- Activate the calendar and task lists functions on your PDA or cell phone. Enter your schedule, important dates, deadlines, and set alert reminders. Since you carry your PDA or cell phone with you regularly, you will always have this information at your fingertips.

Work backward from this long-range plan to:

- Plan your week.
  a. Make a map of your *weekly schedule* that includes times during the week when you are in class, when you typically eat and sleep, and if you are employed, when you work.
  b. If you are a full-time college student, find *at least 25 total hours per week* when you can do academic work outside the classroom. (These 25 hours can be pieced together in any way you like, including time between daytime classes and work commitments, evening time, and weekend time.) When adding these 25 hours to the time you spend in class each week, you will end up with a 40-hour workweek, similar to any full-time job. If you are a part-time student, you should plan on spending at least two hours on academic work outside of class for every hour that you're in class.
  c. Make good use of your *free time between classes* by working on assignments and studying in advance for upcoming exams. See **Do It Now! 4.1** for a summary of how you can use your out-of-class time to improve your academic performance and course grades.

- Plan your day.
  a. Make a *daily to-do list*.

> **Remember**
>
> *If you write it out, you're less likely to block it out and forget about it.*

b. Attack daily tasks in *priority order*.

> **Remember**
>
> *"First things first."* Plan your work by placing the most important and most urgent tasks at the top of your list, and work your plan by attacking tasks in the order in which you have listed them.

- Carry a *small calendar, planner, or appointment book* at all times. This will enable you to record appointments that you may make on the run during the day and will allow you to jot down creative ideas or memories of things you need to do—which can sometimes pop into your mind at the most unexpected times.

- Take *portable work* with you during the day that you can carry with you and do in any place at any time. This will enable you to take advantage of "dead time" during the day. For example, carry material with you that you can read while sitting and waiting for appointments or transportation, allowing you to resurrect this dead time and convert it to "live" work time. (Not only is this a good time-management strategy, it's a good stress-management strategy because it puts you in control of "wait time," enabling you use it to save time later and reducing the likelihood that you'll feel frustrated, anxious, or bored.)

- Wear a *watch* or carry a cell phone that can accurately and instantly tell you what time it is and what date it is. You can't even begin to manage time if you don't know what time it is, and you can't plan a schedule if you don't know what date it is. (Try setting the time on your watch or cell phone slightly ahead of the actual time to help ensure that you arrive to class, work, or meetings on time.)

Reflection 4.4

Do you make a to-do list of things you need to get done each day? (Circle one.)

never   seldom   often   almost always

If you circled "never" or "seldom," why don't you?

2. **A good time-management plan includes planning reserve time to take care of the unexpected.** Always hope for the best, but always be prepared for the worst. Your time-management plan should include a buffer zone or safety net of extra time in case you encounter unforeseen developments or unexpected emergencies. Just as you should plan to have extra funds in your account to pay for unexpected costs (e.g., an auto repair), you should plan to have extra time in your schedule for unexpected events (e.g., a random emergency).

4.1

Making Productive Use of Free Time Outside the Classroom

Unlike in high school, homework in college often does not involve turning things in to your instructor daily or weekly. The academic work you do outside the classroom may not even be collected and graded. Instead, it is done for your own benefit to help prepare yourself for upcoming exams and major assignments (e.g., term papers or research reports). Rather than formally assigning work to you as homework, your professors expect that you will do this work on your own and without supervision. Listed below are strategies for working independently and in advance of college exams and assignments. These strategies will increase the quality of your time management in college and the quality of your academic performance.

Working Independently in Advance of Exams

Use the following strategies to use out-of-class time wisely to prepare for exams:

- **Complete reading assignments** relating to lecture topics before the topic is discussed in class. This will make lectures easier to understand and will prepare you to participate intelligently in class (e.g., ask meaningful questions of your instructor and make informed comments during class discussions).
- **Review your class notes** between class periods so that you can construct a mental bridge from one class to the next and make each upcoming lecture easier to follow. When reviewing your notes before the next class, rewrite any class notes that may be sloppily written the first time. If you find notes related to the same point all over the place, reorganize them by combining them into one set of notes. Lastly, if you find any information gaps or confusing points in your notes, seek out the course instructor or a trusted classmate to clear them up before the next class takes place.
- **Review information** you highlighted in your reading assignments to improve your retention of the information. If certain points are confusing to you, discuss them with your course instructor during office hours or with a fellow classmate outside of class.
- **Integrate key ideas** in your class notes with information that you have highlighted in your assigned reading, which relates to the same major point or general category. In other words, put related information from your lecture notes and your reading in the same place (e.g., on the same index card).
- **Use a part-to-whole study method** whereby you study material from your class notes and assigned reading in small pieces during short, separate study sessions that take place well in advance of the exam; then make your last study session before the exam a longer review session during which you restudy all the small parts together as a whole. It's a myth that studying in advance is a waste of time because you'll forget it all anyway by test time. As you'll see in Chapter 5, information studied in advance of an exam remains in your brain and is still there when you later review it. Even if you cannot recall the previously studied information when you first start reviewing it, you will relearn it faster than you did the first time, thus proving that some memory of it was retained from your earlier study sessions.

Work Independently Well in Advance of Due Dates for Term Papers and Research Reports

Work on large, long-range assignments by breaking them into the following smaller, short-term tasks:

1. Search for and select a topic.
2. Locate sources of information on the topic.
3. Organize the information obtained from these sources into categories.
4. Develop an outline of the report's major points and the order or sequence in which you plan to discuss them.
5. Construct a first draft of the paper (and, if necessary, a second draft).
6. Write a final draft of the paper.
7. Proofread the final draft of your paper for minor mechanical mistakes, such as spelling and grammatical errors, before submitting it to your instructor.

3. **A good time-management plan should balance work and recreation.** Don't only plan work time: plan time to relax, refuel, and recharge. Your overall time-management plan shouldn't turn you into an obsessive-compulsive workaholic. Instead, it should represent a balanced blend of work and play, including activities that promote your mental and physical wellness, such as relaxation, recreation, and reflection. If your schedule makes room for the things you like to do, you're more likely do to the things you have to do. You could also arrange your schedule of work and play as a self-motivation strategy by using your play time to reward completion of your work time. A good time-management plan includes a balanced blend of time planned for both work and recreation.

Reflection **4.5**

What activities do you engage in for fun or recreation?

What do you do to relax or relieve stress?

Do you build these activities into your daily or weekly schedule?

Remember

A good time-management plan should help you stress less, learn more, and earn higher grades while leaving you time for other important aspects of your life. A good plan not only enables you to get your work done on time, but also enables you to attain and maintain balance in your life.

4. **A good time-management plan has some flexibility.** Some students are immediately turned off by the idea of developing a schedule and planning their time because they feel it over-structures their lives and limits their freedom. It's only natural for you to prize your personal freedom and resist anything that appears to restrict your freedom in any way. However, a good time-management plan doesn't limit freedom: it preserves freedom by helping you get done what you must do and reserves free time to do what you want and like to do.

A good time-management plan shouldn't enslave you to a rigid work schedule. The plan should be flexible enough to allow you to occasionally bend it without breaking it. Just as work commitments and family responsibilities can crop up unexpectedly, so, too, can opportunities for fun and enjoyable activities. Your plan should allow you the freedom to modify your schedule so that you can take advantage of these enjoyable opportunities and experiences. However, you should plan to make up the work time you lost. In other words, you can borrow or trade work time for play time, but don't "steal" it; plan to pay back the work time you borrowed by substituting it for play time that was planned for another time. If you can't do something you planned to do, the next best thing is to re-plan when you'll do it.

Remember

When you create a personal time-management plan, remember that it is your *plan—you own it and you run it. It shouldn't run you.*

Converting a Time-Management Plan into an Action Plan

Once you've planned the work, the next step is to work the plan. A good action plan is one that enables you to (1) preview what you intend to accomplish and (2) review what you actually accomplished. You can begin to implement an action plan by constructing a daily to-do list, bringing that list with you as the day begins, and checking off items on the list as you get them done throughout the day. At the end of the day, review your list and identify what was completed and what still needs to be done. The uncompleted tasks should become high priorities for the next day.

Reflection **4.6**

By the end of a typical day, how often do you find that you accomplished most of the important tasks you hoped to accomplish? (Circle one.)

never   seldom   often   almost always

Why?

At the end of the day, if you find many unchecked items remain on your daily to-do list, this may mean that you're spreading yourself too thin by trying to do too many things in a day. You may need to be more realistic about the number of items you can accomplish per day by shortening your daily to-do list.

Being unable to complete many of your intended daily tasks may also mean that you need to modify your time-management plan by adding more work time or subtracting activities that are drawing time and attention away from your work (e.g., responding to phone calls and text messages during your planned work times).

Dealing with Procrastination

Procrastination Defined

The word *procrastination* derives from two roots: *pro* (meaning "forward") plus *crastinus* (meaning "tomorrow"). As these roots suggest, procrastinators don't abide by the proverb "Why put off to tomorrow what can be done today?" Their philosophy is just the opposite: "Why do today what can be put off until tomorrow?" Adopting this philosophy promotes a perpetual pattern of postponing what needs to be done until the last possible moment, forcing a frantic rush to finish the job in time, which results in a product of poorer quality (or not finishing the product at all).

Research shows that 80–95 percent of college students procrastinate (Steel, 2007) and almost 50 percent report that they procrastinate consistently (Onwuegbuzie, 2000). Furthermore, the percentage of people reporting that they procrastinate is on the rise (Kachgal, Hansen, & Nutter, 2001).

Procrastination is such a serious issue for college students that some colleges and universities have opened "procrastination centers" to provide help exclusively for students who are experiencing problems with procrastination (Burka & Yuen, 2008).

Myths That Promote Procrastination

Before there can be any hope of putting a stop to procrastination, procrastinators need to let go of two popular myths (misconceptions) about time and performance.

> "Many people take no care of their money 'til they come nearly to the end of it, and others do just the same with their time."
>
> —Johann Wolfgang von Goethe, German poet, dramatist, and author of the epic *Faust*

Student *Perspective*

"I believe the most important aspect of college life is time management. DO NOT procrastinate because, although this is the easy thing to do at first, it will catch up with you and make your life miserable."

—Advice to new college students from a first-year student

List of Things
To Do Today

1. Write Paper
2. Study for
   Math Test
3. Prepare Speech

List of Things
Due Today

1. Turn in Paper
2. Take Math
   Test
3. Deliver Speech

Next time I'll start sooner!

A procrastinator's idea of planning ahead and working in advance often boils down to this scenario.

Myth 1. "I work better under pressure" (e.g., on the day or night before something is due). Procrastinators often confuse desperation with motivation. Their belief that they work better under pressure is often just a rationalization to justify or deny the reality that they *only* work when they're under pressure—that is, when they've run out of time and have no choice but to do it under the gun of the final deadline.

It's true that some people will only start to work and will work really fast when they're under pressure, but that does not mean they're working more *effectively* and producing work of better quality. Because they're playing "beat the clock," the procrastinator's focus is no longer is on doing the job *well* but is on doing the job *fast* so that it gets done before they run out of time. This typically results in a work product that turns out to be incomplete or inferior to what could have been produced if the work process began earlier.

Myth 2. "Studying in advance is a waste of time because you will forget it all by test time." The misconception that information learned early will be forgotten is commonly used to justify procrastinating with respect to preparing for upcoming exams. As will be discussed in Chapter 5, studying that is distributed (spread out) over time is more effective than massed (crammed) studying. Furthermore, last-minute studying that takes place the night before exams often results in lost sleep time resulting from pulling "late-nighters" or "all-nighters." This fly-by-night strategy interferes with retention of information that has been studied and elevates test anxiety because of lost dream sleep (a.k.a. rapid eye movement, or REM) that the brain needs to store memories and manage stress (Hobson, 1988; Voelker, 2004). Research indicates that procrastinators experience higher rates of stress-related physical disorders, such as insomnia, stomach problems, colds, and flu (McCance & Pychyl, 2003).

Working under time pressure adds to performance pressure because procrastinators are left with no margin of error to correct mistakes, no time to seek help on

"Haste makes waste."
—Benjamin Franklin

Although you may work quickly under pressure, you are probably not working better.

their work, and no chance to handle random catastrophes that may arise at the last minute (e.g., an attack of the flu or a family emergency).

Psychological Causes of Procrastination

Sometimes, procrastination has deeper psychological roots. People may procrastinate for reasons that do not relate directly to poor time-management habits but to emotional issues. For instance, studies show that procrastination is sometimes used as a psychological strategy to protect self-esteem. Referred to as *self-handicapping* (Rhodewalt & Vohs, 2005), this strategy is used, either consciously or unconsciously, by some procrastinators to give themselves a "handicap" or disadvantage. Thus, if their performance turns out to be less than spectacular, they can conclude (rationalize) that it was because they were performing under a handicap—lack of time rather than lack of ability (Chu & Cho, 2005).

Reflection **4.7**

Do you tend to put off work for so long that getting it done turns into an emergency or panic situation?

If your answer is yes, why do you think you find yourself in this position? If your answer is no, what is it that prevents this from happening to you?

"We didn't lose the game; we just ran out of time."

—Vince Lombardi, football coach

"Procrastinators would rather be seen as lacking in effort than lacking in ability."

—Joseph Ferrari, professor of psychology and procrastination researcher

For example, if they receive a low grade on a test or paper, they can "save face" (self-esteem) by concluding that it was because they waited until the last minute and didn't put much time or effort into it. In other words, they had enough ability or intelligence to earn a high grade; they just didn't have enough time. Better yet, if they happened to luck out and get a good grade—despite doing it at the last minute—they can think it proves just how smart they are because they were able to get that good grade without putting in much time at all! Thus, self-handicapping creates a fail-safe or win-win scenario that's guaranteed to protect the procrastinator's self-image. If the work performance or product is less than excellent, it can be blamed on external factors (e.g., lack of time); if it happens to earn them a high grade, they can attribute the result to themselves—their extraordinary ability enabled them to do so well despite working at the last minute.

In addition to self-handicapping, other psychological factors have been found to contribute to procrastination, including the following:

- **Fear of failure.** The procrastinator feels better about not completing the work on time than doing it and experiencing failure (Burka & Yuen, 2008; Solomon & Rothblum, 1984);
- **Perfectionism.** Having unrealistically high personal standards or expectations, which leads to the procrastinator's belief that it's better to postpone work or not do it than to risk doing it less than perfectly (Kachgal et al., 2001);
- **Fear of success.** Fearing that doing well will show others that the procrastinator has the ability to achieve success and will lead others to expect the procrastina-

tor to maintain those high standards in the future (Beck, Koons, & Milgram, 2000; Ellis & Knaus, 2002)

- **Indecisiveness.** The procrastinator has difficulty making decisions, including decisions about what to do first, when to do it, or whether to do it (Anderson, 2003; Steel, 2007);
- **Thrill seeking.** The procrastinator enjoys the adrenaline rush triggered by hurrying to get things done just before a deadline (Szalavitz, 2003).

Reflection 4.8

How often do you procrastinate? (Circle one.)

rarely   occasionally   frequently   consistently

When you do procrastinate, what's the usual cause?

If these underlying psychological issues are at the root of procrastination, they must be dealt with before procrastination can be overcome. Because they have deeper roots, it may take some time and professional assistance to uproot them. A good place to get such assistance is the Counseling Center on campus, where there are counseling psychologists who are professionally trained to deal with emotional issues, including those that may be contributing to procrastination.

Self-Help Strategies for Beating the Procrastination Habit

Once inaccurate beliefs or emotional issues underlying procrastination have been identified and dealt with, the next step is to take direct action on the procrastination habit itself. What follows are seven key strategies for minimizing or eliminating the procrastination habit.

1. **Continually practice effective time-management strategies.** If effective time-management practices, such as those previously cited in this chapter, are implemented consistently, they can turn into a habit. When people repeatedly practice effective time-management strategies, these practices gradually become part of their routine and develop into habits. For instance, when procrastinators repeatedly practice effective time-management strategies with respect to tasks that they procrastinate on, their procrastination tendencies begin to fade and are gradually replaced by good habits of good time management (Ainslie, 1992; Baumeister, Heatherton, & Tice, 1994).

2. **Make the start of work as inviting or appealing as possible.** Getting started can be a stumbling block for many procrastinators. They experience what's called "start-up stress"—when they're about to begin a task, they start to experience negative feelings about the task being unpleasant, difficult, or boring (Burka & Yuen, 2008). If you have trouble starting your work, one way to give yourself a jump-start is to arrange your work tasks in an order that allows you to start with tasks that you're likely to find most interesting or to succeed in. Once you overcome the initial inertia and get going, you can ride the momentum you've created to attack other tasks that you find less appealing or more daunting.

You're also likely to discover that the dreaded work wasn't as difficult, boring, or time-consuming as it appeared to be. When you sense that you're making some

> "Striving for excellence motivates you; striving for perfection is demoralizing."
> —Harriet Braiker, psychologist and bestselling author

> "Just do it."
> —Commercial slogan of Nike, the athletic equipment company named after the Greek goddess of victory

> **Student Perspective**
> "Did you ever dread doing something, then it turned out to take only about 20 minutes to do?"
> —Conversation between two college students overheard in a coffee shop

progress toward getting work done, your anxiety begins to decline. As with many experiences in life that are feared and avoided, the anticipation of the event turns out to be worse than the event itself. Research on students who hadn't started a project until it was about to be due indicates that they experienced anxiety and guilt about delaying their work, but once they begin working these negative emotions subsided and were replaced by more positive feelings of progress and accomplishment (McCance & Pychyl, 2003).

"The secret to getting ahead is getting started."

—Mark Twain (Samuel Clemens), American humorist and author of *The Adventures of Huckleberry Finn* (1885), often called "the Great American Novel"

© marekuliasz, 2013. Under license from Shutterstock, Inc.

For many procrastinators, getting started is often their biggest obstacle.

"To eat an elephant, first cut it into small pieces."

—Author unknown

3. **Make the work manageable.** Work becomes less overwhelming and less stressful when it's handled in small chunks or pieces. You can conquer procrastination for large tasks by using a "divide and conquer" strategy: divide the large task into smaller, more manageable units, and then attack and complete them one at a time.

Don't underestimate the power of short work sessions. They can be more effective than longer sessions because it's easier to maintain momentum and concentration for shorter periods of time. If you're working on a large project or preparing for a major exam, dividing your work into short sessions will enable you to take quick jabs and poke small holes in it, reducing its overall size with each successive punch. This approach will also give you the sense of satisfaction that comes with knowing that you're making steady progress toward completing a big task—by continually jabbing at it in short strokes and gradually reducing the pressure associated with having to go for a big knockout punch right before the final bell (deadline).

Author's Experience

The two biggest projects I've had to complete in my life were writing my doctoral thesis and writing this textbook. The strategy that enabled me to keep going until I competed both of these large tasks was to make up short-term deadlines for myself (e.g., complete 5–10 pages each week). I psyched myself into thinking that these make-believe due dates were real, drop-dead deadlines and if I didn't meet them by completing these smaller tasks on time, I was going to fall so far behind that I'd never get the whole thing done. I think these self-imposed deadlines worked for me because they gave me smaller, more manageable tasks to work on that allowed me to make steady progress toward my larger, long-term goal. It was as if this strategy enabled me to take a huge, hard-to-digest meal and break it into small, bite-sized pieces that I could easily swallow and gradually digest over time—as opposed to trying to devour and digest a monstrous-sized meal right before bedtime (the final deadline).

Joe Cuseo

4. **Organization matters.** Research indicates that disorganization is a factor that contributes to procrastination (Steel, 2007). How well you organize your workplace and manage your work materials can reduce your risk of procrastination. Ask yourself, "Can I just go in and do it?" Having the right materials in the right place at the right time can make it easier to get to your work and get going on your work. Once you've made a decision to start working, you don't want to delay acting on that decision by looking for the tools you need to get started. For procrastinators, this time delay may be just the amount of time they need to change their minds and decide not to start working!

- Organize your work materials to make it easy and convenient for you to start working.
- Organize your work place or space so that you work in a location that minimizes distractions and temptations not to work.
- Intentionally arrange your work tasks so that you're working on more enjoyable or stimulating tasks at times when you're vulnerable to procrastination.
- If you're close to finishing a task, finish it, because it's often harder to restart a task than to complete one you've already started.

Mastering the skill of managing time is critical for success in college and beyond. Time is one of our most powerful personal resources; the better we manage it, the more likely we are to achieve our goals and gain control of our lives.

"Dost thou love life? Then do not squander time, for that is the stuff life is made of."

—Benjamin Franklin, 18th-century inventor, newspaper writer, and signer of the *Declaration of Independence*

Learning More through the World Wide Web
Internet-Based Resources for Further Information on Time Management

For additional information related to the ideas discussed in this chapter, we recommend the following Web sites:

Time-Management Strategies for All Students:

www.studygs.net/timman.htm

www.pennstatelearning.psu.edu/resources/study-tips/time-mgt

Time-Management Strategies for Adult Students:

www.essortment.com/lifestyle/timemanagement_sjmu.htm

Beating Procrastination:

www.mindtools.com

4.1 Term at a Glance

Term _____, Year _____

Review the syllabus (course outline) for all classes you're enrolled in this term, and complete the following information for each course.

Course ↓	Professor ↓	Exams ↓	Projects & Papers ↓	Other Assignments ↓	Attendance Policy ↓	Late & Makeup Assignment Policy ↓

Self-Assessment Questions

1. Is the overall workload what you expected? Are your surprised by the amount of work required in any particular course or courses?

2. At this point in the term, what do you see as your most challenging or demanding course or courses? Why?

3. Do you think you can handle the total workload required by the full set of courses you're enrolled in this term?

4. What adjustments or changes could you make to your personal schedule that would make it easier to accommodate your academic workload this term?

4.2 Taking a Personal Time Inventory

On the blank Week-at-a-Glance Grid that follows, map out your typical or average week for this term. Start by recording what you usually do on these days, including when you have class, when you work, and when you relax or recreate. You can use abbreviations (e.g., J for job and R&R for rest and relaxation) or write tasks out in full if you have enough room in the box. List the abbreviations you created at the bottom of the page so that your instructor can follow them.

If you're a *full-time* student, find 25 *hours* in your week that you could devote to homework (HW). These 25 hours could be found between classes, during the day, in the evenings, or on the weekends. If you can find 25 hours per week for homework (in addition to the time you spend in class), you'll have a 40-hour workweek for coursework, which research has shown to result in good grades and success in college.

If you're a *part-time* student, find two *hours* you could devote to homework *for every hour* that you're in class (e.g., if you're in class nine hours per week, find 18 hours of homework time).

Week-at-a-Glance Grid

	Sunday	Monday	Tuesday	Wednesday	Thursday	Friday	Saturday
7:00 a.m.							
8:00 a.m.							
9:00 a.m.							
10:00 a.m.							
11:00 a.m.							
12:00 p.m.							
1:00 p.m.							
2:00 p.m.							
3:00 p.m.							
4:00 p.m.							
5:00 p.m.							
6:00 p.m.							
7:00 p.m.							
8:00 p.m.							
9:00 p.m.							
10:00 p.m.							
11:00 p.m.							

1. Go to the following Web site: pennstatelearning.psu.edu/resources/study-tips/time-mgt
   Click on the link for the "time-management exercise."

2. Complete the time-management exercise at this site. The exercise asks you to estimate the hours per day or week that you spend doing various activities (e.g., sleeping, employment, and commuting). As you enter the amount of time you engage in these activities, the total number of remaining hours available in the week for academic work will be automatically computed.

3. After completing your entries, look at your Week-at-a-glance Grid and answer the following questions (or provide your best estimate).

    a. How many hours per week do you have available for academic work?

    b. Do you have two hours available for academic work outside of class for each hour you spend in class?

    c. What time wasters do you detect that might be easily eliminated or reduced to create more time for academic work outside of class?

Procrastination: The Vicious Cycle

Delilah has a major paper due at the end of the term. It's now past midterm and she still hasn't started to work on her paper. She tells herself, "I should have started sooner."

However, Delilah continues to postpone starting her work on the paper and begins to feel anxious and guilty about it. To relieve her growing anxiety and guilt, she starts doing other tasks instead, such as cleaning her room and returning e-mails. This makes Delilah feel a little better because these tasks keep her busy, take her mind off the term paper, and give her the feeling that at least she's getting something accomplished. Time continues to pass; the deadline for the paper is growing dangerously close. Delilah now finds herself in the position of having lots of work to do and little time in which to do it.

Source: Burka & Yuen, *Procrastination: Why you do it, and what to do about it.*

Reflection and Discussion Questions

1. What do you predict Delilah will do at this point?

2. Why did you make the above prediction?

3. What grade do you think Delilah will receive on her paper?

4. What do you think Delilah will do on the next term paper she's assigned?

5. Other than starting sooner, what recommendations would you have for Delilah (and other procrastinators like her) to break this cycle of procrastination and prevent it from happening repeatedly?

Strategic Learning and Studying
Learning Deeply and Remembering Longer

LEARNING GOAL

To develop a set of effective strategies for studying smarter, learning deeply, and retaining what you learn longer.

What do you think is the key difference between learning and memorizing?

Stages in the Learning and Memory Process

Learning deeply, and remembering what you've learned, is a process that involves three key stages:

1. **Sensory input (perception).** Taking information into your brain;
2. **Memory formation (storage).** Saving that information in your brain; and
3. **Memory recall (retrieval).** Bringing information back to mind when you need it.

These three stages in the learning-memory process are summarized visually in **Figure 5.1**.

You can consider these stages of the learning and memory process to be similar to the way information is processed by a computer: (1) information is typed onto the screen (input), (2) the information is saved in a file (storage), and (3) the saved information is recalled and used when it's needed (retrieval). This three-stage process can be used to create a systematic set of strategies for effectively using the two major routes through which you acquire information and knowledge in college: taking notes as you listen to lectures, and reading textbooks.

Effective Lecture-Listening and Note-Taking Strategies

The importance of effective listening skills in the college classroom is highlighted by a study of more than 400 first-year students who were given a listening test at the start of their first term in college. At the end of their first year in college, 49 percent of those students who scored low on the listening test were on academic probation, compared to only 4.4 percent of students who scored high on the listening test. On the other hand, 68.5 percent of students who scored high on the listening test were

FIGURE 5.1

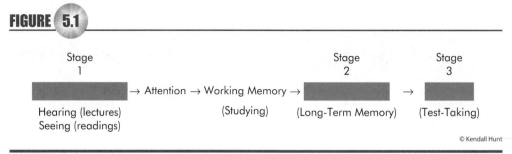

Key Stages in the Learning and Memory Process

eligible for the honors program at the end of their first year—compared to only 4.17 percent of those students who had low listening test scores (Conaway, 1982).

Reflection 5.2

Do you think writing notes in class helps or hinders your ability to pay attention and learn from your instructors' lectures?

Why?

Studies show that information delivered during lectures is the number one source of test questions (and answers) on college exams (Brown, 1988; Kuhn, 1988). When lecture information that hasn't been recorded in the student's notes appears on a test, it has only a 5 percent chance of being recalled (Kiewra et al., 2000). Students who write notes during lectures achieve higher course grades than students who just listen to lectures (Kiewra, 1985, 2005), and students with a more complete set of notes are more likely to demonstrate higher levels of overall academic achievement (Johnstone & Su, 1994; Kiewra & DuBois, 1998; Kiewra & Fletcher, 1984).

Contrary to popular belief that writing while listening interferes with the ability to listen, students report that taking notes actually increases their attention and concentration in class (Hartley, 1998; Hartley & Marshall, 1974). Studies also show that when students write down information that's presented to them, rather than just sitting and listening to it, they're more likely to remember the most important aspects of that information when tested later (Bligh, 2000; Kiewra et al., 1991). One study discovered that students with grade point averages (GPAs) of 2.53 or higher recorded more information in their notes and retained a larger percentage of the most important information than did students with GPAs of less than 2.53 (Einstein, Morris, & Smith, 1985). These findings are not surprising when you consider that *hearing* information, *writing* it, and then *seeing* it after you've written it produces three different memory traces (tracks) in the brain, which combine to multiply your chances of remembering it. Furthermore, students with a good set of notes have a written record of that information, which can be reread and studied later.

These research findings suggest that you should view each lecture as a test-review session during which your instructor is giving out test answers and you're given the opportunity to write all those answers in your notes. Come to class with the attitude that your instructors are dispensing answers to test questions as they speak, and your job is to pick out and pick up these answers.

> **Remember**
>
> *If important points your professor makes in class make it into your notes, they can become points learned; these learned points will turn into earned points on your exams (and higher grades in the course).*

The next sections give strategies for getting the most out of lectures at three stages in the learning process: *before*, *during*, and *after* lectures.

Pre-Lecture Strategies: What to Do before Lectures

1. **Check your syllabus to see where you are in the course and determine how the upcoming class fits into the total course picture.** Checking your syllabus before individual class sessions strengthens learning because you will see how each part (individual class session) relates to the whole (the entire course). This strategy also capitalizes on the brain's natural tendency to seek larger patterns and see the "big picture." Rather than seeing things in separate parts, the brain is naturally inclined to connect parts into a meaningful whole (Caine & Caine, 1991). In other words, the brain looks for meaningful patterns and connections rather than isolated bits and pieces of information (Jensen, 2000). In **Figure 5.2**, notice how your brain naturally ties together and fills in the missing information to perceive a meaningful whole pattern.

FIGURE 5.2

You perceive a white triangle in the middle of this figure. However, if you use three fingers to cover up the three corners of the white triangle that fall outside the other (background) triangle, the white triangle suddenly disappears. What your brain does is take these corners as starting points and fill in the rest of the information on its own to create a complete or whole pattern that has meaning to you. (Also, notice how you perceive the background triangle as a complete triangle, even though parts of its left and right sides are missing.)

© Kendall Hunt

Triangle Illusion

2. **Get to class early so that you can look over your notes from the previous class session and from any reading assignment that relates to the day's lecture topic.** Research indicates that when students preview information related to an upcoming lecture topic, it improves their ability to take more accurate and complete lecture notes (Kiewra, 2005; Ladas, 1980). Thus, a good strategy to help you learn from lectures is to review your notes from the previous class session and read textbook information related to an upcoming lecture topic—*before* hearing the lecture. This strategy will help you better understand and take more detailed notes on the lecture. Reviewing previously learned information also activates your previous knowledge, enabling you to build a mental bridge from one class session to the next, connecting new information to what you already know—a key to deep learning (Bruner, 1990; Piaget, 1978; Vygotsky, 1978). Acquiring

knowledge isn't a matter of simply pouring information into the brain as if it were an empty jar. It's a matter of attaching or connecting new ideas to ideas that are already stored in the brain. When you learn deeply, a physical connection is actually made between nerve cells in your brain (Alkon, 1992), as illustrated in **Figure 5.3.**

FIGURE 5.3

© Jurgen Ziewe, 2013. Under license from Shutterstock, Inc.

When something is learned, it's stored in the brain as a link in an interconnected network of brain cells. Thus, deep learning involves making connections between what you're trying to learn and what you already know.

Network of Brain Cells

3. **Adopt a seating location that maximizes your focus of attention and mini-mizes sources of distraction.** Many years of research show that students who sit in the front and center of class tend to earn higher exam scores and course grades (Tagliacollo, Volpato, & Pereira, 2010; Benedict & Hoag, 2004; Rennels & Chaud-hair, 1988). These results are found even when students are assigned seats by their instructor, so it's not just a matter of more motivated and studious students tending to sit in the front of the room: instead, the better academic performance achieved by students sitting in the front and center of the room likely results from a learning advantage provided by this seating location. Front-and-center seating benefits students' academic performance by improving their vision of material written on the board or screen and their ability to hear the instructor's lectures. In addition, this seating position allows for better eye contact with the instructor, which can increase students' level of attention, reduce their feeling of anonymity, and heighten their sense of involvement in the classroom. Sitting in the front of class can also reduce your level of anxiety about speaking up in class because, when you speak, you will not have numerous classmates sitting in front of you turning around to look at you while you speak.

The bottom line: When you enter a classroom, get in the habit of heading for a seat in the front and center of class. In large classes, it's even more important to get "up close and personal" with your instructors, not only to improve your attention, note taking and participation in class, but also to improve your instructors' ability to remember who you are and how well you performed in class—which will work to your advantage when it comes time to ask your instructors for letters of recommendation.

4. **Sit by people who will enable (not disable) your ability to learn.** Intentionally sit near classmates who will not distract you or interfere with the quality of your

Student
Perspective

"I tend to sit at the very front of my classrooms. It helps me focus and take notes better. It also eliminates distractions."

—First-year college student

Student
Perspective

"[In high school] the teacher knows your name. But in college they don't know your name; they might see your face, but it means nothing to them unless you make yourself known."

—First-year college student

note taking. Attention comes in degrees or amounts; you can give all of your attention or part of it to whatever task you're performing. Trying to grasp complex information in class is a task that demands your undivided attention.

Student
Perspective

"I like to sit up front so I am not distracted by others and I don't have to look around people's heads to see the chalkboard."

—First-year college student

Remember

When you enter a class, you have a choice about where you're going to sit. Choose wisely by selecting a location that will maximize your attentiveness to the instructor and the effectiveness of your note taking.

The evolution of student attention from the back to the front of class.

5. **Adopt a seating posture that screams attention.** Sitting upright and leaning forward increases your attention because these bodily signals will reach your brain and increase mental alertness. If your body is in an alert and ready position, your mind tends to pick up these physical cues and follow your body's lead by also becoming alert and ready (to learn). Just as baseball players assume a ready position in the field before a pitch is delivered to put their bodies in position to catch batted balls, learners who assume a ready position in the classroom put themselves in a better position to catch ideas batted around in the classroom. Studies show that when humans are mentally alert and ready to learn, greater amounts of the brain chemical C-kinase are released at the connection points between brain cells, which increases the likelihood that a learning connection will form between them (Howard, 2000).

There's another advantage to being attentive in class: You send a clear message to your instructor that you're a conscientious and courteous student. This can influence your instructor's perception and evaluation of your academic performance, which can earn you the benefit of the doubt at the end of the term if you're on the border between a lower and higher course grade.

Listening and Note-Taking Strategies: What to Do during Lectures

1. **Take your own notes in class.** Don't rely on someone else to take notes for you. Taking your own notes in your own words focuses your attention and ensures that you're taking notes that make sense to you. Research shows that students who record and review their own notes earn higher scores on memory tests for that information than do students who review the notes of others (Fisher,

Students who take notes during lectures have been found to achieve higher class grades than those who just listen.

Harris, & Harris, 1973; Kiewra, 2005). These findings point to the importance of taking and studying your own notes because they will be most meaningful to you. You can collaborate with classmates to compare notes for completeness and accuracy or to pick up points you may have missed. However, don't routinely rely on someone else to take notes for you.

2. **Focus full attention on the most important information.** Attention is the critical first step to successful learning and memory. Since the human attention span is limited, it's impossible to attend to and make note of (or take notes on) everything. Thus, you need to use your attention *selectively* to focus on, detect, and select information that matters most. Here are some strategies for attending to and recording the most important information delivered by professors in the college classroom:

   - Pay attention to information your instructors put *in print*—on the board, on a slide, or in a handout. If your instructor takes the time and energy to write it out or type it out, that's usually a good clue that the information is important and you're likely to see it again—on an exam.

   - Pay attention to information presented during the first and last few minutes of class. Instructors are more likely to provide valuable reminders, reviews, and previews at these two points in time.

   - Use your instructor's *verbal and nonverbal cues* to detect important information. Don't just tune in when the instructor is writing something down and tune out at other times. It's been found that students record almost 90 percent of information written on the board, but less than 50 percent of important ideas that professors state but don't write on the board (Johnstone & Su, 1994; Locke, 1977; Titsworth & Kiewra, 2004). Don't fall into the reflex-like routine of just writing something in your notes when you see your instructor writing on the board. Listen actively to receive and record important ideas in your notes that you *hear* your instructor saying. In **Do It Now! 5.1**, you'll find strategies for detecting clues to important information that professors deliver during lectures.

3. **Take organized notes**. Keep taking notes in the same paragraph if the instructor is continuing on the same point or idea. When the instructor shifts to a new idea, skip a few lines and shift to a new paragraph. Be alert to phrases that your instructor may use to signal a shift to a new or different idea (e.g., "Let's turn to . . ." or "In addition to . . ."). Use these phrases as cues for taking notes in paragraph form. By recording different ideas in different paragraphs, you improve the organizational quality of your notes, which will improve your comprehension and retention of them. Also, be sure to leave extra space between paragraphs (ideas) to give yourself room to add information later that you may have initially missed, or to translate the professor's words into your own words that are more meaningful to you.

5.1   DO IT **NOW**

Detecting When Instructors Are Delivering Important Information during Class Lectures

1. **Verbal cues**
   - Phrases signal important information (e.g., "The point here is . . ." or "What's most significant about this is . . .").
   - Information is repeated or rephrased in a different way (e.g., "In other words . . .").
   - Stated information is followed with a question to check understanding (e.g., "Is that clear?" "Do you follow that?" "Does that make sense?" or "Are you with me?").

2. **Vocal (tone of voice) cues**
   - Information is delivered in a louder tone or at a higher pitch than usual, which may indicate excitement or emphasis.
   - Information is delivered at a slower rate or with more pauses than usual, which may be your instructor's way of giving you more time to write down these important ideas.

3. **Nonverbal cues**
   - Information is delivered by the instructor with more than the usual
     a. facial expressiveness (e.g., raised or furrowed eyebrows);
     b. body movement (e.g., more gesturing and animation); or
     c. eye contact (e.g., looking more directly and intently at the faces of students to see whether they are following or understanding what's being said).
   - The instructor moves closer to the students (e.g., moving away from the podium or blackboard).
   - The instructor's body is oriented directly toward the class (i.e., both shoulders directly or squarely face the class).

Another popular strategy for taking organized notes, called the Cornell Note-Taking System, is summarized in **Do It Now! 5.2**.

4. **Keep taking notes even if you don't immediately understand what your instructor is saying.** If you are uncertain or confused about what your instructor is saying, don't stop taking notes, because your notes will at least leave you with a record of the information to review later—when you have more time to think about and grasp their meaning. If you still don't understand it after taking time to review it, check it out in your textbook, with your instructor, or with a classmate.

Remember

Your primary goal during lectures is to get important information into your brain long enough to note it mentally and then physically in your notes. Making sense of that information often has to come later, when you have time to reflect on the notes you took in class.

Post-Lecture Strategies: What to Do after Lectures

1. **As soon as class ends, quickly check your notes for missing information or incomplete thoughts.** Since the information is likely to be fresh in your mind immediately after class, a quick check of your notes at this time will allow you to take advantage of your short-term memory. By reviewing and reflecting on it, you can help move the information into long-term memory before forgetting takes place. This quick review can be done alone or, better yet, with a motivated classmate. If you both have gaps in your notes, check them out with your in-

structor before he or she leaves the classroom. Even though it may be weeks before you will be tested on the material, the quicker you address missed points and clear up sources of confusion, the better, because you'll be able to use your knowledge to help you understand and learn upcoming material. Catching confusion early in the game also enables you to avoid the mad last-minute rush of students seeking help from the instructor just before test time. You want to reserve the critical time just before exams for studying a set of notes that you know are complete and accurate, rather than rushing around trying to find missing information and getting cheap fast-food help on concepts that were presented weeks ago.

Reflection 5.3

What do you tend to do immediately after a class session ends?

Why?

5.2

DO IT NOW!

The Cornell Note-Taking System

1. On the page on which you're taking notes, draw a horizontal line about 2 inches from the bottom edge of the paper.
2. If there's no vertical line on the left side of the page, draw one line about 2½ inches from the left edge of the paper (as shown in the scaled-down illustration here).
3. When your instructor is lecturing, use the large space to the right of the vertical line (area A) to record your notes.
4. After a lecture, use the space at the bottom of the page (area B) to summarize the main points you recorded on that page.
5. Use the column of space on the left side of the page (area C) to write questions that are answered in the notes on the right.
6. Quiz yourself by looking at the questions listed in the left margin while covering the answers to them that are found in your class notes on the right.

Note: You can use this note-taking and note-review method on your own, or you could team up with two or more students and do it collaboratively.

© Kendall Hunt

2. **Before the next class session meets, reflect on and review your notes to make sense of them.** Your professors will often lecture on information that you may have little prior knowledge about, so it is unrealistic to expect that you will understand everything that's being said the first time you hear it. Instead, you'll need to set aside time for making notes or taking notes on your own notes (i.e., rewriting them in your own words so that they make sense to you).

During this reflect-and-rewrite process, we recommend that you take notes on your notes by:

- Translating technical information into your own words to make it more meaningful to you; and
- Reorganizing your notes to get ideas related to the same point in the same place.

Studies show that when students organize lecture information into meaningful categories, they demonstrate greater recall for that information on a delayed memory test than do students who simply review their notes without organizing them into categories (Howe, 1970; Kiewra, 2005).

Remember

Look at note taking as a two-stage process: Stage 1 involves actively taking notes in class, and Stage 2 takes place later, when you have time to reflect on your notes and process them more deeply.

Author's Experience My first year in college was mainly spent trying to manipulate my schedule to find some free time. I took all of my classes in a row without a break to save some time at the end of the day for relaxation and hanging out with friends before I went to work. Seldom did I look over my notes and read the material that I was assigned on the day I took the lecture notes and received the assignment. Thus, on the day before the test I was in a panic trying to cram the lecture notes into my head for the upcoming test. Needless to say, I did not perform well on many of these tests. Finally, I had a professor who told me that if I spent time each day after a couple of my classes catching up on reading and rewriting my notes, I would retain the material longer, improve my grades, and decrease my stress at test time. I employed this system, and it worked wonderfully.

— *Aaron Thompson*

Reading Strategically to Comprehend and Retain Textbook Information

Second only to lecture notes as a source of test questions on college exams is information found in assigned readings (Brown, 1988). You're likely to find exam questions containing information that your professors didn't talk about specifically in class (or even mention in class), but that was contained in your assigned reading. College professors often expect you to relate or connect what they lecture about in class with material that you've been assigned to read. Furthermore, they often deliver class lectures with the assumption that you have done the assigned reading, so if you haven't done it, you're likely to have more difficulty following what your instructor is talking about in class.

> **Remember**
>
> *Do the assigned reading and do it according to the schedule your instructor has established. It will help you better understand class lectures, improve the quality of your participation in class, and raise your overall course grade.*

Reflection 5.4

Rate yourself in terms of how frequently you use these note-taking strategies according to the following scale:

4 = always, 3 = sometimes, 2 = rarely, 1 = never

1.	I take notes aggressively in class.	4	3	2	1
2.	I sit near the front of the room during class.	4	3	2	1
3.	I sit upright and lean forward while in class.	4	3	2	1
4.	I take notes on what my instructors say, not just what they write on the board.	4	3	2	1
5.	I pay special attention to information presented at the start and end of class.	4	3	2	1
6.	I take notes in paragraph form.	4	3	2	1
7.	I review my notes immediately after class to check that they are complete and accurate.	4	3	2	1

When completing your reading assignments, use effective reading strategies that are based on sound principles of human learning and memory, such as those listed here.

What follows is a series of research-based strategies for effective reading at three key stages in the learning process: before, during, and after reading.

Pre-Reading Strategies: What to Do before Reading

1. **Before jumping into your assigned reading, look at how it fits into the overall organizational structure of the book and course.** You can do this efficiently by taking a quick look at the book's table of contents to see where the chapter you're about to read is placed in the overall sequence of chapters, especially its relation to chapters that immediately precede and follow it. Using this strategy will give you a sense of how the particular part you're focusing on connects with the bigger picture. Research shows that if learners gain access to advanced knowledge of how information they're about to learn is organized—if they see how its parts relate to the whole—*before* they attempt to start learning the specific parts, they're better able to comprehend and retain the material (Ausubel, Novak, & Hanesian, 1978; Mayer, 2003). Thus, the first step toward improving reading comprehension and retention of a book chapter is to see how it relates to the whole book before you begin to examine the chapter part by part.

Reflection 5.5

When you open a textbook to read a chapter, how do you start the reading process? That is, what's the first thing you do?

2. **Preview the chapter you're about to read by reading its boldface headings and any chapter outline, objectives, summary, or end-of-chapter questions that may be included.** Before jumping right into the content, get in the habit of previewing what's in a chapter to gain an overall sense of its organization. If you dive into the specific details first, you lose sight of how the smaller details relate to the larger picture. The brain's natural tendency is to perceive and comprehend whole patterns rather than isolated bits of information. Start by seeing how the parts of the chapter are integrated into the whole. This will enable you to better connect the separate pieces of information you encounter while you read, similar to seeing the whole picture of a completed jigsaw puzzle before you start assembling is pieces.

3. **Take a moment to think about what you already know that relates to the material in the chapter you're about to read.** By thinking about knowledge you possess about the topic you're about to read, you activate the areas of your brain where that knowledge is stored, thereby preparing it to make meaningful connections with the material you're about to read.

Strategies to Use while Reading

1. **Read selectively to locate the most important information.** Rather than jumping into reading and randomly highlighting, effective reading begins with a plan or goal for identifying what should be noted and remembered. Here are three strategies to use while reading to help you determine what information should be noted and retained.

   - **Use boldface or dark-print headings and subheadings as cues for identifying important information.** These headings organize the chapter's major points; thus, you can use them as "traffic signs" to direct you to the most important information in the chapter. Better yet, turn the headings into questions and then read to find answers to these questions. This question-and-answer strategy will ensure that you read actively and with a purpose. (You can set up this strategy when you preview the chapter by placing a question mark after each heading contained in the chapter.) Creating and answering questions while you read also keeps you motivated; the questions help stimulate your curiosity and finding answers to them serves to reward or reinforce your reading (Walter, Knudsbig, & Smith, 2003). Lastly, answering questions about what you're reading is an effective way to prepare for tests because you're practicing exactly what you'll be expected to do on exams—answering questions. You can quickly write the heading questions on separate index cards and use them as flash cards to review for exams. Use the question on the flash card as a way to flash back and trigger your recall of information from the text that answers the question.

   - **Pay special attention to words that are *italicized*, <u>underlined</u>, or appear in boldface print.** These are usually signs for building-block terms that must be understood and built on before you can proceed to understand higher-level concepts covered later in the reading. Don't simply highlight these words because their special appearance suggests they are important. Read these terms carefully and be sure you understand their meaning before you continue reading.

   - **Pay special attention to the first and last sentences in each paragraph.** These sentences contain an important introduction and conclusion to the ideas covered in the paragraph. It's a good idea to reread the first and last sentences of each paragraph before you move on to the next paragraph, particularly when reading sequential or cumulative material (e.g., science or math) that requires full comprehension of what was previously covered to understand what will be covered next.

Reread your chapter notes and highlights after you've listened to your instructor lecture on the material contained in the chapter. You can use your lecture notes as a guide to help you focus on what information in the chapter your instructor feels is most important. If you adopt this strategy, your reading before lectures will help you understand the lecture and take better class notes, and your reading after lectures will help you locate and learn information in the textbook that your instructor is emphasizing in class—which is likely to be the information your instructor thinks is most important and is most likely to show up on your exams. Thus, it's a good idea to have your class notes nearby when you're completing your reading assignments to help you identify what you should pay special attention to while reading.

Remember

Your goal when reading is not merely to cover the assigned pages, but to uncover the most important information and ideas contained on those pages.

2. **Take written notes on what you're reading.** Just as you should take notes in class, you should take notes in response to the author's words in the text. Writing requires more active thinking than highlighting because you're creating your own words rather than passively highlighting words written by somebody else. Don't get into the habit of using your textbook as a coloring book in which the artistic process of highlighting what you're reading with spectacular kaleidoscopic colors distracts you from the more important process of learning actively and thinking deeply.

> "I would advise you to read with a pen in your hand, and enter in a little book of short hints of what you find that is curious, or that might be useful; for this will be the best method of imprinting such particulars in your memory, where they will be ready."
>
> —Benjamin Franklin, 18th-century inventor, newspaper writer, and signer of the *Declaration of Independence*

Highlighting textbooks in spectacular colors is a very popular reading strategy among college students, but it's a less effective strategy for producing deep learning than taking written notes on what you read.

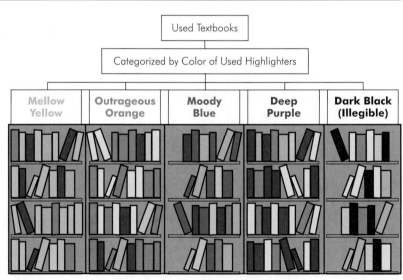

© Kendall Hunt

> "I had the worst study habits and the lowest grades. Then I found out what I was doing wrong. I had been highlighting with a black magic marker."
>
> —Jeff Altman, American comedian

If you can express what someone else has written in words that make sense to you, this means that you're relating it to what you already know—a sign of deep learning (Demmert & Towner, 2003). A good time to pause and summarize what you've read in your own words is when you encounter a boldface heading, because this indicates you've just completed reading about a major concept and are about to begin a new one.

Remember

Effective reading isn't a passive process of covering pages: it's an active process in which you uncover meaning in the pages you read.

3. **Use the visual aids included in your textbook.** Don't fall into the trap of thinking that visual aids can or should be skipped because they're merely secondary supplements to the written words in the body of the text. Visual aids, such as charts, graphs, diagrams, and concept maps, are powerful learning and memory tools for a couple of reasons: (1) they enable you to "see" the information in addition to reading (hearing) it, and (2) they organize and connect separate pieces of information into an integrated whole.

Reflection 5.6

When reading a textbook, do you usually have the following tools on hand?

Highlighter: yes   no

Pen or pencil: yes   no

Notebook: yes   no

Class notes: yes   no

Dictionary: yes   no

Glossary: yes   no

Furthermore, visual aids allow you to experience a form of information input other than repeatedly processing written words. This occasional change of sensory input brings variety to the reading process, which can recapture your attention and recharge your motivation.

Post-Reading Strategies: What to Do after Reading

1. **End a reading session with a short review of the information you've noted or highlighted.** Most forgetting that takes place after you receive and process information occurs immediately after you stop focusing on the information and turn your attention to another task (Baddeley, 1999; Underwood, 1983). (See **Figure 5.4.**) Taking a few minutes at the end of your reading time to review the most important information works to lock that information into your memory before you turn your attention to something else and forget it.

The graph in Figure 5.4 represents the results of a classic experiment on how well information is recalled at various times after it was originally learned. As you can see on the far left of the graph, most forgetting occurs soon after information has been taken in (e.g., after 20 minutes, the participants in the study forgot more than 60 percent of it). The results of this classic study, which have been confirmed multiple times (Schacter, 2001), point to the importance of reviewing information you've acquired through reading immediately after you've read it. When you do so, your memory for that information will improve dramatically because you're intercepting

FIGURE 5.4

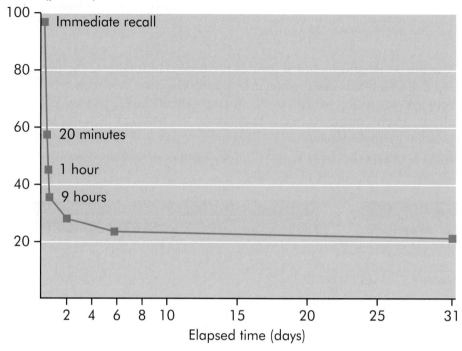

Source: Hermann Ebbinghaus, *Memory: A Contribution to Experimental Psychology*, 1885/1913

The Forgetting Curve

the forgetting curve at its steepest point of memory loss—immediately after information has been read.

2. **For difficult-to-understand concepts, seek out other information sources.** If you find you can't understand a concept explained in your text, even after re-reading and repeatedly reflecting on it, try the following strategies:

   - **Look at how another textbook explains it.** Not all textbooks are created equally: some do a better job of explaining certain concepts than others. Check to see whether your library has other texts in the same subject as your course, or check your campus bookstore for textbooks in the same subject area as the course you're taking. A different text may be able to explain a hard-to-understand concept much better than the textbook you purchased for the course.

   - **Seek help from your instructor.** If you read carefully and made every effort to understand a particular concept but still can't grasp it, most instructors should be willing to assist you. If your instructor is unavailable or unwilling, seek help from the professionals and peer tutors in the Learning Center or Academic Support Center on campus.

Snapshot Summary

5.1 SQ3R: A Method for Improving Reading Comprehension and Retention

A popular reading strategy for organizing and remembering information is the SQ3R method. SQ3R is an acronym for five steps you can take to increase textbook reading comprehension and retention, particularly when reading highly technical or complex material. The following sequences of steps comprise this method:

1. Survey
2. Question
3. Read
4. Recite
5. Review

S = Survey: Get a preview and overview of what you're about to read.

1. Read the title to activate your thoughts about the subject and prepare your mind to receive information related to it.
2. Read the introduction, chapter objectives, and chapter summary to become familiar with the author's purpose, goals, and most important points.
3. Note the boldface headings and subheadings to get a sense of the chapter's organization before you begin to read. This creates a mental structure or framework for making sense of the information you're about to read.
4. Take note of any graphics, such as charts, maps, and diagrams; they provide valuable visual support and reinforcement for the material you're reading.
5. Pay special attention to reading aids (e.g., italics and boldface font) that you can use to identify, understand, and remember key concepts.

Q = Question: Stay active and curious.

As you read, use the boldface headings to formulate questions you think will be answered in that particular section. When your mind is actively searching for answers to questions, it becomes more engaged in the learning process. As you read, add any questions that you have about the reading.

R = Read: Find the answer to the questions you've created.

Read one section at a time, with your questions in mind, and search for answers to these questions. Also, keep an eye out for new questions that need to be asked.

R = Recite: Rehearse your answers.

After you complete reading each section, recall the questions you asked and see whether you can answer them from memory. If not, look at the questions again and practice your answers to them until you can recall them without looking. Don't move on to the next section until you're able to answer all questions in the section you've just completed.

R = Review: Look back and get a second view of the whole picture.

Once you've finished the chapter, review all the questions you've created for different parts or sections. See whether you can still answer them without looking. If not, go back and refresh your memory.

Study Strategies for Learning Deeply and Remembering Longer

The final step in the learning process is to save the information in your brain and bring it back to mind at the time you need it—e.g., test time. Described here is a series of effective study strategies for acquiring knowledge, keeping that knowledge in your brain (memory storage), and accessing that information when you need it (memory retrieval).

The Importance of Undivided Attention

The human attention span has limited capacity; we have only so much of it available to us at any point in time, and we can give all or part of it to whatever task we're working on. If study time is spent engaging in other activities besides studying (e.g., listening to music, watching TV, or text-messaging friends), the attention available for studying is subtracted and divided among the other activities. In other words, studying doesn't receive your undivided attention.

Studies show that when people multitask they don't pay equal attention to all tasks at the same time. Instead, they divide their attention by shifting it back and forth between tasks (Howard, 2000) and their performance on the task that demands the most concentration or deepest thinking is what suffers the most (Crawford & Strapp, 1994). Furthermore, research shows that multitasking can increase boredom for the task that requires the most intense concentration. One study found that with even a low level of stimulation from another source of sensory input, such as a TV turned on a low volume in the next room, students were more likely to describe the mental task they were concentrating on as "boring" (Damrad-Frye & Laird, 1989).

Reflection 5.7

Rate yourself in terms of how frequently you use these reading strategies according to the following scale:

4 = always, 3 = sometimes, 2 = rarely, 1 = never

1.	I read the chapter outlines and summaries before I start reading the chapter content.	4	3	2	1
2.	I preview a chapter's boldface headings and subheadings before I begin to read the chapter.	4	3	2	1
3.	I adjust my reading speed to the type of subject I am reading.	4	3	2	1
4.	I look up the meaning of unfamiliar words and unknown terms that I come across before I continue reading.	4	3	2	1
5.	I take written notes on information I read.	4	3	2	1
6.	I use the visual aids included in my textbooks.	4	3	2	1
7.	I finish my reading sessions with a review of important information that I noted or highlighted.	4	3	2	1

When performing complex mental tasks that cannot be done automatically or mindlessly, other tasks and sources of external stimulation interfere with the quiet internal reflection needed for permanent connections to form between brain cells—which is what must happen if deep, long-lasting learning is to take place (Jensen, 2000).

Studies show that doing challenging academic work while multitasking divides up attention and drives down comprehension and retention.

Remember

Attention must happen first in order for retention to happen later.

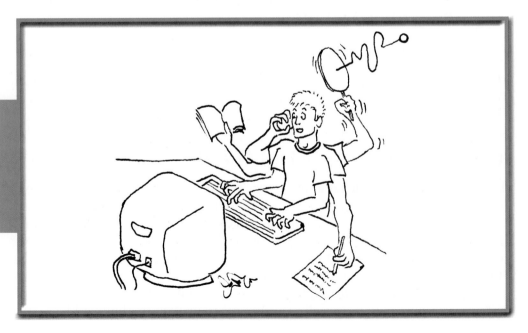

Making Meaningful Associations

Connecting what you're trying to learn to something you already know is a powerful memory-improvement strategy because knowledge is stored in the form of a connected network of brain cells (Coward, 1990; Chaney, 2007). (See Figure 5.3 on p. 114.)

The brain's natural tendency to seek meaningful, connected patterns applies to words as well as images. This is illustrated in the following passage that once appeared anonymously on the Internet. See whether you can read it and grasp its meaning.

> *Aoccdrnig to rscheearch at Cmabridge Uinverstisy, it deos't mattaer in what order the ltteers in a word are, the only iprmoetnt thing is that the frist and lsat ltteer be at the rghit pclae. The rset can be a total mses and you can still raed it wouthit a porbelm. This is bcusae the human mind deos not raed ervey lteter by istlef, but the word as a wlohe. Amzanig huh?*

Notice how easily you found the meaning of the misspelled words by naturally transforming them into correctly spelled words—which you knew because the correctly spelled words were already stored in your brain. Thus, whenever you learn meaningfully, you do so by connecting what you're trying to understand to what you already know.

Learning by making meaningful connections is referred to as *deep learning* (Biggs & Tang, 2007; Entwistle & Ramsden, 1983). It involves moving beyond shallow memorization to deeper levels of understanding. This is a major a shift from the old view that learning occurs by passively absorbing information like a sponge—for example, by receiving it from the teacher or text and studying it in the same prepackaged form as you received it. Instead, you want to adopt an approach to learning that involves actively transforming the information you receive into a form that's meaningful to you (Feldman & Paulsen, 1994; Mayer, 2002). This transforms short-term, surface-level learning (memorization of information) into deep and meaningful long-term learning (acquisition of knowledge).

So, instead of immediately trying to learn something by repeatedly pounding it into your brain like a hammer, your first strategy should be to try hooking or hanging it onto something that's already stored in your brain—something you already know and is meaningful to you. It may take a little while and a little work to find the right hook, but once you've found it, you'll learn the information faster and retain it longer. For instance, here's a meaningful way to learn and remember how to correctly spell one of the most frequently misspelled words in the English language: *separate* (not *seperate*). If you remember that *par* means "to divide," as in the words *par*ts or *par*tition, it makes sense that *separate* should be spelled *separate* because its meaning is "to divide into parts."

Each of the academic subjects that comprise the college curriculum has a specialized vocabulary that can sound like a foreign language to someone who has no experience with the subject area. Before you start to brutally beat these terms into your brain through sheer repetition, try to find some meaning in them. One way you can make a term more meaningful to you is by looking up its word root in the dictionary or by identifying its prefix or suffix, which may give away the term's meaning. For instance, suppose you're taking a biology course and studying the autonomic nervous system—the part of the nervous system that operates without your conscious awareness or voluntary control (e.g., your heart beating and lungs breathing). The meaning of the phrase is given away by the prefix *auto*, which means self-controlling, as in the word *automatic* (e.g., automatic transmission).

"The extent to which we remember a new experience has more to do with how it relates to existing memories than with how many times or how recently we have experienced it."

—Morton Hunt, *The Universe Within: A New Science Explores the Human Mind*

Student *Perspective*

"When you have to do work, and you're getting it. It's linking what I already know to what I didn't know.

—Student's description of a "good class"

If looking up the term's root, prefix, or suffix doesn't give away its meaning, see if you can make it meaningful to you in some other way. For instance, suppose you looked up the root of the term *artery* and nothing about the origins of this term suggested its meaning or purpose. You could create your own meaning for this term by taking its first letter (a), and have it stand for "*away*"—to help you remember that arteries carry blood away from the heart. Thus, you've taken a biological term and made it personally meaningful (and memorable).

Reflection 5.8

Think of a key term or concept you're learning in a course this term that you could form a meaningful association to remember?

What is the information you're attempting to learn?

What is the meaningful association you could use to help you remember it?

Remember

If what you're learning is meaningful to you, you'll learn it more deeply and you'll remember it longer.

Compare and Contrast

When you're studying something new, get in the habit of asking yourself the following questions:

1. Is this idea similar or comparable to something that I've already learned? (Compare)
2. How does this idea differ from what I already know? (Contrast)

Research indicates that this simple strategy is one of the most powerful ways to promote learning of academic information (Marzano, Pickering, & Pollock, 2001). Asking yourself the question "How is this similar to and different from concepts that I already know?" makes learning more personally meaningful because you are relating what you're trying to learn to what you already know.

Integration and Organization

Integrate or connect ideas from your class notes and assigned readings that relate to the same major point by organizing them into the same category. For example, get these related ideas in the same place by recording then on the same index card under the same category heading. Index cards are a good tool for such purposes; you can use each card as a miniature file cabinet for different categories of information. The category heading on each card functions like the hub of a wheel, around which individual pieces of related information are attached like spokes. Integrating information related to the same topic in the same place and studying it at the same time divides the total material you're learning into identifiable and manageable parts. In contrast, when ideas pertaining to the same point or concept are spread all over the place, they're more likely to take that form in your mind—leaving them mentally disconnected and leaving you confused (as well as feeling stressed and overwhelmed).

Remember

Just as important as organizing course materials is organizing course concepts. Ask yourself the following questions: How can this specific concept be categorized or classified? How does this particular idea relate to or "fit into" something bigger?

Divide and Conquer

Effective learning depends not only on *how* you learn (your method), but on *when* you learn (your timing). Although cramming just before exams is better than not studying, it's far less effective than studying that's spread out across time. Rather than cramming all your studying into one long session, use the method of *distributed practice*: spread or distribute your study time over several shorter sessions. Research consistently shows that short, periodic practice sessions are more effective than a single marathon session.

© Arieliona, 2013. Under license from Shutterstock, Inc.

Spreading out your studying into shorter sessions improves your memory by reducing loss of attention due to fatigue.

Distributing study time over several shorter sessions improves your learning and memory by:

- Reducing loss of attention due to fatigue or boredom; and
- Reducing mental interference by giving your brain some downtime to cool down and lock in information it has received before it's interrupted by the need to deal with additional information (Malmberg & Murnane, 2002; Murnane & Shiffrin, 1991).

If the brain's downtime is interfered with by the arrival of additional information, it gets overloaded and its capacity for handling information becomes impaired. This is what cramming does—it overloads the brain with lots of information in a limited period of time. In contrast, distributed study does just the opposite—it uses shorter sessions with downtime between sessions, thereby giving the brain the time and opportunity to retain the information that it has received and processed (studied).

Another major advantage of distributed study is that it's less stressful and more motivating than cramming. Shorter sessions provide you with an incentive to start studying because you know that you're not going to be doing it for a long stretch of time or lose any sleep over it. It's easier to maintain your interest and motivation for any task that's done for a shorter rather than a longer period. Furthermore, distributing studying makes exam preparation easier because you know that if you run into difficulty understanding anything, you'll still have plenty of time to get help with it before you're tested and graded on it.

The "Part-to-Whole" Study Method

The part-to-whole method of studying is a natural extension of the distributed practice just discussed. With the part-to-whole method, you break up the material you need to learn into smaller parts and study those parts in separate sessions in advance of the exam; then you use your last study session just before the exam to review (restudy) all the parts you previously studied in separate sessions. Thus, your last session is not a cram session or even a study session: it's a review session.

Research shows that students of all ability levels learn material in college courses more effectively when it's studied in small units and when progression to the next unit takes place only after the previous unit has been mastered or understood (Pascarella & Terenzini, 1991, 2005). This strategy has two advantages: (1) it reinforces your memory for what you previously learned and (2) it builds on what you already know to help you learn new material. These advantages are particularly important in cumulative subjects that require memory for problem-solving procedures or steps, such as math and science. When you repeatedly practice these procedures, they become more automatic and you're able to retrieve them quicker (e.g., on a timed test). This enables you to use them efficiently without having to expend a lot of mental effort and energy (Samuels & Flor, 1997), freeing your working memory for more important tasks—such as critical thinking and creative problem solving (Schneider & Chein, 2003).

Reflection **5.9**

Are you more likely to study in advance of exams or cram just before exams?

Why?

Don't buy into the myth that studying in advance is a waste of time because you'll forget it all by test time. As discussed in Chapter 4, this is a myth that procrastinators often use to rationalize their habit of putting off studying until the very last moment, which forces them to cram frantically the night before exams. Do not underestimate the power of breaking material to be learned into smaller parts and studying those parts some time before a major exam. Even if you cannot recall what you previously studied, when you start reviewing it you'll find that you will relearn it much faster than when you studied it the first time. This proves that studying in advance is not a waste of time, because it takes less time to relearn the material, indicating that information studied in the earlier sessions was still retained in your brain (Kintsch, 1994).

Build Variety into the Study Process

You can increase your concentration and motivation by using the following strategies to infuse variety and a change of pace into your study routine.

Periodically vary the type of academic work you do while studying. Changing the nature of your work activities or the type of mental tasks you're performing while studying increases your level of alertness and concentration by reducing *habituation*—attention loss that occurs after repeated engagement in the same type of mental task (McGuiness & Pribram, 1980). To combat attention loss due to habituation, occasionally vary the type of study task you're performing. For instance, shift periodically among tasks that involve reading, writing, studying, and problem-solving skills (e.g., math or science problems).

Study different subjects in different places. Studying in different locations provides different environmental contexts for learning, which reduces the amount of interference that normally builds up when all information is studied in the same place (Rankin et al., 2009). In addition to spreading out your studying at different times, it's also a good idea to spread it out in different places. The great public speakers in ancient Greece and Rome used this method of changing places to remember long speeches by walking through different rooms while rehearsing their speech, learning each major part of their speech in a different room (Higbee, 1998).

Changing the nature of the learning task and place provides a change of pace that infuses variety into the learning process, which, in turn, stimulates your attention, concentration, and motivation. Although it's useful to have a set time and place to study for getting you into a regular work routine, this doesn't mean that learning occurs best by habitually performing all types of academic tasks in the same place.

Instead, research suggests that you should periodically change the learning tasks you perform and the environment in which you perform them to maximize attention and minimize interference (Druckman & Bjork, 1991).

Remember

Changes of pace and place while studying can stimulate your attention to what you're studying as well as your interest in and motivation for studying.

Mix long study sessions with short study breaks that involve physical activity (e.g., a short jog or brisk walk). Study breaks that include physical activity not only refresh the mind by giving it a rest from studying, but also stimulate the mind by increasing blood flow to your brain, which will help you retain what you've already studied and regain concentration for what you'll study next.

Learn with all of your senses. When studying, try to use as many sensory channels as possible. Research shows that information perceived through multiple sensory modalities is remembered better because it creates multiple interconnections in long-term memory areas of the brain (Bjork, 1994; Shams & Seitz, 2011; Zull, 2002). When a memory is formed in the brain, different sensory aspects of it are stored in different areas. For example, when your brain receives visual, auditory (hearing), and motor (movement) input while learning, each of these forms of sensory input is stored as memory trace in a different part of the brain. **Figure 5.5** shows a map of the outer surface of the human brain; you can see how different parts of the brain are specialized to receive input from different sensory modalities. When you use all of these sensory modalities while learning, multiple memory traces of what you're studying are recorded in different parts of your brain, which leads to deeper learning and stronger memory for what you have learned (Education Commission of the States, 1996).

Student
Perspective

"I have to *hear* it, *see* it, *write* it, and *talk* about it."

—First-year college student responding to the question "How do you learn best?"

FIGURE 5.5

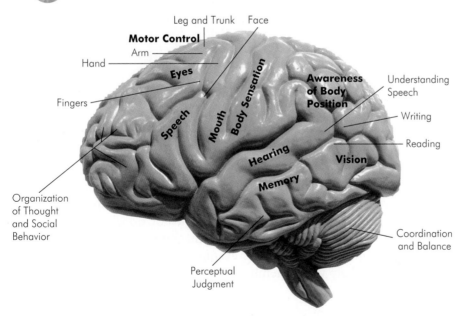

Brain image modified from © David Huntley, 2013. Under license from Shutterstock, Inc.

A Map of the Functions Performed by the Outer Surface of the Human Brain

Reflection **5.10**

Would you say that you're more of a visual learner or verbal learner?

How do you think most people would answer this question?

Learn visually. The human brain consists of two hemispheres (half spheres): the left and the right (see **Figure 5.6**). Each hemisphere of the brain specializes in a different type of learning. In most people, the left hemisphere specializes in verbal learning, dealing primarily with words. In contrast, the right hemisphere specializes in visual-spatial learning, dealing primarily with perceiving images and objects that occupy physical space. If you use both hemispheres while studying, you lay down two different memory traces in your brain: one in the left hemisphere where words are stored, and one in the right hemisphere where images are stored. This process of laying down a double memory trace (verbal and visual) is referred to as *dual coding* (Paivio, 1990). When this happens, memory for what you're learning is substantially strengthened, primarily because two memory traces are better than one.

FIGURE 5.6

The human brain consists of the left hemisphere, which processes words, and the right hemisphere, which processes images.

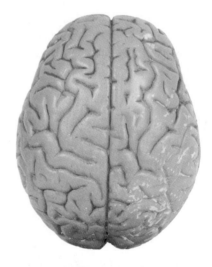

© JupiterImages Corporation.

To capitalize on the advantage of dual coding, be sure to use any visual aids that are available to you, including those provided in your textbook and by your instructor in class. You can also create your own visual aids by drawing pictures, symbols, and concept maps, such as flowcharts, Venn diagrams, spider webs, wheels with spokes, or branching tree diagrams. (For example, see **Figure 5.7** for a tree diagram that could be used to help you remember the parts and functions of the human nervous system.)

FIGURE 5.7

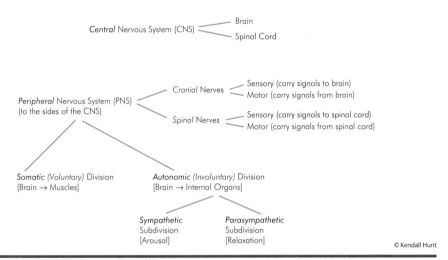

ORGANIZATION OF THE HUMAN NERVOUS SYSTEM

Central Nervous System (CNS) ─── Brain
                                └── Spinal Cord

Peripheral Nervous System (PNS)
(to the sides of the CNS)

Cranial Nerves ─── Sensory (carry signals to brain)
                 └── Motor (carry signals from brain)

Spinal Nerves ─── Sensory (carry signals to spinal cord)
                └── Motor (carry signals from spinal cord)

Somatic (Voluntary) Division
[Brain → Muscles]

Autonomic (Involuntary) Division
[Brain → Internal Organs]

Sympathetic
Subdivision
[Arousal]

Parasympathetic
Subdivision
[Relaxation]

© Kendall Hunt

Concept Map for the Human Nervous System

Remember

Drawing and other forms of visual illustration are not just artistic exercises: they can also be powerful learning tools—you can draw to learn! Drawing keeps you actively involved in the process of learning, and by representing what you're learning in visual form, you're able to dual-code the information you're studying, which doubles the number of memory traces recorded in your brain. As the old saying goes, "A picture is worth a thousand words."

Reflection 5.11

Think of a course you're taking this term in which you're learning related pieces of information that could be joined together to form a concept map. In the space that follows, make a rough sketch of this map that includes the information you need to remember.

Learn by moving or using motor learning (a.k.a. muscle memory). In addition to hearing and seeing, movement is a sensory channel. When you move, your brain receives kinesthetic stimulation—the sensations generated by your muscles. Research shows that memory traces for movement are commonly stored in an area of your brain that plays a major role for all types of learning (Middleton & Strick, 1994). Thus, associating movement with what you're learning can improve your ability to retain it because you add a muscle memory trace in the motor control area of your brain. (See Figure 5.5.)

You can use movement to help you learn and retain academic information by using your body to act out what you're studying or to symbolize it with your hands (Kagan & Kagan, 1998). For example, if you're trying to remember five points about something (e.g., five consequences of the Civil War), when you're studying these points, count them on your fingers as you try to recall each of them. Also, remember that talking involves muscle movement of your lips and tongue. Thus, by speaking aloud when you're studying, either to a friend or to yourself, you can improve your memory of what you're studying by adding kinesthetic stimulation to the auditory or sound stimulation your brain receives from hearing what you're saying.

Remember

Try to make the learning process a total body experience—hear it, see it, say it, and move it.

Learn with emotion. Information reaches the brain through your senses and is stored in the brain as a memory trace; the same is true of emotions. Numerous connections occur between brain cells in the emotional and memory centers (Zull, 1998). For instance, when you're experiencing emotional excitement about what you're learning, adrenaline is released and is carried through the bloodstream to the brain. Once adrenaline reaches the brain, it increases blood flow and glucose production, which stimulates learning and strengthens memory (LeDoux, 1998; Rosenfield, 1988). In fact, emotionally intense experiences can release such a substantial amount of adrenaline into the bloodstream that memories for them can be immediately stored in long-term memory and last an entire lifetime. For instance, most people remember exactly what they were doing at the time they experienced such emotionally intense events as the September 11 terrorist attack on the United States, their first kiss, or their favorite team winning a world championship.

What does this emotion-memory link have to do with helping you remember academic information while studying? Research indicates that emotional intensity, excitement, and enthusiasm strengthen memory of academic information just as they do for memory for life events and personal experiences. If you get psyched up about what you're learning, you have a much better chance of learning and remembering it. When you're passionate or intense about what you're learning and convince yourself that what you're learning is really important to know, you're more likely to remember it (Howard, 2000; Minninger, 1984). So, keep in mind the importance or significance of what you're learning. For instance, if you're learning about photosynthesis, remind yourself that you're not just learning about a chemical reaction, you're learning about the driving force that underlies all plant life on the planet! If you aren't aware of the importance or significance of a particular concept you're studying, ask your instructor or a student majoring in the field. Enthusiasm can be contagious; you may catch it and become more passionate about learning the concept.

Remember

You learn most effectively when you actively involve all your senses (including bodily movement) and when you learn with passion and enthusiasm. In other words, learning grows deeper and lasts longer when you put your whole self into it—your heart, your mind, and your body.

Learn by collaborating with others. Research indicates that college students who work regularly in small groups of four to six become more actively involved in the learning process and learn more (Light, 2001). To maximize the power of study groups, each member should study individually *before* studying in a group and should come prepared with specific information or answers to share with teammates, as well as questions or points of confusion that the team can attempt to help answer or clarify. (For specific team-learning strategies, see Chapter 1.)

"We are born for cooperation, as are the feet, the hands, the eyelids, and the upper and lower jaws."

—Marcus Aurelius, Roman emperor

Author's Experience

When I was in my senior year of college, I had to take a theory course by independent study because the course would not be offered again until after I planned to graduate. Another senior found himself in the same situation. The instructor allowed both of us to take this course together and agreed to meet with us every two weeks. My classmate and I studied independently for the first two weeks.

I prepared for the biweekly meetings by reading thoroughly, yet I had little understanding of what I had read. After our first meeting, I left with a strong desire to drop the course but decided to stick with it. Over the next two weeks, I spent many sleepless nights trying to prepare for our next meeting and was feeling pretty low about not being the brightest student in my class of two. During the next meeting with the instructor, I noticed that the other student was also having difficulty, and so did the instructor. After that meeting, the instructor gave us study questions and asked us to read separately and then get together to discuss the questions. During the next two weeks, my classmate and I met several times to discuss what we were learning (or attempting to learn). By communicating with each other about the issues we were studying, we both ended up gaining greater understanding. Our instructor was delighted to see that he was able to suggest a collaborative learning strategy that worked for both of us.

Aaron Thompson

Self-Monitor Your Learning

Successful learners just don't put in study time; they reflect and check on themselves to see if they're putting in quality time and really understanding what they're attempting to learn. They monitor their comprehension as they go along by asking themselves questions such as "Am I following this?" "Do I really understand it?" and "Do I know it for sure?"

How do you know if you really know it? Probably the best answer to this question is "I find *meaning* in it—that is, I can relate to it personally or put it in terms that make sense to me" (Ramsden, 2003).

Following are some strategies for checking whether you truly understand what you're trying to learn. They help you answer the question "How do I know if I really know it?" These strategies can be used as indicators or checkpoints for determining whether you're just memorizing or learning at a deeper level.

- **Can you paraphrase (restate or translate) what you're learning into your own words?** When you can paraphrase what you're learning, you're able to complete the following sentence: "In other words . . ." If you can complete that sentence in your own words, this is a good indication that you've moved beyond memorization to comprehension because you've transformed what you're learning into

Student Perspective

"I would suggest students get to know [each] other and get together in groups to study or at least review class material. I find it is easier to ask your friends or classmates with whom you are comfortable asking 'dumb' questions."

—Advice to first-year students from a college sophomore (Walsh, 2005)

"When you know a thing, to recognize that you know it; and when you do not, to know that you do not know; that is knowledge."

—Confucius, influential Chinese thinker and educator

words that are meaningful to you. You know you know it if you're not stating it the same way your instructor or textbook stated it, but restating it in words that are your own.

- **Can you explain what you're learning to someone who is unfamiliar with it?** Simply put, if you can't explain it to someone else, you probably don't really understand it yourself. If you can explain to a friend what you've learned, this is a good sign that you've moved beyond memorization to comprehension because you're able to translate it into language that's understandable to anyone. Studies show that students gain deeper levels of understanding for what they're learning when they're asked to explain it to someone else (Chi et al., 1994). Sometimes, we only become aware of how well we know or don't know something until we have to explain it to someone who's never heard it before (just ask any teacher). If you cannot find someone else to explain it to, then explain it aloud as if you were talking to an imaginary friend.

- **Can you think of an example of what you've learned?** If you can come up with an instance or illustration of what you're learning that's your own—not one given by your instructor or textbook—this is a good sign that you truly understand it. It shows you're able to take a general, abstract concept and apply it to a specific real-life experience (Bligh, 2000). Furthermore, a personal example is a powerful memory tool. Studies show that when people retrieve a concept from memory, they first recall an example of it. The example then serves a memory-retrieval cue to trigger their memory of other details about the concept, such as its definition and relationship to other concepts (Norman, 1982; Okimoto & Norman, 2010; Park, 1984).

- **Can you represent or describe what you've learned in terms of an analogy or metaphor that compares it to something with similar meaning, or which works in a similar way?** Analogies and metaphors are basically ways of learning something new by understanding it in terms of its similarity to something you already understand. For instance, the computer can be used as a metaphor for the human brain to get a better understanding of learning and memory as a three-stage process in which information is (1) inputted—perceived or received (through lectures and readings), (2) stored or saved—by studying, and (3) retrieved—recalled from storage at test time. If you can use an analogy or metaphor to represent what you're learning, you're grasping it at a deep level because you're building a mental bridge that connects it to what you already know (Cameron, 2003).

- **Can you apply what you're learning to solve a new problem that you haven't previously seen?** The ability to use knowledge by applying it in a different situation is a good indicator of deep learning (Erickson & Strommer, 2005). Learning specialists refer to this mental process as *decontextualization*—taking what you learned in one context (situation) and applying it to another (Bransford, Brown, & Cocking, 1999). For instance, you know that you've learned a mathematical concept deeply when you can use that concept to solve math problems that are different from the ones used by your instructor or your textbook. This is why your math instructors rarely include on exams the exact problems that they solved in class or were solved in your textbook. They're not trying to trick you at test time: they're trying to see whether you've learned the concept or principle deeply.

Reflection 5.12

Rate yourself in terms of how frequently you use these study strategies according to the following scale:

4 = always,   3 = sometimes,   2 = rarely,   1 = never

1. I block out all distracting sources of outside stimulation when I study.   4   3   2   1

2. I try to find meaning in technical terms by looking at their prefixes or suffixes or by looking up their word roots in the dictionary.   4   3   2   1

3. I compare and contrast what I'm currently studying with what I've already learned.   4   3   2   1

4. I organize the information I'm studying into categories or classes.   4   3   2   1

5. I integrate or pull together information from my class notes and readings that relates to the same concept or general category.   4   3   2   1

6. I distribute or spread out my study time over several short sessions in advance of the exam, and I use my last study session before the test to review the information I previously studied.   4   3   2   1

7. I participate in study groups with my classmates.   4   3   2   1

Summary and Conclusion

Information delivered during lectures is most likely to form questions and answers on college tests. Students who do not record information presented during lectures in their notes have a slim chance of recalling the information at test time. Thus, effective note taking is critical to successful academic performance in college.

Information from reading assignments is the next most common source of test questions on college exams. Professors often don't discuss information contained in assigned reading during class lectures. Thus, doing the assigned reading, and doing it in a way that's most effective for promoting comprehension and retention, plays an important role in your academic success.

The most effective strategies for promoting effective classroom listening, textbook reading, and studying are those that reflect three of the college success principles discussed in Chapter 1: (1) active involvement, (2) collaboration, and (3) self-awareness.

Active involvement is critical for learning from lectures (e.g., actively taking notes while listening to lectures) and learning from reading (e.g., actively taking notes while reading). While active involvement is necessary for learning because it engages your attention and enables information to enter the brain, personal reflection is also necessary for deep learning because it keeps that information in the brain by locking it into long-term memory. Reflection also encourages deep learning by promoting self-awareness. By periodically pausing to reflect on whether you're truly understanding what you're studying, you become a more self-aware learner and a more successful student.

Learning is also deepened when it's a multisensory experience—when you engage as many senses as possible in the learning process, particularly the sense of vision. Lastly, learning is strengthened when it's done collaboratively. You can collaborate with peers to take better notes in class, to identify what's most important in your assigned reading, and to study lecture and reading notes in preparation for course exams.

Learning More through the World Wide Web

Internet-Based Resources for Further Information on Strategic Learning and Memory Improvement

For additional information related to the ideas discussed in this chapter, we recommend the following Web sites:

Strategic Learning and Study Strategies:

www.Dartmouth.edu/~acskills/success/index.html

www.muskingum.edu/~cal/database/general/

Learning Math and Overcoming Math Anxiety:

www.mathacademy.com/pr/minitext/anxiety

www.onlinemathlearning.com/math-mnemonics.html

5.1 Self-Assessment of Note-Taking and Reading Habits

Look back at the ratings you gave yourself for effective note-taking (p. 118), reading (p. 124), and studying (p. 135) strategies. Add up your total score for these three sets of learning strategies (the maximum score for each set is 28):

Note Taking = _____

Reading = _____

Studying = _____

Total Learning Strategy Score = _____

Self-Assessment Questions

1. In which learning strategy area did you score lowest?

2. Do you think that the strategy area in which you scored lowest has anything to do with your lowest course grade at this point in the term?

3. Of the seven strategies listed within the area in which you scored lowest, which ones could you immediately put into practice to improve your lowest course grade this term?

4. What is the likelihood that you will put the preceding strategies into practice this term?

5.2 Consulting with a Learning Center or Academic Development Specialist

Make an appointment to visit your Learning Center or Academic Support Center on campus to discuss the results of your note-taking, reading, and studying self-assessment in Exercise 5.1 (or any other learning self-assessment you may have taken). Ask for recommendations about how you can improve your learning habits in your lowest-score area. After your visit, answer the following questions.

Learning Resource Center Reflection

1. Who did you meet with in the Learning Center? _____

2. Was your appointment useful (e.g., did you gain any insights or acquire any new learning or test-taking strategies)?

3. What steps were recommended to you for improving your academic performance?

4. How likely is it that you will take the steps mentioned in the previous question: (a) definitely, (b) probably, (c) possibly, or (d) unlikely? Why?

5. Do you plan to visit the Learning Center again? If yes, why? If no, why not?

Too Fast, Too Frustrating: A Note-Taking Nightmare

Susan Scribe is a first-year student who is majoring in journalism, and she's enrolled in an introductory course that is required for her major (Introduction to Mass Media). Her instructor for this course lectures at a rapid rate and uses vocabulary words that go right over her head. Since she cannot get all her instructor's words down on paper and cannot understand half the words she does manage to write down, she becomes frustrated and stops taking notes. She wants to do well in this course because it's the first course in her major, but she's afraid she will fail it because her class notes are so pitiful.

Reflection and Discussion Questions

1. Can you relate to this case personally, or do you know any students who are in the same boat as Susan?

2. What would you recommend that Susan do at this point?

3. Why did you make the preceding recommendation?

Test-Taking Skills and Strategies

What to Do before, during, and after Exams

LEARNING GOAL

To strengthen your performance on college exams and tests for admission to professional and graduate programs.

1. On which of the following types of activities do you tend to perform best? (Circle one.) On which do you perform the worst? (Circle one.)

   Taking multiple-choice tests

   Taking essay tests

   Writing papers

   Making oral presentations

2. What do you think accounts for the fact that you perform better on one of these types than the others?

Test-Taking Strategies

Academic learning in college involves three stages: acquiring information from lectures and readings; studying that information and storing it in your brain as knowledge; and demonstrating that knowledge on exams. What follows is a series of strategies related to stage three of this process: test taking. The strategies are divided into three categories:

- Strategies to use in advance of the test,
- Strategies to use during the test, and
- Strategies to use after test results are returned.

Pre-Test Strategies: What to Do in Advance of the Test

Your ability to remember what you've studied depends not only on how much and how well you studied, but also on how you will be tested (Stein, 1978). You may be able to remember what you've studied if you are tested in one format (e.g., multiple-choice questions) but may not remember the material as well if the test is in a different format (e.g., essay questions). You need to be aware of the type of test you'll be taking and adjust your study strategies accordingly.

College test questions fall into two major categories: (1) recognition questions and (2) recall questions. Each of these types of questions requires a different type of memory and a different study strategy.

1. **Recognition test questions.** Recognition questions ask you to select or choose the correct answer from choices that are provided for you. Falling into this category are multiple-choice, true-false, and matching questions. These test questions don't require you to supply or produce the correct answer on your own: instead, you're asked to recognize or pick out the correct answer—similar to picking out the "correct" criminal from a lineup of potential suspects.

2. **Recall test questions.** Recall questions require you to retrieve information you've studied and reproduce it on your own at test time. As the word *recall* implies, you have to "call back" to mind the information you need and supply it yourself, rather than selecting it or picking it out from information that's supplied for you. Recall test questions include essay and short-answer questions, which require a written response.

Since recognition test questions ask you to recognize or identify the correct answer from among answers that are provided for you, repeatedly reading over your class and textbook notes to identify important concepts may be an effective study strategy for multiple-choice and true-false test questions. Doing so matches the type of mental activity you'll be asked to perform on the exam—read over and identify correct answers.

On the other hand, recall test questions, such as essay questions, require you to retrieve information and generate answers on your own. Studying for essay tests by looking over your class notes and highlighted reading will not prepare you to recall information because it does not simulate what you'll be doing on the test itself. However, when you study for essay tests, if you retrieve information without looking at it and write out your answers to questions, you will ensure that your practice (study) sessions match your performance (test) situation because you are rehearsing what you'll be expected to do on the test—write essays.

Two strategies that are particularly effective for practicing the type of memory retrieval you will need to perform on essay tests are recitation and creation of retrieval cues. Each of these strategies is described below.

Recitation

Recitation involves saying the information you need to recall without looking at it. Research indicates that memory for information is significantly strengthened when students study by trying to generate that information on their own, rather than simply looking it over or rereading it (Roediger & Karpicke, 2006). Reciting strengthens recall memory in three ways:

1. Recitation forces you to actively retrieve information, which is what you will have to do on the test, instead of passively reviewing information that's in front of you and in full view, which is not what you will do on the test.

2. Recitation gives you clear feedback on whether you can recall the information you're studying. If you can't retrieve and recite it without looking at it, you know for sure that you won't be able to recall it at test time and that you need to study it further. One way to provide yourself with this feedback is to put the question on one side of an index card and the answer on the flip side. If you find yourself flipping over the index card to look at the answer in order to remember it, you clearly cannot retrieve the information on your own and need to study it further.

3. Recitation encourages you to use your own words; this gives you feedback on whether you can paraphrase it. If you can paraphrase it (rephrase it in your own words), it's a good indication that you really understand it, and if you really understand it, you're more likely to recall it at test time.

Recitation can be done silently, by speaking aloud, or by writing out what you're saying. We recommend speaking aloud or writing out what you're reciting because these strategies involve physical action, which keeps you actively involved in the learning process.

Creation of Retrieval Cues

Suppose you're trying to remember the name of a person you know but just cannot recall it. If a friend gives you a clue (e.g., the first letter of the person's name or a name that rhymes with it), it's likely to suddenly trigger your memory of that person's name. What your friend did was provide you with a retrieval cue. A *retrieval cue* is a type of memory reminder (like a string tied around your finger) that brings back to your mind what you've temporarily forgotten. Since human memories are stored as parts in an interconnected network, if you're able to recall one piece or segment of the network (the retrieval cue), it can trigger recall of the other pieces of information linked to it in the same organizational network (Willingham, 2001).

Reflection 6.2

Think of material in a course you're taking this term that could be easily grouped into categories to help you remember that material. What is the course?

What categories could you use to organize information that's been covered in the course?

Studies show that students who can't remember previously studied information are better able to recall that information if they are given a retrieval cue. In one study, students studied a long list of items that included different animals (e.g., giraffe, coyote, and turkey). When given a blank sheet of paper to write down the names of those animals, they weren't able to recall all of them. However, when the word "animals" was written on top of the answer sheet to provide a retrieval cue, the students were often able to recall many animals they couldn't name without the retrieval cue (Tulving, 1983). Research findings such as these suggest that category names can serve as powerful retrieval cues. By taking information that you need to recall on an essay test and organizing it into categories, you can use these category names as retrieval cues at test time.

Another strategy for creating retrieval cues is to come up with your own catchwords or catchphrases that you can use to "catch" or batch together all related ideas you're trying to remember. For instance, an acronym can serve as a catchword, with each letter acting as a retrieval cue for a batch of related ideas. Suppose you're studying for an essay test in abnormal psychology that will include questions testing your knowledge of different forms of mental illness. You could create the acronym SCOT as a retrieval cue to help you remember to include each of the following elements of mental illness in your essay answers: symptoms (S), causes (C), outcomes (O), and therapies (T). See **Do It Now! 6.1** for ideas on how to create your own memory-retrieval cues.

6.1

Key Questions to Guide Creation of Your Own Retrieval Cues

1. Can you relate or associate what you're trying to remember with something you already know, or can you create a short meaningful story out of it? (Meaningful Association)
2. Can you remember it by visualizing an image of it, or by visually associating the pieces of information you want to recall with familiar places or sites? (Visualization)
3. Can you represent each piece of information you're trying to recall as a letter and string the letters together to form a single word or short phrase? (Acronym)
4. Can you rhyme what you're trying to remember with a word or expression you know well, or can you create a little poem, jingle, or melody out of it that contains the information? (Rhythm and Rhyme)

• Remember

On multiple-choice questions, you're given a list of answers and you pick out the right one. On essay questions, you have a blank sheet of paper and you have to dig out the answer on your own, which means you have to recite (rehearse) your answers before the test and use memory-retrieval cues during the test to dig up the information you need to remember.

Student *Perspective*

"Avoid flipping through notes (cramming) immediately before a test. Instead, do some breathing exercises and think about something other than the test."

—Advice to first-year students from a college sophomore (Walsh, 2005)

Strategies to Use Immediately before a Test

1. **Before the exam, try to take a brisk walk.** Physical activity increases mental alertness by increasing oxygen flow to the brain; it also decreases tension by increasing the brain's production of emotionally "mellowing" brain chemicals (e.g., serotonin and endorphins).

2. **Come fully armed with all the test-taking tools you need.** In addition to the required supplies (e.g., No. 2 pencil, pen, blue book, Scantron, calculator, etc.), bring backup equipment in case you experience equipment failure (e.g., an extra pen in case your first one runs out of ink or extra pencils in case your original one breaks).

3. **Try to get to the classroom a few minutes early.** Arriving at the test ahead of time gives you a chance to review any formulas and equations you may have struggled to remember and any memory-retrieval cues you've created (e.g., acronyms). You want to be sure that you have this information in your working memory when you receive the exam so that you can get it down on paper before you forget it. Arriving early also allows you to take a few minutes to get into a relaxed pre-test state of mind by thinking positive thoughts, taking slow, deep breaths, and stretching your muscles. Also, avoid last-second discussions with unprepared classmates about the test just before the test is handed out; their hurried and harried questions can often cause confusion and elevate your level of test anxiety.

4. **Sit in the same seat that you normally occupy in class.** Research indicates that memory is improved when information is recalled in the same place where it was originally received or reviewed (Sprenger, 1999). Thus, taking the test in the same seat you normally occupy during lectures should improve your test performance because it puts you in the same place where you originally heard much of the information that is going to appear on the test. Studies show that when students take a test in the same environment that they studied in, they tend to remember more of that information at test time than do students who study in one place and take the test in a different place (Smith, Glenberg, & Bjork, 1978). While it is unlikely that you'll be able to do all your studying in the same room that you will take your test in, it may be possible to do your final review in your classroom or in an empty classroom with similar features. This could strengthen your memory for the information you studied, because the features of the room in which you studied the information may become associated with the information, and seeing these features again at test time may help trigger memory of the information (Tulving, 1983).

Studies have shown that if students are exposed to a distinctive or unique aroma while they are studying (e.g., the smell of chocolate) and are exposed to that same smell again during a later memory test, they display better memory for the information they studied than do students who didn't study and take the test with the same aroma present (Schab, 1990). Perhaps one practical application of this finding is to wear a distinctively smelling cologne or perfume while studying, and use it again on the day of the test. This might improve your memory for the information you studied by matching the scent of your study environment with the scent of your test environment. Although this strategy may seem silly, keep in mind that the area of the human brain where smell is perceived has connections with the brain's memory pathways (Jensen, 1998). This may account for why people commonly report that certain smells can trigger memories of past experiences (e.g., the smell of a summer breeze triggering memories of summer games played during childhood). Thus, don't underestimate the sense of smell's potential for promoting memory.

6.2   **DO IT NOW !**

Nutritional Strategies for Strengthening Your Academic Performance

Is there a "brain food" that can strengthen our mental performance? Can we "eat to learn"? Some animal studies suggest that memory may be improved by consumption of foods containing lecithin, which is a substance that helps the brain produce acetylcholine—a brain chemical that plays an important role in memory formation and in learning and cognitive abilities (Ueda et al, 2011; Ulus, Hirsch & Wurtman, 1977). Fish contains high amounts of lecithin, which may have something to do with why some people refer to it as "brain food."

Despite the results of these animal studies, there is not enough research yet available to conclude there are particular foods humans can consume that will dramatically increase their ability to comprehend and retain knowledge. However, there is evidence that the following nutritional strategies can improve mental performance on days when our knowledge is tested.

1. **Eat breakfast on the day of the exam.** Numerous studies show that students who eat a nutritious breakfast on the day they are tested are more likely to achieve higher test scores than students who do not (Martin & Benton, 1999; Smith, Clark, & Gallagher, 1999). Breakfast on the day of an exam should include grains, such as whole-wheat toast, whole-grain cereal, oatmeal, or bran, because those foods contain complex carbohydrates that will deliver a steady stream of energy to the body throughout the day; this should help sustain your test-taking endurance or stamina. Also, these complex carbohydrates should help your brain generate a steady stream of

   > "No man can be wise on an empty stomach."
   > —George Eliot, 19th-century English novelist

   serotonin, which may reduce your level of nervousness or tension on test days.

2. **Make the meal you eat before an exam a light meal.** You don't want to take tests while feeling hungry, but the meal you consume nearest test time should not be a large one. We tend to get sleepy after consuming a large meal because it elevates our blood sugar to such a high level that large amounts of insulin are released into the bloodstream in order to reduce our high blood-sugar level. This draws blood sugar away from the brain, which results in a feeling of mental fatigue.

3. **If you feel you need an energy boost immediately before an exam, eat a piece of fruit rather than a candy bar.** Candy bars are processed sweets that can offer a short burst of energy provided by synthetic sugar. Unfortunately, this short-term rise in blood sugar and quick jolt of energy is typically accompanied by increased bodily tension followed by a sudden drop in energy and a feeling of sluggishness (Haas, 1994). The key is to find a food that can produce a state of elevated energy without elevating tension (Thayer, 1996) and maintains that state of energy at an even level. The best nutritional option for producing a sustained, steady state of energy is the natural sugar contained in a piece of fruit, not processed sugar that's artificially slipped into a candy bar.

4. **Avoid consuming caffeine before an exam.** Even though caffeine is a stimulant that increases alertness, it also qualifies as a legal drug that can significantly increase bodily tension and nervousness; these are feelings you don't want to experience during a test, particularly if you're prone to test anxiety. Also, caffeine is a diuretic, which means it will increase your urge to urinate. This is a distracting urge you certainly want to avoid during an exam when you're confined to a classroom for an extended period of time.

Consuming large doses of caffeine or other stimulants before exams may increase your alertness, but may also increase your level of stress and test anxiety.

Strategies to Use during the Test

1. **As soon as you receive a copy of the test, write down key information you need to remember.** In particular, write down any hard-to-remember terms, formulas, and equations and any memory-retrieval cues you may have created as soon as you start the exam to ensure that you don't forget this information after you begin answering specific test questions.

2. **Answer the easier test questions first.** As soon as you receive the test, before launching into answering the first question listed, check out the layout of the test. Note the questions that are worth the most points and the questions that you know well. You can do this by first surveying the test and putting a checkmark next to questions whose answers you're unsure of; come back to these questions later after you've answered the questions you're sure of, to ensure all their points are added into your final test score.

Reflection **6.3**

During tests, if I experience memory block, I usually . . .

I am most likely to experience memory block in the following subject areas:

3. **Prevent "memory block" from setting in.** If you tend to experience memory block for information that you know is stored in your brain, use the following strategies:

   • Mentally put yourself back in the environment or situation in which you studied the information. Recreate the steps in which you learned the information that you've temporarily forgotten by mentally picturing the place where you first heard or saw it and where you studied it, including sights, sounds, smells, and time of day. This memory-improvement strategy is referred to as *guided retrieval*, and research supports its effectiveness for recalling information, including information recalled by eyewitnesses to a crime (Glenberg, 1997; Glenberg, Bradley, Kraus, & Renzaglia, 1983).

   • Think of any idea or piece of information that may be related to the information you can't remember. Studies show that when students experience temporary forgetting, they're more likely to suddenly recall that information if they first recall a piece or portion of that information that relates to it in some way (Reed, 1996). This related piece of information can trigger your memory for the forgotten information because related pieces of information are typically stored within the same neural network of cells in the brain.

- Take your mind off the question and turn to another question. This may allow your subconscious to focus on the forgotten information, which may trigger your conscious memory of it. Also, you may find some information included in other test questions that can help you remember an answer to a previous test question.

- Before turning in your test, carefully review and double-check your answers. This is the critical last step in the process of effective test taking. Sometimes the rush and anxiety of taking a test can cause test takers to overlook details, misread instructions, unintentionally skip questions, or make absentminded mistakes. When you're done, take time to look over your answers to be sure you didn't make any mindless mistakes. Avoid the temptation to immediately cut out because you're pooped out, or to take off on an ego trip by being among the first and fastest students in class to finish the test. Instead, take the full amount of test time available to you. When you think about the amount of time and effort you put into preparing for the exam, it's foolish not to take a little more time on the exam itself.

Strategies for Answering Multiple-Choice Questions

Multiple-choice questions are commonly used on college tests, on certification or licensing exams to practice in particular professions (e.g., nursing and teaching), and on admissions tests for graduate school (e.g., master's and doctoral degree programs) or professional school (e.g., law school and medical school). Since you're likely to encounter multiple-choice tests frequently in college and beyond, this section of the text is devoted to a detailed discussion of strategies for answering such test questions. These strategies are also applicable to true-false tests, which are really multiple-choice tests that involve two choices (true or false).

Reflection **6.4**

How would you rate your general level of test anxiety during most exams? (Circle one.)

high   moderate   low

What types of tests or subjects tend to produce the most test stress or test anxiety for you?

Why?

1. **Read all choices listed and use a process-of-elimination approach.** You can find an answer by eliminating choices that are clearly wrong and continue to do so until you're left with one answer that is the most accurate option. Keep in mind that the correct answer is often the one that has the highest probability or likelihood of being true; it doesn't have to be absolutely true—just truer than the other choices listed.

2. **Use *test-wise* strategies when you don't know the correct answer.** Your first strategy on any multiple-choice question should be to choose an answer based on your knowledge of the material, rather than trying to outsmart the test or the test maker by guessing the correct answer based on how the question is worded. However, if you've relied on your knowledge and used the process-of-elimination strategy to eliminate clearly wrong choices but you're still left with two or more answers that appear to be correct, then you should turn to being *test wise*, which refers to your ability to use the characteristics of the test question itself (such as its wording or format) to increase your chances of selecting the correct answer (Flippo & Caverly, 2009). Listed here are three test-wise strategies for multiple-choice questions whose answer you don't know or can't remember:

A process-of-elimination approach is an effective test-taking strategy to use when answering difficult multiple-choice questions.

To be or not to be?
(a) Orange Julius
(b) Julius Erving ("Dr. J.")
(c) Julius Caesar
(d) Caesar Salad
(e) Casarean Section

- **Pick an answer that contains qualifying words.** Look for words such as *usually, probably, likely, sometimes, perhaps,* or *may.* Knowledge often doesn't come neatly wrapped in the form of absolute truths, so choices that are stated as broad generalizations are more likely to be false. For example, answers containing words such as *always, never, only, must,* and *completely* are more likely to be false than true.
- **Pick the longest answer.** True statements often require more words to make them true.
- **Pick a middle answer rather than the first or last answer.** For example, on a question with four choices, if you've narrowed down the correct answer to a "b" or "c" versus an "a" or "d" choice, go with the "b" or "c" choice. Studies show that instructors have a tendency to place correct answers as middle choices rather than as the first or last choice (Linn & Gronlund, 1995), perhaps because they think the correct answer will be too obvious or stand out if it's listed at the beginning or end.

3. **Check to be sure that your answers are aligned with the right questions.** When looking over your test before turning it in, search carefully for questions you may have skipped and intended to go back to later. Sometimes you may skip a test question on a multiple-choice test and forget to skip the number of that question on the answer form, which will throw off all your other answers by one space or line. On a computer-scored test, this means that you may get multiple items marked wrong because your answers are misaligned, resulting in a "domino effect" of wrong answers, which can do major damage to your test score. As a

damage-prevention measure, check all of your answers to be sure there are no blank lines or spaces on your answer sheet to set off this damaging domino effect.

4. **Don't feel that you must remain locked in to your first answer.** When checking your answers on multiple-choice and true-false tests, don't be afraid to change an answer after you've given it more thought. There have been numerous studies on the topic of changing answers on multiple-choice and true-false tests dating back to 1928 (Kuhn, 1988). These studies consistently show that most changed test answers go from being incorrect to correct, resulting in improved test scores (Bauer, Kopp, & Fischer, 2007; Benjamin, Cavell, & Shallenberger, 1984; Prinsell, Ramsey, & Ramsey, 1994). In one study of more than 1,500 students' midterm exams in an introductory psychology course, it was found that students who changed answers went from incorrect to correct 75 percent of the time (Kruger, Wirtz, & Miller, 2005). These findings probably reflect the fact that students often catch mistakes when they read the question again or when they find some information later in the test that causes them to reconsider their first answer.

Don't buy into the common belief that your first answer is always your best answer. If you have good reason to think a change should be made, don't be afraid to make it. The only exception to this general rule is when you find yourself changing many of your original answers; this is an indication that you were not well prepared for the exam and are just doing a lot of random second-guessing.

Reflection **6.5**

On exams, do you ever change your original answers?

If you do change answers, what's the usual reason you make changes?

Strategies for Answering Essay Questions

Along with multiple-choice questions, essay questions are among the most commonly used forms on college exams. Following are strategies that will help you achieve peak levels of performance on essay questions.

1. **Focus on main ideas first.** Before you begin answering the question by writing full sentences, make a brief outline or list of bullet points to represent the main ideas you will include in your answers. Outlines are effective for several reasons:
   - **An outline helps you remember the major points.** It prevents you from becoming so wrapped up in the details of constructing sentences and choosing words for your answers that you lose the big picture and forget the most important points you need to make.
   - **An outline improves your answer's organization.** In addition to reminding you of the points you intend to make, an outline gives you a plan for sequencing your ideas in an order that ensures they flow smoothly. One factor that instructors consider when awarding points for an answer to an essay question is how well that answer is organized. An outline makes your answer's organization clearer by calling your attention to its major categories and subcategories.

- **Having an advanced idea of what you will write reduces your test anxiety.** An outline takes care of the answer's organization beforehand so you don't have the added stress of worrying about how to organize your answer at the same time you're writing and explaining your answer.
- **An outline can add points to an incomplete answer's score.** If you run out of test time before writing out your full answer to an essay question, an outline allows your instructor to see what you planned to include in your written answer. Your outline itself is likely to earn you points because it demonstrates your knowledge of the major points called for by the question. In contrast, if you skip an outline and just start writing answers to test questions one at a time, you run the risk of not getting to questions you know well before your time is up; you'll then have nothing on your test to show what you know about those unfinished questions.

Exhibit 1

Identical twins
Adoption
Parents/family tree

6/6

1. *There are several different studies that scientists conduct, but one study that they conduct is to find out how genetics can influence human behavior in <u>identical twins</u>. Since they are identical, they will most likely end up very similar in behavior because of their identical genetic makeup. Although environment has some impact, genetics are still a huge factor and they will, more likely than not, behave similarly. Another type of study is with <u>parents and their family trees</u>. Looking at a subject's family tree will explain why a certain person is bipolar or depressed. It is most likely caused by a gene in the family tree, even if it was last seen decades ago. Lastly, another study is with adopted children. If an <u>adopted child</u> acts a certain way that is unique to that child, and researchers find the parents' family tree, they will most likely see similar behavior in the parents and siblings as well.*

No freewill
No afterlife

2. *The monistic view of the mind-brain relationship is so strongly opposed and criticized because there is a belief or assumption that <u>free will</u> is taken away from people. For example, if a person commits a horrendous crime, it can be argued "monistically" that the chemicals in the brain were the reason, and that a person cannot think for themselves to act otherwise. This view limits responsibility.*

6/6

Another reason that this view is opposed is because it has been said that <u>there is no afterlife</u>. If the mind and brain are one and the same, and there is <u>NO</u> difference, then once the brain is dead and is no longer functioning, so is the mind. Thus, it cannot continue to live beyond what we know today as life. <u>And</u> this goes against many religions, which is why this reason, in particular, is heavily opposed.

Written answers to two short essay questions given by a college sophomore, which demonstrate effective use of bulleted lists or short outlines (in the side margin) to ensure recall of most important points.

---

2. **Get directly to the point on each essay question.** Avoid elaborate introductions that take up your test time (and your instructor's grading time) but don't earn you any points. For example, an answer that begins with the statement "This is an interesting question that we had a great discussion on in class . . ." is pointless because it will not add points to your test score. The time available to you on essay tests is often limited, so you can't afford flowery introductions that waste valuable test time and don't contribute anything to your overall test score.

One effective way to get directly to the point on essay questions is to include part of the question in the first sentence of your answer. For example, suppose the test question asks you to: "Argue for or against capital punishment by explaining how it will or will not reduce the nation's murder rate." Your first sentence could be, "Capital punishment will not reduce the murder rate for the following reasons . . ." Thus, your first sentence becomes your thesis statement, which immediately points you directly to the major points you're going to make in your answer and earns immediate points for your answer.

> **Remember**
>
> *As a rule, it's better to over explain than under explain your answers to essay questions.*

3. **Answer all essay questions with as much detail as possible.** Don't assume that your instructor already knows what you're talking about or will be bored by details. Instead, take the approach that you're writing to someone who knows little or nothing about the subject—as if you're an expert teacher and the reader is a clueless student.

4. **Support your points with evidence—facts, statistics, quotes, or examples.** When taking essay tests, take on the role of a lawyer making a case by presenting concrete evidence (exhibit A, exhibit B, etc.). Since timed essay tests can often press you for time, be sure to prioritize and cite your most powerful points and persuasive evidence. If you have time later, you can return to add other points worth mentioning.

Do It Now! 6.3 contains a list of thinking verbs that you're likely to see in college writing assignments and the type of mental action typically called for by each of these verbs. As you read the list, make a short note after each mental action indicating whether or not you've been asked to use such thinking on any assignments you completed before college.

6.3   **DO IT NOW!**

Ten Mental-Action Verbs Commonly Found in Essay-Test Questions

1. **Analyze.** Break the topic down into its key parts and evaluate the parts in terms of their accuracy, strengths, and weaknesses.
2. **Compare.** Identify the similarities and differences between major ideas.
3. **Contrast.** Identify the differences between ideas, particularly sharp differences and opposing viewpoints.
4. **Describe.** Provide details (e.g., who, what, where, and when).
5. **Discuss.** Analyze (break apart) and evaluate the parts (e.g., strengths and weaknesses).
6. **Document.** Support your judgment and conclusions with references or information sources.
7. **Explain.** Provide reasons that answer the questions "Why?" and "How?"
8. **Illustrate.** Supply concrete examples or specific instances.
9. **Interpret.** Draw your own conclusion about something, and explain why you came to that conclusion.
10. **Support.** Back up your ideas with research findings, factual evidence, or logical arguments.

"I keep six honest serving men. They taught me all I knew. Their names are what and why and how and when and where and who."

—Rudyard Kipling, "The Elephant's Child," *Just So Stories*

Reflection **6.6**

Which of the mental actions in the list in Do It Now! 6.3 were most often required on your high school writing assignments?

Which was least often (or never) required?

5. **Leave space between your answers to each essay question.** This strategy will enable you to easily add information to your original answer if you have time or if you recall something later in the test that you forgot initially.

6. **Proofread your test for spelling and grammar.** Before turning in your test, proofread what you've written and correct any obvious spelling or grammatical errors you find. Eliminating them is likely to improve your test score. Even if your instructor doesn't explicitly state that grammar and spelling will be counted in determining your grade, these mechanical mistakes are still likely to influence your professor's overall evaluation of your written work.

7. **Neatness counts.** Many years of research indicates that neatly written essays tend to be scored higher than sloppy ones, even if the answers are essentially the same (Huck & Bounds, 1972; Klein & Hart, 1968; Hughes, Keeling, & Tuck, 1983; Pai, Sanji, Pai, & Kotian, 2010). These findings are understandable when you consider that grading essay answers is a time-consuming task that requires your instructor to plod through multiple styles of handwriting whose readability may range from crystal-clear to cryptic. Make an earnest attempt to write as clearly as possible, and if you finish the test with time to spare, clean up your work by rewriting any sloppily written words or sentences.

Reflection **6.7**

Rate yourself in terms of how frequently you use these test-taking strategies according to the following scale:

4 = always,   3 = sometimes,   2 = rarely,   1 = never

1.	I take tests in the same seat that I usually sit in to take class notes.	4	3	2	1
2.	I answer easier test questions first.	4	3	2	1
3.	I use a process-of-elimination approach on multiple-choice tests to eliminate choices until I find one that is correct or appears to be the most accurate option.	4	3	2	1
4.	On essay questions, I outline or map out my ideas before I begin to write the answer.	4	3	2	1
5.	I look for information included on the test that may help me answer difficult questions or that may help me remember information I've forgotten.	4	3	2	1
6.	I leave extra space between my answers to essay questions in case I want to come back and add more information later.	4	3	2	1

7. I carefully review my work, double-checking
   for errors and skipped questions before turning
   in my tests.   4   3   2   1

Post-Test Strategies: What to Do after Receiving Test Results

1. **Use your test results as feedback to improve your future performance.** Your test score is not just an end result: it can be used as a means to an end—a higher score on your next test performances and a higher course grade. When you get tests back, examine them carefully and be sure to note any written comments your instructor may have made. If your test results are disappointing, don't get bitter, get better. Use the results as feedback to diagnose where you went wrong so that you can avoid making the same mistakes again. If your test results were positive, see where you went right so you can do it right again.

2. **Seek additional feedback.** In addition to using your own test results as a source of feedback, ask for feedback from others whose judgment you trust and value. Three social resources you can use to obtain feedback on how to improve your performance are your instructors, professionals in your Learning or Academic Support Center, and your peers.

Make appointments with your instructors to visit them during office hours and get their feedback on how you might be able to improve your test performance. You'll likely find it easier to see your instructors after a test than before it, because most students don't realize that it's just as valuable to seek feedback from instructors following an exam as it is to get last-minute help before an exam.

Tutors and other learning support professionals on your campus can also be excellent sources of feedback about what adjustments to make in your study habits or test-taking strategies to improve your future performance. Also, be alert and open to receiving feedback from trusted peers. While feedback from experienced professionals is valuable, don't overlook your peers as another source of information on how to improve your performance. You can review your test with other students in class, particularly with students who did exceptionally well. Their tests can provide you with models of what type of work your instructor expects on exams. You might also consider asking successful students what they did to be successful—for example, what they did to prepare for the test and what they did during the test.

Whatever you do, don't let a bad test grade get you mad, sad, or down, particularly if it occurs early in the course when you're still learning the rules of the game. Look at mistakes in terms of what they can do *for* you, rather than to you. A poor test performance can be turned into a valuable learning experience by using test results as a source of feedback and as an error detector to pinpoint the source of your mistakes. Look back at your mistakes so you can move forward and progress toward future success.

> "People can't learn without feedback. It's not teaching that causes learning. Attempts by the learner to perform cause learning, dependent upon the quality of the feedback and opportunities to use it."
> —Grant Wiggins, *Feedback: How Learning Occurs*

> "When you make a mistake, there are only three things you should do about it: admit it; learn from it; and don't repeat it."
> —Paul "Bear" Bryant, legendary college football coach

> "Failure is not fatal, but failure to change might be."
> —John Wooden, legendary college basketball coach

Remember

Your past mistakes should be neither ignored nor neglected: they should be detected and corrected so that you don't replay them on future tests.

> ### Snapshot Summary
>
> **6.1** **Key Features of Performance-Enhancing Feedback**
>
> When asking for feedback from others on your academic performance, seek feedback that is likely to improve your future performance. Effective performance-enhancing feedback has the following features:
>
> - Performance-enhancing feedback is *specific*—it precisely identifies what you should do to improve your performance and how you should go about doing it. For example, after a test, seek feedback from your instructors that provides you with more than just information about what your grade is, or why you lost points: seek specific information about what you could do to improve your performance next time.
>
> - Performance-enhancing feedback is *prompt*—it comes soon after completing a task, because this is the time when you are most motivated to receive it and most likely to retain it. For example, as soon as possible after completing tests or assignments, review your performance with classmates or your professor.
> - Performance-enhancing feedback is *proactive*—it comes early in the learning process when you still have plenty of time to use it to improve your performance. For example, seek feedback from instructors early in the term, so you have more time to use that feedback to improve your course performance and course grade.

Remember

Just as you learn before tests by preparing for your performance, you can learn after tests by reviewing your performance.

Strategies for Pinpointing the Source of Lost Points on Exams

On test questions where you lost points, identify the stage in the learning process where the breakdown occurred by asking yourself the following questions:

1. **Did you have the information you needed to answer the question correctly?** If you didn't have the information, what was the source of the missing information? Was it information presented in class that didn't get into your notes? If so, look at our strategies for improving listening and note-taking habits. (See p. 109.) If the missing information was contained in your assigned reading, check whether you're using effective reading strategies. (See p. 118.)
2. **Did you have the information but did not study it because you didn't think it was important?** If you didn't realize the information would be on the test, review the study strategies for finding and focusing on the most important information in class lectures and reading assignments.
3. **Did you study it, but did not retain it?** Not remembering information you studied may mean one of three things:
   - You didn't store the information adequately in your brain, so your memory trace wasn't strong enough to recall. This suggests that more study time needs to be spent on recitation or rehearsal.
   - You may have tried to cram in too much information too quickly just before the exam and may have not given your brain time enough to "digest" (consolidate) it and store it in long-term memory. The solution would be to distribute your study time more evenly in advance of the next exam and take advantage of the part-to-whole study method. (See p. 127.)
   - You put in enough study time and you didn't cram, but you didn't study effectively or strategically. For example, you may have studied for essay questions by just reading over your class notes and reading highlights rather than rehearsing and reciting them. The solution would be to adjust your study strategy so that it better matches or aligns with the type of test you're taking.

4. **Did you study the material but not really understand it or learn it deeply?** This suggests you may need to self-monitor your comprehension more carefully while studying to track whether you truly understand the material at a deeper level. (See p. 133.)

5. **Did you know the information but find yourself unable to retrieve it during the exam?** If you had the information on the "tip of your tongue" during the exam, this indicates that you did retain it and it was stored (saved) in your brain, but you couldn't get at it and get it out (retrieve it) when you needed it. This error may be corrected by making better use of memory-retrieval cues. (See p. 141.)

6. **Did you know the answer but just make a careless test-taking mistake?** If your mistake was careless, the solution may be simply to take more time to review your test once you've completed it and check for absentminded errors before turning it in. (See p. 145.) Or, your careless errors may be the result of test anxiety that's interfering with your ability to concentrate during exams.

Strategies for Reducing Test Anxiety

1. **Understand what test anxiety is and what it's not.** Don't confuse anxiety with stress. Stress is a physical reaction that prepares your body for action by arousing and energizing it; this heightened arousal and energy can be used productively to strengthen your performance. In fact, if you're totally stress-free during an exam, it may mean that you're too "laid back" and couldn't care less about how well you're doing. Stress is something that cannot and should not be completely eliminated when you're trying to reach peak levels of performance, whether academic or athletic. Instead of trying to block out stress altogether, your goal should be to control it, contain it, and maintain it at a level that maximizes the quality of your performance. The key is to keep stress at a moderate level, thereby capitalizing on its capacity to help you get psyched up or pumped up, but preventing it from reaching such a high level that you become psyched out or stressed out.

   If you experience the following symptoms during tests, your stress level may be at a level high enough to be accurately called test anxiety.
   - You feel physical symptoms of tension during the test, such as a pounding heartbeat, a rapid pulse, muscle tension, sweating, or an upset stomach.
   - Negative thoughts and feelings rush through your head—for example, fear of failure or self-defeating putdowns such as "I always mess up on exams."
   - You rush through the test just to get it over with (probably because you want to get rid of the anxiety you're experiencing).
   - You have difficulty concentrating or focusing your attention while answering test questions.
   - Even though you studied and know the material, you go blank during the exam and forget what you studied. (However, you're able to remember the information after you turn in your test and leave the test situation.)
   To minimize test anxiety, consider the following practices and strategies:

2. **Avoid cramming for exams.** Research indicates that college students who display greater amounts of procrastination experience higher levels of test anxiety (Rothblum, Solomon, & Murakami, 1986). High levels of pre-test tension associated with rushing and late-night cramming are likely to carry over to the test itself, resulting in higher levels of test-taking tension. Furthermore, loss of sleep caused by previous-night cramming results in lost dream (REM) sleep, which, in turn, elevates anxiety levels the following day—test day.

3. **Use effective test-preparation strategies prior to the exam.** Test-anxiety research indicates that college students who prepare well for exams not only achieve higher test scores, but also experience lower levels of test anxiety (Zohar, 1998). Other research findings demonstrate that using effective study strategies prior to the exam—such as those discussed in Chapter 5—reduces test anxiety during the exam (Benjamin, McKeachie, Lin, & Holinger, 1981; Jones & Petruzzi, 1995; Zeidner, 1995).

4. **During the exam, concentrate on the here and now.** Devote your attention fully to answering the test question that you're currently working on; don't spend time thinking (and worrying) about the test's outcome and what your grade will be.

5. **Stay focused on the test in front of you, not the students around you.** Don't spend valuable test time looking at what others are doing and wondering whether they're doing better than you are. If you came to the test well prepared and still find the test difficult, it's very likely that other students are finding it difficult too. If you happen to notice that other students are finishing before you do, don't assume they breezed through the test or that they're smarter than you. Their faster finish may simply reflect the fact that they didn't know many of the answers and decided to give up and get out, rather than prolong the agony.

6. **Don't spend a lot of time focusing on the amount of time left in the exam.** Repeatedly checking the time during the test can disrupt the flow of your thought process and increase your stress level. Although it's important that you remain aware of how much time remains to complete the exam, only check the time periodically, and do your time-checking after you've completed answering a question so you don't disrupt or derail your train of thought.

7. **Control your thoughts by focusing on what you're getting right, rather than worrying about what answers you don't know and how many points you're losing.** Our thoughts influence our emotions (Ellis, 1995), and positive emotions, such as those associated with optimism and a sense of accomplishment, can improve mental performance by enhancing the brain's ability to process, store, and retrieve information (Rosenfield, 1988). Keep in mind that college exams are often designed to be more difficult than high school tests, so it's less likely that students will get 90 to 100 percent of the total points. You can still achieve a good grade on a college exam without having to achieve a near-perfect test score.

8. **Remember that if you're experiencing a *moderate* amount of stress during the exam, this isn't abnormal or an indication that you're suffering from test anxiety.** If you're experiencing moderate levels of tension, it indicates that you're motivated and want to do well. In fact, research shows that experiencing *moderate* levels of tension during tests and other performance-evaluation situations serves to maximize alertness, concentration, and memory (Sapolsky, 2004).

9. **Don't forget that it's just a test: it's not a measure of your ability or character.** An exam is not a measure of your overall intelligence, your overall academic ability, or your quality as a person. In fact, a test grade may be less of an indication of your effort or ability than of the complexity of the particular content covered by the test material or the nature of the test itself. Furthermore, one low grade on one particular test doesn't mean you're not capable of doing good work and are going to end up with a poor grade in the course, particularly if you use the results as feedback to improve your next test performance. (See p. 151.)

One final note on the topic of test anxiety: if you continue to experience test anxiety after implementing the above strategies, don't hesitate to seek assistance from a professional in your Learning (Academic Support) Center or Personal Counseling Office.

Summary and Conclusion

Improving performance on college exams involves strategies used in advance of the test, during the test, and after test results are returned. Good test performance begins with good test preparation and adjustment of your study strategy to the type of test you'll be taking (e.g., multiple-choice or essay test).

You can learn and improve your grades not only by preparing for tests, but also by reviewing your tests and using them as feedback to apply as you continue in the course. Past mistakes shouldn't be ignored or neglected: they should be detected and corrected so that they're not replayed on future tests.

Learning More through the World Wide Web

Internet-Based Resources for Further Information on Test-Taking Skills

For additional information related to ideas discussed in this chapter, we recommend the following Web sites:

Test-Taking Strategies:

www.muskingum.edu/~cal/database/general/testtaking.html

Overcoming Test Anxiety:

www.studygs.net/tstprp8.htm

www.swccd.edu/~asc/lrnglinks/test_anxiety.html

6.1 Midterm Self-Evaluation

Since you are near the midpoint of this textbook, you may be near the midpoint of your first term in college. At this time of the term, you are likely to experience the midterm crunch—a wave of midterm exams and due dates for certain papers and projects. This may be a good time to step back and assess your academic progress thus far.

Use the form that follows to list the courses you're taking this term and the grades you are currently receiving in each of these courses. If you do not know what your grade is, take a few minutes to check your syllabus for your instructor's grading policy and add up your scores on completed tests and assignments; this should give you at least a rough idea of where you stand in your courses. If you're having difficulty determining your grade in any course, even after checking your course syllabus and returned tests or assignments, then ask your instructor how you could estimate your current grade.

Course No.	Course Title	Instructor	Grade
1.			
2.			
3.			
4.			
5.			

Self-Assessment Questions

1. Were these the grades you were hoping for? Are you pleased or disappointed by them?
2. Were these the grades you expected to get? If not, were they better or worse than expected?
3. Do you see any patterns in your performance that suggest things you are doing well or things that you need to improve?
4. If you had to pinpoint one action you could immediately take to improve your lowest course grades, what would it be?

6.2 Calculating Your Midterm Grade Point Average

Use the information in the **Snapshot Summary 6.2** to calculate what your grade point average (GPA) would be if these grades turn out to be your final course grades for the term.

Snapshot Summary

6.2 How to Compute Your Grade Point Average (GPA)

Most colleges and universities use a grading scale that ranges from 0 to 4.0 to calculate a student's grade point average (GPA) or quality point average (QPA). Some schools use letter grades only, while other institutions use letter grades with pluses and minuses.

Grading System Using Letters Only

Grade = Point Value

A = 4
B = 3
C = 2
D = 1
F = 0

GRADE POINTS Earned Per Course = Course Grade Multiplied by the Number of Course Credits (Units)

GRADE POINT AVERAGE (GPA) = $\dfrac{\text{Total Number of Grade Points for all Courses}}{\text{Divided by Total Number of Course Units}}$

SAMPLE/EXAMPLE

Course	Units	×	Grade	=	Grade Points
Roots of Rock 'n' Roll	3	×	C (2)	=	6
Daydreaming Analysis	3	×	A (4)	=	12
Surfing Strategies	1	×	A (4)	=	4
Wilderness Survival	4	×	B (3)	=	12
Sitcom Analysis	2	×	D (1)	=	2
Love and Romance	3	×	A (4)	=	12
	16				48

$$GPA = \frac{48}{16} = 3.0$$

1. What is your overall GPA at this point in the term?
2. At the start of this term, what GPA were you hoping to attain?
3. Do you think your actual GPA at the end of the term will be higher or lower than it is now? Why?

Notes: It's normal for GPAs to be lower in college than they were in high school, particularly during the first year of college. Here are the results of one study that compared students' high school GPAs with their GPAs after their first year of college:

- 29 percent of beginning college students had GPAs of 3.75 or higher in high school, but only 17 percent had GPAs that high at the end of their first year of college.
- 46 percent had high school GPAs between 3.25 and 3.74, but only 32 percent had GPAs that high after the first year of college (National Resource Center for the First-Year Experience and Students in Transition, 2004).

6.3 Preparing an Oral Presentation on Student Success

1. Scan this textbook and identify a chapter topic or chapter section that you find most interesting or think is most important to you.

2. Create an introduction for a class presentation on this topic that:
    a. provides an overview or sneak preview of what you will cover in your presentation;
    b. grabs the attention of your audience (your classmates); and
    c. demonstrates the topic's relevance or importance for your audience.

3. Create a conclusion to your presentation that:
    a. relates back to your introduction;
    b. highlights your most important point or points; and
    c. leaves a memorable last impression.

Bad Feedback: Shocking Midterm Grades

Joe Frosh has enjoyed his first weeks on campus. He has met lots of interesting people and feels that he fits in socially. He's also very pleased to discover that his college schedule doesn't require him to be in class for five to six hours per day, like it did in high school. This is the good news. The bad news is that unlike in high school, where his grades were all As and Bs, his first midterm grades in college are three Cs, one D, and one F. He's stunned and a bit depressed by his midterm grades because he thought he was doing well. Since he never received grades this low in high school, he's beginning to think that he's not college material and may flunk out.

Reflection and Discussion Questions

1. What factors may have caused or contributed to Joe's bad start?

2. What are Joe's options at this point?

3. What do you recommend Joe do right now to get his grades up and avoid being placed on academic probation?

4. What might Joe do in the future to prevent this midterm setback from happening again?

Three Keys to Academic Success and Lifelong Learning Skills

Information Literacy, Writing, and Speaking

What would you say is the key difference between acquiring factual knowledge and learning a transferable skill?

LEARNING GOAL

To acquire and document ideas of others through effective research, and communicate your own ideas through effective writing and speaking.

The Importance of Research and Communication Skills

We're now living in an era commonly referred to as the "information" and "communication" age because more information is being produced and communicated in today's world than at any other time in history (Breivik, 1998; Cairncross, 2001; Thornburg, 1994). Since information is being generated and disseminated at such a rapid rate, "information literacy"—the ability to search for, locate, and evaluate information for relevance and accuracy—is now an essential 21st-century skill for managing and making sense of the overload of information that's currently available to us. As discussed in Chapter 2, these communication skills are highly transferable to settings beyond the college classroom. Plus, this 21st-century skill makes college graduates very marketable in today's workplace.

Communication skills, such as speaking and writing have become critical for career success (AAC&U, 2007; National Association of Colleges & Employers, 2012); college graduates with well-developed communication skills have a clear advantage in today's job market (Mackes, 2003). If you dedicate yourself to improving your information literacy, writing, and speaking skills, you'll improve not only your academic performance in college, but also your career performance beyond college. This chapter is designed to strengthen your skills in each of these three key areas.

Information Literacy: Strategies for Researching (Locating and Evaluating) Information

In addition to assignments relating to material covered in course readings and class lectures, you are likely to be assigned research projects that involve writing in response to information you locate and evaluate on your own. If you recall from Chapter 2, a key outcome of a college education is for students to become self-reliant, lifelong learners. One key characteristic of a self-reliant, lifelong learner is *information literacy*—the ability to locate, evaluate, and use information. When you're information literate, you become a critical consumer of information: you know where and

Student
Perspective

"Information literacy is knowing how, where, why to get information. You can quickly and easily find information on anything. You have no fear of something you don't know, because you know you can easily find information about it."

—First-year college student (Watts, 2005)

how to find credible information whenever you need it (National Forum on Information Literacy, 2005).

Following is a six-step process for locating, evaluating, and using information to write research papers and reports in college (and beyond). This process can also be used to research information for oral presentations and group projects.

1. Define Your Research Topic or Question

Be sure that your research topic is relevant to the assignment and that its scope is neither too *narrow*, leaving you with too little available information on the topic, or too *broad*, leaving you with too much information to cover within the maximum number of pages allowed for your paper or report.

If you have any doubts about your topic's relevance or scope, before going any further, seek feedback from your instructor or from a professional in your college library.

2. Locate Potential Sources of Information

© photogl, 2013. Under license from Shutterstock, Inc.

There are two main types of resources you can use to locate and access information: print resources and on-line resources.

You have two major types of resources you can use to search for and locate information:

- Print resources—e.g., card catalogs, published indexes, and guidebooks; and
- Online resources—e.g., online card catalogs, Internet search engines, and electronic databases.

Since different information-search tools are likely to generate different types of information, it's best not to rely exclusively on just one research tool. See Snapshot Summary 7.1 for a summary of key information-search tools and terms.

Snapshot Summary

7.1   Key Information-Search Tools and Terms

As you read the following list of terms, make a note after each item indicating (1) whether you've heard of it before and (2) whether you've used it before.

Abstract. A concise summary of the source's content, usually appearing at the beginning of an article, which can help you to decide quickly whether the source is relevant to your research topic.

Catalog. A library database containing information about what information sources the library owns and where they are located. Libraries may still have some or all parts of their catalogs available on

cards (i.e., in a *card catalog*); however, most catalogs are now in electronic form and can be searched by typing in a topic heading, author, topic, or keyword.

Citation. A reference to an information source (e.g., book, article, Web page) that provides enough information to allow the reader to retrieve the source. Citations used in a college research paper must be given in a standard format, such as APA or MLA format.

Database. A collection of data (information) that has been organized to make the information easily accessible and retrievable. A database may include:

1. *Reference citations*—e.g., author, date, and publication source,
2. *Abstracts*—summaries of the contents of scholarly articles,
3. *Full-length documents*, or
4. A combination of 1, 2, and 3.

Descriptor (a.k.a. subject heading). A keyword or key phrase in the index of a database (card or catalog) that describes the subjects or content areas found within it, enabling you to quickly locate sources relevant to your research topic. For example, *emotional disorders* may be a descriptor for a psychology database to help researchers find information related to anxiety and depression. (Some descriptors or subject headings will be accompanied by suggestions for different words or phrases that you can use in your search.)

Index. An alphabetical listing of topics contained in a database.

Keyword. A word used to search multiple databases by matching the search word to items found in different databases. Keywords are very specific, so if the exact word is not found in the database, any information related to the topic you're researching that doesn't exactly match the keyword will be missed. For example, if the keyword is *college*, it will not pick up relevant sources that may have *university* instead of *college* in their titles.

Search engine. A computer-run program that allows you to search for information across the entire Internet or at a particular Web site. For regularly updated summaries of different electronic search engines, how they work, and the types of information they generate, check the Web sites searchenginewatch.com/reports and researchbuzz.com.

Search thesaurus: A list of words or phrases with similar meaning, allowing you to identify which of these words or phrases could be used as keywords, descriptors, or subject headings in the database. This feature enables you to choose the best search terms before beginning the search process.

Subscription database. A database that can only be accessed only through a paid subscription. You may be able to access through your college or university library because most electronic databases available in libraries are paid for through subscriptions.

URL (Uniform Resource Locator). An Internet address consisting of a series of letters and/or numbers that pinpoints the exact location of an information resource (e.g., www. thrivingincollege.com)

Wildcard. A symbol, such as an asterisk (*), question mark (?), or exclamation point (!), that may be used to substitute different letters into a search word or phrase, so that an electronic search will be performed on all variations of the word represented by the symbol. For example, an asterisk at the end of the keyword *econom** may be used to search for all information sources containing the words *economy, economical,* or *economist*.

Source: Hacker, D., & Fister, B. (2010). *Research and documentation in the electronic age* (5th ed.). Boston, MA: Bedford/St. Martin's.

For a more extensive glossary of Internet terms, see "Matisse's Glossary of Internet Terms" at www.matisse.net/files/glossary.html.

Reflection 7.2

Look back at the terms listed in Snapshot Summary 7.1 and make note of those terms that you hadn't heard of or whose meaning you weren't sure of.

When you locate a source, your first step is to evaluate its relevance to your paper's topic. One strategy for efficiently determining the relevance of a source is to ask if it will help you answer one or more of the following questions about your topic: Who? What? When? Where? Why? How?

However, the first important question to ask yourself about potential sources is whether they are acceptable to the instructor who assigned your research paper. Before you even begin the information-search process, be sure you know what sources your instructor requires or prefers.

3. Evaluate the Credibility and Quality of Your Sources

The primary purpose of your sources is to provide *documentation*—references that support or confirm your conclusions. Since sources of information can vary widely in terms of their accuracy and quality, you'll need to think critically and make sound judgments about what are solid sources to select and use as documentation. The Internet has made this selection process more challenging because most of its posted information is self-published and not subjected to the same quality control measures as information published in journals and books—which go to press only after they are reviewed for acceptance by a neutral panel of experts and are carefully edited by a professional editor. Listed below are some criteria to help you critically evaluate the quality of the sources you locate:

Credibility. Is the source written by an authority or expert in the field, such as someone with an advanced educational degree or professional experience relating to the topic? For example, if your topic relates to an international issue, a highly credible source would be an author who has an advanced degree in international relations or professional experience in international affairs.

Scholarly. Is the source a scholarly publication that has been reviewed by a panel or board of impartial experts in the field before being published? If the source is written in formal style and includes references to other published sources, this is a good indication that it's a scholarly reference. Journal articles that have been "peer-reviewed" or "peer-refereed" have been reviewed, evaluated, and approved for publication by other experts in the field. This is a good indication that the source is a scholarly publication. Professional journals (e.g., the *New England Journal of Medicine*) are peer-reviewed, but popular magazines (e.g., *Newsweek*) and popular Web sites (e.g., Wikipedia) are not. Subscription databases accessible through your college or university library are more likely to contain scholarly information sources that are peer-reviewed and closely monitored for quality than free databases available to you on the World Wide Web. You may, however, use Web sites like Google Scholar (scholar.google.com) to find some scholarly sources that can be accessed for free.

Currency. Is it a recent or current source of information? In certain fields of study, such as the natural and social sciences, recent references may be strongly preferred because new data is generated rapidly in these fields and information can become quickly outdated. In other fields, such as history and philosophy,

Wikipedia isn't considered a scholarly source, but you can use its cited references as a "citation trail" for leading you to scholarly works.

older references may be viewed as classics, and citing them is perfectly acceptable. If you're not sure whether current references are strongly preferred, check with your instructor before you begin the search process.

Objectivity. Is the author likely to be impartial or unbiased toward the subject? One way to answer this question is to consider how the professional positions or personal backgrounds of the authors may influence their ideas or their interpretation of evidence. Scholars should be impartial pursuers of truth who attempt to maximize their objectivity and minimize their level of emotional and political involvement with the topic. They should also not be in a position to gain personally or fiscally from favoring a certain conclusion about the topic. You should always be very skeptical about the objectivity of Web-based information sources whose addresses end with *.com*, because these are *com*mercial sites whose primary purpose is to sell products and make money, rather than educate the public and engage in the objective pursuit of truth. To assess the objectivity of a Web site, always ask yourself why the site was created, what its objective or purpose is, and who sponsors it.

Research articles you locate may also demonstrate a lack of objectivity. Suppose your topic relates to a controversial political issue such as global warming and you find an article written by a researcher who works for or consults with an industry that would incur significant costs to switch to more ecologically efficient sources of energy. It would be reasonable to suspect that this researcher has a conflict of interest and may be biased toward reaching a conclusion that financially benefits his employer (and himself). In this case, the objectivity of the article may be questionable, and you may not want to use it as a source in your paper. If scholars are not neutral, it increases the risk that they will find what they *want* to find. In scientific research, this risk is referred to as *experimenter bias*, and it stems from the natural tendency for people to see what they expect to see, or what they hope to see (King, 2010; Rosenthal, 1966). When evaluating an article, ask yourself the following questions to check for bias: (1) Is the author a member of a special-interest group or political or religious organization that could affect the article's objectivity? (2) Does the author consider alternative and opposing viewpoints and deal with those viewpoints fairly? (3) Does the author use words that convey a sense of rationality and objectivity, or are they characterized by emotionality and an inflammatory tone?

If you think an article may lack complete objectivity, but still find that it's well written and contains good information and arguments, you can cite it in your paper; however, be sure you demonstrate critical thinking by noting that its conclusions may have been biased by the author's background or position.

4. Evaluate the Quantity and Variety of Your Sources

Your research will be judged not only in terms of the quality of your individual sources, but also in terms of the overall set or total collection of references you used throughout your paper. Your total set of references is likely to be judged in terms of the following two criteria:

Quantity of references. Have you cited a sufficient number of references? As a general rule, it is better to use a larger rather than smaller number of references because it will provide your paper with a stronger research foundation and a greater number of perspectives. In addition, using multiple sources allows more opportunity to demonstrate the higher-level thinking skill of synthesis because you can demonstrate your ability to integrate information from different sources.

Variety of references. Have you used different *types* of sources? For some research papers and some professors, the variety of references you use matters as much as (or more than) the sheer quantity. You can intentionally vary your sources by drawing on different types of references, such as:

- Books,
- Scholarly journal articles written by professionals and research scholars in the field,
- Magazine or newspaper articles written by journalists,
- Course readings or class notes, and
- Personal interviews or personal experiences.

You can also vary your references in terms of using *primary sources*—firsthand information or original documents (e.g., research experiments or novels)—and *secondary sources*—publications that rely on or respond to primary sources (e.g., a textbook or a newspaper article that critically reviews a novel or movie). Lastly, varying your references by including a balanced blend of older, classic sources and newer, cutting-edge references may also be desirable. This combination will enable you to demonstrate how certain ideas have changed or evolved over time, or how certain ideas have withstood the test of time and continue to remain important.

5. Use Your Sources as Stepping Stones to Your Own Ideas and Conclusions

> **Remember**
>
> *A good research paper places your own ideas in a larger context that includes the ideas of others. You not only want to show that you've done your research by citing the ideas of others, but also want to demonstrate higher-level thinking by connecting, evaluating, and expanding on those ideas to create ideas of your own.*

Your paper should represent something more than an accumulation of ideas gathered from other people. Simply collecting and compiling the ideas of others will result in a final product that reads more like a high school book report than a college research paper. It's your name that appears on the front cover of the paper. Your sources just provide the raw material for your paper; it's your job to shape that raw material into a finished product that's uniquely your own. Do not just report or describe information you've drawn from your sources: instead, react to them, draw conclusions from them, and use them as evidence to support your reactions and conclusions.

Reflection **7.3**

Prior to college, did you write papers in which you had to cite references? If so, do you remember the reference style you were required to use?

6. Cite Your Sources with Integrity

By citing and referencing your sources, you demonstrate intellectual honesty by giving credit where credit is due. You credit others whose ideas you've borrowed and you credit yourself for the careful research you've done.

When should sources be cited? You should cite the source of *anything you include in your paper that does not represent your own work or thoughts.* This includes other people's words, ideas, statistics, research findings, and visual work (e.g., diagrams, pictures, or drawings). There is only one exception to this rule: You don't need to cite sources for information that's *common knowledge*—i.e., information that most people already know. For example, common knowledge includes well-known facts (e.g., the earth is the third planet from the sun) and familiar dates (e.g., the Declaration of Independence was signed in 1776).

The Internet has allowed us to gain easy access to an extraordinary amount of information and has made research much easier—that's the good news. The bad news is that it has also made proper citation more challenging. Determining the true "owner" or original author of information posted online isn't as clear-cut as it is for published books and articles. If you have any doubt, print it out and check it out with your instructor or a professional librarian. If you don't have the time or opportunity to consult with either one of them, then play it safe and cite the source in your paper. If you cannot find the name of an author, at least cite the Web site, the date of the posted information (if available), and the date you accessed or downloaded it.

Remember

As a general rule, whenever you're unsure about the need to cite a source, it's better to cite it and risk being corrected for over-citing than it is to run the risk of being accused of plagiarism—a serious violation of academic integrity that can have grave consequences (e.g., probation, suspension, or expulsion). See Snapshot Summary 7.2 for details about what constitutes plagiarism and specific strategies for demonstrating academic integrity in your research papers and reports.

Where and how should sources be cited? Sources should be cited into two places: (1) the body of your paper, and (2) the reference section at the end of your paper (also known as a "bibliography" or "works cited" section).

How you should cite your sources depends on the referencing style of the particular academic field or discipline in which you are writing your paper, so be sure that you know the citation style your instructor prefers. It's likely that you will be expected to use one of two referencing styles during your first year of college:

1. *MLA* style—standing for the *Modern Language Association*—the citation style commonly used in the humanities and fine arts (e.g., English and theatre arts); or
2. *APA* style—standing for the *American Psychological Association*—the citation style most commonly used in the social and natural sciences (e.g., sociology and anthropology).

It's also possible that you may be asked to use other styles in advanced courses in specialized fields, such as *The Chicago Manual of Style* for papers in history, or the Council of Biology Editors (CBE) style for papers in the biological sciences. Be sure you're aware of the referencing style that is expected or preferred by your instructor before you begin to write your paper. There is software now available for automatically formatting references according to a particular citation style, such as CiteFast (www.citefast.com) and EasyBib (www.easybib.com). If you use these programs, be sure to proofread the results, because they can sometimes generate inaccurate or incomplete citations (Hacker & Fister, 2010).

When you use someone else's *exact words* in the body of your paper, place quotation marks around those words and cite the specific page number of your source. If you're using someone else's ideas rather than their exact words, put their ideas in your own words—known as paraphrasing. To ensure that you're paraphrasing, not plagiarizing your source, write your summary without looking directly at the source itself. After you've completed your summary, check the source to see if you accurately captured the author's main ideas without copying the author's actual words (Purdue University Online Writing Lab, 2012). If you paraphrase several ideas from

Student Perspective

"Although it may seem like a pain to write a works cited page, it is something that is necessary when writing a research paper. You must acknowledge every single author of whose information you used. The authors spent much time and energy writing their book or article, [so] you must give them the credit that they deserve."

—First-year student reflection on a plagiarism violation

Student Perspective

"Students can avoid plagiarism by getting help from someone who knows how to cite correctly. I know now to have my citations double-checked."

—First-year student reflection on a plagiarism violation

Student Perspective

"I really had no clue I was doing anything wrong because I didn't put it in word for word. I learned that plagiarism is not just copying it word for word, but it is also about [using] the idea."

—First-year student reflection on a plagiarism violation

the same source within the same paragraph, you don't need to cite the author after every single sentence; cite the source only once, at the end of the paragraph.

Snapshot Summary

7.2 Plagiarism: A Violation of Academic Integrity

What Is Academic Integrity?

There are ethical as\pects of writing papers and reports. Academic integrity involves avoiding the unethical practice of stealing the ideas of others, whether they are the ideas of peers (e.g., cheating on exams) or the words and ideas of authorities that have been used in a written paper (plagiarism). When writing papers and reports, students with academic integrity give credit where credit is due: they carefully cite and reference their sources.

What Exactly Is Plagiarism?

Plagiarism is a violation of academic integrity that involves intentional or unintentional use of someone else's work without acknowledging it, giving the reader the impression that it's the writer's original work.

Student Perspective

"My intent was not to plagiarize. I realize I was unclear [about] the policy and am actually thankful for now knowing exactly what I can and cannot do on assignments and how to prevent academic dishonesty in the future."

—First-year college student's reflection on a plagiarism violation

Common Forms of Plagiarism

1. Paying someone, or paying for a service, for a paper and turning it in as your own work
2. Submitting an entire paper, or portion thereof, that was written by someone else.
3. Copying sections of someone else's work and inserting it into your own work.
4. Cutting paragraphs from separate sources and pasting them into the body of your own paper.
5. Paraphrasing (rewording) someone else's words or ideas without citing that person as a source.

Student Perspective

"When a student violates an academic integrity policy no one wins, even if the person gets away with it. It isn't right to cheat and it is an insult to everyone who put the effort in and did the work, and it cheapens the school for everyone. I learned my lesson and have no intention of ever cheating again."

—First-year college student's reflection on an academic integrity violation

6. Not placing quotation marks around someone else's exact words that appear in the body of your paper.
7. Failing to cite the source of factual information in your paper that's not common knowledge.

Note: If the source for information included in your paper is listed at the end of your paper in your reference (works cited) section but is not cited in the body of your paper, this still qualifies as plagiarism.

Final Note: Only include sources in your reference section that you actually used and cited in the body of your paper. Including sources in your reference section that aren't cited in your paper isn't technically a form of plagiarism; however, it can be perceived as being deceitful because you're "padding" your reference section, giving the reader the impression that you incorporated more sources of information into your paper than you actually did.

Sources: Academic Integrity at Princeton (2011); Purdue University Online Writing Lab (2012).

Reflection **7.4**

Take a look back at the definition and forms of plagiarism described in Snapshot Summary 7.2. List those forms of plagiarism that you were not aware of, or weren't sure actually represented plagiarism.

Writing Skills and Strategies
The Power of Writing

Writing is a powerful, transferable skill that you can use to promote your success across the curriculum, including both general education courses and courses in your academic major. Writing is a major route through which you can communicate your ideas, and it is a route of communication that your instructors will rely on to judge the extent of your knowledge and the quality of your thinking. You may have many great ideas in your head, but unless you can get them out of your head and onto paper, your instructors will never know you have them and you'll never receive full credit for them in your college courses. If you improve your writing skills, you will improve your ability to demonstrate your knowledge, communicate your ideas, and elevate your grades. Research indicates that writing is positively related to deep learning and student gains in personal development (National Survey of Student Engagement, 2008).

Your ability to write clearly, concisely, and persuasively is not only a skill that will help you succeed academically, it's also a skill that will help you succeed professionally. In a study of college alumni who were asked about the importance of different skills to their current work responsibilities up to 10 years after they graduated, more than 90 percent of them ranked "need to write effectively" as a skill they considered to be of "great importance" to their current work (Worth, as cited in Light, 2001). In fact, the first contact and first impression you will make on future employers is likely to be the letter of application or cover letter you write when applying for positions. Constructing a well-written letter of application may be your first step toward converting your college experience and college degree into a future career.

> "Want one more reason for developing strong writing skills? Money. Good writing skills are consistently one of the most sought-after skills by employers."
>
> —Karen Brooks, career counselor and author of *You Majored in What? Mapping Your Path from Chaos to Career*

Writing to Learn

As we mentioned in Chapter 1, humans learn most effectively from experience when they're actively involved in the learning experience and when they reflect on that experience after it has taken place. Writing can help you learn from any experience—either inside or outside the classroom—by increasing both active involvement and personal reflection. The phrase *writing to learn* has been coined by scholars to capture the idea that writing is not only a communication skill learned in English composition classes, but a learning skill that can deepen understanding of any academic subject or life experience (Ackerman, 1993; Applebee, 1984; Elbow, 1973; Zinsser, 1993). Just as you can learn to write better, you can write to learn better.

Writing-to-learn activities differ from traditional writing assignments, such as essays or term papers, in two key major ways:

1. They're shorter—requiring less amount of time to complete.
2. They're written primarily for the benefit of the writer—as an aid to thinking and learning (Tchudi, 1986).

> **Remember**
>
> *Writing skills will contribute to your academic success across all courses you take throughout your time in college, and they will promote your professional success in any career you may pursue beyond college.*

Writing-to-learn activities can be used for a wide variety of learning tasks and purposes in college, such as those listed below. As you read the following list of different writing activities and purposes, make a short note in the margin indicating whether you do each type of writing. If you don't do it, indicate whether you think it would be worth doing.

Writing to Listen

You can use writing to improve your attention and listening skills during classroom lectures, study group sessions, or office visits with your instructors. For instance, immediately after each class session, you could write a "one-minute paper" that only takes a minute or less to complete, yet enables you to assess whether you've actively listened to and grasped the most important message delivered in class that day (e.g., "What was the most significant concept I learned in class today?" or "What was the most confusing thing that I experienced in today's class that I should ask my instructor to clarify?")

Writing to Read

Just as writing can promote active listening, it can also promote active reading. Taking notes on what you're reading while you're reading implements the effective learning principle of active involvement because it requires more mental and physical energy than merely reading and highlighting sentences.

Writing to Remember

Writing lists of ideas generated at a group meeting, definitions, terms, or key concepts that you need to remember is an old-fashioned but surefire way not to forget them. When you've recorded an idea in print, you've created a permanent record of it that will enable you to access it and review it at any time. Furthermore, the act of writing itself creates motor (muscle) memory for the information you're writing, which enables you to better retain and retrieve the information you've written. Writing also improves memory by allowing you to *see* the information, which registers it in your brain as a visual memory trace.

Author's Experience Whenever I have trouble remembering the spelling of a word, I take a pen or pencil and start to write the word out. I'm surprised at how many times the correct spelling comes back to my mind once I begin to write the word. However, the more I think about this, it's not surprising that my ability to remember the spelling immediately returns when I start writing it. This memory "flashback" is probably due to the fact that when I start using the muscles in my hand to write the word, it activates the "muscle memories" in my brain that were previously formed when I wrote that word with its correct spelling.

— *Joe Cuseo*

Writing to Organize

Constructing summaries and outlines, or writing ideas on different index cards that relate to the same category or concept, are effective ways of organizing and learning information. This type of organizational writing deepens learning because it requires synthesis of different ideas and restatement of ideas in your own words, both of which are deep-learning strategies.

Writing to Study

Writing study guides or practice answers to potential test questions is an effective strategy that can be used when studying alone or when preparing for study groups. This is particularly effective preparation for essay tests because it enables you to study in a way that closely matches what you will be expected to do on an essay test, which requires you to write out answers (not pick out answers as you would on a multiple-choice test).

Writing to Understand

Paraphrasing or restating what you're attempting to learn by writing it in your own words is an effective way to get feedback about whether you've truly understood it (not just memorized it) because you transform what you're learning into words that are meaningful to you.

Also, writing deepens learning because it requires physical action, which implements the effective learning principle of active involvement: writing essentially forces you to focus attention on your own thoughts and activate your thinking. In addition, writing slows down your thought process, allowing you to think in a more careful, systematic fashion that makes you more consciously aware of specific details. Lastly, the act of writing results in a visible product you can review and use as feedback to improve the quality of your thoughts (Applebee, 1984; Langer & Applebee, 1987). In other words, writing allows you to "think out loud on paper" (Bean, 2003, p. 102).

"I write to understand as much as to be understood."

—Elie Wiesel, world-famous American novelist, Nobel Prize winner, and Holocaust survivor

"How can I know what I think 'til I see what I say?"

—Graham Wallas, *The Art of Thought*

Writing to Create

Writing can also stimulate your discovery of ideas because new ideas are likely to emerge in your mind during the act or process of writing. Thus, writing is not just an end result or final product of your thinking: it's is also a means or process of stimulating your thinking.

You can generate creative ideas through the process of *freewriting*, whereby you quickly jot down free-floating thoughts on paper without worrying about spelling and grammar. Freewriting can be used as a warm-up exercise to help you generate ideas for a research topic, to keep track of original ideas you happen to discover while brainstorming, or to record creative ideas that suddenly pop into your mind at unexpected times (before you forget them).

"There is in writing the constant joy of sudden discovery, of happy accident."

—H. L. Mencken, 20th-century American journalist and social critic

"There are some kinds of writing that you have to do very fast, like riding a bicycle on a tightrope."

—William Faulkner, Nobel Prize-winning author

Writing to Discuss

Prior to participating in class discussions or small-group work, you can gather your thoughts in writing to prepare for expressing them orally. This will ensure that you've carefully reflected on your ideas, which, in turn, should improve the quality of ideas you contribute. Gathering your thoughts in writing before speaking should also make you a less anxious, more confident speaker because you have a better idea about what you're going to say before you start to say it. Your written notes also give you a script to build on, or fall back on, in case you experience speech anxiety (or memory loss) while expressing your ideas.

Writing for Problem Solving

Writing can be used to capture your thought process while solving math and science problems. By writing down the thoughts going through your mind at each major step in the problem-solving process, you increase self-awareness of how your thinking progressed and you're left with a written record of your train of thought. You can review this written record later to help you retrieve the path of thought that led you to solve the problem successfully, allowing you to reuse the same path to solve similar problems in the future.

Reflection **7.5**

Which of the above-listed writing activities have you done? For those you haven't done, which would you strongly consider doing?

Try to get into the habit of periodically stepping back to reflect on your thinking process. Ask yourself what type of thinking you are doing (such as analysis, synthesis, or evaluation) and record your personal reflections in writing. You could even keep a "thinking log" or "thinking journal" to increase self-awareness of the thinking strategies you develop across time, or how your thinking strategies may vary across different courses and academic fields.

Writing Papers and Reports

Studies show that a small percentage of high school students' class and homework time is spent on writing assignments that are as lengthy and demanding as those given in college. In high school, most writing assignments involve summaries or descriptive reports; in college, students are expected to engage in expository (persuasive) writing, which requires the writer to make or prove a case by supporting it with sound evidence (Applebee et al., 1990).

Completing papers and written reports almost always takes more time than you think it will. Writing is a multistep process that cannot be completed in one night. Breaking down the writing process into smaller steps that are completed in advance of the paper's due date is an effective way to strengthen the quality of your final product. What follows is a sequence of steps that divides the writing process into different parts (planning, writing, rewriting, and editing), which should make your writing of papers and reports more manageable, less stressful, and more successful.

Dividing large writing assignments into smaller, manageable steps can reduce late-night frustration and the risk of permanent computer damage.

1. **Be sure you know the purpose or objective of the writing assignment.** You can't begin to take the right steps toward doing anything well until you know why you're doing it. Having a clear understanding of the purpose or goal of the writing assignment is the critical first step to completing it successfully. It helps you stay on track and moving in the right direction. It also helps you to get going in the first place, because one major cause of writer's block is uncertainty about the goal or purpose of the writing task (Knaus, 2010; Rennie & Brewer, 1987).

   Before you begin to write anything, be sure you have a clear understanding of what your instructor expects you to accomplish. You can do this by asking yourself these three questions about the writing assignment:

   - What is its objective or intended outcome?
   - What type of thinking am I being asked to demonstrate?
   - What criteria (standards) will my instructor use to evaluate and grade my performance?

2. **Generate ideas.** At this stage of the writing process, the only thing you're concerned about is getting the ideas you have in your head out of your head and onto paper. Don't worry about how good or bad the ideas may be. Writing scholars refer to this process as *focused freewriting*—you write freely for a certain period just to generate ideas—without worrying about writing complete or correct sentences (Bean, 2011). Remember that the act of writing itself can stimulate ideas, so if you're not sure what ideas you have, start writing because it will likely trigger ideas, which, in turn, will lead to additional ideas. One way to overcome writer's block is to start writing something (Zinsser, 1993). It could be anything, as long as it jump-starts the process. The creative thinking strategy of *brainstorming*, described in Chapter 8 (p. 202), can be an effective way to jump-start the freewriting process. Sometimes, even changing your working environment or format may stimulate new ideas, such as shifting from writing ideas in pen or pencil to typing them on your computer. Also, generating ideas with a friend or testing your ideas with a classmate can make the brainstorming stage more stimulating and productive.

3. **Organize your ideas.** After all your ideas have been laid out, the next step is to sort them out and figure out how they can be pieced together. There are two key sub-steps in the process of organizing your ideas for a paper or written report.

   First step: Connect separate pieces of information related to the same general idea by organizing them into categories. For instance, if your topic is terrorism and you find three ideas on your list referring to different causes of terrorism, group those ideas together under the category of "causes." Similarly, if you find ideas on your list that relate to possible solutions to the problem of terrorism, group those ideas under the category of "solutions." You could record your separate ideas on sticky notes and stick the notes with ideas pertaining to the same general category on index cards, with the category heading written at the top of the card.

   Second step: Organize your categories of ideas into an order that flows smoothly or logically from start to finish. Arrange your different categories of ideas in an orderly sequence that has a meaningful beginning, middle, and end. Index cards come in handy when trying to find the best progression of your major ideas because the cards can be arranged and rearranged easily until you discover an order that produces the smoothest, most logical sequence. You can use your sequence of index cards to create an outline for your paper that lists the major categories of your ideas and the order in which they will appear in your paper.

"Begin with the end in mind."

—Stephen Covey, *The Seven Habits of Highly Effective People*

"A writer is not so much someone who has something to say as he is someone who has found a process that will bring about new things he would not have thought of if he had not started to say [write] them."

—William Stafford, American author and recipient of the National Book Award for Poetry

Another effective way to organize and sequence your ideas is to map them out by creating a concept map that depicts your main categories of ideas in a visual-spatial format similar to a road map. **Figure 7.1** shows a concept map that was used to organize and sequence the main ideas covered in Chapter 8 on higher-level thinking. This type of concept map is called a clock map because its main ideas are organized like the numbers of a clock, beginning at the top and then moving sequentially in a clockwise direction.

Reflection 7.6

When you attempt to organize your ideas, are you more likely to use a map (diagram) format or an outline format—in which you list major ideas as headings (A, B, C, etc.) and related minor ideas as subheadings (1, 2, 3, etc.)?

Why do you think you tend to favor one method over the other?

FIGURE 7.1

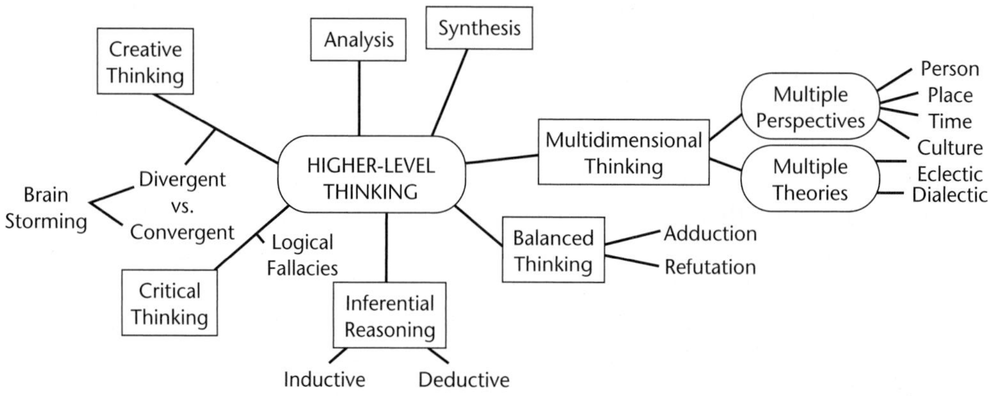

© Kendall Hunt

Concept Map Used to Organize and Sequence Major Ideas Relating to Higher-Level Thinking

4. **Write a first draft in which you identify your main idea and supporting ideas.** The previous steps in the writing process are referred to as *prewriting* because they focus on generating and organizing your ideas before communicating them to anyone else (Murray, 2002). In a *first draft*, you begin the formal writing process of converting your major ideas into sentences, but you do so without worrying about the mechanics of writing (e.g., punctuation, grammar, or spelling). The purpose of your first draft is to simply "talk through" your key ideas on paper. In your later drafts, you can convert your informal writing into more formal and polished prose.

At this stage in the process, you transform your major ideas into written paragraphs and arrange your paragraphs in a logical sequence. Here are some strategies for accomplishing each of these steps.
- Use your first paragraph to provide a meaningful introduction, overview, or preview of the major points you will make in the remainder (body) of the

paper. Pay particular attention to your opening paragraph because it creates the all-important first impression and sets the stage for what will follow. Your introduction should include a *thesis statement*—a short summary (one to three sentences) of your key point or central idea—which you will follow up in the body of your paper with evidence to support it. Your thesis statement is the most important sentence in your introduction; it's the compass that will guide your thinking and keep you and your audience moving in the direction toward the same destination (conclusion). You may also phrase your thesis statement in the form of a question, and use the body of your paper as a quest or journey to reach an answer to that question.

- Keep different points (ideas) in different paragraphs. A paragraph should represent a chain of sentences that are linked to the same thought or idea. If you shift to a different idea, shift to a different paragraph.

- Whenever possible, start new paragraphs with a *topic sentence* that introduces the new point you're about to make and relates it to the major point being made in your paper—your thesis statement. Topic sentences help bring cohesion to your paper by organizing the points you make in separate paragraphs and by integrating your separate paragraphs into the body of the paper as a whole.

- Use your final paragraph to "tie it all together" and drive home your paper's major points. This will leave your paper with three distinctive parts:
  a. *Introduction*. An opening paragraph that includes a thesis statement;
  b. *Body*. A series of paragraphs that follows the introduction, each of which contains one of your paper's major points or ideas, and
  c. *Conclusion*. A final paragraph that summarizes your major points and relates them to the thesis statement in your introduction.

After you've completed your first draft, it's often a good idea to step away from it for a while and give your mind some time to cool off and incubate. When you return to it later, you're likely to think of new ideas and better ways to express the ideas you previously generated.

5. **Write more than one draft.** Don't expect to write a perfect draft of your paper on the first try. Even professional writers report that it takes them more than one draft (often three or four) before they produce their final draft. Although the final product of award-winning writers may look spectacular, what precedes it is a messy process that includes lots of revisions between the first try and the final product (Bean, 2011). Just as actors and actresses need multiple takes (take two, take three, etc.) to get their spoken lines right, writers need multiple takes (drafts) to get their written lines right.

> "I'm not a writer; I'm a rewriter."
>
> —James Thurber, award-winning American journalist and author

It may be a particularly good idea to review your thesis statement because, in the process of rewriting, you're likely to discover new thoughts and better ideas. If this happens, you can modify your opening thesis statement so that it more closely matches your concluding statement (Bean, 2011). However, if you find yourself making radical changes to your thesis statement, this may indicate that you radically changed directions while writing the body of your paper and you didn't accomplish what you said you were going to do in your introduction.

6. **Critique and edit your writing.** After completing each draft of your paper, take your mind off it for a while and come back to look it from a different perspective—as a reader and editor, rather than a writer. Read your own words as if they were written by someone else and critically evaluate the paper's ideas, organization, and writing style. If you find words and sentences that aren't clearly capturing or reflecting what you meant to say, this is the stage in the writing process when you make your major revisions. (At this stage, make sure your

paper is double-spaced so that you have enough room for making changes and additions.)

When critiquing and editing your paper, critically evaluate each of the following features:

- **Documentation.** Are its major points and final conclusion well supported by evidence, such as:
  a. Direct quotes from authoritative sources,
  b. Specific examples,
  c. Statistical data,
  d. Scientific research findings, or
  e. Firsthand experiences?

- **Overall organization.** Take a *panoramic* or aerial view of your paper to see if you can clearly identify its three major parts: the beginning (introduction), the middle (body), and the end (conclusion). Do these three parts unite to form a connected whole? Also, check to see if there is *continuity* from one paragraph to the next throughout your paper: Does your train of thought stay on track from start to finish? If you find yourself getting off track at certain points in your paper, eliminate that information or rewrite it in a way that reroutes your thoughts back onto their main track (your thesis statement).

- **Sentence structure.** Do the sentences within each paragraph make sense and flow smoothly from one to another? Check for sentences that are too long—rambling sentences that go on and on without any punctuation or pauses that allow readers to catch their breath. You can correct rambling sentences by (1) punctuating them with a comma, signaling a short pause, (2) punctuating them with a semicolon, signaling a longer pause than a comma (but not as long as a period), or (3) dividing them into two shorter sentences (separated by a period). Also, check for sentences that are too short—choppy sentences that "chop up" what you've written into such short statements that they interfere with the natural flow or rhythm of reading. Correct choppy sentences by joining them to form a larger sentence, punctuated by a comma or semicolon.

- A good strategy for helping you determine if your written sentences flow smoothly is to read them aloud. Note the places where you naturally tend to pause and where you tend to keep going. Your natural pauses may serve as cues for places where your sentences need punctuation, and your natural runs may indicate sentences that are flowing smoothly and should be left alone. Reading your writing out loud can help you find run-on sentences and choppy sentences.

- **Word selection.** Are certain words or phrases showing up so frequently in your paper that they sound repetitious? If so, try to add variety to your vocabulary by substituting words that have the same or similar meaning. This substitution process can be made easier by using a thesaurus, which may be conveniently available on your computer's word processing program.

7. **Get feedback on your writing from a trusted peer or writing professional.** You're always the first reader of your paper, but you don't have to be the only reader before you submit to your instructor and receive a grade. Sometimes, no matter how honest or objective we try to be about our own work, we may still be blind to its weaknesses. All of us may have a natural tendency to see what we hope or want to see in our work, rather than what's really there—especially after we've put a great deal of time, effort, and energy into the process of creating it. Consider getting a second opinion on your paper by asking a trusted friend or a tutor in the Writing or Learning Center to read it.

You can seek feedback at any stage of the writing process—whether it be for help with understanding the assignment, brainstorming ideas, writing your first draft, or writing your final draft. Seeking help from the Writing or Learning Center is not limited to students experiencing writing problems or writer's block. Help may be sought by all students who want to push the quality of their writing to a higher level. Even if you consider yourself to be a good writer, your writing can get even better if you seek and receive feedback from others before submitting your final product. Consider pairing up with a partner to exchange and assess each other's papers, using a checklist of criteria that your instructor will use to evaluate and grade your papers. Studies show that when students with different levels of writing ability receive feedback from others prior to submitting a paper, it improves their quality of writing as well as their grade (Patchan, Charney, & Schunn, 2009; Thompson, 1981).

8. **In your final draft, be sure that your conclusion and introduction are connected or aligned.** The most important component of your conclusion involves revisiting or restating your original thesis and answering the question you originally posed in your introduction. Connecting your thesis statement and concluding statement provides a pair of meaningful bookends to your paper, anchoring it at its two most pivotal points: beginning and end. This ensures you end up at the destination you intended to reach when you started, and enables you to maximize the power of the two most important impressions you can make: the first impression and the last impression.

"End with the beginning in mind."

—Joe Cuseo, non-award-winning author of the book you're now reading

9. **Carefully proofread your paper for structural and technical mistakes before submitting it.** Proofreading is a critical last step in the editorial process because small, technical errors are likely to have been overlooked during earlier stages of the writing process when your attention was focused on larger issues related to your paper's content and organizational structure. Proofreading may be viewed as a micro form of editing, during which you shift the focus of your editorial attention to the minute mechanics of your paper and detection of details related to referencing, grammar, punctuation, and spelling. For instance, check to be sure that none of your sentences are *sentence fragments*—missing either a noun or a verb—or *run-on sentences*—two sentences that are not separated by a period or conjunction word (e.g., *and* or *but*). Also, don't forget that your computer's spell-checker doesn't check whether words are correctly spelled in the context (sentence) in which you're using them. For instance, a spell-checker would not detect the three "correctly" spelled words that are actually misspelled words in the context of the following sentence: "*Ware* your high-*heal* sneakers because you're going out *two night.*"

Student *Perspective*

"Spell checkers aren't always reliable, so ask someone for suggestions or read papers out loud to yourself."

—Advice to first-year students from a college sophomore (Walsh, 2005)

Remember

Careful proofreading is the key, final step in the process of writing a high-quality paper. Earlier stages of the writing process involve generating, organizing, and expressing your ideas, which are more mentally demanding and time-consuming than proofreading. To overlook or underestimate this simple last step of proofreading and lose valuable points for a written product that you spent so much time creating would be a downright shame.

10. **After the paper has been graded and returned to you, carefully review your instructor's written comments.** Sometimes, no matter how hard you try to anticipate and demonstrate everything your instructor expects, particularly on the first major assignment, there are some things that can only be learned and corrected *after* you've received feedback from your instructor on your first perfor-

mance. Review your paper closely when you get it back and pay special attention to any written comments provided by your instructor. If the grade you receive is lower than you expected, try not to get emotional or defensive. Instead, learn from your mistakes and use your instructor's comments as constructive feedback to improve your performance on future assignments.

If your instructor's written feedback still leaves you unclear about what went wrong or what needs to be improved, make an appointment for an office visit. Receiving personalized feedback from the very person who has evaluated your work, and who will be evaluating your future work, may be the most powerful way to improve your future performance and final grade. If your instructor is willing to meet with you during office hours and review your paper with you, take full advantage of this opportunity. Besides receiving personalized performance-improving feedback, you will send a clear message to the instructor that you're a serious student who wants to learn from mistakes and achieve excellence.

Reflection 7.7

Reflect back on your writing assignments in high school.

1.   What was the longest paper you wrote?

2.   What type of thinking were you usually asked to do on your writing assignments (e.g., memorize, summarize, analyze, criticize, or compare and contrast)?

Public Speaking: Making Oral Presentations and Delivering Speeches

The Importance of Oral Communication

In addition to writing, the second major channel you'll use to convey ideas and demonstrate your knowledge is oral communication. Developing your ability to speak in a clear, concise, and confident manner will strengthen your performance in college and in your career. In fact, the oral communication skills you demonstrate during your job interviews are likely to play a pivotal role in determining whether you're initially hired. In addition, your ability to speak effectively at meetings and while making professional presentations will increase your prospects for career advancement and promotion. Research repeatedly shows that employers place high value on oral communication skills and rank them among the top characteristics they seek in prospective employees (AC Nielsen Research Services, 2000; National Association of Colleges & Employers, 2012; Conference Board of Canada, 2000; Peter D. Hart Research Associates, 2006).

"As you move up through your career path, you're judged on your ability to articulate a point of view."

—Donald Keogh, former president of the Coca-Cola Company

Reflection 7.8

Before college, had you ever made an oral presentation or delivered a speech?

Does your college include a course in speech or public speaking as a graduation requirement?

If your college doesn't require it, would you consider taking an elective course in public speaking?

Strategies for Making Effective Oral Presentations and Speeches

In the following section of this chapter, you'll find strategies you can use immediately to improve your ability to make oral presentations and speeches. Since speaking and writing both involve communicating thoughts in the form of words, you'll find that many of the strategies suggested here for improving oral reports will also be useful for improving written reports. You should be able to "double dip" and transfer the effective strategies you learn for oral presentations to improve your written presentations, and vice versa.

1. **Know the purpose of your presentation.** Knowing the intended outcome of your oral presentation is the critical first step toward making an effective presentation. If you have any doubt about what your oral presentation should accomplish, seek clarification from your instructor before proceeding.

   Oral presentations usually fall into one of the following two categories, depending on their purpose or objective:
   - **Informative presentations** that are intended to provide the audience with accurate information and explanations.
   - **Persuasive (expository) presentations** that are intended to persuade (convince) the audience to agree with a certain position by supporting it with solid evidence and sound arguments.

   In college, most of your oral presentations will fall into the persuasive category, which means that you will search for information, draw conclusions about your research, and document your conclusions with evidence. Similar to research papers, persuasive presentations usually require you to think at a higher level, cite sources, and demonstrate academic integrity.

2. **Identify your topic.** If you're given a choice about the topic of your presentation, seize this opportunity to pursue a subject that captures your interest and enthusiasm. If you do, your interest and enthusiasm are likely to show through in your delivery, which should increase your self-confidence, get your audience's attention, and improve your overall grade for the presentation.

3. **Rehearse and revise.** Just as you should write several drafts of a paper before turning it in, your oral presentation should be rehearsed and revised before delivering it. Rehearsal will improve your memory and increase the clarity of your presentation by reducing long pauses, the need to stop and re-start, and the use of distracting "fillers" (e.g., *uh, um, like, you know*) that fill up your listeners' time without filling them in on any information. Rehearsal also helps reduce speech anxiety. Studies show that fear of public speaking is often really a fear of failure—fear of being negatively evaluated by the audience. So, if your oral presentation is well prepared and well rehearsed, your fear of receiving a negative evaluation should decrease, which, in turn, will decrease your speech anxiety.
   - Rehearse the total time it takes to complete your presentation to see if it falls within the time range set by your instructor, making sure that it's neither too short nor too long.
   - During rehearsal, pay special attention to the following parts of your presentation:
     a. The introduction: this part should be rehearsed carefully because it sets

"Enthusiasm is everything."

—Pelé, Brazilian soccer player; arguably the most famous player in the sport's history

Student *Perspective*

"The only time I get nervous is when I am not very familiar with my topic or if I'm winging my assignment and I'm not prepared."

—First-year student commenting on her previous oral presentations

the stage and creates a powerful first impression. As in a written report, your introduction should include a thesis statement in which you state (orally) what you propose to accomplish in your presentation.

b.   Statements that signal your transition from one major category of ideas to another (e.g., statements that move you from one index card to another): these statements serve to highlight your presentation's organization, showing how its separate parts are connected.

c.   Your conclusion should be carefully rehearsed because this is your chance to finish strong and create a powerful last impression by driving home your presentation's most important point or most memorable idea. Your conclusion should include a statement that refers back to and reinforces your original thesis statement, thereby connecting your ending with your beginning.

4.   **Get feedback on your presentation before officially delivering it.** Ask a friend or group of friends to listen to your presentation and ask for their input. Not only can peers provide valuable feedback, they can also provide a live audience that makes your rehearsal more realistic and effective because it more closely matches what you will do during your actual performance.

Another way to obtain feedback prior to your actual presentation is to have a friend video-record your delivery of it. This allows you to view your presentation as if you were a member of the audience. Viewing yourself on video is almost like having an "out-of-body experience" because it enables you to step outside of your body and view yourself as others view you. This provides you with a unique form of feedback that can dramatically increase awareness of your behavior while you are communicating, particularly your nonverbal communication (body language).

Just as writing provides you with a visible product of your thoughts that can be reviewed and used to improve the quality of your thinking, video recordings provide a visible product of your spoken thoughts, which can be reviewed and used as feedback to improve the quality of your thinking as well as the quality of your speaking. You may be a bit shocked when you first see how you look and hear how you sound on video, but that's a normal reaction. After a while, the initial shock will fade and you will feel more comfortable viewing and reviewing your presentations.

> "First, I tell 'em what I'm gonna tell 'em; then I tell 'em; then I tell 'em what I told 'em."
>
> —Anonymous country preacher's formula for successful sermons

Reflection 7.9

Have you ever received feedback on the quality of your speaking skills from a teacher or a peer, or by observing yourself on videotape?

If you have, did you learn anything about your speaking habits and how to improve them?

If you haven't, would you be willing to seek feedback from others on your speaking skills?

5.   **During your speech, minimize reading time and maximize speaking time.** You can occasionally look at your notes or slides during your presentation and use them as cue cards to help you recall the key points you intend to make; however, they shouldn't be used as a script that's read verbatim. This is the major

danger associated with PowerPoint presentations, where the speaker ends up looking at and reading from the slides rather than speaking to an audience. (See *Snapshot Summary 7.3* for tips on how to use, not abuse, PowerPoint.)

An oral presentation should not be something that's written out entirely in advance and read (or memorized) word for word (Luotto, Stoll, & Hoglund-Kettmann, 2001), nor should it be an impromptu speech—something spontaneously delivered off the top of your head. Instead, it should be an *extemporaneous* presentation—something in between a formal reading and an impromptu speech that involves advanced preparation and use of notes or slides as memory-retrieval cues. Extemporaneous speaking is not reading, and it allows you some freedom to ad-lib or improvise. For instance, if you forget the exact words you intended to use, some improvising can prevent you from getting struck by silence, and it can prevent your audience from even noticing that you forgot what you were planning to say.

Snapshot Summary

7.3 Tips for Using (Not Abusing) PowerPoint®

- List information on your slides as bulleted points, not as complete sentences. Wordiness will result in your audience spending more time reading your slides than listening to you. You can further focus your audience's eye contact on you rather than your slides by showing only one point on your slide at a time. This will keep the audience members focused on the point you're discussing and prevent them from reading ahead.
- Avoid reading your slides. Keep eye contact primarily with your audience.

Remember

The words or images on your PowerPoint slides are not your entire presentation: they are merely the launching pad for more elaborate ideas that you'll deliver orally.

"A presentation is about explaining things to people that go above and beyond what they get in the slides. If it weren't, they might just as well get your slides and read them in the comfort of their own office, home, boat, or bathroom."

—Jesper Johansson, senior security strategist for Microsoft and author of *Death by PowerPoint* (personal blog) (2005)

- List only three to five points on each slide. Research indicates that the number of points or bits of information that humans can hold in their short-term memory is about four (Cowan, 2001).
- Use the title of the slide as a general heading for organizing or connecting the bulleted points on the slide.

- Use a font size of at least 18 points, or else people in the back of the room will have difficulty reading what's printed on the slide.
- Color should be not be used for decoration or distraction, but as a visual aid to highlight the organization of points included on the slide. For example, a dark or bold blue heading could be used to highlight each major category, and related subcategories could be distinguished by presenting them in a lighter (but still visible) shade of blue.
- Use your slides to deliver pictures or visual images that relate to and reinforce the points you're making verbally. This may be the true power of PowerPoint.

Remember

Probably the most powerful advantage of PowerPoint is its ability to enhance your verbal presentation with visual images, which can increase the impact of your spoken message and expand the attention span of your audience.

- If you include words or an image on a slide that's not your own work, acknowledge its source at the bottom of the slide.
- Before going public with your slides, proofread them with the same care as you would a written paper.

Sources: Johansson (2005); "Ten Commandments of PowerPoint Presentations" (2005); University of Wisconsin, La Crosse (2001).

6. **Incorporate visual elements into your presentation.** Visual aids can be a powerful way to illustrate and reinforce your points, as well as stimulate audience interest. Don't hesitate to use pictures, images, graphs, cartoons, and objects or artifacts that relate to the verbal points you're making during your presentation.

Remember

The more organized and prepared you are for speaking in public, the less anxiety you'll experience when speaking in public.

7. **During your speech, don't remain motionless.** Research shows that some movement and gesticulation on the part of the speaker help hold the audience's attention and interest more effectively than standing still (Andersen, 1985; Lucas, 2003). Perhaps this is because movement suggests energy, which may send the message that you're not emotionless but passionate about the topic you're talking about. When you're experiencing even moderate stress, your body releases adrenaline—an energy-generating hormone. Thus, it may be natural for your body to want to move during your speech, so move it. Trying to inhibit your body's natural tendency to move can increase your level of tension.

Reducing Speech Anxiety

National surveys show that fear of public speaking is very common among people of all ages, including adolescents and adults (Brewer, 2001). Studies also show that many college students experience *classroom communication apprehension*—anxiety about speaking in classroom settings (Morreale, 2007; Richmond & McCloskey, 1997). So, if you get at least somewhat nervous when speaking in public, don't feel bad, because it's a feeling that's so common, it could be considered normal. Listed below are specific strategies for reducing speech anxiety:

1. When practicing your speech, try to match your practice situation to the actual performance situation. For instance, speak out loud and at the same volume that you'll use during your actual speech, and try to practice delivering your presentation at least once in the same room where you will actually deliver it. The more familiar you become with the environment in which you'll be delivering your speech and the sound of your own voice while delivering it, the less speech anxiety you're likely to experience.

2. Focus attention on the *message* you're delivering (the content of your speech), not the *messenger* who's delivering it (yourself). By remaining conscious of the ideas you're communicating to your listeners, you become less self-conscious about the impression you're making on them and their impression (evaluation) of you.

3. Practice and learn your introduction especially well. This will enable you to get off to a smooth start and give you an early sense of confidence, which should reduce your anxiety for the remainder of your presentation.

4. Carefully observe presentations made by other students and note the things that the more relaxed and effective speakers did during their speeches for clues about what you could do to be equally relaxed and successful when you speak.

5. Prepare your body and brain for the speech by getting adequate sleep the night before your presentation and eating well on the day of the presentation. Avoid consuming caffeine or other stimulating substances prior to speaking because an elevated level of arousal during your speech may also elevate your level of tension.

6. Come prepared with all the equipment you can use to support your presentation (e.g., notes, index cards to jog your memory, and visual aids to illustrate your points). Knowing that you're fully equipped should reduce your worries about something going wrong, and if something does go wrong, you'll have a plan to deal with it immediately and you'll avoid the anxiety-producing hassle of trying to figure out what to do on the spur of the moment. Simply stated, the more organized and prepared you are for a public performance of any kind, the less anxiety you're likely to experience during the performance.

7. Try to get to the site of your speech early, so you have time to settle in and settle down before delivering your presentation. In the minutes just prior to delivering your speech, relax yourself by taking deep breaths and visualizing a successful performance.

8. Since thoughts can influence our emotions and positive thoughts trigger positive emotions (Ellis, 2000), come to your speech with a positive mindset. For example:

    - Keep in mind that it's natural to experience at least some anxiety in any performance situation, especially in a public speaking situation. This is not necessarily a bad thing; if your anxiety is kept at a moderate level, it will actually increase your enthusiasm, energy, concentration, and memory (Rosenfield, 1988; Sapolsky, 2004).

    - Don't expect to give "the perfect speech" as if you're a TV reporter rattling off (actually reading) the nightly news. A few verbal mistakes or lapses of memory are common during speeches, just as they are during normal conversations. You can still receive an excellent grade on an oral presentation without delivering a flawless performance.

    - If you happen to realize you forgot to make a point or two, keep in mind that the audience will not know and notice you forgot those points: only you will. Similarly, keep in mind that much of the anxiety you may be feeling internally during your speech will not be externally visible to your audience and will often go unnoticed as they focus on the points you're making.

    - conversation; the only difference is that you're speaking to more than one person at a time and for a somewhat longer period of time. However, it's a longer conversation that you've had the opportunity to prepare for in advance. To help get into this more informal and conversational mindset, look at one person at a time while you're delivering different parts of your speech. However, periodically change your focus to people in different sections of the room to ensure that you're making eye contact with different sections of your audience.

    - Keep in mind that the audience to whom you are speaking is not made up of expert speakers. Most of them have no more public speaking experience than you do, nor are they experienced critics. These are your peers, and they are very much aware that getting up in front of a class is a stressful thing to do. They're likely to be very accepting of any mistakes you happen to make, just as they hope you will be for them when it's their turn to stand and deliver.

Final Note: If you continue to experience high levels of speech anxiety after implementing these strategies, seek advice and help from a professional in your Learning Center or Counseling Center.

"Be prepared."
—Motto of the Boy Scouts and Girl Scouts

Student
Perspective

"I was really nervous during the entire thing, but I felt so relieved and proud afterwards."
—First-year college student commenting on her first public speech

Summary and Conclusion

We began this chapter by asking you what the difference was between learning factual knowledge and learning a transferable skill. You may have known the answer to the question before reading this chapter, or discovered it while reading the chapter; either way, you know now that a transferable skill has more flexibility than factual knowledge because it can be applied or transferred to different situations or contexts. The three key skills discussed in this chapter—research (information literacy), writing, and speaking—are powerful, transferable skills that can be applied across different academic subjects that you encounter in college and across different work situations you encounter beyond college.

Research, writing, and speaking are interrelated and complementary sets of success tools. Research skills are needed to acquire high-quality ideas from others, and both writing and speaking skills are needed to actively stimulate your own thinking about the ideas you acquire and as vehicles for communicating your ideas to others. Said in another way, *research* skills enable you to locate, evaluate, and integrate information, while *writing* and *speaking* skills enable you to comprehend, communicate, and demonstrate your mastery of that information to others.

These three key skills have always been relevant to the educational and professional success of college students and college alumni, but they are even more critical for success in today's information and communication age. Furthermore, as discussed in Chapter 2, they are valued highly by employers.

We strongly encourage you to work hard at developing the transferable skills that were discussed in this chapter and take full advantage of the campus resources that have been intentionally designed to help you develop them, such as your College Library and Academic Support Center. The time and energy you invest in developing your research, writing, and speaking skills will pay huge dividends toward promoting your success in college and beyond.

Learning More through the World Wide Web

Internet-Based Resources for Further Information on Research, Writing, and Speaking

For additional information related to ideas discussed in this chapter, we recommend the following Web sites:

Information Search Strategies:

http://libguides.reynolds.edu/content.php?pid=151660&sid=3009481

Writing Strategies:

www.enhancemywriting.com/

Academic Integrity:

http://www.academicintegrity.org/icai/home.php

Public Speaking Skills:

www.public-speaking.org/public-speaking-articles.htm

7.1 Internet Research

Go to www.itools.com/search. This Web site allows you to conveniently access multiple search engines, Web directories, and newsgroups. Type in the name of a subject or topic you'd like to research and select three of the multiple search engines listed at this site.

1. What were the major differences in the types of information that was generated by these three searches?

2. Was the information provided by any one of these searches more useful than the others?

3. Would you return to this Web site again to conduct future research?

7.2 Is It or Is It Not Plagiarism?

The following are four incidents that were actually brought to a judicial review board to determine if plagiarism had occurred and, if so, what the penalty should be. After you read each case, answer the questions listed below it.

Case 1. A student turned in an essay that included substantial material copied from a published source. The student admitted that he didn't cite the sources properly, but argued that it was because he misunderstood the directions, not because he was attempting to steal someone else's ideas.

Is this plagiarism?

How severe is it? (Rate it on a scale from 1 = low to 10 = high)

What should the consequence or penalty be for the student?

How could the suspicion of plagiarism have been avoided in this case?

_____

Case 2. A student turned in a paper that was identical to a paper submitted by another student for a different course.

Is this plagiarism?

How severe is it? (Rate it on a scale from 1 = low to 10 = high)

What should the consequence or penalty be for the student?

How could the suspicion of plagiarism have been avoided in this case?

_____

Case 3. A student submitted a paper he wrote in a previous course as an extra-credit paper for a course.

Is this plagiarism?

How severe is it? (Rate it on a scale from 1 = low to 10 = high)

What should the consequence or penalty be for the student?

How could the suspicion of plagiarism have been avoided in this case?

_____

Case 4. A student submitted a paper in an art history course that contained some ideas from art critics that she read about and whose ideas she agreed with. The student claimed that not citing these critics' ideas wasn't plagiarism because their ideas were merely their own subjective judgments or opinions, not facts or findings, and, furthermore, they were opinions that she agreed with.

Is this plagiarism?

How severe is it? (Rate it on a scale from 1 = low to 10 = high)

What should the consequence or penalty be for the student?

Looking back at these four cases, which of them do you think represent the most severe and least severe violation of academic integrity? Why?

7.3 Preparing an Oral Presentation on Student Success

1. Scan this textbook and identify a chapter topic or chapter section that you find most interesting or most important.

2. Create an introduction for a class presentation on this topic that:

    a. provides an overview or sneak preview of what you will cover in your presentation;

    b. grabs the attention of your audience (your classmates); and

    c. demonstrates the topic's relevance or importance for your audience.

3. Create a conclusion to your presentation that:

    a. relates back to your introduction;

    b. highlights your most important point or points; and

    c. leaves a memorable last impression.

Crime and Punishment: Plagiarism and Its Consequences

Because of the ease with which internet sources can be copied and pasted, it is now common for college students to submit assignments using text that has been lifted off the Web. In response to this trend many college professors now subscribe to Web sites that match the content of students' papers with content from books and online sources. To monitor plagiarism in their classes, these faculty members require students to submit their papers through these Web sites. If students are caught plagiarizing, for a first offense, they typically receive an F for the assignment or the course. A second offense can result in dismissal or expulsion from college, which has already happened to a few students.

Source: http://www.plagiarism.org/index.html

Reflection and Discussion Questions

1. Why do you think students plagiarize? What do you suspect are the primary motives, reasons, or causes?

2. What do you think is a fair or just penalty for those found guilty of a first plagiarism violation? What is fair for those who commit a second violation?

3. How do you think plagiarism could be most effectively reduced or prevented from happening in the first place?

Higher-Level Thinking

Moving Beyond Basic Knowledge to Critical and Creative Thinking

ACTIVATE YOUR THINKING *Reflection* **8.1**

LEARNING GOAL

To increase awareness of what it means to think at a higher level and how higher-level thinking can be used to achieve excellence in college and beyond.

To me, critical thinking means . . .

(At a later point in this chapter, we'll discuss critical thinking and ask you to flash back to the response you made here.)

What Is Higher-Level Thinking?

The term *higher-level thinking* (or *higher-order thinking*) refers to a more advanced level of thought than that used for learning basic skills and acquiring factual knowledge. Higher-level thinking involves reflecting on the knowledge you've acquired and taking additional mental action on it, such as evaluating its validity, integrating it with something else you've learned, or creating new ideas.

Contestants performing on TV quiz shows such as *Jeopardy!* or *Who Wants to Be a Millionaire?* respond to questions asking for knowledge about who, what, when, and where. If game-show contestants were asked higher-level thinking questions, they'd be responding to questions such as "Why?" "How?" and "What if?"

Remember

The focus of higher-level thinking is not just to answer questions, but also to question answers.

As its name implies, higher-level thinking involves raising the bar and jacking up your thinking to levels that go beyond merely remembering, reproducing, or regurgitating factual information. "Education is what's left over after you've forgotten all the facts" is an old saying that carries a lot of truth. Studies show that students' memory of facts learned in college often fades with time (Pascarella & Terenzini, 1991, 2005). Memory for factual information has a short lifespan; the ability to think at a higher level is a durable, lifelong learning skill that lasts a lifetime.

Compared to high school, college courses focus less on memorizing information and more on thinking about issues, concepts, and principles (Conley, 2005). Remembering information in college may get a grade of "C," demonstrating comprehension of that information may get you a "B," and going beyond comprehension to demonstrate higher-level thinking will earn you an "A." In national surveys of college professors teaching freshman- through senior-level courses in various fields, more than 95 percent of them report that the most important goal of a college education is to develop students' ability to think critically (Gardiner, 2005; Milton, 1982). Simi-

Student Perspective

"To me, thinking at a higher level means to think and analyze something beyond the obvious and find the deeper meaning."

—First-year college student

"What is the hardest task in the world? To think."

—Ralph Waldo Emerson, 19th-century American essayist and lecturer

larly, college professors teaching introductory courses to freshmen and sophomores indicate that the primary educational purpose of their courses is to develop students' critical thinking skills (Higher Education Institute, 2009; Stark et al., 1990).

Simply stated, college professors are often more concerned with teaching you *how* to think than with teaching you *what* to think (i.e., what facts to remember).

Remember

Your college professors will often expect you to do more than just retain or reproduce information; they'll ask you to demonstrate higher levels of thinking with respect to what you've learned, such as analyze it, evaluate it, apply it, or connect it with other concepts that you've learned.

This is not to say that acquiring knowledge and basic comprehension are unimportant. They are important because they supply you with the raw material needed to manufacture higher-level thinking. Deep learning and a broad base of knowledge provide the stepping stones you need to climb to higher levels of thinking (as illustrated in Figure 8.1).

FIGURE 8.1

Higher-Level Thinking

Comprehension

Basic Knowledge

© Kendall Hunt

The Relationship between Knowledge, Comprehension, and Higher-Level Thinking

Defining and Describing the Major Forms of Higher-Level Thinking

When your college professors ask you to "think critically," they're usually asking you to use one or more of the eight forms of thinking listed in the Snapshot Summary 8.1. As you read the description of each form of thinking, note whether or not you've heard of it before.

Application (Applied Thinking)

When you learn something deeply, you transform information into knowledge; when you translate knowledge into action, you're engaging in a higher-level thinking process known as *application*. Applied thinking moves you beyond simply knowing something to actually doing something with the knowledge you possess; you use the knowledge you've acquired to solve a problem or resolve an issue. For example, if you use knowledge you've acquired in a human relations course (or from Chapter 9 of this text) to resolve an interpersonal conflict, you're engaging in application. Simi-

Snapshot Summary

8.1

Major Forms of Higher-Level Thinking

1. **Application (applied thinking).** Putting knowledge into practice to solve problems and resolve issues;
2. **Analysis (analytical thinking).** Breaking down information to identify its key parts and underlying elements;
3. **Synthesis.** Building up ideas by integrating them into a larger whole or more comprehensive system;
4. **Multidimensional thinking.** Taking multiple perspectives (i.e., viewing issues from different vantage points);

5. **Inferential reasoning.** Making arguments or judgments by inferring (stepping to) a conclusion that's supported by empirical (observable) evidence or logical consistency;
6. **Balanced thinking.** Carefully considering arguments for and against a particular position or viewpoint;
7. **Critical thinking.** Evaluating (judging the quality of) arguments, conclusions, and ideas; and
8. **Creative thinking.** Generating ideas that are unique, original, or distinctively different.

larly, when you use knowledge acquired in a math course to solve a problem that you haven't seen before, you're using applied thinking. Application is a powerful form of higher-level thinking because it allows you to transfer your knowledge to new situations or contexts and put it into practice.

Reflection **8.2**

Look back at the eight forms of thinking described in the **Snapshot Summary 8.1**. Which of these forms of thinking had you heard of before? Did you use any of these forms of thinking on high school exams or assignments?

Always be on the lookout for ways to apply the knowledge you acquire to your personal life experiences and current events or issues. When you use your knowledge for the practical purpose of doing something good, such as bettering yourself or others, you not only demonstrate application, you also demonstrate *wisdom* (Staudinger, 2008).

Analysis (Analytical Thinking)

The mental process of analysis is similar to the physical process of peeling an onion. When you analyze something, you take it apart or break it down and pick out its key parts, main points, or underlying elements. For example, if you were to analyze a textbook chapter, you would go beyond reading just to cover the content; instead, you would read it to uncover the author's main ideas, detecting its core ideas and distinguishing them from background information and incidental details.

In an art course, you would use analysis to identify the components or elements of a painting or sculpture (e.g., its structure, texture, tone, and form). In the natural and social sciences, you would use analysis to identify underlying reasons or causes for natural (physical) phenomena and social events, which is commonly referred to as *causal analysis*. For instance, causal analysis of the September 11, 2001, attack on the United States would involve identifying the factors that led to the attack or the underlying reasons for why the attack took place.

Student Perspective

"In physics, you have to be analytical and break it [the problem] down into its parts, and not look at the question all at once."

—Physics student (Donald, 2002)

Synthesis

A form of higher-level thinking that's basically the opposite of analysis is *synthesis*. When you analyze, you break information into its parts; when you synthesize, you build it up by taking separate parts or pieces of information and connect them to form an integrated whole (like piecing together parts of a puzzle). You engage in synthesis when you connect ideas presented in different courses: for instance, when you integrate ethical concepts learned in a philosophy course with marketing concepts learned in a business course to produce a set of ethical guidelines for marketing and advertising products.

Reflection **8.3**

A TV commercial for a particular brand of liquor (which shall remain nameless) once showed a young man getting out of his car in front of a house where a party is going on. The driver gets out of his car, takes out a knife, slashes his tires, and goes inside to join the party. Using the higher-level thinking skill of analysis, what would you say are the underlying or embedded messages in this commercial?

Synthesis involves more than a summary. It goes beyond just condensing information to a higher level of thinking that involves finding and forming meaningful connections across separate pieces of information and weaving them together to form a cohesive picture. When you're synthesizing, you're thinking conceptually by converting isolated facts and separate bits of information and integrating them into a *concept*—a larger system or network of related ideas.

Although synthesis and analysis are virtually opposite thought processes, they complement each other. When you analyze, you disassemble information into its key parts. When you synthesize, you reassemble information into a whole. For instance, when writing this book, we analyzed published material in many fields (e.g., psychology, history, philosophy, and biology) and identified information from parts of these fields that were most relevant to promoting the success of beginning college students. We then synthesized or reassembled these parts to create a new whole—the textbook you're now reading.

Multidimensional Thinking

When you engage in multidimensional thinking, you view yourself and the world around you from different angles or vantage points. In particular, a multidimensional thinker is able to think from four key perspectives and determine how each of them influences, and is influenced by, the issue under discussion.

1. **Person (self).** How does this issue affect me as an individual? (The perspective of person.)
2. **Place.** What impact does this issue have on people living in different countries? (The perspective of place.)
3. **Time.** How will future generations of people be affected by this issue? (The perspective of time.)
4. **Culture.** How is this issue likely to be interpreted or experienced by groups of people who share different social customs and traditions? (The perspective of culture.)

Each of these four general perspectives has specific elements embedded within it. The four major perspectives, along with the key elements that comprise each of them, are listed and described in the **Snapshot Summary 8.2**. Note how these perspectives are consistent with those developed by the liberal arts (discussed in Chapter 2).

Snapshot Summary

8.2 Perspectives Associated with Multidimensional Thinking

Perspective 1: PERSON (Perspectives on different dimension of oneself)

Key Components
- **Intellectual (cognitive):** Knowledge, style of thinking, and self-concept
- **Emotional:** Feelings, emotional adjustment, and mental health
- **Social:** Interpersonal relationships and social interactions
- **Ethical:** Values and moral convictions
- **Physical:** Health and wellness
- **Spiritual:** Beliefs about the meaning or purpose of life and the hereafter
- **Vocational (occupational)**—Means of making a living and earning an income

Perspective 2: PLACE (Perspectives beyond the self that include progressively wider social and spatial distance)

Key Components
- **Family:** Parents, children, and other relatives
- **Community:** Local communities and neighborhoods
- **Society:** Societal institutions (e.g., schools, churches, and hospitals) and groups within society (e.g., social groups differing in age, gender, race, or socioeconomic status)
- **Nation:** One's own country or place of citizenship
- **International:** Citizens of different nations and territories
- **Global:** Planet earth (e.g., its life forms and natural resources)
- **Universe:** The galaxy that includes earth, other planets, and celestial bodies

Perspective 3: TIME (Chronological perspective)

Key Components
- **Historical:** The past
- **Contemporary:** The present
- **Futuristic:** The future

Perspective 4: CULTURE (Perspective of particular groups of people who share the same social heritage and traditions)

Key Components
- **Linguistic (language):** How group members communicate via spoken and written words and through nonverbal communication (body language)
- **Political:** How the group organizes societal authority and uses it to govern itself, make collective decisions, and maintain social order
- **Economic:** How the material wants and needs of the group are met through allocation of limited resources, and how wealth is distributed among its members
- **Geographical:** How the group's physical location influences the nature of social interactions and the way its members adapt to and use their environment
- **Aesthetic:** How the group appreciates and expresses artistic beauty and creativity through the arts (e.g., visual art, music, theater, literature, and dance)
- **Scientific:** How the group views, understands, and investigates natural phenomena through research (e.g., scientific tests and experiments)
- **Ecological:** How the group views its relationship to the surrounding biological world (e.g., other living creatures) and the physical environment
- **Anthropological:** How the group's culture originated, evolved, and developed over time
- **Sociological:** How the group's society is structured and organized into social subgroups and social institutions
- **Psychological:** How group members tend to think, feel, and interact with each other, and how their attitudes, opinions, or beliefs have been acquired
- **Philosophical:** The group's ideas or views on the nature of truth, goodness, wisdom, beauty, and the meaning or purpose of life
- **Theological:** Group members' ideas and beliefs about a transcendent, supreme being, and how they express their shared faith in a supreme being

Important human issues don't exist in isolation but as parts of complex, interconnected systems that involve the interplay of multiple factors and perspectives. For example, global warming is a current issue that involves the earth's atmosphere gradually thickening and trapping more heat due to a collection of greenhouse gases, which are being produced primarily by the burning of fossil fuels. It's theorized that this increase of manmade pollution is causing temperatures to rise (and sometimes fall) around the world and is contributing to natural disasters, such as droughts, wildfires, and dust storms (Joint Science Academies Statement, 2005; National Resources Defense Council, 2012). Understanding and addressing this issue involves interrelationships among a variety of perspectives, as depicted in **Figure 8.2**.

FIGURE 8.2

Person   Global warming involves us on an individual level because our personal efforts at energy conservation in our homes and our willingness to purchase energy-efficient products can play a major role in solving this problem.

Place   Global warming is an international issue that extends beyond the boundaries of one's own country to all countries in the world, and its solution will require worldwide collaboration.

Time   If the current trend toward higher global temperatures caused by global warming continues, it could seriously threaten the lives of future generations of people who inhabit our planet.

Culture   The problem of global warming has been caused by industries in technologically advanced cultures, yet the problem of rising global temperatures is likely to have its most negative impact on less technologically advanced cultures that lack the resources to respond to it (Joint Science Academies Statement, 2005). To prevent this from happening, technologically advanced cultures will need to use their advanced technology to devise alternative methods for generating energy that don't release heat-trapping gases into the atmosphere.

Understanding Global Warming from Four Key Perspectives

Addressing the issue of global warming also involves different components of our culture, including: (1) ecology: understanding the delicate interplay between humans and their natural environment, (2) science: need for research and development of alternative sources of energy, (3) economics: managing the cost incurred by industries to change their existing sources of energy, (4) politics: devising incentives or laws to encourage changes in industries' use of energy sources, and (5) international relations: collaboration between our nation and other nations that are currently contributing to this worldwide problem and that play pivotal roles in its future solution.

Reflection 8.4

Briefly explain how each of the perspectives of person, place, time, and culture may be involved in causing and solving one the following problems:

1. War and terrorism

2. Poverty and hunger

3. Prejudice and discrimination

4. Any world issue of your choice

Inferential Reasoning

When people make arguments or arrive at conclusions, they do so by starting with a premise (a statement or an observation) and use it to infer (step to) a conclusion. The following sentence starters demonstrate the process of inferential reasoning:

"Because this is true, it follows that . . ."

"Based on this evidence, I can conclude that . . ."

Inferential reasoning is the primary thought process humans use to reach conclusions about themselves and the world around them. This is also the form of thinking that you will use to make arguments and reach conclusions about ideas presented in your college courses. You'll often be required to take positions and draw conclusions by supporting them with solid evidence and sound reasoning. In a sense, you'll be asked to take on the role of a courtroom lawyer trying to prove a case by supplying supporting arguments and evidence (exhibit A, exhibit B, etc.).

The following are two major ways in which you use inferential reasoning to support your points or arguments:

1. **Citing empirical (observable) evidence.** Supporting your point with specific examples, personal experiences, facts, figures, statistical data, scientific research findings, expert testimonies, supporting quotes, or statements from leading authorities in the field.

2. **Using principles of logical consistency.** Showing that your conclusion follows or flows logically from an established premise or proposition. The following is an example of logical consistency:
   - The constitution guarantees all U.S. citizens the right to vote (established premise);
   - U.S. citizens include women and people of color; therefore,
   - Granting women and people of color the right to vote was logically consistent (and constitutional).

Both empirical evidence and logical consistency can be used to support the same argument. For instance, advocates for lowering the legal drinking age to 18 have argued that: (1) in other countries where drinking is allowed at age 18, statistics show fewer binge-drinking and drunk-driving problems than in the United States (empirical evidence), and (2) 18-year-olds in the United States are considered to be legal adults with respect to such rights and responsibilities as voting, serving on juries, joining the military, and being held responsible for committing crimes; therefore, 18-year-olds should have the right to drink.

Reflection **8.5**

Can you think of any arguments *against* lowering the drinking age to 18 that are based on empirical (observable) evidence or logical consistency?

Unfortunately, errors can be made in the inferential reasoning process, often referred to as *logical fallacies*. Some of the more common logical fallacies are summarized in the Snapshot Summary 8.3. As you read each of these reasoning errors, briefly note in the margin whether you've ever witnessed it or experienced it.

Snapshot Summary

8.3 Logical Fallacies: Inferential Reasoning Errors

- **Dogmatism.** Stubbornly clinging to a personally held viewpoint that's unsupported by evidence and remaining closed-minded (non-receptive) to other viewpoints that are better supported by evidence (for instance, those who believe that America's form of capitalism is the only economic system that can work in a successful democracy, while refusing to acknowledge that there are other successful democratic countries with different types of capitalistic economies).

"Facts do not cease to exist because they are ignored."

—Aldous Huxley, English writer and author of Brave New World.

- **Selective perception.** Seeing only examples and instances that support a position while overlooking or ignoring those that contradict it (e.g., believers in astrology who only notice and point out people whose personalities happen to fit their astrological signs, while overlooking those who don't).

"A very bad (and all too common) way to misread a newspaper: To see whatever supports your point of view as fact, and anything that contradicts your point of view as bias."

—Daniel Okrent, first public editor of *The New York Times* and inventor of Rotisserie League Baseball, the best-known form of fantasy baseball

- **Double standard.** Having two sets of standards for judgment: a higher standard for judging others and a lower standard for judging oneself. This is the classic "do as I say, not as I do" hypocrisy (e.g., critically evaluating and challenging the opinions of others but not our own).
- **Wishful thinking.** Thinking that something is true not on the basis of logic or evidence, but because the person wants it to be true (for instance, a teenage girl who believes she will not become pregnant, even though she and her boyfriend always have sex without using any form of contraception).

"Belief can be produced in practically unlimited quantity and intensity, without observation or reasoning, and even in defiance of both by the simple desire to believe."

—George Bernard Shaw, Irish playwright and Nobel Prize winner for literature

- **Hasty generalization.** Reaching a conclusion prematurely on the basis of a limited number of instances or experiences (e.g., concluding that people belonging to a group are all or nearly all "that way" on the basis of personal experiences with only one or two individuals).
- **Jumping to a conclusion.** Making a leap of logic to reach a conclusion that's based on only one reason or factor while ignoring other possible reasons and contributing factors (e.g., immediately concluding that "I must be a real loser" after being rejected for a date or a job)
- **Glittering generality.** Making a positive general statement without supplying details or evidence to back it up (e.g., writing a letter of recommendation describing someone as a "wonderful person" with a "great personality" but not providing any reasons or evidence to support these claims).
- **Straw man argument.** Distorting an opponent's position and then attacking it (e.g., attacking an opposing political candidate for supporting censorship and restricting civil liberties when the opponent supported only a ban on violent pornography).
- **Ad *hominem* argument.** Aiming an argument at the person rather than the person's argument (e.g., telling a younger person, "You're too young and inexperienced to know what you're talking about," or telling an older person, "You're too old-fashioned to understand this issue"). Literally translated, the term *ad hominem* means "to the man."
- **Red herring.** Bringing up an irrelevant issue that disguises or distracts attention from the real issue being discussed or debated (e.g., responding to

criticism of former President Richard Nixon's involvement in the Watergate scandal by arguing, "He was a good president who accomplished many good things while he was in office"). The term *red herring* derives from an old practice of dragging a herring—a strong-smelling fish—across a trail to distract the scent of pursuing dogs. (In the example, Nixon's effectiveness as a president is an irrelevant issue or a red herring; the real issue being discussed is Nixon's behavior in the Watergate scandal.)

- **Smoke screen.** Intentionally disguising or covering up true reasons or motives with reasons that confuse or mislead others (e.g., opposing gun control legislation by arguing that it is a violation of the constitutional right to bear arms without revealing that the opponent of the legislation is receiving financial support from gun manufacturing companies).

- **Slippery slope.** Using fear tactics by arguing that not accepting a position will result in a "domino effect"—one bad thing happening after another, like a series of falling dominoes (e.g., "If someone experiments with marijuana, it will automatically lead to loss of motivation, harder drugs, and withdrawal from college").

- **Rhetorical deception.** Using deceptive language to conclude that something is true without providing reasons or evidence (e.g., glibly making statements such as: "Clearly this is . . ." "It is obvious that . . ." or "Any reasonable person can see . . ." without explaining why it's so clear, obvious, or reasonable).

- **Circular reasoning (a.k.a. "begging the question").** Drawing a conclusion that's merely a rewording or restatement of one's position without any supporting reasons or evidence, leaving the original question still unanswered and the issue still unsolved. This form of reasoning basically draws conclusion logically by claiming "it's true because it's true" (e.g., "Stem cell research shouldn't be legal because it shouldn't be done").

- **Appealing to authority or prestige.** Believing that if an authority figure or celebrity says it's true then it must be true or should be done (e.g., buying product X simply because a famous actor or athlete uses it, or believing that if someone in authority, such as the U.S. president, says something should be done, then it must be the right or best thing to do).

- **Appealing to tradition or familiarity.** Concluding that if something has always been thought to be true or has always been done in a certain way, then it must be true or the best way to do it (e.g., "This is the way it's always been done, so it must be right").

- **Appealing to popularity or the majority (a.k.a. jumping on the bandwagon).** Believing that if it's popular or held by the majority of people, it must be true (e.g., "So many people believe in psychics, it has to be true; they can't all be wrong").

- **Appealing to emotion.** Believing in something based on the emotional intensity experienced when the claim is made, rather than the quality of reasoning or evidence used to support the claim (e.g., "If I feel strongly about something, it must be true"). The expressions "Always trust your feelings" and "Just listen to your heart" may not always lead to the most accurate conclusions and the best decisions because they could be driven more by emotion than by reason.

"Political talk shows have become shouting matches designed to push emotional hot buttons and drive us further apart. We desperately need to exchange ideas with one another rationally and courteously."

—David Boren, president of the University of Oklahoma and longest-serving chairman of the U.S. Senate Intelligence Committee

Note: For evaluations of the factual accuracy of statements made by politicians in TV ads, debates, speeches, interviews, and news releases, go to www.factcheck.org or www.politifact.com.

Reflection **8.6**

Glance back at the reasoning errors summarized in the Snapshot Summary 8.3. Identify the two most common errors you've witnessed or experienced.

What was the situation in which these errors took place?

Why do you think they occurred?

Author's Experience   Soon after my wife and I were married, we moved to a new city and tried to find a place to live. We got up early one morning, skipped breakfast, and drove to the town where we were planning to move. We were determined to find an apartment to rent before lunch, but we found ourselves still driving around town from place to place in the middle of the afternoon. By this time, both of us were famished because we hadn't eaten anything since the night before; we decided to stop looking for a place to live and start looking for a place to eat.

Unfortunately, we had about as much luck finding a place to eat as we did finding a place to live. It was approaching 4 p.m. and we were now beginning to hear lion-like growls coming from our stomachs. While I was driving, my wife suddenly elbowed me (hard) and exclaimed, "Joe, look—fried chicken!" She pointed to a flashing sign in the distance; I couldn't read the sign clearly, but figured her long-range vision was better than me. So, I hit the accelerator and sped up to get there as fast as was legally possible. As we continued down the road, I still couldn't see any flashing sign that read "fried chicken." Finally, I did see a sign flashing sign and thought to myself, "That must be it!" However, as I drove closer and closer to the flashing sign, it became clearer and clearer to me that it didn't spell FRIED CHICKEN at all. Instead, it was a sign flashing the words: FREE CHECKING! FREE CHECKING!

We had a great laugh about my wife's perceptual error. She wasn't joking when she first saw the flashing sign in the distance; she really did think it was flashing the words "fried chicken." That experience proved to me beyond a doubt that human beings engage in selection perception—we tend to see what we *want* (or hope) to see, rather than reality.

Joe Cuseo

Reflection 8.7

Have you ever had the experience of seeing what you hoped or expected to see, rather than seeing things accurately (objectively)? Or, have you ever observed this happen to someone else?

What was the situation?

Why do you think that you (or the person you observed) did not view the situation accurately or objectively?

Balanced Thinking

Balanced thinking involves seeking out and carefully considering evidence for and against a particular position. The process of supporting a position with evidence is technically referred to as *adduction*; when you adduce, you offer reasons for a position. The process of arguing against a position by presenting contradictory evidence or reasons is called *refutation*; when you refute, you provide a rebuttal by supplying evidence *against* a particular position. The opposing position's stronger arguments are acknowledged, and its weaker ones are refuted (Fairbairn & Winch, 1996).

Balanced thinking involves both adduction and refutation. The goal of a balanced thinker is not to stack up evidence for one position or the other, but to be an impartial investigator who looks at supporting and opposing evidence for both sides of an issue and attempts to reach a conclusion that's not biased or one-sided. Thus, the first step in the process of seeking truth should not be to immediately jump in and take an either-or (for or against) stance on a debatable issue. Instead, your first step should be to look at arguments for and against each position, acknowledge the strengths and weaknesses of both sides of the argument, and identify what additional information may still be needed to make a fair judgment or reach a reasonable conclusion.

Balanced thinking requires more than just adding up the number of arguments for and against a position; it also involves weighing the strength of those arguments, because arguments can vary in terms of their level of importance and degree of support. When evaluating arguments, ask yourself, "How sure am I about the conclusion made by this argument?" Determine whether the evidence is:

1. **Definitive.** So strong or compelling that a definite conclusion should be reached;
2. **Suggestive.** Strong enough to suggest that a tentative conclusion may be reached; or
3. **Inconclusive.** Too weak to reach any conclusion.

"The more you know, the less sure you are."

—Voltaire, French historian, philosopher, and advocate for civil liberty

Remember

A characteristic of balanced thinking is being mindful of the weight (degree of importance) you assign to different arguments and articulating how their weight has been factored into your final conclusion (e.g., in a written report or class presentation).

In some cases, after you review both supporting and contradictory evidence for opposing positions, balanced thinking may lead you to suspend judgment and to withhold making a firm decision that favors one position over the other. A balanced thinker may occasionally reach the following conclusions: "Right now, I can't be sure; the evidence doesn't strongly favor one position over the other," or "More information is needed before I can make a final judgment or reach a firm conclusion." This isn't being wishy-washy: these are legitimate conclusions to draw, as long as they are informed conclusions supported by sound reasons and solid evidence. In fact, it's better to hold an undecided but informed viewpoint based on balanced thinking than to hold a definite opinion that's uninformed, biased, or based on emotion—such as the opinions offered loudly and obnoxiously by people on radio and TV talk shows.

"Too often we enjoy the comfort of opinion without the discomfort of thought."

—John F. Kennedy, 35th president of the United States

Reflection 8.8

Consider the following positions:

1. Course requirements should be eliminated; college students should be allowed to choose the classes they want to take for their degree.

2. Course grades should be eliminated; college students should take classes on a pass-fail basis.

Using balanced thinking, identify one or more arguments *for* and *against* each of these positions.

"I always seemed to stand in the no man's land between opposing arguments, yearning to be won over by one side or the other but finding instead degrees of merit in both. But in time I came to accept, even embrace, what I called 'my confusion.' I preferred to listen rather than speak; to inquire, not crusade."

—"In Praise of the 'Wobblies'" by Ted Gup, journalist who has written for *Time Magazine, National Geographic,* and *The New York Times*

Remember

When you combine balanced thinking with multidimensional thinking, you become a more complex and comprehensive thinker who is capable of viewing any issue from opposing sides and different angles.

Critical Thinking

Critical thinking is a form of higher-level thinking that involves *evaluation* or *judgment*. The evaluation can be either positive or negative: for example, a movie critic can give a good (thumbs up) or bad (thumbs down) review of a film. However, critical thinking involves much more than simply stating, "I liked it," or "I didn't like it." Specific reasons or evidence must be supplied to support the critique; failure to do so makes the criticism unfounded—i.e., it has no foundation or basis of support.

Reflection **8.9**

Flash back to the journal entry at the start of this chapter. How does your response to the incomplete sentence compare with the definition of critical thinking we just provided?

How are they similar?

How do they differ?

(If you wrote that critical thinking means "being critical" or negatively criticizing something or somebody, don't feel bad. Many students think that critical thinking has this negative meaning or connotation.)

Critical thinking is used to evaluate many things besides films, art, or music: it's also used to judge the quality of ideas, beliefs, choices, and decisions—whether they be your own or those of others. It's also a skill that's highly valued by professors teaching students at all stages in the college experience and all subjects in the college curriculum (Higher Education Institute, 2009; Stark et al., 1990). By working on developing these skills now, you'll significantly improve your academic performance throughout your college experience. You can start developing the mental habit of critical thinking by regularly asking yourself the following questions as criteria for evaluating any idea or argument:

1. **Validity (truthfulness).** Is it true or accurate?
2. **Morality (ethics).** Is it fair or just?
3. **Beauty (aesthetics).** Is it beautiful or artistic?
4. **Practicality (usefulness).** Can it be put to use for practical purposes?
5. **Priority (order of importance or effectiveness).** Is it the best option or alternative?

Author's Experience   When I teach classes or give workshops, I often challenge students or participants to debate me on either politics or religion. For their debate topic, I ask them to choose a political party affiliation, a religion or a branch of religion, or a stance on a social issue for which there are political or religious viewpoints. The ground rules are as follows: they choose the topic for debate; they can only use facts to pose their argument, rebuttal, or both; and they can only respond in a rational manner, without letting emotions drive their answers. This exercise usually reveals that the topics people feel strongly about are often topics that they have not critically evaluated. People often say they are Democrat, Republican, independent, and so on, and argue from this position. However, few of them have taken the time to critically examine whether their stated affiliation is actually consistent with their personal viewpoints. For example, they almost always answer "no" to the following questions: "Have you read the core document (e.g., party platform) that outlines the party stance?" and "Have you engaged in self-examination of your party affiliation through reasoned discussions with others who say they have the same or a different political affiliation?"

Aaron Thompson

Creative Thinking

When you think creatively, you generate something new or different, whether that may be a novel idea, strategy, or work product. Creative thinking leads you to ask the question, "Why not?" (e.g., "Why not do it a different way?"). It could be said that when you think critically you look "inside the box" and evaluate the quality of its content. When you think creatively, you look "outside the box" to imagine other packages containing different content.

Any time you combine two existing ideas to generate a new idea, you're engaging in creative thinking. Creative thinking can be viewed as an extension or higher form of synthesis, whereby parts of separate ideas are combined or integrated to create a final product that turns out to be different (and better) than what previously existed (Anderson & Krathwohl, 2001). Even in the arts, what's created isn't totally original or unique. Instead, artistic creativity typically involves a combination or rearrangement of previously existing elements to generate a new "whole"—a final product that is distinctive or noticeably different. For instance, hard rock was created by combining elements of blues and rock and roll, and folk rock took form when Bob Dylan combined musical elements of acoustic blues and amplified rock (Shelton et al., 2003). Robert Kearns (subject of the film *Flash of Genius*) combined preexisting mechanical parts to create the intermittent windshield wiper (Seabrook, 2008).

Creative and critical thinking are two of the most important forms of higher-level thinking, and they work well together. We use creative thinking to ask new questions and generate new ideas; we use critical thinking to evaluate or critique the ideas we create (Paul & Elder, 2004). A creative idea must not only be different or original: it must also be effective (Sternberg, 2001; Runco, 2004). If critical thinking reveals that the quality of what we've created is poor, we then shift back to creative thinking to generate something new and improved. Or, we may start by using critical thinking to evaluate an old idea or approach and come to the judgment that it's not very good. This unfavorable evaluation naturally leads to and turns on the creative thinking process, which tries to come up with a new idea or different approach that's better than the old one.

"The principal mark of genius is not perfection but originality, the opening of new frontiers."

–Arthur Koestler, Hungarian novelist and philosopher

"The blues are the roots. Everything else are the fruits."

–Willie Dixon, blues songwriter; commenting on how all forms of contemporary American music contain elements of blues music, which originated among African American slaves

Brainstorming is a problem-solving process that effectively illustrates how creative and critical thinking complement each other. The steps or stages involved in the process of brainstorming are summarized in **Do It Now! 8.1**. As the brainstorming process suggests, creativity doesn't just happen suddenly or effortlessly, like the so-called stroke of genius; instead, it takes considerable mental effort (Paul & Elder, 2004; De Bono, 2007). Although creative thinking initially involves some spontaneous and intuitive leaps; it also involves careful reflection and evaluation of whether any of those leaps actually land you on a good idea.

8.1   DO IT **NOW** !

The Process of Brainstorming

1. List as many ideas as you can, generating them rapidly without stopping to evaluate their validity or practicality. Studies show that worrying about whether an idea is correct often blocks creativity (Basadur, Runco, & Vega, 2000). So, at this stage of the process, just let your imagination run wild; don't worry about whether the idea you generate is impractical, unrealistic, or outrageous.

2. Use the ideas on your list as a springboard to trigger additional ideas, or combine them to create new ideas.

3. After you run out of ideas, review and critically evaluate the list of ideas you've generated and eliminate those that you think are least effective.

4. From the remaining list of ideas, choose the best idea or best combination of ideas.

Note: The first two steps in the brainstorming process involve *divergent thinking*—a form of creative thinking that allows you to go off in different directions and generate diverse ideas. In contrast, the last two steps in the process involve *convergent thinking*—a form of critical thinking in which you converge (focus in) and narrow down the ideas, evaluating each of them for their effectiveness.

Author's Experience

Several years ago, I was working with a friend to come up with ideas for a grant proposal. We started out by sitting at his kitchen table, exchanging ideas while sipping coffee; then we both got up and began to pace back and forth, walking all around the room while bouncing different ideas off each other. Whenever a new idea was thrown out, one of us would jot it down (whoever was pacing closer to the kitchen table at the moment).

After we ran out of ideas, we shifted gears, slowed down, and sat down at the table again to critique each of the ideas we'd just generated during our "binge-thinking" episode. After some debate, we finally settled on an idea that we judged to be the best of all the ideas we produced, and we used this idea for the grant proposal.

"Creativity is allowing oneself to make mistakes; art is knowing which ones to keep."

—Scott Adams, creator of the comic strip *Dilbert* and author of *The Dilbert Principle*

Although I wasn't fully aware of it at the time, the stimulating thought process we were using was called brainstorming because it involved both of its key stages: we first engaged in creative thinking—our fast-paced walking and idea-production stage; we followed that with critical thinking—our slower-paced sitting and idea-evaluation stage.

Joe Cuseo

Lastly, keep in mind that creative thinking is not restricted to the arts: it can occur in all subject areas, even in fields that seek precision and definite answers. For example, in math, creative thinking may involve using new approaches or strategies for arriving at a correct solution to a problem. In science, creative thinking takes place when a scientist first uses imaginative thinking to create a hypothesis or logical hunch ("What might happen if . . . ?"), then conducts an experiment to test whether that hypothesis proves to be true.

Strategies for Developing Higher-Level Thinking Skills and Using Them to Improve Academic Performance

Thus far, this chapter has been devoted primarily to helping you get a clear idea about what higher-level thinking is and what its major forms are. The remainder of this chapter focuses on helping you develop habits of higher-level thinking and apply these habits to improve your performance in the first year of college and beyond.

1. **Cross-reference and connect any ideas you acquire in class with related ideas you acquire from your assigned reading.** When you discover information in your reading that relates to something you've learned about in class (or vice versa), make a note of it in the margin of your textbook or your class notebook. By integrating knowledge you've obtained from these two major sources, you're using synthesis—a higher-level thinking skill that you can then demonstrate on course exams and assignments to improve your course grades.

2. **When listening to lectures and completing reading assignments, pay attention not only to the content being covered, but also to the thought process that accompanies the content.** Periodically ask yourself what form of higher-level thinking your instructors are using during major segments of a class presentation and what your textbook authors are using in different sections of a chapter. The more conscious you are of the types of higher-level thinking skills you're being exposed to, the more likely you are to acquire those thinking skills and demonstrate them on exams and assignments.

3. **Periodically pause to reflect on your own thinking process.** When working on your courses, ask yourself what type of thinking you're doing (e.g., analysis, synthesis, or evaluation) during the work process. When you think about your own thinking, you're engaging in a mental process known as *metacognition*—that is, you're aware of how you're thinking while you're thinking (Flavell, 1979; Hartman, 2001). Metacognition is a mental habit that's associated with higher-level thinking and improved problem-solving skills (Halpern, 2003; Resnick, 1986).

4. **Develop habits of higher-level thinking by asking yourself higher-level thinking questions.** One simple but powerful way to think about your thinking is through self-questioning. Since questions have the power to activate and elevate your thinking and since thinking often involves talking silently to yourself, if you make an intentional attempt to ask yourself good questions, you can train your mind to think at a higher level. A good question can serve as a launching pad that propels you to higher levels of thinking in your quest to answer it. The higher the level of thinking called for by the questions you regularly ask yourself, the higher the level of thinking you will display in class discussions, on college exams, and in written assignments.

"Imagination should give wings to our thoughts, but imagination must be checked and documented by the factual results of the experiment."

—Louis Pasteur, French microbiologist, chemist, and inventor of pasteurization (a method for preventing milk and wine from going sour)

"To think is to talk to oneself."

—Immanuel Kant, German philosopher

"If you do not ask the right questions, you do not get the right answers."

—Edward Hodnett, British poet

Asking yourself a good question can stimulate your higher-level thinking about almost any experience, whether it takes place inside or outside the classroom.

Happy Hour, 4–6 PM
All Drinks—$2

Reflection Hour, Anytime
"What Is Happiness?"
All Thoughts—Priceless

Pub & Grub

© Kendall Hunt

In **Do It Now! 8.2** you'll find numerous questions that have been intentionally designed to promote higher-level thinking. The questions are constructed in a way that will allow you to easily fill in the blank and apply the type of thinking called for by the question to ideas or issues being discussed in any course you may take. Considerable research indicates that students can learn to use questions such as these to improve their higher-level thinking ability in various subject areas (King, 1990, 1995; 2002).

As you read each set of trigger questions, place a checkmark next to one question in the set that could be applied to a concept or issue being covered in a course you're taking this term.

Reflection **8.10**

Look back at the forms of thinking described in Snapshot Summary 8.3. Identify one question listed under each set of trigger questions in Do It Now! 8.2 and fill in the blank with an idea or issue being covered in a course you're taking this term.

8.2   DO IT **NOW** !

Self-Questioning Strategies for Triggering Different Forms of Higher-Level Thinking

Application (applied thinking). Putting knowledge into practice to solve problems and resolve issues.

Trigger Questions

- How can this idea be used to _____?
- How could this concept be implemented to _____?
- How can this theory be put into practice to _____?
- What could be done to prevent or reduce _____?

Analysis (analytical thinking). Breaking down information into its essential elements or parts.

Trigger Questions

- What are the main ideas contained in _____?
- What are the important aspects of _____?
- What are the issues raised by _____?
- What are the major purposes of _____?
- What assumptions or biases lie hidden within _____? _____
- What are the reasons behind _____?

Synthesis. Integrating separate pieces of information to form a more complete product or pattern.

Trigger Questions

- How can this idea be joined or connected with _____ to create a more complete or comprehensive understanding of _____?
- How could these different _____ be grouped together into a more general class or category?
- How could these separate _____ be reorganized or rearranged to produce a more comprehensive understanding of the big picture?

Multidimensional thinking. Thinking that involves viewing yourself and the world around you from different angles or vantage points.

Trigger Questions

- How would _____ affect different dimensions of myself (emotional, physical, etc.)?
- What broader impact would _____ have on the social and physical world around me?
- How might people living in different times (e.g., past and future) view _____?

- How would people from different cultural backgrounds interpret or react to _____?
- Have I taken into consideration all the major factors that could influence _____ or be influenced by _____?

Inferential reasoning. Making an argument or judgment by inferring (stepping to) a conclusion that's supported by empirical (observable) evidence or logical consistency.

Trigger Questions Seeking Empirical Evidence

- What examples support the argument that _____?
- What research evidence is there for _____?
- What statistical data document that this _____ is true?

Trigger Questions Seeking Logical Consistency

- Since _____ is true, why shouldn't _____ also be true?
- If people believe in _____, shouldn't they practice _____?
- To make the statement that _____, wouldn't it have to be assumed that _____?

Balanced thinking. Carefully considering reasons for and against a particular position or viewpoint.

Trigger Questions

- Have I considered both sides of _____?
- What are the strengths (advantages) and weaknesses (disadvantages) of _____?
- What evidence supports and contradicts _____?
- What are arguments for and counterarguments against _____?

Trigger Questions for Adduction (arguing for a particular idea or position by supplying supporting evidence)

- What proof is there for _____?
- What are logical arguments for _____?
- What research evidence supports _____?

Trigger Questions for Refutation (arguing against a particular idea or position by supplying contradictory evidence)

- What proof is there against _____?
- What logical arguments indicate that _____ is false?
- What research evidence contradicts _____?
- What counterarguments would provide an effective rebuttal to _____?

(continued)

Critical thinking. Making well-informed evaluations or judgments.

Trigger Questions for Evaluating Validity (Truthfulness)

- Is _____ true or accurate?
- Is there sufficient evidence to support the conclusion that _____?
- Is the reasoning behind _____ strong or weak?

Trigger Questions for Evaluating Morality (Ethics)

- Is _____ fair?
- Is _____ just?
- Is this action consistent with the professed or stated values of _____?

Trigger Questions for Evaluating Beauty (Aesthetics)

- What is the artistic merit of _____?
- Does _____ have any aesthetic value?
- Does _____ contribute to the beauty of the world?

Trigger Questions for Evaluating Practicality (Usefulness)

- Will _____ work?
- How can _____ be put to good use?
- What practical benefit would result from _____?

Trigger Questions for Evaluating Priority (Order of Importance or Effectiveness)

- Which one of these _____ is the most important?
- Is this _____ the best option or choice available?
- How should these _____ be ranked from first to last (best to worst) in terms of their effectiveness?

Creative thinking. Generating ideas that are unique, original, or distinctively different.

Trigger Questions

- What could be invented to _____?
- Imagine what would happen if _____?
- What might be a different way to _____?
- How would this change if _____?
- What would be an ingenious way to _____.

Note: Save these higher-level thinking questions so that you can use them when completing different academic tasks required by your courses (e.g., preparing for exams, writing papers or reports, and participating in class discussions or study-group sessions). Try to get into the habit of periodically stepping back to reflect on your thinking process. Ask yourself what type of thinking you are doing (such as analysis, synthesis, or evaluation) and record your personal reflections in writing. You could even keep a "thinking log" or "thinking journal" to increase self-awareness of the thinking strategies you develop across time, or how your thinking strategies may vary across different courses and academic fields. This strategy will not only help you acquire higher-level thinking skills: it will also help you describe the thinking skills you have acquired during job interviews and in letters of application for career positions.

5. **To stimulate creative thinking, use the following strategies.**

- **Be flexible.** Think about ideas and objects in unusual or unconventional ways. The power of flexible and unconventional thinking is well illustrated in the movie *Apollo 13*, which is based on the real story of an astronaut saving his life by creatively using duct tape as an air filter. The inventor of the printing press (Johannes Gutenberg) made his groundbreaking discovery while watching a machine being used to crush grapes at a wine harvest. He thought that the same type of machine could be used to press letters onto paper (Dorfman, Shames, & Kihlstrom, 1996).

- **Be experimental.** Play with ideas, trying them out to see whether they'll work and work better than the status quo. Studies show that creative people tend to be mental risk-takers who experiment with ideas and techniques (Sternberg, 2001). Consciously resist the temptation to settle for the security of familiarity. Doing things the way they've always been done doesn't mean you're doing them the best way possible. It may mean that it's just the most habitual (and mindless) way to do them. When people cling rigidly or stubbornly to what's conventional or traditional, what they're doing is clinging to the comfort or security of what's most familiar and predictable, which blocks originality, ingenuity, and openness to change.

- **Get mobile.** Get up and move around. Studies show that the brain gets approximately 10 percent more oxygen when we stand up than it does when we're sitting down (Sousa, 2006). Since oxygen provides fuel for the brain, our ability to think creatively is stimulated when we think on our feet and move around, rather than sitting on our butts for extended periods of time.

- **Get it down.** Carry a pen and a small notepad or packet of sticky notes (or a portable electronic recording device) with you at all times to record creative ideas, because these ideas often come to mind at the most unexpected times. The process of creative ideas suddenly popping into your mind is sometimes referred to as *incubation*—just like incubated eggs can hatch at any time, ideas can suddenly hatch and pop into consciousness after you've sat on them for a while. Unfortunately, however, just as an idea can suddenly come into mind, it can just as suddenly slip out of mind when you start thinking about something else. You can prevent this from happening by having the right equipment on hand to record your creative ideas as soon as you have them.

- **Get diverse.** Seek ideas from diverse social and informational sources. Bouncing your ideas off of different people and getting their ideas about your idea is a good way to generate energy, synergy, and serendipity (accidental discoveries). Studies show that creative people venture well beyond the boundaries of their particular area of training or specialization (Baer, 1993; Kaufman & Baer, 2002). They have wide-ranging interests and knowledge, which they draw upon and combine to generate new ideas (Riquelme, 2002). Be on the lookout to combine the knowledge and skills you acquire from different subject areas and different people to create bridges to new ideas.

- **Take a break.** When working on a problem that you can't seem to solve, stop working on it for a while and come back to it later. Creative solutions often come to mind after you stop thinking about the problem. When you're trying so hard and working so intensely on a problem or challenging task, your attention may become mentally set or rigidly fixed on one aspect of it (German & Barrett, 2005; Maier, 1970). Taking your mind off of it and returning to it at a later point allows the problem to incubate in your mind at a lower level of consciousness and stress. This can sometimes give birth to a sudden solution. Furthermore, when you come back to the task later, your focus of attention is likely to shift to a different feature or aspect of the problem. This new focus may enable you to view the problem from a different angle or vantage point, which can lead to a breakthrough idea that was blocked by your previous perspective (Anderson, 2000).

- **Reorganize the problem.** When you're stuck on a problem, try rearranging its parts or pieces. Rearrangement can transform the problem into a different pattern that provides you with a new perspective. The new perspective may position you to suddenly see a solution that was previously overlooked, much like changing the order of letters in a word jumble can suddenly enable you to see the hidden scrambled word. By changing the wording of any problem you're working on, or by recording ideas on index cards (or sticky notes) and laying them out in different orders and arrangements, you may suddenly see a solution.

- If you're having trouble solving problems that involve a sequence of steps (e.g., math problems), try reversing the sequence and start by working from the end or middle. The new sequence changes your approach to the problem by forcing you to come at it from a different direction, which can sometimes provide you with an alternative path to its solution.

"I make progress by having people around who are smarter than I am—and listening to them. And I assume that everyone is smarter about something than I am."

—Henry Kaiser, successful industrialist, known as the father of American shipbuilding

"Eureka!" (Literally translated, "I have found it!")

—Attributed to Archimedes, ancient Greek mathematician and inventor, when he suddenly discovered (while sitting in a bathtub) how to measure the purity of gold

"Creativity consists largely of re-arranging what we know in order to find out what we do not know."

—George Keller, prolific American architect and originator of the Union Station design for elevated train stations

"Genius is 1% inspiration and 99% perspiration."

—Thomas Edison, scientist and creator of more than 1,000 inventions, including the light bulb, phonograph, and motion picture camera

- **Be persistent.** Studies show that creativity takes time, dedication, and hard work (Ericsson, 2006; Ericsson & Charness, 1994). Creative thoughts often do not emerge in one sudden stroke of genius, but evolve gradually after repeated reflection and persistent effort.

Summary and Conclusion

Since higher-level thinking is the number one educational goal of college professors, developing this skill is crucial for achieving academic excellence. In addition to improving academic performance in college, developing higher-level thinking skills have three other critical benefits.

Reflection **8.11**

The popularity of sticky notes is no doubt due to their versatility—you can post them on almost anything, remove them from where they were stuck (without a mess), and re-stick them somewhere else.

Think creatively for a minute. In what ways could college students use sticky notes to help complete the academic tasks they face in college? Think of as many ways as possible.

1. **Higher-level thinking is essential in today's "information age," in which new information is being generated at faster rates than at any other time in human history.** The majority of new workers in the information age will no longer work with their hands but will instead work with their heads (Miller, 2003), and, as discussed in Chapter 2, employers will value college graduates who have inquiring minds and possess higher-level thinking skills (Harvey, Moon, Geall, & Bower, 1997; Peter D. Hart Research Associates, 2006).
2. **Higher-level thinking skills are vital for citizens in a democracy.** Authoritarian political systems, such as dictatorships and fascist regimes, suppress critical thought and demand submissive obedience to authority. In contrast, citizens living in a democracy are expected to control their political destiny by choosing (electing) their political leaders; thus, judging and choosing wisely are crucial civic responsibilities in a democratic nation. Citizens living and voting in a democracy must use higher-level reasoning skills, such as balanced and critical thinking, to make wise political choices.
3. **Higher-level thinking is an important safeguard against prejudice, discrimination, and hostility.** Racial, ethnic, and national prejudices often stem from narrow, self-centered, or group-centered thinking (Paul & Elder, 2002). Prejudice often results from oversimplified, dualistic thinking that can lead individuals to categorize other people into either "in" groups (us) or "out" groups (them). This type of dualistic thinking can lead, in turn, to ethnocentrism—the tendency to view one's own racial or ethnic group as the superior "in" group and see other groups as inferior "out" groups. Development of higher-level thinking skills, such as taking multiple perspectives and using balanced thinking, counteracts the type of dualistic, ethnocentric thinking that leads to prejudice, discrimination, and hate crimes.

Learning More through the World Wide Web

Internet-Based Resources for Further Information on Higher-Level Thinking

For additional information related to the ideas discussed in this chapter, we recommend the following Web sites:

Critical Thinking:

www.criticalthinking.org

Creative Thinking:

www.amcreativityassoc.org

Higher-Level Thinking Skills:

www.wcu.edu/ceap/houghton/Learner/think/thinkhigherorder.html

Chapter 8 Exercises

8.1 Self-Assessment of Higher-Level Thinking Characteristics

Listed here are four general characteristics of higher-level thinkers accompanied by a set of traits related to each characteristic. When you read the traits listed beneath each of the general characteristics, place a checkmark next to any trait that you think is true of you.

Characteristics of Higher-Level Thinkers

1. **Tolerant and Accepting**
   - Keep emotions under control when someone criticizes their viewpoint
   - Do not tune out ideas that conflict with their own
   - Feel comfortable with disagreement
   - Are receptive to hearing different points of view

2. **Inquisitive and Open-Minded**
   - Are eager to continue learning new things from different people and different experiences
   - Have an inquiring mind that's genuinely curious, inquisitive, and ready to explore new ideas
   - Find differences of opinion and opposing viewpoints interesting and stimulating
   - Attempt to understand why people hold different viewpoints and try to find common ground between them

3. **Reflective and Tentative**
   - Suspend judgment until all the evidence is in, rather than making snap judgments before knowing the whole story
   - Acknowledge the complexity, ambiguity, and uncertainty associated with certain issues, and are willing to perhaps say, "I need to give this more thought," or "I need more evidence before I can draw a conclusion"
   - Take time to think things through before drawing conclusions, making choices, and reaching decisions
   - Periodically reexamine personal viewpoints to see whether they should be maintained or changed as a result of new experiences and evidence

4. **Honest and Courageous**
   - Give fair consideration to ideas that others may instantly disapprove of or find distasteful
   - Are willing to express personal viewpoints that may not conform to those of the majority
   - Are willing to change old opinions or beliefs when they are contradicted by new evidence
   - Are willing to acknowledge the limitations or weaknesses of their attitudes and beliefs

Look back at the list and count the number of checkmarks you placed in each of the four general areas:

1. Tolerant and Accepting = _____

2. Inquisitive and Open-Minded = _____

3. Reflective and Tentative = _____

4. Honest and Courageous = _____

For which characteristic did you have (a) the *most* checkmarks, (b) the *least* checkmarks?

What do you think accounts for this difference?

8.2 Demonstrating Higher-Level Thinking in Your Current Courses

Look at the syllabus for three courses you're enrolled in this term and find an assignment or exam that carries the greatest weight (counts the most) toward your final course grade. If you're taking fewer than three courses, you can choose more than one assignment or exam from the same course.

Course	Major Assignment or Test
1.	
2.	
3.	

On the grid that follows, place a checkmark in each box that represents the form of higher-level thinking you think will be required on each of these major assignments or tests. (For a quick review of the major forms of higher-level thinking, see the higher-level thinking definitions on p. 191.)

Major Assignment or Test

	Course 1	Course 2	Course 3
Applied Thinking			
Analysis			
Synthesis			
Multidimensional Thinking			
Inferential Reasoning			
Balanced Thinking			
Critical Thinking			
Creative Thinking			

Choose one box you checked for each course and describe how you would demonstrate that particular form of higher-level thinking on that particular assignment or test. For instance, if you checked a box indicating that you will use multidimensional thinking, describe what perspectives or factors you will take into consideration.

Course 1 exam or assignment: _____

Form of higher-level thinking required:

How I plan to demonstrate this form of thinking:

Course 2 exam or assignment: _____

Form of higher-level thinking required:

How I plan to demonstrate this form of thinking:

Course 3 exam or assignment: _____

Form of higher-level thinking required:

How I plan to demonstrate this form of thinking:

Case Study

Trick or Treat: Confusing or Challenging Test?

Students in Professor Plato's philosophy course just got their first exam back and they're going over the test together in class. Some students are angry because they feel that Professor Plato deliberately included "trick questions" to confuse them. Professor Plato responds by saying that his test questions were not designed to trick the class but to "challenge them to think."

Reflection and Discussion Questions

1. Why do you think that some students thought that Professor Plato was trying to trick or confuse them?

2. What do you think the professor meant when he told his students that his test questions were designed to "challenge them to think"?

3. On future tests, what might the students do to reduce the likelihood that they will feel tricked again?

4. On future tests, what might Professor Plato do to reduce the likelihood that students will complain about being asked "trick questions"?

Social and Emotional Intelligence

Relating to Others and Regulating Our Emotions

ACTIVATE YOUR THINKING — *Reflection* **9.1**

When you think about someone who's "intelligent," what personal characteristics come to mind? Why?

LEARNING GOAL

To acquire social and emotional knowledge and skills to enhance the quality of your interpersonal relationships and mental health.

Social intelligence (a.k.a. interpersonal intelligence) refers to the ability to communicate and relate effectively to others (Gardner, 1993, 1999). It's a major type of human intelligence, which research indicates is a better predictor of personal and professional success than intellectual ability (Goleman, 2006). *Emotional intelligence* refers to the ability to identify and monitor our emotions and to remain aware of how our emotions affect our thoughts and actions (Salovey & Mayer, 1990). Emotional intelligence has been found to be a better predictor of personal and occupational success than performance on intellectual intelligence tests (Goleman, 1995). These two important elements of human intelligence and personal success are the focus points of this chapter.

"The most important single ingredient in the formula of success is knowing how to get along with people."

—Theodore (Teddy) Roosevelt, 26th president of the United States and winner of the Nobel Peace Prize

"I will pay more for the ability to deal with people than any other ability under the sun."

—John D. Rockefeller, American industrialist and philanthropist and once the richest man in the world

Social Intelligence

Our interpersonal relationships may be a source of social support that promotes success, or they may serve as a source of social conflict that distracts us from focusing on and achieving your personal goals. As a new college student, you may find yourself surrounded by multiple social opportunities. One of the college adjustments you'll need to make is finding a healthy middle ground between too much and too little socializing, as well as forming solid interpersonal relationships that support rather than sabotage your educational success.

Studies show that people with stronger social support networks have a longer life expectancy (Giles, Glonek, Luszcz, & Andrews, 2005) and are more likely to report being happy (Myers, 1993, 2000). Development of a strong social support system is particularly important in today's high-tech world of virtual reality and online (vs. in-person) communication, both of which make it easier to avoid direct contact, neglect connections with others, and increase the risk of isolation, loneliness, and social avoidance (Putman, 2000).

Student *Perspective*

"I have often found conflict in living a balanced academic and social life. I feel that when I am enjoying and succeeding in one spectrum, I am lagging in the other."

—First-year college student

The quality of our interpersonal relationships rests on two types of personal skills: our communication skills, or how well we send and receive information when interacting with others (verbally and nonverbally), and our human relations skills, or how well we relate to and treat others (i.e., people skills).

Following are our top recommendations for strengthening your interpersonal communication skills. Some strategies may appear to be very basic, but they're also very powerful. It may be that because they are so basic, people overlook them or forget to use them consistently. Don't be fooled by the seeming simplicity of the following suggestions, and don't underestimate their impact on your social interactions and relationships.

Reflection **9.2**

Who are the people in your life that you tend to turn to for social support when you are experiencing stress or need personal encouragement?

Strategies for Improving the Quality of Interpersonal Communication

"We have been given two ears and but a single mouth in order that we may hear more and talk less."

—Zeno of Citium, ancient Greek philosopher and founder of Stoic philosophy

1. **Work hard at being a good listener.** When the term *communication* is used, the skills of speaking and writing usually come to mind. However, the etymological root of the word *communicate* is *communicare*, meaning "to share or divide out." The prefix *co* in communication implies that it's a two-way process that involves not only the art of delivering ideas, but also receiving them. In fact, studies show that listening is the most frequent human communication activity, followed, in order, by reading, speaking, and writing (Newton, 1990; Purdy & Borisoff, 1996). One study found that college students spend an average of 52.5 percent of each day listening (Barker & Watson, 2000). Being a good listener is one of the top characteristics mentioned by people when they cite the positive features of their best friends (Berndt, 1992). Listening is also one of the top skills employers look for when hiring and promoting employees (Maes, Weldy, & Icenogle, 1997; Winsor, Curtis, & Stephens, 1997).

   Human relations experts often recommend that we spend less time talking and more time listening and listening well (Nichols, 1995). Because we're not actively doing something while listening, it's easy to lapse into *passive listening*—we hear their words, but our mind isn't actively and fully processing the message because it's partially somewhere else. While listening, we need to remain aware of this natural tendency to drift off and actively combat it by devoting our full attention to others when they're speaking. Two key strategies for doing so are to: (1) focus your attention on what the speaker is saying rather than on what you're going to say next, and (2) actively engage with the speaker's message by occasionally asking questions or seeking clarification about what is being said.

Remember

When you listen closely to those who speak to you, you send them the message that you respect their ideas and that they're worthy of your undivided attention.

2. **Remain conscious of the nonverbal messages you send while listening.** It's estimated that more than two-thirds of all communication is nonverbal because human body language often communicates stronger and truer messages than spoken language (Driver, 2010; Navarro, 2008).

   When it comes to listening, body language may be the best way to communicate interest in the message, as well as interest in and respect for the speaker. Similarly, if you are speaking, awareness of your listeners' body language can provide you with important clues about whether you're holding or losing their interest.

"Give every man thine ear, but few thy voice."

—William Shakespeare, English poet, playwright, and the most quoted writer in the English-speaking world

A good mnemonic device (memory-improvement method) for the nonverbal signals you should send others while listening is the acronym SOFTEN, in which each letter stands for an effective nonverbal message:

S = **Smile.** Smiling suggests interest and acceptance, but do it periodically, not continually. (A permanent smile can come across as an artificial pose.)
Sit still. Fidgeting and squirming send the message that the speaker is making you feel anxious or bored.

O = **Open posture.** Avoid closed-posture positions, such as crossing your arms or folding your hands; they can send a message that you're not open to what the speaker is saying or passing judgment on what's being said.

F = **Forward lean.** Leaning back can send a signal that you're not "into" what the person is saying or evaluating (psychoanalyzing) the person saying it. **Face the speaker directly.** Line up both shoulders with the speaker rather than turning one shoulder away, as if to give the speaker the cold shoulder.

T = **Touch.** A light touch on the arm or hand can be a good way to communicate warmth, but no rubbing, stroking, or touching in ways that could be interpreted as inappropriate intimacy (or sexual harassment).

E = **Eye contact.** Lack of eye contact sends the message that you're looking around for something more interesting or stimulating than the speaker. However, don't make continual or relentless eye contact, because that borders on staring or glaring. Instead, strike a happy medium by making *periodic* eye contact.

N = **Nod your head.** Slowly and periodically, not rapidly and repeatedly—this sends the message that you want the speaker to hurry up and finish up so you can start talking.

An interesting exercise you can use to gain greater awareness of your nonverbal communication habits is to choose a couple of people whom you trust, and who know you well, and ask them to imitate your body language. This is an exercise that can frequently be revealing (and occasionally entertaining).

3. **Be open to different topics of conversation.** Don't be a closed-minded or selective listener who listens to others like you're listening to a radio—selecting or tuning into only those stations that immediately capture your special interests and reinforce your opinions, but tuning out or turning off everything else.

> **Remember**
> *People learn most from others whose interests and viewpoints don't necessarily match or mimic their own. Ignoring or blocking out information and ideas about topics that don't immediately interest you or support your particular perspective is not only a poor social skill: it's also a poor learning strategy.*

If people express viewpoints that you don't agree with, you don't have to nod in agreement; however, you still owe them the courtesy of listening to what they have to say (rather than shaking your head, frowning, or interrupting them). This isn't just a matter of social etiquette: it's a matter of social ethics. Only after others finish expressing their point of view should you then feel free to express your own. Your informed opinions are worth expressing, as long as you don't express them in an opinionated way—stating them so strongly that it sounds like your viewpoints are the only rational or acceptable ones while all others are inferior or insane. Opinionated expression is likely to immediately end a potentially useful discussion or a possible future relationship.

"The most important thing in communication is to hear what isn't being said."

—Peter F. Drucker, Austrian author and founder of the study of "management"

On what topics do you hold strong opinions?

When you express these opinions, how do others usually react to you?

Human Relations Skills (a.k.a. "People Skills")

In addition to communicating and conversing well with others, another aspect of social intelligence is how well you relate to and treat others. Here are three key strategies for strengthening your human relations skills.

> "We should be aware of the magic contained in a name. The name sets that individual apart; it makes him or her unique among all others. Remember that a person's name is to that person the sweetest and most important sound in any language."
>
> —Dale Carnegie, author of the best-selling book *How to Win Friends and Influence People* and founder of The Dale Carnegie Course, a worldwide program for business based on his teachings

1. **Remember the names of people you meet.** When you remember others' names, you acknowledge their uniqueness and individuality. It makes them feel less like anonymous faces in a crowd and more like special individuals with distinctive identities.

    You've likely heard people claim they don't have a good memory for names; however, there's no evidence that ability to remember names is a natural talent or inherited trait that people are born with or without. Instead, it's a habit and skill that can be developed through personal effort and consistent use of effective memory-improvement strategies.

    You can use the following strategies for remembering names:

    -   Consciously pay attention to the name of each person you meet. Listen for the person's name rather than focusing on the impression you're making on that person, the impression that person is making on you, or what you're going to say next. When people say, "I forgot that person's name," what they really mean is they never *got* that person's name in the first place because they weren't paying attention to it when they first heard it.

    -   Reinforce your memory of the person's name by saying it or rehearsing it within a minute or two after you first hear it. For instance, if your friend Gertrude has just introduced you to Geraldine, you might say: "Geraldine, how long have you known Gertrude?" By using a person's name soon after you've heard it, you intercept memory loss when forgetting is most likely to occur—immediately after information is first received and processed.

    -   Strengthen your memory of an individual's name by associating it with other information, you've learned or know about the person. For instance, you can associate the person's name with (1) your first impression of the individual's personality, (2) a physical characteristic of the person, (3) your topic of conversation, (4) the place where you met, or (5) a familiar word that rhymes with the person's name. By making a mental connection between the person's name and some other piece of information, we make learning of the name more meaningful and memorable.

    -   People write down things that they want to be sure to remember. We can do the same for remembering names by keeping a name journal that includes the names of new people we meet plus some information about them (e.g., what they do and what their interests are). Make it a goal to meet one new person every day or week and remember that person's name by recording it in a name journal, along with the situation or circumstances in which you met.

> "When I joined the bank, I started keeping a record of the people I met and put them on little cards, and I would indicate on the cards when I met them, and under what circumstances, and sometimes [make] a little notation which would help me remember a conversation."
>
> —David Rockefeller, prominent American banker, philanthropist, and former CEO of the Chase Manhattan Bank

Remember

Developing the habit of remembering names is not only a social skill that can improve your social life and bring you friends, but also a powerful professional tool that can promote your career success in whatever field you may pursue.

In business, remembering names can help recruit and retain customers; in politics, it can win votes; and in education, it can build effective teacher-student relationships that can increase learning.

2. **Refer to people by name when you greet and interact with them.** When you greet a person, be sure to use the person's name in your greeting. Saying, "Hi, Waldo," will mean a lot more to Waldo than simply saying "Hi" or "Hi, there," which sounds like you just detected somebody "out there," or addressing a letter "to whom it may concern" rather than using the name of an actual person. By continuing to use people's names after you've learned them, you continue to send them the message that you haven't forgotten who they are and you continue to strengthen your memory for their names.

3. **Show interest in others by remembering information about them.** Ask people questions about their personal interests, plans, and experiences. Listen closely to their answers, especially to what seems most important to them, what they care about, or what interests them, and use this information as topics of conversation with them. For one person that topic may be politics, for another it may be sports, and for another it may be relationships.

When you see that person again, ask about something that was brought up in your last conversation. Try to get beyond the standard, generic questions that people routinely ask after they say "Hello" (e.g., "What's going on?"). Instead, ask about something specific you discussed with them last time you spoke (e.g., "How did that math test go that you were worried about last week?"). This sends a clear message to others that you remember them and care about them. Our memories often reflect our priorities—we're likely to remember what's important to us. When we remember people's names and something about them, it lets them know that they're a high priority to us.

Furthermore, you're likely to find that others start showing more interest in you after you show interest in them. When you ask questions that show interest in others, you're also likely to discover another surprising thing may happen: You'll hear people say that you're an excellent listener, a great conversationalist, and a good friend.

> "If we obey this law, [it] will bring us countless friends. The law is this: Always make the person feel important."
> —Dale Carnegie, *How to Win Friends and Influence People*

> "You can make more friends in two months by becoming interested in other people than you can in two years by trying to get other people interested in you."
> —Dale Carnegie, *How to Win Friends and Influence People*

Strategies for Meeting People and Forming Friendships

An important aspect of the college experience is meeting new people, learning from them, and forming lifelong friendships. Here are some practical strategies for increasing the quantity and variety of the people you meet and the quality of friendships you form.

1. **Place yourself in situations and locations where you will come into regular contact with others.** Social psychologists have found that the origin of friendships is physical propinquity—people are more likely to become friends if they continually find themselves in the same place at the same time (Latané, Liu, Nowak, Bonevento, & Zheng, 1995). You can apply this principle by spending as much time on campus as possible and spending time in places where others are likely to be present (e.g., by eating your meals in the student cafeteria and studying in the college library). If you have the opportunity to live on campus, do so;

studies show that it helps students make social connections and increases their satisfaction with the college experience (Pascarella & Terenzini, 2005; Tinto, 1993). If you are a commuter student, try to make your college experience as similar as possible to that of a residential student: for example, try to spend more than just class time on campus by spending study time and social time on campus (e.g., attending campus social or cultural events).

2. **Put yourself in social situations where you're likely to meet people who have similar interests, goals, and values.** Research supports the proverb, "Birds of a feather flock together." People tend to form friendships with others who share similar interests, values, or goals (AhYun, 2002). When two people have something in common, they're more likely to become friends because they're more likely to enjoy spending time together doing things that relate to their common interests. They're also more likely to get along with each other because they reinforce or validate each other's personal interests and values (Festinger, 1954; Suls, Martin, & Wheeler, 2002).

An important aspect of the college experience is meeting new people and forming lasting friendships.

One straightforward way to find others with whom you have something in common is by participating in clubs and organizations on campus that reflect your interests and values. If you cannot find one, start one of your own. Also, regularly check your college newspaper, posted flyers on campus, and the Student Information Desk in your Student Activities Center to keep track of social events that are more likely to attract others who share your interests, values, or goals.

3. **Meeting others through a social website.** Facebook and other social websites are another type of venue through which you can network with other college students. You can use this electronic medium to meet new people, join groups on campus, and check for announcements of parties or other social events. However, be careful about the people you respond to, and be careful about what you post on your page or "wall." Reports indicate that both schools and employers are checking students' Facebook entries and using that information to help them decide whether to accept or reject applicants (Palank, 2006).

Student
Perspective

"I have observed different kinds of people. There are the ones that party and flunk, then there are the kind that party rationally and don't flunk, and the kinds that just don't party."

—First-year college student

Reflection **9.4**

Have you been to college parties on or off campus?

If yes, what were they like?

If no, are there any reasons you have not gone?

Dating and Romantic Relationships

Romantic relationships begin through the process of dating. Research shows that college students take different approaches to dating, ranging from not dating at all to dating with the intent of exploring or cementing long-term relationships. Listed below is a summary of the major forms or purposes of college dating.

Snapshot Summary

9.1

Approaches to Dating

Postpone dating. Students who adopt this approach feel that the demands of college work and college life are too time-consuming to take on the additional social and emotional burden of dating while in college.

Student Perspectives

> "Relationships take time and patience, and in college, both of these can be very limited."
>
> —College student quoted in Kucewicz (2001)

> "It's hard enough to have fun here with all the work you have to do. There's no reason to have the extra drama [of dating] in your life."
>
> —College sophomore quoted in Sax (2003)

Hooking up. Students who prefer this approach believe that formal dating is unnecessary; they feel that their social and sexual needs are better met more casually by associating with friends and acquaintances. Instead of going out on one-on-one dates, they prefer to first meet and connect with romantic partners in larger group settings, such as college parties.

> "Now all a guy has to do to hook up on a Saturday night is to sit on the couch long enough at a party. Eventually a girl will plop herself down beside him . . . he'll make a joke, she'll laugh, their eyes will meet, sparks will fly, and the mission is accomplished. And you want me to tell this guy to call a girl, spend $100 on dinner and hope for a goodnight kiss."
>
> —College student quoted in Beckett (2003)

Casual dating. Students taking this approach go out on dates primarily for the purpose of enjoying themselves, but not getting "tied down" to any particular person. These "casual daters" prefer to go out on a series of successive dates with different partners, and they may date different individuals at the same time. Their primary goal is to meet new people and discover what characteristics they find attractive in others.

Exclusive dating. Students adopting this approach prefer to date only one person for an extended period of time. Although marriage is not the goal, exclusive dating takes casual dating one step further. This form of dating may help the partners develop a clearer idea of what characteristics they may seek in an ideal spouse or long-term mate.

Courtship. This form of dating is intended to continue the relationship until it culminates in marriage or a formal, long-term commitment.

Source: Adapted from research reviewed by Seirup (2004).

The different approaches to dating described in **Snapshot Summary 9.1** don't always occur separately or independently: they may be blended or combined. Romantic relationships may also evolve or grow into different stages with the passage of time. Following are the characteristics of two major stages that often take place in the evolution or maturation of romantic love.

Reflection 9.5

How would you define love?

Would you say that love is a feeling? An action? Both?

What do you think are the best signs that two people are "in love"?

What would you say are the most common reasons why people "fall out of love"?

Romantic Relationships

Research on romantic love indicates that it comes in two major stages (Bassham, Irwin, Nardone, & Wallace, 2005; Ruggiero, 2004; Wade & Tavris, 1990).

Stage 1. Passionate Love (Infatuation)

This represents the very first stage of a romantic relationship, and it's often characterized by the following features.

- Heavy emphasis placed on physical elements of the relationship. Lots of attention is focused on the partner's physical appearance or attractiveness, and the partners experience a high level of physical arousal and passion—they experience "erotic love" in which lust and love are closely connected.
- Impulsive: Partners quickly or suddenly "fall" into love or are "swept off their feet"—i.e., "love at first sight."
- Obsessive: Partners can't stop thinking about each other ("madly in love").
- Intense emotion characterized by a "rush" of chemical changes in the body, similar to a drug-induced state—namely:
  a. Release of the hormone adrenaline, which triggers faster heartbeat and breathing, and
  b. Increased production of the brain chemical dopamine, which triggers feelings of excitement, euphoria, joy, and general well-being (Bartels & Zeki, 2000).

The intensity of this emotional and chemical experience decreases with the passage of time, typically leveling off within a year after the couple has been together. The leveling off of emotional intensity experienced by romantic partners after their relationship continues for an extended period of time is similar to the buildup of tolerance to a drug after the drug continues to be used for an extended period of time (Fisher, 2004; Peele & Brodsky, 1991).

- **Idealism.** The partner and the relationship are perceived as "perfect." The partners may say things like "We're perfect for each other," "Nobody else has a relationship like ours," "We'll be together forever." This is the stage where love can be

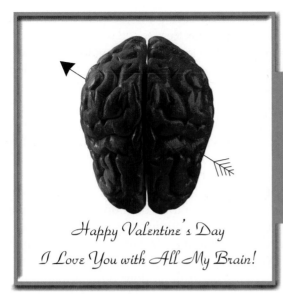

Happy Valentine's Day
I Love You with All My Brain!

Despite expressions like "I love you with all my heart," romantic love takes place in the human brain and is accompanied by major changes in the production of brain chemicals.

"blind"—the partners may not "see" each other's obvious flaws and weaknesses. As in the psychological defense mechanism of *denial*, the partner's personal shortcomings, or any problems that may threaten the security of the relationship, are pushed out of consciousness.

- **Attachment and dependency.** The lover feels insecure without the partner and cannot bear being separated from him or her (e.g., "I can't live without him"). This type of attachment and dependence follows the principle "I love you because I am loved" and "I love you because I need you." Thus, it may be difficult to determine whether the person is in love with the other person or is in love with the process of being in love or the feeling of being loved (Fromm, 1970).

- **Possessiveness and jealousy.** The lover feels that he or she has exclusive rights to the partner and may become very suspicious of the partner's fidelity, or very jealous of those who interact with the partner in a friendly or affectionate manner, which can be totally illogical or irrational ("insanely jealous"): the lover may suspect the partner is "cheating" when there's no real evidence that any cheating is taking place.

- **"Love sickness."** If the relationship breaks up, intense depression or "love withdrawal" may follow the breakup, similar to the feeling of withdrawing from a pleasure-producing drug. Studies show that the most common cause of despair or depression among college students is a romantic breakup (Foreman, 2009).

Stage 2. Mature Love

At this more advanced stage of the relationship, the partners gradually "fall out" of first-stage (puppy) love, and gradually grow into a more mature stage of love that has the following characteristics.

- The partners become less selfish and self-centered (egocentric), and become more selfless and other-centered (altruistic). Love moves beyond being just a noun, an emotion or feeling within the person (e.g., "I am in love"), and becomes an action verb, a way in which the partners act toward one another (e.g., "we love each other"). More emphasis is placed on caring for the partner, rather than being cared for. Mature love follows two principles:

1. "I am loved because I love"—not "I'm in love because I am loved" and
2. "I need you because I love you"—not "I love you because I need you." (Fromme, 1980)

- There's less of an emotional high experienced at this stage than during early stages of the relationship. For example, the mad rush of hormones and mass production of euphoria-producing brain chemicals is replaced by feelings of emotional serenity (mellowness) and emotional evenness (versus the emotional "ups and downs" of early-stage love). The love "rush" is replaced by a less intense, but more consistently pleasant emotional state characterized by slightly elevated levels of different brain chemicals (endorphins, rather than dopamine). Unlike infatuation or early-stage love, this pleasant emotional state doesn't decline with time: in fact, it may actually grow stronger as the partners' relationship continues and matures (Bartels & Zeki, 2000).

- Physical passion decreases. The "flames of the flesh" don't burn as intensely as in first-stage love, but a romantic afterglow continues. This afterglow is characterized by more emotional intimacy or psychological closeness between the partners, greater self-disclosure, mutual trust, and interpersonal honesty, which enhances both the physical and psychological quality of the relationship (Viorst, 1998).

At this more advanced stage of love, interest is focused broadly on the partner as a whole person, rather than narrowly on the partner's physical qualities. Each partner has a realistic (not idealistic) view of the other: their respective strengths and weaknesses are recognized and accepted. The partners genuinely like one another as individuals and consider each other to be their "best" or "closest" friend.

- The partners have mutual trust and confidence in each other's commitment and aren't plagued by feelings of suspicion, distrust, or petty jealousy. Each partner continues to have interests and close friends outside the relationship without the other becoming jealous (Hatfield & Rapson, 1993; Hatfield and Walster, 1985).

- The partners have mutual concern for each other's growth and fulfillment. Rather than being envious or competitive, they take joy in each other's personal success and accomplishments.

- The partners maintain a balanced blend of independence and interdependence in their relationship—sometimes referred to as the "paradox (contradiction) of love"—both partners maintain their independence and individuality yet feel more complete and fulfilled when they're together. The partners maintain their own sense of personal identity and self-worth; however, together, their respective identities become more complete.

Reflection 9.6

Rate your degree of agreement or disagreement with the following statements:

"All you need is love."

   strongly agree   agree   not sure   disagree   strongly disagree

Reason for rating:

"Love is just a four-letter word."

    strongly agree   agree   not sure   disagree   strongly disagree

Reason for rating:

"Love stinks."

    strongly agree   agree   not sure   disagree   strongly disagree

Reason for rating:

Unhealthy Relationships

When a relationship becomes unhealthy, there are often clear warning signs telling you it's time to end things for your own well-being. If you are feeling disrespected or controlled, or you are concerned for your safety, it's essential that you acknowledge and act upon these signals. Relationship violence—whether emotional, psychological, physical, or sexual—is *never* appropriate or acceptable. Neither is it an effective means for dealing with a dating conflict. If you are in such a situation, or you have a friend who is, addressing the violence immediately is of primary importance.

Sometimes victims and perpetrators don't recognize that they are in fact in a violent relationship because they don't identify the behaviors as abusive. Behaviors that characterize relationship violence include, but are not limited to, degrading language, dominating or dictating a partner's actions, and physical and/or sexual assault (Murray & Kardatzke, 2007). Without such recognition, victims and perpetrators are likely to remain in their current relationships or have relationships that are more violent in the future (Miller, 2011).

Unfortunately, this type of violence is highly common among college-aged women and men. In fact, recent studies have reported that 13 to 42 percent of college students have experienced and/or perpetrated physical relationship violence (Beyers, Leonard, Mays, & Rosen, 2000; Luthra & Gidycz, 2006; Miller, 2011; Perry & Fromuth, 2005; Shook, Gerrity, Jurich, & Segrist, 2000). In another study, 88 percent of females and 81 percent of males reported being victims and/or perpetrators of psychological and/or emotional relationship violence (White & Koss, 1991). Also important to note is that relationship violence occurs among all segments of the college-aged population. When looking at the demographics of victims and perpetrators, studies show comparable rates among men and women and among members of all races, ethnicities, and socioeconomic groups (Malik, Sorenson, & Aneshensel, 1997). Comparable levels of occurrence have also been found among victims and perpetrators who are gay, bisexual, and straight (Freedner, Freed, Yang, & Austin, 2002). Taken together, these data highlight the unfortunate fact that relationship violence is all too common. Furthermore, they emphasize the need for such cases to be stopped before they escalate to even more dangerous levels.

Since victims of relationship violence often experience distress, and perhaps even trauma, it is critical that they seek help. Victims tend to be reluctant to do so however for fear of embarrassment or retribution. If you find yourself in a violent relationship, it is important that you tell someone what is going on and get support. Don't let fear immobilize you. Talking to a trusted friend who has your health and safety in mind is a good place to start. Also, connecting with your college's Counseling Center is especially helpful so that you can get the trained assistance you might need. Counseling Centers are often staffed with professionals who have experience working with victims—and perpetrators—of relationship violence and will explain to you your rights as a victim. If the center on your campus is not staffed with such experienced professionals, they are likely to help connect you to a center in your community that is.

Snapshot Summary

9.2 Examples of Emotional, Psychological, Physical, and Sexual Abuse and Violence

This list explains various forms of abuse and violence experienced by both men and women. Note that these examples are not just physical or sexual in nature; emotional and psychological violence can be just as harmful to victims.

Sexual Harassment

Sexual harassment may be defined as unwelcome sexual advances or requests for sexual favors in exchange for a grade, job, or promotion. Harassment can take the following forms:

- **Verbal** (e.g., sexual comments about your body or clothes; sexual jokes or teasing)
- **Nonverbal** (e.g., staring or glaring at your body or obscene gestures)
- **Physical** (e.g., contact by touching, pinching, or rubbing up against your body)

Recommendations for Dealing with Sexual Harassment

- Make your objections clear and firm. Tell the harasser directly that you are offended by the unwanted behavior and that you consider it sexual harassment.
- Keep a written record of any harassment. Record the date, place, and specific details about the harassing behavior.
- Become aware of the sexual harassment policy at your college, which is likely to be found in the Student Handbook or may be available from the Office of Human Resources on your campus.
- If you're unsure about whether you are experiencing sexual harassment or what to do, seek help from the Counseling Center on campus.

Abusive Relationships

Abusive relationships may be described as relationships in which one partner abuses the other sexually, physically, verbally, psychologically, or emotionally. Abusive individuals are often dependent on their partners for a sense of self-worth. They commonly have low self-esteem and fear their partners will abandon them, so they attempt to prevent this abandonment by over-controlling their partners. Frequently, abusers feel powerless or weak in other areas of life and overcompensate by attempting to gain and exert power and personal strength over their partners.

Potential Signs of Abuse

- Abuser tries to dominate or control all aspects of the partner's life
- Abuser frequently yells, shouts, intimidates, or makes physical threats
- Abuser constantly checks up on the partner
- Abuser constantly puts down the partner and damages the partner's self-esteem
- Abuser displays intense and irrational jealousy
- Abuser demands affection or sex when the partner is not interested
- The abused partner behaves differently and is more inhibited when the abuser is around
- The abused partner fears the abuser
- The abuser blames the partner for their abusive behavior

Strategies for Avoiding or Escaping Abusive Relationships

- Avoid isolation by continuing to maintain social ties with others outside the relationship.
- To help you see your relationship more clearly, ask friends for feedback on how they see it (love can sometimes be "blind"; it's possible to be in denial about the abusive relationship and not see what's really going on).
- Speak with a professional counselor on campus to help you see your relationship more objectively and to help you cope or escape from any relationship that you sense is becoming abusive.

Sexual Violence and Sexual Assault

Rape is a form of sexual assault, which is legally defined as "the penetration, no matter how slight, of the vagina or anus with any body part or object, or oral penetration by a sex organ of another person, without the consent of the victim" (Office of Public Affairs, 2012). Rape occurs in two major forms:

1. **Stranger Rape:** When a total stranger forces sexual intercourse on the victim.

2. **Acquaintance Rape or Date Rape:** When the victim knows or is dating the person who forces unwanted sexual intercourse. It's estimated that 63 percent of completed rapes against women in 2008 were committed by perpetrators known to the victims (Bureau of Justice Statistics, 2009). Alcohol is frequently associated with acquaintance rapes because it lowers the rapist's inhibitions and reduces the victim's ability to judge whether he or she is in a potentially dangerous situation. (Most acquaintance rape is committed by men against women; however, men are also victims of acquaintance rape.) Since the victim is familiar with the offender, he or she may feel at fault or conclude that what happened is not sexual assault.

Recommendations to Reduce the Risk of Rape and Sexual Assault

- Don't drink to excess or associate with others who drink to excess.

- Go to parties with at least one friend so you can keep an eye out for each other.
- Clearly and firmly communicate your sexual intentions and limits (e.g., if you say no, make absolutely sure that the other individual knows that you mean what you say and you say what you mean).
- Distinguish lust from love. If you just met someone who makes sexual advances toward you, that person lusts for you but doesn't love you.
- Take a self-defense class.
- Carry Mace or pepper spray.

Recommendations for Men

- Don't assume a woman wants to have sex just because she's:
  - Very friendly
  - Dressed in a certain way
  - Drinking alcohol
- If a woman says no, don't assume that she really means yes.
- Don't interpret sexual rejection as personal rejection.

Sources: Evans (2010); Smith & Segal (2012);

Handling Interpersonal Conflict

Disagreement and conflict among people are inevitable aspects of social life. Research shows that even the most happily married couples don't live in continual marital bliss: they have occasional disagreements and conflicts (Gottman, 1994, 1999). Thus, conflict is something you cannot expect to escape or eliminate; you can only hope to contain it, defuse it, and prevent it from reaching unmanageable levels. The interpersonal communication and human relations skills already discussed in this chapter can help minimize conflicts. In addition to these general social skills, the following specific set of strategies may be used to handle interpersonal conflict constructively and compassionately.

1. **Pick the right place and time to resolve the conflict.** Don't discuss sensitive issues when you're fatigued, in a fit of anger, or in a hurry (Daniels & Horowitz, 1997). Also, don't discuss them in front of others: deal with them only with the person involved. As the expression goes, "Don't air your dirty laundry in public." Criticizing someone in public is akin to a public stoning; it's likely to embarrass or humiliate the person and will cause him or her to resist or resent you.

2. **Decompress yourself before you express yourself.** When you have a conflict with a person, your ultimate objective should be to solve the problem, not unload your anger and enjoy an emotionally cathartic experience. Impulsively dumping on the other person and saying the first thing that comes to your mind may give you an immediate sense of relief, but it's not likely to produce permanent improvement in the other person's attitude or behavior toward you. Instead

Remember

Sometimes things are better left unsaid until you find the right time and place to say them.

of unloading, take the load off—cool down and give yourself a little downtime to reflect rationally before you react emotionally. For example, count to 10 and give your emotions time to settle down and your rational mind time to reflect on what you're going to say before you say it. Pausing for reflection also communicates to the other person that you've given careful thought and focused attention to the matter, rather than blasting away randomly like a loose cannon.

If the conflict is so intense that you're feeling incensed or enraged, it may be a good idea to slow things down by writing out your thoughts ahead of time before you confront the person. This strategy supplies you with time to organize and clarify your ideas by first talking silently to yourself (on paper) before talking out loud to the other person (in person).

3. **Give the person a chance to respond.** Just because you're angry doesn't mean that the person you're angry with must forfeit the right to free speech and self-defense. Giving the other person a chance to speak and be heard increases the likelihood that you'll receive a cooperative response to your request. It will also prevent you from storming in, jumping the gun, and pulling the trigger before being sure you've got all the facts straight.

After listening to the other person's response, check your understanding by summarizing it in your own words (e.g., "What I hear you saying is . . ."). This is an important first step in the conflict resolution process because conflicts often revolve around a simple misunderstanding, a failure to communicate, or a communication breakdown. Sometimes just taking the time to hear where the other person is coming from before launching into a full-scale complaint or criticism can reduce or resolve the conflict.

4. **Acknowledge the person's perspectives and feelings.** After listening to the person's response, if you disagree with it, don't dismiss or discount the person's feelings. For instance, don't say, "That's ridiculous," or "You're not making any sense." Instead, say, "I see how you might feel that way, but . . ." or "I feel bad that you are under pressure, but . . ."

5. **If things begin to get nasty, call for a time-out or cease-fire and postpone the discussion to allow both of you time to cool off.** When emotion and adrenaline run high, logic and reason tend to run low. This can result in one person saying something during a fit of anger that triggers an angry response from the other person; then the anger of both combatants continues to escalate and turns into an intense volley of verbal punches and counterpunches. For example, an emotionally heated conversation may end up going something like this:
Person A: "You're way out of control."
Person B: "I'm not out of control; you're the one that's overreacting."
Person A: "*I'm* overreacting? You're the one who's acting like a jerk!"
Person B: "I might be acting like a jerk but *you're* a real jerk!"

Blow-by-blow exchanges such as these are likely to turn up the emotional heat to a level so high that focusing on the issue and resolving the conflict take a back seat to winning the argument. Both fighters need to back off, retreat to their respective corners, cool down, and try again later when neither one of them is ready to throw a knockout punch.

6. **Make your point assertively (not passively, aggressively, or passive-aggressively).** When you're passive, you don't stand up for your personal rights: you allow others to take advantage of you and push you around. You say nothing when you should say something. You say yes when you want to say no. People who handle conflict passively tend to become angry, anxious, or resentful about doing nothing and keeping it all inside (Alberti & Emmons, 2001).

"Seek first to understand, then to be understood."

—Stephen Covey, international bestselling author of *The Seven Habits of Highly Effective People*

When you're aggressive, you stand up for your rights, but you also violate the rights of the other person by threatening, dominating, humiliating, or bullying that person. You use intense, emotionally loaded words to attack the person (e.g., "You spoiled brat" or "You're a sociopath"). You may manage to get what you want, but at the other person's expense and at the risk of losing a friend. Later, you tend to feel guilty about overreacting or coming on too strong (e.g., "I knew I shouldn't have said that").

When you're passive-aggressive, you get back at or get even with the other person by either (1) withholding or taking away something (e.g., not speaking to the other person or withdrawing all attention and affection), or (2) indirectly hinting that you're angry (e.g., by making cynical comments or using sarcastic humor).

In contrast, when you're assertive, you strike a happy medium between being too aggressive or too passive. You handle conflict in a way that protects or restores your rights without taking away or stepping on the rights of the other person. You approach conflict in an even-tempered way rather than in an angry or agitated manner; you speak in a normal volume rather than yelling or screaming; and you communicate at a normal distance rather than getting up close and into the face of the other person involved in the conflict. You can resolve conflicts assertively by using the following strategies.

- **Focus on the specific behavior causing the conflict, not the person's general character.** Avoid labeling the person as "selfish," "mean," "inconsiderate," etc. For instance, if you're upset because your roommate doesn't do his share of cleaning, stay away from aggressive labels such as "slacker" or "lazy bum." Attacking others with such negative labels does to the other person just what it sounds like: It makes the person feel like he's being verbally assaulted. This is likely to put him on the defensive and provoke a counterattack aimed at one of your personal characteristics. Before you know it, you're likely to find yourself in a full-out war of words and mutual character assassinations that has escalated well beyond a small-scale skirmish about the specific behavior in question.

  Rather than focusing on the person's general character, focus on the action that's causing the problem (e.g., failing to do the dishes or leaving dirty laundry around the room). This will enable the other person to know exactly what behavior needs to be changed to resolve the conflict. Furthermore, it's much easier to change a specific behavior than it is to change one's entire character, which would require a radical change in personality (or frontal lobotomy surgery).

- **Use "I" messages to focus on how the other person's behavior or action affects you.** "I" messages focus on what you're perceiving and feeling, which sends a message that's less accusatory and threatening to the other person. In contrast, "you" messages are more likely to make the other person defensive and put that person on the offensive—ready to retaliate rather than cooperate (Bippus & Young, 2005).

  Suppose you've received a course grade that's lower than what you think you earned or deserved and you decide to question your instructor about it. Don't begin by saying to the instructor, "You made a mistake," or "You gave me the wrong grade." These messages are likely to make your professor immediately ready to defend the grade you received. Your professor will be less threatened and more likely to listen to and consider your complaint if you initiate the conversation with an "I" statement, such as "I don't believe I received the correct grade" or "I think an error may have been made in my final grade."

"I" messages are less aggressive because you're targeting an issue, not a person (McKay, Davis, & Fanning, 2009). Saying, "I feel angry when . . ." rather than "You make me angry when . . . " sends the message that you're taking responsibility for the way you feel rather than guilt-tripping the individual for making you feel that way (perhaps without the person even being aware of how you feel). When using "I" messages:

a. Be specific about what emotion you're experiencing. For example, saying, "I feel neglected when you don't write or call" identifies what you're feeling more specifically than saying, "I wish you'd be more considerate." Describing what you feel in specific terms increases the persuasive power of your message and reduces the risk that the other person will misunderstand or discount it.

b. Be specific about what you're requesting of the other person to resolve the conflict. For example, "I would like for you to call me at least once a day" is more specific than "I want you to keep in touch with me."

c. Express what you want the other person to do in the form of a firm request rather than a demand or ultimatum. For example, saying, "I would like you to . . ." is less likely to put the person on the defensive than saying, "I insist . . ." or "I demand . . ."

> "Precision of communication is important, more important than ever, in our era of hair-trigger balances, when a false or misunderstood word may create as much disaster as a sudden thoughtless act."
>
> —James Thurber, U.S. author, humorist, and cartoonist

7. **Avoid absolute judgments or blanket statements.** Compare the following three pairs of statements:

a. "You're no help at all" versus "You don't help me enough"

b. "You never try to understand how I feel" versus "You don't try hard enough to understand how I feel"

c. "I always have to clean up" versus "I'm doing more than my fair share of the cleaning"

The first statement in each of the preceding pairs is an absolute statement that covers all times, situations, and circumstances: it leaves no room for any possible exceptions. Such extreme, blanket criticisms are likely to put the criticized person on the defensive because they suggest the person is totally lacking or deficient with respect to the behavior in question (a character flaw). The second statement in each pair states the criticism in terms of degree or amount, which is less likely to threaten the person's self-esteem (and is probably closer to the truth).

> "Don't find fault. Find a remedy."
>
> —Henry Ford, founder of Ford Motor Company and one of the richest people of his generation

Reflection 9.7

Your teammates aren't carrying their weight on a group project that you're all supposed to be working on together, and you're getting frustrated and angry because you're doing most of the work.

Construct an "I" message you could use to communicate your concern in a non-threatening way.

8. **Focus on solving the problem, not winning the argument.** Don't approach conflict with the attitude that you're going to get even or prove that you're right. Winning the argument but not persuading the person to change the behavior that's causing the conflict is like winning a battle but losing the war. Instead, approach conflict resolution as a problem to be solved in a way that allows both parties to win—i.e., both of you can end up with a better relationship in the long run.

9. **Conclude your discussion of the conflict on a warm, constructive note.** End on a positive note by ensuring that there are no hard feelings, and let the person know you're optimistic that the conflict can be resolved and your relationship improved.

10. **If the conflict is resolved because of some change made by the other person, express your appreciation for the individual's effort.** Even if your complaint was legitimate and your request was justified, the person's effort to accommodate your request shouldn't be taken for granted. At the least, you shouldn't react to a positive change in behavior by rubbing it in with sarcastic comments such as "That's more like it" or "It's about time!"

Expressing appreciation to the other person for making a change in response to your request is not only a socially sensitive thing to do but also a self-serving thing to do. By recognizing or reinforcing the other person's changed behavior, you increase the likelihood that the positive change in behavior will continue and you'll continue to benefit from the change.

> "To keep your marriage brimming with love . . . when you're wrong, admit it; when you're right, shut up."
>
> —Ogden Nash, American poet

Emotional Intelligence

Research shows that college students who score higher on tests of emotional intelligence, such as the ability to identify their emotions and moods, are (1) less likely to experience boredom (Harris, 2006) and (2) more able to focus their attention and get absorbed (in the zone) when completing challenging tasks (Wiederman, 2007). Excelling in college is a challenging task that will test your emotional strength and your ability to persist to task completion (graduation).

Research also indicates that experiencing positive emotions, such as optimism and excitement, promotes learning by increasing the brain's ability to take in, store, and retrieve information (Rosenfield, 1988). In one study involving nearly 4,000 first-year college students, it was found that students' level of optimism or hope for success during their first term on campus was a more accurate predictor of their first-year grades than was their SAT score or high school grade point average (Snyder, Harris, Anderson, Holleran, Irving, Sigmon, et al., 1991). In contrast, negative emotion—such as anxiety and fear—can interfere with the brain's ability to (1) store and retrieve memories, and (2) engage in higher-level thinking (Caine & Caine, 1991; Hertel & Brozovich, 2010).

Following are research-based strategies for minimizing the impact of negative emotions that sabotage success, as well as strategies for maximizing the impact of positive emotions that promote success.

Stress and Anxiety

Among the most common emotions that humans must monitor, manage, and regulate is stress. Students report experiencing higher levels of stress in college than they did in high school (Bartlett, 2002; Sax, 2003).

What exactly is stress? The biology of stress originates from the fight-or-flight reaction that's been wired into your body for survival purposes. This automatic reaction prepares us to handle danger or threat by flooding our bodies with chemicals (e.g., adrenaline) in the same way that ancient humans had to handle threats by engaging in fight or flight (escape) when confronted by life-threatening predators. The word *stress* derives from a Latin root that means "to draw tight." Thus, stress isn't necessarily bad; in the right amount, it can actually be productive. For example, a tightened guitar string generates better sound than a string that's too lax or loose, a tightened bow delivers a more powerful arrow shot, and a tightened muscle provides more strength or speed. Such productive stress is sometimes referred to as *eustress*—deriving from the root *eu* meaning "good" (as in the words *euphoria*, meaning a good mood, and *eulogy*, meaning good words).

If you keep college stress at a moderate level, it can be a productive emotion that promotes learning and personal development. Moderate stress can improve your:

1. Physical performance (e.g., strength and speed);
2. Mental performance (e.g., attention and memory); and
3. Mood (e.g., hope and optimism).

Reflection 9.8

Can you think of a situation in which you performed at a higher level because you were slightly nervous or experienced a moderate amount of stress?

However, if stress becomes extreme and continues for a prolonged period, it moves from being productive to destructive. Using the guitar string as an analogy, if it's strung too tightly, the string is likely to snap or break, which isn't productive. Unproductive stress is often referred to as *distress*—from the root *dis* meaning "bad" (as in the words *discomfort* and *disease*). Extreme stress can create the negative feeling of anxiety and contribute to anxiety disorders (e.g., panic attacks). If stress persists at a high level for a prolonged period, it can trigger psychosomatic illnesses—tension-induced bodily disorders (from *psyche*, meaning "mind," and *soma*, meaning "body"). For instance, prolonged distress can trigger indigestion by increasing secretion of stomach acids or contribute to high blood pressure, a.k.a. hypertension. Prolonged stress can also suppress the immune system, leaving you more vulnerable to flu, colds, and other infectious diseases. Studies show that the immune systems of college students are suppressed (produce fewer antibodies) at stressful times during the aca-

Research indicates that college students' stress levels tend to rise when they are experiencing a wave of exams, such as midterms and finals.

demic term, such as during midterms and finals (Bosch, de Geus, Ring, & Nieuw-Amerongen, 2004; Deinzer, Kleineidam, Stiller-Winkler, Idel, & Bachg, 2000).

Excess stress interferes with mental performance because anxious feelings and thoughts begin to preoccupy our mind, taking up valuable space in our working memory, leaving it with less capacity to process information we're trying to learn and retain. Studies also show that students experiencing higher levels of academic stress and performance anxiety are more likely to use ineffective surface approaches to learning that rely on memorization (Biggs & Tang, 2007; Ramsden, 2003) rather than effective deep-learning strategies that involve seeking meaning and understanding. Furthermore, high levels of test anxiety are more likely to interfere with memory for information that's been studied and to result in careless concentration errors on exams—e.g., overlooking key words in test questions (Tobias, 1985, 1993). Although considerable research points to the negative effects of excess stress, you still need to keep in mind that stress can work either for or against you: you can be either energized or sabotaged by stress depending on its level of intensity and the length of time it continues. You can't expect to stop or eliminate stress completely, nor should you want to: you can only hope to contain it and maintain it at a level where it's more productive than destructive. Many years of research indicate that personal performance is best when it takes place under conditions of moderate stress because this creates a sense of challenge. On the other hand, too much stress creates performance anxiety, and too little stress results in loss of intensity or indifference (Sapolsky, 2004; Yerkes & Dodson, 1908). (See **Figure 9.1**.)

Reflection 9.9

How would you rate your level of anxiety in the following situations?

1. Taking tests or exams	high	moderate	low
2. Interacting in social situations	high	moderate	low
3. Making decisions about the future	high	moderate	low

FIGURE 9.1

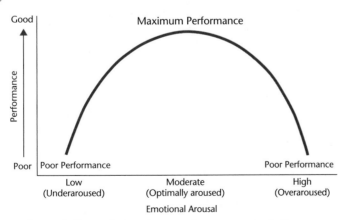

Moderate challenge that produces moderate stress typically promotes maximum (peak) performance.

Source: Williams, Landers, & Boutcher (1993).

Relationship between Arousal and Performance

Snapshot Summary 9.3 provides a short summary of the signs or symptoms of extreme stress that indicate stress has climbed to a level where it's creating distress or anxiety. If these symptoms are experienced for an extended period (e.g., longer than a week), deliberate action should be taken to reduce them.

Snapshot Summary

9.3 High Anxiety: Recognizing the Symptoms (Signs) of Distress

- **Jitteriness or shaking,** especially in the hands
- **Accelerated heart rate or heart palpitations:** irregular heartbeat
- **Muscle tension:** tightness in the chest or upper shoulders or a tight feeling (lump) in the throat (the expressions "uptight" and "choking" stem from these symptoms of upper-body tension)
- **Body aches:** heightened muscle tension leading to tension headaches, backaches, or chest pain (in extreme cases, it can feel as if a heart attack is taking place)
- **Sweating,** especially sweaty (clammy) palms
- **Cold, pale hands or feet,** symptoms that have led to the expressions "white knuckles" and "cold feet" to describe someone who is very anxious
- **Dry mouth:** decreased production of saliva (leading to the expression

"cotton mouth" and the need for very nervous speakers to have water nearby)
- **Stomach discomfort or indigestion** due to increased secretion of stomach acid (the expression "feeling butter-flies in my stomach" relates to this symptom)
- **Gastrointestinal discomfort,** e.g., stomach cramps, constipation, or diarrhea
- **Feeling faint or dizzy** due to constriction of blood vessels that decreases oxygen flow to the brain
- **Weakness and fatigue:** a sustained (chronic) state of arousal and prolonged muscle tension becomes tiring
- **Menstrual changes:** missing or irregular menstrual periods
- **Difficulty sleeping:** insomnia or interrupted (fitful) sleep
- **Increased susceptibility to colds, flu, and other infections** due to suppression of the body's immune system

---

Effective Methods for Managing Stress

If you perceive your level of stress to be reaching a point where it's beginning to interfere with the quality of your academic performance or personal life, you need to take steps to reduce it. Listed here are three stress-management methods whose positive effects have been well documented by research in psychology and biology (Benson & Klipper, 1990; Lehrer et al., 2007).

Deep (Diaphragmatic) Breathing

The type of breathing associated with excessive stress is hyperventilation—fast, shallow, and irregular breathing through the mouth rather than the chest. Breathing associated with relaxation is just the opposite—slow, deep, and regular breathing that originates from the stomach.

Breathing is something you usually do automatically (involuntarily) without conscious awareness. However, with some concentration and effort, you can gain voluntary control of your breathing by controlling your diaphragm—the muscle that enables you to expand and contract your lungs. By voluntarily controlling the diaphragm muscle, you can slow your breathing rate, which, in turn, can bring down your stress level.

Progressive Muscle Relaxation

This is a stress-management method similar to stretching exercises that are used to relax and loosen muscles before and after physical exercise. Total body (head-to-toe) muscle relaxation can be achieved by progressively tensing and releasing the five sets of muscles listed below. For each muscle area listed, hold the tension for about five seconds and then release it slowly.

1. Wrinkle your forehead muscles, then release them.
2. Shrug your shoulders up as if to touch your ears, then drop them.
3. Make a fist with each hand, then open both.
4. Tighten your stomach muscles, then release them.
5. Tighten your toes by curling them under your feet, and then raise them as high as you can.

To help tense your muscles before releasing them, imagine using your muscles to push or lift a heavy object. When relaxing your muscles, take a deep breath and think or say, "Relax." By breathing deeply and thinking or hearing "Relax" each time you release your muscles, you come to associate the word with your muscles becoming relaxed. Thus, if you find yourself in a stressful situation, you can take a deep breath, think or say, "Relax," and immediately reduce tension because your muscles have been conditioned to relax in response to that word. You can do this at any time and in any place: for example, when you're stuck in traffic, waiting in line, or waiting to take a test.

Mental Imagery

Create visual images to generate relaxation. You can create your own relaxing mental movie or imaginary DVD by visually placing yourself in a calm, comfortable, and soothing setting. Visualize images such as ocean waves, floating clouds, sitting in a warm sauna, or any sensory experience that tends to relax you. The more senses you use, the more real the scene will seem and the more powerful its relaxing effects will be (Fezler, 1989). Try to use all of your senses—not only to see it, but try to hear it, smell it, touch it, and feel it. You can also use musical imagination to create calming background music that accompanies your visual image.

Author's Experience My wife, Mary, is a kindergarten teacher. Whenever her young students start misbehaving and the situation becomes stressful (e.g., during lunchtime when the kids are running wildly, arguing vociferously, and screaming at maximum volume), Mary "plays" relaxing songs in her head. She reports that her musical imagination always works to soothe her nerves, enabling her to remain calm and even-tempered when she must confront children who need to be scolded or disciplined.

Joe Cuseo

Reflection 9.10

What are your most common sources or causes of stress?

What strategies do you use to cope with stress?

Would you say that you cope with stress well?

Simple Stress-Reduction Strategies and Habits

In addition to formal stress-management techniques of diaphragmatic breathing, progressive muscle relaxation, and mental imagery, stress may be managed by simpler strategies and habits, such as those discussed below.

1. **Exercise.** Exercise reduces stress by increasing release of serotonin—a mellowing brain chemical that reduces feelings of tension (anxiety) and depression. Studies also show that people who exercise regularly tend to report feeling happier (Myers, 1993). Exercise also elevates mood by improving people's sense of self-esteem because it gives them a sense of accomplishment by improving their physical self-image. It is for these reasons that counselors and psychotherapists recommend exercise for patients experiencing milder forms of anxiety or depression (Johnsgard, 2004).

2. **Keep a journal of feelings and emotions.** Writing about our feelings in a personal journal can serve as an effective way to identify our emotions (one form of emotional intelligence) and provide a safe outlet for releasing steam and coping with stress. Writing about our emotions also enables us to become more aware of them, reducing the risk that we'll deny them and push them out of consciousness.

3. **Take time for humor and laughter.** Research on the power of humor for reducing tension is clear and convincing. In one study, college students were suddenly told they had to deliver an impromptu (off the top of their head) speech. This unexpected assignment caused students' heart rate to elevate to an average of 110 beats per minute during delivery of the speech. However, students who watched humorous episodes of sitcoms before delivering their impromptu speeches had an average heart rate during the speech that was significantly lower (80–85 beats per minute), suggesting that humor reduces anxiety (O'Brien, as cited in Howard, 2000). Research also shows that if our immune system is suppressed or weakened by stress, humor strengthens it by blocking the body's production of the stress hormone cortisol—a biochemical responsible for suppressing our immune system when we're stressed (Berk, as cited in Liebertz, 2005b).

> "There are thousands of causes for stress, and one antidote to stress is self-expression. That's what happens to me every day. My thoughts get off my chest, down my sleeves, and onto my pad."
>
> —Garson Kanin, American writer, actor, and film director

> "The arrival of a good clown exercises a more beneficial influence upon the health of a town than the arrival of twenty asses laden with drugs."
>
> —Thomas Sydenham, 17th-century physician

Depression

Along with anxiety, depression is the emotional problem that most commonly afflicts humans and needs to be managed. Depression may be succinctly described as an emotional state characterized by loss of optimism, hope, and energy. As the term implies, when we're depressed, our mood is lowered or pushed down (like depressing the accelerator in a car). In contrast to anxiety, which typically involves worrying about something that is currently happening or is about to happen (e.g., experiencing test anxiety before an upcoming exam), depression more often relates to something that has already happened. In particular, depression is often related to a loss, such as a lost relationship (e.g., a departed friend, a broken romance, or the death of a family member) or a lost opportunity (e.g., losing a job, failing a course, or failing to be accepted into a major) (Bowlby, 1980; Price, Choi, & Vinokur, 2002). It is natural and normal to feel dejected after losses such as these. However, if dejection reaches a point where we can't concentrate and complete our day-to-day tasks, and if this continues for an extended period, we may be experiencing what psychologists call *clinical depression*—i.e., depression so serious that it requires professional help.

Research indicates that depression is a significant predictor of lower college GPA and higher probability of withdrawing from college, even among highly motivated and academically well-prepared students (Eisenberg, Golberstein, & Hunt, 2009).

9.1   DO IT **NOW** !

Recognizing the Symptoms (Signs) of Depression

- Feeling low, down, dejected, sad, or blue
- Pessimistic feelings about the future (e.g., expecting failure or feeling helpless or hopeless)
- Decreased sense of humor
- Difficulty finding pleasure, joy, or fun in anything
- Lack of concentration
- Loss of motivation or interest in things previously found to be exciting or stimulating
- Stooped posture (e.g., hung head or drawn face)
- Slower and softer speech rate
- Decreased animation and slower bodily movements
- Loss of energy

- Changes in sleeping patterns (e.g., sleeping more or less than usual)
- Changes in eating patterns (e.g., eating more or less than usual)
- Social withdrawal
- Neglect of physical appearance
- Consistently low self-esteem (e.g., thinking "I'm a loser")
- Strong feelings of worthlessness or guilt (e.g., thinking "I'm a failure")
- Suicidal thoughts (e.g., thoughts such as "I can't take it anymore," "People would be better off without me," or "I don't deserve to live")

Do It Now! 9.1 provides a summary of symptoms or signs of depression. If these symptoms continue to occur for two or more weeks, action should be taken to relieve them.

Remember

There is a difference between feeling despondent or down and being depressed. When psychologists use the word depression, *they're usually referring to clinical depression—a mood state so low that it's interfering with a person's ability to cope with day-to-day life tasks, such as getting to school or going to work.*

Reflection 9.11

Have you, or a member of your family, ever experienced clinical depression?

What do you think was the primary cause or factor that triggered it?

Strategies for Coping with Depression

Depression can vary widely in intensity. Moderate and severe forms of depression often require professional counseling or psychotherapy, and their cause often lies in genetic factors that involve inherited imbalances in brain chemistry.

The following strategies are offered primarily for milder cases of depression that are manageable through self-help and self-control. These strategies may also be used in conjunction with professional help or psychiatric medication to reduce the intensity and frequency of depression.

1. **Focus on the present and the future, not the past.** We should consciously fight the tendency to dwell on past losses or failures, because we can no longer change or control them. Instead, focus on things you can still control, which are occurring now and will occur in the future. This can be a challenging task because when you have an experience, your response to it passes through emotional areas of the brain before it reaches areas of the brain involved in rational thinking and reasoning (LeDoux, 1998, 2003). (See **Figure 9.2**.)

   Thus, your brain reacts to events emotionally before it does rationally. If an experience triggers intense emotions (e.g., anger, anxiety, or sadness after receiving a bad test grade), your emotional reaction has the potential to short-circuit or wipe out rational thinking. Thus, if you find yourself beginning to feel overwhelmed by negative emotions following a setback, you need to consciously and quickly block them with rational thoughts (e.g., thinking or saying to yourself, "Before I get carried away emotionally, let me think this through rationally"). This involves more than simply saying, "I have to stay positive." Instead, you should develop a set of specific counter-thinking strategies ready to use as soon as you begin to think negatively.

2. **Increase effort to engage in positive or emotionally uplifting behavior.** If our behavior is upbeat, our mind (mood) often follows suit. "Put on a happy face" may be an effective depression-reduction strategy because smiling induces certain changes in our facial muscles, which, in turn, trigger changes in brain chemistry that improve our mood (Liebertz, 2005a). In contrast, frowning activates a different set of facial muscles that tend to reduce production of mood-elevating brain chemicals (Myers, 1993).

3. **Continue to engage in activities that are fun and enjoyable.** Falling into the downward spiral of withdrawing from doing the things that bring you joy because you're too down to do them will bring you even lower by taking away the very things that bring you up. You should continue to socialize with friends and engage in your usual recreational activities. Interestingly, the root of the word *recreation* means "to re-create" (create again), which suggests that recreation can revive, restore, and renew us—physically and emotionally.

4. **Continue trying to get things done.** By staying busy and getting things done when we're feeling down, helps boost our mood because we experience a sense of accomplishment that boosts our self-esteem. Doing things for others less fortunate than yourself can be a particularly effective way to elevate your mood because it helps you realize that your issues are often far less serious and more manageable than the problems faced by others.

> "Yesterday is gone. Tomorrow has not yet come. We have only today. Let us begin."
>
> —Mother Teresa of Calcutta, Albanian Catholic nun and winner of the Nobel Peace Prize

> "The best way to cheer yourself up is to try to cheer somebody else up."
>
> —Samuel Clemens, a.k.a. Mark Twain, writer, lecturer, and humorist

FIGURE 9.2

Information passes through the emotional center of the brain (lower, shaded area) before reaching the center responsible for rational thinking (upper area). Thus, people need to counteract their tendency to respond emotionally and irrationally to personal setbacks by making a conscious attempt to respond rationally and positively.

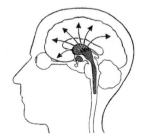

© Kendall Hunt

The Human Brain First Processes Information Emotionally before It Reaches Higher Areas of Rational Thinking

5. **Intentionally seek out humor and opportunities to laugh.** In addition to reducing anxiety, laughter can lighten and brighten a dark mood. In addition, humor improves memory (Nielson, as cited in Liebertz, 2005a), which is an important benefit because depression tends to impair concentration and memory. Research supporting the benefits of humor for the body and mind is so well established that humor has become a legitimate academic field of study known as *gelontology*—the study of laughter (from the Greek word *gelos* for "laughter" and *ology*, meaning "study of").

6. **Make a conscious effort to focus on your personal strengths and accomplishments.** Another way to drive away the blues is by keeping track of the positive developments in your life. You can do this by keeping a positive events journal in which you note the good experiences in your life, including things you're grateful for, as well as your accomplishments and achievements. Positive journal entries will leave you with a visible uplifting record that you can review any time you're feeling down. Furthermore, a positive events journal can provide a starting point for developing a resume, portfolio, and personal strengths sheet, which can be provided to those who serve as your personal references and those who write letters of recommendation for you.

7. **If you're unable to overcome depression on your own, seek help from others.** Compared to previous generations, today's college students are more likely to seek professional help if they're feeling depressed (Kadison & DiGeronimo, 2004). This is good news because it suggests that seeking help is no longer viewed as a source of embarrassment or a sign of personal weakness: instead, college students are more willing to share their feelings with others and improve the quality of their emotional life.

"If you can laugh at it, you can survive it."

—Bill Cosby, American comedian, actor, and activist

One strategy for coping with depression is to write down the positive events in your life in a journal.

In some cases, students may be able to help themselves overcome emotional problems through personal effort and effective coping strategies. This is particularly true if they experience depression or anxiety in milder forms and for limited periods. However, overcoming more serious and long-lasting episodes of clinical depression or anxiety isn't as simple as people make it out to be when they glibly and insensitively say, "Just deal with it," "Get over it," or "Snap out of it." More serious cases of depression and anxiety are often strongly associated with genetic factors, which are not completely within the person's ability to control.

Reflection **9.12**

If you thought you were experiencing a serious episode of anxiety or depression, would you feel comfortable seeking help from a professional?

If yes, why? If no, why not?

Summary and Conclusion

The quality of our interpersonal relationships is strengthened by communication skills (verbal and nonverbal) and human relations (people) skills. We can improve our interactions and relationships by working hard at remembering the names and interests of people we meet, being good listeners, and being open to different topics of conversation.

Interpersonal conflict is an inevitable aspect of social life; we can't completely eliminate it, but we can minimize and manage it with effective strategies that enable us to resolve conflicts assertively rather than aggressively, passively, or passive–aggressively.

Today's college students report higher levels of stress than students in years past. Strategies for reducing excess stress include formal stress-management techniques (e.g., diaphragmatic breathing and progressive muscle relaxation), good physical habits (e.g., exercising and reducing intake of caffeine or other stimulants), and positive ways of thinking (e.g., focusing on the present and the future, rather than the past, and making a conscious effort to focus on our personal strengths and accomplishments).

Intellectual ability is only one form of human intelligence. Social and emotional intelligence are at least as important for being successful, healthy, and happy. The strategies discussed in this chapter are not merely "soft skills": they're actually "hardcore" skills essential for success in college and beyond.

Learning More through the World Wide Web

Internet-Based Resources for Further Information on Social and Emotional Intelligence

For additional information related to the ideas discussed in this chapter, we recommend the following Web sites:

Social Intelligence and Interpersonal Relationships:

www.articles911.com/Communication/Interpersonal_Communication/hodu.com/ECS-Menu1.shtml

Emotional Intelligence and Mental Health:

www.eqi.org/eitoc.htm

www.nimh.nih.gov/health/publications/index.shtml (National Institute of Mental Health)

www.activeminds.org (national, student-run organization that supports mental health awareness)

9.1 Identifying Ways of Handling Interpersonal Conflict

Think of a social situation or relationship that's currently causing the most conflict in your life. Describe how this conflict could be approached in each of the following ways:

1. Passively:
2. Aggressively:
3. Passive-aggressively:
4. Assertively:

(See pp. 227–231 for descriptions of each of these four approaches.)

Practice the assertive approach by role-playing it with a friend or classmate and consider applying it to the actual situation or relationship in your life that's currently causing you the most conflict.

9.2 College Stress: Identifying Potential Sources and Possible Solutions

Read through the following 29 college stressors and rate them in terms of how stressful each one is for you on a scale from 1 to 5 (1 = lowest, 5 = highest):

Potential Stressors	*Stress Rating*				
Tests and exams	1	2	3	4	5
Assignments	1	2	3	4	5
Class workload	1	2	3	4	5
Pace of courses	1	2	3	4	5
Performing up to expectations	1	2	3	4	5
Handling personal freedom	1	2	3	4	5
Time pressure (e.g., not enough time)	1	2	3	4	5
Organizational pressure (e.g., losing things)	1	2	3	4	5
Living independently	1	2	3	4	5
The future	1	2	3	4	5
Decisions about a major or career	1	2	3	4	5
Moral and ethical decisions	1	2	3	4	5
Finding meaning in life	1	2	3	4	5
Emotional issues	1	2	3	4	5
Physical health	1	2	3	4	5
Social life	1	2	3	4	5
Intimate relationships	1	2	3	4	5
Sexuality	1	2	3	4	5

Family responsibilities	1	2	3	4	5
Family conflicts	1	2	3	4	5
Family pressure	1	2	3	4	5
Peer pressure	1	2	3	4	5
Loneliness or isolation	1	2	3	4	5
Roommate conflicts	1	2	3	4	5
Conflict with professors	1	2	3	4	5
Campus policies or procedures	1	2	3	4	5
Transportation	1	2	3	4	5
Technology	1	2	3	4	5
Safety	1	2	3	4	5

Review your ratings and write down three of your top (highest-rated) stressors. Identify: (1) a coping strategy you may use on your own to deal with each source of stress, and (2) a campus resource you could use to obtain help with each source of stress.

Stressor: _____

Personal coping strategy:

Campus resource:

Stressor: _____

Personal coping strategy:

Campus resource:

Stressor: _____

Personal coping strategy:

Campus resource:

9.3 Transforming Pessimistic Thought into Optimistic Thoughts

In *Hamlet*, Shakespeare wrote, "There is nothing good or bad, but thinking makes it so." His point was that our experiences have the potential to be positive or negative, depending on how we interpret them and react to them.

Listed below is a series of statements representing negative interpretations and reactions to a bad situation or personal setback.

1. "I'm just not good at this."

2. "There's nothing I can do about it."

3. "Things will never be the same."

4. "This always happens to me."

5. "This is unbearable."

6. "Everybody is going to think I'm a loser."

For each of the above statements, replace the negative statement with a statement that reflects a more positive interpretation or reaction—i.e., one that would decrease anxiety and increase the person's sense of optimism or hope.

Caught between a Rock and a Hard Place: Romantic versus Academic Commitments

Lauren has been dating her boyfriend (Nick) for about two months. She's convinced this is the real thing and that she's definitely in love. Lately, Nick has been asking her to skip class to spend more time with him. He tells Lauren, "If you really love me, you would do it for our relationship." Lauren feels that Nick truly loves her and wouldn't do anything to hurt her or interfere with her goals. So she figures that skipping a few classes to spend time with her boyfriend is the right choice. However, Lauren's grades soon start to slip; at the same time, Nick starts to demand that she spend even more time with him.

Reflection and Discussion Questions

1. What concerns you most about Lauren's behavior?

2. What concerns you most about Nick's behavior?

3. Would you agree with Lauren's decision to start skipping classes?

4. What might Lauren do to keep her grades up and still keep her relationship with Nick strong?

5. If you were Lauren's friend, what advice would you give her?

6. If you were Nick's friend, what advice would you give him?

10

Diversity
Learning about and from Human Differences

ACTIVATE YOUR THINKING | *Reflection* **10.1**

LEARNING GOAL

To further your appreciation of human differences and develop skills for making the most of diversity in college and beyond.

Complete the following sentence:

When I hear the word *diversity,* the first thoughts that come to my mind are . . .

The Spectrum of Diversity

The word *diversity* derives from the Latin root *diversus,* meaning "various." Thus, human diversity refers to the variety of differences that exist among the people who comprise humanity (the human species). In this chapter, we use *diversity* to refer primarily to differences among the major groups of people who, collectively, comprise humankind or humanity. The relationship between diversity and humanity is represented visually in **Figure 10.1**.

The relationship between humanity and human diversity is similar to the relationship between sunlight and the spectrum of colors. Just as sunlight passing through a prism is dispersed into all groups of colors that make up the visual spectrum, the human species spread across the planet is dispersed into all groups of people that make up the human spectrum (humanity). As you can see in Figure 10.1, human diversity expresses itself in numerous ways, including differences in physical features, religious beliefs, mental and physical abilities, national origins, social backgrounds, gender, and sexual orientation.

Since diversity has been interpreted (and misinterpreted) in different ways by different people, we begin by defining some key terms related to diversity that should lead to a clearer understanding of its true meaning and value.

> "We are all brothers and sisters. Each face in the rainbow of color that populates our world is precious and special. Each adds to the rich treasure of humanity."
>
> —Morris Dees, civil rights leader and cofounder of the Southern Poverty Law Center

What Is Race?

A racial group (race) is a group of people who share some distinctive physical traits, such as skin color or facial characteristics. The U.S. Census Bureau (2010) identifies four races: White, Black, Asian, and American Indian or Alaska Native. However, as Anderson and Fienberg (2000) caution, racial categories are social-political constructs (concepts) that are not based on scientific research, but on classifications constructed by people. There continues to be disagreement among scholars about what groups of people constitute a human race or whether distinctive races exist (Wheelright, 2005). No identifiable set of genes distinguishes one race from another.

245

FIGURE 10.1

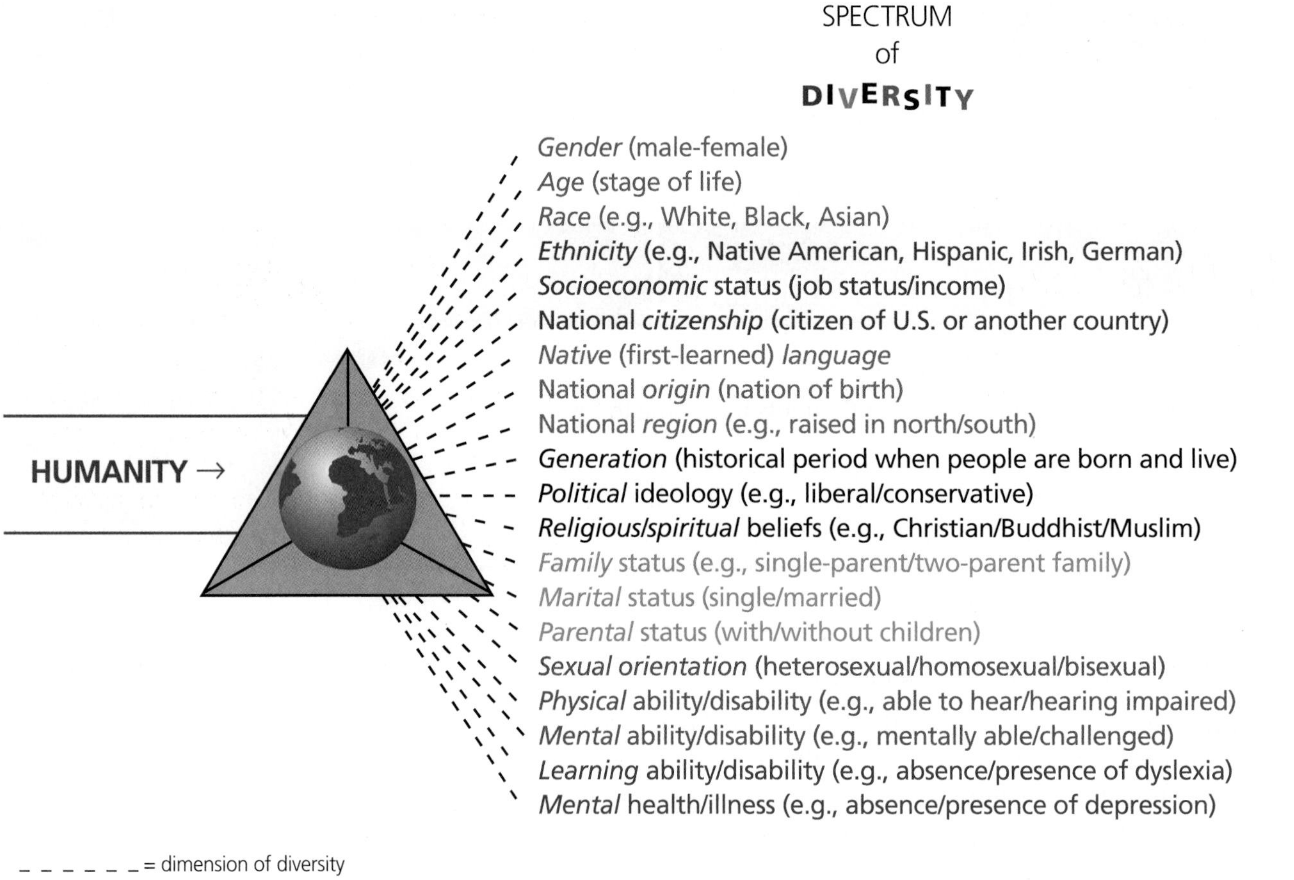

SPECTRUM
of
DIVERSITY

HUMANITY →

Gender (male-female)
Age (stage of life)
Race (e.g., White, Black, Asian)
Ethnicity (e.g., Native American, Hispanic, Irish, German)
Socioeconomic status (job status/income)
National *citizenship* (citizen of U.S. or another country)
Native (first-learned) *language*
National *origin* (nation of birth)
National *region* (e.g., raised in north/south)
Generation (historical period when people are born and live)
Political ideology (e.g., liberal/conservative)
Religious/spiritual beliefs (e.g., Christian/Buddhist/Muslim)
Family status (e.g., single-parent/two-parent family)
Marital status (single/married)
Parental status (with/without children)
Sexual orientation (heterosexual/homosexual/bisexual)
Physical ability/disability (e.g., able to hear/hearing impaired)
Mental ability/disability (e.g., mentally able/challenged)
Learning ability/disability (e.g., absence/presence of dyslexia)
Mental health/illness (e.g., absence/presence of depression)

_ _ _ _ _ _ = dimension of diversity

*This list represents some of the major dimensions of human diversity; it does not represent a complete list of all possible forms of human diversity. Also, disagreement exists about certain dimensions of diversity (e.g., whether certain groups should be considered races or ethnic groups).

Humanity and Diversity

In other words, you can't do a blood test or some type of internal genetic test to determine a person's race. Humans have simply decided to categorize people into races on the basis of certain external differences in physical appearance, particularly the color of their outer layer of skin. The U.S. Census Bureau could just as easily have divided people into categories based on such physical characteristics as eye color (blue, brown, and green) or hair texture (straight, wavy, curly, and frizzy).

Reflection **10.2**

Look at the diversity spectrum in Figure 10.1 and look over the list of groups that make up the spectrum. Do you notice any groups missing from the list that should be added, either because they have distinctive backgrounds or because they've been targets of prejudice and discrimination?

The differences in skin color we now see among different human beings are largely due to biological adaptations that evolved over thousands of years among groups of humans living in different regions of the world under different climatic conditions. Darker skin tones developed among humans inhabiting and reproducing in hotter regions nearer the equator (e.g., Africans) because darker skin helped them adapt and survive by providing their bodies with better protection from the potentially damaging effects of the sun (Bridgeman, 2003). In contrast, lighter skin tones developed over time among humans inhabiting colder climates that were farther from the equator (e.g., Scandinavia) to enable their bodies to absorb greater amounts of vitamin D supplied by sunlight, which was in shorter supply in their region of the world (Jablonski & Chaplin, 2002).

Author's Experience My mother was from Alabama and was dark in skin color, with high cheekbones and long curly black hair. My father stood approximately six feet and had light brown straight hair. His skin color was that of a Western European with a slight suntan. If you didn't know that my father was of African American descent, you would not have thought of him as Black. All of my life I've thought of myself as African American, and all of the people who are familiar with me thought of me as African American. I've lived half of a century with that as my racial description. Several years ago, after carefully looking through records available on births and deaths in my family history, I discovered that fewer than 50 percent of my ancestors were of African lineage. Biologically, I'm not Black; socially and emotionally, I still am. Clearly, race is more of a social concept than a biological fact.

Aaron Thompson

While humans may display diversity in the color or tone of their outer layer of skin, the biological reality is that all members of the human species are remarkably similar. More than 98 percent of the genes that make up humans from different racial groups are exactly the same (Bridgeman, 2003; Molnar, 1991). This large amount of genetic overlap among humans accounts for the many similarities that exist, regardless of differences in skin color. For example, all people have similar external features that give them a human appearance and clearly distinguish people from other animal species, all humans have internal organs that are similar in structure and function, and regardless of the color of their outer layer of skin, when it's cut, all humans bleed in the same color.

Reflection 10.3

What race do you consider yourself to be? Would you say you identify strongly with your race, or are you rarely conscious of it?

What Is Culture?

"Culture" may be defined as a distinctive pattern of beliefs and values learned by a group of people who share the same social heritage and traditions. In short, culture is the whole way in which a group of people has learned to live (Peoples & Bailey, 2008): it includes their style of speaking (language), fashion, food, art, music, values, and beliefs. Cultural differences can exist within the same society (multicultural society), within a single nation (domestic diversity), or across different nations (international diversity).

A major advantage of culture is that it helps bind its members together into a supportive, tight-knit community; however, it can blind them to other cultural perspectives. Since culture shapes the way people think, it can cause groups of people to view the world solely through their own cultural lens or frame of reference (Colombo, Cullen, & Lisle, 2010). Optical illusions are a good example of how cultural perspectives can blind people, or lead them to inaccurate perceptions. For instance, compare the lengths of the two lines in Figure 10.2.

Author's Experience

Being African American and living in southeastern Kentucky, the heart of Appalachia, did not provide for the grandest of living styles. Even though my father worked 12 hours a day in the coal mines, he earned only enough pay to supply staples for the table. Our family also worked as tenant farmers to have enough vegetables for my mother to can for the winter and to provide a roof over our heads.

My mother was a direct descendent of slaves and moved with her parents from the deep south at the age of 17. My father lived in an all-Black coal mining camp, into which my mother and her family moved in 1938. My dad would say to me, "Son, you will have opportunities that I never had. Many people, White and Black alike, will tell you that you are no good and that education can never help you. Don't listen to them because soon they will not be able to keep you from getting an education like they did me. Just remember, when you do get that education, you'll never have to go in those coal mines and have them break your back. You can choose what you want to do, and then you can be a free man."

My father lived through a time when freedom was something he dreamed his children might enjoy someday, because before the civil rights movement succeeded in changing the laws, African Americans were considerably limited in educational opportunities, job opportunities, and much else in what was definitely a racist society. My father remained illiterate because he was not allowed to attend public schools in eastern Kentucky.

In the early 1960s, my brother, my sister, and I were integrated into the White public schools. Physical violence and constant verbal harassment caused many other Blacks to forgo their education and opt for jobs in the coal mines at an early age. But my father remained constant in his advice to me: "It doesn't matter if they call you n_____, but don't you ever let them beat you by walking out on your education."

Being poor, Black, and Appalachian did not offer me great odds for success, but constant reminders from my parents that I was a good and valuable person helped me to see beyond my deterrents to the true importance of education. My parents, who could never provide me with monetary wealth, truly made me proud of them by giving me the gift of insight and an aspiration for achievement.

Aaron Thompson

FIGURE 10.2

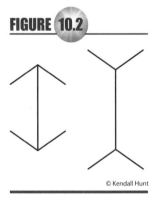

© Kendall Hunt

Optical Illusion

If you perceive the line on the right to be longer than the line on the left, welcome to the club. Virtually all Americans and people from Western cultures perceive the line on the right to be longer. Actually, both lines are equal in length. (If you don't believe it, take out a ruler and check it out.) Interestingly, this perceptual error isn't made by people from non-Western cultures whose architectural structures consist primarily of circular structures, rather than rectangular buildings with angled corners that have been constructed in Western cultures (Segall, Campbell, & Herskovits, 1996).

The key point underlying this optical illusion is that cultural experiences shape and sometimes distort perceptions of reality. People think they are seeing things objectively or as they really are, but they're really seeing things subjectively from their particular cultural vantage point. Being open to the viewpoints of diverse people who perceive the world from different cultural vantage points widens our range of perception and helps us overcome our cultural blind spots. As a result, we tend to perceive the world around us with greater clarity and accuracy.

• Remember

The reality of our own culture is not the reality of other cultures. Our perceptions of the outside world are shaped (and sometimes distorted) by our prior cultural experiences.

What Is an Ethnic Group?

An ethnic group (ethnicity) is a group of people who share the same culture. Thus, *culture* refers to what an ethnic group has in common and *ethnic group* refers to people who share the same culture. Unlike a racial group, whose members share physical characteristics that they are born with and that have been passed on to them biologically, an ethnic group's shared characteristics have been passed on through socialization—their common characteristics have been learned or acquired through shared social experiences.

The major cultural (ethnic) groups found within the United States include:

- Native Americans (American Indians)
  - Cherokee, Navajo, Hopi, Alaska Natives, Blackfoot, etc.
- African Americans (Blacks)
  - Americans whose cultural roots lie in the continent of Africa (e.g., Ethiopia, Kenya, Nigeria) and the Caribbean Islands (e.g., Bahamas, Cuba, Jamaica).
- Hispanic Americans (Latinos)
  - Americans with cultural roots in Mexico, Puerto Rico, Central America (e.g., El Salvador, Guatemala, Nicaragua), and South America (e.g., Brazil, Colombia, Venezuela).
- Asian Americans
  - Americans who are cultural descendants of East Asia (e.g., Japan, China, Korea), Southeast Asia (e.g., Vietnam, Thailand, Cambodia), and South Asia (e.g., India, Pakistan, Bangladesh).
- Middle Eastern Americans
  - Americans with cultural roots in Iraq, Iran, Israel, etc.
- European Americans (Whites)
  - Americans with roots in Western Europe (e.g., the United Kingdom, Ireland, the Netherlands), Eastern Europe (e.g., Hungary, Romania, Bulgaria), Southern Europe (e.g., Italy, Greece, Portugal), and Northern Europe or Scandinavia (e.g., Denmark, Sweden, Norway).

© neelsky, 2013. Under license from Shutterstock, Inc.

Culture is a distinctive pattern of beliefs and values that develops among a group of people who share the same social heritage and traditions.

Currently, European Americans are the majority ethnic group in the United States because they account for more than 50 percent of the American population. Native Americans, African Americans, Hispanic Americans, and Asian Americans are considered to be ethnic minority groups because each of these groups represents less than 50 percent of the American population.

Reflection **10.4**

Which ethnic group or groups do you belong to or identify with?

What are the most common cultural values shared by your ethnic group or groups?

Ethnic groups can be comprised of Whites or people of color. For people of color, their ethnicity is immediately visible to other people; in contrast, members of White ethnic groups have the option of choosing whether they want to identify with their ethnicity or share it with others, because it is not visible to the naked eye. Members of ethnic minority groups with European ancestry can more easily "blend into" or become assimilated into the majority (dominant) culture because their minority status can't be visibly detected. Minority White immigrants of European ancestry have even changed their last names to appear to be Americans of English descent. In contrast, the immediately detectable minority status of African Americans, darker-skinned Hispanics, and Native Americans doesn't allow them the option of presenting themselves as members of an already-assimilated majority group (National Council for the Social Sciences, 1991).

Author's Experience   My mother's family changed their name from the very Italian-sounding DeVigilio to the more American-sounding Vigilis, and my mother's first name was changed from the Italian-sounding Carmella to Mildred. My father's first name was also changed from Biaggio to Blase; he chose to list his first name, not his last name (Cuseo), on the sign outside his watch-repair cubicle in New York City because he feared that would reveal his Italian ethnicity and people would not bring him their business.

Thus, my parents were able to minimize their risk of appearing "different" and encountering discrimination, while maximizing their chances of being assimilated (absorbed) into American culture. If my parents were members of a non-White ethnic group, they would not have been able to "hide" their ethnicity and reduce their risk of encountering prejudice or discrimination. I learned later that some Jewish Americans used the same name-changing strategies as my parents and grandparents: for example, changing their last name from Greenbaum to Green in order to avoid anti-Semitic treatment.

Joe Cuseo

As with racial grouping, classifying humans into different ethnic groups can also be very arbitrary and subject to different interpretations by different groups of people. Currently, there are three racial categories used by the U.S. Census Bureau: White, Black, and Asian. Hispanics are not defined as a race, but are classified as an ethnic group. However, among those who checked "some other race" in the 2000 Census, 97 percent were Hispanic. This finding suggests that Hispanic Americans consider themselves to be a racial group, probably because this is how they feel they're perceived and treated by non-Hispanics (Cianciotto, 2005). Supporting the Hispanic viewpoint that others perceive them as a race, rather than an ethnic group, is the recent use of the term *racial profiling* in the American media to describe Arizona's controversial 2010 law that allows police to target people who "look" like illegal aliens from Mexico, Central America, and South America. Again, this illustrates how race and ethnicity are subjective, socially constructed concepts that depend on how society perceives and treats certain social groups, which, in turn, affect how these groups perceive themselves.

This disagreement illustrates how difficult it is to conveniently categorize groups of people into particular racial or ethnic groups. The United States will continue to struggle with this issue because the ethnic and racial diversity of its population is growing and members of different ethnic and racial groups are forming cross-ethnic and interracial families. Thus, it is becoming progressively more difficult to place people into distinct categories based on their race or ethnicity. For example, by 2050, the number of people who will identify themselves as being of two or more races is projected to more than triple, growing from 5.2 million to 16.2 million (U.S. Census Bureau, 2008).

What Is Humanity?

It's important to realize that human variety and human similarity coexist and complement each other. Diversity is a "value that is shown in mutual respect and appreciation of similarities and differences" (Public Service Enterprise Group, 2009). Experiencing diversity not only enhances appreciation of the unique features of different cultures, but also provides a larger perspective on the universal aspects of the human experience that are common to all humans, no matter what their particular cultural background may be. For example, despite racial and cultural differences, all people express the same emotions with the same facial expressions. (See Figure 10.3.)

Other human characteristics that anthropologists have found to be shared by all groups of people in every corner of the world include storytelling, poetry, adornment of the body, dance, music, decoration of artifacts, families, socialization of children by elders, a sense of right and wrong, supernatural beliefs, and mourning of the dead (Pinker, 2000). Although different ethnic groups may express these shared experiences in different ways, these universal experiences are common to all humans.

> **Remember**
> *Diversity represents variations on the common theme of humanity. Although groups of humans may have different cultural backgrounds, they're still cultivated from the same soil—we're all grounded in the common experience of being human.*

Reflection 10.5

List three human experiences you think are universal—i.e., experienced by all humans in all cultures:

1.

2.

3.

"As the child of a Black man and a White woman, someone who was born in the racial melting pot of Hawaii, with a sister who's half Indonesian but who's usually mistaken for Mexican or Puerto Rican and a brother-in-law and niece of Chinese descent, with some blood relatives who resemble Margaret Thatcher and others who could pass for Bernie Mac, family get-togethers over Christmas take on the appearance of a UN General Assembly meeting. I've never had the option of restricting my loyalties on the basis of race, or measuring my worth on the basis of tribe."

—Barack Obama, 44th president of the United States and winner of the Nobel Peace Prize

"Above all nations is humanity."

—Motto of the University of Hawaii

FIGURE 10.3

Humans all over the world display the same facial expressions when experiencing certain emotions. See if you can detect the emotions being expressed in the following faces. (To find the answers, turn your book upside down.)

  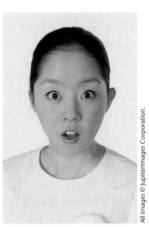

Answers: The emotions shown, Top, left to right: anger, fear, and sadness. Bottom, left to right: disgust, happiness, and surprise.

"We are all the same, and we are all unique."

—Georgia Dunston, African American biologist and research specialist in human genetics

Different cultures associated with different ethnic groups may be viewed simply as variations on the same theme: being human. You may have heard the question, "We're all human, aren't we?" The answer to this important question is "yes and no." Yes, humans are all the same, but not in the same way.

A good metaphor for understanding this apparent contradiction is to visualize humanity as a quilt in which we are all joined by the common thread of humanity—by the common bond of being human. The different patches that make up the quilt represent diversity—the distinctive or unique cultures that comprise our common humanity. The quilt metaphor acknowledges the identity and beauty of all cultures. It differs from the old American "melting pot" metaphor, which viewed differences as something that should be melted down or eliminated, or the salad bowl metaphor, which suggested that America is a hodgepodge or mishmash of cultures thrown together without any common connection. In contrast, the quilt metaphor suggests that the cultures of different ethnic groups are to be recognized and celebrated, but

can be woven together to create a unified whole, as in the Latin expression *E pluribus unum* ("Out of many, one")—the motto of the United States, which you'll find printed on its coins.

To appreciate diversity and its relationship to humanity is to capitalize on the power of our differences (diversity) while still preserving our collective strength through unity (humanity).

> "We have become not a melting pot but a beautiful mosaic."
>
> —Jimmy Carter, 39th president of the United States and winner of the Nobel Peace Prize

Remember

When we learn about human differences (diversity), we simultaneously learn about our commonalities (humanity).

Author's Experience

When I was 12 years old and living in New York City, I returned from school one Friday afternoon and my mother asked me if anything interesting happened at school that day. I mentioned to her that the teacher went around the room, asking students what we had for dinner the night before. At that moment, my mother began to become a bit agitated and nervously asked me, "What did you tell the teacher?" I said, "I told her and the rest of the class that I had pasta last night because my family always eats pasta on Thursdays and Sundays." My mother exploded and fired back at me, "Why couldn't you tell her that we had steak or roast beef?" For a moment, I was stunned and couldn't figure out what I had done wrong or why I should have lied about eating pasta. Then it suddenly dawned on me: my mom was embarrassed about being Italian American. She wanted me to hide our family's ethnic background and make it sound like we were very "American."

I never forgot this incident because it was such an emotionally intense experience. For the first time in my life, I became aware that my mother was ashamed of being a member of the same group to which every other member of my family belonged, including me. After her outburst, I felt a combined rush of astonishment and embarrassment. However, these feelings eventually faded and my mother's reaction ended up having the opposite effect on me. Instead of making me feel inferior or ashamed about being Italian American, her reaction that day caused me to become more aware of, and take more pride in, my Italian heritage.

As I grew older, I also grew to understand why my mother felt the way she did. She grew up in America's melting pot era—a time when different American ethnic groups were expected to melt down and melt away their ethnicity. They were not to celebrate diversity: they were to eliminate it.

Joe Cuseo

Student Perspective

When you see me, do not
    look at me with disgrace.
Know that I am an
    African-American
Birthed by a woman of style
    and grace.
Be proud
To stand by my side.
Hold your head high
Like me.
Be proud. To say you know
    me.
Just as I stand by you, proud
    to be me.

—Poem by Brittany Beard, first-year student

What Is Individuality?

It's important to keep in mind that individual differences within the same racial or ethnic group are greater than the average differences between different groups. For example, differences in physical attributes (e.g., height and weight) and behavior patterns (e.g., personality characteristics) among individuals within the same racial group are greater than the average differences between racial groups (Caplan & Caplan, 2009).

As you proceed through this chapter, keep in mind the following distinctions among humanity, diversity, and individuality:

- **Diversity.** We are all members of *different groups* (e.g., different gender and ethnic groups).
- **Humanity.** We are all members of the *same group* (the human species).
- **Cultural competence.** The ability to *appreciate and capitalize* on human differences by interacting effectively with people from diverse cultural backgrounds.
- **Individuality.** We are all *unique individuals* who differ from other members of any group to which we may belong.

> "Every human is, at the same time, like all other humans, like some humans, and like no other human."
>
> —Clyde Kluckhohn, American anthropologist

Major Forms or Types of Diversity in Today's World

Ethnic and Racial Diversity

America is rapidly becoming a more racially and ethnically diverse nation. In 2008, the minority population in the United States reached an all-time high of 34 percent of the total population. The population of ethnic minorities is now growing at a much faster rate than the White majority. This trend is expected to continue, and by the middle of the 21st century, the minority population will have grown from one-third of the U.S. population to more than one-half (54 percent), with more than 60 percent of the nation's children expected to be members of what we now call minority groups (U.S. Census Bureau, 2008).

By 2050, the U.S. population is projected to be more than 30 percent Hispanic (up from 15 percent in 2008), 15 percent Black (up from 13 percent), 9.6 percent Asian (up from 5.3 percent), and 2 percent Native American (up from 1.6 percent). The native Hawaiian and Pacific Islander population is expected to more than double between 2008 and 2050. During this same time period, the percentage of White Americans will drop from 66 percent (2008) to 46 percent (2050). As a result of these population trends, ethnic and racial minorities will become the new majority because they will constitute the majority of Americans by the middle of the 21st century. (See **Figure 10.4**.)

Socioeconomic Diversity

Diversity also appears in the form of socioeconomic status or social class, which is typically stratified (divided) into lower, middle, and upper classes, based on level of education and income. Groups occupying lower social strata have significantly fewer social and economic opportunities or privileges (Feagin & Feagin, 2007).

According to U.S. Census figures, the wealthiest 20 percent of the American population controls approximately 50 percent of the country's total income, and the 20 percent of Americans with the lowest income controls only 4 percent of the nation's income. Sharp discrepancies also exist in income level among different racial, ethnic, and gender groups. In 2007, Black households had the lowest median income

FIGURE **10.4**

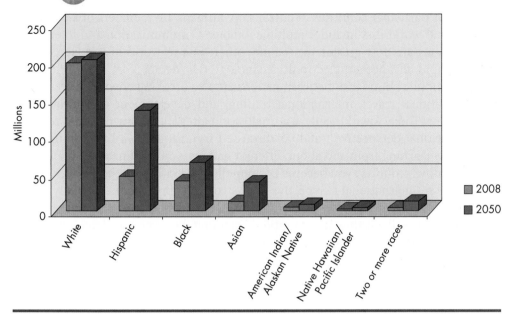

The "New Majority"

($33,916), compared to a median income of $54,920 for non-Hispanic White house-holds (Annual Social and Economic Supplement, 2008).

Poverty continues to be a problem in America. In 2007, 12.5 percent of Americans (37.3 million people) lived below the poverty line, making the United States one of the most impoverished of all developed countries in the world (Shah, 2008). Although all ethnic and racial groups experience poverty, minority groups experience poverty at significantly higher rates than the White majority. In 2007, poverty rates for different ethnic and racial groups were as follows:

- Whites: 8.2 percent
- Asians: 10.2 percent
- Hispanics: 21.5 percent
- Blacks: 24.5 percent
  Source: U.S. Census Bureau, 2008.

It's estimated that 600,000 families and 1.25 million children are now homeless, accounting for roughly 50 percent of the homeless population. Typically, these families are comprised of a mother and two children under the age of five (National Alliance to End Homelessness, 2007).

Reflection **10.6**

What do you think is the factor that is most responsible for poverty in:

1. the United States?

2. the world?

International Diversity

Beyond our particular countries of citizenship, humans are members of a common, international world that includes multiple nations. Communication and interaction across nations are now greater than at any other time in world history, largely because of rapid advances in electronic technology (Dryden & Vos, 1999; Friedman, 2005). Economic boundaries between nations are also breaking down due to increasing international travel, international trading, and development of multinational corporations. Today's world really is a small world after all, and success in it requires an international perspective—and, as discussed in Chapter 2, a 21st-century perspective. By learning from and about different nations, you become more than a citizen of your own country: you become cosmopolitan—a citizen of the world.

Taking an international perspective allows you to appreciate the diversity of humankind. If it were possible to reduce the world's population to a village of precisely 100 people, with all existing human ratios remaining the same, the demographics of this world village would look something like this:

- 61 would be Asians, 13 Africans, 12 Europeans, 9 Latin Americans, and 5 from the USA and Canada
- 50 would be male, 50 would be female
- 75 would be non-White; 25 White
- 67 would be non-Christian; 33 would be Christian
- 80 would live in substandard housing
- 16 would be unable to read or write
- 50 would be malnourished and 1 dying of starvation
- 33 would be without access to a safe water supply
- 39 would lack access to improved sanitation
- 24 would not have any electricity (and of the 76 that do have electricity, most would only use it for light at night)
- 8 people would have access to the Internet
- 1 would have a college education
- 1 would have HIV
- 2 would be near birth; 1 near death
- 5 would control 32 percent of the entire world's wealth; all 5 would be US citizens
- 48 would live on less than US$2 a day
- 20 would live on less than US$1 a day
  Source: Family Care Foundation (1997–2012).

Generational Diversity

Humans are also diverse with respect to the generation in which they grew up. "Generation" refers to a group of individuals born during the same historical period whose attitudes, values, and habits have been shaped by events that took place in the world during their formative years of development. Each generation experiences different historical events, so it's likely that generations will develop different attitudes and behaviors as a result.

Snapshot Summary 10.1 provides a brief summary of the major generations, the key historical events that occurred during the formative periods of the people in each generation, and the personal characteristics that have been associated with particular generations (Lancaster & Stillman, 2002).

Snapshot Summary

10.1   Generational Diversity

- **The Traditional Generation, a.k.a. the Silent Generation (born 1922–1945).** This generation was influenced by events such as the Great Depression and World Wars I and II. Characteristics associated with this generation include loyalty, patriotism, respect for authority, and conservatism.

- **The Baby Boomer Generation (born 1946–1964).** This generation was influenced by events such as the Vietnam War, Watergate, and the human rights movement. Characteristics associated with this generation include idealism, importance of self-fulfillment, and concern for equal rights.

- **Generation X (born 1965–1980).** This generation was influenced by Sesame Street, the creation of MTV, AIDS, and soaring divorce rates that produced the first "latchkey children"—youngsters who let themselves into their homes after school with their own keys

because their mother (or single mother) was working outside the home. Characteristics associated with this generation include self-reliance, resourcefulness, and being comfortable with change.

- **Generation Y, a.k.a. Millennials (born 1981–2002).** This generation was influenced by the September 11, 2001, terrorist attack on the United States, the shooting of students at Columbine High School, and the collapse of the Enron Corporation. Characteristics associated with this generation include a preference for working and playing in groups, being technologically savvy, and a willingness to provide volunteer service in their community (the civic generation). They are also the most ethnically diverse generation, which may explain why they are more open to diversity and see it as a positive experience.

"I don't even know what that means."

—Comment made by 38-year-old basketball coach after hearing one of his younger players say, "I'm trying to find my mojo and get my swag back." *Source:* Lancaster & Stillman (2002).

Reflection **10.7**

Look back at the characteristics associated with your generation. Which of these characteristics most accurately reflect your attitudes, values, or personality traits? Which clearly do not?

Gender Diversity

Recent research has shown that the concept of gender is quite complex and cannot be limited to the categories of "men" and "women." Other groups, such as transgender and gender queer, have emerged as gender diversity has become more recognized and accepted. The term "gender" has been used interchangeably with the word "sex;" however, "sex" is associated with categories that are biologically determined by external genitalia, such as male, female, intersex, etc. Gender, on the other hand, refers to one's identification along a continuum of masculine and feminine traits and roles, regardless of external genitalia (Muehlenhard & Peterson, 2011). These traits and roles are reflective of social and cultural conventions, interests, and customs. Certainly, there is interplay between sex and gender as they both contribute to our individual identity. Therefore, while the characteristics associated with masculinity and femininity are socially ascribed, how rigidly we adhere to these definitions depends on the level at which we see these qualities in ourselves (Priest et al., 2012).

Gender characteristics are not exclusive to a single gender or set in stone. For example, would you consider a woman not feminine if she were a semi-professional football player? Would you consider a man not to be masculine if he were a nanny?

These questions give us pause because there are certain behaviors and qualities that socially define what is masculine and feminine, but these definitions are also open to our individual interpretation. A woman can be very feminine and also enjoy playing a sport that is typically played by men, and a man can be very masculine and also enjoy fulfilling duties that are typically thought to be maternal. The characteristics we associate with gender also change over time and vary between cultures. Consider how these same two questions might have been answered 50 years ago and how the responses of different cultural groups might vary even today. In sum, our interpretation of femininity and masculinity depends on how strictly we personally adhere to the social definitions of gender (Parker, 2009).

Sexual Diversity

Sexuality is another aspect of our human identity that contributes to diversity. We all express our sexuality in our own ways and come into various aspects of our sexuality throughout our lives. "Sexual diversity" refers to the full continuum of the human sexual experience and identity. Represented in this range include lesbians, gay men, bisexuals, transgendered people, and heterosexuals. When we accept individuals who self-identify within this range of sexual diversity, we look beyond heterosexuality as the norm and recognize the variation that contributes to the human experience (Dessel, Woodford, & Warren, 2012).

Campuses are increasing their support for LGBTQIA (lesbian, gay, bisexual, transgendered, questioning, intersexed, and asexual) students and creating centers and support services to assist them with their adjustment to campus life. These offices also play an important role in helping to reduce homophobia in the campus community and promote mutual respect for all types of sexual diversity.

Diversity and the College Experience

There are more than 3,000 public and private colleges in the United States. They vary in size (small to large) and location (urban, suburban, and rural), as well as in their purpose or mission (research universities, comprehensive state universities, liberal arts colleges, and community colleges). This variety makes America's higher education system the most diverse and accessible in the world. The diversity of educational opportunities in American colleges and universities reflects the freedom of opportunity in the United States as a democratic nation (American Council on Education, 2008).

America's system of higher education is also becoming more diverse with respect to the variety of people enrolled in it. College students in the United States are growing more diverse with respect to age; almost 40 percent of all undergraduate students in America are 25 years of age or older, compared to 28 percent in 1970 (U.S. Department of Education, 2002). The ethnic and racial diversity of students in American colleges and universities is also rapidly rising. In 1960, Whites made up almost 95 percent of the total college population; in 2005, that percentage had decreased to 69 percent. At the same time, the percentage of Asian, Hispanic, Black, and Native American students attending college increased (*Chronicle of Higher Education*, 2003). First-year college students are more likely than sophomores, juniors, and seniors to have contact with students from different racial and ethnic backgrounds, probably because first-year students are more likely to live on campus and in close proximity to other students (Kuh, 2005).

Reflection 10.8

1. What diverse groups do you see represented on your campus?

2. Are there groups on campus that you did not expect to see or to see in such large numbers?

3. Are there groups on your campus that you expected to see but do not see or see in smaller numbers than you expected?

The Benefits of Experiencing Diversity

Diversity Promotes Self-Awareness

Learning from people with diverse backgrounds and experiences sharpens our self-knowledge and self-insight by allowing us to compare and contrast our life experiences with others whose experiences differ sharply from our own. This comparative perspective gives us a reference point for viewing our own lives, placing us in a better position to see how our unique cultural background has influenced the development of our personal beliefs, values, and lifestyle. By viewing our lives in relation to the lives of others, we see more clearly what is distinctive about ourselves and how we may be uniquely advantaged or disadvantaged.

When students around the country were interviewed about their diversity experiences in college, they reported that these experiences often helped them learn more about themselves and that their interactions with students from different races and ethnic groups produced unexpected or jarring self-insights (Light, 2001).

Remember

The more opportunities you create to learn from others different than yourself, the more opportunities you create to learn about yourself.

Diversity Enriches a College Education

Diversity magnifies the power of a college education by liberating students from the tunnel vision of ethnocentricity (culture-centeredness) and egocentricity (self-centeredness), enabling them to get beyond themselves and view the world from a multicultural perspective. Just as the various subjects you take in the college curriculum open your mind to multiple perspectives, so does your experience with people from varied backgrounds. A multicultural perspective helps us become aware of our "cultural blind spots" and avoid the dangers of *groupthink*—the tendency for tight-knit groups of people to think so much alike that they overlook flaws in their thinking (Baron, 2005; Janis, 1982).

Diversity Strengthens Learning and Critical Thinking

Research consistently shows that we learn more from people who are different than ourselves than we do from people similar to ourselves (Pascarella, 2001; Pascarella & Terenzini, 2005). When our brain encounters something that is unfamiliar or different from what we're accustomed to, we must stretch beyond our mental comfort zone and work harder to understand it, because doing so forces us to compare and

Student Perspective

"I remember that my self-image was being influenced by the media. I got the impression that women had to look a certain way. I dyed my hair, wore different clothes, more makeup . . . all because magazines, TV, [and] music videos 'said' that was beautiful. Luckily, when I was 15, I went to Brazil and saw a different, more natural beauty and came back to America more as myself. I let go of the hold the media image had on me."

—First-year college student

Student Perspective

"I am very happy with the diversity here, but it also frightens me. I have never been in a situation where I have met people who are Jewish, Muslim, atheist, born-again, and many more."

—First-year college student (Erickson, Peters, & Strommer, 2006)

"Without exception, the observed changes [during college] involve greater breadth, expansion, and appreciation for the new and different."

—Ernest Pascarella and Pat Terenzini, *How College Affects Students*

"When all men think alike, no one thinks very much."

—Walter Lippmann, distinguished journalist and originator of the term *stereotype*

"Research indicates the equality of men and women—socially, educationally, occupationally, and within the family—becomes more accepted by students of both sexes during the college years."

—Ernest Pascarella & Patrick Terenzini, *How College Affects Students*

"When the only tool you have is a hammer, you tend to see every problem as a nail."

—Abraham Maslow, psychologist, best known for his theory of human self-actualization

"What I look for in musicians is generosity. There is so much to learn from each other and about each other's culture. Great creativity begins with tolerance."

—Yo-Yo Ma, French-born, Chinese-American virtuoso cellist, composer, and winner of multiple Grammy Awards

"The benefits that accrue to college students who are exposed to racial and ethnic diversity during their education carry over in the work environment. The improved ability to think critically, to understand issues from different points of view, and to collaborate harmoniously with co-workers from a range of cultural backgrounds all enhance a graduate's ability to contribute to his or her company's growth and productivity."

—Business-Higher Education Forum, 2002

contrast it to what we are already familiar with (Acredolo & O'Connor, 1991; Nagda, Gurin, & Johnson, 2005). Stretching our minds to understand something that's unfamiliar to us requires extra psychological effort and energy, which produces a deeper, more powerful learning experience.

Diversity Promotes Creative Thinking

Experiences with diversity supply you with a broader base of knowledge and wider range of thinking styles that better enable you to think outside your own cultural box or boundaries. In contrast, limiting your number of cultural vantage points is akin to limiting the variety of mental tools you can use to solve new problems, thereby limiting your creativity. When like-minded people only associate with other like-minded people, they're unlikely to think outside the box.

Drawing on different ideas from people with diverse backgrounds and bouncing your ideas off them is a great way to generate energy, synergy, and serendipity—unanticipated discoveries and creative solutions. People who approach problems from diverse perspectives are more likely to look for and discover "multiple partial solutions" (Kelly, 1994). Diversity expands students' capacity for viewing issues or problems from multiple vantage points, equipping them with a wider variety of approaches to solving unfamiliar problems they may encounter in different contexts and situations.

Furthermore, ideas acquired from diverse people and diverse cultures may combine or "cross-fertilize," giving birth to new approaches for solving old problems. When ideas are generated openly and freely in groups comprised of people from diverse backgrounds, powerful "cross-stimulation" effects can occur, whereby one group member's idea can trigger different ideas from other group members (Brown, Dane, & Durham, 1998). Drawing on different ideas from people of diverse backgrounds and bouncing ideas off them serves to stimulate divergent (expansive) thinking, which can lead to synergy (idea multiplication) and serendipity (unexpected discoveries of innovative solutions).

In contrast, when different cultural perspectives are not sought out or tolerated, the variety of lenses available to students for viewing new problems is reduced, which, in turn, limits or shrinks one's capacity for creative thinking. Creativity tends to be replaced by conformity or rigidity because ideas do not flow freely and divergently (in different directions): instead, ideas tend to converge and merge into the same cultural channel—the one shared by the homogeneous group of people doing the thinking.

Diversity Education Promotes Career Preparation for the 21st Century

Learning about and from diversity has a very practical benefit: it better prepares students for their future work roles. Whatever line of employment students may eventually pursue, they're likely to find themselves working with employers, co-workers, customers, and clients from diverse cultural backgrounds. America's workforce is now more diverse than at any other time in the nation's history and it will grow ever more diverse throughout the 21st century. The proportion of America's working-age population comprised of workers from minority ethnic and racial groups will jump from 34 percent in 2008 to 55 percent in 2050 (U.S. Census Bureau, 2008).

A national survey revealed that policymakers, business leaders, and employers were seeking college graduates who were more than just "aware" or "tolerant" of diversity; they wanted graduates who had actual *experience* with diversity (Education Commission of the States, 1995). These findings are reinforced by a national survey of American voters, the overwhelming majority of who agreed that diversity education helps students learn practical skills that are essential for success in today's world, such as communication skills, teamwork, and problem-solving skills. Almost one-half of the surveyed voters also thought that the American school system should "put more emphasis on teaching students about others' cultures, backgrounds and lifestyles" (National Survey of Voters, 1998). Thus, both employers and the American public agree that diversity education is *career preparation*. Intercultural competence is now a highly valued skill and one that is essential for success in today's work world.

The current "global economy" also requires intercultural skills relating to international diversity. Work in today's global economy is characterized by economic interdependence among nations, international trading (imports/exports), multinational corporations, international travel, and almost instantaneous worldwide communication—due to advances in the World Wide Web (Dryden & Vos, 1999; Friedman, 2005). As a result, employers now seek job candidates with the following skills and attributes: sensitivity to human differences, ability to understand and relate to people from different cultural backgrounds, international knowledge, and ability to communicate in a second language (Fixman, 1990; National Association of Colleges & Employers, 2007; Office of Research, 1994). Thus, learning about and from diversity is not only good education: it's also good career preparation.

> **Remember**
>
> *The wealth of diversity on college campuses today represents an unprecedented educational opportunity. You may never again be a member of a community that includes so many people from such a rich variety of backgrounds. Seize this opportunity! You're in the right place at the right time to experience the variety of people and programs that will enrich the breadth and depth of your learning.*

Stumbling Blocks and Barriers to Experiencing Diversity

Stereotypes

The word *stereotype* derives from a combination of two roots: *stereo* (to look at in a fixed way) and *type* (to categorize or group together, as in the word *typical*). Thus, stereotyping is viewing individuals of the same type (group) in the same (fixed) way.

In effect, stereotyping ignores or disregards individuality; instead, all people sharing the same group characteristic (e.g., race or gender) are viewed as having the same personal characteristics—as in the expression, "You know what they're like: they're all the same." Stereotypes involve bias, which literally means "slant." A bias can be slanted either positively or negatively. Positive bias results in a favorable stereotype (e.g., "Italians are great lovers"); negative bias produces an unfavorable stereotype (e.g., "Italians are in the Mafia"). Snapshot Summary 10.2 lists some common stereotypes.

"Only a well educated, diverse work force, comprised of people who have learned to work productively and creatively with individuals from a multitude of races and ethnic, religious, and cultural backgrounds, can maintain America's competitiveness in the increasingly diverse and interconnected world economy."
—Spokesman for General Motors Corporation, quoted in Chatman (2008).

"The federal government and private organizations with extensive international interests will require the services of increasing numbers of specialists who are fluent in foreign languages and highly knowledgeable about countries, regions, and international problems."
—Derek Bok, president emeritus and research professor at Harvard University, and author of *Our Underachieving Colleges*

"Empirical evidence shows that the actual effects on student development of emphasizing diversity and of student participation in diversity activities are overwhelmingly positive."
—Alexander Astin, *What Matters in College?* (1993)

Reflection 10.9

Have you ever been stereotyped, such as based on your appearance or group membership? If so, how did it make you feel and how did you react?

Have you ever unintentionally perceived or treated someone in terms of a group stereotype rather than as an individual? What assumptions did you make about that person? Was that person aware of, or affected by, your stereotyping?

Snapshot Summary

10.2   Examples of Common Stereotypes

Muslims are terrorists.

Whites can't jump (or dance).

Blacks are lazy.

Asians are brilliant in math.

Irish are alcoholics.

Gay men are feminine; lesbian women are masculine.

Jews are cheap.

Hispanic men are abusive to women.

Men are strong.

Women are weak.

Whether you are male or female, don't let gender stereotypes limit your career options.

Author's Experience When I was six years old, I was told by another six-year-old from a different racial group that all people of my race could not swim. Since I couldn't swim at that time and she could, I assumed she was correct. When I asked a boy, who happened to be of the same racial group as that little girl, if that statement were true, he responded emphatically, "Yes, it's true!" Since I was from an area where few other African Americans were around to counteract this belief about Blacks, I bought into this stereotype until I finally took swimming lessons as an adult. I am now a lousy swimmer after many lessons because I didn't even attempt to swim until I was an adult. The moral of this story is that group stereotypes can limit the confidence and potential of individuals who are members of the stereotyped group..

Aaron Thompson

Prejudice

If virtually all members of a stereotyped group are judged or evaluated in a negative way, the result is prejudice. (The word *prejudice* literally means to "pre-judge.") Technically, prejudice may be either positive or negative; however, the term is most often associated with a negative prejudgment that involves *stigmatizing*—associating inferior or unfavorable traits with people who belong to the same group. Thus, prejudice may be defined as a negative judgment, attitude, or belief about another person or group of people that's formed before the facts are known. Stereotyping and prejudice often go hand in hand because individuals who are placed in a negatively stereotyped group are commonly prejudged in a negative way.

Someone with a prejudice toward a group typically avoids contact with individuals from that group. This enables the prejudice to continue unchallenged because there's little chance for the prejudiced person to have positive experiences with any member of the stigmatized group that could contradict or disprove the prejudice. Thus, a vicious cycle is established in which the prejudiced person continues to avoid contact with individuals from the stigmatized group, which, in turn, continues to maintain and reinforce the prejudice.

Discrimination

Literally translated, the term *discrimination* means "division" or "separation." Whereas prejudice involves a belief or opinion, discrimination involves an action taken toward others. Technically, discrimination can be either negative or positive—for example, a discriminating eater may be careful about eating only healthy foods. However, the term is most often associated with a negative action that results in a prejudiced person treating another person, or group of people, in an unfair way. Thus, it could be said that discrimination is prejudice put into action. Hate crimes are examples of extreme discrimination because they are acts motivated solely by prejudice against members of a stigmatized group.

Other forms of discrimination are more subtle and may be practiced by society's institutional systems rather than particular individuals. These forms of *institutional racism* are less flagrant or visible, and they are rooted in societal policies and practices that discriminate against members of certain ethnic groups. For instance, *redlining*, a term coined in the late 1960s, refers to the practice of banks marking a red line on a map to indicate an area where they will not invest or lend money; many of those areas are neighborhoods in which African Americans live (Shapiro, 1993). Studies also show that compared to White patients, Black patients of the same socioeconomic status are less likely to receive breast cancer screenings, eye exams if they have diabetes, and follow-up visits after hospitalization for mental illness (Schneider, Zaslavsky, & Epstein, 2002).

"Let us all hope that the dark clouds of racial prejudice will soon pass away and the deep fog of misunderstanding will be lifted from our fear-drenched communities, and in some not too distant tomorrow the radiant stars of love and brotherhood will shine over our great nation."
—Martin Luther King Jr., civil rights activist and clergyman

"'See that man over there?'
'Yes.'
'Well, I hate him.'
'But you don't know him.'
'That's why I hate him.'"
—Gordon Allport, *The Nature of Prejudice* (1954)

Thus, trying to be "race blind" and getting along with people of all colors with whom we interact on an *individual* basis is not all there is to eliminating discrimination. Racial discrimination is an issue that goes beyond individual interactions to larger institutional policies and societal systems. One goal of multicultural education is to empower students to eventually change these societal systems by "laying a foundation for the transformation of society and the elimination of oppression and injustice" (Gorski, 2010, p. 1).

Reflection 10.10

Prejudice and discrimination can be subtle and only begin to surface when the social or emotional distance among members of different groups grows smaller. Honestly rate your level of comfort with the following situations.

Someone from another racial group:

1.	going to your school	high	moderate	low
2.	working in your place of employment	high	moderate	low
3.	living on your street as a neighbor	high	moderate	low
4.	living with you as a roommate	high	moderate	low
5.	socializing with you as a personal friend	high	moderate	low
6.	being your most intimate friend or romantic partner	high	moderate	low
7.	being your partner in marriage.	high	moderate	low

For any item you rated "low," what caused you to give it such a low rating?

Snapshot Summary 10. 3 contains a summary of biased attitudes, prejudicial beliefs, and discriminatory behaviors that must be overcome if humankind is to experience the full benefits of diversity. As you read through the list, place a checkmark next to any form of prejudice that you, a family member, or friend has experienced.

Reflection 10.11

Have you, a family member, or friend experienced any of the form(s) of prejudice in the above list? Why do you think it occurred?

Snapshot Summary

10.3 **Blocks to Learning from Diversity: Biased Attitudes, Prejudicial Beliefs, and Discriminatory Behaviors**

- **Stereotyping.** Viewing all (or virtually all) individuals of the same group in the same way—as having the same qualities or characteristics.
  Example: "If you're Italian, you must be in the Mafia, or have a family member who is."
- **Prejudice.** A negative pre-judgment of another group of people.
  Example: Women do not make good leaders because they're too emotional.
- **Discrimination.** Unequal and unfair treatment of a person or group of people, i.e., prejudice put into action.
  Example: People of color being paid less for performing the same job, even though they have the same level of education and job qualifications as whites performing the same job.
- **Segregation.** A conscious decision made by a group to separate itself (socially or physically) from another group.
  Example: "White flight"—White people moving out of neighborhoods when people of color move in.
- **Racism.** A belief that one's racial group is superior to another group and expressing that belief in the form of an attitude (prejudice) or action (discrimination).
  Example: Cecil Rhodes—Englishman and empire builder of British South Africa—once claimed: "We [the British] are the finest race in the world and the more of the world we inhabit the better it is for the human race."
- **Institutional racism.** Racism rooted in organizational policies and practices that disadvantage certain racial groups.
  Example: Race-based discrimination in mortgage lending, housing, and bank loans.
- **Slavery.** Forced labor in which people are considered to be the property of others, are held against their will, and are deprived of the right to leave, to refuse to work, or to demand wages.
  Example: Enslavement of Blacks was legal in the United States until 1865.
- **"Jim Crow" laws.** Formal and informal laws created by Whites after the abolition of slavery to segregate Blacks. (The term *Jim Crow* likely derived from a song-and-dance character named "Jump Jim Crow," who was played by a White man in blackface.)
  Example: Laws in the U.S. that once required Blacks and Whites to use separate bathrooms and be educated in separate schools.
- **Apartheid.** An institutionalized system of "legal racism" supported by a nation's government. (*Apartheid* derives from a word in the Afrikaan language meaning "apartness.")
  Example: The national system of racial segregation and discrimination that existed in South Africa from 1948 to 1994.
- **Hate crimes.** Criminal action motivated solely by prejudice toward the crime victim.
  Example: Acts of vandalism or assault aimed at members of a particular ethnic group or persons with a particular sexual orientation.
- **Hate groups.** Organizations whose primary purpose is to stimulate prejudice, discrimination, or aggression toward certain groups of people based on their ethnicity, race, religion, etc.
  Example: The Ku Klux Klan, an American terrorist group that perpetrates hatred toward all non-white races.
- **Genocide.** Mass murdering of a particular ethnic or racial group by another group.
  Example: The Holocaust during World War II, in which millions of Jews were systematically murdered. Other examples include the murdering of Cambodians under the Khmer Rouge regime, the murdering of Bosnian Muslims in the former country of Yugoslavia, and the slaughter of the Tutsi minority by the Hutu majority in Rwanda.
- **Classism.** Prejudice or discrimination based on social class, particularly toward people of low socioeconomic status.
  Example: Acknowledging the contributions made by politicians and wealthy industrialists to America, while ignoring the contributions of poor immigrants, farmers, slaves, and pioneer women.
- **Religious bigotry.** Denying the fundamental human right of people to hold religious beliefs, or to hold religious beliefs that differ from one's own.
  Example: An atheist who forces non-religious (secular) beliefs on others, or a member of a religious group who believes that people who hold different religious beliefs are immoral "sinners."

Student
Perspective

"Most religions dictate that theirs is the only way, and without believing in it, you cannot enter the mighty kingdom of heaven. Who are we to judge? It makes more sense for God to be the only one mighty enough to make that decision. If other people could understand and see from this perspective, then many religious arguments could be avoided."

—First-year college student

"Rivers, ponds, lakes and streams—they all have different names, but they all contain water. Just as religions do—they all contain truths."

—Muhammad Ali, three-time world heavyweight boxing champion, member of the International Boxing Hall of Fame, and recipient of the Spirit of America Award as the most recognized American in the world

Student
Perspective

"I would like to change the entire world, so that we wouldn't be segregated by continents and territories."

—College sophomore

- **Anti-Semitism.** Prejudice or discrimination toward Jews or people who practice the religion of Judaism.
  Example: Hating Jews because they're the ones who "killed Christ."
- **Xenophobia.** Extreme fear or hatred of foreigners, outsiders, or strangers.
  Example: Believing that immigrants should be banned from entering the country because they'll increase the crime rate or ruin our economy.
- **Regionalism.** Prejudice or discrimination based on the geographical region in which an individual has been born and raised.
  Example: A northerner thinking that all southerners are racists.
- **Jingoism.** Excessive interest and belief in the superiority of one's own nation without acknowledging its mistakes or weaknesses; it's often accompanied by an aggressive foreign policy that neglects the needs of other nations, or the common needs of all nations.
  Example: "Blind patriotism"—not seeing the shortcomings of one's own nation and viewing any questioning or criticism of it as disloyalty or being "unpatriotic." (As in the slogans "America: right or wrong" or "America: love it or leave it!")
- **Terrorism.** Intentional acts of violence against civilians that are motivated by political or religious prejudice.

- **Example:** The September 11th attacks on the United States.
- **Sexism:** Prejudice or discrimination based on sex or gender.
  Example: Believing that women should not pursue careers in fields traditionally filled only by men (e.g., engineering) because they lack the natural qualities or skills to do them.
- **Heterosexism.** Belief that heterosexuality is the only acceptable sexual orientation.
  Example: Using the word *fag* or *queer* as an insult or put-down, or believing that gays should not have the same legal rights and opportunities as heterosexuals.
- **Homophobia.** Extreme fear or hatred of homosexuals.
  Example: People who engage in "gay bashing" (acts of violence toward gays), or who create and contribute to anti-gay websites.
- **Ageism.** Prejudice or discrimination based on age, particularly toward the elderly.
  Example: Believing that all "old" people are bad drivers with bad memories who should not be allowed on the road.
- **Ableism.** Prejudice or discrimination toward people who are disabled or handicapped (physically, mentally, or emotionally).
  Example: Avoiding social contact or interaction with people in wheelchairs.

What Is Cultural Competence?

Research suggests (Thompson & Cuseo, 2012) that when we focus on differences alone, we create cultural environments in which some groups will feel excluded. Authentic appreciation of diversity takes place when members from different groups interact, work together, and learn from one another (Smith, 1997). Someone who merely tolerates diversity, or simply coexists with diverse groups, might say things like "Let's just get along," "Live and let live," or "To each his own." Cultural competence moves us beyond diversity tolerance to a higher level of diversity *appreciation*, which involves learning about, with, and from diverse people. It empowers us to be culturally sensitive and responsive individuals who recognize, appreciate, and capitalize on human differences (Etsy, Griffin, & Hirsch, 1995). Therefore, when we attain cultural competence, we move beyond mere acceptance or tolerance of diversity to a deeper, more authentic appreciation of diversity.

Achieving this level of diversity appreciation requires us to not only be introspective and reflective, but to regularly step out of our usual comfort zones. This is because we develop insights about ourselves and others in relation to diversity through interaction and experience. By acknowledging and accepting your own cultural identity as well as the cultural identities of others, you open yourself up to the human experience. Maintaining this level of diversity appreciation requires that you engage in *action* (Thompson & Cuseo, 2012). Examples of such action include, but are not limited to:

- Attending meetings and activities on campus or in your community to gain a deeper understanding of your peers' cultural backgrounds
- Enrolling in courses that expand your knowledge of the culture, history, and language of various ethnic and cultural groups, including your own
- Participating in a service-learning or community activity
- Meeting and interacting with students in your residence hall or in the Student Center who are from various cultural backgrounds
- Forming study groups in your classes comprised of diverse members
- Participating in a study abroad experience
- Becoming an advocate for diversity on your campus and in your community.

Strategies for Diversity Appreciation

The following practices and strategies may be used to help us open up to and appreciate individuals from other groups toward whom we may hold prejudices, stereotypes, or subtle biases that bubble beneath the surface of our conscious awareness.

1. **Consciously avoid preoccupation with physical appearances.** Go deeper and get beneath the surface of appearances to judge people not in terms of how they look, but in terms of who they are and how they act. Remember the old proverb: "It's what inside that counts." Judge others by their inner qualities, not by the familiarity of their outer features.

2. **Perceive each person with whom you interact as a unique human being.** Make a conscious effort to interact with people as individuals, not as group members, and form your impressions of others on a case-by-case basis, not according to some general rule of thumb. This may seem like an obvious and easy thing to do, but research shows that humans have a natural tendency to perceive individuals from unfamiliar groups as being more alike (or all alike) than members of their own group (Taylor, Peplau, & Sears, 2006). Thus, we need to make a conscious effort to counteract this tendency.

> "The common eye sees only the outside of things, and judges by that. But the seeing eye pierces through and reads the heart and the soul, finding there capacities which the outside didn't indicate or promise."
>
> —Samuel Clemens, a.k.a. Mark Twain, writer, lecturer, and humorist

• Remember

While it's valuable to learn about different cultures and the common characteristics shared by members of the same culture, it shouldn't be done at the expense of ignoring individual differences among members of the same culture. Don't assume that all individuals who share the same cultural background share the same personal characteristics.

3. **Make an intentional attempt to interact and collaborate with members of diverse groups.** Once we've overcome our biases and begin to perceive members of diverse groups as unique individuals, we move into a position to take the next step of interacting, collaborating, and forming friendships with members of diverse groups. Interpersonal contact between diverse people takes us beyond simple awareness and acceptance, and moves us up to a higher level of diversity appreciation that involves intercultural interaction. When we take this step to cross cultural boundaries, we transform diversity appreciation from an internal attitude or personal conviction into an observable action or interpersonal commitment.

> "Stop judging by mere appearances, and make a right judgment."
>
> —John 7:24

> "You can't judge a book by the cover."
>
> —Title of the 1962 hit song by Elias Bates, a.k.a. Bo Diddley (Note: A bo diddley is a one-stringed African guitar)

Student
Perspective

"I would change how people judge others before knowing them. I would change it so that there weren't cliques based on race. I would change it so people are more open to ideas and different thoughts."

—College sophomore, responding to the question "If there's anything in the world you could change, what would it be?"

Your initial comfort level with interacting with people from diverse groups is likely to depend on how much experience you have had with diversity before college. If you've had little or no prior experience interacting with members of diverse groups, it may be more challenging for you to initiate interactions with diverse students on campus. However, the good news is that you have the most to gain from interacting and collaborating with those of other ethnic or racial groups. Research consistently shows that when we have social experiences that differ radically from our prior experiences, we gain the most in terms of learning and cognitive development (Acredolo & O'Connor, 1991; Piaget, 1985).

Reflection 10.12

Rate the amount or variety of diversity you have experienced in the following settings:

1. The high school you attended	high	moderate	low
2. The college or university you now attend	high	moderate	low
3. The neighborhood in which you grew up	high	moderate	low
4. Places where you have worked or been employed	high	moderate	low

Which setting had the *most* and the *least* diversity?

What do you think accounts for this difference?

Following are specific strategies for meeting, interacting with, and learning from people of diverse backgrounds.

1. **Intentionally create opportunities for interaction and conversation with individuals from diverse groups.** Studies show that stereotyping and prejudice can be sharply reduced if contact between members of different racial or ethnic groups is frequent enough to allow time for the development of friendships (Pettigrew, 1998). Make an intentional attempt to fight off the tendency to associate only with people who are similar to you. One way to do this is by intentionally placing yourself in situations where individuals from diverse groups are nearby so that interaction can potentially take place. Research indicates that meaningful interactions and friendships are more likely to form among people who are in physical proximity with one another (Back, Schmukle, & Egloff, 2008; Latané et al., 1995). You can create this condition in the college classroom by sitting near students from different ethnic or racial groups or by joining them if you are given the choice to select whom you will work with in class discussion groups and group projects.

2. **Take advantage of the Internet to chat with students from diverse groups.** Electronic communication can be a more convenient and more comfortable way to initially interact with members of diverse groups with whom you have had little prior experience. After you've communicated successfully *online*, you may then feel more comfortable about interacting with them *in person*. Online and

in-person interaction with students from other cultures deepens your understanding of your own culture and elevates your awareness of cultural customs and values that you may have overlooked or taken for granted (Bok, 2006).

3. **Seek out the views and opinions of classmates from diverse backgrounds.** During or after class discussions, ask students from different backgrounds if there was any point made or position taken in class that they would strongly question or challenge. Seeking out divergent (diverse) viewpoints has been found to be one of the best ways to develop critical thinking skills (Inoue, 2005; Kurfiss, 1988).

4. **Join or form discussion groups with students from diverse backgrounds.** You can gain exposure to diverse perspectives by joining or forming discussion groups with students who differ from you in terms of such characteristics as gender, age, race, or ethnicity. You might begin by forming study groups with students who are different than you in one way but similar to you in other ways. For instance, you can form learning teams with students who have the same major as you, but who differ from you in terms of race, ethnicity, or age. This strategy gives the diverse members of your team some common ground for discussion (your major) and can raise your team's awareness that although you may be members of different groups, you can share similar educational goals and life plans.

> **Remember**
>
> *Including diversity in your learning groups not only provides social variety: it also promotes the quality of the group's work by giving its members access to diverse perspectives and life experiences of people from different backgrounds.*

5. **Form collaborative learning teams.** A learning team is more than a discussion group or a study group. It moves beyond discussion to collaborative learning—its members become teammates who "co-labor" (work together) as part of a joint and mutually supportive effort to reach the same team goal. Studies show that when individuals from different ethnic and racial groups work collaboratively toward the attainment of a common goal, racial prejudice is reduced and interracial friendships are promoted (Allport, 1954; Amir, 1976; Dovidio, Eller, & Hewstone, 2011). These positive developments probably take place because individuals from diverse groups working on the same team creates a social environment in which no one is a member of an "out" group ("them"): they're all members of the same "in" group ("us") (Pratto et al., 2000; Sidanius, Levin, Liu, & Pratto, 2000). For specific strategies on how to form diverse and effective learning teams, see Do It Now! 10.1.

10.1   DO IT **NOW** !

Tips for Teamwork: Creating Diverse and Effective Learning Teams

1. **Intentionally form diverse learning teams comprised of individuals with different cultural backgrounds and life experiences.** If you team up only with friends or classmates whose lifestyles and experiences are similar to your own, it can actually impair your team's performance. Your similar experiences can cause your learning to get off track and onto topics that have nothing to do with the learning task (for example, what you did last weekend or what you are planning to do next weekend).

2. **Your team should identify and pursue a common goal.** Your team should create the same final product that represents their unified effort and accomplishment (e.g., a completed sheet of answers to questions, a list or chart of specific ideas). A collectively created end product helps individual members function as "we" rather than "me," and helps the team stay on task and moving in the same direction toward their common goal.

3. **Each teammate should have equal opportunity and assume personal responsibility for contributing to the team's final product.** For example, all team members should be equally responsible for making a specific contribution to the team's final product, such as contributing a different piece of information to the team's overall topic or project (e.g., a specific chapter from the textbook or a particular section of class notes), as if each teammate is bringing a different piece or part that's needed to complete the whole puzzle.

4. **All teammates should work interdependently—that is, they should depend on or rely upon each other to achieve their common goal.** Like members of a sports team, each member of a learning team should have a specific role to play. For instance, each teammate could assume one of the following roles:
   - Manager, whose role is to ensure that the team stays on track and moving toward their goal.
   - Moderator, whose role is to ensure that all members have equal opportunity to contribute.
   - Summarizer, whose role is to monitor the team's progress and identify what has been accomplished and what still needs to be done.
   - Recorder, whose role is to keep a written record of the team's ideas.

   "We are born for cooperation, as are the feet, the hands, the eyelids, and the upper and lower jaws."
   —Marcus Aurelius, Roman emperor, 161–180 AD

Teammates may also assume roles that involve contributing a particular type of thinking to the learning task (e.g., analysis, synthesis, or application) or bringing a specific perspective to the final product (e.g., cultural, national, or international).

5. **Before delving into the work task, teammates should take some social "warm-up" time to interact informally with each other.** Getting the opportunity to learn each other's names, backgrounds, and interests will enable group members to become comfortable with one another and develop a sense of team solidarity or identity, particularly if they come from diverse (and unfamiliar) cultural backgrounds. Once they get to know each other as individuals, they should become more comfortable sharing their personal thoughts and viewpoints during teamwork.

6. **Teamwork should take place in a friendly, informal setting.** The context or atmosphere in which group work takes place can influence the nature and quality of interaction among team members. People are more likely to work openly and collaboratively when they are in an environment that is conducive to relationship building. For example, a living room or a lounge area would provide a warmer and friendlier team-learning atmosphere than a sterile classroom.

7. **Learning teams should occasionally divide into smaller subgroups (e.g., pairs or trios) so that teammates get an opportunity to work with each other on a more personal level, particularly if they are from different ethnic or racial groups.** The smaller the group size, the greater the level of participation, involvement, and interaction between group members. For example, it's much easier not to participate in a group of six than in a group of two. If opportunities are created for different team members to work together, everyone gets at least one opportunity to work closely with every other member of the team. This can promote diversity appreciation by allowing each team member to experience working at a personal level with an individual from a minority group that's not represented in large numbers at your school.

When contact among people from diverse groups takes place under the above conditions, it has the greatest potential for having positive impact on learning and diversity appreciation. A win-win scenario is created: learning is strengthened, and at the same time, prejudice is weakened.

References: Allport (1979); Amir (1969); Aronson, Wilson, & Akert (2009); Brown & Hewstone (2005); Cook (1984); Sherif, Harvey, White, Hood, & Sherif (1961).

Summary and Conclusion

Diversity refers to differences among groups of people who, together, comprise humanity. Experiencing diversity increases appreciation of the features unique to different cultures and provides a panoramic perspective on the human experience that is shared by all people, no matter what their particular culture happens to be.

Culture is formed by the beliefs and values of a group with the same traditions and social heritage. It helps bind people into supportive, tight-knit communities. However, culture can also lead its members to view the world solely through their own cultural lens (known as ethnocentrism), which can blind them to other cultural perspectives. Ethnocentrism can contribute to stereotyping—viewing individual members of a group in the same way and seeing all of them as having the same personal characteristics.

Evaluating members of a stereotyped group negatively results in prejudice—a biased prejudgment about another person or group of people that's formed before the facts are known. Stereotyping and prejudice often go hand in hand, because if the stereotype is negative, individual members of the stereotyped group are then prejudged negatively. Discrimination takes prejudice one step further by converting the negative prejudgment into action that results in treating others unfairly. Thus, discrimination is prejudice in action.

Once stereotyping and prejudice are overcome, we are positioned to experience diversity and reap its multiple benefits, which include sharper self-awareness, broadened personal perspectives, deeper learning, higher-level thinking, and career success.

The increasing diversity of students on campus, combined with the wealth of diversity-related educational experiences found in the college curriculum and cocurriculum, presents you with an unprecedented opportunity to infuse diversity into your college experience. Seize this opportunity and capitalize on the power of diversity to increase the quality of your college education and your prospects for success in the 21st century.

Learning More through the World Wide Web

Internet-Based Resources for Further Information on Diversity

For additional information related to the ideas discussed in this chapter, we recommend the following Web sites:

www.tolerance.org

www.amnesty.org

www.intercultural.org

10.1 Gaining Awareness of Multi-Group Identities

We can be members of multiple groups at the same time, and our membership in these overlapping groups can influence our personal development and self-identity. In the figure that follows, consider the shaded center circle to be yourself and the six non-shaded circles to be six groups you belong to that you think have influenced your personal development or personal identity.

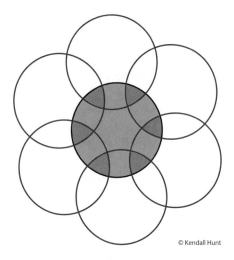

© Kendall Hunt

Fill in the non-shaded circles with the names of groups to which you belong that have had the most influence on your personal development. You can use the diversity spectrum that appears on the second page of this chapter to help you identify different groups. You don't have to come up with six groups and fill all six circles. What's important is to identify those groups that have had a major influence on your development and identity.

Self-Assessment Questions

1. Which one of the groups you identified has had the greatest influence on your personal identity? Why?

2. Have you ever felt limited or disadvantaged by being a member of any particular group or groups?

3. Have you ever felt that you experienced advantages or privileges because of your membership in any group or groups?

10.2 Intercultural Interview

Find a student, faculty member, or administrator on campus whose cultural background differs from your own and ask if you can interview that person about his or her culture. Use the following questions in your interview:

1. How is "family" defined in your culture, and what are the traditional roles and responsibilities of different family members?

2. What are the traditional gender (male vs. female) roles associated with your culture? Are they changing?

3. What is your culture's approach to time? Is there an emphasis on punctuality? Is moving quickly and getting things done rapidly valued more than reflection and deliberation?

4. What are your culture's staple foods and favorite beverages?

5. What cultural traditions or rituals are highly valued and commonly practiced?

6. What special holidays are celebrated?

10.3 Hidden Bias Test

Go to www.tolerance.org/activity/test-yourself-hidden-bias and take one or more of the hidden bias tests on the Web site. These tests assess subtle bias with respect to gender, age, Native Americans, African Americans, Asian Americans, religious denominations, sexual orientations, disabilities, and body weight. The site allows you to assess whether you have a bias toward any of these groups.

Self-Assessment Questions

1. Did the results reveal any bias that you were unaware of?

2. Did you think the assessment results were accurate or valid?

3. What do you think best accounts for or explains your results?

4. If your closest family member and best friend took the test, how do you think their results would compare with yours?

Hate Crime: A Racially Motivated Murder

Jasper County, Texas, has a population of approximately 31,000 people. In this county, 80 percent of the people are White, 18 percent are Black, and 2 percent are of other races. The county's poverty rate is considerably higher than the national average, and its average household income is significantly lower. In 1998, the mayor, the president of the chamber of commerce, and two councilmen were Black. From the outside, Jasper appeared to be a town with racial harmony, and its Black and White leaders were quick to state that there was no racial tension in Jasper.

However, on June 7, 1998, James Byrd Jr., a 49-year-old African American man, was walking home along a road one evening and was offered a ride by three White men. Rather than taking Byrd home, Lawrence Brewer (age 31), John King (age 23), and Shawn Berry (age 23), three individuals linked to White supremacist groups, took Byrd to an isolated area and began beating him. They dropped his pants to his ankles, painted his face black, chained Byrd to their truck, and dragged him for approximately three miles. The truck was driven in a zigzag fashion to inflict maximum pain on the victim. Byrd was decapitated after his body collided with a culvert in a ditch alongside the road. His skin, arms, genitalia, and other body parts were strewn along the road, while his torso was found dumped in front of a Black cemetery. Medical examiners testified that Byrd was alive for much of the dragging incident.

While in prison awaiting trial, Brewer wrote letters to King and other inmates. In one letter, Brewer wrote: "Well, I did it and am no longer a virgin. It was a rush and I'm still licking my lips for more." Once the trials were completed, Brewer and King were sentenced to death. Both Brewer and King, whose bodies were covered with racist tattoos, had been on parole before the incident, and they had previously been cellmates. King had spent an extensive amount of time in prison, where he began to associate with White males in an environment in which each race was pitted against the other.

As a result of the murder, Byrd's family created the James Byrd Foundation for Racial Healing in 1998. On January 20, 1999, a wrought iron fence that separated Black and White graves for more than 150 years in Jasper Cemetery was removed in a special unity service. Members of the racist Ku Klux Klan have since visited the gravesite of Byrd several times, leaving racist stickers and other marks that have angered the Jasper community and Byrd's family.

Sources: *Houston Chronicle* (June 14, 1998); *San Antonio Express News* (September 17, 1999); *Louisiana Weekly* (February 3, 2003).

Reflection and Discussion Questions

1. What factors do you think were responsible for causing this incident to take place?

2. Could this incident have been prevented? If yes, how? If no, why not?

3. How likely do you think it is that an incident like this could take place in your hometown or near your college campus?

4. If this event took place in your hometown, how would you and members of your family and community react?

Educational Planning and Academic Decision Making

Making Wise Choices about College Courses and a College Major

11

Reflection **11.1**

LEARNING GOAL

To develop effective strategies for exploring different academic fields and for choosing an educational path that best enables you to achieve your personal and occupational goals.

At this point in your college experience, are you decided or undecided about your major?

If you're undecided, what subjects might be possibilities?

If you're decided:

1. What is your choice?

2. How sure are you about your choice? (Circle one.)

    absolutely sure   fairly sure   not too sure   likely to change

To Be or Not to Be Decided about a College Major: What the Research Shows

Studies of student decisions about a college major show that:

- Less than 10 percent of new college students feel they know a great deal about the fields in which that they intend to major in.
- As students proceed through the first year of college, they grow more uncertain about the majors they chose when they began college.
- More than two-thirds of new students change their minds about their majors during the first year of college.
- Only one in three college seniors eventually major in the same field that they chose during their first year of college (Cuseo, 2005).

These findings demonstrate that the vast majority of students entering college are not certain about their college majors. Many students don't reach their final decision about a major *before* starting their college experience; instead, they make that decision *during* their college experience. Being uncertain about a major is nothing to be embarrassed about. Being "undecided" and "undeclared" doesn't mean that you're irresponsible, clueless, or lost. Beginning college students may be undecided for very good reasons. For instance, you may be undecided simply because you have interests in various subjects; this is a healthy form of indecision because it shows that you

275

Student *Perspective*

Student *Perspective*

have a range of interests and a high level of motivation to learn about different subjects. You may also be undecided simply because you're a careful, reflective thinker whose decision-making style is to gather more information before making a firm and final commitment.

In one study of students who were undecided about a major at the start of college, 43 percent had several ideas in mind but were not yet ready to commit to one of them (Gordon & Steele, 2003). These students were not lacking direction. In fact, they had some ideas but still wanted to explore them and keep their options open, which is an effective way to go about making decisions.

As a first-year student, it's only natural to be at least somewhat uncertain about your educational goals because you haven't yet experienced the variety of subjects and academic programs that make up the college curriculum, some of which you didn't know existed. In fact, one purpose of general education courses is to help new students develop the critical thinking skills needed to make wise choices and well-informed decisions, such as their choice of a college major. The liberal arts curriculum is designed to introduce you to various academic subjects, and as you progress through this curriculum, you may discover subjects that captivate you and capture your interest. Some of these subjects may represent fields of study that you never experienced before, and all of them represent possible choices for a college major.

As you gain experience with the college curriculum, you will also gain more self-awareness about your academic strengths and weaknesses. This is important knowledge to take into consideration when choosing a major, because you want to be sure to select a field that builds on your academic abilities and talents.

It's true that some people take too long and sometimes procrastinate when it comes to making important decisions. However, it's also true that they can make decisions too quickly, resulting in premature choices made without sufficient reflection and careful consideration of all options. Judging from the large number of students who end up changing their minds about a college major, it's probably safe to say that more students make the mistake of reaching a decision about a major too quickly rather than procrastinating indefinitely. "What's your major?" is a question that students hear over and over again, even before they've set foot on a college campus. You probably also saw this question on your college applications, and you're likely to hear it often during your very first term in college. Family members are also likely to ask you the same question, particularly if they're paying or helping to pay the high cost of a college education. They want assurance that their investment will pay off, and they're likely to feel more assured if they know you have a definite commitment to a major and are on your way to a self-supporting career.

Reflection **11.2**

If you've selected a major or are strongly considering one, what or who led you to select or consider this option?

If you're undecided and are feeling pressure to make an early decision, we encourage you to respectfully resist it until you've gain more self-knowledge and more experience with the college curriculum and co-curriculum. Even if you think you're sure about your choice of major, before you make a formal and final commitment to it, take a course or two in the major to test it and confirm whether it's a good fit for your personal interests, talents, and values.

When Should Students Reach a Firm Decision about a College Major?

It's okay to start off not knowing what your major will be and to give yourself some time and college experience before reaching a decision. You can take courses that will count toward your degree and stay on track for graduation, even if you haven't yet decided on or declared your college major. If you're undecided, you can still enjoy the educational journey even if you aren't completely sure about your final destination; however, at the same time, you want to make progress (not mark time).

If you've entered college with a major in mind, there's still time to change your mind without falling behind. If you realize that your first choice of a major isn't a good choice, don't think you're "locked in" to your original plan and your only option is to stick with it throughout college or drop out of college. Changing your original educational plans is not necessarily a bad thing. It may mean that you have discovered another field that's more interesting to you or that's more compatible with your personal interests and talents. Your college, however, may require you to declare a major by a certain point in your academic career, so be sure to check your college catalog and speak with your academic advisor.

The one drawback to changing your major is making that change *late* in your college experience. Late major-changing can lengthen your time to college graduation, and increase the cost of your college education, because you'll likely need to complete additional courses for your newly chosen major—particularly if it's in a very different field than your previous major. The key to preventing this scenario from happening late in your college experience is to engage in long-range educational planning *early* in your college experience.

Changing your major this close to graduation will add to the time it takes for you to earn your college degree; it will also add to the cost of your college education.

> ● **Remember**
>
> *As a general rule, you should reach a fairly firm decision about your major during your second (sophomore) year in college. However, to reach a good decision within this time frame, the process of exploring and planning should begin now—during your*
> ● *first term in college.*

The Importance of Long-Range Educational Planning

"When you have to make a choice and don't make it, that is in itself a choice."

—William James, philosopher and one of the founders of American psychology

College allows you choices about courses to enroll in and fields to specialize in. By looking beyond your first year of college and developing a tentative long-range educational plan, you're able to get a sneak preview and big-picture overview of your college experience. In contrast, looking at and scheduling your classes one term at a time—just before each registration period when—limits the view your college to as a choppy series of short, separate snapshots that lacks continuity, connection, and direction.

Long-range educational planning also enables you to take a *proactive* approach to your education: you take charge by taking early and preemptive action that anticipates your future, rather than passively allowing the future to sneak up on you and taking a reactive approach—i.e., reacting to your future without a strategic plan of attack. As the old saying goes, "If you fail to plan, you plan to fail." Through advanced planning, you can actively take charge of your academic future and make it happen *for* you, rather than waiting and passively letting it happen *to* you.

"Education is our passport to the future, for tomorrow belongs to the people who prepare for it today."

—Malcolm X, African American Muslim minister, public speaker, and human rights activist

> ● **Remember**
>
> *Any long-range educational plan you develop is not set in stone: it can change depending on changes in your academic interests and future plans. The purpose of long-range planning is not to lock you into a rigid plan, but to free you from short-*
> ● *sightedness, procrastination, and denial about making decisions on your future.*

Don't take the avoidance and denial approach to planning your educational future.

Factors to Consider When Choosing a Major

Self-awareness is the critical first step in making decisions about a college major, or any important personal decision. You must know yourself before you can know what choice is best for you. While this may seem obvious, self-awareness and self-discovery are often overlooked aspects of the decision-making process. In particular, when choosing a major you should be aware of:

- Your *interests*, what you like doing;
- Your *abilities*, what you're good at doing; and
- Your *values*, what you feel good about doing.

Research indicates that students are more likely to continue in college and graduate when they choose majors that reflect their personal interests and talents (Leuwerke, Robbins, Sawyer, & Hovland, 2004).

Reflection 11.3

In Chapter 3 (pp.68–70), you answered self-awareness questions related to three elements of "self": interests, abilities (talents), and values. Review your answers to these questions. Do you notice any patterns across your answers suggesting that a certain major would provide a nice "fit" or "match" with your personal interests, abilities, and values?

Multiple Intelligences: Identifying Personal Abilities and Talents

One element of the self that you should be aware of when choosing a major is your mental strengths, abilities, or talents. Intelligence was once considered to be one general trait that could be detected and measured by a single intelligence test score. The singular word "intelligence" has now been replaced by the plural word "intelligences" to reflect the fact that humans can display intelligence (mental ability) in many forms other than performance on an IQ test.

Listed in Snapshot Summary 11.1 are forms of intelligence identified by Howard Gardner (1993, 1999, 2006) based on studies of gifted and talented individuals, experts in different lines of work, and various other sources. As you read through the types of intelligence, place a checkmark next to the type that you think represents your strongest ability or talent. (You can possess more than one type.) Keep your type(s) of intelligence in mind when you're choosing a college major, because different majors emphasize different thinking skills (Brooks, 2009). Ideally, you want to select an academic field that allows you to utilize your strongest skills and talents. Choosing a major that's compatible with your abilities should enable you to master the concepts and skills required by your major more easily and more deeply. If you follow your academic talents, you're also more likely to succeed or excel in what you do, which will bolster your academic self-confidence and motivation.

Snapshot Summary

11.1   Multiple Forms of Intelligence

- **Linguistic intelligence.** Ability to communicate through language—e.g., verbal skills in the areas of speaking, writing, listening, and reading.
- **Logical-mathematical intelligence.** Ability to reason logically and succeed in tasks that involve mathematical problem solving—e.g., making logical arguments and following logical reasoning, or ability to work well with numbers and make quantitative calculations.
- **Spatial intelligence.** Ability to visualize relationships among objects arranged in different spatial positions and the ability to perceive or create visual images—e.g., forming mental images of three-dimensional objects; detecting detail in objects or drawings; artistic talent for drawing, painting, sculpting, and graphic design; and skills related to sense of direction and navigation.
- **Musical intelligence.** Ability to appreciate or create rhythmical and melodic sounds—e.g., playing, writing, and arranging music.
- **Interpersonal (social) intelligence.** Ability to relate to others, to accurately identify others' needs, feelings, or emotional states of mind, and to effectively express emotions and feelings to others—e.g., interpersonal communication skills and ability to accurately read the feelings of others and meet their emotional needs.
- **Intrapersonal (self) intelligence.** Ability to introspect and understand one's own thoughts, feelings, and behavior—e.g., capacity for personal reflection, emotional self-awareness, and self-insight.
- **Bodily-kinesthetic (psychomotor) intelligence.** Ability to use one's own body skillfully and learn through bodily sensations or movements—e.g., skilled at tasks involving physical coordination, ability to work well with hands, mechanical skills, talent for building models, assembling things, and using technology.

> "I used to operate a printing press. In about two weeks I knew how to run it and soon after I could take the machine apart in my head and analyze what each part does, how it functioned, and why it was shaped that way."
>
> —Response of college sophomore to the questions "What are you really good at? What comes easily or naturally to you?"

- **Naturalist intelligence.** Ability to carefully observe and appreciate features of the natural environment—e.g., keen awareness of nature or natural surroundings, and ability to understand causes and consequences of events occurring in the natural world.
- **Existential intelligence.** Ability to conceptualize phenomena and experiences that require one to go beyond sensory or physical evidence, such as questions and issues involving the origin of the universe and human life, and the purpose of human existence.

Source: Gardner (1993, 1999, 2006).

Learning Styles: Identifying Your Learning Preferences

Your learning style is another important personal characteristic you should be aware of when choosing your major. Learning style refers to the way in which individuals prefer to perceive information (receive or take it in) and process information (deal with it after taking it in). Individuals may differ in terms of whether they prefer to take in information by reading about it, listening to it, seeing an image or diagram of it, or physically touching and manipulating it. Individuals can vary in terms of whether they like to receive information in structured and orderly formats or prefer more unstructured formats that allow them the freedom to explore, play with, and restructure it in their own way. Once information has been received, individuals may also differ in terms of how they prefer to process or deal with it mentally. Some might like to think about it on their own; others may prefer to discuss it with someone else, some prefer to outline it, while others may prefer to map it out or draw a diagram of it.

Reflection 11.4

Which type or types of intelligence listed in Snapshot Summary 11.1 represent your strongest area or areas?

Which majors or fields of study do you think may be the best match for your natural talents?

Author's Experience In my family, whenever there's something that needs to be assembled or set up (e.g., a ping-pong table or new electronic equipment), I've noticed that my wife, my son, and myself have different learning styles in terms of how we go about doing it. I like to read the manual's instructions carefully and completely before I even attempt to touch anything. My son prefers to look at the pictures or diagrams in the manual and uses them as models to find parts; then he begins to assemble those parts. My wife seems to prefer not to look at the manual at all! Instead, she likes to figure things out as she goes along by grabbing different parts from the box and trying to assemble those parts that look like they should fit together—piecing them together as if she were completing a jigsaw puzzle.

Joe Cuseo

You can take specially designed tests to assess your particular learning style and how it compares with others. If you're interested in assessing your learning style, the Learning Center or Career Development Center are the two most likely sites on campus where you will be able to do so.

Probably the most frequently used learning styles test is the Myers-Briggs Type Indicator (MBTI), which is based on the personality theory of psychologist Carl Jung. The test consists of four pairs of opposing traits and assesses how people vary on a scale (low to high) for each of these four sets of traits. The four sets of opposing traits are illustrated in Figure 11.1.

As you read about the four pairs of opposite traits, place a mark along the line where you think you fall with respect to each set of traits. For example, place a mark in the middle of the line if you think you are midway between these opposing traits, or place a mark at the far left or far right if you think you lean strongly toward the trait listed on either end.

FIGURE 11.1

Extraversion	**Introversion**
Prefer to focus on "outer" world of persons, actions, or objects	Prefer to focus on "inner" world of thoughts and ideas
Sensing	**Intuition**
Prefer interacting with the world directly through concrete, sensory experiences	Prefer dealing with symbolic meanings and imagining possibilities
Thinking	**Feeling**
Prefer to rely on logic and rational thinking when making decisions	Prefer to rely on human needs and feelings when making decisions
Judging	**Perceiving**
Prefer to plan for and control events	Prefer flexibility and spontaneity

Traits and Learning Styles Measured by the Myers-Briggs Type Indicator (MBTI)

Reflection 11.5

For each of the following four sets of opposing traits, make a note about where you fall—low, middle, or high.

MBTI Personality Traits	Low	Middle	High
Extraversion–Introversion			
Sensing–Intuition			
Thinking–Feeling			
Judging–Perceiving			

What majors or fields of study do you think are most compatible with your personality traits?

It's been found that college students who score high on the introversion scale of the MBTI are less likely to become bored than extroverts while engaging in mental tasks that involve repetition and little external stimulation (Vodanovich, Wallace, & Kass, 2005). Students who score differently on the MBTI also have different learning preferences when it comes to writing and types of writing assignments (Jensen & Ti Tiberio, as cited in Bean, 2001). These findings are depicted below.

FIGURE 11.2

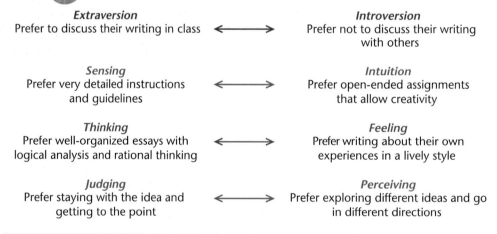

Extraversion
Prefer to discuss their writing in class ⟷ **Introversion**
Prefer not to discuss their writing with others

Sensing
Prefer very detailed instructions and guidelines ⟷ **Intuition**
Prefer open-ended assignments that allow creativity

Thinking
Prefer well-organized essays with logical analysis and rational thinking ⟷ **Feeling**
Prefer writing about their own experiences in a lively style

Judging
Prefer staying with the idea and getting to the point ⟷ **Perceiving**
Prefer exploring different ideas and go in different directions

Students with Each MBTI Learning Style Have a Preferred Style of Writing

These results clearly indicate that students have different learning styles, which, in turn, influence the type of writing assignments they feel most comfortable performing. This may be important to keep in mind when choosing your major because different academic fields emphasize different styles of writing. Some fields place heavy emphasis on writing that is structured and tightly focused (e.g., science and business), while other fields may encourage writing with personal style, flair, and creativity (e.g., English). How your writing style meshes with the style emphasized by an academic field may be an important factor to consider when making decisions about your college major.

Another popular learning styles test is the Learning Styles Inventory (Dunn, Dunn, & Price, 1990), originally developed by David Kolb, a professor of philosophy (Kolb, 1976, 1985). It's based on how individuals differ with respect to the following two elements of the learning process:

How Information Is *Perceived* (Taken in)

Concrete Experience
Learning through direct involvement
or personal experience

⟵⟶

Reflective Observation
Learning by watching
or observing

How Information Is *Processed* (Dealt with after it has been taken in)

Abstract Conceptualization
Learning by thinking about things
and drawing logical conclusions

⟵⟶

Active Experimentation
Learning by taking chances
and trying things out

When these two dimensions are crisscrossed to form intersecting lines, four sectors (areas) are created, each of which represents a different learning style, as illustrated in Figure 11.3. As you read the characteristics associated with each of these four areas (styles) in the figure, circle the style that you think reflects your most preferred way of learning.

FIGURE 11.3

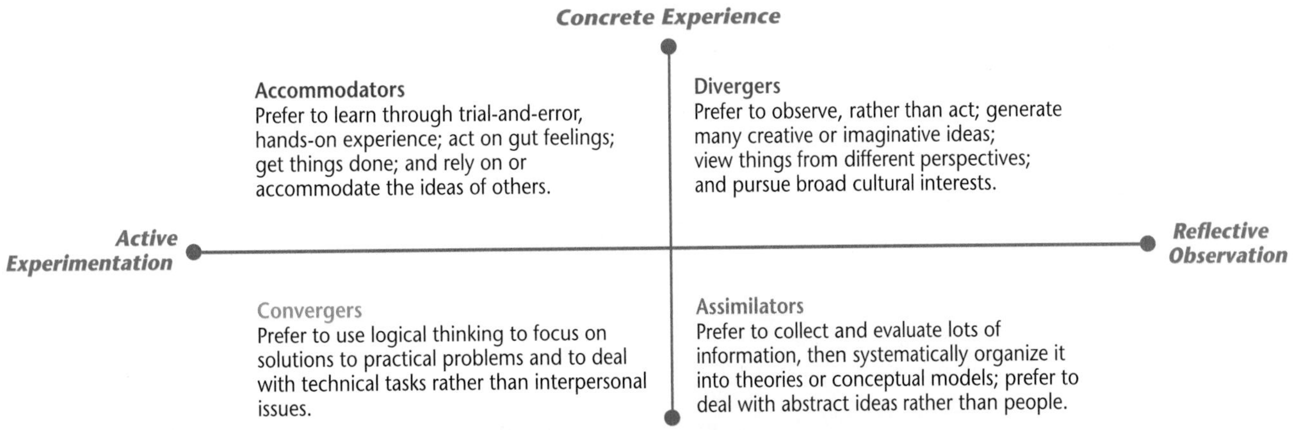

Concrete Experience

Accommodators
Prefer to learn through trial-and-error, hands-on experience; act on gut feelings; get things done; and rely on or accommodate the ideas of others.

Divergers
Prefer to observe, rather than act; generate many creative or imaginative ideas; view things from different perspectives; and pursue broad cultural interests.

Active Experimentation

Reflective Observation

Convergers
Prefer to use logical thinking to focus on solutions to practical problems and to deal with technical tasks rather than interpersonal issues.

Assimilators
Prefer to collect and evaluate lots of information, then systematically organize it into theories or conceptual models; prefer to deal with abstract ideas rather than people.

Learning Styles Measured by the Learning Styles Inventory (LSI)

Reflection **11.6**

Which one of the four learning styles appears to most closely match your learning style? (Check one of the following boxes.)

☐ Accommodator

☐ Diverger

☐ Converger

☐ Assimilator

What majors or fields of study do you think would be a good match for your learning style?

Research indicates that students majoring in different fields tend to display differences in these four learning styles (Svinicki, 2004; Svinicki & Dixon, 1987). For instance, "assimilators" are more often found majoring in mathematics and natural sciences (e.g., chemistry and physics), probably because these subjects stress reflection and abstract thinking. In contrast, academic fields where "accommodators" tend to be more commonly found are business, accounting, and law, perhaps because these fields involve taking practical action and making concrete decisions. "Divergers" are more often attracted to majors in the fine arts (e.g., music, art, and drama), humanities (e.g., history and literature), or social sciences (e.g., psychology and political science), possibly because these fields emphasize appreciating multiple viewpoints and perspectives. In contrast, "convergers" are more often found in fields such as engineering, medicine, and nursing, probably because these fields focus on finding solutions to practical and technical problems (Kolb, 1976). These same clusters of fields are found when faculty are asked to classify academic fields in terms of what learning styles they emphasize (Biglan, 1973; Schommer-Aikins, Duell, & Barker, 2003).

The engineering and humanities majors settle their differences in the fine arts quad!

Since students have different learning styles and academic fields emphasize different styles of learning, it's important to consider how your learning style meshes with the style of learning emphasized by the field you're considering as a major. If the match seems to be close and compatible, then the marriage between you and that major could be one that leads to a satisfying and successful learning experience.

We recommend taking a trip to the Learning Center or Career Development Center on your campus to take a learning styles test, or you could try the learning styles inventory that accompanies this text (see the inside of the front cover for details). Even if the test doesn't help you choose a major, it will at least help you become more aware of your particular learning style. This alone could contribute to your academic success, because studies show that when college students gain greater self-awareness of their learning styles, their academic performance improves (Claxton & Murrell, 1987; Hendry et al., 2005).

Reflection 11.7

In addition to taking formal tests to assess your learning style, you can gain awareness of your learning style through some simple self-reflection. Take a moment to reflect on your learning style by completing the following statements:

I learn best if . . .

I learn most from . . .

I enjoy learning when . . .

Author's Experience I first noticed that students in different academic fields may have different learning styles when I was teaching a psychology course required for students majoring in nursing and social work. Some students seemed to lose interest (and patience) when we got involved in lengthy class discussions about controversial issues or theories, while others seemed to love it. On the other hand, whenever I lectured or delivered information for an extended period, some students seemed to lose interest (and attention), while others seemed to get "into it" and took great notes.

After one class period that involved quite a bit of class discussion, I thought about which students seemed most involved and which seemed to drift off or lose interest. I suddenly realized that the students who did most of the talking and seemed most enthused during the class discussion were the students majoring in social work. On the other hand, most of the students who appeared disinterested or a bit frustrated were the nursing majors. The more I thought about this, it dawned on me that the nursing students were accustomed to gathering factual information and learning practical skills in their major courses and were expecting to use that learning style in my psychology course. They felt more comfortable with structured class sessions in which they received lots of factual, practical information from the professor. On the other hand, the social work majors were more comfortable with unstructured class discussions because courses in their major often emphasized debating social issues and listening to different viewpoints.

As I left class that day, I wondered if the nursing and social work students had just become accustomed to learning in different ways because of the different teaching methods they were exposed to, or if they had chosen their majors because the teaching methods best matched their learning styles.

Joe Cuseo

To sum up, the most important factors to consider when reaching decisions about a major are whether it is compatible with four characteristics of the self: (1) your learning style, (2) your abilities, (3) your personal interests, and (4) your values (see Figure 11.4). These four pillars provide the foundation for effective decision-making about a college major.

FIGURE 11.4

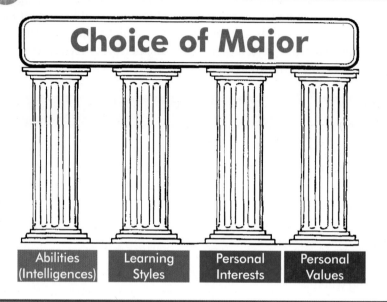

© Kendall Hunt

Personal Characteristics That Provide an Effective Foundation for Choice of a College Major

Reflection **11.8**

Consider the following statement: "Choosing a major is a life-changing decision because it will determine what you do for the rest of your life."

Would you agree or disagree with this statement?

Why?

Myths about the Relationship between Majors and Careers

Good decisions are based on accurate or valid information, rather than misconceptions or myths. Good decisions about a college major are built on accurate or valid information about the relationship between majors and careers. Unfortunately, numerous misconceptions exist about the relationship between majors and careers that often lead students to make uninformed or unrealistic choices of a college major. Following are four common myths about the major-career relationship that you should be aware of and factor into your decisions about a college major.

Myth 1. When you choose your major, you're choosing your career. While some majors lead directly to a particular career, most do not. Majors leading directly to specific careers are called pre-professional or pre-vocational majors; they include such fields as accounting, engineering, and nursing. However, the vast majority of college majors don't channel you straight to one particular career: instead, they leave you with a variety of career options. All physics majors don't become physicists, all philosophy majors don't become philosophers, all history majors don't become historians, and all English majors don't become Englishmen (or Englishwomen).

As we discussed and illustrated in Chapter 2, the truth is that the trip from your college major to your eventual career(s) is less like climbing a pole and more like climbing up a tree. You begin with the tree's trunk (the foundation provided by general education), which leads to separate limbs (choices for college majors), which, in turn, leads to different branches (different career paths or options). Just as a cluster of branches grow from the same limb, so does a "family" of related careers grow from the same major. For example, an English major typically leads to careers that involve use of the written language, such as editing, journalism, and publishing, while a major in art leads to careers that involve use of visual media, such as illustration, graphic design, and art therapy. (The Web site mymajors.com provides useful and free information on groups or families of jobs that tend to be related to different majors.)

Furthermore, different majors can also lead to the same career. For instance, a variety of majors can lead a student to law school and to an eventual career as a lawyer; there really isn't a law or pre-law major. Similarly, pre-med really isn't a major. Although most students interested in going into medical school graduate with a four-year degree in some field in the natural sciences (e.g., biology or chemistry), it's possible for students to go to medical school with majors in other fields, particularly if they take and do well in a cluster of science courses that are emphasized in medical school (e.g., general biology, general chemistry, organic and inorganic chemistry).

So, don't assume that your major *is* your career, or that your major automatically turns into your career field. It's this belief that can result in some students procrastinating about choosing a major; they think they're making a lifelong decision and fear that if they make the "wrong" choice, they'll be stuck doing something they hate for the rest of their lives. The belief that your major becomes your career may also account for the fact that 58 percent of college graduates major in a pre-professional or pre-vocational field—e.g., nursing, accounting, and engineering (Association of American Colleges and Universities, 2007). These majors have a career that's obviously connected to them, which reassures students (and their family members) that they will have a job after graduation. However, the truth is that students in pre-professional majors may be more likely to be hired *immediately* after graduation, but within six months after graduation, college graduates with other college majors are just as likely to have jobs and aren't any more likely to be unemployed (Pascarella & Terenzini, 2005).

> **Remember**
>
> *Don't assume that when you choose your college major, you're choosing what you'll be doing for the remainder of your working life.*

Additional research on college graduates indicates that they change careers numerous times, and the further they continue along their career paths, the more likely they are to work in fields unrelated to their college majors (Millard, 2004). Remember that the general education curriculum is an important and influential part of a college education. It allows students to acquire knowledge in diverse subjects and to develop durable, transferable skills (e.g., writing, speaking, organizing) that qualify

"Linear thinking can keep you from thinking broadly about your options and being open-minded to new opportunities."
—Karen Brooks, *You Majored in What?*

Student *Perspective*

"Things like picking majors and careers really scare me a lot! I don't know exactly what I want to do with my life."
—First-year student

them for a diversity of careers, regardless of what their particular majors happened to be. Thus, for the vast majority of college majors, students first make decisions about majors, and later, make decisions about careers. Although it's important to think about the relationship between your choice of major and your initial career choice, for most college students these are different choices made at different times. Both choices relate to your future goals, but they involve different timeframes: choosing your major is a more immediate or short-range goal, whereas choosing your career is an intermediate or long-range goal.

Remember

Deciding on a major and deciding on a career are not identical decisions: they're often different decisions made at different times.

Myth 2. If you want to continue your education after a bachelor's degree, you must continue in the same field as your college major. After college graduation, you have two main options or alternative paths available to you:

1. You can enter a career immediately, or
2. You can continue your education in graduate school or professional school. (See Figure 11.5 for a visual map of the signposts or stages in the college experience and the primary paths available to you after college graduation.)

Once you complete a bachelor's degree, it's possible to continue your education in a field that's not directly related to your college major. This is particularly true for students who are majoring in pre-professional careers that funnel them directly into a particular career after graduation (Pascarella & Terenzini, 2005). For example, if you major in English, you can still go to graduate school in a subject other than English, or go to law school, or get a master's degree in business administration. In fact, it's common to find that the majority of graduate students in master's of business administration (MBA) programs were not business majors in college (Dupuy & Vance, 1996).

Myth 3. You should major in business because most college graduates work in business settings. Studies show that college graduates with a variety of majors end up working in business settings. For instance, engineering majors are likely to work in accounting, production, and finance. Liberal arts majors are likely to move on to positions in business settings that involve marketing, human resources, or public affairs (Bok, 2006; Useem, 1989). So, don't restrict your choices of a major to business by believing in the myth that you must major in business to work for a business after graduation. Research shows that in the long run, the career mobility and career advancement of non-business majors in the business world are equal to those attained by business majors (Pascarella & Terenzini, 1991; 2005).

Myth 4. If you major in a liberal arts field, the only career available to you is teaching. Liberal arts majors are not restricted to teaching careers. Many college graduates with majors in liberal arts fields have proceeded to, and succeeded in, careers other than teaching. Among these graduates are such notable people as:

- Jill Barad (English major), CEO, Mattel Toys
- Steve Case (political science major), CEO, America Online
- Brian Lamb (speech major), CEO, C-Span
- Willie Brown (liberal studies major), mayor, San Francisco
  Source: Indiana University (2004).

FIGURE 11.5

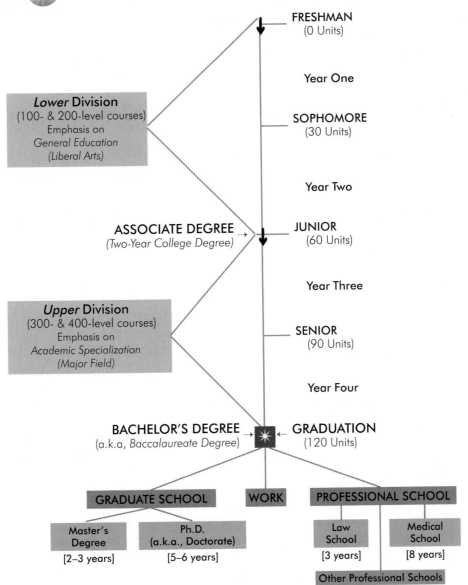

Notes

1. The total number of *general education* units and the total number of units needed to **graduate** with a bachelor's degree may vary somewhat from school to school. Also, the total number of units required for a *major* will vary somewhat from major to major and from school to school.

2. It often takes college students longer than four years to graduate due to a variety of reasons, such as working part-time and taking fewer courses per term, needing to repeat courses that were failed or dropped, or making a late change to a different major and needing to fulfill additional requirements for the new major.

3. *Graduate* and *professional* schools are options for continuing to higher levels of education after completion of an undergraduate (college) education.

4. Compared to graduate school, *professional* school involves advanced education in more "applied" professions (e.g., pharmacy or public administration).

Timeline to the Future: A Snapshot of the College Experience and Beyond

In fact, studies show that college graduates with liberal arts majors are just as likely to advance to the highest levels of corporate leadership as graduates majoring in pre-professional fields, such as business and engineering (Pascarella & Terenzini, 2005). If you are considering a major in a liberal arts field, you shouldn't be dismayed or discouraged by those who may question your choice by asking, "What are you going to do with a degree in *that* major?" (Brooks, 2009).

Strategies for Discovering a Major That's Compatible with Your Interests, Talents, and Values

If you're undecided about a major, there's no need to feel anxious or embarrassed, because you're just beginning your college experience. Although you haven't officially declared a major, this doesn't mean you're a clueless procrastinator. Just be sure that you don't put all thoughts about your major on the back burner and simply drift along until you have no choice but to make a choice. Now is the time to start exploring and developing a game plan for narrowing down your options that will eventually lead to a well-informed choice of a college major.

Similarly, if you've already chosen a major, this doesn't mean that you'll never have to give any more thought to that decision or that you can just shift into cruise control and motor along a mindless ride in the major you've selected. Instead, you should continue the exploration process by carefully testing your first choice, making sure it's a choice that's compatible with your abilities, interests, and values. In other words, take the approach that this is your *current* choice. Whether it becomes your firm and *final* choice will depend on how well you perform (and how interested you are) in the first courses you take in the field.

Following are specific strategies for exploring and identifying majors that may be most compatible with your personal strengths and interests.

Reflect on successful and enjoyable learning experiences you've had in the past. Think about your high school courses and out-of-class learning experiences. If you have done well and continue to do well in a certain field of study, this may indicate that your natural abilities and learning style correspond well with the academic skills required by that particular field. This could translate into future success and satisfaction in the field if you decide to pursue it as a college major. As the old saying goes, "Nothing succeeds like success itself."

You can enter information about your academic performance in high school courses at mymajors.com, which will analyze it and provide you with college majors that may be a good match for you based on your experiences in high school.

Use your elective courses to test your interests and abilities in subjects that you might consider as a major. As its name implies, "elective" courses are those that you elect or choose to take. Your college electives come in two forms: free electives and restricted electives. *Free electives* are courses that you may elect (choose) to enroll in; they count toward your college degree but are not required for general education or your major. *Restricted electives* are courses that you must take, but you choose them from a restricted list of possible courses that have been specified by your college as fulfilling a requirement in general education or your major. For example, your campus may have a general education requirement in social or behavioral sciences that requires you to take two courses in this field, but you're allowed to choose what those two courses are from a menu of options in the field, such as anthropology, economics, political science, psychology, or sociology. If you're considering one of these subjects as a possible major, you can take an introductory course in that subject to test your interest in it while simultaneously fulfilling a general education requirement needed for graduation. This strategy will allow you to use general education as the main highway for travel toward your final destination (a college degree) while using your electives to explore side roads (potential majors) along the way. If you find one that's compatible with your talents and interests, you may have found yourself a major.

Naturally, you don't have to use all your electives for the purpose of exploring majors. Depending on your major, as many as one-third of your courses in college may be electives; this leaves you with a significant amount of freedom to shape your college experience that best meets your educational and personal goals. For suggestions on how to make the best use of your free electives, see Do It Now! 11.1.

11.1   DO IT **NOW**!

Top 10 Suggestions for Making the Most of Your College Electives

Your elective courses give you some academic freedom and sense of personal control over your college coursework. Exercise this freedom responsibly and strategically by selecting electives in a way that enables you to make the most of your college experience and college degree.

Listed below are 10 recommendations for making effective use of your college electives. As you read them, identify three strategies that appeal most to you and that you'd most likely put into practice.

Electives may be used strategically for the following purposes.

1. **To complete a minor or build an area of concentration.** Your electives can complement and strengthen your major or allow you to pursue a field of interest other than your major.
2. **To help you choose a career path.** Just as you can use electives to test your interest in a college major, you can use them to test your interest in a career. For instance, you could enroll in:
   - career planning or career development courses; and
   - courses that include internships or service learning experiences in a field that you're considering as a possible career (e.g., health, education, or business).
3. **To strengthen your skills in areas that may appeal to future employers.** For example, courses in foreign language, leadership development, and argumentation or debate can develop skills that are attractive to future employers.

4. **To develop practical life skills that you can use now or in the near future.** Courses in managing personal finances, marriage and family, or child development can help you manage your money and your future family.
5. **To seek balance in your life and develop yourself as a whole person.** You can use your electives strategically to cover all key dimensions of self-development. For instance, you could take courses that promote your emotional development (e.g., stress management), social development (e.g., interpersonal relationships), mental development (e.g., critical thinking), physical development (e.g., nutrition, self-defense), and spiritual development (e.g., world religions or death and dying).

> **Remember**
> *Choose courses that contribute not only to your particular major and career, but also to your overall quality of life.*

6. **To make connections across different academic disciplines (subject areas).** Courses designed specifically to integrate two or more academic disciplines are referred to as interdisciplinary courses. For example, psychobiology is an interdisciplinary course that integrates the fields of psychology (focusing on the mind) and biology (focusing on the body), thus helping you see how the mind influences the body and vice versa. Making connections across subjects and seeing how they can be combined to create a more complete understanding of a personal

(continued)

or societal issue can be a stimulating mental experience. Furthermore, the presence of interdisciplinary courses on your college transcript may be attractive to future employers because responsibilities and issues in the work world are not neatly packaged into separate majors: they require the ability to combine skills acquired from different fields of study.

7. **To help you develop broader perspectives on the human condition and the world around you.** You can take courses that progressively widen your perspectives. For example, you could select courses that provide you with a societal perspective (e.g., sociology), a national perspective (e.g., political science), an international perspective (e.g., cultural geography), a global perspective (e.g., ecology), and a cosmological perspective (e.g., astronomy). These broadening perspectives widen your scope of knowledge and deepen your understanding of the world.

8. **To appreciate different cultural viewpoints and improve your ability to communicate with people from diverse cultural backgrounds.** You could take courses related to differences across nations (international diversity), such as international relations, and courses related to ethnic and racial differences in America (domestic diversity).

9. **To stretch beyond your familiar or customary learning style to experience different ways of learning and acquire new skills.** Your college curriculum is likely to include courses that were never previously available to you and that focus on skills you've never had the opportunity to test or develop. These courses can stretch your mind and allow you to explore new ideas and add to your repertoire of skills.

10. **To learn something you were always curious about or know little about.** For instance, if you've always been curious about how members of the other sex think and feel, you could take a course on the psychology of men and women. Or if you've always been fascinated by movies and how they are made, you might elect to take a course in filmmaking or cinematography.

"Try not to take classes because they fit neatly into your schedule. Start by identifying classes that are most important to you and fit your schedule to accommodate them."

—Karen Brooks, *You Majored in What?*

• Remember

Your elective course in college will give you the opportunity to shape and create an academic experience that is uniquely your own. Seize this opportunity by exercising your freedom reflectively and responsibly. Don't make your elective choices randomly or merely on the basis of scheduling convenience (e.g., choosing courses to create a schedule with no early morning or late afternoon classes). Instead, make strategic choices of courses that will contribute most to your educational, personal, and professional development.

Choosing courses that best enable you to achieve your long-term educational and personal goals should take precedence over creating a schedule that leaves your Fridays free for three-day weekends.

Be sure you know what courses are required for the major you're considering. In college, students are expected to know the requirements for the majors they've chosen. These requirements vary considerably from one field to the next. Review your college catalog carefully to determine what courses are required for the major you're considering. College catalogs are often written in a technical and legalistic manner that can sometimes be hard to interpret. If you're having some trouble identifying and understanding the requirements for a major that you are considering, don't be embarrassed about seeking assistance from a professional in your school's Academic Advising Center.

Reflection 11.9

What three strategies on the list in **Do It Now! 11.1** most appealed to you and which are you most likely to implement?

Write a short explanation about why you chose each of these strategies.

Keep in mind that college majors often require courses in fields outside of the major that are designed to support the major. For instance, psychology majors are often required to take at least one course in biology, and business majors are often required to take calculus. If you're interested in majoring in a particular field, be sure you are fully aware of such outside requirements and are comfortable with them.

Once you've accurately identified all courses required for the major you're considering, ask yourself the following two questions:

1. Do the course titles and descriptions appeal to my interests and values?
2. Do I have the abilities or skills needed to do well in these courses?

Take a look at introductory textbooks in the field you're considering as a major. You can find introductory textbooks for all courses in your college bookstore, in the college library, or with a faculty member in that field. Review their tables of contents and read a few pages of each text to get some sense of the writing style used in the field and whether the topics are compatible with your educational interests and talents.

Speak with students majoring in the field you're considering and ask them about their experiences. Talk to several students in the field you're considering to get a different and balanced perspective on what the field is like. A good way to find students in the major you're considering is to visit student clubs on campus related to the major (e.g., psychology club or history club). You could also check the class schedule to see when and where classes in your major are meeting and then go to the rooms where these classes meet and speak with students about the major, either before or after class. The following questions may be good ones to ask students in a major that you're considering:

- What first attracted you to this major?
- What would you say are the advantages and disadvantages of majoring in this field?
- Knowing what you know now, would you choose the same major again?

Also, ask students about the quality of teaching and advising in the department. Studies show that different departments within the same college or university can vary greatly in terms of the quality of teaching, as well as their educational philosophy and attitude toward students (Pascarella & Terenzini, 1991; 2005).

Sit in on some classes in the field you're considering as a major. If the class you want to visit is large, you probably could just slip into the back row and listen. However, if the class is small, you should ask the instructor's permission. When visiting a class, focus on the content or ideas being covered rather than the instructor's personality or teaching style. Don't forget that you're trying to decide whether you'll major in the subject, not the teacher.

Discuss the major you're considering with an academic advisor. To get unbiased feedback about the pros and cons of majoring in that field, it's probably best to speak with an academic advisor who advises students in various majors, rather than someone who advises only students in that particular academic department or field.

Speak with faculty members in the department. Consider asking the following questions:

- What academic skills or qualities are needed for a student to be successful in your field?
- What are the greatest challenges faced by students majoring in your field?
- What do students seem to like most and least about majoring in your field?
- What can students do with a major in your field after graduation?
- What types of graduate programs or professional schools would a student in your major be well prepared to enter?

Surf the Web site of the professional organization associated with the field you're considering as a major. The Web site of a professional organization often contains useful information for students who are considering that field as a major. For example, if you're thinking about becoming an anthropology major, check out the Web site of the American Anthropological Association. If you're considering history as a major, look at the Web site of the American Historical Association. The Web site of the American Philosophical Association contains information about nonacademic careers for philosophy majors, and the American Sociological Association's Web site identifies various careers that sociology majors are qualified to pursue after college graduation. To locate the professional Web site of the field that you might want to explore as a possible major, ask a faculty member in that field or complete a search on the Web by simply entering the name of the field followed by the word "association."

Be sure you know whether the major you're considering is impacted or oversubscribed and whether it requires certain academic standards to be met before you can be admitted. Certain college majors may be "impacted" or "oversubscribed," meaning that more students are interested in majoring in these fields than there are openings for them. Some majors that are often oversubscribed are pre-professional fields that lead directly to a particular career (e.g., engineering, pre-med, nursing, or physical therapy). On some campuses, these majors are called "restricted" majors, meaning that departments control their enrollment by restricting the number of students they let into the major. For example, departments may restrict entry to their major by admitting only students who have achieved an overall GPA of 3.0 or higher in certain introductory courses required by the majors, or they may take all students who apply for the major, rank them by GPA, and then count down until they have filled their maximum number of available spaces.

If you intend to major in a restricted field of study, be sure to check whether you're meeting the acceptance standards of the major as you continue to complete courses and earn grades. If you find yourself failing to meet these standards, you may need to increase the amount of time and effort you devote to your studies and seek assistance from your campus Learning Center. If you're working at your maximum level of effort and are regularly using the learning assistance services available on your campus but are still not meeting the academic standards of your intended major, consult with an academic advisor to help you identify an alternative field that may be closely related to the restricted major you were hoping to enter.

Reflection **11.10**

Do you think that the major you're considering is likely to be oversubscribed or restricted—i.e., a major in which there are more students trying to enter it than there are available openings?

Consider the possibility of a college minor in a field that complements your major. A college minor usually requires about half the number of credits (units) required for a major. Most campuses allow you the option of completing a minor with your major. Check the course catalog or consult with an academic advisor to see if your school offers a minor that interests you and what courses are required to complete it.

If you have strong interests in two different fields, a minor will allow you to major in one of these fields while minoring in the other. Thus, you can pursue two fields that interest you without having to sacrifice one for the other. Furthermore, a minor can usually be completed along with a major without delaying your time to graduation. In contrast, a double major is likely to lengthen your time to graduation because you must complete the separate requirements for both majors.

You can also pursue a second field of study in addition to your major without increasing your time to graduation by completing a "concentration" or "cognate area"—an academic specialization that requires fewer courses to complete than a minor (e.g., three to five courses vs. seven to eight courses). A concentration area may have even fewer requirements (only two to three courses).

Taking a cluster of courses in a field outside your major can be an effective way to strengthen your resume and increase your employment prospects; it demonstrates your versatility and enables you to develop skills and acquire knowledge in areas that may be missing or underemphasized in your major. For example, students majoring in the fine arts (e.g., music or theater) or humanities (e.g., English or history) may take a cluster of courses in the fields of mathematics (e.g., statistics), technology (e.g., computer science), or business (e.g., economics)—none of which are strongly emphasized by their majors and all of which are very likely to increase their prospects for employment after graduation.

Visit your Career Development Center. Ask if there's information available on college graduates who've majored in the field you're considering and what they've gone on to do with that major after graduation. This will give you an idea about the types of careers the major can lead to and what graduate or professional school programs students often enter after completing the major.

Summary and Conclusion

Here's a snapshot of the points that were made in this chapter:

Changing your educational goal is not necessarily a bad thing; it may represent your discovery of another field that's more interesting to you or more compatible with your personal interests and talents.

Two important characteristics to be aware of when choosing your major are:

1. Your intelligences, your mental strengths or talents, and
2. Your learning styles, your preferred ways of learning.

Several myths exist about the relationship between college majors and careers that need to be dispelled:

- Myth 1. When you choose your major, you're choosing your career.
- Myth 2. After a bachelor's degree, any further education must be in the same field as your college major.
- Myth 3. You should major in business because most college graduates work in business settings.
- Myth 4. If you major in a liberal arts field, the only career available is teaching.

Strategically select your college courses in a way that maximizes your educational, personal, and professional development. In particular, choose your elective courses with one or more of the following purposes in mind:

- To explore or confirm your choice of a college major.
- To acquire a minor or build a concentration to complement and augment your major.
- To broaden your perspectives on the world around you.
- To become a more balanced or complete person.
- To handle the practical life tasks that face you now and in the future.
- To strengthen your career development and employment prospects after graduation.

Compared to high school, higher education supplies you with more freedom of choice and greater opportunity to determine your own academic course of action. Enjoy and employ this freedom responsibly to make the most of your college experience and college degree.

Learning More through the World Wide Web
Internet-Based Resources for Further Information on Educational Planning and Decision Making

We recommend the following Web sites for additional information related to the ideas discussed in this chapter.

Identifying and Choosing College Majors:
www.mymajors.com
www.princetonreview.com/majors.aspx

Careers for Liberal Arts Majors:
http://www.bls.gov/opub/ooq/2007/winter/art01.pdf

11.1 Planning for a College Major

The point of this exercise is not to force you to commit to a major now, but to develop a tentative plan that will put you in a position to apply the knowledge you gain while completing this assignment to reach a well-informed final decision about your major. Even if you don't yet know what your final destination may be with respect to a college major, creating this educational plan will help keep you moving in the right direction.

1. Go to your college catalog and use its index to locate pages containing information related to the major you have chosen or are considering. If you're undecided, select a field that you might consider as a possibility. (To help you identify possible majors, peruse your catalog or go online and complete the short interview at the www.mymajors.com Web site.)

2. Once you've selected a major for this assignment, look at your college catalog and identify the courses that are required for the major you've selected. Use the form on the following page to list the number and title of each course required by the major.

   Note: You'll find that you must take specific courses for a major. For instance, all business majors are required to take microeconomics. You're also likely to discover that other required courses can be chosen from a menu or list of options (e.g., "choose any three courses from the following list of six courses"). Such courses are often called "major electives." When you find that you have a choice of electives in the major you've selected, read their course descriptions and choose those that most interest you now to include in your plan. Simply list the numbers and titles of these courses on the planning form. (You don't need to write down all choices listed in the catalog.)

   College catalogs can sometimes be tricky to navigate or interpret, so if you run into any difficulty, don't panic. Seek help from an academic advisor. Your campus may also have a degree audit program available, which allows you to track major requirements electronically. If so, take advantage of it.

College Major Planning Form

Major Selected:_____

Requirements in the Major
(Courses in your major that you must take)

Course #	Course Title	Course #	Course Title

Major Electives
(Courses required for your major that you choose to take from a specified list)

Course #	Course Title	Course #	Course Title

Self-Assessment Questions

1. Looking over the courses required for the major you've selected, would you still be interested in majoring in this field?

2. Were there courses required by the major that you were surprised to see or that you did not expect would be required?

3. Are there questions that you still have about this major?

11.2 Developing a Comprehensive Graduation Plan

A comprehensive, long-range graduation plan includes all three types of courses you need to complete a college degree:

1. General education requirements

2. Major requirements

3. Free electives

In Exercises 2.1 and 2.2 (p. 61) you planned for your required general education courses and required courses in your major. The third set of courses you'll take in college are called *free electives*—courses that are not required for general education or your major but that you freely choose from any of the courses listed in your college catalog. By combining your general education courses, major courses, and free elective courses, you can create a comprehensive, long-range graduation plan.

Use the "Long-Range Graduation Planning Form" on pp. 301–302 to develop this complete educational plan. Use the slots to pencil in the general education courses you're planning to take to fulfill your general education requirements, your major requirements, and your free electives. (For ideas on choosing free electives, see Do It Now! 11.1 on pp. 291–292.) Since this may be a tentative plan, it's probably best to complete it in pencil or electronically, in case you need to modify it later.

Notes

1. If you haven't decided on a major, a good strategy might be to concentrate on taking liberal arts courses to fulfill your general education requirements during your first year of college. This will open more slots in your course schedule during your sophomore year. By that time, you may have a better idea of what you want to major in, and you can fill these open slots with courses required by your major. This may be a particularly effective strategy if you choose to major in a field that has many lower-division (first year and sophomore) requirements that must be completed before you can take upper-division (junior and senior) courses in the major. (These lower-division requirements are often referred to as *premajor requirements*.)

2. Keep in mind that the course number indicates the year in the college experience when the course is usually taken. Courses numbered in the 100s (or below) are typically taken in the first year of college, 200-numbered courses in the sophomore year, 300-numbered courses in the junior year, and 400-numbered courses in the senior year. Also, be sure to check whether the course you're planning to take has any *prerequisites*—courses that need to be completed *before* you can enroll in the course you're planning to take. For example, if you are planning to take a course in literature, it's likely that you cannot enroll in it until you have completed at least one prerequisite course in writing or English composition.

3. To complete a college degree in four years (approximately 120 units), you should complete about 30 credits each academic year.

> **Remember**
>
> *Unlike in high school, taking summer courses in college isn't something you do because you've failed or forgotten to do something during the "normal" school year (fall and spring terms). Instead, it's an additional term that you can use to make further progress toward your college degree and reduce the total time it takes to complete your degree. Adopt the attitude that summer term is a regular part of the college academic year, and make strategic use of it to keep you on a four-year timeline to graduation.*

4. Check with an academic advisor to see whether your college has developed a projected plan of scheduled courses that shows the academic terms when courses are scheduled to be offered (e.g., fall, spring, or summer) for the next two to three years. If such a long-range plan of scheduled courses is available, take advantage of it because it will enable you to develop a personal educational plan that includes not only

what courses you will take, but also *when* you will take them. This can be an important advantage because some courses you may need for graduation may not be offered every term. We strongly encourage you to inquire about and acquire any long-range plan of scheduled courses that may be available, and use it when creating your long-range graduation plan.

5. Don't forget to include out-of-class learning experiences as part of your educational plan, such as volunteer service, internships, and study abroad. (For more detailed information on these learning experiences, see Chapter 12.)

Your long-range graduation plan doesn't have to be set in stone and inflexible. Consider your plan to be built with clay, not concrete, so its shape may be molded and changed into final form as you gain more experience with the college curriculum. Your development of this initial plan provides the important blueprint for guiding the construction of your educational future. Once you've built slots into the educational plan for your general education requirements, your major courses, and your electives, you've created structures for all the three key categories of courses you need to graduate. If you need to make changes to your original plan, they can be easily accommodated by simply substituting different specific courses into the general slots you've already created.

Remember

Long-range educational planning shouldn't rigidly and prematurely lock you into a final product that you're not yet fully prepared or committed to. Instead, it's a process that supplies you with a telescope for viewing your educational future and a map for guiding you toward your educational goals.

Long-Range Graduation Planning Form

STUDENT: ID NO:

MAJOR: MINOR:

TERM		TERM		TERM		TERM	
Course	Units	Course	Units	Course	Units	Course	Units
TOTAL		TOTAL		TOTAL		TOTAL	

TERM		TERM		TERM		TERM	
Course	Units	Course	Units	Course	Units	Course	Units
TOTAL		TOTAL		TOTAL		TOTAL	

TERM		TERM		TERM		TERM	
Course	Units	Course	Units	Course	Units	Course	Units
TOTAL		TOTAL		TOTAL		TOTAL	

TERM		TERM		TERM		TERM	
Course	Units	Course	Units	Course	Units	Course	Units
TOTAL		TOTAL		TOTAL		TOTAL	

		Student Leadership & Development Experiences	Service Learning & Internship Experiences
Advisor's Signature:	Date:		
Student's Signature:	Date:		

Self-Assessment Questions

1. Do you think this was a useful assignment? Why or why not?

2. Do you see any way in which this assignment could be improved or strengthened?

3. Did completing this long-range graduation plan influence your educational plans in any way?

Whose Choice Is It Anyway?

Ursula, a first-year student, was in tears when she showed up at the Career Center. She had just returned from a weekend visit home, during which she informed her parents that she was planning to major in art or theater. When Ursula's father heard about her plans, he exploded and insisted that she major in something "practical," like business or accounting, so that she could earn a living after she graduates. Ursula replied that she had no interest in these majors, nor did she feel she had the skills needed to complete the level of math required by them, which included calculus. Her father shot back that he had no intention of "paying four years of college tuition for her to end up as an unemployed artist or actress!" He went on to say that if she wanted to major in art or theater, she'd "have to figure out a way to pay for college herself."

Reflection and Discussion Questions

1. What options (if any) do you think Ursula has at this point in her college experience?

2. If Ursula were your friend, what would you recommend she do?

3. Do you see any way(s) in which Ursula might pursue a major that she's interested in and, at the same time, ease her father's concern that she'll end up jobless after college graduation?

Finding a Path to Your Future Profession

Career Exploration, Preparation, and Development

LEARNING GOAL

To acquire strategies you can use now and throughout the remaining years of your college experience for effective career exploration, preparation, and development.

Before you start to dig into this chapter, take a moment to answer the following questions:

1. Have you decided on a career, or are you leaning strongly toward one?

2. If yes, why have you chosen this career? (Was your decision strongly influenced by anybody or anything?)

3. If no, what careers are you considering as possibilities?

The Importance of Career Planning

College graduates in the 21st century are likely to continue working until age 75 (Herman, 2000). Once you enter the workforce full time, most of the remaining waking hours of your life will be spent working. The only other single activity you'll spend more time on in your entire life is sleeping. When you consider that such a sizable portion of life is spent working, it's understandable how your career can have such a strong influence on your personal identity and self-esteem. Given the importance of career choice, the process of career exploration and planning should begin now—during the first year of your college experience.

Even if you've decided on a career that you were dreaming about since you were a preschooler, you still need to engage in the process of career exploration and planning because you still need to decide on what specialization within that career you'll pursue. For example, if you're interested in pursuing a career in law, you'll need to eventually decide what branch of law you wish to practice (e.g., criminal law, corporate law, or family law). You'll also need to decide what employment sector or type of industry you would like to work in, such as nonprofit, for-profit, education, or government. Thus, no matter how certain or uncertain you are about your career path, you still need to explore career options and start taking your first steps toward formulating a career development plan.

Remember

When you're doing career planning, you're doing life planning because you're planning how you will spend most of the waking hours of your future life.

Becoming a 21st-Century Graduate

Although graduation seems to be in the far and distant future, it's never too soon to plan for the demands that will await you once you have your degree in hand. What will those demands be specifically? Well, that may be hard to anticipate right now when you think about how quickly our world is changing. When you consider the list of jobs in Snapshot Summary 12.1 that didn't exist 10 years ago, you can see how these careers express the global changes have occurred in the past decade. While planning for the future seems to be full of uncertainties, you can work now with your advisor and the Career Development Center on identifying your abilities, interests, and values and then factor this information into your educational plan, as discussed in Chapter 11. Be sure to take full advantage of the curricular and co-curricular opportunities that align with the components of your plan. In doing so, you will prepare yourself to become a 21st-century graduate who is ready for an ever-changing world.

Snapshot Summary

12.1 Jobs That Didn't Exist 10 Years Ago

1. **App developer.** When you hear "there's an app for that," that's because a career track emerged for program developers who expanded their professional knowledge and skills into the world of mobile devices.

2. **Market research data miner.** Ever wonder how retailers know how to market to you? Market research data miners collect data on consumer behaviors and predict trends for advertisers to use to develop marketing strategies.

3. **Educational or admissions consultant.** Some parents take extra steps to make sure their children are accepted into the "right" schools (from preschool to college). Educational or admissions consultants are hired to guide families through the application and interview process.

4. **Millennial generation expert.** It's very common to find members of different generations who are working together in the same organization. Millennial generation experts help employers maximize the potential of their staff by providing advice on working with their youngest employees and how to mentor them for future success.

5. **Social media manager.** The business world has made great use of social media to market and advertise their products and services. Social media managers target their marketing to the users of the various social media sites.

6. **Chief listening officer.** Similar to a social media manager, a chief listening officer uses social media to monitor consumer discussions and shares this information with marketing agents so they can design strategies that appeal to various segments of the population.

7. **Cloud computing services.** Most Web sites used every day by consumers store incredibly large amounts of data. These computer engineers, who have an expertise in data management, store and index tremendous volumes of bytes for companies (in the area of a quadrillion!).

8. **Elder care.** As life expectancy in the U.S. has increased, so has the need for individuals who have the knowledge, abilities, and compassion to serve the elderly, their families, and the agencies and companies that assist them.

9. **Sustainability expert.** For environmental and economic reasons, companies are seeking ways to minimize their carbon footprints. Sustainability experts have an expertise in the science of sustainability and the know-how to develop "green" business practices that are also cost-effective.

10. **User experience designer.** User experience designers do exactly what their titles suggest—they create experiences for consumers through technology. These designers bring to life color, sound, and images using HTML, Photoshop, and CSS.

Source: Casserly (2012)

Another important point to consider is that it is common for Americans to change jobs throughout their working lives. In fact, studies show that Americans change jobs 10 times in the two decades following college and that such change is even more frequent for younger workers (AAC&U, 2007). So, while you might be focused on a particular career, it's also important that you widen your focus and acquire a breadth of skills and knowledge that will make you marketable for a variety of career paths. The transferability of experiences offered by your major, the liberal arts, and the co-curricular programs offered on your campus is the key to your success. As mentioned in Chapter 2, not only are employers seeking job candidates with a strong foundation in their field, they want their new hires to have the 21st-century skills that will propel their companies and organizations forward. That is, their new hires need to be adaptable, innovative problem-solvers who have strong communications skills and are culturally competent when interacting with people from diverse backgrounds.

Strategies for Career Exploration and Preparation

Reaching an effective decision about a career involves the same four steps involved in setting and reaching any personal goal:

1. **Awareness of yourself.** Your abilities, interests, needs, and values.
2. **Awareness of your options.** The variety of career fields available to you.
3. **Awareness of what options provide the best "fit" for you.** What career best matches your personal abilities, interests, needs, and values.
4. **Awareness of the process.** How to prepare for and gain entry into the career of your choice.

Step 1. Self-Awareness

The more you know about yourself, the more effective your personal choices and decisions will be. Self-awareness is a particularly important step to take when making career decisions because your career choice says a lot about who you are and what you want from life. Your career choice should be based on and built around your personal identity and life goals, not the other way around.

© Stephen Coburn, 2013. Under license from Shutterstock, Inc.

Your career choice should lead you to work that provides you with a sense of personal satisfaction and fulfillment.

One way to gain greater self-awareness of where your career interests may lie is by taking psychological tests or assessments. There are assessment instruments that allow you to see how your interests in certain career fields compare with those of other students and professionals who've experienced career satisfaction and success in particular careers. These comparative perspectives provide you with an important reference point for assessing whether your level of interest in a career is high, average, or low relative to other students and working professionals. You can find these career interest tests, as well as other instruments for assessing your career-related abilities and values, in the Career Development Center on your campus.

When making choices about a career, in addition to your interests, abilities, and values, you should also be aware of your personal needs. A *need* may be described as something stronger than an interest. When you do something that satisfies a per-

"Don't expect a recluse to be motivated to sell, a creative thinker to be motivated to be a good proofreader day in and day out, or a sow's ear to be happy in the role of a silk purse."

—Pierce Howard, *The Owner's Manual for the Brain* (2000)

sonal need, you're doing something that makes your life more personally satisfying and fulfilling (Melton, 1995). Psychologists have identified several important human needs that vary in strength or intensity from person to person. Listed in **Do It Now! 12.1** are personal needs that are especially important to consider when making a career choice.

12.1 DO IT NOW

Personal Needs to Consider When Making Career Choices

As you read the needs in this box, make a note after each one indicating how strong the need is for you (high, moderate, or low).

1. **Autonomy.** Need for working independently without close supervision or control. Individuals with a high need for autonomy would experience greater fulfillment working in careers that allow them to be their own boss, make their own decisions, and control their own work schedule. Individuals low in this need may experience greater satisfaction working in careers that are more structured and involve working with a supervisor who provides direction, assistance, and frequent feedback.

2. **Affiliation.** Need for social interaction, a sense of belonging, and the opportunity to collaborate with others. Individuals with a high need for affiliation would experience greater fulfillment working in careers that involve frequent interpersonal interaction and teamwork with colleagues or co-workers. Individuals low in this need are more likely to be satisfied working alone or in competition with others.

Student Perspective

"To me, an important characteristic of a career is being able to meet new, smart, interesting people."

—First-year student

3. **Achievement.** Need to experience challenge and a sense of personal accomplishment. Individuals with high achievement needs would feel a stronger sense of fulfillment working in careers that push them to solve problems, generate creative ideas, and continually learn new information or master new skills. Individuals with a low need for achievement are likely to be more satisfied with careers that don't continually test their abilities and don't repeatedly challenge them to

stretch their skills with new tasks and different responsibilities.

Student Perspective

"I want to be able to enjoy my job and be challenged by it at the same time. I hope that my job will not be monotonous and that I will have the opportunity to learn new things often."

—First-year student

4. **Recognition.** Need for prestige, status, and respect from others. Individuals with high recognition needs are likely to feel satisfied working in careers that are perceived by family, friends, and society to be prestigious or high-ranking. Individuals with a low need for recognition would feel comfortable working in a career that they find satisfying, regardless of how impressive or enviable their career appears to others.

5. **Sensory stimulation.** Need for experiencing variety, change, and risk. Individuals with a high need for sensory stimulation are more likely to be satisfied working in careers that involve frequent changes of pace and place (e.g., travel), unpredictable events (e.g., work tasks that vary considerably), and moderate stress (e.g., working under pressure of competition or deadlines). Individuals with a low need for sensory stimulation may feel more comfortable working in careers that involve regular routines, predictable situations, and minimal amounts of risk or stress.

Student Perspective

"For me, a good career is very unpredictable and interest-fulfilling. I would love to do something that allows me to be spontaneous."

—First-year student

Sources: Baumeister & Leary (1995); Chua & Koestner (2008); Deci & Ryan (2002); Ryan (1995)

Reflection 12.2

Which of the five needs in **Do It Now! 12.1** did you indicate as being strong personal needs?

What career or careers do you think would best match your strongest needs?

Author's Experience I was enrolled in my third year of college with half of my degree completed when I had an eye-opening experience. I wish this experience had happened in my first year, but better late than never. Although I had chosen a career during my first year of college, my decision-making process was not systematic and didn't involve critical thinking. I chose a major based on what sounded prestigious and would pay me the most money. Although these are not necessarily bad factors, my failure to use a systematic and reflective process to evaluate my career choice was bad. In my junior year of college, I asked one of my professors why he decided to get his Ph.D. and become a professor. He simply answered, "I wanted autonomy." This was an epiphany for me. He explained that when he reflected on what mattered most to him, he realized that he needed a career that offered independence. So, he began looking at career options that would offer that. After hearing his explanation, *autonomy* became my favorite word, and this story became a guiding force in my life. After going through a critical self-awareness process, I determined that autonomy was exactly what I desired, and a professor is what I became.

—Aaron Thompson

In summary, four key personal characteristics should be considered when exploring and choosing a career: abilities, interests, values, and needs. As illustrated in **Figure 12.1**, these core characteristics are the pillars that provide the foundational support for making effective career choices and decisions. You want to choose a career that you're good at, interested in, and passionate about and that fulfills your personal needs.

Lastly, since a career choice is a long-range decision that involves life beyond college, self-awareness should involve not only reflection on where you are now but also self-projection—reflecting on how you see yourself in the future. When you engage in the process of self-projection, you begin to see a connection between where you are now and where you want or hope to be.

Ideally, your choice of a career should be one that leads to the best-case future scenario in which your typical day goes something like this: You wake up in the morning and hop out of bed enthusiastically, eagerly looking forward to what you'll be doing at work that day. When you're at work, time flies by; before you know it, the day's over. When you go to bed at night and reflect on your day, you feel good about what you did and how well you did it. In order for this ideal scenario to have any chance of becoming (or even approaching) reality, you should make every attempt to select a career path that's is true to yourself and leads you to a career that's "in sync" with your abilities (what you do well), your interests (what you like to do), your values (what you feel good about doing), and your needs (what provides you with a sense of satisfaction and personal fulfillment).

Student *Perspective*

"I believe following my passion is more crucial than earning money. I think that would come itself eventually."

—College sophomore responding to the question "What are you looking for in a career?"

"To love what you do and feel that it matters—how could anything be more fun?"

—Katharine Graham, former CEO of the *Washington Post* and Pulitzer Prize–winning author

"Make your vocation your vacation."

—Mark Twain

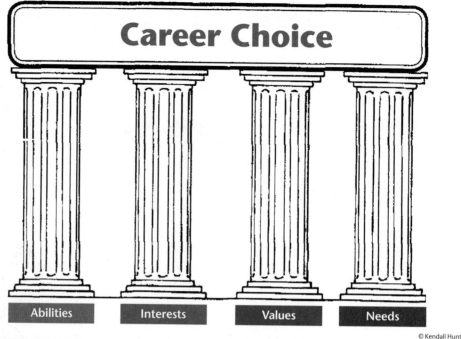

Personal Characteristics Providing the Foundation for Effective Career Choice

Step 2. Awareness of Your Options

In addition to self-awareness and self-knowledge, making an effective decision about your career path also requires knowledge about the nature of different careers and the realities of the work world. The first place to go for information on and help with career exploration and planning is the Career Development Center. Besides helping you explore your personal career interests and abilities, this is your campus resource for learning about the nature of different careers and for strategies on locating career-related work experiences.

Reflection **12.3**

Project yourself 10 years into the future and visualize your ideal career and your ideal life.

1.   What are you spending most of your time doing during your typical workday?

2.   Where and with whom are you working?

3.   How many hours are you working per week?

4.   Where are you living?

5.   Are you married or in a committed relationship? Do you have children?

6.   How does your work influence your home life?

If you were to ask people to name as many careers as they could, they wouldn't come close to naming the 900 career titles listed by the federal government in its Occupational Information Network. Many of these careers you may have never heard of, yet some of them may be good career choices for you. You can learn more about the multitude of careers available to you in the following ways:

- Reading about careers (in books or online)
- Becoming involved in co-curricular programs on campus related to career development
- Taking career development courses
- Interviewing people in different career fields
- Observing (shadowing) people at work in different careers
- Volunteering or service learning
- Part-time work (on or off campus)
- Internships (paid or unpaid)
- Co-op programs

Resources on Careers

Your Career Development Center and your College Library are campus resources where you can find a wealth of reading material on careers, either in print or online. Listed below are some of the best sources of written information on careers.

Dictionary of Occupational Titles (DOT) (www.occupationalinfo.org). This is the largest printed resource on careers; it contains concise definitions of more than 17,000 jobs. It also includes information on:

- Work tasks typically performed by people in different careers
- Background experiences of people working in different careers that qualified them for their positions
- Types of knowledge, skills, and abilities that are required for different careers
- Interests, values, and needs of individuals who find working in particular careers to be personally rewarding

Occupational Outlook Handbook (OOH) (www.bls.gov/oco). This is one of the most widely available and used resources on careers. It contains descriptions of approximately 250 positions, including information on the nature of work, work conditions, places of employment, training or education required for career entry and advancement, salaries, careers in related fields, and additional sources of information about particular careers (e.g., professional organizations and governmental agencies). A distinctive feature of this resource is that it contains information about the *future employment outlook* for different careers.

Encyclopedia of Careers and Vocational Guidance (Chicago: Ferguson Press). As the name suggests, this is an encyclopedia of information on qualifications, salaries, and advancement opportunities for a wide variety of careers.

© Monkey Business Images, 2013. Under license from Shutterstock, Inc.

Multiple resources exist for finding information on careers, many of which can be accessed through the Internet.

Occupational Information Network (O*NET) Online (www.online.onetcenter. org). This is America's most comprehensive source of online information about careers. It contains an up-to-date set of descriptions for almost 1,000 careers, plus lots of other information similar to what you would find in print in the *Dictionary of Occupational Titles*.

In addition to these general sources of information, your Career Development Center and College Library should have other books and published materials related to specific careers or occupations (e.g., careers for English majors). You can also learn a lot about careers by simply reading advertisements for position openings in your local newspaper or online at such sites as www.careerbuilder.com and college. monster.com. When reading position descriptions, make special note of the tasks, duties, or responsibilities they involve and ask yourself whether these positions are compatible with your personal abilities, interests, needs, and values.

Career Planning and Development Programs

Periodically during the academic year, co-curricular programs devoted to career exploration and career preparation are likely to be offered on your campus. For example, the Career Development Center may sponsor career exploration or career planning workshops that you can attend for free. Research conducted on career development workshops indicate that they're effective in helping students plan for and choose careers (Brown & Krane, 2000; Hildenbrand & Gore, 2005). Your Career Center may also organize career fairs, at which professionals working in different career fields are given booths on campus where you can visit with them and ask questions about their careers.

Career Development Courses

Many colleges offer career development courses for elective credit. These courses typically include self-assessment of your career interests, information about different careers, and strategies for career preparation. You need to do career planning while you're enrolled in college, so why not do it by enrolling in a career development course that rewards you with college credit for doing it? Studies show that students who participate in career development courses benefit significantly from them (Pascarella & Terenzini, 2005).

It might also be possible for you to take an independent study course that will give you the opportunity to investigate issues in a career field you're considering. An independent study is a project that you work out with a faculty member, which usually involves writing a paper or detailed report. It allows you to receive academic credit for an in-depth study of a topic of your choice without having to enroll with other students in a traditional course that has regularly scheduled classroom meetings. You could use this independent study option to choose a project related to a career. To see whether this independent study option is available at your campus, check the college catalog or consult with an academic advisor.

You may be able to explore a career of interest to you in a writing or speech course that allows you to choose the topic that you'll write or speak about. If you can choose to research any topic, consider researching a career that interests you and make that the topic of your paper or presentation.

Information Interviews

One of the best and most overlooked ways to get accurate information about a career is to interview professionals working in that career. Career development specialists refer to this strategy as information interviewing. Don't assume that working professionals aren't interested in taking time to speak with a student; most are open to being interviewed and many report that they enjoy it (Crosby, 2002).

Information interviews provide you inside, realistic information about what careers are like because you're getting that information directly from the horse's mouth. The interview process also helps you gain experience and confidence in interview situations, which may help you prepare for future job interviews. Furthermore, if you make a good impression during information interviews, the people you interview may suggest that you contact them again after graduation to see if there are position openings. If there is an opening, you might find yourself being the interviewee instead of the interviewer (and you might find yourself a job).

Because interviews are a valuable source of information about careers and provide possible contacts for future employment, we strongly recommend that you complete the information interview assignment included at the end of this chapter.

Career Observation (Shadowing)

In addition to learning about careers from reading and interviews, you can experience careers more directly by placing yourself in workplace situations and work environments that allow you to observe workers performing their daily duties. Two college-sponsored programs may be available on your campus that will allow you to observe working professionals:

- **Job shadowing programs.** These programs enable you to follow (shadow) and observe a professional during a typical workday.
- **Externship programs.** These programs are basically an extended version of job shadowing that lasts for a longer time period (e.g., two or three days).

Visit your Career Development Center to learn about what job shadowing or externship programs may be available on your college campus. If you're unable to find any in a career field that interests you, consider finding one on your own by using strategies similar to those we recommend for information interviews at the end of this chapter. It's basically the same process; the only difference is that instead of asking the person for an interview, you're asking if you can observe that person at work. In fact, the same person who granted you an information interview may also be willing to be observed at work. Just one or two days of observation can give you some great information about a career.

Reflection **12.4**

If you were to observe or interview a working professional in a career that interests you, what position would that person hold?

Information interviewing, job shadowing, and externships can supply great information about a career. However, information is not experience. To get career-related work *experience*, you have four major options:

- Internships
- Cooperative education programs
- Volunteer work or service learning
- Part-time work

Each of these options for gaining work experience is discussed on the following page.

Internships

In contrast to job shadowing or externships, where you observe someone at work, an internship actively involves you in the work itself and gives you the opportunity to perform career-related work duties. A distinguishing feature of internships is that you can receive academic credit and sometimes financial compensation for the work you do. An internship usually totals 120 to 150 work hours, which may be completed at the same time you're enrolled in a full schedule of classes or when you're not taking classes (e.g., during summer term). A major advantage of internships is that they enable college students to avoid the classic catch-22 situation they often run into when interviewing for their first career position after graduation. The interview scenario usually goes something like this: The potential employer asks the college graduate, "What work experience have you had in this field?" The recent graduate replies, "I haven't had any work experience because I've been a full-time student." You can avoid this scenario by completing an internship during your college experience. We strongly encourage you to participate in at least one internship while you're enrolled in college because it will enable you to beat the "no experience" rap after graduation and distinguish yourself from many other college graduates. Surveys show that more than 75 percent of employers prefer candidates with internships (National Association of Colleges & Employers, 2010), and students who have internships while in college are more likely to develop career-relevant work skills and find employment immediately after college graduation (Pascarella & Terenzini, 2005; Peter D. Hart Research Associates, 2006).

Internships are typically available to college students during their junior or senior year; however, some campuses offer internships for first- and second-year students. Check with your Career Center if this option may be available to you. You can also pursue internships on your own by consulting published guides that describe various career-related internships, along with information on how to apply for them (e.g., *Peterson's Internships* and the *Vault Guide to Top Internships*). Consider searching for internships on the Web as well (for example, go to www.internships.com or www.vaultreports.com). Information on internships may also be available from the local chamber of commerce in the town or city where your college is located or in your hometown.

Cooperative Education (Co-op) Programs

A co-op program is similar to an internship but involves work experience that lasts longer than one academic term and often requires students to stop their coursework temporarily to participate in the program. However, some co-op programs allow you to continue to take classes while working part time at a co-op position; these are sometimes referred to as "parallel co-ops." Students are paid for participating in co-op programs but don't receive academic credit; however, their co-op experience is officially noted on their college transcript (Smith, 2005).

Typically, co-ops are only available to juniors or seniors, but you can begin now to explore co-op programs by reviewing your college catalog and visiting your Career Development Center to see whether your school offers co-op programs in career areas that may interest you. If you find one, build it into your long-range educational plan because it can provide you with authentic and extensive career-related work experience.

The value of co-ops and internships is strongly supported by research, which indicates that students who have these experiences during college:

- Are more likely to report that their college education was relevant to their career
- Receive higher evaluations from employers who recruit them on campus

- Have less difficulty finding an initial position after graduation
- Are more satisfied with their first career position after college
- Obtain more prestigious positions after graduation
- Report greater job satisfaction (Gardner, 1991; Knouse, Tanner, & Harris, 1999; Pascarella & Terenzini, 1991; 2005).

In surveys that ask employers to rank various factors they considered important when hiring new college graduates, internships or cooperative education programs receive the highest ranking (National Association of Colleges & Employers, 2012a). Furthermore, employers report that when full-time positions open up in their organization or company, they usually turn first to their own interns and co-op students (National Association of Colleges & Employers, 2003).

Volunteer Work or Service Learning

Volunteering not only provides a service to your community, it also serves you by giving you the opportunity to explore different work environments and gain work experience in career fields that relate to your area of service. For example, volunteer work performed for different age groups (e.g., children, adolescents, or the elderly) and in different work environments (e.g., hospital, school, or laboratory) provides you with firsthand work experience and simultaneously allows you to test your interest in careers related to these age groups and work environments.

Author's Experience

I was once advising two first-year students: Kim and Christopher. Kim was thinking about becoming a physical therapist and Chris was thinking about becoming an elementary school teacher. I suggested to Kim that she visit the hospital near our college to see whether she could do volunteer work in the physical therapy unit. The hospital did need volunteers, so she volunteered in the physical therapy unit and loved it. That volunteer experience confirmed for her that physical therapy was what she should pursue as a career. She completed a degree in physical therapy and is now a professional physical therapist.

I suggested to Chris, the student who was thinking about becoming an elementary school teacher, that he visit some local schools to see whether they could use a volunteer teacher's aide. One of the schools did need his services, so Chris volunteered as a teacher's aide for about 10 weeks. At the halfway point during his volunteer experience, he came into my office to tell me that the kids were just about driving him crazy and that he no longer had any interest in becoming a teacher! He ended up majoring in communications.

Kim and Chris were the first two students I advised to get involved in volunteer work to test their career interests. Their volunteer experiences turned out to be so valuable for helping them identify their career paths that I continue to encourage all students I advise to get volunteer experience in the fields they're considering for future careers.

Joe Cuseo

Volunteer work also enables you to network with professionals outside of college who may serve as excellent references and resources for letters of recommendation for you. Furthermore, if these professionals are impressed with your volunteer work, they may become interested in hiring you part-time while you're still in college or full time when you graduate.

It may be possible to do volunteer work on campus by serving as an informal teaching assistant or research assistant to a faculty member. Such experiences are particularly valuable for students intending to go to graduate school. If you have a good relationship with any faculty members who are working in an academic field that interests you, consider asking them whether they would like some assistance with their teaching or research responsibilities. You might also check out your professors' Web pages to find out what type of research projects they're working on; if any of these projects interest you or relate to a career path you're considering, contact the professor and offer your help. Volunteer work for a college professor could lead to making a presentation with your professor at a professional conference or even result in your name being included as a coauthor on an article published by the professor.

Volunteer work may also be available to you through college courses. Some courses may integrate volunteer service into the course as a required or optional assignment, where you participate in the volunteer experience and then reflect on it in a written paper or class presentation. When volunteer work is integrated into an academic course and involves reflection on the volunteer experience through writing or speaking, it's referred to as *service learning*.

Another course-integrated option for gaining work experience that may be available to you is to enroll in courses that include a *practicum* or *field work*. For instance, if you're interested in working with children, courses in child psychology or early childhood education may offer experiential learning opportunities in a preschool or daycare center on campus. Similarly, you could take a course in a field you may want to pursue as a career to enable you to get work experience in that field. For instance, taking a class in child psychology may help you get a part-time or summer job that involves working with children.

Reflection 12.5

Have you done volunteer work? If you have, did you learn anything about yourself or anything from your volunteer work that might help you identify careers that best match your interests, talents, and values?

Part-Time Work

Jobs that you hold during the academic year or during summer break should not be overlooked as potential sources of career information and as resume-building experience. Part-time work can provide opportunities to learn or develop skills that may be relevant to your future career, such as organizational skills, communication skills, and ability to work effectively with co-workers from diverse backgrounds and cultures.

It's also possible that work in a part-time position may eventually turn into a full-time career. The following personal story illustrates how this can happen.

Author's Experience   A former student of mine was an English major who worked part-time for an organization that provides special assistance to mentally handicapped children. After he completed his English degree, he was offered a full-time position in this organization, which he accepted. While working at his full-time position with handicapped children, he decided to go to graduate school part time and eventually completed a master's degree in special education, which qualified him for a promotion to a more advanced position in the organization, which he also accepted. This student's professional career path opened up for him as a result of the type of part-time work he did while attending college.

Joe Cuseo

It might also be possible for you to obtain part-time work experience on campus through your school's work-study program. Work-study jobs can be done in a variety of campus settings (e.g., Financial Aid Office, Library, Public Relations Office, or Computer Services Center) and they typically allow you to build your employment schedule around your course schedule. On-campus work can provide you with valuable career-exploration and resume-building experiences, and the professionals for whom you work can also serve as excellent references for letters of recommendation to future employers. To see whether you are eligible for your school's work-study program, visit the Financial Aid Office on your campus. If you're not eligible for work-study jobs, ask about other campus jobs that are not funded through the work-study program.

Learning about careers through firsthand experience in actual work settings (e.g., shadowing, internships, volunteer services, and part-time work) is critical to successful career exploration and preparation. You can take a career-interest test, or you can test your career interest through actual work experiences. There is simply no substitute for direct, hands-on experience for gaining knowledge about careers. These firsthand experiences represent the ultimate career reality test. They allow you direct access to information about what careers are like, as opposed to how they are portrayed on TV or in the movies, which often paint an inaccurate or unrealistic picture of careers and make them appear more exciting or glamorous than they are.

Remember

One key characteristic of effective goal setting is to create goals that are realistic. In the case of careers, getting firsthand experience in actual work settings (e.g., shadowing, internships, volunteer services, and part-time work) allows you to get a much more realistic view of what work is like in certain careers, as opposed to the idealized or fantasized way they are portrayed on TV and in the movies.

In summary, firsthand experiences in actual work settings equip you with five powerful career advantages:

- Learn about what work is like in a particular field.
- Test your interest and skills for certain types of work.
- Strengthen your resume by adding experiential learning to academic (classroom) learning.
- Acquire contacts who may serve as personal references and sources for letters of recommendation.
- Network with employers who may hire you or refer you for a position after graduation.

Furthermore, gaining firsthand work experience early in college not only promotes your job prospects after graduation, but also makes you a more competitive candidate for internships and part-time positions that you may apply for during college.

Be sure to use your campus resources (e.g., the Career Development Center and Financial Aid Office), local resources (e.g., Chamber of Commerce), and your personal contacts (e.g., family and friends) to locate and participate in work experiences that relate to your career interests. When you land a work experience, work hard at it, learn as much as you can from it, and build relationships with as many people there as possible, because these are the people who can provide you with future contacts, references, and referrals. Research indicates that as many as 75 percent of all jobs are obtained through interpersonal relationships, i.e., "networking" (Brooks, 2009).

"Give me a history major who has done internships and a business major who hasn't, and I'll hire the history major every time."

—William Ardery, senior vice president, Investor Communications Company

Step 3. Awareness of What Best Fits You

Effective decision making requires identifying all relevant factors that need to be considered and determining how much weight (influence) each of these factors should carry. As we've emphasized throughout this chapter, the factor that should carry the greatest weight in career decision making is the match between your career choice and your personal abilities, interests, needs, and values.

Reflection 12.6

Have you had firsthand work experiences that may influence your future career plans?

If you could get firsthand work experience in any career field right now, what would it be?

A good career decision should involve more than salary and should take into consideration how the career will affect different dimensions of yourself (social, emotional, physical, etc.) at different stages of your future life: young adulthood, middle age, and late adulthood. It's almost inevitable that your career will affect your identity, the type of person you become, how you balance the demands of work and family, and how well you serve others beyond yourself. An effective career decision-making process requires you to make tough and thoughtful decisions about what matters most to you.

Reflection 12.7

Answer the following questions about a career you're considering or have chosen:

1. Why attracted you to this career? (What led or caused you to become interested in it?)

2. Would you say that your interest in this career is characterized primarily by *intrinsic* motivation—something "inside" of you, such as your personal abilities, interests, needs, and values? Or, would you say that your interest in the career is driven by *extrinsic* motivation—something "outside" of you, such as starting salary, pleasing parents, or meeting expectations of your gender (i.e., an expected career role for a male or female)?

3. If money wasn't an issue and you could earn a comfortable living working in any career, would you choose the same career that you're currently considering?

Step 4. Awareness of the Process

Whether you're keeping your career options open or you think you've already decided on a particular career, you can start taking early steps for successful entry into any career by using the following strategies.

Remember

A good career choice should bring your more than just personal wealth: it should also provide you with personal fulfillment.

Student
Perspective

"I think that a good career has to be meaningful for a person. It should be enjoyable for the most part [and] it has to give a person a sense of fulfillment."

—First-year student

"It's easy to make a buck. It's a lot tougher to make a difference."

—Tom Brokaw, award-winning television journalist and author

Self-Monitoring: Watching and Tracking Your Personal Skills and Positive Qualities

Don't forget that the learning skills you acquire in college become the earning skills in your career after college. It may appear that you're just developing *academic* skills, but you're also developing *career* skills. When you're engaged in the process of completing academic tasks (such as note-taking, reading, writing papers, and taking tests), you're strengthening career-relevant skills (such as analysis, synthesis, communication, and problem solving).

The general education skills and qualities developed by the liberal arts component of your college education are critical to *career advancement* (your ability to move up the career ladder) and *career mobility* (your ability to move into different career paths). General educational skills enable workers to move into and take on different positions, which is important in today's work world. On average, Americans now change jobs ten times by the time they're 40 years old (Association of American Colleges and Universities, 2007). Specific technical skills are important for getting you into a particular career, but general educational skills enable you to move into different careers and move up the career ladder. These skills are growing more important for college graduates entering the workforce in the 21st century because the demand for upper-level positions in management and leadership will exceed the supply of workers available to fill these positions (Herman, 2000). The courses you take as part of your general education will prepare you for advanced career positions, not just your first one (Boyer, 1987; Miller, 2003).

Students often think it's the final product (a college diploma) that provides them with the passport to a good job and career success (AAC&U, 2007; Sullivan, 1993). However, for most employers of college graduates, what matters much more than the credential are the skills and personal qualities the job applicant brings to the job (Education Commission of the States, 1995; Figler & Bolles, 2007). You can start building these skills and qualities through effective *self-monitoring*—monitoring (watching) yourself and keeping track of the skills you're using and developing during your college experience. Skills are mental habits, and like all other habits that are repeatedly practiced, their development can be so gradual that you may not even notice how much growth is taking place—perhaps somewhat like watching grass grow. Thus, career development specialists recommend that you consciously reflect on the skills you're using so that you remain aware of them and are ready to "sell" them to potential employers (Lock, 2004).

The key to discovering career-relevant skills and positive personal qualities is to get in the habit of stepping back from your academic and out-of-class experiences to reflect on what skills and qualities these experiences involved and then get them down in writing before they slip your mind. One strategy you can use to track your developing skills is to keep a *career development journal* in which you note academic tasks and assignments you've completed, along with the skills you used to complete them. Also, don't forget to record skills in your journal that you've developed in nonacademic situations, such as skills used while performing part-time jobs, personal hobbies, co-curricular activities, and volunteer services. Since skills are actions, it's best to record them as action verbs in your career development journal. You're likely to find that many personal skills you develop in college will be the same ones that employers will seek in the workforce. Do It Now! 12.2 contains a sample of important, action-oriented career skills that you're likely to develop during your college experience.

"If you want to earn more, learn more."

—Tom Hopkins, internationally acclaimed trainer of business and sales professionals

"Employers are far more interested in the prospect's ability to think and to think clearly, to write and speak well, and how (s)he works with others than in his major or the name of the school(s) he went to. Several college investigating teams found that these were the qualities on which all kinds of employers, government and private, base their decisions."

—Lauren Pope, *Looking Beyond the Ivy League*

Student *Perspective*

"They asked me during my interview why I was right for the job and I told them because I can read well, write well and I can think. They really liked that because those were the skills they were looking for."

—English major hired by a public relations firm (Source: *Los Angeles Times,* April 4, 2004)

12.2

DO IT NOW!

Personal Skills Relevant to Successful Career Performance

The following behaviors represent a sample of useful skills that are relevant to success in various careers (Figler & Bolles, 2007; Bolles, 1998). As you read these skills, underline or highlight any of them that you have performed, either inside or outside of school.

advising	creating	initiating	operating	resolving
assembling	delegating	measuring	planning	sorting
calculating	designing	mediating	presenting	summarizing
coaching	evaluating	motivating	producing	supervising
coordinating	explaining	negotiating	researching	synthesizing

Author's Experience

After class one day, I had a conversation with a student (Max) about his personal interests. He said he was considering a career in the music industry and was working part time as a disc jockey at a nightclub. I asked him what it took to be a good disc jockey, and in less than five minutes of talking about his part-time work, we discovered there were many more skills involved in doing his job than either of us had realized. He was responsible for organizing three to four hours of music each night he worked; he had to read the reactions of his audience (customers) and adapt or adjust his selections to their musical tastes; he had to arrange his selections in a sequence that periodically varied the tempo of the music he played throughout the night; and he had to continually research and update his music collection to track the latest trends in hits and popular artists. Max also said that his job required him to deliver public announcements, which enabled him to overcome his fear of public speaking.

Although we were just having a short, friendly conversation after class about his part-time work, Max ended up reflecting on and identifying multiple skills he was developing on the job. We both agreed that it would be a good idea to get these skills down in writing so that he could use them as selling points for future jobs in the music field (or any career field).

— *Joe Cuseo*

In addition to tracking your developing skills, track the positive traits, attitudes, and attributes you may be developing. In contrast to skills, which are best recorded in a career journal as action verbs because they represent actions that you can perform for anyone who hires you, personal attributes are best recorded as adjectives because they describe who you are and what positive qualities you can bring to the job. Do It Now! 12.3 supplies an assortment of personal traits and qualities that are relevant to successful performance in any career.

Remember

Keeping track of your developing skills and positive qualities is as important to your successful entry into a future career as completing courses and compiling credits.

12.3

DO IT NOW!

Personal Traits and Qualities Relevant to Successful Career Performance

The following personal attributes are important for success in any career. As you read these traits, underline or highlight any of them that you feel you possess or will soon possess.

conscientious	energetic	loyal	positive	reflective
considerate	enthusiastic	observant	precise	sincere
courteous	ethical	open-minded	prepared	tactful
curious	flexible	outgoing	productive	team player
dependable	imaginative	patient	prudent	thorough
determined	industrious	persuasive	punctual	thoughtful

Self-Marketing: Packaging and Presenting Your Personal Strengths and Achievements

One way to help convert your college degree into gainful employment is to view yourself (a college graduate) as a product and future employers as customers who may be interested in purchasing your product (your skills and attributes). As a first-year student, it could be said that you're in the early stages of developing your product. Begin the process now of developing and packaging your skills and attributes so that by the time you graduate, you've developed into a high-quality product that potential employers will notice and be interested in purchasing.

An effective self-marketing plan is one that gives employers a clear idea of what you can bring to the table and do for them. You can effectively market or advertise your personal skills, qualities, and achievements to future employers through the following channels.

Reflection 12.8

Look back at the personal skills and traits listed in **Do It Now! 12.3** and **12.4** that you noted you possess or will soon possess.

1. Are your personal skills and traits relevant to the career(s) that you're considering?

2. Do you see your skills and traits as being relevant to any other career(s) that you haven't yet considered?

Course Transcript

Your course transcript is a listing of all courses you enrolled in and the grades you received in those courses. Two pieces of information included on your college transcript can strongly influence employers' hiring decisions or admissions committee decisions about your acceptance to a graduate or professional school: (1) the grades you earned in your courses, and (2) the types of courses you completed.

Simply stated, the better grades you earn in college, the better are your employment prospects after college. Research on college graduates indicates that higher grades improve the following:

- The prestige of their first job
- Their total earnings (salary and fringe benefits)
- Their job mobility (ability to change jobs or positions)

This relationship between higher college grades and greater career success exists for students at all types of colleges and universities; regardless of the reputation or prestige of the institution they attend (Pascarella & Terenzini, 1991; 2005).

Co-curricular Experiences

Participation in student clubs, campus organizations, and other types of co-curricular activities is a valuable source of experiential learning that can complement classroom-based learning and contribute to your career preparation and development. A sizable body of research supports the power of co-curricular experiences for career success (Astin, 1993; Kuh, 1993; Pascarella & Terenzini, 1991, 2005; Peter D. Hart Research Associates, 2006). Get involved with co-curricular experiences on your campus, especially those that:

- Allow you to develop leadership and helping skills—e.g., leadership retreats, student government, college committees, peer counseling, or peer tutoring.
- Enable you to interact with others from diverse ethnic and racial groups—e.g., multicultural or international clubs and organizations.
- Provide you with out-of-class experiences related to your academic major or career interests—e.g., student clubs in your college major or intended career field.

Keep in mind that co-curricular experiences are also resume-building experiences that provide solid evidence of your commitment to the college community outside the classroom. Be sure to showcase these experiences to prospective employers. Also, don't forget that the campus professionals with whom you may interact while participating in co-curricular activities (e.g., the director of student activities or dean of students) can serve as valuable references for letters of recommendation to future employers or graduate and professional schools.

Personal Portfolio

You may have heard the word "portfolio" in reference to a collection of artwork that professional artists put together to showcase or advertise their artistic talents. However, a portfolio can be a collection of any materials or products that illustrate skills and talents or demonstrate educational and personal development. For example, a portfolio could include such items as:

- Outstanding papers, exam performances, research projects, or lab reports
- Artwork and photos from study abroad, service learning, or internship experiences
- Video footage of oral presentations or theatrical performances
- Recordings of musical performances
- Assessments from employers or coaches
- Letters of recognition or commendation

You can start the process of portfolio development right now by saving your best work and performances. Store them in a traditional portfolio folder, or save them on a computer disc to create an electronic portfolio. Another option would be to create a Web site and upload your materials there. Eventually, you'll be able to build a well-stocked portfolio that documents your skills and demonstrates your development to future employers or future schools. You can start to develop an electronic portfolio now by completing Exercise 12.2 at the end of this chapter.

Reflection **12.9**

What do you predict will be your best work products in college—those that you're most likely to include in a portfolio?

Why?

Personal Resume

Unlike a portfolio, which contains actual products or samples of your work, a resume may be described as a listed summary of your most important accomplishments, skills, and credentials. If you have just graduated from high school, you may not have accumulated enough experiences to construct a fully developed resume. However, you can start to build a skeletal resume that contains major categories or headings (the skeleton) under which you'll eventually include your experiences and

The ritual of burning completed coursework in high school is not recommended in college. Instead, save your best work, and include it in a personal portfolio.

accomplishments, as well as skills you developed and problems you solved. (See Do It Now! 12.4 for a sample skeleton resume.) As you acquire experiences, you can flesh out the resume by gradually filling in its general categories with your skills, accomplishments, and credentials.

12.4   DO IT NOW

Constructing a Resume

Use this skeletal resume as an outline or template for beginning construction of your own resume and for setting your future goals. (If you have already created a resume, use this template to identify and add categories that may be missing from your current one.)

NAME
(First, Middle, Last)

Current Addresses: Permanent Addresses:
Postal address   Postal address
E-mail address   E-mail address (be sure it's professional)
Phone number   Phone number

EDUCATION: Name of College or University, City, State
Degree Name (e.g., Bachelor of Science)
College Major (e.g., Accounting)
Graduation Date
GPA

RELATED WORK   Position Title, City, State   Start and stop dates
EXPERIENCES: (Begin the list with the most recent position
                                                          dates held.)

(List skills you used or developed.)

VOLUNTEER (COMMUNITY SERVICE) EXPERIENCES:
(List skills you used or developed.)

NOTABLE COURSEWORK
(e.g., leadership, interdisciplinary, or intercultural courses; study abroad experiences)

CO-CURRICULAR EXPERIENCES:
(e.g., student government or peer leadership)
(List skills you used or developed.)

PERSONAL SKILLS AND POSITIVE QUALITIES:
(List as bullets; be sure to include those that are especially relevant to the position for which you're applying.)

HONORS AND AWARDS:
(In addition to those received in college, you may include those received in high school.)

PERSONAL INTERESTS:
(Include special hobbies or talents that may not be directly tied to school or work experiences.)

Letters of Recommendation (Letters of Reference)

Letters of recommendation can serve to support and document your skills and strengths. To maximize the power of your personal recommendations, give careful thought to (1) who should serve as your references, (2) how to approach them, and (3) what to provide them.

Strategies for improving the quality of your letters of recommendation are suggested in **Do It Now! 12.5.**

12.5   DO IT NOW!

The Art and Science of Requesting Letters of Recommendation: Effective Strategies and Common Courtesies

1. **Select recommendations from people who know you well.** Think about individuals with whom you've had an ongoing relationship, who know you by name, and who know about your personal strengths and skills (e.g., an instructor you've had for more than one class, an academic advisor whom you see often, or an employer with whom you've worked for an extended period).

2. **Seek a balanced blend of letters from people who have observed your performance in different settings or situations.** The following are settings in which you may have performed well and people who may have observed your performance in these settings:
   - The classroom—a professor who can speak to your academic performance
   - On campus—a student life professional who can comment on your contributions outside the classroom
   - Off campus—a professional for whom you've performed volunteer service, part-time work, or an internship

3. **Pick the right time and place to make your request.** Be sure to request your letter well in advance of the letter's deadline date (e.g., at least two weeks). First, ask the person if he or she is willing to write the letter, and come back at a later time with forms and envelopes. Don't approach the person with these materials in hand because it may send the message that you've already assumed or presumed the person will automatically say "yes." This isn't the most socially sensitive message to send someone whom you're about to ask for a favor.

Also, pick a place and time where the person can give full attention to your request. For instance, make a personal visit to the person's office, rather than making the request in a busy hallway or in front of a classroom full of students.

4. **Waive your right to see the letter.** If the school or organization to which you're applying has a reference-letter form that asks whether or not you want to waive (give up) your right to see the letter, waive your right—as long as you feel reasonably certain that you will be receiving a good letter of recommendation. By waiving your right to see your letter of recommendation, you show confidence that the letter to be written about you will be positive, and you assure the person who reads the letter that you didn't inspect or screen it to make sure it was a good one before sending it.

5. **Provide your references with a fact sheet about yourself.** Include your experiences and achievements—both inside and outside the classroom. This will help make your references' job a little easier by providing points to focus on. More importantly, it will help you because your letter becomes more powerful when it contains concrete examples or illustrations of your positive qualities and accomplishments. On your fact sheet, be sure to include any exceptionally high grades you may have earned in certain courses, as well as volunteer services, leadership experiences, special awards or forms of recognition, and special interests or talents relevant to your academic major and career choice. Your fact sheet is the place and time for you to "toot your own horn," so don't be afraid of coming across as a braggart or egotist. You're not being conceited; you're just showcasing your strengths.

6. **Provide your references with a stamped, addressed envelope.** This is a simple courtesy that makes their job a little easier and demonstrates your social sensitivity.

(continued)

7. **Follow up with a thank-you note.** Send this note at about the time your letter of recommendation should be sent. This is the right thing to do because it shows your appreciation; it's also the smart thing to do, because if the letter hasn't been written yet, the thank-you note serves as a gentle reminder for your reference to write the letter.

8. **Let your references know the outcome of your application.** If you've been offered the position or been admitted to the school to which you applied, let those know who wrote letters on your behalf. This is the socially sensitive thing to do, and your references are likely to remember your social sensitivity, which is likely to strengthen the quality of future letters of recommendation they may write for you.

Reflection 12.10

Have you met a faculty member or other professional on campus who knows you well enough to write a letter of recommendation for you?

If yes, who is this person, and what position does he or she hold on campus?

Summary and Conclusion

In national surveys, employers rank attitude of the job applicant as the number one factor in making hiring decisions. They rate this higher in importance than such factors as reputation of the applicant's school, previous work experience, and recommendations of former employers (Education Commission of the States, 1995; Institute for Research on Higher Education, 1995; National Association of Colleges & Employers, 2012b). However, many college students think that it's the degree itself—the credential or piece of paper—that will get them the career they want (AAC&U, 2007).

Graduating from college with a diploma in hand may make you a more competitive job candidate, but you still have to compete by documenting and selling your strengths and skills. Your diploma doesn't work like a merit badge or passport that you flash to gain automatic access to your dream job. Your college experience opens career doors for you, but it's your attitude, initiative, and effort that enable you to step through those doors and into a successful career.

Your career success *after* college depends on what you do *during* college. Touching all the bases that lead to *college* success will also lead to *career* success:

> "Life just doesn't hand you things. You have to get out here and make things happen."
>
> —Emeril Lagasse, award-winning American chef, cookbook author, and TV celebrity

1. **Get actively involved in the college experience.** Get good grades in your classes and get work-related experiences outside the classroom.
2. **Use your campus resources.** Capitalize on the career preparation and development opportunities that your Career Development Center has to offer.
3. **Interact and collaborate with others.** Network with students in your major, college alumni, and career professionals.
4. **Take time for self-awareness and personal reflection.** Deepen your self-awareness so that you choose a career path that's compatible with your personal interests, talents, values, and needs, and maintain awareness of your developing skills and personal qualities so that you can successfully "sell yourself" to future employers.

Learning More through the World Wide Web
Internet-Based Resources for Further Information on Careers

For additional information related to the ideas discussed in this chapter, we recommend the following Web sites:

Assessing Your Strengths, Talents, and Values:

www.authentichappiness.sas.upenn.edu

www.viacharacter.org

Developing a Personalized Career Plan:

www.mappingyourfuture.org

Navigating the Job Market:

www.youmajoredinwhat.com

Career Descriptions and Future Employment Outlook:

www.bls.gov

Internships:

www.internships.com

www.vaultreports.com

Position Openings and Opportunities:

www.rileyguide.com

www.monster.com

Resume and Interview Resources:

www.quintcareers.com

12.1 Conducting an Information Interview

One of the best ways to acquire accurate information about a career that interests you is to interview a working professional in that career. This career exploration strategy is known as an *information interview*. An information interview enables you to (1) get an insider's view of what the career is really like, (2) network with a professional in the field, and (3) gain confidence in interview situations that prepares you for later future job interviews.

Steps in the Information Interview Process

1. Select a career that you may be interested in pursuing. Even if you're currently keeping your career options open, pick a career that might be a possibility. You can use the resources cited on pp. 311–312 in this chapter to help you identify a career that may be most appealing to you.

2. Find someone who is working in the career you selected and set up an information interview with that person. To locate possible interview candidates, consider members of your family, friends of your family members, and family members of your friends. Any of these people may be working in the career you selected and may be good interview candidates, or they may know others who could be good candidates. The Career Development Center on your campus and the Alumni Association (or the Rotaract Club) may also be able to connect you with graduates of your college, or professionals working in the local community near your college, who are willing to talk about their careers with students.

   The Yellow Pages or the Internet may also be used to locate names and contact information for interview candidates. Send candidates a short letter or e-mail asking about the possibility of scheduling a short interview, and mention that you would be willing to conduct the interview in person or by phone, whichever would be more convenient for them. If you don't hear back within a reasonable period (e.g., within a couple of weeks), send a follow-up message. If you don't receive a response to the follow-up message, then consider contacting someone else.

3. Conduct an information interview with the professional who has agreed to speak with you. Consider using the following suggested strategies.

Tips for Conducting Information Interviews

- **Thank the person for taking the time to speak with you.** This should be the first thing you do after meeting the person—before you officially begin the interview.
- **Prepare your interview questions in advance.** Here are some questions that you might consider asking:

1. During a typical day's work, what do you spend most of your time doing?

2. What do you like most about your career?

3. What are the most difficult or frustrating aspects of your career?

4. What personal skills or qualities do you see as being critical for success in your career?

5. How did you decide on your career?

6. What personal qualifications or prior experiences enabled you to enter your career?

7. How does someone find out about openings in your field?

8. **What steps did you take to find your current position?**

9. What advice would you give first-year students about what they might do at this stage of their college experience to help prepare them to enter your career?

10. How does someone advance in your career?

11. Are there any moral issues or ethical challenges that tend to arise in your career?

12. Are members of diverse groups likely to be found in your career? (This is an especially important question to ask if you're a member of an ethnic, racial, or gender group that is underrepresented in the career field.)

13. What impact does your career have on your home life or personal life outside of work?

14. If you had to do it all over again, would you choose the same career?

15. Would you recommend that I speak with anyone else to obtain additional information or a different perspective on this career field? (If the answer is "Yes," you may follow up by asking, "May I mention that you referred me?") It's always a good idea to obtain more than one person's perspective before making an important choice, especially one that can have a major influence on your life, such as your career choice.

- **Take notes during the interview.** This not only benefits you by helping you remember what was said, but also sends a positive message to the persons you interview because it shows them that their ideas are important and worth writing down.

Final Note: If the interview goes well, you might ask whether you could observe or shadow your interviewee during a day at work.

Self-Assessment Questions

After completing your interview, take a moment to reflect on it and answer the following questions:

1. What information did you receive that impressed you about this career?
2. What information did you receive that distressed (or depressed) you about this career?
3. What was the most useful thing you learned from conducting this interview?
4. Knowing what you know now, would you still be interested in pursuing this career? (If yes, why?) (If no, why not?)

12.2 Creating a Skeletal Resume

Review the headings of a skeletal resume described on p. 324.

1. Under each heading, list any experiences or skills that you've already acquired.

2. Return to each heading and add (in a different color) any experiences or skills you plan to acquire during your college experience.

3. Review your entries under each heading and identify any experiences or skills that may result in work products or artifacts that you can include in a personal portfolio. (See p. 322 for samples of work products that could be included in a portfolio.)

Career Choice: Conflict and Confusion

Josh is a first-year student whose family has made a great financial sacrifice to send him to college. He deeply appreciates the tremendous commitment his family members have made to his education and wants to pay them back as soon as possible. Consequently, he has been looking into careers that offer the highest starting salaries to college students immediately after graduation. Unfortunately, none of these careers seem to match Josh's natural abilities and personal interests, so he's conflicted, confused, and starting to get stressed out. He knows he'll have to make a decision soon because the careers with high starting salaries involve majors that have many course requirements, and if he expects to graduate in a reasonable period, he'll have to start taking some of these courses during his first year.

Reflection and Discussion Questions

1. If you were Josh, what would you do?

2. Do you see any way that Josh might balance his desire to pay back his family as soon as possible with his desire to pursue a career that's compatible with his interests and talents?

3. What other questions or factors do you think Josh should consider before making his decision?

Fiscal Literacy

Managing Money and Minimizing Debt

Complete the following sentence with the first thought that comes to your mind:

For me, money is . . .

LEARNING GOAL

To become more self-aware, knowledgeable, and strategic with respect to managing money and financing a college education.

The beginning of college often marks the beginning of greater personal independence and greater demands for effective financial self-management and fiscal decision making. The importance of money management for college students is growing for two major reasons. The first reason is the rising cost of a college education, which has resulted in more students working more hours while they're in college (Levine & Cureton, 1998; Perna & DuBois, 2010). The rising cost of a college education is also requiring students to make more difficult decisions about what options (or combination of options) to use to meet their college expenses. Unfortunately, research indicates that many students today are not making the most effective decisions about how to finance their college education in a way that best contributes to their academic success in college and their financial success beyond college (King, 2005).

A second reason money management is growing in importance for college students is the availability and convenience of credit cards. It has never been easier for college students to get access to, use, and abuse credit cards. A college graduate today can do everything right in college, such as earn good grades, get involved on campus, and get work experience before graduating, but a poor credit history resulting from irresponsible credit card use while in college can reduce that student's chances of obtaining credit after college as well as their job prospects after graduation (Mae, 2005). Credit reporting agencies and bureaus collect information about how faithfully college students make credit-card payments and report their "credit scores" to credit-card companies and banks. Employers check these credit scores and use them as indicators or predictors of how responsible students will be as employees, because there's a statistical relationship between using credit cards responsibly and being a responsible employee (Ring, 1997; Susswein, 1995). Thus, being irresponsible with credit while you're in college can affect your ability to land a job after (or during) college. Your credit score report will also affect your likelihood of qualifying for car loans and home loans, as well as your ability to rent an apartment (Pratt, 2008).

Furthermore, research indicates that accumulating high levels of debt while in college is associated with higher levels of stress (Nelson, Lust, Story, & Ehlinger,

"If we command our wealth, we shall be rich and free; if our wealth commands us, we are poor indeed."

—Edmund Burke, 18th-century author, political philosopher, and supporter of the American Revolution

2008), lower academic performance (Susswein, 1995), and greater risk of withdrawing from college (Ring, 1997). On the positive side of the ledger, studies show that when students learn to use effective money-management strategies, they reduce unnecessary spending, minimize accumulation of debt, and lower their level of stress (Health & Soll, 1996; Kidwell & Turrisi, 2004; Walker, 1996).

Student *Perspective*

"My money-management skills are poor. If I have money, I will spend it unless somebody takes it away from me. I am the kind of person who lives from paycheck to paycheck."

—First-year student

Strategies for Managing Money Effectively

Developing Financial Self-Awareness

Developing any good habit begins with the critical first step of self-awareness. The habit of effective money management begins with awareness of your *cash flow*—the amount of money you have flowing in and flowing out. As illustrated in **Figure 13.1**, you can track your cash flow by monitoring:

- The amount of money you have coming in (income) versus the amount going out (expenses or expenditures), and
- The amount of money you've earned and not spent (savings) versus the amount you've borrowed and not yet paid back (debt).

FIGURE 13.1

Income ⟷ Expenses

Savings ⟷ Debt

Two Key Avenues of Cash Flow

Income for college students typically comes from one or more of the following sources:

- Scholarships or grants, which don't have to be paid back
- Loans, which must be repaid
- Salary earned from part-time or full-time work
- Personal savings
- Gifts or other forms of monetary support from parents and other family members

Your sources of expenses or expenditures may be classified into three categories:

1. Basic needs or essential necessities—expenses that tend to be fixed because you cannot do without them (e.g., expenses for food, housing, tuition, textbooks, phone, transportation to and from school, and health-related costs)
2. Incidentals or extras—expenses that tend to be flexible because spending money on them is optional or discretionary, i.e., you choose to spend at your own discretion or judgment; these expenses typically include:
   a. money spent on entertainment, enjoyment, or pleasure (e.g., music, movies, and spring-break vacations), and
   b. money spent primarily for reasons of promoting personal status or self-image (e.g., buying expensive brand-name products, fashionable clothes, jewelry, and other personal accessories)
3. Emergency expenses—unpredicted, unforeseen, or unexpected costs (e.g., money paid for doctor visits and medicine needed to treat illnesses or injuries)

Reflection 13.2

What are your two or three most expensive incidentals (optional purchases)?

Do you think you should reduce these expenses or eliminate them?

Developing a Money-Management Plan

Once you're aware of the amount of money you have coming in (and from what sources) plus the amount of money you're spending (and for what reasons), the next step is to develop a plan for managing your cash flow. The bottom line is to ensure that the money coming in (income) is equal to or greater than the money going out (expenses). If the amount of money going out exceeds the amount coming in, you're "in the red" or have "negative cash flow."

Strategic Selection and Use of Financial Tools for Tracking Cash Flow

To track your cash flow and manage your money, there are a variety of tools available to you .These cash-flow tools include:

- Checking accounts
- Credit cards
- Charge cards
- Debit cards

What follows is a description of these different tools, along with specific strategies for using them effectively.

Checking Account

Long before credit cards were created, a checking account was the method most people used to keep track of their money. Many people still use checking accounts in addition to (or instead of) credit cards. A checking account may be obtained from a bank or credit union; its typical costs include a deposit ($20–$25) to open the account, a monthly service fee (e.g., $10), and small fees for checks. Some banks charge customers a service fee based on the number of checks written, which is a good option if you don't plan to write many checks each month. If you maintain a high enough balance of money deposited in your account, the bank may not charge any extra fees, and if you're able to maintain an even higher balance, the bank may also pay you interest—known as an interest-bearing checking account.

In conjunction with your checking account, banks usually provide you with an automatic teller machine (ATM) card that you can use to get cash. Look for a checking account that doesn't charge a separate fee for ATM transactions, but offers it as a free service along with your checking account. Also, look for a checking account that doesn't charge you if your balance drops below a certain minimum figure.

Strategies for Using Checking Accounts Effectively

Apply the following strategies to make the best use of your checking account:

- Whenever you write a check or make an ATM withdrawal, immediately subtract its amount from your *balance* (the amount of money remaining in your account) to determine your new balance.
- Keep a running balance in your checkbook; it will ensure that you know exactly how much money you have in your account at all times. This will reduce your risk of writing a check that *bounces*—a check that you don't have enough money in the bank to cover. If you do bounce a check, you'll probably have to pay a

charge to the bank and possibly to the business that attempted to cash your bounced check.

- Double-check your checkbook balance with each monthly statement you receive from the bank. Be sure to include the service charges your bank makes to your account that appear on your monthly statement. This practice will make it easier to track errors—on either your part or the bank's part. (Banks can and do occasionally make mistakes.)

Advantages of a Checking Account

A checking account has several advantages:

- You can carry checks instead of cash.
- You have access to cash at almost any time through an ATM.
- It allows you to keep a visible track record of income and expenses in your checkbook.
- A properly managed checking account can serve as a good credit reference for future loans and purchases.

Credit Card (e.g., MasterCard®, Visa®, or Discover®)

A credit card is basically money loaned to you by the credit-card company that issues you the card, which you pay back to the company monthly. You can pay the whole bill or a portion of the bill each month, as long as some minimum payment is made. However, for any remaining (unpaid) portion of your bill, you are charged a high interest rate, which is usually about 18 percent.

© stefanolunardi, 2013. Under license from Shutterstock, Inc.

Don't let peer pressure determine your spending habits.

Strategies for Selecting a Credit Card

If you decide to use a credit card, pay attention to *its annual percentage rate (APR)*—the interest rate you pay for previously unpaid monthly balances. This rate can vary from one credit-card company to the next. Credit-card companies also vary in terms of their annual service fee. You will likely find companies that charge higher interest rates tend to charge lower annual fees, and vice versa. As a rule, if you expect to pay the full balance every month, you're probably better off choosing a credit card that does not charge you an annual service fee. On the other hand, if you think you'll need more time to make the full monthly payments, you may be better off with a credit-card company that offers a low interest rate.

Another feature that differentiates one credit-card company from another is whether or not you're allowed a *grace period*—a certain period after you receive your monthly statement during which you can pay back the company without paying added interest fees. Some companies may allow you a grace period of a full month, while others may provide none and begin charging interest immediately after you fail to pay on the bill's due date.

Credit cards may also differ in terms of their *credit limit* (also called a *credit line* or *line of credit*), which refers to the maximum amount of money the credit-card company will make available to you. If you're a new customer, most companies will set a credit limit beyond which no additional credit is granted.

Advantages of a Credit Card

If a credit card is used responsibly, it has some key advantages as a money-management tool, such as those listed below.

- It helps you track your spending habits because the credit card company sends you a monthly statement that provides an itemized list of all your card-related purchases. This list supplies you with a "paper trail" of what you purchased that month and when you purchased it.
- It provides the convenience of making purchases online, which can save time and money that would otherwise be spent traveling to and from stores.
- It allows access to cash whenever and wherever you need it, because any bank or ATM that displays your credit card's symbol will give you cash up to a certain limit (usually for a small transaction fee). Keep in mind that some credit card companies charge a higher interest rate for cash advances than credit card purchases.
- It enables you to establish a personal credit history. If you use a credit card responsibly, you can establish a good credit history that you can use later in life for big-ticket purchases such as a car or home. In effect, responsible use of a credit card shows others from whom you wish to seek credit (or borrow money) that you're financially responsible.

Remember

Don't buy into the belief that the only way you can establish a good credit history is by using a credit card. It's not your only option; you can establish a good credit history through responsible use of a checking account and by paying your bills on time.

Strategies for Using Credit Cards Responsibly

While there may be advantages to using a credit card, you only reap those advantages if you use your card strategically. If not, the advantages of a credit card can be quickly and greatly outweighed by its disadvantages. Listed here are some strategies for using a credit card in a way that maximizes its advantages and minimizes its disadvantages.

1. **Use a credit card only as a convenience for making purchases and tracking the purchases you make; don't use it as a tool for obtaining a long-term loan.** A credit card's main money-management advantage is that it enables you to make purchases with plastic instead of cash. A credit card saves you the inconvenience of having to carry around cash and it provides you with a monthly statement of your purchases from the credit card company, which makes it easier for you to track and analyze your spending habits.

   The credit provided by a credit card should be seen simply as a short-term loan that must be paid back at the end of every month. Do not use credit cards for long-term credit or long-term loans because their interest rates are outrageously high. Paying such a high rate of interest for a loan represents an ineffective (and irresponsible) money-management strategy.

2. **Limit yourself to one credit card.** The average college student has 2.8 credit cards (United College Marketing Service, cited in Pratt, 2008). More than one credit card just means more accounts to keep track of and more opportunities to accumulate debt. You don't need additional credit cards from department stores, gas stations, or any other profit-making business because they duplicate what your personal credit card already does (plus they charge extremely high interest rates for late payments).

3. **Pay off your balance each month in full and on time.** If you pay the full amount of your bill each month, this means that you're using your credit card effectively to obtain an interest-free, short-term (one-month) loan. You're just paying principal—the total amount of money borrowed and nothing more. However, if your payment is late and you need to pay interest, you end up paying more for the items you purchased than their actual ticket price. For instance, if you have an unpaid balance of $500 on your monthly credit bill for merchandise purchased the previous month and you are charged the typical 18 percent credit card interest rate for late payment, you end up paying $590: $500 (merchandise) + $90 (18 percent interest to the credit card company).

Credit card companies make their profit from the interest they collect from cardholders who don't pay back their credit on time. Just as procrastinating about completing schoolwork is a poor time-management habit that can hurt your grades, procrastinating about paying your credit-card bills is a poor money-management habit that can hurt your pocketbook by forcing you to pay high interest rates.

Don't allow credit card companies to make profit at your expense. Pay your total balance on time and avoid paying exorbitantly high interest rates. If you can't pay the total amount owed at the end of the month, rather than making the minimum monthly payment, pay off as much of it as you possibly can. If you keep making only the minimum payment each month, you'll begin to pile up huge amounts of debt.

> **Remember**
>
> *If you keep charging on your credit card while you have an unpaid balance or debt, you no longer have a grace period to pay back your charges; instead, interest is charged immediately on all your purchases.*

Charge Card

A charge card works similar to a credit card in that you're given a short-term loan for one month; the only difference is that you must pay your bill in full at the end of each month and you cannot carry over any debt from one month to the next. Its major disadvantage relative to a credit card is that it has less flexibility—no matter what your expenses may be for a particular month, you must still pay up or lose your ability to acquire credit for the next month. For people who habitually fail to pay their monthly credit card bills on time, this makes a charge card a smarter money-management tool than a credit card because the cardholder cannot continue to accumulate debt.

Reflection **13.3**

Do you have a credit card? Do you have more than one?

If you have at least one credit card, do you pay off your entire balance each month?

If you don't pay off your entire balance each month, what's your average unpaid balance per month?

What changes would you have to make in your money-management habits to be able to pay off your entire balance each month?

Debit Card

A debit card looks almost identical to a credit card (e.g., it has a MasterCard or Visa logo), but it works differently. When you use a debit card, money is immediately taken out or subtracted from your checking account. Thus, you're only using money that's already in your account (rather than borrowing money), and you don't receive a bill at the end of the month. If you attempt to purchase something with a debit card that costs more than the amount of money you have in your account, your card will not allow you to do so. Just like a bounced check, a debit card will not permit you to pay out any money that is not in your account. Like a check or ATM withdrawal, any purchase you make with a debit card should immediately be subtracted from your balance.

Like a credit card, a major advantage of the debit card is that it provides you with the convenience of plastic; however, unlike a credit card, it prevents you from spending beyond your means and accumulating debt. For this reason, financial advisors often recommend using a debit card rather than a credit card (Knox, 2004; Tyson, 2003).

> "Never spend your money before you have it."
>
> —Thomas Jefferson, third president of the United States and founder of the University of Virginia

Sources of Income for Financing Your College Education

Free Application for Federal Student Aid (FAFSA)

The Free Application for Federal Student Aid (FAFSA) is the application used by the U.S. Department of Education to determine financial aid eligibility for students. A formula is used to determine each student's *estimated family contribution (EFC)*—the amount of money the government has determined a family can contribute to the educational costs of the family member who is attending college. No fee is charged to complete the application, so you should complete one every year to determine your eligibility to receive financial aid, whether you believe you're eligible or not. See the Financial Aid Office on your campus for the FAFSA form and for help in completing it.

13.1

Snapshot Summary

Financial Literacy: Understanding the Language of Money Management

As you can tell from the number of financial terms used in this chapter, there is a fiscal vocabulary or language that we need to master in order to fully understand our financial options and transactions. In other words, we need to become *financially literate*. As you read the financial terms listed below, place a checkmark next to any term whose meaning you didn't already know.

Account. A formal business arrangement in which a bank provides financial services to a customer (e.g., checking account or savings account).

Annual percentage rate (APR). The interest rate that must be paid when monthly credit card balances are not paid in full.

Balance. The amount of money in a person's account or the amount of unpaid debt.

Bounced check. A check written for a greater amount of money than the amount contained in a personal checking account, which typically requires the person to pay a charge to the bank and possibly to the business that attempted to cash the bounced check.

Budget. A plan for coordinating income and expenses to ensure that sufficient money is available to cover personal expenses or expenditures.

Cash flow. Amount of money flowing in (income) and flowing out (expenses). "Negative cash flow" occurs when the amount of money going out exceeds the amount coming in.

Credit. Money obtained with the understanding that it will be paid back, either with or without interest.

Credit line (a.k.a. credit limit). The maximum amount of money (credit) made available to a borrower.

Debt. Amount of money owed.

Default. Failure to meet a financial obligation (e.g., a student who fails to repay a college loan "defaults" on that loan).

Emergency student loan. Immediate, interest-free loans provided by a college or university to help financially strapped students cover short-term expenses (e.g., cost of textbooks) or deal with financial emergencies (e.g., accidents and illnesses). Emergency student loans are typically granted within 24–48 hours, sometimes even the same day, and usually need to be repaid within two months.

Deferred student payment plan. A plan that allows student borrowers to temporarily defer or postpone loan payments for some acceptable reason (e.g., to pursue an internship or to do volunteer work after college).

Estimated family contribution (EFC). The amount of money the government has determined a family can contribute to the educational costs of the family member who is attending college.

Fixed interest rate. A loan with an interest rate that will remain the same for the entire term of the loan.

Grace period. The amount of time after a monthly credit card statement has been issued during which the credit card holder can pay back the company without paying added interest fees.

Grant. Money received that doesn't have to be repaid.

Gross income. Income generated before taxes and other expenses are deducted.

Insurance premium. The amount paid in regular installments to an insurance company to remain insured.

Interest. The amount of money paid to a customer for deposited money (as in a bank account) or money paid by a customer for borrowed money (e.g., interest on a loan). Interest is usually calculated as a percentage of the total amount of money deposited or borrowed.

Interest-bearing account. A bank account that earns interest if the customer keeps a sufficiently large sum of money in the bank.

Loan consolidation. Consolidating (combining) separate student loans into one larger loan to make the process of tracking, budgeting, and repayment easier. Loan consolidation typically requires the borrower to pay slightly more interest.

Loan premium. The amount of money loaned without interest.

Merit-based scholarship. Money awarded to a student on the basis of performance or achievement that doesn't have to be repaid.

Need-based scholarship. Money awarded to a student on the basis of financial need that doesn't have to be repaid.

Net income. Money earned or remaining after all expenses and taxes have been paid.

Principal. The total amount of money borrowed or deposited, not counting interest.

Variable interest rate. An interest rate on a loan that can vary or be changed by the lender.

Yield. Revenue or profit produced by an investment beyond the original amount invested. For example, the higher lifetime income and other monetary benefits acquired from a college education that exceed the amount of money invested in or spent on a college education.

Reflection 13.4

Which of the terms in Snapshot Summary 13.1 were unfamiliar to you?

Which of the terms apply to your current financial situation or money-management plans?

Scholarships

Scholarships are available from many sources besides the institution you've chosen to attend. Typically, scholarships are awarded at the time of admission to college, but some scholarships may be awarded to students at a later point in their college experience. To find out about scholarships that you may still be eligible to receive, visit your Financial Aid Office. You can also conduct an Internet search to find many sites that offer scholarship information. (However, don't enter your credit card or bank account information on any site.)

Also, keep in mind that scholarships are very competitive and deadlines are strictly enforced.

Grants

Grants are considered to be gift aid, which typically does not have to be repaid. About two-thirds of all college students receive grant aid, which, on average, reduces their tuition bills by more than half (College Board, 2009). The Federal Pell Grant is the largest grant program; it provides need-based aid to low-income undergraduate students. The amount of the grant depends on criteria such as (1) the anticipated contribution of the family to the student's education (EFC), (2) the cost of the post-secondary institution that the student is attending, and (3) the enrollment status of the student (part-time or full-time).

Loans

Student loans need to be repaid once a student graduates from college. Listed below are some of the more common student loan programs.

- **The Federal Perkins Loan** is a 5 percent simple-interest loan awarded to exceptionally needy students. The repayment for this loan begins nine months after a student is no longer enrolled at least half-time.
- **The Federal Subsidized Stafford Loan** is available to students enrolled at least half-time and has a fixed interest rate that's established each year on July 1. The federal government pays the interest on the loan while the student is enrolled. The repayment for this loan begins six months after a student is no longer enrolled half-time.
- **The Federal Unsubsidized Stafford Loan** is a loan that's not based on need and has the same interest rate as the Federal Subsidized Stafford Loan. Students are responsible for paying the interest on this loan while they're enrolled in college. The loan amount limits for Stafford loans are based on the classification of the student (e.g., freshman or sophomore).

Snapshot Summary

13.2 Federal Loan versus Private Loan: A Critical Difference

Private loans and federal loans are different, unrelated types of loans. Here are the key differences:

Federal loans have fixed interest rates that are comparatively low (currently less than 7 percent).

Private loans have variable interest rates that are very high (currently more than 15 percent) and can go higher at any time.

Note: Despite the high cost of private loans, they are the fastest-growing type of loans taken out by college students, largely because of aggressive, misleading, and sometimes irresponsible or unethical advertising on loan-shopping Web sites. Students sometimes think they're getting a federal loan only to find out later they have taken on a more expensive private loan.

"Apply for as much grant aid as possible before borrowing, and then seek lower-interest federal student loans before tapping private ones. There is a lot of student aid that can help make the expense [of college] more manageable."

—Sandy Baum, senior policy analyst, College Board (Gordon, 2009)

"Borrow money from a pessimist. He won't expect it back."

—Steven Wright, American comedian and first inductee to the Boston Comedy Hall of Fame

Source: Hamilton (2012); Kristof (2008).

Remember

Not all loans are created equally. Federally guaranteed student loans are relatively low-cost compared to private loans, and they may be paid off slowly after graduation. On the other hand, private lenders of student loans are like credit-card companies: they charge extremely high interest rates (that can go even higher at any time), and must be paid off as quickly as possible. They should not to be used as a primary loan to help pay for college, and they should only be used as a last resort when no other options are available for covering your college expenses.

Keep in mind that federal and state regulations require that if you're receiving financial aid, you must maintain "satisfactory academic progress." In most cases this means you must do the following:

1. **Maintain a satisfactory GPA.** Your entire academic record will be reviewed, even if you have paid for any of the classes with your own resources.
2. **Make satisfactory academic progress.** Your academic progress will be evaluated at least once per year, usually at the end of each spring semester.
3. **Complete a degree or certificate program within an established period of time.** Check with your institution's Financial Aid Office for details.

Salary Earnings

If you find yourself relying on your salary to pay for college tuition, check with your employer to see whether the company offers tuition reimbursement. Also, check with the Billing Office on your campus to determine whether payment plans are available for tuition costs. These plans may differ in terms of how much is due, deadlines for payments, and how any remaining debt owed to the institution is dealt with at the end of the term. You may find that the college you're attending will not allow you to register for the following term until the previous term is completely paid for.

Research shows that when students work on campus (versus off campus) they're more likely to succeed in college (Astin, 1993; Pascarella & Terenzini, 1991; 2005), probably because they become more connected to the college when they work on campus (Cermak & Filkins, 2004; Tinto, 1993) and also because on-campus employers are more flexible than off-campus employers in allowing students to meet their academic commitments (Leonard, 2008). For instance, campus employers are more willing to schedule students' work hours around their class schedule and allow students to modify their work schedules when their academic workload increases (e.g., at midterm and finals). Thus, if at all possible, rather than seeking work off campus, try to find work on campus and capitalize on its proven capacity to promote college success.

Money-Saving Strategies and Habits

The ultimate goal of money management is to save money and dodge debt. Here are some strategies for accomplishing this goal.

Prepare a personal budget. A budget is simply a plan for coordinating income and expenses to ensure that your cash flow leaves you with sufficient money to cover your expenses. A budget helps you maintain awareness of your financial state or condition, and enables you to be your own accountant who keeps an accurate account of your own money.

Just like managing and budgeting time, the first step in managing and budgeting money involves prioritizing. Money management requires identifying your most important expenses (indispensable necessities you can't live without) and distinguishing them from incidentals (dispensable luxuries you can live without). People can easily confuse essentials (what they need) and desirables (what they want). For instance, if a piece of merchandise happens to be on sale, it may be a desirable purchase at that time because of its reduced price, but it's not an essential purchase unless the person really needs that piece of merchandise at that particular time.

Postponing immediate or impulsive satisfaction of material desires is a key element of effective college financing and long-term financial success. We need to remain aware of whether we're spending money on impulse and out of habit or out of need and after thoughtful reflection. The truth is that humans spend money for a host of psychological reasons (conscious or subconscious), many of which are unrelated to actual need. For example, some people spend money to build their self-esteem or self-image, to combat personal boredom, or to seek an emotional "high" (Dittmar, 2004; Furnham & Argyle, 1998). Furthermore, people can become obsessed with spending money, shop compulsively, and develop an addiction to purchasing products. Just as Alcoholics Anonymous (AA) exists as a support group for alcoholics, Debtors Anonymous exists as a support group for shopaholics and includes a 12-step recovery program similar to AA.

Author's Experience   I was a student who had to manage my own college expenses, so I soon became an expert in managing small budgets. The first thing I always took care of was my tuition. I was going to go to school even if I starved. The next thing I budgeted for was my housing, food, clothing, and transportation needs. If I ran out of money, I would then work additional hours if it didn't interfere with my academics. I clearly understood that I was working to make a better future life for myself, rather than making and spending money while I was in college. To be successful, I had to be a great money manager because there was so little of it to manage. This took a lot of focus and strong will, but did it ever pay off? Absolutely.

Aaron Thompson

Make all your bills visible and pay them off as soon as possible. When your bills remain in your sight, they remain on your mind; you're less likely to forget to pay them or forget to pay them on time. Increase the visibility of your bill payments by keeping a financial calendar on which you record key fiscal deadlines for the academic year (e.g., due dates for tuition payments, residential bills, and financial aid applications). Also, try to get in the habit of paying a bill as soon as you open it and have it in your hands, rather than setting it aside and running the risk of forgetting to pay it (or losing it altogether).

Live within your means. To state it simply: Don't purchase what you can't afford. If you're spending more money than you're taking in, it means you're living *beyond* your means. To begin living *within* your means, you have two options:

1. Decrease your expenses (reduce your spending), or
2. Increase your income (earn more money).

"We choose to spend more money than we have today. Choose debt, or choose freedom, it's your choice."

—Bill Pratt, *Extra Credit: The 7 Things Every College Student Needs to Know About Credit, Debt & Cash*

Since most college students are already working while attending college (Orszag, Orszag, & Whitmore, 2001) and working so many hours that it's interfering with their academic performance or progress (King, 2005), the best option for most college students who find themselves in debt is to reduce their spending and begin living within their means.

Economize. By being intelligent consumers who use critical thinking skills when purchasing products, we can be frugal or thrifty without compromising the quality of our purchases. For example, we could pay less to see the same movie in the late afternoon than we could to see it at night. Why pay more for brand-name products that are the same as products with a different name? Why pay 33 percent more for Advil or Tylenol when the same amount of pain-relieving ingredient (ibuprofen or acetaminophen) is contained in generic brands? Often, what we're paying for when we buy brand-name products is all the advertising these companies pay to the media and to celebrities to publicly promote their products.

Reflection 13.5

Are you working for money while attending college?

If you're not working, are you sacrificing anything you want or need because you don't have the money to buy it?

If you are working:

1. How many hours per week do you currently work?
2. Do you think that working is interfering with your academic performance or progress?
3. Would it be possible for you to reduce the number of weekly hours you now work and still be able to make ends meet?

Remember

Advertising creates product familiarity, not product quality. The more money manufacturers pay for advertising and creating a well-known brand, the more money we pay for the product—not necessarily because we're acquiring a product of higher quality, but more likely because we're covering its high cost of advertising.

Downsize. Cut down or cut out spending for products that you don't need. Don't engage in conspicuous consumption just to keep up with the "Joneses" (your neighbors or friends), and don't allow peer pressure to determine your spending habits. Let your spending habits reflect your ability to think critically rather than your tendency to conform socially.

Save money by living with others rather than living alone. Although you lose privacy when you share living quarters with others, you save money. Living with others also has the fringe social benefit of spending time with roommates or housemates whom you've chosen to live with and whose company you enjoy.

Give gifts of time rather than money. Spending money on gifts for family, friends, and romantic partners isn't the only way to show that you care. The point of gift giving isn't to show others you aren't cheap or show off by being a big-time spender; instead, show off your social sensitivity by doing something special or by making something meaningful for them. Gifts of time and kindness can often be more personal and more special than store-bought gifts.

> "It is preoccupation with possessions, more than anything else, that prevents us from living freely and nobly."
>
> —Bertrand Russell, British philosopher and mathematician

> "The richer your friends, the more they will cost you."
>
> —Elisabeth Marbury, legal agent for theatrical and literary stars in the late 19th and early 20th centuries

Author's Experience When my wife (Mary) and I were first dating, I was trying to gain weight because I was on the thin side. (All right, I was skinny.) One day when I came home from school, I found this hand-delivered package in front of my apartment door. I opened it up and there was a homemade loaf of whole wheat bread made from scratch by Mary. That gift didn't cost her much money, but she took the time to do it and she remembered to do something that was important to me (gaining weight). That gift really touched me; it's a gift I've never forgotten. Since I eventually married Mary and we're still happily married, I guess you could say that inexpensive loaf of bread was a "gift that kept on giving."

Joe Cuseo

Develop your own set of money-saving strategies and habits. You can save money by starting to develop little money-saving habits that eventually add up to big savings over time. Consider the following list of habit-forming tips for saving money that were suggested by students in a first-year seminar class:

> "If you would be wealthy, think of saving as well as getting."
>
> —Benjamin Franklin, 18th-century inventor, newspaper writer, and signer of the Declaration of Independence

- Don't carry a lot of extra money in your wallet. (It's just like food; if it's easy to get to, you'll be more likely to eat it up.)
- Shop with a list—get in, get what you need, and get out.
- Put all your extra change in a jar.
- Put extra cash in a piggy bank that requires you to smash the piggy to get at it.
- Seal your savings in an envelope.
- When you get extra money, get it immediately into the bank (and out of your hands).
- Bring (don't buy) your lunch.
- Take full advantage of your meal plan—you've already paid for it, so don't pay twice for your meals by buying food elsewhere.
- Use e-mail instead of the telephone.
- Hide your credit card or put it in the freezer so that you don't use it on impulse.
- Use cash (instead of credit cards) because you can give yourself a set amount of cash and clearly see how much of it you have at the start of a week (and how much is left at any point during the week).

Reflection **13.6**

"The safest way to double your money is to fold it over and put it in your pocket."

—Kin Hubbard, American humorist, cartoonist, and journalist

Do you use any of the strategies on the above list?

Have you developed any effective strategies that do not appear on the list?

"Ask yourself how much of your income is being eaten up by car payments. It may be time to admit you made a mistake . . . sell it [and] replace it with an older or less sporty model."

—Bill Pratt, *Extra Credit: The 7 Things Every College Student Needs to Know About Credit, Debt & Cash*

When making purchases, always think in terms of their long-term total cost. It's convenient and tempting for consumers to think in the short term ("I see it; I like it; I want it; and I want it now.") However, long-term thinking is one of the essential keys to successful money management and financial planning. Those small (monthly) installment plans that businesses offer to get you to buy expensive products may make the cost of those products appear attractive and affordable in the short run. However, when you factor in the interest rates you pay on monthly installment plans, plus the length of time (number of months) you're making installment payments, you get a more accurate picture of the product's total cost over the long run. This longer-range perspective can quickly alert you to the reality that a product's sticker price represents its partial and seemingly affordable short-term cost but its long-term total cost is much less affordable (and perhaps out of your league).

Furthermore, the long-term price for purchases sometimes involves additional "hidden costs" that don't relate directly to the product's initial price but must be paid to keep using the product. For example, the sticker price you pay for clothes doesn't include the hidden, long-term costs that may be involved if those clothes require dry cleaning. By just taking a moment to check the inside label, you can save yourself this hidden, long-term cost by purchasing clothes that are machine washable. To use an example of a big-ticket purchase, the extra money spent to buy a new car (instead of a used car) includes not only paying a higher sticker price but also paying the higher hidden costs of licensing and insuring the new car, as well as any interest fees if the new car was purchased on an installment plan. When you add in these hidden, long-term costs to a new car's total cost, buying a good used car is clearly a much more effective money-management strategy than buying a new one.

Author's Experience

When I was four years old and living in the mountains of Kentucky, it was safe for a young lad to walk the railroad tracks and roads alone. So, my mother would send me on long walks to the general store to buy various small items we needed for our household. Since we had little money, she was very cautious about spending money only on the essential necessities we needed to survive. I could only purchase items from the general store that my mother strictly ordered me to purchase. Most of these items cost less than a dollar, and in many cases multiple items could be bought for a dollar in the early 1960s. At the store I would hand my mother's handwritten list to the owners. They would pick the items for me, and we would exchange the items for my money. On the checkout counter jars were different kinds of candy or gum. You could buy two pieces for a penny. As a hardworking boy who was doing a good deed for his parents, I didn't think there would be any harm in rewarding myself with two pieces of candy after doing a good deed. After all, I could devour the evidence of my disobedience on my slow walk home. Upon my return, my mother, being the protector of the vault and the sergeant-of-arms in our household, would count each item I brought home to make sure I had been charged correctly. She always found that I had either been overcharged by one cent or that I had spent one cent. In those days, parents believed in behavior modification. After she gave me a scolding, she would say "Boy, you better learn how to count your money if you're ever going to be successful in life." I learned the value of saving money and the danger of overspending at a young age!

Aaron Thompson

Long-Range Fiscal Planning: Financing Your College Education

An effective money-management plan should be time-sensitive and include the following time frames:

- Short-range financial planning (e.g., weekly income and expenses)
- Mid-range financial planning (e.g., monthly income and expenses)
- Long-range financial planning (e.g., projected or anticipated income and expenses for the entire college experience)
- Extended long-range financial planning (e.g., expected income and debt after graduation, including a plan for repayment of college loans)

Thus far, our discussion has focused primarily on short-range and mid-range financial planning strategies that will keep you out of debt on a monthly or yearly basis. We turn now to issues involving long-term financial planning for your entire college experience. While no one "correct" strategy exists for financing a college education, there are some important research findings on the effectiveness of different financing strategies that you should be aware of when doing long-range financial planning for college and beyond.

Research shows that obtaining a student loan and working no more than 15 hours per week is an effective long-range strategy for students at all income levels to finance their college education and meet their personal expenses. Students who use this strategy are more likely to graduate from college, graduate in less time, and graduate with higher grades than students who work part-time for more than 15 hours per week while attending college full-time, or students who work full-time and attend college part-time (King, 2002; Perna & DuBois, 2010). Unfortunately, less than 6 percent of all first-year students use this strategy. Instead, almost 50 percent of first-year students choose a strategy that research shows to be least associated with college success: borrowing nothing and trying to work more than 15 hours per week. Students who use this strategy increase their risk of lowering their grades significantly and withdrawing from college altogether (King, 2005)—probably because they have difficulty finding enough time to handle the amount of academic work required by college on top of the more than 15 hours they're working per week. Thus, a good strategy for balancing learning and earning is to try to limit work for pay to 15 hours per week (or as close to 15 hours as possible). Working longer hours increases the temptation to switch from full-time to part-time enrollment, which can increase the risk of delaying graduation or not graduating at all.

Remember

Avoid buying costly items impulsively. Instead, take time to reflect on the purchase you intend to make, do a cost analysis of its hidden and long-term costs, and then integrate these invisible costs with the product's sticker price to generate an accurate synthesis and clearer picture of the product's total cost.

"People don't realize how much work it is to stay in college. It's its own job in itself, plus if you've got another job you go to, too. I mean, it's just a lot."

—College student (quoted in Engle & Bermeo, 2006)

"I work two jobs and go to school and it's hard, real hard. I go home at like 9 or 10, and I'm too tired to do my homework."

—College student (quoted in Engle & Bermeo, 2006)

Reflection 13.7

Do you need to work part-time to meet your college expenses?

If you answered "yes" to the above question, are you working more than 15 hours per week?

If you answered "yes" to the above question, can you reduce your work time to 15 or fewer hours per week and still make ends meet?

Some students decide to finance their college education by working full-time and going to college part-time. These students believe it will be less expensive in the long run to attend college part-time because it will allow them to avoid any debt from student loans. However, studies show that when students use this strategy, it lengthens their time to degree completion and increases the risk that they will never complete a degree (Orszag et al., 2001).

Students who manage to eventually graduate from college but take longer to do so because they have worked more than 15 hours per week will lose money in the long run. The longer they take to graduate, the longer they must wait to "cash in" on their college degrees and enter higher-paying, full-time positions that a college diploma would qualify them to enter. The hourly pay for most part-time jobs students hold while going to college is less than half what they will earn from working in full-time positions as college graduates (King, 2005).

Furthermore, studies show that two out of three college students have at least one credit card and nearly one of every two students with credit cards carries an average balance of more than $2,000 per month (Mae, 2005). A debt level this high is likely to push many students into working more than 15 hours a week to pay it off ("I owe, I owe, so off to work I go"). This often results in their taking longer to graduate and start earning a college graduate's salary because they end up taking fewer courses per term so they can work more hours to pay off their credit card debt.

Instead of paying almost 20 percent interest to credit card companies for their monthly debt, these students would be better off obtaining a student loan at a much lower interest rate, which they will not start paying back until 6 months after graduation—when they'll be making more money in full-time positions as college graduates. Despite this clear advantage of student loans compared to credit card loans, only about 25 percent of college students who use credit cards take out student loans (King, 2002).

> ### Remember
> *Student loans are provided by the American government with the intent of helping its citizens become better educated. In contrast, for-profit businesses such as credit-card companies lend students money with no intent of helping them become better educated, but with the clear intent of helping themselves make money—from the high rates of interest they collect from students who do not pay off their debt in full at the end of each month.*

> "Unlike a car that depreciates in value each year that you drive it, an investment in education yields monetary, social, and intellectual profit. A car is more tangible in the short term, but an investment in education (even if it means borrowing money) gives you more bang for the buck in the long run."
>
> —Eric Tyson, financial counselor and national bestselling author of *Personal Finance for Dummies*

> "The cynic knows the price of everything and the value of nothing."
>
> —Oscar Wilde, Irish playwright, poet, and author of numerous short stories

Keep in mind that not all debt is bad. Debt can be good if it represents an investment in something that will appreciate with time—i.e., something that will gain in value and eventually turn into profit for the investor. Purchasing a college education on credit is a good investment because, over time, it appreciates in the form of higher salaries for the remainder of the life of the investor (the college graduate). In contrast, purchasing a new car is a bad long-term investment because it immediately begins to depreciate or lose monetary value once it's purchased. The instant you drive that new car off the dealer's lot, you immediately become the proud owner of a used car that's worth much less than what you just paid for it.

> ### Remember
> *What you're willing to sacrifice and save for, and what you're willing to go into debt for, say a lot about who you are and what you value.*

You may have heard the expression that "time is money." One way to interpret this expression is that the more money you spend, the more time you must spend making money. If you're going to college, spending more time on earning money to cover your spending habits often means spending less time studying, learning, completing classes, and earning good grades. You can avoid this vicious cycle by viewing academic work as work that "pays" you back in terms of completed courses and higher grades. If you put in more academic time to complete more courses in less time and with higher grades, you're paid back by graduating and earning the full-time salary of a college graduate sooner—which will pay you about twice as much money per hour than you'll earn doing part-time work without a college degree (not to mention fringe benefits such as health insurance and paid vacation time). Furthermore, the time you put into earning higher grades in college should pay off immediately in your first full-time position after college, because research shows that students graduating in the same field who have higher grades receive higher starting salaries (Pascarella & Terenzini, 2005).

Reflection 13.8

In addition to college, what might be other good long-term investments you could make now in the near future?

> "If a man empties his purse into his head, no one can take it away from him. An investment in knowledge always pays the best interest."
> —Benjamin Franklin, 18th-century scientist, inventor, and a founding father of the United States

> "I invested in myself—in study, in mastering my tools, in preparation. Many a man who is putting a few dollars a week into the bank would do much better to put it into himself."
> —Henry Ford, founder of the Ford Motor Company and one of the richest people of the 20th century

Summary and Conclusion

The following strategies for effectively managing money were recommended in this chapter:

- **Develop financial self-awareness.** Become aware of your cash flow—the amount of money flowing in and flowing out of your hands.
- **Develop a money-management plan.** Ensure that your income is equal to or greater than your expenses.
- **Manage your money effectively.** Use available financial tools and instruments to track and maximize your cash flow, such as checking accounts, credit cards, charge cards, or debit cards.
- **Finance your education wisely.** Explore all sources of income for financing your college education, including the FAFSA, scholarships, grants, loans, monetary gifts from family or friends, salary earnings, and personal savings.
- **Prepare a personal budget.** A budget helps you keep an accurate account of your money and ensures you have sufficient money to cover your expenses.
- **Pay your bills when they arrive.** Paying bills when you first lay your hands on them serves to reduce the risk that you'll forget to pay them or pay them late.
- **Live within your means.** Don't purchase what you can't afford.
- **Economize.** Be an intelligent consumer who uses critical thinking skills to evaluate and prioritize your purchases.
- **Downsize.** Don't buy products you don't need, and don't let peer pressure determine your spending habits.
- **Live with others, rather than live alone.** The reduction in privacy can be offset by the financial savings. Living with others can also bring the fringe social benefit of having roommates or housemates whom you've chosen to live with and whose company you enjoy.
- **Work for better grades now and better pay later.** Research shows that taking out a student loan and working part-time for 15 or fewer hours per week is the most effective financial and educational strategy for students at all income levels.

- **Take full advantage of your Financial Aid Office.** Check periodically to see if you qualify for additional sources of income, such as part-time employment on campus, low-interest loans, grants, or scholarships.

Money management is a personal skill that can either support or sabotage your success in college and life beyond college. As with time management, if you effectively manage your money and gain control of how you spend it, you gain greater control over the quality of your life. Research shows that accumulating high levels of debt while in college is associated with higher levels of stress, lower academic performance, and greater risk of withdrawing from college. The good news is that research demonstrates that students who learn to use effective money-management strategies are able to reduce unnecessary spending, decrease their risk of debt and stress, and increase the quality of their academic performance.

Learning More through the World Wide Web

Internet-Based Resources for Further Information on Money Management

For additional information related to the ideas discussed in this chapter, we recommend the following Web sites:

Fiscal Literacy and Money Management:

www.360financialliteracy.org

www.cashcourse.org

www.loveyourmoney.org

Financial Aid and Federal Funding Sources for a College Education:

studentaid.ed.gov

13.1 Self-Assessment of Financial Attitudes and Habits

Answer the following questions as accurately and honestly as possible.

	Agree	Disagree
1. I pay my rent or mortgage on time each month.	_____	_____
2. I avoid maxing out or going over the limit on my credit cards.	_____	_____
3. I balance my checkbook each month.	_____	_____
4. I set aside money each month for savings.	_____	_____
5. I pay my phone and utility bills on time each month.	_____	_____
6. I pay my credit card bills in full each month to avoid interest charges.	_____	_____
7. I believe it's important to buy the things I want when I want them.	_____	_____
8. Borrowing money to pay for college is a smart thing to do.	_____	_____
9. I have a monthly or weekly budget that I follow.	_____	_____
10. The thing I enjoy most about making money is spending money.	_____	_____
11. I limit myself to one credit card.	_____	_____
12. Getting a degree will get me a good job and a good income.	_____	_____

Sources: Cude et al. (2006); Niederjohn (2008).

Give yourself one point for each item that you marked "agree"—except for items 7, 9, and 10. For these items, give yourself a point if you marked "disagree."

A perfect score on this short survey would be 12.

Self-Assessment Questions

1. What was your total score?

2. Which items lowered your score?

3. Do you detect any pattern across the items that lowered your score?

4. Do you see any realistic way(s) for improving your score on this test?

13.2 Financial Self-Awareness: Monitoring Money and Tracking Cash Flow

1. Use the worksheet that follows to *estimate* your income and expenses per month, and enter them in column 2.

2. *Track* your actual income and expenses for a month and enter them in column 3. (To help you do this accurately, keep a file of your cash receipts, bills paid, and credit card or checking account records for the month.)

3. After one month of tracking your cash flow, answer the self-assessment questions.

   a. Were your estimates generally accurate?

   b. For what specific items were there the largest discrepancies between your estimated cost and the actual cost?

   c. Comparing your bottom-line totals for income and expenses, are you satisfied with how your monthly cash flow is going?

   d. What changes could you make to create more positive cash flow—i.e., to increase your income or savings and reduce your expenses or debt?

   e. How likely is it that you'll make the changes you mentioned in the previous question?

Financial Self-Awareness Worksheet

	Estimate	Actual
Income Sources		
Parents/Family		
Work/Job		
Grants/Scholarships		
Loans		
Savings		
Other:		
TOTAL INCOME		
Essentials (Fixed Expenses)		
Living Expenses:		
Food/Groceries		
Rent/Room & Board		
Utilities (gas/electric)		
Clothing		
Laundry/Dry Cleaning		
Phone		
Computer		
Household Items (dishes, etc.)		
Medical Insurance Expenses		
Debt Payments (loans/credit cards)		
Other:		
School Expenses:		
Tuition		
Books		
Supplies (print cartridges, etc.)		
Special Fees (lab fees, etc.)		
Other:		
Transportation:		
Public Transportation (bus fees, etc.)		
Car Insurance		
Car Maintenance		
Fuel (gas)		
Car Payments		
Other:		
Incidentals (Variable Expenses)		
Entertainment:		
Movies/Concerts		
DVDs/CDs		
Restaurants (eating out)		
Other:		
Personal Appearance/Accessories:		
Haircuts/Hairstyling		
Cosmetics/Manicures		
Fashionable Clothes		
Jewelry		
Other:		
Hobbies:		
Travel (trips home, vacations)		
Gifts		
Other:		
TOTAL EXPENSES		

Problems Paying for College

A college student posted the following message on the Internet:

"I went to college for one semester, failed some my classes, and ended with 900 dollars in student loans. Now I can't even get financial aid or a loan because of some stupid thing that says if you fail a certain amount of classes you can't get aid or a loan. And now since I couldn't go to college this semester they want me to pay for my loans already, and I don't even have a job. Any suggestions?"

Reflection and Discussion Questions

1. What suggestions would you offer this student? Which of your suggestions should the student do immediately? Which should the student do eventually?

2. What should the student have done to prevent this from happening in the first place?

3. Do you think that this student's situation is common or unusual? Why?

Health and Wellness

Body, Mind, and Spirit

ACTIVATE YOUR THINKING | *Reflection* **14.1**

LEARNING GOAL

To acquire strategies for physical wellness that can be applied to promote success during the first year of college and beyond.

What would you say are the three most important things that college students could do to maintain reserve their health and promote peak performance?

1.

2.

3.

What Is Wellness?

Wellness may be described as a state of high-quality health and personal well-being that promotes peak physical and mental performance.

There's still some debate about the exact number and nature of the components that define or comprise wellness (Miller & Foster, 2010; President's Council on Physical Fitness and Sports, 2001). However, the following key dimensions of holistic (whole-person) development provide a comprehensive foundation for achieving total wellness.

- **Physical.** Applying knowledge about how the human body functions to prevent disease, maintain wellness, and promote peak performance.
- **Intellectual (mental).** Acquiring knowledge, learning how to learn, and how to think deeply and positively.
- **Social development.** Enhancing the quality and depth of interpersonal relationships.
- **Emotional development.** Strengthening skills for coping with, controlling, and expressing emotions.
- **Vocational (occupational) development.** Exploring career options, making career choices wisely, and developing skills needed for lifelong career success.
- **Ethical (character) development.** Acquiring a clear value system for guiding life choices and personal decisions, and developing consistency between moral convictions (beliefs) and moral commitments (actions).

> "To keep the body in good health is a duty, otherwise we shall not be able to keep our mind strong and clear."
>
> —Buddha, founder of Buddhism

- **Spiritual development.** Developing an appreciation for introspection and contemplation about the meaning or purpose of life and death, and a capacity for exploring ideas that transcend human life and the physical or material world.
- **Personal development.** Developing a coherent self-concept, personal identity, self-direction, and self-determination.

As can be seen in **Figure 14.1**, these elements of self join together to form the spokes of the "wellness wheel." Development of all these elements is a primary goal of wellness and being a well-rounded person.

FIGURE 14.1

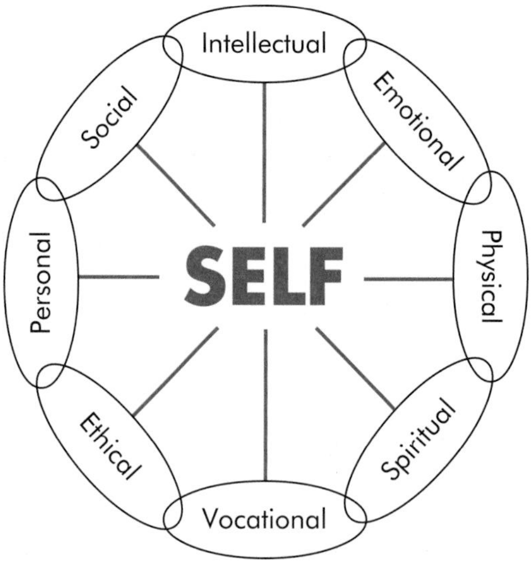

© Kendall Hunt

Components of the Wellness Wheel

Author's Experience When I was writing this chapter of the book, I told myself that I needed to post the wellness wheel in a very visible spot in my house to remind me to devote time to each element of the wheel, each day, to ensure that I seek balance in my life and strike to develop myself as a "whole person." The wheel is now posted on the front door of my refrigerator.

Joe Cuseo

The physical component of wellness is the primary focus of this chapter. It could be said that physical health is a necessary precondition or prerequisite that enables all other elements of wellness to be experienced. For instance, it's hard to develop intellectually and socially if you're not well physically, and it's hard to become wealthy and wise unless you're first healthy.

Physical wellness means more than simply avoiding illness or disease, nor is it something done in response or reaction to illness (e.g., getting well after being sick); instead, it's engaging in health-promoting behavior proactively to prevent illness from happening in the first place (Corbin, Pangrazi, & Franks, 2000). Wellness puts into practice two classic proverbs: "Prevention is the best medicine" and "An ounce of prevention is worth a pound of cure."

As depicted in **Figure 14.2**, there are three potential interception points for preventing illness, maintaining health, and promoting peak performance that range from the reactive (after illness) to proactive (before illness). Wellness goes beyond merely maintaining physical health to attaining a high quality of life that includes personal satisfaction, happiness, vitality (energy and vigor), and longevity (a longer life span).

Buono salute é la vera ricchezza. ("Good health is true wealth.")
—Italian proverb

FIGURE 14.2

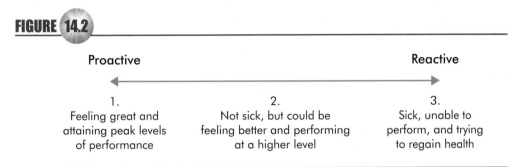

Proactive		Reactive
1.	2.	3.
Feeling great and attaining peak levels of performance	Not sick, but could be feeling better and performing at a higher level	Sick, unable to perform, and trying to regain health

Potential Points for Preventing Illness, Preserving Health, and Promoting Peak Performance

The Relevance of Wellness for Today's College Students

When students move directly from high school to college, and when they move from life at home to life on campus, they're moving toward taking personal responsibility for their wellness. Mom, Dad, and other family members are no longer around to monitor their health habits and to remind them about what to eat, what hours to keep, or when to go to sleep.

In addition to receiving less parental guidance and supervision, new college students are making a major life transition. When anyone undergoes significant change or experiences a major life transition, stress tends to increase. Unhealthy habits, such as eating poorly, further increases stress and moodiness (Khoshaba & Maddi, 2005). In contrast, maintaining good health habits is an effective stress-management strategy.

In the introduction to this book, we noted research that pointed to the advantages of the college experience. Among the advantages experienced by college graduates are that they lead physically healthier and longer lives and experience higher levels of psychological well-being (mental health) and personal happiness (life satisfaction). These findings show that students are learning something about wellness and how to promote it by the time they graduate from college. This chapter is designed to help you learn more about wellness at the very start of your college experience, so you can experience its benefits immediately and continually throughout your college years.

Reflection **14.2**

If you could single out one thing about your physical health that you'd like to improve or learn more about, what would it be?

Elements of Physical Wellness

A healthy physical lifestyle includes four elements:

1. Supplying the body with effective fuel (nutrition)
2. Transforming the fuel we consume into bodily energy (exercise)
3. Giving the body adequate rest (sleep) so that it can recover and replenish the energy it has expended
4. Avoiding risky substances (alcohol and drugs) and risky behaviors that can threaten our health and safety

Nutrition

Your body needs nutrients to replenish its natural biochemicals and repair its tissues. The food you put into your body supplies it with energy much like fuel does for a car. Just as high-quality gasoline can improve how well and how long your car runs, so can high-quality (nutritious) food improve the performance of your body and mind, allowing them to function at peak capacity. Unfortunately, however, people often pay more attention to the quality of fuel they put in their cars than to the quality of food they put into their bodies. Humans often eat without any intentional planning about what they eat. They eat at places where they can get access to food fast, where they can pick up food conveniently while they're on the go, and where they can consume it without having to step out of their cars (or get off their butts) to consume it. America has become a fast-food nation, accustomed to consuming food that can be accessed quickly, conveniently, cheaply, and in large (super-sized) portions (Schlosser, 2005).

Studies show that the least nutritious and healthy foods are the very ones that receive the most media advertising, and the most frequently advertised food items that people are consuming in the largest quantities tend to be junk food—i.e., the food with the least nutrients, the most calories, and the highest health risks (Caroli, Argentieri, Cardone, & Masi, 2004; Hill, 2002). The advertising, availability, and convenience of high-calorie, low-cost food contribute to the fact that Americans today are heavier now than at any other time in our nation's history. In 2003, approximately 65 percent of Americans 20 years and older were either overweight (20 percent more than the ideal body weight for their height and age) or obese (30 percent more than their ideal weight) (World Health Organization, 2012). In 1976, the percentage of Americans who were overweight or obese was only 26 percent (Hill, Wyat, Reed, & Peters, 2003). The most telling piece of evidence is the finding that when people from other countries move to America and begin to adopt American eating habits, they typically put on a significant amount of weight (Sundquist & Winkleby, 2000).

National surveys of first-year college students indicate that less than 40 percent report that they maintain a healthy diet (Sax, Lindholm, Astin, Korn, & Mahoney, 2004). The phrase "freshman 15" is commonly used to describe the 15-pound weight gain that some students experience during their first year of college (Brody, 2003; Levitsky, Nussbaum, Halbmaier, & Mrdjenovic, 2003). This weight gain may be temporary and associated with the initial transition to the college eating lifestyle (e.g., all-you-can-eat dining halls, late-night pizzas, and junk-food snacks). However, for other students, it may signal the start of a longer-lasting pattern of gaining and carrying excess weight. The disadvantage of being overweight isn't merely a matter of appearance: it's also a matter of health and survival because excess weight increases susceptibility to the leading life-threatening diseases, such as diabetes, heart disease, and certain forms of cancer.

Reflection 14.3

Have your eating habits changed since you've begun college? If yes, in what ways have they changed?

We should eat in a thoughtful, nutritionally conscious way, rather than solely out of convenience, habit, or pursuit of what's most pleasant to our taste buds. We should also "eat to win" by eating the types of food that will best equip us to defeat disease and allow us to reach peak levels of physical and mental performance.

Chi mangia bene, vive bene.
("Who eats well, lives well.")
—Italian proverb

Snapshot Summary

14.1 Eating Disorders

While some students experience the "freshman 15," others experience eating disorders related to weight loss and loss of control of their eating habits. The disorders described in this box are more common among females (National Institute of Mental Health, 2011). Studies show that approximately one of every three college females indicates that she worries about her weight, body image, or eating habits. Western cultures place more emphasis and pressure on females than males to maintain lighter body weight and body size.

What follows is a short summary of the major eating disorders experienced by college students. These disorders are often accompanied by emotional issues (e.g., depression and anxiety) that are serious enough to require professional treatment. The earlier these disorders are identified and treated, the better the prognosis or probability of complete and permanent recovery. The Counseling Center and Student Health Center are the key campus resources where students can seek help and treatment for any of the following eating disorders.

Anorexia Nervosa

The self-esteem of people who experience anorexia nervosa disorder is often tied closely to their body weight or shape. They see themselves as overweight and have an intense fear of gaining weight, even though they're dangerously thin. Anorexics typically deny that they're severely underweight, and even if their weight drops to the point where they may look like walking skeletons, they may continue to be obsessed with losing weight, eating infrequently, and eating in extremely small portions. Anorexics may also use other methods to lose weight, such as compul-

sive exercise, diet pills, laxatives, diuretics, or enemas.

Bulimia Nervosa

The eating disorder known as bulimia nervosa is characterized by repeated episodes of binge eating—consuming excessive amounts of food within a limited period of time. Bulimics tend to lose all sense of self-control during their binges, then try to compensate for overeating by engaging in behavior to purge their guilt and prevent weight gain. For example, they may purge by self-induced vomiting, consuming excessive amounts of laxatives or diuretics, using enemas, and fasting. The binge-purge pattern typically takes place at least twice a week and continues for three or more months.

Unlike anorexia, bulimia is harder to detect because bulimics' binges and purges take place secretly and their body weight looks about normal for their age and height. However, similar to anorexics, bulimics fear gaining weight, aren't happy with their bodies, and have an intense desire to lose weight.

Binge-Eating Disorder

Like bulimia, binge-eating disorder involves repeated, out-of-control binging on large quantities of food. However, unlike bulimics, binge eaters don't purge after binging episodes. For someone to be diagnosed as suffering from binge-eating disorder, that person must demonstrate at least three of the following symptoms, two or more times per week, for several months:

1. Eating more rapidly than normal
2. Eating until becoming uncomfortably full

Student *Perspective*

"I've had a friend who took pride in her ability to lose 30 lbs. in one summer because of not eating and working out excessively. I know girls that find pleasure in getting so ill that they throw up and can't eat because the illness causes them to lose weight."

—Comments written in a first-year student's journal

3. Eating large amounts of food when not physically hungry
4. Eating alone because of embarrassment about others seeing how much they eat
5. Feeling guilty, disgusted, or depressed after overeating.

Since individuals suffering from these eating disorders usually don't recognize or admit their illness, friends and family members play a key role in helping them receive help before the disorder progresses to a life-threatening level. If someone you know is experiencing an eating disorder, consult with a professional at the Student Health Center or Counseling Center about strategies for approaching and encouraging this person to seek help.

Nutrition-Management Strategies

The following nutrition-management strategies may be used to enhance your body's ability to stay well and perform well.

1. **Develop a nutrition management plan to ensure your diet has variety and balance.** Planning what you eat is essential to ensure you eat what's best for preserving health and promoting wellness. If you don't plan ahead to acquire the food you should eat, you're more likely to eat food that can be accessed conveniently and doesn't require advanced preparation. Unfortunately, the types of foods that are readily available, easily accessible, and immediately consumable are usually fast food and packaged food, which are the least healthy foods. If you're serious about eating in a way that's best for your health and performance, you need to do some nutritional planning in advance.

   Figure 14.3 depicts the MyPlate chart, which is the new version of the former Food Guide Pyramid and created by the United States Department of Agriculture (USDA). Since foods vary in terms of the nature of nutrients they provide (carbohydrates, protein, and fat), no single food group can supply all the

FIGURE 14.3

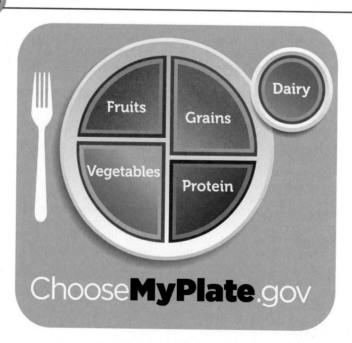

Source: USDA

MyPlate

nutrients your body needs. Therefore, your diet should be balanced and include all of these food groups, but you should include them in different proportions or percentages. To find the daily amount of food you should be consuming from each of these major food groups (e.g., your age and gender), go to www.choose myplate.gov or www.cnpp.usda.gov/dietaryguidelines.htm. You can use these guidelines to create a dietary plan that ensures you consume each of these food groups every day, resulting in a balanced diet that minimizes your risk of experiencing any nutritional deficits or deficiencies. If this guide to nutrition is followed, there should be no need for you to take vitamins or dietary supplements.

Reflection 14.4

What type of junk food (if any) do you currently eat? Why?

If you do eat junk food, what's the likelihood that you'll continue to do so? Why?

2. **Maintain self-awareness of your eating habits.** A key step toward effective nutrition management is to become fully aware of your current eating habits. People often make decisions about what to eat without giving it much thought or even without conscious awareness. You can increase awareness of your eating habits by simply taking a little time to read the labels on the food products before you put them into your shopping cart and into your body. Keeping a nutritional log or journal of what you eat in a typical week to track its nutrients and caloric content is also an effective way to become self-aware of your eating habits.

Another thing to be aware of is your family history. Are there members of your immediate and extended family who have shown tendencies toward heart disease, diabetes, or cancer? If so, intentionally adopt a diet that reduces your risk for developing the types of illnesses that you may have the genetic potential to develop. (For regularly updated information on dietary strategies for reducing the risk of common diseases, see the following Web site: fnic.nal.usda.gov/diet-and-disease.)

Reflection 14.5

Are you aware of any disease or illness that tends to run in your family?

If yes, are you aware of how you may decrease your risk of experiencing this disease or illness through your diet?

Exercise and Fitness

Wellness depends not only on fueling the body but also on moving it. The benefits of physical exercise for improving the longevity and quality of human life are simply extraordinary. Physical activity was something that our early ancestors did daily to stay alive. They had no motorized vehicles to move them from point A to point B, and no one sold or served them food. Exercise was part of their daily survival routine of roaming and rummaging for fruit, nuts, and vegetables, as well as running after and tracking down animals for meat to eat. Just as eating natural (unprocessed) food is better for your health because it's long been part of human history and has

"If exercise could be packaged into a pill, it would be the single most widely prescribed and beneficial medicine in the nation."

—Robert N. Butler, former director of the National Institute of Aging

contributed to the survival of the human species, so too is exercise a "natural" health-promoting activity that has contributed to the survival of our species (Booth & Vyas, 2001). If done regularly, exercise may well be the most effective "medicine" available to humans for preventing disease and preserving lifelong health.

Author's Experience   I kept in shape when I was young by playing sports such as basketball and baseball. Every time my schedule would allow it, I'd play these sports for hours at a time. I enjoyed it so much that I didn't even realize I was exercising. My body fat was practically nonexistent, energy was ever flowing, and my skills in basketball were always growing. Age has caught up with me, and I can no longer play these sports. At this point in my life, I attempt to remain active through regularly scheduled workouts to keep my body fat in a reasonable double-digit category. This takes good scheduling, forethought, and strong will.

— Aaron Thompson

Benefits of Exercise for the Body

1. **Exercise promotes cardiovascular health.** Exercise makes for a healthy heart. The heart is a muscle, and like any other muscle in the body, its size and strength are increased by exercise. A bigger and stronger heart pumps more blood per beat, reducing the risk for heart disease and stroke (loss of oxygen to the brain) by increasing circulation of oxygen-carrying blood throughout the body and by increasing the body's ability to dissolve blood clots (Khoshaba & Maddi, 2005).

   Exercise further reduces the risk of cardiovascular disease by decreasing the level of triglycerides (clot-forming fats) in the blood, increasing the level of "good" cholesterol (high-density lipoproteins), and preventing "bad" cholesterol (low-density lipoproteins) from sticking to and clogging up blood vessels.

2. **Exercise stimulates the immune system.** Exercise improves the functioning of the immune system, enabling you to better fight off infectious diseases (e.g., colds and the flu) for the following reasons:
   - Exercise reduces stress, which normally weakens the immune system.
   - Exercise increases breathing rate and blood flow throughout the body, which helps flush out germs from your system by increasing the circulation of antibodies carried through the bloodstream.
   - Exercise increases body temperature, which helps kill germs—similar to how a low-grade fever kills germs when you're sick.

3. **Exercise strengthens muscles and bones.** Exercise reduces muscle tension, which helps prevent muscle strain and pain. For example, strengthening abdominal muscles reduces the risk of developing lower back pain. Exercise also maintains bone density and reduces the risk of osteoporosis (brittle bones that bend and break easily). It's noteworthy that bone density before age 20 affects a person's bone density for the remainder of life. Thus, engaging in regular exercise early in life pays long-term dividends by preventing bone deterioration throughout life.

Reflection 14.6

Have your exercise habits changed (for better or worse) since you've begun college?

If yes, why do you think this change has taken place?

---

4. **Exercising promotes weight loss and weight management.** The increasing national trend toward weight gain is due not only to Americans consuming more calories but also to reduced levels of physical activity. Much of this reduction in physical activity results from the emergence of modern technological conveniences that have made it easier for humans to go about their daily business without exerting themselves in the slightest. For example, almost all TVs now come with remote controls so that you don't have to move to change channels, change volume, or turn the TV on and off. Children now have video games galore that are played virtually so that they can have fun playing without getting up, running around, or jumping up and down. Consequently, people today are playing double jeopardy with their health by eating more and moving less.

Exercise is superior to dieting in one major respect: It raises the body's rate of metabolism (i.e., the rate at which consumed calories are burned as energy rather than stored as fat). In contrast, low-calorie dieting lowers the body's rate of metabolism (Leibel, Rosenbaum, & Hirsch, 1995) and slows the rate at which calories are burned. After two to three weeks of low-calorie dieting without exercising, the body saves more of the limited calories it's getting by storing them as fat. This happens because long-term low-calorie dieting makes the body "think" it's starving; therefore, it tries to compensate and increase its chances of survival by conserving more calories as fat so that they can be used for future energy (Bennet & Gurin, 1983). In contrast, exercise speeds up basal metabolism—the body's rate of metabolism when it's resting. So, in addition to burning fat directly while exercising, exercise burns fat by continuing to keep the body's metabolic rate higher after you stop exercising and move on to do more sedentary things.

Benefits of Exercise for the Mind

In addition to the multiple benefits of exercise for the body, it has numerous benefits for the mind. What follows is a summary of the powerful benefits of physical exercise for mental health and mental performance.

1. **Exercise increases mental energy and improves mental performance.** Have you ever noticed how red your face gets when you engage in strenuous physical activity? This rosy complexion occurs because physical activity pumps enormous amounts of blood into your head region, resulting in more oxygen reaching your brain. Exercise increases the heart's ability to pump blood throughout the body, and since the brain needs more oxygen to function at peak capacity than any other part of the body, it's the bodily organ that benefits most from exercise. Moreover, aerobic exercise, i.e., exercise that increases respiratory rate and circulates oxygen throughout the body, has been found to (1) enlarge the frontal lobe, the part of the brain responsible for higher-level thinking (Colcombe et al., 2006; Kramer & Erickson, 2007), and (2) increase the production of chemicals in the brain that create neurological connections between brain cells (Howard, 2000; Ratey, 2008). As noted in Chapter 5, these are the connections that provide

Student Perspective

"I'm less active now than before college because I'm having trouble learning how to manage my time."

—First-year student

the biological basis of learning and memory. Furthermore, exercise is a stimulant—it stimulates both the mind and the body. In fact, its stimulating effects are similar to those provided by popular energy drinks (e.g., Red Bull, Full Throttle, and Monster) but without the sugar, caffeine, and negative side effects such as nervousness, irritability, increased blood pressure, and a crash (sharp drop in energy) after the stimulating effects of these drinks wear off (Malinauskas, Aeby, Overton, Carpenter-Aeby, & Barber-Heidal, 2007).

2. **Exercise elevates mood.** Exercise increases the release of endorphins (morphine-like chemicals found in the brain that produce a natural high) and serotonin (a mellowing brain chemical that reduces feelings of tension, anxiety, and depression). It is for these reasons that psychotherapists prescribe exercise for patients who are experiencing mild cases of anxiety and depression (Johnsgard, 2004). Studies show that people who exercise regularly report feeling happier (Myers, 1993).

3. **Exercise strengthens self-esteem.** Exercise can improve self-esteem by giving us a sense of personal achievement or accomplishment and by improving our physical self-image (e.g., improved weight control, body tone, and skin tone).

4. **Exercise deepens and enriches the quality of sleep.** Research on the effects of exercise on sleep indicates that exercise at least three hours before bedtime helps us fall asleep, stay asleep, and sleep more deeply (Singh, Clements, & Fiatarone, 1997). For these reasons, exercise is a common component of treatment programs for people seeking help with insomnia (Dement & Vaughan, 2000).

"It is exercise alone that supports the spirits, and keeps the mind in vigor."

—Marcus Cicero, ancient Roman orator and philosopher

Physical exercise provides benefits for the body and the mind.

Guidelines and Strategies for Maximizing the Effectiveness of Exercises

Specific types of exercises benefit the body and mind in different ways. Nevertheless, there are general guidelines and strategies that can be applied to improve the positive impact of any exercise routine or personal fitness program, such as those discussed below.

1. **Warm up before exercising and cool down after exercising.** Start with a 10-minute warm-up of low-intensity movements similar to the ones you'll be using in the actual exercise. This increases circulation of blood to the muscles that you'll be exercising and reduces muscle soreness and your risk of muscle pulls. End your exercise routine with a 10-minute cool-down, during which you stretch the muscles that were strenuously used while exercising. Stretch the muscle until it burns a little bit, and then release it. Cooling down after exercise improves circulation to the exercised muscles and enables them to return more gradually to a tension-free state, which will minimize the risk of muscle tightness, cramps, pulls, or tears.

2. **Engage in cross-training to attain total body fitness.** A balanced, comprehensive fitness program is one that involves cross-training—a combination of different exercises to achieve overall bodily fitness. For instance, you can combine exercises that promote:
   - Endurance and weight control (e.g., running, cycling, or swimming);
   - Muscle strength and tone (e.g., weight training, push-ups, or sit-ups); and
   - Flexibility (e.g., yoga, Pilates, or tai chi).

   A total fitness plan also includes exercising various muscle groups on a rotational basis (e.g., upper-body muscles one day, lower-body muscles the next). This gives different sets of muscle tissue extra time to rest, repair, and recover before they're exercised again.

3. **Exercising with regularity and consistency is as important as exercising with intensity.** Doing exercise regularly, and allowing strength and stamina to increase gradually, is the key to attaining fitness and avoiding injury. One strategy you can use to be sure that you're training your body, rather than straining or overextending it, is to see whether you can talk while you're exercising. If you can't continue speaking without having to catch your breath, you may be overdoing it. Drop the intensity level and allow your body to adapt or adjust to a less strenuous level. After continuing at this lower level awhile, try again at the higher level while trying to talk simultaneously. If you can do both, then you're ready to continue at that level for some time. By continuing to use this strategy, you can gradually increase the intensity, frequency, or duration of your exercise routine to a level that produces maximum benefits with minimal post-exercise strain or pain.

Author's Experience — I had a habit of exercising too intensely—to the point where I over-fatigued my muscles and left my body feeling sore for days after I worked out. Like many people, I exercise while listening to music to make the exercise routine more stimulating. I've since discovered that listening to music through headphones while exercising may help me determine whether I'm overdoing it. If I can't sing along with the music without having to stop and catch my breath, then I know I'm overextending myself. This strategy has helped me manage my exercise intensity level and reduce my day-after-exercise soreness. (Plus, I've gained more confidence as a singer, because my voice singing sounds a lot better to me when my ears are covered with headphones!).

Joe Cuseo

4. **Take advantage of exercise and fitness resources on your campus.** You paid for use of the campus gym or recreation center with your college tuition, so take advantage of this and other exercise resources on campus. Also, consider taking physical education courses offered by your college. They count toward your college degree, and typically they carry one unit of credit so that they can be easily added to your course schedule. If exercise-related groups or clubs meet on campus, consider joining them; they can provide motivational support and convert your exercise routine from one that's done in isolation to one done in conjunction with others. (This is also a good way to meet and form friendships with other people.)

5. **Take advantage of natural opportunities for physical activity that present themselves during the day.** Exercise can take place outside a gym or fitness center and outside scheduled workout times. Opportunities for exercise often occur naturally as you go about your daily activities. For example, if you can walk or ride your bike to class, do that instead of driving a car or riding a bus. If you can climb some stairs instead of taking an elevator, take the route that requires more bodily activity and generates the most physical exercise.

Reflection **14.7**

Do you have a regular exercise routine?

1. If not, why not?

2. If yes, what do you do and how often do you do it?

What more could you do to improve your:

1. endurance?

2. strength?

3. flexibility?

Rest and Sleep

Sleep experts agree that humans in today's information-loaded, multitasking world aren't getting the quantity and quality of sleep needed to perform at peak levels (Mitler, Dinges, & Dement, 1994).

The Value and Purpose of Sleep

Resting and reenergizing the body are the most obvious purposes of sleep (Dement & Vaughan, 1999). However, other benefits of sleep are less well known but equally important for physical and mental health (Dement & Vaughan, 2000; Horne, 1988). Some of these equally important, but less apparent benefits of sleep are described here.

1. **Sleep restores and preserves the power of the immune system.** Studies show that when humans and other animals lose sleep, it lowers their production of disease-fighting antibodies and make them more susceptible to illness, such as common colds and the flu.
2. **Sleep helps you cope with daily stress.** Sleep research shows that the amount of time people spend in dream sleep increases when they're experiencing stress. When we lose dream sleep, emotional problems such as anxiety and depression worsen (Voelker, 2004). It's thought that the biochemical changes that take place in our brain during dream sleep help to restore imbalances in brain chemistry that occur when we experience anxiety or depression. Getting quality sleep, especially dream sleep, is essential for recovering and maintaining our emotional stability and keeping us in a positive frame of mind. Indeed, research reveals that people who sleep better report feeling happier (Myers, 1993).
3. **Sleep helps the brain form and store memories.** Studies show that loss of dream sleep at night results in poorer memory for information learned earlier in the day (Peigneux, Laureys, Delbeuck, & Maquet, 2001). For instance, adolescents who get minimal sleep have more difficulty retaining new information learned in school (Horne, 1988).

The Importance of Sleep for College Students

College students, in particular, tend to have poor sleep habits and experience more sleep problems. Heavier academic workloads, more opportunities for late-night socializing, and more frequent late-night (or all-night) study sessions often lead to more irregular sleep schedules and more sleep deprivation among college students.

How much sleep do you need and should you get? The answer lies on your genes and varies from person to person. On average, adults need seven to eight hours of sleep each day and teenagers need slightly more—about nine hours (Roffwarg,

Muzio, & Dement, 1966). Research shows that college students get an average of less than seven hours of sleep each night (Hicks, as cited in Zimbardo, Johnson, & Weber, 2006); this means that they're not getting the amount of sleep needed for optimal academic performance.

Attempting to train your body to sleep less is likely to be an exercise in futility because you're trying to force your body to do something that it's not naturally (genetically) inclined or "wired up" to do. When your body is deprived of the amount of sleep it's genetically designed to receive, it accumulates "sleep debt," which, like financial debt, must be eventually paid back at a later time (Dement & Vaughan, 1999). If your sleep debt isn't repaid, it catches up with you and you pay the price with lower energy, lower mood, poorer health, and poorer performance (Van Dongen, Maislin, Mullington, & Dinges, 2003). For example, studies show that the effects of sleep loss on automobile-driving performance are similar to the effects of drinking alcohol (Arnedt, Wilde, Munt, & MacLean, 2001; Fletcher, Lamond, Van Den Heuvel, & Dawson, 2003), and sleep-deprived students' academic performance is poorer than that of students who get sufficient sleep (Spinweber, as cited in Zimbardo et al., 2006).

Student Perspective

"I'm not getting enough sleep. I've been getting roughly 6–7 hours of sleep on weekdays. In high school, I would get 8–9 hours of sleep."

—First-year student

Student Perspective

"First of all, you should probably know that your body will not function without sleep. I learned that the hard way."

—Words written by a first-year student in a letter of advice to incoming college students

14.1   DO IT NOW!

Adjusting Your Academic Work to Your Biological Rhythms

Attaining peak performance in colleges required attention to and integration of two types of self-management: time management and energy management. Listed below are strategies for connecting both these forms of self-management to maximize your academic performance.

- When planning your daily work schedule, be aware of your "biological rhythms"—i.e., your natural *peak periods* and *down times*. Studies show that humans vary in terms of when they naturally prefer to fall asleep and wake up; some are "early birds" who prefer to go to sleep early and wake up early, and others are "night owls" who prefer to stay up late at night and get up late in the morning. (Teenagers more often fall into the category of night owls.) As a result of these differences in sleeping patterns, individuals will vary with respect to the times of day when they experience their highest and lowest levels of physical energy. Naturally, early birds are more likely to be "morning people" whose peak energy period occurs before noon; night owls are likely to be more productive in the late afternoon and evening. Most people, whether they are night owls or early birds, tend to experience a post-lunch dip in energy in the early afternoon (Monk, 2005).

- Become aware of your most productive hours of the day and schedule your highest-priority work and most challenging tasks at times when you tend to work at peak effectiveness. For example, schedule your out-of-class work so that you're tackling academic tasks that require intense thinking (e.g., technical writing or complex problem solving) at times of the day when you tend to be most productive, and schedule lighter work (e.g., light reading or routine tasks) at times when your energy level tends to be lower. Also, keep your natural peak and down times in mind when you schedule your courses. Try to arrange your class schedule in such a way that you experience your most challenging courses at times of the day when your body and mind are most ready to accept that challenge.

Strategies for Improving Sleep Quality

Since sleep has powerful benefits for both the body and the mind, if you can improve the quality of your sleep, you can improve your physical and mental well-being. Listed here is a series of strategies for improving sleep quality that should also improve your health and performance.

Reflection **14.8**

How much sleep per night do you think you need to perform at peak level?

How many nights per week do you typically get this amount of sleep?

If you're not getting this optimal amount of sleep each night, what's preventing you from getting it?

---

1. **Increase awareness of your sleep habits by keeping a sleep log or sleep journal.** Make note of what you did what you before going to bed on night when you slept well or poorly. Tracking your sleep experiences in a journal may enable you to detect patterns that reveal relationships between certain things you do (or don't do) during the day on those nights you sleep well. If you find such a pattern, you may have found yourself a routine you can follow to ensure that you consistently get a good night's sleep.

2. **Try to get into a regular sleep schedule by going to sleep and getting up at about the same times each day.** Irregular sleep schedules can disrupt the quality of sleep. This is what happens to people who experience jet lag. Traveling to a new time zone often requires travelers to change their sleep schedule to accommodate the time shift, which can disrupt the quality of their sleep. Your body likes to work on a biological rhythm of set cycles; if you can get your body on a regular sleep schedule, you're more likely to establish a biological rhythm that makes it easier for you to fall asleep, stay asleep, and wake up naturally from sleep according to your internal alarm clock.

   Establishing a stable sleep schedule is particularly important around midterms and finals. Unfortunately, these are the times during the term when students often disrupt their normal sleep patterns by cramming in last-minute studying, staying up later, getting up earlier, or not going to sleep at all. Sleep research shows that if you want to be at your physical and mental best for upcoming exams, you should get yourself on a regular sleep schedule of going to bed at about the same time and getting up at about the same time for at least one week before your exams (Dement & Vaughan, 1999).

3. **Attempt to get into a relaxing bedtime ritual each night.** Taking a hot bath or shower, consuming a hot (non-caffeinated) beverage, or listening to relaxing music are bedtime rituals that can get you into a worry-free state and help you fall asleep sooner. Making a list of things you intend to do the next day before going to bed may help you relax and fall asleep because you can go bed with the peace of mind that comes from being organized and ready to handle the following day's tasks.

   Light reading or reviewing notes at bedtime might also be a good ritual to adopt because sleep helps you retain what you experienced just before going to sleep. Many years of studies show that the best thing you can do after attempting

Student *Perspective*

"I 'binge' sleep. I don't sleep often and then I hibernate for like a day or two."

—First-year student

Student *Perspective*

"Something I noticed when playing guitar: I would play a song better the first time I tried to in the morning than the last time I played it before I went to bed. This made me think that my brain must be strengthening what I'd been learning while I was asleep."

—College sophomore

to learn something is to sleep on it, probably because your brain can then focus on processing it without interference from outside distractions (Jenkins & Dallenbach, 1924).

Reflection 14.9

What do you do on most nights immediately before going to bed? Do you think this helps or hinders the quality of your sleep?

4. **Make sure the temperature of your sleep room is not too warm (no higher than 70 degrees Fahrenheit).** Warm temperatures often make people feel sleepy, but they usually don't help them stay asleep or sleep deeply. This is why people have trouble sleeping on hot summer evenings. High-quality, uninterrupted sleep is more likely to take place at cooler, more comfortable room temperatures (Coates, 1977).

5. **Avoid intense mental activity just before going to sleep.** Light mental work may serve as a relaxing pre-sleep ritual, but cramming intensely for a difficult exam or doing intensive writing before bedtime is likely to generate a state of mental arousal, which can interfere with your ability to wind down and fall asleep.

6. **Avoid intense physical exercise before going to sleep.** Physical exercise generates an increase in muscle tension and mental energy (by increasing oxygen flow to the brain), which energizes you and keeps you from falling asleep. If you're going to exercise in the evening, it should be done at least three hours before bedtime (Hauri & Linde, 1996).

7. **Avoid consuming sleep-interfering foods, beverages, or drugs in the late afternoon or evening.** In particular, avoid the following substances near bedtime:
   - **Caffeine.** It works as a stimulant drug for most people, so it's likely to stimulate your nervous system and keep you awake.
   - **Nicotine.** This is a stimulant drug that's also likely to reduce the depth and quality of your sleep. (Note: Smoking hookah through a water pipe delivers the same amount of nicotine as a cigarette.)
   - **Alcohol.** It's a drug that will make you feel sleepy in larger doses, but smaller doses can have a stimulating effect. Furthermore, alcohol in all doses disrupts the quality of sleep by reducing the amount of time you spend in dream-stage sleep. (Marijuana does the same.)
   - **High-fat foods.** Eating anything right before bedtime isn't a good idea because the internal activity your body engages in to digest the food is likely to interfere with the quality of your sleep, but particularly peanuts, beans, fruits, raw vegetables, and high-fat snacks should be avoided because your stomach has to work hard to digest them; this extra internal and combustion (and noise) can interrupt or disrupt your sleep.

Remember

Substances that make you feel sleepy or cause you to fall asleep (e.g., alcohol and marijuana) reduce the overall quality of your sleep by interfering with dream sleep.

Wellness is built on a balanced foundation of nutrition, exercise, and rest.

Alcohol, Drugs, and Risky Behavior

In addition to putting healthy nutrients into your body, exercising it, and resting it, two other elements can help you maintain physical wellness: (1) keeping risky substances out of your body and (2) keeping away from risky behaviors that jeopardize your body. New college students are often confronted with new choices to make about what risks to take, or not to take, during their first year of college.

Alcohol Use among College Students

In the United States, alcohol is a legal beverage (drug) for people 21 years of age and older. However, whether you're of legal age or not, it's likely that alcohol has already been available to you and will continue to be available to you when you're in college. Since it's a substance commonly accessible at college parties and social gatherings, you'll be confronted with two sets of decisions about alcohol:

1. To drink or not to drink
2. To drink responsibly or irresponsibly

   If you decide to drink, here are some quick tips for drinking responsibly:

- Don't drink with the intention of getting drunk; set a limit about how much you will drink. (Use alcohol as a beverage, not as a mind-altering drug.)
- Drink slowly. (Sip, don't gulp, and avoid "shotgunning" or "chug-a-lugging" drinks.)
- Space out your drinks over time. (This gives your body time to metabolize the alcohol and keeps your blood alcohol level manageable.)
- Eat well before you drink and snack while you're drinking. (This will lower the peak blood alcohol level in your bloodstream.)

Naturally, the best way to avoid irresponsible drinking is to not to drink at all. This is the safest option, particularly if your family has a history of alcohol abuse. If you choose to drink, make sure that it's *your* choice, not a choice imposed on you through social pressure or the need to conform. Research indicates that first-year college students drink more than they did in high school and that alcohol abuse is higher among first-year college students than students at more advanced stages of their college experience (Bergen-Cico, 2000). The most common reason why first-year students drink is to "fit in" or to feel socially accepted (Meilman & Presley, 2005). However, college students overestimate the number of their peers who drink and the total amount they drink; this overestimation can lead them to believe that if they don't conform to this "norm," they're not "normal" (DeJong & Linkenback, 1999). Student beliefs that college partying and college drinking go hand in hand may also be exaggerated by media portrayals of college students as wild party animals. Popular magazines rank the "top party schools," television programs and movies depict female college students who've "gone wild," and popular movies have been made whose entire plots revolve around the drunken escapades of college students (*Animal House, Spring Break I, II*, etc.).

College students' expectations that they should drink (and drink to excess) account, at least in part, for the fact that the number one drug problem on college campuses is *binge drinking*—periodic drinking episodes during which a large amount of alcohol (four or five drinks) is consumed in a short period of time, resulting in an acute state of intoxication—i.e., a drunken state (Marczinski, Estee, & Grant, 2009). Although alcohol is a legal substance (if you're 21 or older) and it's consumed as a beverage rather than injected, smoked, or snorted, alcohol is still a mind-altering substance when consumed in large quantities (doses). Just as THC is the mind-altering ingredient in marijuana, ethyl alcohol is the mind-altering ingredient in beer, wine, and hard liquor (see **Figure 14.4**).

Also, like any other drug, alcohol abuse is a form of drug abuse. Approximately 7 to 8 percent of people who drink develop alcohol addiction or dependency, i.e., alcoholism (Julien, 2004).

Although binge drinking may not be alcoholism, it's still a form of alcohol abuse because it has direct, negative effects on the drinker's:

- Behavior—e.g., drunk driving accidents and deaths,
- Body—e.g., acute alcohol withdrawal syndrome, better known as a hangover, and
- Mind—e.g., memory loss ("blackouts").

Research indicates that repeatedly getting drunk can reduce the size and effectiveness of the part of the brain involved with memory formation (Brown, Tapert, Granholm, & Delis, 2000), which has led some researchers to the conclusion that the more often a person gets drunk, the dumber that person gets (Weschsler & Wuethrich, 2002).

Furthermore, binge drinking can have indirect negative effects on health and safety by reducing the drinker's inhibitions about engaging in risk-taking behavior, which, in turn, increases the risk of personal accidents, injuries, and illnesses. Arguably, no other drug reduces a person's inhibitions as dramatically as alcohol. After consuming a significant amount of alcohol, people can become much less cautious about doing things they normally wouldn't do. This chemically induced sense of courage (sometimes referred to as "liquid courage") can override the process of logical thinking and decision making, increasing the drinker's willingness to engage in irrational risk-taking behavior. Typically, binge drinkers become less inhibited about engaging in reckless driving, increasing the risk of accidental injury or death, and

"Drunken State University"

—Logo once appearing on T-shirts sold at a state university

FIGURE 14.4

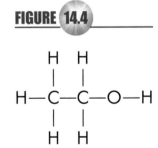

Ethyl Alcohol: The Mind-Altering Ingredient Contained in Alcohol

"If you drink, don't park. Accidents cause people."

—Steven Wright, American comedian

less cautious about engaging in reckless (unprotected) sex, increasing the risk of accidental pregnancy or contracting sexually transmitted infections (STIs). It could be said that binge drinkers think they've become invincible, immortal, and infertile.

Motor vehicle accidents are the leading cause of death of Americans between the ages of 16 and 19 (Center for Disease Control and Prevention, 2012). When teenagers gain independence and acquire their first taste of new freedoms, they often take the new found freedom beyond moderation and push it to the outer limits—for example, driving as fast as they can and drinking as much as they can—perhaps to prove to themselves and others how much freedom they now have. It's as if the more risks they take with their new freedom, the more of it they think they have. In the case of freedom to drink and freedom to drive, they can be a dangerous (or deadly) combination. It's noteworthy that the legal age for consuming alcohol was once lowered to 18 years; it was raised back to 21 because the number of drunk-driving accidents and deaths among teenage drinkers increased dramatically when the legal age was lowered (Mothers Against Drunk Driving, 2012).

Since alcohol is a depressant drug, it depresses (slows) the nervous system. This can increase the probability of aggressive and sexual behavior by slowing signals normally sent from the upper, front part of the brain (the "human brain") that's responsible for rational thinking and inhibits or controls the lower, middle part of the brain (the "animal brain") that is responsible for basic animal drives, such as sex and aggression (see **Figure 14.5**). When the upper (rational) brain's messages are slowed by alcohol, the animal brain is freed from the signals that normally restrain or inhibit it, allowing its basic drives to be released or expressed. Thus, the less inhibited drinker is more likely to engage in aggressive or sexual behavior.

Reflection 14.10

During the Prohibition years (1920–1933), laws were passed in America that made alcohol illegal for anyone to consume at any age.

Why do you think prohibition laws were passed?

Why do you think alcohol still continued to be produced illegally during the Prohibition era (as bootleg liquor) and prohibition laws were eventually eliminated?

FIGURE 14.5

Alcohol slows down or suppresses signals sent from out upper "human" brain that normally control or inhibit the lower "animal" brain.

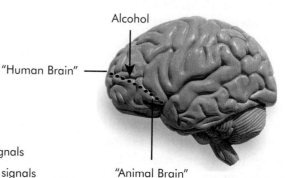

"Human Brain"

Alcohol

"Animal Brain"

•••••• = controlling (inhibiting) signals

↓ = slows down (suppresses) signals

Brain image modified © David Huntley, 2013. Under license from Shutterstock, Inc.

How Alcohol Works in the Brain to Reduce Personal Inhibitions

The Connection between Alcohol and Aggressive Behaviors

This is the underlying biological reason why excessive alcohol use increases the risk of aggressive behaviors, such as those discussed in Chapter 9: fighting, damaging property, sexual harassment, assault, and abuse (Abbey, 2002; Bushman & Cooper, 1990). See Snapshot Summary 9.2 in Chapter 9 for a summary of sexually aggressive behaviors, all of which are more likely to occur when a person is under the influence of alcohol.

Illegal Drugs

In addition to alcohol, other substances are likely to be encountered on college campuses that are illegal for anyone to use at any age. Among the most commonly used illegal drugs are the following:

- **Marijuana (weed, pot).** Primarily a depressant or sedative drug that slows the nervous system and produces a mellow feeling of relaxation
- **Ecstasy (X).** A stimulant typically taken in pill form that speeds up the nervous system and reduces social inhibitions
- **Cocaine (coke, crack).** A stimulant that's typically snorted or smoked and produces a strong rush of euphoria
- **Amphetamines (speed, meth).** A strong stimulant that increases energy and general arousal; it is usually taken in pill form but may also be smoked or injected
- **Hallucinogens (psychedelics).** Drugs that alter or distort perception and are typically swallowed—e.g., LSD or acid and hallucinogenic mushrooms ("shrooms")
- **Narcotics (e.g., heroin and prescription pain pills).** Depressant or sedative drugs that slow the nervous system and produce feelings of relaxation (heroin is a particularly powerful narcotic that can be either be injected or smoked and produces an intense rush of euphoria)

All of these drugs are potentially habit-forming, especially if they're injected intravenously (directly into a vein) or smoked (inhaled through the lungs). These routes of drug delivery are particularly dangerous because they allow the drug to reach the brain faster and with more intense impact, resulting in the drug's effect being experienced more rapidly and at a higher peak effect. However, this is followed by a rapid and sharp drop (crash) after the drug's peak effect has been experienced (see **Figure 14.6**). This peak-to-valley, roller-coaster effect creates a greater risk for

 FIGURE 14.6

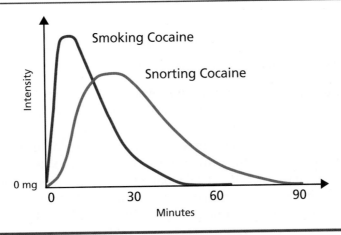

Drugs Smoked Produce a Higher and More Rapid Peak Effect

craving and desire to use the drug again, thereby increasing the user's risk of dependency (addiction).

When a drug is smoked (or injected), it reaches the brain faster and produces a higher peak effect, followed by a sharper drop or "crash," which increases the risk of addiction.

Listed here are common signs that use of any drug (including alcohol) is moving in the direction of *dependency* (*addiction*):

- Steadily using more of the drug and/or using it more often
- Difficulty cutting back (e.g., unable to use the drug less frequently or in smaller amounts)
- Difficulty controlling or limiting the amount taken after starting
- Keeping a steady supply of the drug on hand
- Spending more on the drug than you can afford
- Using the drug alone
- Hiding or hoarding the drug
- Lying about your drug use to family and friends
- Reacting angrily or defensively when questioned about drug use
- Being in denial about abusing the drug (e.g., "I don't have a problem")
- Rationalizing drug abuse (e.g., "It's no big deal; it's just part of the college experience")
- Continuing to use the drug matters more to you than the personal and interpersonal problems caused by its use

Addiction is one major motive for repeated use of any drug. However, there are other motives underlying the desire to do drugs. A summary of the major motives for drug use is provided in **Snapshot Summary 14.2.**

Reflection 14.11

What drugs (if any) have you seen being used on your campus?

How would the types and frequency of drug use on your campus compare to what you saw in high school?

What motives for drug use listed in Snapshot Summary 14.2 would you say are the most common reasons for drug use on your campus?

Strategies for Minimizing or Eliminating the Negative Effects of Alcohol and Other Drugs

1. **Don't let yourself be pressured into drinking.** Keep in mind that college students tend to overestimate how much their peers drink, so don't feel you're uncool, unusual, or abnormal if you prefer not to drink.
2. **If you drink, maintain awareness of how much you're drinking while you're drinking by monitoring your physical and mental state.** Don't continue to drink after you've reached a state of moderate relaxation or a mild loss of inhibition. Drinking to the point where you're drunk or bordering on intoxication doesn't improve your physical health or your social life. You're not exactly the life

Snapshot Summary

14.2 Drug Use among College Students: Common Causes and Major Motives

1. **Social pressure.** To fit in or be socially accepted (e.g., smoking marijuana because lots of college students seem to be doing it)
2. **Recreational (party) use.** For fun, stimulation, or pleasure (e.g., drinking alcohol at parties to loosen inhibitions and to have a good time)
3. **Experimental use.** Doing drugs out of curiosity—to test out their effects (e.g., experimenting with LSD to see what it's like to have a psychedelic or hallucinogenic experience)
4. **Therapeutic use.** Using prescription or over-the-counter drugs for medical purposes (e.g., taking Prozac for depression or Ritalin to treat attention deficit disorder)

5. **Performance enhancement.** To improve physical or mental performance (e.g., taking steroids to improve athletic performance or stimulants to stay awake all night and cram for an exam)
6. **Escapism.** To temporarily escape a personal problem or an unpleasant emotional state (e.g., taking ecstasy to escape depression or boredom)
7. **Addiction.** Physical or psychological dependence resulting from habitual use of a drug (e.g., continuing to use nicotine or cocaine because stopping will result in withdrawal symptoms such as anxiety or depression).

Student
Perspective

"For fun." "To party." "To fit in." "To become more talkative, outgoing, and flirtatious."

"To try anything once." "To become numb." "To forget problems." "Being bored."

—Responses of freshmen and sophomores to the question "Why do college students take drugs?"

of the party if you're slurring your speech, vomiting in the restroom, nodding out, or on the verge of falling sound asleep.

The key to drinking responsibly and in moderation is to have a plan for managing your drinking. Your plan should include strategies such as:

- Drinking slowly
- Eating while drinking
- Alternating between drinking alcoholic and nonalcoholic beverages
- Tapering off your drinking after the first hour of a party or social gathering (Vogler & Bartz, 1992).

Lastly, don't forget that alcohol is costly, both in money and in calories. Thus, reducing or eliminating your drinking is not only a good way to manage your health, but also a good money-management and weight-management strategy.

3. **If you're a woman who drinks, or who frequents places where others drink, remain aware of the possibility of date-rape drugs being dropped into your drink.** Drugs such as gamma-hydroxybutyric acid (a.k.a. GHB or G) and Rohypnol (a.k.a. roofies or roaches) induce sleep and memory loss, and their effects are particularly powerful when taken with alcohol. To guard against this risk, don't

There are safer and more productive ways to blow your mind than using mind-altering substances.

Don't Blow It on Drugs

let others give you drinks, and hold onto your drink at all times (e.g., don't leave it, go to the restroom, and come back to drink it again).

4. **If you find yourself in a situation where an illegal drug is available to you, our bottom-line recommendation is this: If you're in doubt, keep it out—don't put anything into your body that you're unsure about.** We acknowledge that the college years are a time for exploring and experimenting with different ideas, experiences, feelings, and states of consciousness. However, doing illegal drugs just isn't worth the risk. Even if you're aware of how an illegal drug affects people in general, you don't know how it will affect you in particular, because each individual has a unique genetic makeup. Furthermore, unlike legal drugs that have to pass through rigorous testing by the Food and Drug Administration before they're approved for public consumption, you can't be sure how an illegal drug has been produced and packaged from one time to the next, and you don't know if it may have been "cut" (mixed) with other substances during the production process. Thus, you're not just taking a criminal risk by using a drug that's illegal: you're also taking a health risk by consuming an unregulated substance whose effects on your body and mind are likely to be more unpredictable and potentially detrimental.

Minimize Your Risk of Contracting Sexually Transmitted Infections (STIs)

STIs are a group of contagious infections that are spread through sexual contact. Latex condoms provide the best protection against STIs (Holmes, Levine, & Weaver, 2004). You can also reduce your risk of contracting an STI by having sex with fewer partners. Naturally, not engaging in sexual intercourse is the most foolproof way to eliminate the risk of an STI (and unwanted pregnancy). When it comes to sexual intercourse, you've got three basic options: do it recklessly, do it safely, or just don't do it. If you choose the last option (abstinence), it doesn't mean you're an unaffectionate prude. It simply means that you're electing not to have sexual intercourse at this particular time in your life.

More than 25 types of STIs have been identified, and virtually all of them are effectively treated if detected early. However, if they're ignored, some STIs can progress to the point where they result in infection and possibly infertility (Cates, Herndon, Schulz, & Darroch, 2004). Pain during or after urination or unusual discharge from the penis or vaginal areas are often the early signs of an STI. However, sometimes the symptoms can be subtle and undetectable; if you have any doubt, play it safe and check it out immediately by visiting the Health Center on your campus. Any advice or treatment you receive there will remain confidential. If you happen to contract a form of STI, immediately inform anyone you've had sex with, so that he or she may receive early treatment before the disease progresses. This isn't just the polite thing to do: it's the right (ethical) thing to do.

Summary and Conclusion

Research findings and advice from professionals indicate that physical wellness is most effectively promoted if we adopt the following strategies with respect to our bodies:

- **Pay more attention to nutrition.** In particular, we should increase consumption of natural fruits, vegetables, legumes, whole grains, fish, and water and decrease consumption of processed, fatty, and fried foods. Although the expression "you are what you eat" may be a bit of an exaggeration, it contains a kernel of truth because the food we consume does influence our health, our emotions, and our performance.
- **Become more physically active.** To counteract the sedentary lifestyle created by life in modern society and to attain total fitness, we should engage in a balanced blend of exercises that build stamina, strength, and flexibility.
- **Don't cheat on sleep.** Humans typically do not get enough sleep to perform at their highest levels. College students, in particular, need to get more sleep and develop more regular (consistent) sleeping habits.
- **Drink alcohol responsibly or not at all.** We should avoid excessive consumption of alcohol or other mind-altering substances that can threaten our physical health, impair our mental judgment, and increase our tendency to engage in dangerous, risk-taking behavior.
- **Minimize the risk of contracting sexually transmitted infections.** College students have basically three options for doing so: using latex condoms during sex, limiting the number of sexual partners they have, or choosing not to be sexually active.

In the introduction to this book, research was cited about the advantages of the college experience and college degree. Among the many benefits experienced by college graduates are health and wellness benefits: they live healthier, longer lives. This suggests that students manage to learn something about physical wellness and how to promote it by the time they graduate from college. The strategies discussed in this chapter can be implemented immediately to promote optimal health and peak performance throughout your college experience and beyond.

Learning More through the World Wide Web

Internet-Based Resources for Further Information on Health and Wellness

For additional information related to the ideas discussed in this chapter, we recommend the following Web sites:

Nutrition:

www.eatright.org

Fitness:

www.fitness.gov/resource-center/

Sleep:

www.sleepfoundation.org

Alcohol and Drugs:

www.nida.nih.gov

Sexual Harassment, Assault, and Abuse

www.princeton.edu/uhs/healthy-living/hot-topics/sexual-harassment-assault

14.1 Wellness Self-Assessment and Self-Improvement

For each aspect of wellness listed here, rate yourself in terms of how close you are to doing what you should be doing.

	Nowhere Close to What I Should Be Doing	Not Bad but Should Be Better	Right Where I Should Be
Nutrition			
Exercise			
Sleep			
Alcohol and Drugs			

For each area where there's a gap between where you are now and where you should be, identify the best action you could take to reduce or eliminate this gap.

14.2 Nutritional Self-Assessment and Self-Improvement

1. Go to p. 358 and review the MyPlate chart in Figure 14.3.

2. For each of the five food groups listed below, record the amount recommended for you to consume daily, and next to it, estimate the amount you consume on a daily basis.

Basic Food Type	Amount Recommended	Amount Consumed
Fruits		
Vegetables		
Grains		
Protein Foods		
Dairy		

3. For any food group for which you're consuming less than the recommended amounts, click on that group at www.choosemyplate.gov/food-groups/ and find foods you would be willing to consume to meet the recommended daily amount. Write down those items, and answer the following questions about each of them:

   a. How likely is it that you'll actually add this food item to your regular diet?

   very likely   possibly   very unlikely

   b. If you did not answer "very likely," what would prevent you from adding this food item to your regular diet?

Drinking to Death: College Partying Gone Wild

At least 50 college students nationwide die each year as a result of drinking incidents on or near campus. During a one-month period in fall 1997, three college students died as a result of binge drinking at college parties. One was an 18-year-old first-year student at a private university who collapsed after drinking a mixture of beer and rum, fell into a coma at his fraternity house, and died three days later. He had a blood-alcohol level of more than .40, which is about equal to gulping down 20 shots of liquor in one hour.

The second incident involved a student from a public university in the South who died of alcohol poisoning (overdose). The third student died at another public university in the Northeast United States where, after an evening of partying and heavy drinking, he accidentally fell off a building in the middle of the night and fell through the roof of a greenhouse. Some colleges in the Northeast now have student volunteers roaming the campus on cold winter nights to make sure that no students freeze to death after passing out from an intense bout of binge drinking.

Listed below are some strategies that have been suggested by politicians to stop or reduce the problem of dangerous binge drinking:

1. A state governor announced that he was going to launch a series of radio ads designed to discourage underage drinking.

2. A senator filed bills to toughen penalties for those who violate underage drinking laws, such as producing and using fake identification cards.

3. A group of city council members was going to look into stiffening penalties for liquor stores that deliver directly to fraternity houses.

Source: Los Angeles Times (1997; 2000).

Reflection and Discussion Questions

1. Rank the effectiveness of these three strategies for stopping or reducing the problem of binge drinking mentioned in the last paragraph (1 = the most effective strategy, 3 = the least effective).

2. Comparing your highest-ranked and lowest-ranked choices:

    a. Why did you rank the first one as most effective?

    b. Why did you rank the last one as least effective?

3. What other strategies do you think would be effective for stopping or reducing dangerous binge drinking among college students?

Glossary

Ability (Aptitude): the capacity to do something well or to have the potential to do it well.

Academic Advisor: a professional who advises college students on course selection, helps students understand college procedures, and helps guide their academic progress toward completion of a college degree.

Academic Dismissal: denying a student to continue enrollment at a college because of a cumulative GPA that is below a minimum standard (e.g., below 2.0).

Academic Probation: a period of time (usually one term) during which students with a GPA that is too low (e.g., less than 2.0) are given a chance to improve their grades; if the student's GPA does not meet or exceed the college's minimum requirement after this probationary period, they may be academically dismissed from the college.

Academic Support Center: place on campus where students can obtain individual assistance from professionals and trained peers to support and strengthen their academic performance.

Active Involvement: the amount of personal *time* you devote to learning in the college experience and the degree of personal *effort* or *energy* (mental and physical) you put into the learning process.

Administrators: college personnel whose primary responsibility is the governance of the college or a unit within the college, such as an academic department or student support service.

Career: the sum total of vocational experiences throughout an individual's work life.

Career Advancement: working up the career ladder to higher levels of decision-making responsibility and socioeconomic status.

Career Development Center: key campus resource for learning about the nature of different careers and for strategies on how to locate career-related work experiences.

Career Development Courses: college courses that typically include self-assessment of career interests, information about different careers, and strategies for career preparation.

Career Entry: gaining entry into a career and beginning a career path.

Citation: an acknowledgment of the source of any piece of information included in a written paper or oral report that doesn't represent the writer's original work.

Co-curricular Experiences: student learning and development from experiences that take place outside the classroom.

Collaboration: the process of two or more people working interdependently toward a common goal that involves true teamwork, whereby teammates support each other's success and take equal responsibility for helping the team move toward its shared goal.

Communication Skills: skills necessary for accurate comprehension and articulate expression of ideas, which include reading, writing, speaking, listening, and multimedia skills.

Commuter Students: college students who do not live on campus.

Concentration: a cluster of approximately three courses in the same subject area.

Concept: a larger system or network of related ideas.

Concept (Idea) Map: a visual diagram that represents or maps out main categories of ideas and depicts their relationships in a visual-spatial format.

Cooperative Education (Co-op) Programs: programs in which students gain work experience relating to their college major, either by stopping their course work temporarily to work full-time at the co-op position, or by continuing to take classes while working part-time at the co-op position.

Core Courses: courses required of all students, regardless of their particular major.

Cover (Application) Letter: letter written by an applicant who is applying for an employment position or admission to a school.

Cramming: packing study time into one study session immediately before an exam.

Creative Thinking: a form of higher-level thinking skill that involves producing a unique idea, method, strategy, or work product.

Critical Thinking: a form of higher-level thinking that involves making well-informed evaluations or judgments.

Cultural Competence: the ability to appreciate and capitalize on human differences by interacting effectively with people from diverse cultural backgrounds.

Culture: a distinctive pattern of beliefs and values learned by a group of people who share the same social heritage and traditions.

Cum Laude: graduating "with honors" (e.g., achieving a cumulative GPA of 3.3).

Cumulative GPA: a student's grade point average for all academic terms combined.

Curriculum: the total set of courses offered by a college or university.

Dean's List: achieving an outstanding GPA for a particular term (e.g., 3.5 or higher).

Diversity: interacting with and learning from others who have varied backgrounds and lifestyles.

Diversity Appreciation: valuing the experiences of different groups of people and interest in learning more about them.

Diversity (Multicultural) Courses: courses designed to promote diversity awareness and appreciation of multiple cultures.

Documentation: sources of information that serve as references to support or reinforce conclusions in a written paper or oral presentation.

Electives: courses that students are not required to take, but which they elect or choose to take.

Ethnic Group (Ethnicity): a group of people who share the same culture.

Experiential Learning: out-of-class experiences that promote learning and development.

Faculty: a collection of instructors on campus whose primary role is to teach courses in the college curriculum.

Free Electives: courses that students may elect to enroll in, which count toward your college degree, but are not required for general education or an academic major.

Freshman Fifteen: a phrase commonly used to describe the 15-pound weight gain that some students experience during their first year of college.

Grade Points: number of points earned for a course, which is calculated by multiplying the course grade multiplied by the number of credits carried by the course.

Grade Point Average (GPA): translation of students' letter grades into a numeric system, whereby the total number of grade points earned in all courses is divided by total number of course units.

Graduate School: education pursued after completing a four-year bachelor's degree.

Grant: money received that does not have to be repaid.

Higher-Level Thinking: thinking at a higher or more complex level than merely acquiring factual knowledge or memorizing information.

Holistic (Whole Person) Development: development of the total self, which includes intellectual, social, emotional, physical, spiritual, ethical, vocational, and personal development.

Human Diversity: the variety of differences that exist among people who comprise the human species.

Humanity: common elements of the human experience shared by all human beings.

Hypothesis: an informed guess that might be true, but still needs to be tested to confirm or verify its truth.

Illustrate: to provide concrete examples or specific instances.

Independent Study: a project in which a student receives academic credit for in-depth study of a topic of his or her choice by working independently with a faculty member, rather than enrolling in a classroom-based course.

Information Interview: an interview with a professional currently working in a career to obtain inside information on what the career is really like.

Information Literacy: the ability to access, retrieve, and evaluate information.

Intellectual (Cognitive) Development: acquiring knowledge, learning how to learn, and learning how to think deeply.

Interdisciplinary: courses or programs that are designed to help students integrate knowledge from two or more academic disciplines (fields of study).

International Student: a student attending college in one nation who is a citizen of another nation.

International Study (Study Abroad) Program: completing coursework at a college or university in another country for one or two terms.

Internship: work experience related to a college major for which students receive academic credit and, in some cases, financial compensation.

Interpret: to draw a conclusion about something, and support that conclusion with evidence.

Job Shadowing: a program that allows a student to follow (shadow) and observe a professional during a typical workday.

Justify: to back up one's arguments and viewpoints with evidence.

Leadership: ability to influence people in a positive way (e.g., motivating your peers to do their best) or to produce positive change in an organization or institution (e.g., improving the quality of a school, business, or a political organization).

Leadership Course: course in which students learn how to advance and eventually assume important leadership positions in an organization.

Learning Community: a program in which the same group of students takes the same block of courses together during the same academic term.

Learning Habits: the usual approaches, methods, or techniques a student uses while attempting to learn.

Learning Style: the way in which individuals prefer to perceive information (receive or take it in), and process information (deal with it once it has been taken in).

Liberal Arts: the component of a college education that represents the essential foundation or backbone for the college curriculum, which is designed to equip students with a versatile set of skills to promote their success in any academic major or career.

Lifelong Learning Skills: skills that include learning how to learn and how to continue learning that can be used throughout the remainder of one's personal and professional life.

Magna Cum Laude: graduating with "high honors" (e.g., achieving a cumulative GPA of 3.5).

Major: the academic field students choose to specialize in while in college.

Mentor: someone who serves as a role model and personal guide to help you reach your educational or occupational goals.

Merit-Based Scholarship: money awarded on the basis of performance or achievement that does not have to be repaid.

Meta-Cognition: thinking about the process of thinking.

Midterm: the midpoint of an academic term.

Minor: a field of study that is designed to complement and strengthen a major, which usually consists of about half the number of courses required for a college major (e.g., six or seven courses for a minor).

Mnemonic Devices (Mnemonics): specific memory-improvement methods designed to prevent forgetting, which often involve such memory-improvement principles as meaning, organization, visualization, or rhythm and rhyme.

MLA Style: a style of citing references endorsed by the Modern Language Association (MLA) and commonly used by academic fields in the humanities and fine arts (e.g., English and philosophy).

Multicultural Center: place on campus designed to provide a place for interaction among and between members of diverse cultural groups.

Multicultural Competence: ability to understand cultural differences and to interact effectively with people from multiple cultural backgrounds.

Multidimensional Thinking: a form of higher-level thinking that involves taking multiple perspectives and considering multiple theories.

Multiple Intelligences: the theory that humans display intelligence or mental skills in many other forms besides their ability to perform on intellectual tests, such as the IQ or SAT.

Need: a key element of life planning that represents something stronger than an interest and makes a person's life more satisfying or fulfilling.

Need-Based Scholarship: money awarded to students on the basis of financial need that does not have to be repaid.

Netiquette: applying the principles of social etiquette and interpersonal sensitivity when communicating online.

Non-Traditional Age Student (a.k.a. Re-Entry Student): a student entering college not directly out of high school.

Online Resources: resources that can be used to search for and locate information, including online card catalogs, Internet search engines, and electronic databases.

Oral Communication Skills: ability to speak in a concise, confident, and eloquent fashion.

Oversubscribed (Impacted) Major: a major that has more students interested in it than there are openings for students to be accepted.

Paraphrase: restating or rephrasing information in your own words.

Part-to-Whole Study Method: a study strategy in which material to be learned is divided into smaller parts and studied in a series of short sessions in advance of an exam, then the day before the exam, all the previously studied parts are reviewed as a whole.

Personal Reflection: the process of deliberate and thoughtful review of what you've learned and connecting it to what you already know.

Persuasive Speech: an oral presentation intended to persuade or convince the audience to agree with a certain conclusion or position by providing supporting evidence.

Plagiarism: intentional or unintentional use of someone else's work without acknowledging it, giving the impression that it is one's own work.

Portfolio: a collection of work materials or products that illustrates an individual's skills and talents, or demonstrates educational and personal development.

Prewriting: an early stage in the writing process where the focus is on generating and organizing ideas, rather than expressing or communicating ideas to someone else.

Primary Sources: firsthand sources or original documents.

Process-of-Elimination Method: test-taking strategy for multiple-choice exams that involves "weeding out" or eliminating choices that are clearly wrong and continuing to do so until the choices are narrowed down to one answer that seems to be the best choice available.

Procrastination: the tendency to postpone making decisions or taking action until the very last moment.

Professional School: formal education pursued after a bachelor's degree in a school that prepares students for an "applied" profession (e.g., pharmacy, medicine, or law).

Prerequisite Course: a course that must be completed before students can enroll in a more advanced course.

Proofreading: editing that focuses on detecting mechanical errors relating to such things as referencing, grammar, punctuation, and spelling.

Recall Test Question: a type of test question that requires students to generate or produce the correct answer on their own, such as a short-answer question or an essay question.

Recitation (Reciting): a study strategy that involves verbally stating information to be remembered without looking at it.

Recognition Test Question: a type of test question that requires students to select or choose a correct answer from answers that are provided to them (e.g., multiple-choice, true-false, and matching questions).

Reconstruction: a process of recalling information by building back its memory part-by-part or piece-by-piece.

Reference (Referral) Letter: a letter of reference typically written by a faculty member, adviser, or employer, for students who are applying for entry into positions or schools after college, or for students applying for special academic programs, student leadership positions on campus, or part-time employment.

Reflection: a thoughtful review of what one has already done, is in the process of doing, or is planning to do.

Research Skills: ability to locate, access, retrieve, organize, and evaluate information from a variety of sources, including library and technology-based (computer) systems.

Restricted Electives: courses that students must take, but have the option of choosing from a restricted set or list of possible courses that have been specified by the college.

Resume: a written summary or outline that effectively organizes and highlights an individual's strongest qualities, personal accomplishments, skills, credentials, and awards.

Rough Draft: an early stage in the writing process whereby a first (rough) draft is created that converts the writer's major ideas into sentences without worrying about the mechanics of writing (e.g., punctuation, grammar, or spelling).

Scholarly: a criterion or standard for critically evaluating the quality of an information source; typically, a source is considered to be "scholarly" if it has been reviewed by a panel or board of impartial experts in the field before being published.

Secondary Source: a publication that relies on or responds to a primary source that has been previously published: for example, a textbook is a secondary source because it draws its information from published research studies or journal articles.

Self-Assessment: the process of reflecting on and evaluating your personal characteristics, such as your personality traits, learning habits, and personal strengths or weaknesses.

Self-Monitoring: "watching" yourself and maintaining self-awareness of what you're doing and how effectively you're doing it.

Semester (Term) GPA: GPA calculated for one semester or academic term.

Service Learning: a form of experiential learning in which students serve or help others while also acquiring skills through hands-on experience that can be used to strengthen their resumes and explore fields of work that may lead to a future career path.

Sexually Transmitted Infections (STIs): a group of contagious infections that are spread through sexual contact.

Shallow (Surface-Oriented) Learning: an approach to learning in which students spend most of their study time repeating and memorizing information in the exact form it was presented to them.

Socially Constructed Knowledge: knowledge built through interaction and dialogue with others.

Summa Cum Laude: graduating with "highest honors" (e.g., achieving a cumulative GPA of 3.8 or higher).

Syllabus: an academic document that outlines course requirements, attendance policies, grading scale, course topic outlines by date, test dates, and dates for completing reading and other assignments, as well as information about the instructor (e.g., office location and office hours), and serves as a contract between instructor and student.

Synthesis: a form of higher-level thinking that involves integrating (connecting) smaller, separate pieces of information into a more comprehensive and coherent product.

Test Anxiety: a state of emotional tension that can weaken test performance by interfering with concentration, memory, and higher-level thinking.

Test-Wise: having the ability to use the characteristics of the test question itself (such as its wording or format) to increase the probability of choosing the correct answer.

Theory: a body of conceptually related concepts and general principles that help organize, understand, and apply knowledge that has been acquired in a particular field of study.

Thesis Statement: a one- to three-sentence statement contained in the introduction to a paper that serves as a summary of the key point or main argument the writer intends to make and support with evidence in the remainder of the paper.

Transferable Skills: skills that can be transferred or applied across different subjects, careers, and life situations.

Value: what a person strongly believes in, is passionate about, and thinks should be done.

Visual Aids: charts, graphs, diagrams, or concept maps that improve learning and memory by enabling the learner to visualize information as a picture or image and connect separate pieces of information to form a meaningful whole.

Visual Memory: memory that relies on the sense of vision.

Visualization: a memory-improvement strategy that involves creating a mental image or picture of what is to be remembered or imagining it being placed at a familiar site or location.

Vocational (Occupational) Development: exploring career options, making career choices wisely, and developing skills needed for career success.

Waive: to give up a right to access information (e.g., waiving the right to see a letter of recommendation).

Wellness: a state of optimal health, peak performance, and positive well-being that results from balancing and integrating different dimensions of the "self" (body, mind, and spirit).

Work-Study Program: a federal program that supplies colleges and universities with funds to provide on-campus employment for students who are in financial need.

Written Communication Skills: ability to write in a clear, creative, and convincing manner.

Learning the Language of Higher Education

A Dictionary of College Vocabulary

Academic Affairs the unit or division of the college that deals primarily with the college curriculum, course instruction, and campus services that support academic success (e.g., library and learning center).

Academic Calendar the scheduling system used by a college or university to divide the academic year into shorter terms (e.g., semesters, trimesters, or quarters).

Academic Credits (Units) what students are credited with after completing courses that are counted toward completion of their college degree; course credit is typically counted in terms of how many hours the class meets each week (e.g., a course that meets for three hours per week counts for three credits).

Academic Standing where a student stands academically (cumulative grade point average) at a given point in their college experience (e.g., after a term or a year).

Academic Transcript a list of all courses a student has enrolled in, the grades received in those courses, and the student's grade point average.

Advanced Placement (AP) Tests tests designed to measure college-level work that are taken while a student is in high school; if the student scores high enough, then college credit is awarded in the subject area tested or the student is granted advanced placement in a college course.

American Psychological Association (APA) Style a particular style of citing references in a research report or term paper that is endorsed by the APA and is most commonly used in fields that comprise the behavioral sciences (e.g., psychology and sociology) and natural sciences (e.g., biology and chemistry).

Analysis (Analytical Thinking) a form of higher-level thinking that involves breaking down information, identifying its key parts or underlying elements, and detecting what is most important or relevant.

Associate (A.A. or A.S.) Degree a two-year college degree that represents completion of general education requirements and prepares students for transfer to a four-year college or university.

Bachelor's (Baccalaureate) Degree a degree awarded by four-year colleges and universities, which represents the completion of general education requirements plus completion of an academic specialization in a particular major.

Breadth Requirements the required general education courses that span a range of subject areas.

Certificate a credential received by students at a community college or technical college who have completed a one- or two-year vocational or occupational training program, which allows them entry into a specific occupation or career.

College Catalog (a.k.a. College Bulletin) an official publication of a college or university that identifies its mission, curriculum, and academic policies and procedures, as well as the names and educational backgrounds of the faculty members.

Combined Bachelor-Graduate Degree Program a program offered by some universities that allows students to apply for simultaneous admission to both undergraduate and graduate school in a particular field and to receive both a bachelor's degree and a graduate degree in that field after completing the combined program (e.g., a bachelor's and master's degree in physical therapy).

Counseling Services the personal counseling provided by professionals on campus that is designed to promote self-awareness and self-development in emotional and social aspects of life.

Cross-Registration a collaborative program offered by two colleges or universities that allows students who are enrolled at one institution to register for and take courses at another institution.

Dean a college or university administrator who is responsible for running a particular unit of the college.

Distance Learning enrolling in and completing courses online rather than in person.

Doctoral Degree an advanced degree obtained after completion of the bachelor's (baccalaureate) degree, which typically requires five to six years of full-time study in graduate school, including completion of a thesis or doctoral dissertation.

Double Major attaining a bachelor's degree in two majors by meeting the course requirements of both academic fields.

Drop-Add the process of changing an academic schedule by dropping courses or adding courses to a preexisting schedule; at most colleges and universities, adding and dropping courses can be done during the first week of the academic term.

Fine Arts a division of the liberal arts curriculum that focuses largely on artistic performance and appreciation of artistic expression by pursuing such questions as "What is beautiful?" and "How do humans express and appreciate aesthetic (sensory) experiences, imagination, creativity, style, grace, and elegance?"

Full-Time Student a student who typically enrolls in and completes at least 24 units per academic year.

General Education Curriculum a collection of courses designed to provide a broad rather than narrow education and develop skills needed for success in any major or career.

Graduate Record Examination (GRE) a standardized test for admission to graduate schools, which is used in a manner similar to the way that the SAT and ACT tests are used for admission to undergraduate colleges and universities.

Graduate Student a student who has completed a four-year (bachelor's) degree and is enrolled in graduate school to obtain an advanced degree (e.g., master's degree or Ph.D.).

Health Services on-campus services provided to help students who are experiencing physical illnesses or injuries and to educate students on matters relating to health and wellness.

Higher Education formal education beyond high school.

Honors Program a special program of courses and other learning experiences designed for college students who have demonstrated exceptionally high levels of academic achievement.

Humanities a division of the liberal arts curriculum that focuses on the human experience, human culture, and questions that arise in a human's life, such as "Why are we here?" "What is the meaning or purpose of our existence?" "How should we live?" "What is the good life?" and "Is there life after death?"

Impacted Major an academic major in which there are more students wishing to enter the program than there are spaces available in the program; thus, students must formally apply and qualify for admission to the major by going through a competitive screening process.

Interterm (a.k.a. January Interim or Maymester) a short academic term, typically running three to four weeks, during which students enroll in only one course that is studied intensively.

Learning Habits the usual approaches, methods, or techniques a student uses while attempting to learn.

Living-Learning Environment an on-campus student residence that is designed and organized in such a way that students' learning experiences are integrated into their living environment (e.g., study groups, tutoring, and student development workshops).

Lower-Division Courses courses taken by college students during their freshman and sophomore years.

Master's Degree a degree obtained after completion of the bachelor's (baccalaureate) degree, which typically requires two to three years of full-time study in graduate school.

Matriculation the process of initially enrolling in or registering for college. (The term is derived from the term *matricula,* a list or register of people belonging to a society or community.)

Multicultural Center a place on campus that is designed for interaction among and between members of diverse cultural groups.

Natural Sciences a division of the liberal arts curriculum that focuses on observing the physical world and explaining natural phenomena, asking such questions as "What causes physical events in the natural world?" and "How can we predict and control physical events and improve the quality of interaction between humans and the natural environment?"

Nonresident Status the status of out-of-state students who typically pay higher tuition than in-state students because they are not residents of the state in which their college is located.

Orientation an educational program designed to help students make a smooth transition to college that is delivered to students before their first academic term.

Part-Time Student a student who typically enrolls in and completes less than 24 units per academic year.

Pass-Fail (Credit-No Credit) Grading a grading option offered in some courses whereby students do not receive a letter grade (A–F) but only a grade of pass (credit) or fail (no credit).

Phi Beta Kappa a national honor society that recognizes outstanding academic achievement of students at 4-year colleges and universities.

Phi Theta Kappa a national honor society that recognizes outstanding academic achievement of students at two-year colleges.

Placement Tests tests administered to new students upon entry to a college or university designed to assess their basic academic skills (e.g., reading, writing, and mathematics) to place them in courses that are neither too advanced nor too elementary for their particular level of skill development.

Postsecondary Education formal education beyond secondary (high school) education.

Preprofessional Coursework undergraduate courses that are required or strongly recommended for gaining entry into professional school (e.g., medical school or law school).

Proficiency Tests tests given to college students before graduation that are designed to assess whether they can perform certain academic skills (e.g., writing) at a level advanced enough to qualify them for college graduation.

Quarter System a system for scheduling courses in which the academic year is divided into four quarters (fall, winter, spring, and summer terms), each of which lasts approximately 10 or 11 weeks.

Registrar's Office the campus office that maintains college transcripts and other official records associated with student coursework and academic performance.

Resident Assistant a undergraduate student (sophomore, junior, or senior) whose role is to enforce rules in student residences and help new students adjust successfully to residence hall life.

Resident Director a student development professional who is in charge of residential (dormitory) life and the person to whom resident assistants report.

Resident Status the status of in-state students who typically pay lower tuition than out-of-state students because they are residents of the state in which their college is located.

Residential Students students who live on campus or in a housing unit owned and operated by the college.

Semester System a system for scheduling courses in which the academic year is divided into two terms (fall and spring) that are approximately 15 or 16 weeks long.

Self-Regulation adjusting learning strategies in a way that best meets the specific demands of the subject being learned.

Social and Behavioral Sciences a division of the liberal arts curriculum that focuses on the observation of human behavior, individually and in groups, asking such questions as "What causes humans to behave the way they do?" and "How can we predict, control, or improve human behavior and interpersonal interaction?"

Student Activities cocurricular experiences offered outside the classroom that are designed to promote student learning and student involvement in campus life.

Student-Designed (Interdisciplinary) Major an academic program offered at some colleges and universities in which a student works with a college representative or committee to develop a major that is not officially offered by the institution.

Student Development Services (Student Affairs) the division of the college that provides student support on issues relating to social and emotional adjustment, involvement in campus life outside the classroom, and leadership development.

Student Handbook an official publication of a college or university that identifies student roles and responsibilities, violations of college rules and policies, and opportunities for student involvement in cocurricular programs, such as student clubs, campus organizations, and student leadership positions.

Summer Session courses offered during the summer between spring and fall terms that typically run for four to six weeks.

Transfer Program a two-year college program that provides general education and premajor coursework to prepare students for successful transfer to a four-year college or university.

Trimester System a system for scheduling courses in which the academic year is divided into three terms (fall, winter, and spring) that are approximately 12 or 13 weeks long.

Undeclared students who have not committed to a college major.

Undergraduate a student who is enrolled in a two- or four-year college.

University an educational institution that offers not only undergraduate degrees but graduate degrees as well.

Upper-Division Courses courses taken by college students during their junior and senior years.

Vocational-Technical Programs community college programs of study that train students for a particular occupation or trade and immediate employment after completing a two-year associate degree (e.g., Associate of Applied Science) or a one-year certificate program.

Volunteerism volunteering personal time to help others.

Withdrawal dropping a class after the drop-add deadline, which results in a student receiving a W for the course and no academic credit.

Writing Center a campus support service where students can receive assistance at any stage of the writing process, whether it be collecting and organizing ideas, composing a first draft, or proofreading a final draft.

References

Abbey, A. (2002). Alcohol-related sexual assault: A common problem among college students. *Journal of Studies on Alcohol, 14,* 118–128.

AC Nielsen Research Services. (2000). *Employer satisfaction with graduate skills.* Retrieved October 25, 2006, from http://www.dest.gov.au/ty/publications/employability_skills/final_report.pdf

Academic Integrity at Princeton. (2011). *Examples of plagiarism.* Retrieved October 21, 2011, from http://www.princeton.edu/pr/pub/integrity/

Ackerman, J. M. (1993). The promise of writing to learn. *Written Communication, 10*(3), 334–370.

Acredolo, C., & O'Connor, J. (1991). On the difficulty of detecting cognitive uncertainty. *Human Development, 34,* 204–223.

Agus, M. S., Swain, J. F., Larson, C. L., Eckert, E. A., & Ludwig, D. S. (2000). Dietary composition and physiologic adaptations to energy restriction. *American Journal of Clinical Nutrition, 74*(4), 901–907.

AhYun, K. (2002). Similarity and attraction. In M. Allen, R. W. Preiss, B. M. Gayle, & N. A. Burrell (Eds.), *Interpersonal communication research* (pp. 145–167). Mahwah, NJ: Erlbaum.

Ainslie, G. (1975). Specious reward: A behavioral theory of impulsiveness and impulse control. *Psychological Bulletin, 82,* 463–496.

Ainslie, G. (1992). Picoeconomics: *The strategic interaction of successive motivational states within the person.* New York, NY: Cambridge University Press.

Alberti, R. E., & Emmons, M. L. (2001). *Your perfect right: Assertiveness and equality in your life and relationships.* Atascadero, CA: Impact.

Alkon, D. L. (1992). *Memory's voice: Deciphering the brain-mind code.* New York, NY: HarperCollins.

Allport, G. W. (1954). *The nature of prejudice.* Cambridge, MA: Addison-Wesley.

Allport, G. W. (1979). *The nature of prejudice* (3rd ed.). Reading, MA: Addison-Wesley.

American College Testing. (2012). *College student retention and graduation rates from 2000 through 2011.* Retrieved April 15, 2012, from http://www.act.org/research/policymakers/reports/graduation.html

American Council on Education. (2008). *Making the case for affirmative action.* Retrieved October, 2008, from http://www.acenet.edu/bookstore/descriptions/making_the_case/works/research/ctm

American Heart Association. (2010). Understanding Childhood Obesity. Retrieved October 30, 2012, from http://www.heart.org/idc/groups/heart-public/@wcm/@fc/documents/downloadable/ucm_304175.pdf

American Psychiatric Association. (1994). *Diagnostic and statistical manual of mental disorders* (4th ed.). Washington, DC: Author.

American Psychiatric Association. (2000). *Diagnostic and statistical manual of mental disorders, DSM-IV-TR* (4th ed.). Washington, DC: Author.

American Psychiatric Association Work Group on Eating Disorders. (2000). Practice guideline for the treatment of patients with eating disorders (revision). *American Journal of Psychiatry, 157,* 1–39.

Amir, Y. (1969). Contact hypothesis in ethnic relations. *Psychological Bulletin, 71,* 319–342.

Amir, Y. (1976). The role of intergroup contact in change of prejudice and ethnic relations. In P. A. Katz (Ed.), *Towards the elimination of racism* (pp. 245–308). New York, NY: Pergamon Press.

Andersen, P. A. (1985). Nonverbal immediacy in interpersonal communication. In A. W. Siegmean & S. Feldstein (Eds.), *Multichannel integrations of nonverbal behavior* (pp. 1–36). Hillsdale, NJ: Lawrence Erlbaum.

Anderson, C. J. (2003). The psychology of doing nothing: Forms of decision avoidance result from reason and emotion. *Psychological Bulletin, 129,* 139–167.

Anderson, J. R. (2000). *Cognitive psychology and its implications.* New York, NY: Worth.

Anderson, C. J., & Gates, C. (2002, August 8). Freshman absence-based intervention at the University of Mississippi [Electronic mailing list message]. *First-Year Assessment Listserv (FYA) Series.*

Anderson, L. W., & Krathwohl, D. R. (Eds.). (2001). *A taxonomy for learning, teaching, and assessing: A revision of Bloom's taxonomy of educational objectives.* New York, NY: Addison Wesley Longman.

Anderson, M., & Fienberg, S. E. (2000). Race and ethnicity and the controversy over the U.S. census. *Current Sociology, 48*(3), 87–110.

Andres, L., & Wyn, J. (2010). *The making of a generation: The children of the 1970s in adulthood.* Buffalo, NY: University of Toronto Press.

Annual Social and Economic Supplement (ASEC). (2008). *Current population survey (CPS).* Retrieved January 18, 2010, from http://www.census.gov/hhes/www/poverty/data/incpovhlth/2008/index.html

Applebee, A. N. (1984). Writing and reasoning. *Review of Educational Research, 54*(4), 577–596.

Applebee, A. N., Langer, J. A., Jenkins, L. B., Mullis, I. V. S., & Foertsch, M. A. (1990). *Learning to write in our nation's schools: Instruction and achievement in 1988 at grades 4, 8, and 12.* Princeton, NJ: The National Assessment of Educational Progress.

Appleby, D. C. (2008, June). *Diagnosing and treating the deadly 13th grade syndrome.* Paper presented at the Association of Psychological Science Convention, Chicago, IL.

Arnedt, J. T., Wilde, G. J. S., Munt, P. W., & MacLean, A. W. (2001). How do prolonged wakefulness and alcohol compare in the decrements they produce on a simulated driving task? *Accident Analysis and Prevention, 33,* 337–344.

Aronson, E., Wilson, T. D., & Akert, R. M. (2009). *Social psychology* (7th ed.). Upper Saddle River, NJ: Pearson/Prentice Hall.

Association of American Colleges & Universities (AAC&U). (2002). *Greater expectations: A new vision for learning as a nation goes to college.* Washington, DC: Author.

Association of American Colleges and Universities (AAC&U). (2007). *College learning for the new global century.* Washington, DC: Author.

Astin, A. W. (1993). *What matters in college?* San Francisco, CA: Jossey-Bass.

Astin, A. W., Parrot, S. A., Korn, W. S., & Sax, L. J. (1997). *The American freshman: Thirty year trends, 1966–1996.* Los Angeles, CA: Higher Education Research Institute, University of California.

Ausubel, D., Novak, J., & Hanesian, H. (1978). *Educational psychology: A cognitive view* (2nd ed.). New York, NY: Holt, Rinehart & Winston.

Back, M. D., Schmukle, S. C., & Egloff, B. (2008). Becoming friends by chance. *Psychological Science, 19,* 339–440.

Baddeley, A. D. (1999). *Essentials of human memory.* Hove UK: Psychology.

Baer, J. M. (1993). *Creativity and divergent thinking.* Hillsdale, NJ: Erlbaum.

Bandura, A. (1986). *Social foundations of thought and action: A social cognitive theory.* Englewood Cliffs, NJ: Prentice Hall.

Bandura, A. (1994). Self-efficacy. In V. S. Ramachaudran (Ed.), *Encyclopedia of human behavior* (vol. 4, pp. 71–81). New York, NY: Academic Press.

Bandura, A. (1997). *Self-efficacy: The exercise of control.* New York, NY: Freeman.

Bandura, A., & Cervone, D. (1983). Self-evaluative and self-efficacy mechanisms governing the motivational effects of goal systems. *Journal of Personality and Social Psychology, 45*(5), 1017–1028.

Barefoot, B. O., Warnock, C. L., Dickinson, M. P., Richardson, S. E., & Roberts, M. R. (Eds.). (1998). *Exploring the evidence: Vol. 2. Reporting outcomes of first-year seminars* (Monograph No. 29). Columbia, SC: National Resource Center for the First-Year Experience and Students in Transition, University of South Carolina.

Bargdill, R. W. (2000). A phenomenological investigation of being bored with life. *Psychological Reports, 86,* 493–494.

Barker, L., & Watson, K. W. (2000). *Listen up: How to improve relationships, reduce stress, and be more productive by using the power of listening.* New York, NY: St. Martin's Press.

Baron, R. S. (2005). So right it's wrong: Groupthink and the ubiquitous nature of polarized group decision making. In M. P. Zanna (Ed.), *Advances in experimental social psychology* (vol. 37, pp. 219–253). San Diego, CA: Elsevier Academic Press.

Bartlett, T. (2002). Freshman pay, mentally and physically, as they adjust to college life. *Chronicle of Higher Education, 48,* 35–37.

Basadur, M., Runco, M. A., & Vega, L. A. (2000). Understanding how creative thinking skills, attitudes, and behaviors work together. *Journal of Creative Behavior, 34*(2), 77–100.

Bassham, G., Irwin, W., Nardone, H., & Wallace, J. M. (2005). *Critical thinking* (2nd ed.). New York, NY: McGraw-Hill.

Bates, G. A. (1994). *The next step: College.* Bloomington, IN: Phi Delta Kappa.

Bauer, D., Kopp, V., & Fischer, M. R. (2007). Answer changing in multiple choice assessment change that answer when in doubt—and spread the word! *BMC Medical Education, 7,* 28–32.

Baumeister, R. F., Heatherton, T. F., & Tice, D. M. (1994). *Losing control: How and why people fail at self-regulation.* San Diego, CA: Academic Press.

Baumeister, R. F., & Leary, M. R. (1995). The need to belong: Desire for interpersonal attachments as a fundamental human motivation. *Psychological Bulletin, 117,* 497–529.

Bean, J. C. (2001). *Engaging ideas: The professor's guide to integrating writing, critical thinking and active learning in the classroom.* San Francisco, CA: Jossey-Bass.

Bean, J. C. (2003). *Engaging ideas: The professor's guide to integrating writing, critical thinking and active learning in the classroom.* San Francisco, CA: Jossey-Bass.

Bean, J. C. (2011). *Engaging ideas: The professor's guide to integrating writing, critical thinking and active learning in the classroom* (2nd ed.). San Francisco, CA: Jossey-Bass.

Beck, B. L., Koons, S. R., & Milgram, D. L. (2000). Correlates and consequences of behavioral procrastination: the effects of academic procrastination, self-consciousness, self-esteem, and self-handicapping. *Journal of Social Behavior and Personality, 15,* 3–13.

Beckett, W. (2003, September 5). What lies between the hookup and marriage? *The Chronicle.* Retrieved January 6, 2004, from http://www.dukechronicle.com/article/column-what-lies-between-hookup-and-marriage

Bellah, R. N., Madsen, R., Sullivan, W. M., Swidler, A., & Tipton, S. M. (1985). *Habits of the heart: Individualism and commitment in American life.* Berkeley, CA: University of California Press.

Benedict, M. E., & Hoag, J. (2004). Seating location in large lectures: Are seating preferences or location related to course performance? *Journal of Economics Education, 35,* 215–231.

Benjamin, L. T., Jr., Cavell, T. A., & Shallenberger, W. R., III. (1984). Staying with initial answers on objective tests: Is it a myth? *Teaching of Psychology, 11,* 133–141.

Benjamin, M., McKeachie, W. J., Lin, Y. G., & Holinger. D. (1981). Test anxiety: Deficits in information processing. *Journal of Educational Psychology, 73,* 816–824.

Bennet, W., & Gurin, J. (1983). *The dieter's dilemma.* New York, NY: Basic Books.

Benson, H., & Klipper, M. Z. (1990). *The relaxation response.* New York, NY: Avon.

Bergen-Cico, D. (2000). Patterns of substance abuse and attrition among first-year students. *Journal of the First-Year Experience and Students in Transition, 12*(1), 61–75.

Berndt, T. J. (1992). Friendship and friends' influence in adolescence. *Current Directions in Psychological Science, 1*(5), 156–159.

Beyers, J. M., Leonard, J. M., Mays, V. K., & Rosen, L. A. (2000). Gender differences in the perception of courtship abuse. *Journal of Interpersonal Violence, 15,* 451–466.

Biggs, J., & Tang, C. (2007). *Teaching for quality learning at university* (3rd ed.) Buckingham England: SRHE and Open University Press.

Biglan, A. (1973). The characteristics of subject matter in different academic areas. *Journal of Applied Psychology, 57,* 195–203.

Bippus, A. M., & Young, S. L. (2005). Owning your emotions: Reactions to expressions of self- versus other-attributed positive and negative emotions. *Journal of Applied Communication Research, 33*(1), 26–45.

Bishop, S. (1986). Education for political freedom. *Liberal Education, 72*(4), 322–325.

Bjork, R. (1994). Memory and metamemory considerations in the training of human beings. In J. Metcalfe & A. P. Shimamura (Eds.), *Metacognition: Knowing about knowing* (pp. 185–206). Cambridge, MA: MIT Press.

Blakeslee, S. (1993). Mystery of sleep yields as studies reveal immune tie. *The New York Times.*

Bligh, D. A. (2000). *What's the use of lectures?* San Francisco, CA: Jossey-Bass.

Boekaerts, M., Pintrich, P. R., & Zeidner, M. (2000). *Handbook of self-regulation.* San Diego, CA: Academic Press.

Bok, D. (2006). *Our underachieving colleges.* Princeton, NJ: Princeton University Press.

Bolles, R. N. (1998). *The new quick job-hunting map.* Toronto, Canada: Ten Speed Press.

Booth, F. W., & Vyas, D. R. (2001). Genes, environment, and exercise. *Advances in Experimental Medicine and Biology, 502,* 13–20.

Boren, D. (2008). *A letter to America.* Norman, OK: University of Oklahoma Press.

Bosch, J. A., De Geus, E. J., Ring, C., & Nieuw-Amerongen, A. V. (2004). Academic examinations and immunity: Academic stress or examination stress? *Psychosomatic Medicine, 66*(4), 625–627.

Boudreau, C., & Kromrey, J. (1994). A longitudinal study of the retention and academic performance of participants in a freshman orientation course. *Journal of College Student Development, 35,* 444–449.

Bowen, H. R. (1977). Investment in learning: *The individual and social value of American higher education.* San Francisco, CA: Jossey-Bass.

Bowen, H. R. (1997). Investment in learning: *The individual and social value of American higher education* (2nd ed.). Baltimore, MD: Johns Hopkins Press.

Bowlby, J. (1980). *Attachment and loss: Vol. 3. Loss, sadness, and depression.* New York, NY: Basic Books.

Boyer, E. L. (1987). *College: The undergraduate experience in America.* New York, NY: Harper & Row.

Bradshaw, D. (1995). Learning theory: Harnessing the strength of a neglected resource. In D. C. A. Bradshaw (Ed.), *Bringing learning to life: The learning revolution, the economy and the individual* (pp. 79–92). London, England: Falmer Press.

Bransford, J. D., Brown, A. L., & Cocking, R. R. (1999). *How people learn: Brain, mind, experience and school.* Washington, DC: National Academy Press.

Braskamp, L. A. (2008). Developing global citizens. *Journal of College & Character, 10*(1), 1–5.

Breivik, P. S. (1998). *Student learning in the information age.* Phoenix, AZ: The Oryx Press.

Brewer, G. (2001, March 19). Snakes top list of Americans' fears: Public speaking, heights and being closed in small spaces also create fear in many Americans. *Gallup News Service.* Retrieved June 3, 2010, from http://www.gallup.com/poll/1891/snakes-top-list-americans-fears.aspx

Bridgeman, B. (2003). *Psychology and evolution: The origins of mind.* Thousand Oaks, CA: Sage.

Brissette, I., Cohen, S., & Seeman, T. E. (2000). Measuring social integration and social networks. In S. Cohen, L. G. Underwood, & B. H. Gottlieb (Eds.), *Social support measurement and intervention* (pp. 53–85). New York, NY: Oxford University Press.

Brody, J. E. (2003, August 18). Skipping a college course: Weight gain 101. *The New York Times,* p. D7.

Brookings Institute. (2008). Demographic keys to the 2008 election. Washington, DC: Brookings Institute. www.brookings.edu/~/media/Files/events/2008/1020_demographics/ 20081020_demographics.pdf.

Brooks, K. (2009). *You majored in what? Mapping your path from chaos to career.* New York, NY: Penguin.

Brown, R. D. (1988). Self-quiz on testing and grading issues. *Teaching at UNL (University of Nebraska–Lincoln), 10*(2), 1–3.

Brown, K. T., Brown, T. N., Jackson, J. S., Sellers, R. M., & Manuel, W. J. (2003). Teammates on and off the field? Contact with Black teammates and the racial attitudes of White student athletes. *Journal of Applied Social Psychology, 33,* 1379–1403.

Brown, R., & Hewstone, M. (2005). An integrative theory of intergroup contact. In M. P. Zanna (Ed.), *Advances in experimental social psychology* (vol. 37, pp. 255–343). San Diego, CA: Elsevier Academic Press.

Brown, S. D., & Krane, N. E. R. (2000). Four (or five) sessions and a cloud of dust: Old assumptions and new observations about career counseling. In S. D. Brown

& R. W. Lent (Eds.), *Handbook of counseling psychology* (3rd ed., pp. 740–766). New York, NY: Wiley.

Brown, S. A., Tapert, S. F., Granholm, E., & Delis, D. C. (2000). Neurocognitive functioning of adolescents: Effects of protracted alcohol use. *Alcoholism: Clinical & Experimental Research, 24*(2), 164–171.

Bruffee, K. A. (1993). *Collaborative learning: Higher education, interdependence, and the authority of knowledge.* Baltimore, MD: Johns Hopkins University Press.

Bruner, J. (1990). *Acts of meaning.* Cambridge, MA: Harvard University Press.

Bureau of Justice Statistics, U.S. Department of Justice. (2009). *Criminal victimization in the United States.* Retrieved June 23, 2012, from http://bjs.ojp. usdoj.gov/content/pub/pdf/cv08.pdf

Bryant, P. A., Trinder, J., & Curtis, N. (2004). Sick and tired: does sleep have a vital role in the immune system? *Nature Reviews Immunology, 4,* 457–467.

Burka, J. B., & Yuen, L. M. (2008). *Procrastination: Why you do it, what to do about it now.* Cambridge, MA: De Capo Press.

Bushman, B. J., & Cooper, H. M. (1990). Effects of alcohol on human aggression: An integrative research review. *Psychological Bulletin, 107*(3), 341–354.

Business/Higher Education Forum. (2002). *Developing all of America's talent on campus and in the workplace.* Retrieved February 17, 2007, from http://www. bhef.com/publications/pubs.asp

Business/Higher Education Round Table. (1991). *Aiming higher: The concerns and attitudes of leading business executives and university heads to education priorities in Australia in the 1990s* (Commissioned Report No. 1). Melbourne, Australia.

Business/Higher Education Round Table. (1992). *Educating for excellence part 2: Achieving excellence in university professional education* (Commissioned Report No. 2). Melbourne, Australia.

Caine, R. N., & Caine, G. (1991). *Teaching and the human brain.* Alexandria, VA: Association for Supervision and Curriculum Development.

Cairncross, F. C. (2001). *The death of distance: How the communication revolution is changing our lives.* Cambridge, MA: Harvard Business School Press.

Cameron, L. (2003). *Metaphor in educational discourse.* London, England: Continuum.

Campbell, T. A., & Campbell, D. E. (1997, December). Faculty/student mentor program: Effects on academic performance and retention. *Research in Higher Education, 38,* 727–742.

Caplan, P. J., & Caplan, J. B. (2009). *Thinking critically about research on sex and gender* (3rd ed.). New York, NY: HarperCollins College.

Carlson, N. R., Buskist, W., Heth, D. H., & Schmaltz, G. (2007). *Psychology: The science of behaviour* (4th ed.). Toronto, Canada: Pearson Education Canada.

Caroli, M., Argentieri, L., Cardone, M., & Masi, A. (2004). Role of television in childhood obesity prevention. *International Journal of Obesity Related Metabolic Disorders, 28*(Suppl. 3), S104–S108.

Casserly, M. (2012). 10 jobs that didn't exist 10 years ago. *Forbes.* Retrieved June 10, 2012, from http://www.forbes.com/sites/meghancasserly/2012/05/11/10-jobs-that-didnt-exist-10-years-ago

Cates, J. R., Herndon, N. L., Schulz, S. L., & Darroch, J. E. (2004). *Our voices, our lives, our futures: Youth and sexually transmitted diseases.* Chapel Hill, NC: University of North Carolina at Chapel Hill School of Journalism and Mass Communication.

Center of Inquiry. (2011). *Wabash National Study, 2010.* Retrieved October 4, 2011, from http://www.liberalarts.wabash.edu

Centers for Disease Control & Prevention. (2012). *Teen drivers: Fact sheet*. Retrieved October 30, 2012 from http://www.cdc.gov/motorvehiclesafety/teen_drivers/teendrivers_factsheet.html

Cermak, K., & Filkins, J. (2004). *On-campus employment as a factor of student retention and graduation*. DePaul University. Retrieved June 2, 2011, from http://oipr.depaul.edu/open/gradereten/oce.asp

Chaney, W. (2007). *Dynamic mind*. Las Vegas, NV: Houghton-Brace Publishing.

Chaskes, J. (1996). The first-year student as immigrant. *Journal of the Freshman Year Experience & Students in Transition, 8*(1), 79–91.

Chatman, S. (2008). *Does diversity matter in the education process?* (Research & Occasional Paper Series: CSHE.5.08). Berkeley, CA: Center for Studies in Higher Education (CSHE). Retrieved March 30, 2010, from http://cshe.berkeley.edu/publications/docs/ROPS.Chatman.Exploring.3.5.08.pdf

Chi, M., De Leeuw, N., Chiu, M. H., & LaVancher, C. (1994). Eliciting self-explanations improves understanding. *Cognitive Science, 18*, 439–477.

Chickering, A. W., & Schlossberg, N. K. (1998). Moving on: Seniors as people in transition. In J. N. Gardner, G. Van der Veer, et al. (Eds.), *The senior year experience* (pp. 37–50). San Francisco, CA: Jossey-Bass.

Chronicle of Higher Education. (2003, August 30). Almanac 2003–04. *Chronicle of Higher Education, 49*(1).

Chu, A. H. C., & Cho, J. N. (2005). Rethinking procrastination: Positive effects of "active" procrastination behavior on attitudes and performance. *The Journal of Social Psychology, 145*(3), 245–264.

Chua, S. N., & Koestner, R. (2008). A self-determination theory perspective on the role of autonomy in solitary behavior. *The Journal of Social Psychology, 148*(5), 645–647.

Ciancotto, J. (2005). *Hispanic and Latino same-sex couple households in the United States: A report from the 2000 Census*. New York, NY: The National Gay and Lesbian Task Force Policy Institute and the National Latinao/a Coalition for Justice.

Claxton, C. S., & Murrell, P. H. (1987). *Learning styles: Implications for improving practice* (ASHE-ERIC Educational Report No. 4). Washington, DC: Association for the Study of Higher Education.

Coates, T. J. (1977). *How to sleep better: A drug-free program for overcoming insomnia*. Englewood Cliffs, NJ: Prentice Hall.

Colcombe, S. J., Erickson, K., Scalf, P. E., Kim, J. S., Prakash, R., & McAuley, E. (2006). Aerobic exercise training increases brain volume in aging humans. *Journal of Gerontology: Medical Sciences, 61A*(11), 1166–1170.

College Board. (2008). *Coming to our senses: Education and the American future* (Report of the Commission on Access, Admissions and Success in Higher Education). Retrieved August 5, 2009, from http://advocacy.collegeboard.org/college-admission-completion/access-admissions-success-education-and-american-future/publications/co

College Board. (2009). *Economic challenges lead to lower non-tuition revenues and higher prices at colleges and universities*. Retrieved November 4, 2009, from http://www.collegeboard.com/press/releases/208962.html

College Board. (2010). *Education pays 2010*. Washington, DC: Author. Retrieved December 3, 2010, from http://trends.collegeboard.org/education_pays

Colombo, G., Cullen, R., & Lisle, B. (2010). *Rereading America: Cultural contexts for critical thinking and writing* (8th ed.). Boston, MA: Bedford Books of St. Martin's Press.

Conaway, M. S. (1982). Listening: Learning tool and retention agent. In A. S. Algier & K. W. Algier (Eds.), *Improving reading and study skills* (pp. 51–63). San Francisco, CA: Jossey-Bass.

Conference Board of Canada (2000). *Employability skills 2000+*. Retrieved January 7, 2010, from http://www.conferenceboard.ca/Libraries/educ_public/esp2000.sflb

Conley, D. T. (2005). *College knowledge: What it really takes for students to succeed and what we can do to get them ready*. San Francisco, CA: Jossey-Bass.

Cook, S. W. (1984). Cooperative interaction in multiethnic contexts. In N. Miller & M. B. Brewer (Eds.), *Groups in contact: The psychology of desegregation*. New York, NY: Academic Press.

Corbin, C. B., Pangrazi, R. P., & Franks, B. D. (2000). Definitions: Health, fitness, and physical activity. *President's Council on Physical Fitness and Sports Research Digest, 3*(9), 1–8.

Covey, S. R. (2004). *The seven habits of highly effective people* (3rd ed.). New York, NY: Fireside.

Cowan, N. (2001). The magical number 4 in short-term memory: A reconsideration of mental storage capacity. *Behavioral and Brain Sciences, 24*, 87–114.

Coward, A. (1990). *Pattern thinking*. New York, NY: Praeger.

Crawford, H. J., & Strapp, C. H. (1994). Effects of vocal and instrumental music on visuospatial and verbal performance as moderated by studying preference and personality. *Personality and Individual Differences, 16*(2), 237–245.

Credé, M., Roch, S. G., & Kieszczynka, U. M. (2010). Class attendance in college: A meta-analytic review of the relationship of class attendance with grades and student characteristics. *Review of Educational Research, 80*(2), 272–295.

Cronon, W. (1998, Autumn). "Only connect": The goals of a liberal education. *The American Scholar*, 73–80.

Crosby, O. (2002, Summer). Informational interviewing: Get the scoop on careers. *Occupational Outlook Quarterly*, 32–37.

Cross, K. P. (1982). Thirty years passed: Trends in general education. In B. L. Johnson (Ed.), *General education in two-year colleges* (pp. 11–20). San Francisco, CA: Jossey-Bass.

Cross, K. P., Barkley, E. F., & Major, C. H. (2005). *Collaborative learning techniques: A handbook for college faculty*. San Francisco, CA: Jossey-Bass.

Cude, B. J., Lawrence, F. C., Lyons, A. C., Metzger, K., LeJeune, E., Marks, L., & Machtmes, K. (2006). College students and financial literacy: What they know and what we need to learn. *Proceedings of the Eastern Family Economics and Resource Management Association Conference* (pp. 102–109).

Cuseo, J. B. (1996). *Cooperative learning: A pedagogy for addressing contemporary challenges and critical issues in higher education*. Stillwater, OK: New Forums Press.

Cuseo, J. B. (2003). Comprehensive academic support for students during the first year of college. In G. L. Kramer et al. (Eds.), *Student academic services: An integrated approach* (pp. 271–310). San Francisco, CA: Jossey-Bass.

Cuseo, J. B. (2005). "Decided," "undecided," and "in transition": Implications for academic advisement, career counseling, and student retention. In R. S. Feldman (Ed.), *Improving the first year of college: Research and practice* (pp. 27–50). Mahwah, NJ: Lawrence Erlbaum.

Cuseo, J. B. (2011, February). *The potential power of the first-year experience course: Holistic outcomes & systemic impact*. Paper presented at the 30th Annual Conference on the First-Year Experience, Atlanta, GA.

Cuseo, J. B., & Barefoot, B. O. (1996). A natural marriage: The extended orientation seminar and the community college. In J. Henkin (Ed.), *The community college:*

Opportunity and access for America's first-year students (pp. 59–68). Columbia, SC: National Resource Center for the First-Year Experience and Students in Transition, University of South Carolina.

Cuseo, J. B., Fecas, V. S., & Thompson, A. (2007). *Thriving in college & beyond: Research-based strategies for academic success and personal development.* Dubuque, IA: Kendall Hunt.

Cuseo, J. B., & Thompson, A. (2010). *Humanity, diversity, and the liberal arts: The foundation of a college education.* Dubuque, IA: Kendall Hunt.

Csikszentmihalyi, M. (1990). *Flow: The psychology of optimal experience.* New York, NY: Harper and Row.

Dalton, J. C., Eberhardt, D., Bracken, J., & Echols, K. (2006). Inward journeys: Forms and patterns of college student spirituality. *Journal of College & Character, 7*(8), 1–21. Retrieved December 17, 2006, from http://www.collegevalues.org/pdfs/Dalton.pdf

Daly, W. T. (1992, July/August). The academy, the economy, and the liberal arts. *Academe,* 10–12.

Damrad-Frye, R., & Laird, J. (1989). The experience of boredom: The role of self-perception of attention. *Journal of Personality & Social Psychology, 57,* 315–320.

Daniels, D., & Horowitz, L. J. (1997). *Being and caring: A psychology for living.* Prospect Heights, IL: Waveland Press.

De Bono, E. (2007). *How to have creative ideas.* London, England: Vermilion.

Deci, E., & Ryan, R. (Eds.). (2002). *Handbook of self-determination research.* Rochester, NY: University of Rochester Press.

Dee, T. (2004). Are there civic returns to education? *Journal of Public Economics, 88,* 1697–1720.

Deinzer, R., Kleineidam, C., Stiller-Winkler, R., Idel, H., & Bachg, D. (2000). Prolonged reduction of salivary immunoglobulin A (S-IgA) after a major academic exam. *International Journal of Psychophysiology, 37,* 219–232.

DeJong, W., & Linkenback, J. (1999). Telling it like it is: Using social norms marketing campaigns to reduce student drinking. *AAHE Bulletin, 52*(4), 11–13, 16.

Dement, W. C., & Vaughan, C. (1999). *The promise of sleep.* New York, NY: Delacorte Press.

Dement, W. C., & Vaughan, C. (2000). *The promise of sleep: A pioneer in sleep medicine explores the vital connection between health, happiness, and a good night's sleep.* New York, NY: Dell.

Demmert, W. G., Jr., & Towner, J. C. (2003). *A review of the research literature on the influences of culturally based education on the academic performance of Native American students.* Retrieved from the Northwest Regional Educational Laboratory, Portland, Oregon, Web site: http://www.nrel.org/indianaed/cbe.pdf

Dessel, A. B., Woodford, M. R., & Warren, N. (2012). Intergroup dialogue courses on sexual orientation: Lesbian, gay, and bisexual student experiences and outcomes. *Journal of Homosexuality, 58*(8), 1132–1150.

Dittmar, H. (2004). Understanding and diagnosing compulsive buying. In R. Coombs (Ed.), *Handbook of addictive disorders: A practical guide to diagnosis and treatment* (pp. 411–450). New York, NY: Wiley.

Donald, J. G. (2002). *Learning to think: Disciplinary perspectives.* San Francisco, CA: Jossey-Bass.

Doran, G. T. (1981). There's a S.M.A.R.T. way to write management's goals and objectives. *Management Review, 70*(11), 35–36.

Dorfman, J., Shames, J., & Kihlstrom, J. F. (1996). Intuition, incubation, and insight. In G. Underwood (Ed.), *Implicit cognition.* New York, NY: Oxford University Press.

Douglas, K. A., Collins, J. L., Warren, C., Kahn, L., Gold, R., Clayton, S., Ross, J. G., & Kolbe, L. J. (1997). Results from the 1995 National College Health Risk Behavior Survey. *Journal of American College Health, 46,* 55–66.

Dovidio, J. F., Eller, A., & Hewstone, M. (2011). Improving intergroup relations through direct, extended and other forms of indirect contact. *Group Processes & Intergroup Relations, 14,* 147–160.

Doyle, S., Edison, M., & Pascarella, E. (1998). *The "seven principles of good practice in undergraduate education" as process indicators of cognitive development in college: A longitudinal study.* Paper presented at the annual meeting of the Association for the Study of Higher Education, Miami, FL.

Driver, J. (2010). *You say more than you think.* New York, NY: Crown.

Druckman, D., & Bjork, R. A. (Eds.). (1991). *In the mind's eye: Enhancing human performance.* Washington, DC: National Academy Press.

Dryden, G., & Vos, J. (1999). *The learning revolution: To change the way the world learns.* Torrance, CA: Learning Web.

Dunn, R., Dunn, K., & Price, G. (1990). *Learning style inventory.* Lawrence, KS: Price Systems.

Dupuy, G. M., & Vance, R. M. (1996, October). *Launching your career: A transition module for seniors.* Paper presented at the Second National Conference on Students in Transition, San Antonio, TX.

Eble, K. E. (1966). *The perfect education.* New York, NY: Macmillan.

Eckman, P., & Friesen, W. V. (1969). Nonverbal leakage and clues to deception. *Psychiatry, 32,* 88–106.

Education Commission of the States. (1995). *Making quality count in undergraduate education.* Denver, CO: ECS Distribution Center.

Education Commission of the States. (1996). *Bridging the gap between neuroscience and education.* Denver, CO: Author.

Einstein, G. O., Morris, J., & Smith, S. (1985). Note-taking, individual differences, and memory for lecture information. *Journal of Educational Psychology, 77*(5), 522–532.

Eisenberg, D., Golberstein, E., & Hunt, J. (2009). Mental health and academic success in college. *B.E. Journal of Economic Analysis & Policy, 9*(1), 1–40.

Elbow, P. (1973). *Writing without teachers.* New York, NY: Oxford University Press.

Ellis, A. (1995). Changing rational-emotive therapy (RET) to rational emotive behavior therapy (REBT). *Journal of Rational-Emotive & Cognitive Behavior Therapy, 13*(2), 85–89.

Ellis, A. (2000). *How to control your anxiety before it controls you.* New York, NY: Citadel Press/Kensington Publishing.

Ellis, A., & Knaus, W. J. (2002). *Overcoming procrastination* (Rev. ed.). New York, NY: New American Library.

Elster, J., & Loewenstein, G. (Eds.). (1992). *Choice over time.* New York, NY: Russell Sage.

Encrenaz, T., Bibring, J.-P., Blanc, M., Barucci, M.-A., Roques, F., & Zarka, P. (2004). *The solar system.* Berlin, Germany: Springer.

Engle, J., Bermeo, A., & O'Brien, C. (2006). *Straight from the source: What works for first-generation college students.* Washington, DC: The Pell Institute for the Study of Opportunity in Higher Education.

Entwistle, N. J., & Ramsden, P. (1983). *Understanding student learning.* London, England: Croom Helm.

Epstein, L., & Mardon. S. (2007). *The Harvard medical school guide to a good night's sleep*. New York, NY: McGraw-Hill.

Ericsson, K. A. (2006). The influence of experience and deliberate practice on the development of superior expert performance. In K. A. Ericsson, N. Charness, P. Feltovich, and R. R. Hoffman (Eds.), *Cambridge handbook of expertise and expert performance* (pp. 685–706). Cambridge, UK: Cambridge University Press.

Ericsson, K. A., & Charness, N. (1994). Expert performance: Its structure and acquisition. *American Psychologist, 49*(8), 725–747.

Erickson, B. L., Peters, C. B., & Strommer, D. W. (2006). *Teaching first-year college students*. San Francisco, CA: Jossey-Bass.

Erickson, B. L., & Strommer, D. W. (1991). *Teaching college freshmen*. San Francisco, CA: Jossey-Bass.

Erickson, B. L., & Strommer, D. W. (2005). Inside the first-year classroom: Challenges and constraints. In J. L. Upcraft, J. N. Gardner, & B. O. Barefoot (Eds.), *Challenging and supporting the first-year student* (pp. 241–256). San Francisco, CA: Jossey-Bass.

ETR Associates. (2000). *Acquaintance rape*. Santa Cruz, CA: Author.

ETR Associates. (2001). *Sexual harassment*. Santa Cruz, CA: Author.

Etsy, K., Griffin, R., & Hirsch, M. S. (1995). *Workplace diversity: A managers' guide to solving problems and turning diversity into a competitive advantage*. Holbook, MA: Adams Media Corporation.

Evans, M. (2010). Abusive relationships. *University of Oregon Counseling and Testing Center*. Retrieved June 24, 2012, from http://counseling.uoregon.edu/dnn/SelfhelpResources/SexualAssaultSexualAbuse/AbusiveRelationships/tabid/388/Default.aspx

Ewell, P. T. (1997). Organizing for learning. *AAHE Bulletin, 50*(4), 3–6.

Fairbairn, G. J., & Winch, C. (1996). *Reading, writing and reasoning: A guide for students* (2nd ed.). Buckingham England: OU Press.

Family Care Foundation. (2012). *If the world were a village of 100 people*. Retrieved May 29, 2012, from http://www.familycare.org/special-interest/if-the-world-were-a-village-of-100-people

Feagin, J., & Feagin, C. (2007). *Racial and ethnic relations* (3rd ed.). Upper Saddle River, NJ: Prentice Hall.

Feldman, K. A., & Newcomb, T. M. (1997). *The impact of college on students*. New Brunswick, NJ: Transaction. (Original work published 1969.)

Feldman, K. A., & Paulsen, M. B. (Eds.). (1994). *Teaching and learning in the college classroom*. Needham Heights, MA: Ginn Press.

Festinger, L. (1954). A theory of social comparison processes. *Human Relations, 7,* 117–140.

Fidler, P., & Godwin, M. (1994). Retaining African-American students through the freshman seminar. *Journal of Developmental Education, 17,* 34–41.

Figler, H., & Bolles, R. N. (2007). *The career counselor's handbook*. Berkeley, CA: Ten Speed Press.

Fisher, E. E. (2004). *Why we love: The nature and chemistry of romantic love*. New York, NY: Henry Holt.

Fisher, J. L., Harris, J. L., & Harris, M. B. (1973). Effect of note-taking and review on recall. *Journal of Educational Psychology, 65*(3), 321–325.

Fixman, C. S. (1990). The foreign language needs of U.S. based corporations. *Annals of the American Academy of Political and Social Science, 511,* 25–46.

Flavell, J. H. (1979). Metacognition and cognitive monitoring: A new area of cognitive-developmental inquiry. *American Psychologist, 34*(10), 906–911.

Fletcher, A., Lamond, N., Van Den Heuvel, C. J., & Dawson, D. (2003). Prediction of performance during sleep deprivation and alcohol intoxication using a quantitative model of work-related fatigue. *Sleep Research Online, 5,* 67–75.

Flippo, R. F., & Caverly, D. C. (2009). *Handbook of college reading and study strategy research* (2nd ed.). New York, NY: Lawrence Erlbaum Associates.

Flowers, L., Osterlind, S., Pascarella, E., & Pierson, C. (2001). How much do students learn in college? Cross-sectional estimates using the College Basic Academic Subjects Examination. *Journal of Higher Education, 72,* 565–583.

Ford, P. L. (Ed.). (1903). *The works of Thomas Jefferson.* New York, NY: Knickerbocker Press.

Foreman, J. (2009, June 22). Dear, I love you with all my brain. *Los Angeles Times.* Retrieved January 6, 2011, from http://www.latimes.com/features/health/la-he-love22-2009jun22,0,6897401.column

Franklin, K. F. (2002). Conversations with Metropolitan University first-year students. *Journal of the First-Year Experience and Students in Transition, 14*(2), 57–88.

Freedner, N., Freed, L. H., Yang, Y. W., & Austin, S. B. (2002). Dating violence among gay, lesbian, and bisexual adolescents: Results from a community survey. *Journal of Adolescent Health, 21,* 469–474.

Friedman, T. L. (2005). *The world is flat: A brief history of the twenty-first century.* New York, NY: Farrar, Straus & Giroux.

Fromm, E. (1970). *The art of loving.* New York, NY: Bantam.

Fromme, A. (1980). *The ability to love.* Chatsworth, CA: Wilshire Book Company.

Frost, S. H. (1991). *Academic advising for student success: A system of shared responsibility* (ASHE-ERIC Higher Education Report No. 3). Washington, DC: School of Education and Human Development, George Washington University.

Furnham, A., & Argyle, M. (1998). *The psychology of money.* New York, NY: Routledge.

Gamson, Z. F. (1984). *Liberating education.* San Francisco, CA: Jossey-Bass.

Gardner, H. (1983). *Frames of mind: The theory of multiple intelligences.* New York, NY: Basic Books.

Gardner, H. (1993). *Frames of mind: The theory of multiple intelligences* (2nd ed.). New York, NY: Basic Books.

Gardner, H. (1999). *Intelligence reframed: Multiple intelligences for the 21st century.* New York, NY: Basic Books.

Gardner, H. (2006). *Changing minds: The art and science of changing our own and other people's minds.* Boston, MA: Harvard Business School Press.

Gardner, P. D. (1991, March). *Learning the ropes: Socialization and assimilation into the workplace.* Paper presented at the Second National Conference on the Senior Year Experience, San Antonio, TX.

German, T. P., & Barrett, H. C. (2005). Functional fixedness in a technologically sparse culture. *Psychological Science, 16,* 1–5.

Giles, L. C., Glonek, F. V., Luszcz, M. A., & Andrews, G. R. (2005). Effect of social networks on 10-year survival in very old Australians: The Australia longitudinal study of aging. *Journal of Epidemiology and Community Health, 59,* 574–579.

Gilles, R. M., & Adrian, F. (2003). *Cooperative learning: The social and intellectual outcomes of learning in groups.* London, England: Farmer Press.

Gladwell, M. (2008). *Outliers: The story of success.* New York, NY: Little, Brown.

Glass, J., & Garrett, M. (1995). Student participation in a college orientation course: Retention and grade point average. *Community College Journal of Research and Practice, 19,* 117–132.

Glenberg, A. M. (1997). What memory is for. *Behavioral and Brain Sciences, 20,* 1–55.

Glenberg, A. M., Bradley, M. M., Kraus, T. A., & Renzaglia, G. J. (1983). Studies of the long-term recency effect: Support for a contextually guided retrieval hypothesis. *Journal of Experimental Psychology: Learning, Memory, & Cognition, 9,* 231–255.

Glenberg, A. M., Schroeder, J. L., & Robertson, D. A. (1998). Averting the gaze disengages the environment and facilitates remembering. *Memory & Cognition, 26*(4), 651–658.

Goldstein, W. M. & Hogarth, R. M. (Eds.). (1997). *Research on judgment and decision making,* Cambridge, UK: Cambridge University Press.

Goldsmith, E. B. (2010). *Resource management for individuals and families* (4th ed.). Upper Saddle River, NJ: Prentice Hall.

Goleman, D. (1992, October 27). Voters assailed by unfair persuasion. *The New York Times,* pp. C1–C3.

Goleman, D. (1995). *Emotional intelligence: Why it can matter more than IQ.* New York, NY: Random House.

Goleman, D. (2006). *Social intelligence: The new science of human relationships.* New York, NY: Dell.

Godden, D., & Baddeley, A. (1975). Context dependent memory in two natural environments. *British Journal of Psychology, 66*(3), 325–331.

Gordon, L. (2009, October 21). College costs up in hard times. *Los Angeles Times,* p. A13.

Gordon, V. N., & Steele, G. E. (2003). Undecided first-year students: A 25-year longitudinal study. *Journal of the First-Year Experience and Students in Transition, 15*(1), 19–38.

Gorski, P. C. (2009). Key characteristics of a multicultural curriculum. *Critical Multicultural Pavilion: Multicultural Curriculum Reform.* Retrieved June 12, 2011, from http://www.edchange.org/multicultural/curriculum/characteristics.html

Gottman, J. (1994). *Why marriages succeed and fail.* New York, NY: Fireside.

Gottman, J. (1999). *The seven principles for making marriage work.* New York, NY: Three Rivers Press.

Grandpre, E. (2000, September 21). First year attendance [Electronic mailing list message]. Retrieved from the First-Year Experience Listserv: fye-list@vm.sc.edu

Green, M. G. (Ed.). (1989). *Minorities on campus: A handbook for enhancing diversity.* Washington, DC: American Council on Education.

Greenberg, R., Pillard, R., & Pearlman, C. (1972). The effect of dream (stage REM) deprivation on adaptation to stress. *Psychosomatic Medicine, 34*(3), 257–262.

Grigg-Damberger, M. (2007). Normal sleep: Impact of age, circadian rhythms, and sleep debt. *Continuum Neurology, 13*(3), 31–84.

Grunder, P., & Hellmich, D. (1996). Academic persistence and achievement of remedial students in a community college's success program. *Community College Review, 24,* 21–33.

Haas, R. (1994). *Eat smart, think smart.* New York:HarperCollins.

Haberman, S., and Luffey, D. (1998). Weighing in college students' diet and exercise behaviors. *Journal of American College Health, 46,* 189–191.

Hacker, D., & Fister, B. (2010). *Research and documentation in the electronic age* (5th ed.). Boston, MA: Bedford/St. Martin's.

Halpern, D. F. (2003). *Thought & knowledge: An introduction to critical thinking* (4th ed.). Mahwah, NJ: Lawrence Erlbaum Associates.

Hamilton, H. (2012, March 13). Student loan blues. *Los Angeles Times*, pp. B1, B8.

Hamilton, W. (2011, December 29). College still worth it, study says. *Los Angeles Times*, p. B2.

Harriott, J., & Ferrari, J. R. (1996). Prevalence of chronic procrastination among samples of adults. *Psychological Reports, 73*, 873–877.

Harris, M. B. (2006). Correlates and characteristics of boredom and proneness to boredom. *Journal of Applied Social Psychology, 30*(3), 576–598.

Hartley, J. (1998). *Learning and studying: a research perspective*. London, England: Routledge.

Hartley, J., & Marshall, S. (1974). On notes and note taking. *Universities Quarterly, 28*, 225–235.

Hartman, H. J. (2001). *Metacognition in learning and instruction: Theory, research and practice*. Dordrecht Holland: Kluwer Academic.

Harvey, L., Moon, S., Geall, V., & Bower, R. (1997). *Graduates Work: Organizational change and students' attributes*. Birmingham, England: Centre for Research into Quality, University of Central England.

Hashaw, R. M., Hammond, C. J., & Rogers, P. H. (1990). Academic locus of control and the collegiate experience. *Research & Teaching in Developmental Education, 7*(1), 45–54.

Hatfield, E., & Rapson, R. L. (1993). *Love, sex, and intimacy: Their psychology, biology, and history*. New York, NY: HarperCollins.

Hauri, P., & Linde, S. (1996). *No more sleepless nights*. New York, NY: John Wiley & Sons.

Health, C., & Soll, J. (1996). Mental budgeting and consumer decisions. *Journal of Consumer Research, 23*, 40–52.

Heath, H. (1977). *Maturity and competence: A transcultural view*. New York, NY: Halsted Press.

Hendry, G., Heinrich, P., Lyon, P., Barratt, A. L., Simpson, J. M., Hyde, S. J., . . . Mgaieth, S. (2005). Helping students understand their learning styles: Effects on study self-efficacy, preference for group work, and group climate. *Journal of Educational Psychology, 25*(4), 395–407.

Herman, R. E. (2000, November). Liberal arts: The key to the future. *USA Today Magazine, 129*, 34.

Hersh, R. (1997). Intentions and perceptions: A national survey of public attitudes toward liberal arts education. *Change, 29*(2), 16–23.

Hertel, P. T., & Brozovich, F. (2010). Cognitive habits and memory distortions in anxiety and depression. *Current Directions in Psychological Science, 19*, 155–160.

Higbee, K. L. (2001). *Your memory: How it works and how to improve it*. New York, NY: Marlowe.

Higher Education Institute (HERI). (2009). *The American college teacher: National norms for 2007–2008*. Los Angeles, CA: Author.

Hildenbrand, M., & Gore, P. A., Jr. (2005). Career development in the first-year seminar: Best practice versus actual practice. In P. A. Gore (Ed.), *Facilitating the career development of students in transition* (Monograph No. 43, pp. 45–60). Columbia, SC: National Resource Center for the First-Year Experience and Students in Transition, University of South Carolina.

Hill, A. J. (2002). Developmental issues in attitudes toward food and diet. *Proceedings of the Nutrition Society, 61*(2), 259–268.

Hill, J. O., Wyat, H. R., Reed, G. W., & Peters, J. C. (2003). Obesity and environment: Where do we go from here? *Science, 299*, 853–855.

Hobson, J. A. (1988). *The dreaming brain*. New York, NY: Basic Books.

Hollenbeck, J. R., Williams, C. R., & Klein, H. J. (1989). An empirical examination of the antecedents of commitment to difficult goals. *Journal of Applied Psychology, 74*(1), 18–23.

Holmes, K. K., Levine, R., & Weaver, M. (2004). Effectiveness of condoms in preventing sexually transmitted infections. *Bulletin of the World Health Organization, 82,* 254–464.

Horne, J. (1988). *Why we sleep: The functions of sleep in humans and other mammals.* New York, NY: Oxford University Press.

Howard, P. J. (2000). *The owner's manual for the brain: Everyday applications of mind-brain research* (2nd ed.). Atlanta, GA: Bard Press.

Howe, M. J. (1970). Note-taking strategy, review, and long-term retention of verbal information. *Journal of Educational Psychology, 63,* 285.

Huck, S., & Bounds, W. (1972). Essay grades: An interaction between graders' handwriting clarity and the neatness of examination papers. *American Educational Research Journal, 9*(2), 279–283.

Hughes, D. C., Keeling, B., & Tuck, B. F. (1983). Effects of achievement expectations and handwriting quality on scoring essays. *Journal of Educational Measurement, 20*(1), 65–70.

Hunter, M. A., & Linder, C. W. (2005). First-year seminars. In M. L. Upcraft, J. N. Gardner, B. O. Barefoot, et al. (Eds.), *Challenging and supporting the first-year student: A handbook for improving the first year of college* (pp. 275–291). San Francisco, CA: Jossey-Bass.

Indiana University. (2004). *Selling your liberal arts degree to employers.* Retrieved July 7, 2004, from http://www.indiana.edu/~career/fulltime/selling_liberal_arts.html

Institute for Research on Higher Education. (1995). Connecting schools and employers: Work-related education and training. *Change, 27*(3), 39–46.

Internal Revenue Service. (2004). *Statistics of income 2001–2003.* Washington, DC: Author.

Inoue, Y. (2005, April). *Critical thinking and diversity experiences: A connection.* Paper presented at the Annual Meeting of the American Educational Research Association, Montreal, Canada.

Jaasma, M. A. (1997). Classroom communication apprehension: Does being male or female make a difference? *Communication Reports, 10,* 219–229.

Jablonski, N. G., & Chaplin, G. (2002, October). Skin deep. *Scientific American,* 75–81.

Jakubowski, P., & Lange, A. J. (1978). *The assertive option: Your rights and responsibilities.* Champaign, IL: Research Press.

Janis, I. L. (1982). *Groupthink: Psychological studies of policy decisions and fiascoes* (2nd ed.). Boston, MA: Houghton Mifflin.

Jenkins, J. G., & Dallenbach, K. M. (1924). Oblivescence during sleep and waking. *American Journal of Psychology, 35,* 605–612.

Jensen, E. (1998). *Teaching with the brain in mind.* Alexandria, VA: Association for Supervision and Curriculum Development.

Jensen, E. (2000). *Brain-based learning.* San Diego, CA: The Brain Store.

Jernigan, C. G. (2004). What do students expect to learn? The role of learner expectancies, beliefs, and attributions for success and failure in student motivation. *Current Issues in Education, 7*(4). Retrieved January 16, 2012, from http://cie.ed.asu.edu/volume7/number4

Johansson, J. (2005). *Death by PowerPoint.* Retrieved November 11, 2009, from http://articles.tech.republic.com5100-22_11-5875608.html

Johnsgard, K. W. (2004). *Conquering depression and anxiety through exercise.* New York, NY: Prometheus.

Johnson, D., Johnson, R., & Smith, K. (1998). Cooperative learning returns to college: What evidence is there that it works? *Change, 30,* 26–35.

Johnston, L. D., O'Malley, P. M., Bachman, J. G., & Schulenberg, J. E. (2005). *Monitoring the future national survey results on drug use, 1975–2004: Vol. 2. College students and adults ages 19–45* (NIH Publication No. 05-5728). Bethesda, MD: National Institute on Drug Abuse.

Johnstone, A. H., & Su, W. Y. (1994). Lectures: A learning experience? *Education in Chemistry, 31*(1), 65–76, 79.

Joint Science Academies Statement. (2005). *Global response to climate change.* Retrieved August 29, 2005, from http://nationalacademies.org/onpi/06072005.pdf

Jones, L., & Petruzzi, D. C. (1995). Test anxiety: A review of theory and current treatment. *Journal of College Student Psychotherapy, 10*(1), 3–15.

Julien, R. M. (2004). *A primer of drug action.* New York, NY: Worth.

Kachgal, M. M., Hansen, L. S., & Nutter, K. T. (2001). Academic procrastination prevention/intervention: Strategies and recommendations. *Journal of Developmental Education, 25*(1), 2–12.

Kadison, R. D., & DiGeronimo, T. F. (2004). *College of the overwhelmed: The campus mental health crisis and what to do about it.* San Francisco, CA: Jossey-Bass.

Kagan, S., & Kagan, M. (1998). *Multiple intelligences: The complete MI book.* San Clemente, CA: Kagan Cooperative Learning.

Karjane, H. K., Fisher, B. S., & Cullen, F. T. (2002). *Campus sexual assault: How America's institutions of higher education respond* (Final Report, NIJ Grant #1999-WA-VX-0008). Newton, MA: Education Development Center.

Katz, S. N. (2008, May 23). Taking the true measure of liberal education. *Chronicle of Higher Education,* 32.

Kaufman, J. C., & Baer, J. (2002). Could Steven Spielberg manage the Yankees? Creative thinking in different domains. *Korean Journal of Thinking & Problem Solving, 12*(2), 5–14.

Kearns, D. (1989, November). Getting schools back on track. *Newsweek,* pp. 8–9.

Kelly, K. (1994). *Out of control: The new biology of machines, social systems, and the economic world.* Reading, MA: Addison-Wesley.

Khoshaba, D., & Maddi, S. R. (2005). *HardiTraining: Managing stressful change* (4th ed.). Newport Beach, CA: Hardiness Institute.

Kidwell, B., & Turrisi, R. (2004). An examination of college student money management tendencies. *Journal of Economic Psychology, 25*(5), 601–616.

Kiewra, K. A. (1985). Students' note-taking behaviors and the efficacy of providing the instructor's notes for review. *Contemporary Educational Psychology, 10,* 378–386.

Kiewra, K. A. (2000). Fish giver or fishing teacher? The lure of strategy instruction. *Teaching at UNL (University of Nebraska–Lincoln), 22*(3), 1–3.

Kiewra, K. A. (2005). *Learn how to study and SOAR to success.* Upper Saddle River, NJ: Pearson Prentice Hall.

Kiewra, K. A., & DuBois, N. F. (1998). *Learning to learn: Making the transition from student to lifelong learner.* Needham Heights, MA: Allyn and Bacon.

Kiewra, K. A., DuBois, N., Christian, D., McShane, A., Meyerhoffer, M., & Roskelley, D. (1991). Note-taking functions and techniques. *Journal of Educational Psychology, 83*(2), 240–245.

Kiewra, K. A., & Fletcher, H. J. (1984). The relationship between notetaking variables and achievement measures. *Human Learning, 3,* 273–280.

Kiewra, K. A., Hart, K., Scoular, J., Stephen, M., Sterup, G., & Tyler, B. (2000). Fish giver or fishing teacher? The lure of strategy instruction. *Teaching at UNL (University of Nebraska–Lincoln), 22*(3).

King, A. (1990). Enhancing peer interaction and learning in the classroom through reciprocal questioning. *American Educational Research Journal, 27*(4), 664–687.

King, A. (1995). Guided peer questioning: A cooperative learning approach to critical thinking. *Cooperative Learning and College Teaching, 5*(2), 15–19.

King, A. (2002). Structuring peer interaction to promote high-level cognitive processing. *Theory into Practice, 41*(1), 33–39.

King, G. (2010, April). *A hard unsolved problem? Post-treatment bias in big social science questions.* Presentation made at the Hard Problems in Social Science Symposium, Institute for Quantitative Social Science, Harvard University, Cambridge, MA.

King, J. E. (2002). *Crucial choices: How students' financial decisions affect their academic success.* Washington, DC: American Council on Education.

King, J. E. (2005). Academic success and financial decisions: Helping students make crucial choices. In R. S. Feldman (Ed.), *Improving the first year of college: Research and practice* (pp. 3–26). Mahwah, NJ: Lawrence Erlbaum.

King, P. N., Brown, M. K., Lindsay, N. K., & VanHencke, J. R. (2007, September/October). Liberal arts student learning outcomes: An integrated approach. *About Campus,* 2–9.

Kintsch, W. (1970). *Learning, memory, and conceptual processes.* Hoboken, NJ: John Wiley & Sons.

Kintsch, W. (1994). Text comprehension, memory, and learning. *American Psychologist, 49,* 294–303.

Klein, S. P., & Hart, F. M. (1968). Chance and systematic factors affecting essay grades. *Journal of Educational Measurement, 5,* 197–206.

Knapp, J. R., & Karabenick, S. A. (1988). Incidence of formal and informal academic help-seeking in higher education. *Journal of College Student Development, 29*(3), 223–227.

Knaus, B. (2010, June 18). Ten top tips to end writer's block procrastination. *Psychology Today.* Retrieved March 7, 2012, from http://www.psychologytoday.com/blog/science-and-sensibility/201006ten-top-tips-end-writer-s-block-procrastination

Knoll, A. H. (2003). *Life on a young planet: The first three billion years of evolution on earth.* Princeton, NJ: Princeton University Press.

Knouse, S., Tanner, J., & Harris, E. (1999). The relation of college internships, college performance, and subsequent job opportunity. *Journal of Employment Counseling, 36,* 35–43.

Knox, S. (2004). *Financial basics: A money management guide for students.* Columbus, OH: Ohio State University Press.

Kolb, D. A. (1976). Management and learning process. *California Management Review, 18*(3), 21–31.

Kolb, D. A. (1985). *Learning styles inventory.* Boston, MA: McBer.

Kowalewski, D., Holstein, E., & Schneider, V. (1989). The validity of selected correlates of unexcused absences in a four-year private college. *Educational and Psychological Measurement, 49,* 985–991.

Kramer, A. F., & Erickson, K. I. (2007). Capitalizing on cortical plasticity: Influence of physical activity on cognition and brain function. *Trends in Cognitive Sciences, 11*(8), 342–348.

Kristof, K. M. (2008, December 27). Hooked on debt: Students learn too late the costs of private loans. *Los Angeles Times,* pp. A1, A18–A19.

Kruger, J., Wirtz, D., & Miller, D. (2005). Counterfactual thinking and the first instinct fallacy. *Journal of Personality and Social Psychology, 88,* 725–735.

Kucewicz, N. (2001, August 15). Ins and outs of the college dating game: fun or forever? *The Rocky Mountain Collegian.* Retrieved January 3, 2004, from http://www.collegian.com/vnews/display.v/ART/2001/08/15/3d78c7cd538ef?in_archive=1

Kuh, G. D. (1993). In their own words: What students learn outside the classroom. *American Educational Research Journal, 30,* 277–304.

Kuh, G. D. (1995). The other curriculum: Out-of-class experiences associated with student learning and personal development. *Journal of Higher Education, 66*(2), 123–153.

Kuh, G. D. (2005). Student engagement in the first year of college. In M. L. Upcraft, J. N. Gardner, B. O. Barefoot, et al. (Eds.), *Challenging and supporting the first-year student: A handbook for improving the first year of college* (pp. 86–107). San Francisco, CA: Jossey-Bass.

Kuh, G. D., Douglas, K. B., Lund, J. P., & Ramin-Gyurnek, J. (1994). *Student learning outside the classroom: Transcending artificial boundaries* (ASHE-ERIC Higher Education Report No. 8). Washington, DC: George Washington University, School of Education and Human Development.

Kuh, G. D., Kinzie, J., Schuh, J. H., Whitt, E. J., et al. (2005). *Student success in college: Creating conditions that matter.* San Francisco, CA: Jossey-Bass.

Kuh, G. D., Shedd, J. D., & Whitt, E. J. (1987). Student affairs and liberal education: Unrecognized (and unappreciated) common law partners. *Journal of College Student Personnel, 28,* 252–260.

Kuhn, L. (1988). What should we tell students about answer changing? *Research Serving Teaching, 1*(8).

Kurfiss, J. G. (1988). *Critical thinking: Theory, research, practice, and possibilities* (ASHE-ERIC Report No. 2). Washington, DC: Association for the Study of Higher Education.

Kuriyama, K., Mishima, K., Suzuki, H., Aritake, S., & Uchiyama, M. (2008). Sleep accelerates improvement in working memory performance. *The Journal of Neuroscience, 28*(4), 10145–10150.

Lack, L. C., Gradisar, M., Van Someren, E. J. W., Wright, H. R., & Lushington, K. (2008). The relationship between insomnia and body temperatures. *Sleep Medicine Reviews, 12*(4), 307–317.

Ladas, H. S. (1980). Note-taking on lectures: An information-processing approach. *Educational Psychologist, 15*(1), 44–53.

Lakein, A. (1973). *How to get control of your time and your life.* New York, NY: New American Library.

Lancaster, L., & Stilman, D. (2002). *When generations collide: Who they are. Why they clash.* New York, NY: HarperCollins.

Langer, J. A., & Applebee, A. N. (1987). *How writing shapes thinking* (NCTE Research Report No. 22). Urbana, IL: National Council of Teachers of English.

Latané, B., Liu, J. H., Nowak, A., Bonevento, N., & Zheng, L. (1995). Distance matters: Physical space and social impact. *Personality and Social Psychology Bulletin, 21,* 795–805.

Launius, M. H. (1997). College student attendance: Attitudes and academic performance. *College Student Journal, 31*(1), 86–93.

Lay, C. H., & Silverman, S. (1996). Trait procrastination, time management, and dilatory behavior. *Personality & Individual Differences, 21,* 61–67.

Leavy, P., Gnong, A., & Ross, L. S. (2009). Femininity, masculinity, and body image issues among college-age women: An in-depth and written interview study of the mind-body dichotomy. *The Qualitative Report, 14*(2), 261–292.

LeDoux, J. (1998). *The emotional brain: The mysterious underpinnings of emotional life.* New York, NY: Simon & Schuster.

LeDoux, J. (2003). The emotional brain, fear, and the amygdala. *Cellular and Molecular Neurobiology, 23*(4–5), 727–738.

Lehrer, P., Barlow, D. H., Woolfolk, R. L., & Sime, W. E. (Eds.). (2007). *Principles and practice of stress management* (3rd ed.*). New York, NY: The Guilford Press.

Leibel, R. L., Rosenbaum, M., & Hirsch, J. (1995). Changes in energy expenditure resulting from altered body weight. *New England Journal of Medicine, 332,* 621–628.

Leonard, G. (2008). *A study on the effects of student employment on retention.* Retrieved June 17, 2010, from http://uc.iupui.edu/Portals/155/uploadedFiles/Deans/StudEmpRetentionRprt.pdf

Levitin, D. J. (2006). *This is your brain on music: The science of a human obsession.* New York, NY: Dutton.

Leuwerke, W. C., Robbins, S. B., Sawyer, R., & Hovland, M. (2004). Predicting engineering major status from mathematics achievement and interest congruence. *Journal of Career Assessment, 12,* 135–149.

Levine, A., & Cureton, J. S. (1998). *When hopes and fears collide.* San Francisco, CA: Jossey-Bass.

Levitsky, D. A., Nussbaum, M., Halbmaier, C. A., & Mrdjenovic, G. (2003, July). *The freshman 15: A model for the study of techniques to curb the "epidemic" of obesity.* Paper presented at the annual meeting of the Society of the Study of Ingestive Behavior, University of Groningen, Haren, The Netherlands.

Levitz, R., & Noel, L. (1989). Connecting student to the institution: Keys to retention and success. In M. L. Upcraft, J. N. Gardner, et al. (Eds.), *The freshman year experience* (pp. 65–81). San Francisco, CA: Jossey-Bass.

Liebertz, C. (2005a). A healthy laugh. *Scientific American Mind, 16*(3), 90–91.

Liebertz, C. (2005b). Want clear thinking? Relax. *Scientific American Mind, 16*(3), 88–89.

Light, R. L. (1990). *The Harvard assessment seminars.* Cambridge, MA: Harvard University Press.

Light, R. L. (1992). *The Harvard assessment seminars, second report.* Cambridge, MA: Harvard University Press.

Light, R. J. (2001). *Making the most of college: Students speak their minds.* Cambridge, MA: Harvard University Press.

Linn, R. L., & Gronlund, N. E. (1995). *Measurement and assessment in teaching* (7th ed.). Englewood Cliffs, NJ: Prentice Hall.

Lock, R. D. (2004). *Taking charge of your career direction* (5th ed.). Belmont, CA: Brooks Cole.

Locke, E. (1977). An empirical study of lecture note-taking among college students. *Journal of Educational Research, 77,* 93–99.

Locke, E. A. (2000). Motivation, cognition, and action: An analysis of studies of task goals and knowledge. *Applied Psychology: An International Review, 49,* 408–429.

Locke, E. A., & Latham, G. P. (1990). *A theory of goal setting and task performance.* Englewood Cliffs, NJ: Prentice Hall.

Locke, E.A., & Latham, G. P. (2005). Goal setting theory: Theory building by induction. In K. G. Smith & M. A. Mitt (Eds.), *Great minds in management: The process of theory development.* New York, NY: Oxford.

Love, P., & Love, A. G. (1995). *Enhancing student learning: Intellectual, social, and emotional integration* (ASHE-ERIC Higher Education Report No. 4). Washington, DC: Graduate School of Education and Human Development, George Washington University.

Lucas, S. E. (2003). *The art of public speaking* (8th ed.). New York, NY: McGraw-Hill.

Luthra, R., & Gidycz, C. A. (2006). Dating violence among college men and women: Evaluation of a theoretical model. *Journal of Interpersonal Violence, 21*, 717–731.

Luotto, J. A., Stoll, E. L., & Hoglund-Kettmann, N. (2001). *Communication skills for collaborative learning* (2nd ed.). Dubuque, IA: Kendall Hunt.

Mackes, M. (2003). Employers describe perfect job candidate. *NACEWeb Press Releases.* Retrieved July 13, 2004, from http://www.naceweb.org/press

Maddi, S. R. (2002). The story of hardiness: Twenty years of theorizing, research, and practice. *Consulting Psychology Journal: Practice and Research, 54*(3), 175–185.

Mae, N. (2005). *Undergraduate students and credit cards in 2004: An analysis of usage rates and trend.* Wilkes-Barre, PA: Nellie Mae.

Maes, J. D., Weldy, T. G., & Icenogle, M. L. (1997). A managerial perspective: Oral communication competency is most important for business students in the workplace. *Journal of Business Communication, 34*(1), 67–80.

Maier, N. R. F. (1970). *Problem solving and creativity in individuals and groups.* Belmont, CA: Brooks/Cole.

Malik, S., Sorenson, S. B., & Aneshensel, C. S. (1997). Community and dating violence among adolescents: Perpetration and victimization. *Journal of Adolescent Health, 21*(5), 291–302.

Malinauskas, B. M., Aeby, V. G., Overton, R. F., Carpenter-Aeby, T., & Barber-Heidal, K. (2007). A survey of energy drink consumption patterns among college students. *Nutrition Journal, 6*(1), 35.

Malmberg, K. J., & Murnane, K. (2002). List composition and the word-frequency effect for recognition memory. *Journal of Experimental Psychology: Learning, Memory, and Cognition, 28*, 616–630.

Malvasi, M., Rudowsky, C., & Valencia, J. M. (2009). *Library Rx: Measuring and treating library anxiety, a research study.* Chicago, IL: Association of College and Research Libraries.

Marczinski, C., Estee, G., & Grant, V. (2009). *Binge drinking in adolescent and college students.* New York, NY: Nova Science.

Martin, P. Y., & Benton, D. (1999). The influence of a glucose drink on a demanding working memory task. *Physiology and Behavior, 67*(1), 69–74

Marzano, R. J., Pickering, D. J., & Pollock, J. (2001). *Classroom instruction that works: Research-based strategies for increasing student achievement.* Alexandria, VA: Association for Supervision and Curriculum Development.

Maslow, A. H. (1954). *Motivation and personality.* New York, NY: Harper & Row.

Matsui, T., Okada, A., & Inoshita, O. (1983). Mechanism of feedback affecting task performance. *Organizational Behavior and Human Performance, 31*, 114–122.

Mayer, R. E. (2002). Rote versus meaningful learning. *Theory Into Practice, 41*(4), 226–232.

Mayer, R. (2003). *Learning and instruction.* Upper Saddle River, NJ: Pearson Education.

McCance, N., & Pychyl, T. A. (2003, August). *From task avoidance to action: An experience sampling study of undergraduate students' thoughts, feelings and coping strategies in relation to academic procrastination.* Paper presented at the Third Annual Conference for Counseling Procrastinators in the Academic Context, University of Ohio, Columbus, OH.

McGuiness, D., & Pribram, K. (1980). The neurophysiology of attention: Emotional and motivational controls. In M. D. Wittrock (Ed.), *The brain and psychology* (pp. 95–139). New York, NY: Academic Press.

McKay, M., Davis, M., & Fanning, P. (2009). *Messages: The communication skills book* (2nd ed.). Oakland, CA: New Harbinger.

Meilman, P. W., & Presley, C. A. (2005). The first-year experience and alcohol use. In M. L. Upcraft, J. N. Gardner, B. O. Barefoot, et al. (Eds.), *Challenging and supporting the first-year student: A handbook for improving the first year of college* (pp. 445–468). San Francisco, CA: Jossey-Bass.

Melton, G. B. (1995). *The individual, the family, and social good: personal fulfillment in times of change.* Lincoln, NE: University of Nebraska Press.

Meyer, P. J. (2003). *Attitude is everything: If you want to succeed above and beyond.* Waco, TX: Meyer Resource Group.

Middleton, F., & Strick, P. (1994). Anatomical evidence for cerebellar and basal ganglia involvement in higher brain function. *Science, 226*(51584), 458–461.

Millard, B. (2004, November 7). *A purpose-based approach to navigating college transitions.* Preconference workshop presented at the Eleventh National Conference on Students in Transition, Nashville, TN.

Miller, G. (1988). *The meaning of general education.* New York, NY: Teachers College Press.

Miller, L. M. (2011). Physical abuse in a college setting: A study of perceptions and perceptions in abusive dating relationships. *Journal of Family Violence, 26*(1), 71–80.

Miller, M. A. (2003, September/October). The meaning of the baccalaureate. *About Campus,* 2–8.

Miller, G. D., & Foster, L. T. (2010). *Critical synthesis of wellness literature.* Retrieved November 12, 2011, from http://www.geog.uvic.ca/wellness

Miller, W. R., & Munoz, R. G. (2005). *Controlling your drinking: Tools to make moderation work for you.* New York, NY: Guilford Press.

Milton, O. (1982). *Will that be on the final?* Springfield, IL: Charles C. Thomas.

Minninger, J. (1984). *Total recall: How to boost your memory power.* Emmaus, PA: Rodale.

Mitler, M. M., Dinges, D. F., & Dement, W. C. (1994). Sleep medicine, public policy, and public health. In M. H. Kryger, T. Roth, & W. C. Dement (Eds.), *Principles and practice of sleep medicine* (2nd ed.). Philadelphia, PA: Saunders.

Molnar, S. (1991). *Human variation: race, type, and ethnic groups* (3rd ed.). Englewood Cliffs, NJ: Prentice Hall.

Monk, T. H. (2005). The post-lunch dip in performance. *Clinical Sports Medicine, 24*(2), 15–23.

Morgenstern, J. (2004). *Time management from the inside out: The foolproof system for taking control of your schedule—and your life* (2nd ed.). New York, NY: Henry Holt.

Morreale, S. P. (Ed.). (2007). *Assessing motivation to communicate: Willingness to communicate and personal report of communication apprehension* (2nd ed.). Washington, DC: National Communication Association.

Mothers Against Drunk Driving. (2012). Why 21?: Addressing underage drinking. Retrieved October 30, 2012, from http://www.madd.org/underage-drinking/why21

Muehlenhard, C. L., & Peterson, Z. D. (2011). Distinguishing between *sex* and *gender*: History, current conceptualizations, and implications. *Sex Roles, 64*(11/12), 791–803.

Multon, K. D., Brown, S. D., & Lent, R. W. (1991). Relation of self-efficacy beliefs to academic outcomes: A meta-analytic investigation. *Journal of Counseling Psychology, 38*(1), 30–38.

Murnane, K., & Shiffrin, R. M. (1991). Interference and the representation of events in memory. *Journal of Experimental Psychology: Learning, Memory, & Cognition, 17,* 855–874.

Murray, C. E., & Kardatzke, K. N. (2007). Dating violence among college students: Key issues for college counselors. *Journal of College Counseling, 10*(1), 79–89.

Murray, D. M. (2002). *Write to learn* (7th ed.). Fort Worth, TX: Harcourt Brace.

Myers, D. G. (1993). *The pursuit of happiness: Who is happy—and why?* New York, NY: Morrow.

Myers, D. G. (2000). The funds, friends, and faith of happy people. *American Psychologist, 55,* 56–67.

Myers, N. (1997). Environmental Refugees. Population and Environment: A Journal of Interdisciplinary Studies **19**(2): 167–182.

Nagda, B. R., Gurin, P., & Johnson, S. M. (2005). Living, doing and thinking diversity: How does pre-college diversity experience affect first-year students' engagement with college diversity? In R. S. Feldman (Ed.), *Improving the first year of college: Research and practice* (pp. 73–110). Mahwah, NJ: Lawrence Erlbaum.

Naisbitt, J. (1982). *Megatrends: Ten new directions transforming our lives.* New York, NY: Warner Books.

Natale, V., & Cicogna, P. (1996). Circadian regulation of subjective alertness in morning and evening "types". *Personality and Individual Differences, 20*(4), 491–497.

National Alliance to End Homelessness. (2007). *Homelessness counts.* Retrieved from http:www.endhomelessness.org/content/general/detail/1440

National Associatio of Colleges & Employers. (2003). *Job Outlook 2003 survey.* Bethlehem, PA: Author.

National Association of Colleges & Employers. (2007). *Developing the diverse college-educated work force.* Retrieved May 12, 2011, from http://www.naceweb.org/Journal/2007october/Diverse_Work_Force

National Association of Colleges & Employers. (2010). *2009 experiential education survey.* Bethlehem, PA: Author.

National Association of Colleges & Employers. (2012a). *Internship and co-op survey.* Bethlehem, PA: Author.

National Association of Colleges & Employers. (2012b). *Job outlook: The candidate skills/qualities employers want.* Bethlehem, PA: Author.

National Center for Victims of Crime. (2008). *Sexual assault.* Retrieved May 12, 2011, from http://www.ncvc.org/ncvc/main.aspx?dbName=DocumentViewer&DocumentID=32369

National Council for the Social Sciences (NCSS). (1991). *Curriculum guidelines for multicultural education.* Retrieved January 12, 2011, from http://www.socialstudies.org/positions/multicultural

National Forum on Information Literacy. (2005). *Forum overview.* Retrieved October 17, 2005, from http://www.infolit.org

National Institute of Diabetes & Digestive Kidney Diseases (NIDDK). (2010). *Overweight and obesity statistics.* Washington, DC: U.S. Department of Health and Human Services.

National Institute of Mental Health. (2008). *The numbers count: Mental disorders in America.* Retrieved June 9, 2012, from http://wwwapps.nimh.nih.gov/health/publications/the-numbers-count-mental-disorders-in-america.shtml#Eating

National Institute of Mental Health. (2011). *Eating disorders.* Washington, DC: U.S. Department of Health and Human Services.

National Resource Center for the First-Year Experience and Students in Transition. (2004). *The 2003 Your First College Year (YFCY) Survey.* Columbia, SC: Author.

National Resources Defense Council. (2012). *Global warming: An introduction to climate change.* Retrieved May 11, 2012, from http://www.nrdc.org/globalwarming

National Survey of Student Engagement. (2008). *NSSE Annual Results 2008. Promoting engagement for all students: The imperative to look within.* Bloomington, IN: Author.

National Survey of Student Engagement. (2009). *NSSE Annual Results 2009. Assessment for improvement: Tracking student engagement over time.* Bloomington, IN: Author.

Navarro, J. (2008). *What every body is saying.* New York, NY: HarperCollins.

Nelson, M. C., Lust, K., Story, M., & Ehlinger, E. (2008). Credit card debt, stress and key health risk behaviors among college students. *American Journal of Health Promotion, 22*(6), 400–407.

Newell, A., & Simon, H. A. (1959). *The simulation of human thought.* Santa Monica, CA: Rand Corporation.

Newton, T. (1990, September). *Improving students' listening skills* (IDEA Paper No. 23). Manhattan, KS: Center for Faculty Evaluation and Development.

NHTSA/FARS & U.S. Census Bureau. (2012). *Underage drunk driving fatalities.* Retrieved June 2, 2012, from http://www.centurycouncil.org/drunk-driving/underage-drunk-driving-fatalities

Nichols, M. P. (1995). *The lost art of listening.* New York, NY: Guilford Press.

Niederjohn, M. S. (2008). First-year experience course improves students' financial literacy. *ESource for College Transitions* [Electronic newsletter published by the National Resource Center for the First-Year Experience and Students in Transition], 6(1), 9–11.

Nieman, D. C. & Nehlsen-Cannarella, S. L. (1994). The immune response to exercise. *Seminars in Hematology, 31,* 166–179.

Niles, S. G., & Harris-Bowlsbey, J. (2002). *Career development interventions in the 21st century.* Upper Saddle River, NJ: Pearson Education.

Norman, D. A. (1982). *Learning and memory.* San Francisco, CA: W. H. Freeman.

Nuñez, A. (2005). Negotiating ties: A qualitative study of first-generation female students' transitions to college. *Journal of the First-Year Experience & Students in Transition, 17*(2), 97–118.

Obama, B. (2006). *The audacity of hope: Thoughts on reclaiming the American dream.* New York, NY: Three Rivers Press.

Office of Public Affairs. (2012, January 6). Attorney General Eric Holder announces revisions to the Uniform Crime Report's definition of rape. *United States Department of Justice.* Retrieved June 23, 2012, from http://www.justice.gov/opa/pr/2012/January/12-ag-018.html

Office of Research. (1994). *What employers expect of college graduates: International knowledge and second language skills.* Washington, DC: Office of Educational Research and Improvement, U.S. Department of Education.

Ohayon, M. M., Carskadon, M. A., Guilleminault, C., & Vitiello, M. V. (2004). Meta-analysis of quantitative sleep parameters from childhood to old age in healthy individuals: developing normative sleep values across the human lifespan. *Sleep, 27,* 1255–1273.

Okimoto, M., & Norman, D. A. (2010). *A comprehensive strategy for better reading, cognition and emotion.* Tokyo, Japan: Kaitakusha.

Onwuegbuzie, A. J. (2000). Academic procrastinators and perfectionistic tendencies among graduate students. *Journal of Social Behavior and Personality, 15,* 103–109.

Orszag, J. M., Orszag, P. R., & Whitmore, D. M. (2001). *Learning and earning: Working in college.* Retrieved July 19, 2006, from http://www.brockport.edu/career01/upromise.htm

Ottens, A. J., & Hotelling, K. (2001). *Sexual violence on campus: Policies, programs, and perspectives.* New York, NY: Springer.

Pace, C. (1990). *The undergraduates: A report of their activities.* Los Angeles, CA: University of California, Center for the Study of Evaluation.

Pace, C. (1995, May). *From good processes to good products: Relating good practices in undergraduate education to student achievement.* Paper presented at the meeting of the Association for Institutional Research, Boston, MA.

Pai, P., Sanji, N. et al. (2010). Student performances in MCQ versus essay questions. *Journal of Clinical and Diagnostic Research, 4,* 2515–2520.

Pai, M. R., Sanji, N., Pai, P. G., & Kotian, S. (2010). Comparative assessment in pharmacology multiple choice questions versus essay with focus on gender differences. *Journal of Clinical and Diagnostic Research, 4*(3), 2515–2520.

Paivio, A. (1990). *Mental representations: A dual coding approach.* New York, NY: Oxford University Press.

Palank, J. (2006, July 17). *Face it: "Book" no secret to employers.* Retrieved August 21, 2006, from http://www.washtimes.com/business/20060717-12942-1800r.htm

Park, O. (1984). Example comparison strategy versus attribute identification strategy in concept learning. *American Educational Research Journal, 21*(1), 145–162.

Parker, R. (2009). Sexuality culture, and society: Shifting paradigms in sexuality research. *Culture, Health, & Society, 11*(3), 251–266.

Pascarella, E. T. (2001, November/December). Cognitive growth in college: Surprising and reassuring findings from the National Study of Student Learning. *Change,* 21–27.

Pascarella, E. T., & Terenzini, P. (1991). *How college affects students: Findings and insights from twenty years of research.* San Francisco, CA: Jossey-Bass.

Pascarella, E. T., & Terenzini, P. (2005). *How college affects students: A third decade of research* (Vol. 2). San Francisco, CA: Jossey-Bass.

Patchan, M. M., Charney, D., & Schunn, C. D. (2009). A validation study of students' end comments: Comparing comments by students, a writing instructor, and a content instructor. *Journal of Writing Research, 1*(2) 124–152.

Paul, R., & Elder, L. (2002). *Critical thinking: Tools for taking charge of your professional and personal life.* Upper Saddle River, NJ: Pearson Education.

Paul, R., & Elder, L. (2004). *The nature and functions of critical and creative thinking.* Dillon Beach, CA: Foundation for Critical Thinking.

Peigneux, P. P., Laureys, S., Delbeuck, X., & Maquet, P. (2001, December 21). Sleeping brain, learning brain: The role of sleep for memory systems. *NeuroReport, 12*(18), A111–A124.

Penfold, R. B. (2006). *Dragonslippers: This is what an abusive relationship looks like.* New York, NY: Grove/Atlantic.

Peoples, J., & Bailey, G. (2008). *Humanity: An introduction to cultural anthropology.* Independence, KY: Cengage Learning.

Perna, L. W., & DuBois, G. (Eds.). (2010). *Understanding the working college student: New research and its implications for policy and practice.* Sterling, VA: Stylus.

Perry, A. B. (2004). Decreasing math anxiety in college students. *College Student Journal, 38*(2), 321–324.

Perry, A. R., & Fromuth, M. E. (2005). Courtship violence using couple data. *Journal of Interpersonal Violence, 20,* 1078–1095.

Perry, W. G. (1970, 1999). *Forms of intellectual and ethical development during the college years: A scheme.* New York: Holt, Rinehart & Winston.

Peter D. Hart Research Associates. (2006). *How should colleges prepare students to succeed in today's global economy?* Washington, DC: Author.

Peterson, C., & Seligman, M. E. P. (2004). *Character strengths and virtues: A handbook and classification.* New York, NY: Oxford University Press.

Pettigrew, T. F. (1998). Intergroup contact theory. *Annual Review of Psychology, 49,* 65–85.

Pew Internet & American Life Project. (2002). *The Internet goes to college: How students are living in the future with today's technology.* Retrieved January 30, 2005, from http://www. perinternet.org/reports/pdfs/Report1.pdf

Piaget, J. (1978). *Success and understanding.* Cambridge, MA: Harvard University Press.

Piaget, J. (1985). *The equilibration of cognitive structures: The central problem of intellectual development.* Chicago, IL: University of Chicago Press.

Pinker, S. (2000). *The language instinct: The new science of language and mind.* New York, NY: Perennial.

Pintrich, P. R. (Ed.). (1995). *Understanding self-regulated learning* (New Directions for Teaching and Learning, No. 63). San Francisco, CA: Jossey-Bass.

Pintrich, P. R., & Schunk, D. H. (2002). *Motivation in education: Theory, research, and applications.* Upper Saddle River, NJ: Merrill-Prentice Hall.

Plagiarism.org. (2012). Plagiarism FAQs. Retrieved October 25, 2012, from http://www.plagiarism.org/plag_article_plagiarism_faq.html.

Pope, L. (1990). *Looking beyond the Ivy League.* New York, NY: Penguin Press.

Porter, S. R., & Swing, R. L. (2006). Understanding how first-year seminars affect persistence. *Research in Higher Education, 47*(1), 89–109.

President's Council on Physical Fitness and Sports. (2001). Toward a uniform definition of wellness: A commentary. *Research Digest, 3*(15), 1–8.

Pratt, B. (2008). *Extra credit: The 7 things every college student needs to know about credit, debt & cash.* Keedysville, MD: ExtraCreditBook.com.

Pratto, F., Liu, J. H., Levin, S., Sidanius, J., Shih, M., Bachrach, H., & Hegarty, P. (2000). Social dominance orientation and the legitimization of inequality across cultures. *Journal of Cross-Cultural Psychology, 31,* 369–409.

Price, R. H., Choi, J. N., & Vinokur, A. D. (2002). Links in the chain of adversity following job loss: How financial strain and loss of personal control lead to depression, impaired functioning, and poor health. *Journal of Occupational Health Psychology, 7*(4), 302–312.

Priest, J. B., Edwards, A. B., Wetchler, J. L., Gillotti, C. M., Cobb, R. A., & Borst, C. W. (2012). An exploratory evaluation of the cognitive-active gender role identification continuum. *The American Journal of Family Therapy, 40*(2), 152–168.

Prinsell, C. P., Ramsey, P. H., & Ramsey, P. P. (1994). Score gains, attitudes, and behaviour changes due to answer-changing instruction. *Journal of Educational Measurement, 31,* 327–337.

Pryor, J. H., De Angelo, L., Palucki-Blake, B., Hurtado, S., & Tran, S. (2012). *The American freshman: National norms fall 2011.* Los Angeles, CA: Higher Education Research Institute, UCLA.

Public Service Enterprise Group (PSEG). (2009). *Diversity.* Retrieved January 6, 2009, from http://www.pseg.com/info/environment/sustainability/2009/people/diversity.jsp

Purdue University Online Writing Lab. (2012). *Writing a research paper.* Retrieved May 18, 2012, from http://owl.english.purdue.edu

Purdy, M., & Borisoff, D. (Eds.). (1996). *Listening in everyday life: A personal and professional approach.* Lanham, MD: University Press of America.

Putman, R. D. (2000). *Bowling alone: The collapse and revival of American community.* New York, NY: Simon & Schuster.

Rader, P.E., & Hicks, R.A. (1987, April). *Jet lag desynchronization and self-assessment of business-related performance.* Paper presented at the Western Psychological Association, Long Beach, CA.

Ramsden, P. (2003). *Learning to teach in higher education* (2nd ed.). London, England: RoutledgeFalmer.

Rankin, H. A., Abrams, T., Barry, R. J., Bhatnagar, S., Clayton, D. F., Colombo, J., & Thompson, R. F. (2009). Habituation revisited: An updated and revised description of the behavioral characteristics of habituation. *Neurobiology of Learning and Memory, 92*(2), 135–138.

Ratcliff, J. L. (1997). What is a curriculum and what should it be? In J. G. Gaff, J. L. Ratcliff, et al. (Eds.), *Handbook of the undergraduate curriculum: A comprehensive guide to purposes, structures, practices, and change* (pp. 5–29). San Francisco, CA: Jossey-Bass.

Ratey, J. J. (2008). *Spark: The revolutionary new science of exercise and the brain.* New York, NY: Little, Brown.

Reed, S. K. (1996). *Cognition: Theory and applications* (3rd ed.). Pacific Grove, CA: Brooks/Cole.

Rennels, M. R., & Chaudhair, R. B. (1988, October). Eye-contact and grade distribution. *Perceptual and Motor Skills, 67,* 627–632.

Rennie, D., & Brewer, L. (1987). A grounded theory of thesis blocking. *Teaching of Psychology, 14*(1), 10–16.

Rhoads, J. (2005). *The transition to college: Top ten issues identified by students.* Retrieved June 30, 2006, from http://advising.wichita.edu/lasac/pubs/aah/trans.htm

Rhodewalt, F., & Vohs, K. D. (2005). Defensive strategies, motivation, and the self. In A. Elliot & C. Dweck (Eds.), *Handbook of competence and motivation* (pp. 548–565). New York, NY: Guilford Press.

Richmond, V. P., & McCloskey, J. C. (1997). *Communication apprehension: Avoidance and effectiveness* (5th ed.). Boston, MA: Allyn & Bacon.

Riesman, D., Glazer, N., & Denney, R. (2001). *The lonely crowd: A study of the changing American character* (Rev. ed.). New Haven, CT: Yale University Press.

Ring, T. (1997, October). Issuers face a visit to the dean's office. *Credit Card Management, 10,* 34–39.

Riquelme, H. (2002). Can people creative in imagery interpret ambiguous figures faster than people less creative in imagery? *Journal of Creative Behavior, 36*(2), 105–116.

Roediger, H. L., Dudai, Y., & Fitzpatrick, S. M. (2007). *Science of memory: concepts.* New York, NY: Oxford University Press.

Roediger, H., & Karpicke, J. (2006). The power of testing memory: Basic research and implications for educational practice. *Perspectives on Psychological Science. 1*(3), 181–210.

Roffwarg, H. P., Muzio, J. N., & Dement, W. C. (1966). Ontogenetic development of the human sleep-dream cycle. *Science, 152,* 604–619.

Roos, L. L., Wise, S. L., Yoes, M. E., & Rocklin, T. R. (1996). Conducting self-adapted testing using MicroCAT. *Educational and Psychological Measurement, 56,* 821–827.

Rosenberg, M. (2009). *The number of countries in the world.* Retrieved November 18, 2009, from http://geography.about.com/cs/countries/a/numbercountries.htm

Rosenfield, I. (1988). *The invention of memory: A new view of the brain.* New York, NY: Basic Books.

Rosenthal, R. (1966). *Experimenter effects in behavioral research.* New York, NY: Appleton-Century-Crofts.

Rothblum, E. D., Solomon, L. J., & Murakami, J. (1986). Affective, cognitive, and behavioral differences between high and low procrastinators. *Journal of Counseling Psychology, 33*(4), 387–394.

Rotter, J. (1966). Generalized expectancies for internal versus external controls of reinforcement. *Psychological Monographs: General and Applied, 80*(609), 1–28.

Ruggiero, V. R. (2004). *Beyond feelings: A guide to critical thinking.* New York, NY: McGraw-Hill.

Runco, M. A. (2004). Creativity. *Annual Review of Psychology, 55,* 657–687.

Ryan, R. (1995). Psychological needs and the facilitation of integrative processes. *Journal of Personality, 63,* 397–427.

Sadker, M., & Sadker, D. (1994). *Failing at fairness: How America's schools cheat girls.* New York, NY: Charles Scribner's Sons.

Salovey, P., & Mayer, J. D. (1990). Emotional intelligence. *Imagination, Cognition, and Personality, 9,* 185–211.

Samuels, S. J., & Flor, R. F. (1997). The importance of automaticity for developing expertise in reading. *Reading & Writing Quarterly, 13*(2), 107–121.

Sapolsky, R. (2004). *Why zebras don't get ulcers.* New York, NY: W. H. Freeman.

Sax, L. J. (2003, July–August). Our incoming students: What are they like? *About Campus,* 15–20.

Sax, L. J., Astin, A. W., Korn, W. S., & Mahoney, K. M. (1999). *The American freshman: National norms for fall 1999.* Los Angeles, CA: Higher Education Research Institute, Graduate School of Education & Information Studies, University of California.

Sax, L. J., Bryant, A. N., & Gilmartin, S. K. (2004). A longitudinal investigation of emotional health among male and female first-year college students. *Journal of the First-Year Experience and Students in Transition, 16*(2), 29–65.

Sax, L. J., Lindholm, J. A., Astin, A. W., Korn, W. S., & Mahoney, K. M. (2004). *The American freshman: National norms for fall 2004.* Los Angeles, CA: Higher Education Research Institute, University of California.

Schab, F. R. (1990). Odors and the remembrance of things past. *Journal of Experimental Psychology: Learning, Memory, and Cognition, 16*(4), 648–655.

Schacter, D. L. (1992). Understanding implicit memory. *American Psychologist, 47*(4), 559–569.

Schacter, D. L. (2001). *The seven sins of memory: how the mind forgets and remembers.* Boston, MA: Houghton Mifflin.

Schilling, K. (2001, August). *Plenary address.* Presented at The Summer Institute on First-Year Assessment, Asheville, NC.

Schlosser, E. (2005). *Fast food nation: The dark side of the all-American meal.* New York, NY: Harper Perennial.

Schneider, E. C., Zaslavsky, A. M., & Epstein, A. M. (2002). Racial disparities in the quality of care for enrollees in Medicare managed care. *Journal of the American Medical Association, 287,* 1288–1294.

Schneider, C. G., & Shoenberg, R. (1998). *Contemporary understandings of liberal education.* Washington, DC: Association of American Colleges & Universities.

Schneider, W., & Chein, J. M. (2003). Controlled and automatic processing: Behavior, theory, and biological mechanisms. *Cognitive Science, 27,* 525–559.

Schommer-Aikins, M., Duell, O. K., & Barker, S. (2003). Epistemological beliefs across domains using Biglan's classification of academic disciplines. *Research in Higher Education, 44*(3), 347–366.

Schunk, D. H. (1995). Self-efficacy and education and instruction. In J. E. Maddux (Ed.), *Self-efficacy, adaptation, and adjustment: Theory, research, and application* (pp. 281–303). New York, NY: Plenum Press.

Seabrook, J. (2008). *Flash of genius and other true stories of invention.* New York, NY: St. Martin's Press.

SECFHE. (2006). *A national dialogue: The Secretary of Education's Commission on the future of higher education* (U.S. Department of Education Boards and Commissions: A Draft Panel Report). Retrieved January 11, 2012, from http://www.ed.gov/about/bdscomm/list/hiedfuture/reports/0809-draft.pdf

Secretary's Commission on Achieving Necessary Skills. (1992). *Learning a living: A blueprint for high performance. SCANS Report for America 2000.* Washington, DC: U.S. Department of Labor.

Sedlacek, W. (1987). Black students on White campuses: 20 years of research. *Journal of College Student Personnel, 28,* 484–495.

Segall, M. H., Campbell, D. T., & Herskovits, M. J. (1996). *The influence of culture on visual perception.* Indianapolis, IN: Bobbs-Merrill.

Seirup, G. E. (2004). *College dating.* Retrieved January 2, 2004, from http://writing.colostate.edu/gallery/talkingback/v3.1/seirup.htm

Seligman, M. E. P. (1991). *Learned optimism.* New York, NY: Knopf.

Shah, A. (2008). Causes of poverty. *Global Issues.* Retrieved January 22, 2010, from http://www.globalissues.org/issue/2/causes-of-poverty

Shams, W., & Seitz, K. (2011). Influences of multisensory experience on subsequent unisensory processing. *Frontiers in Perception Science, 2*(264), 1–9.

Shanley, M., & Witten, C. (1990). University 101 freshman seminar course: A longitudinal study of persistence, retention, and graduation rates. *NASPA Journal, 27,* 344–352.

Shapiro, S. R. (1993). *Human rights violations in the United States: A report on U.S. compliance.* New York, NY: Human Rights Watch, American Civil Liberties Union.

Shelton, J. T., Elliott, E. M., Matthews, R. A., Hill, B. D., Gouvier, W. D. (2010). The relationships of working memory, secondary memory, and general fluid intelligence: Working memory is special. *Journal of Experimental Psychology: Learning, Memory, & Cognition, 36,* 813–820.

Sherif, M., Harvey, D. J., White, B. J., Hood, W. R., & Sherif, C. W. (1961). *The robbers' cave experiment.* Norman, OK: Institute of Group Relations.

Shimoff, E., & Catania, C. A. (2001). Effects of recording attendance on grades in Introductory Psychology. *Teaching of Psychology, 23*(3), 192–195.

Shook, N. J., Gerrity, D. A., Jurich, J., & Segrist, A. E. (2000). Courtship violence among college students: A comparison of verbally and physically abusive couples. *Journal of Family Violence, 15,* 1–22.

Sidanius, J., Levin, S., Liu, H., & Pratto, F. (2000). Social dominance orientation, anti-egalitarianism, and the political psychology of gender: An extension and cross-cultural replication. *European Journal of Social Psychology, 30,* 41–67.

Sidle, M., & McReynolds, J. (1999). The freshman year experience: Student retention and student success. *NASPA Journal, 36,* 288–300.

Singh, N. A., Clements, K. M., & Fiatarone, M. A. (1997). A randomized controlled trial of the effect of exercise on sleep. *Sleep, 20,* 95–101.

Smith, A. P., Clark, R., and Gallagher, J. (1999). Breakfast cereal and caffeinated coffee: Effects on working memory, attention, mood and cardiovascular function. *Physiology & Behavior, 67*(1), 9–17.

Smith, D. (1997). How diversity influences learning. *Liberal Education, 83*(2), 42–48.

Smith, D. D. (2005). Experiential learning, service learning, and career development. In P. A. Gore (Ed.), *Facilitating the career development of students in transition* (Monograph No. 43, pp. 205–222). Columbia, SC: National Resource Center for the First-Year Experience and Students in Transition, University of South Carolina.

Smith, J. B., Walter, T. L., & Hoey, G. (1992). Support programs and student self-efficacy: Do first-year students know when they need help? *Journal of the Freshman Year Experience, 4*(2), 41–67.

Smith, M., & Segal, J. (2012, April). Domestic violence and abuse. *HelpGuide.org.* Retrieved June 24, 2012 from http://www.helpguide.org/mental/domestic_violence_abuse_types_signs_causes_effects.htm

Smith, S. M., Glenberg, A., & Bjork, R. A. (1978). Environmental context and human memory. *Memory & Cognition, 6,* 342–353.

Smolensky, M., & Lamberg, L. (2001). *The body clock guide to better health: How to use your body's natural clock to fight illness and achieve maximum health.* New York, NY: Henry Holt.

Snyder, C. R. (1994). *Psychology of hope: You can get from here to there.* New York, NY: Free Press.

Snyder, C. R., Harris, C., Anderson, J. R., Holleran, S. A., Irving, L. M., Sigmon, S. T., et al. (1991). The will and the ways: Development and validation of an individual-differences measure of hope. *Journal of Personality and Social Psychology, 60,* 570–585.

Solomon, L. J., & Rothblum, E. D. (1984). Academic procrastination: Frequency and cognitive-behavioral correlates. *Journal of Counseling Psychology, 31*(4), 503–509.

Sousa, D. A. (2006). *How the brain learns.* Thousand Oaks, CA: Corwin Press.

Spiegel, J. (2011). *On the purpose of a liberal arts education.* Retrieved April 8, 2012, from http://wisdomandfollyblog.com/2011/09/12/seven-reasons-for-the-liberal-arts-part-2

Sprenger, M. (1999). *Learning and memory: The brain in action.* Alexandria, VA: Association for Supervision and Curriculum Development.

Stark, J. S., Lowther, R. J., Bentley, M. P., Ryan, G. G., Martens, M. L., Genthon, P. A., et al. (1990). *Planning introductory college courses: Influences on faculty.* Ann Arbor, MI: National Center for Research to Improve Postsecondary Teaching and Learning, University of Michigan. (ERIC Document Reproduction Services No. 330 277 370).

Starke, M. C., Harth, M., & Sirianni, F. (2001). Retention, bonding, and academic achievement: Success of a first-year seminar. *Journal of the First-Year Experience and Students in Transition, 13*(2), 7–35.

Staudinger, U. M. (2008). A psychology of wisdom: History and recent developments. *Research in Human Development, 5,* 107–120.

Steel, P. (2007). The nature of procrastination: A meta-analytic and theoretical review of quintessential self-regulatory failure. *Psychological Bulletin, 133*(1), 65–94.

Stein, B. S. (1978). Depth of processing reexamined: The effects of the precision of encoding and testing appropriateness. *Journal of Verbal Learning and Verbal Behavior, 17,* 165–174.

Sternberg, R. J. (2001). What is the common thread of creativity? *American Psychologist, 56*(4), 360–362.

Strommer, D. W. (1993). Not quite good enough: Drifting about in higher education. *AAHE Bulletin, 45*(10), 14–15.

Suchecki, D., Tiba, P. A., & Machado, R. B. (2012). REM sleep rebound as an adaptive response to stressful situations. *Frontiers in Neurology, 3*, 41.

Sullivan, R. E. (1993, March 18). Greatly reduced expectations. *Rolling Stone*, 2–4.

Suls, J., Martin, R., & Wheeler, L. (2002). Social comparison: Why, with whom and with what effect? *Current Directions in Psychological Science, 11*(5), 159–163.

Sundquist, J., & Winkleby, M. (2000, June). Country of birth, acculturation status and abdominal obesity in a national sample of Mexican-American women and men. *International Journal of Epidemiology, 29*, 470–477.

Susswein, R. (1995). College students and credit cards: A privilege earned? *Credit World, 83*, 21–23.

Svinicki, M. D. (2004). *Learning and motivation in the postsecondary classroom.* Bolton, MA: Anker.

Svinicki, M. D., & Dixon, N. M. (1987). The Kolb model modified for classroom activities. *College Teaching, 35*(4), 141–146.

Szalavitz, M. (2003, July/August). Tapping potential: Stand and deliver. *Psychology Today*, 50–54.

Tagliacollo, V. A., Volpato, G. L., & Pereira, A., Jr. (2010). Association of student position in classroom and school performance. *Educational Research, 1*(6), 198–201.

Taylor, S. E., Peplau, L. A., & Sears, D. O. (2006). *Social psychology* (12th ed.). Upper Saddle River, NJ: Pearson/Prentice-Hall.

Tchudi, S. N. (1986). *Teaching writing in the content areas: College level.* New York, NY: National Educational Association.

Ten Commandments of PowerPoint Presentations. (2005). Retrieved November 15, 2009, from http://power-points.blogspot.com/2005/09/10-commandments-of-powerpoint.html

Thayer, R. E. (1996). *The origin of everyday moods: Managing energy, tension, and stress.* New York, NY: Oxford University Press.

Thompson, A., & Cuseo, J. (2012). *Infusing diversity and cultural competence into teacher education.* Dubuque, IA: Kendall Hunt.

Thompson, R. F. (1981). Peer grading: some promising advantages for composition research and the classroom. *Research in the Teaching of English, 15*(2), 172–174.

Thomson, R. (1998). University of Vermont. In B. O. Barefoot, C. L. Warnock, M. P. Dickinson, S. E. Richardson, & M. R. Roberts (Eds.), *Exploring the evidence: Vol. 2. Reporting outcomes of first-year seminars* (Monograph No. 29, pp. 77–78). Columbia, SC: National Resource Center for the First-Year Experience and Students in Transition, University of South Carolina.

Thornburg, D. D. (1994). *Education in the communication age.* San Carlos, CA: Starsong.

Tinto, V. (1993). *Leaving college: Rethinking the causes and cures of student attrition* (2nd ed.). Chicago, IL: University of Chicago Press.

Titsworth, S., & Kiewra, K. A. (2004). Organizational lecture cues and student notetaking. *Contemporary Educational Psychology, 29*, 447–461.

Tobias, S. (1985). Test anxiety: Interference, defective skills, and cognitive capacity. *Educational Psychologist, 20*(3), 135–142.

Tobias, S. (1993). *Overcoming math anxiety.* New York, NY: W.W. Norton.

Topping, K. (1998). Peer assessment between students in colleges and universities. *Review of Educational Research, 68*(3), 249–276.

Torrance, E. P. (1963). *Education and the creative potential.* Minneapolis, MN: University of Minnesota Press.

Tubbs, N. (2011). Know thyself: Macrocosm and microcosm. *Studies in Philosophy and Education, 30*(1), 53–66.

Tulving, E. (1983). *Elements of episodic memory.* Oxford, England: Clarendon Press/ Oxford University Press.

Tyson, E. (2003). *Personal finance for dummies.* Indianapolis, IN: IDG Books.

Ueda, Y., Wang, M. F., Irei, A., V., Sarukura, N., Sakai, T., & Hsu, T. F. (2011). Effect of dietary lipids on longevity and memory in the SAMP8 mice. *Journal of Nutrition and Vitaminology, 57*(1). 36–41.

Ulus, I. H., Hisrch, M. J., Wurtman, R. J. (1977). Trans-synaptic induction of adrenomedullary tyrosine hydroxylase activity by choline: Evidence that choline administration can increase cholinergic transmission. *Proceedings of the National Academy of Sciences, 74*(2), 798–800.

Underwood, B. J. (1983). *Attributes of memory.* Glenview, IL: Scott, Foresman.

University of Wisconsin, La Crosse. (2001). *Strategies for using presentation software (PowerPoint).* Retrieved November 13, 2009, from http://www.uwlax.edu/biology/communication/PowerpointStrategies.html

U.S. Census Bureau. (2004). *The face of our population.* Retrieved December 12, 2006, from http://factfinder.census.gov/jsp/saff/SAFFInfojsp?_pageId=tp9_race_ethnicity

U.S. Census Bureau. (2008). *Current population survey's annual social and economic supplement.* Washington, DC: United States Census Bureau.

U.S. Census Bureau. (2010). *2010 census redistricting data (public law 94-171) summary file.* Retrieved April 7, 2012, from http://factfinder2 .census.gov/main. html

U.S. Department of Education. (1999). *The new college course map and transcripts files: Changes in course-taking and achievement, 1972–1993* (2nd ed.). Washington, DC: Author.

U.S. Department of Education. (2002). *Profile of undergraduate students in U.S. postsecondary institutions: 1999–2000.* Washington, DC: Government Printing Office.

Useem, M. (1989). *Liberal education and the corporation: The hiring and advancement of college graduates.* Piscataway, NJ: Aldine Transaction.

Van Dongen, H. P. A., Maislin, G., Mullington, J. M., & Dinges, D. F. (2003). The cumulative cost of additional wakefulness: Dose–response effects on neurobehavioral functions and sleep physiology from chronic sleep restriction and total sleep deprivation. *Sleep, 26,* 117–126.

Van Overwalle, F. I., Mervielde, I., & De Schuyer, J. (1995). Structural modeling of the relationships between attributional dimensions, emotions, and performance of college freshmen. *Cognition and Emotion, 9*(1), 59–85.

Viorst, J. (1998). *Necessary losses.* New York, NY: Fireside.

Vodanovich, S. J., Wallace, J. C., & Kass, S. J. (2005). A confirmatory approach to the factor structure of the boredom proneness scale: Evidence for a two-factor sort form. *Journal of Personality Assessment, 85*(3), 295–303, 305.

Voelker, R. (2004). Stress, sleep loss, and substance abuse create potent recipe for college depression. *Journal of the American Medical Association, 291,* 2177–2179.

Vogler, R. E., & Bartz, W. R. (1992). *Teenagers and alcohol: When saying no isn't enough.* Philadelphia, PA: The Charles Press.

Vygotsky, L. S. (1978). Internalization of higher cognitive functions. In M. Cole, V. John-Steiner, S. Scribner, & E. Souberman (Eds. & Trans.), *Mind in society: The development of higher psychological processes* (pp. 52–57). Cambridge, MA: Harvard University Press.

Waddington, P. (1996). *Dying for information: An investigation into the effects of information overload in the USA and worldwide.* London, England: Reuters.

Wade, C., & Tavris, C. (1990). Thinking critically and creatively. *Skeptical Inquirer, 14*, 372–377.

Walker, C. M. (1996). Financial management, coping, and debt in households under financial strain. *Journal of Economic Psychology, 17*, 789–807.

Walsh, K. (2005). *Suggestions from more experienced classmates.* Retrieved June 12, 2006, from http://www.uni.edu/walsh/introtips.html

Walsh, N. P., Gleeson, M., Shephard, R. J., Woods, J. A., Bishop, N. C., Fleshner, M., Simon, P. (2011). Position statement. Part one: Immune function and exercise. *Exercise Immunology Review, 17*, 6–63.

Walter, T. W., Knudsbig, G. M., & Smith, D. E. P. (2003). *Critical thinking: Building the basics* (2nd ed.). Belmont, CA: Wadsworth.

Walter, T. L., & Smith, J. (1990, April). *Self-assessment and academic support: Do students know they need help?* Paper presented at the annual Freshman Year Experience Conference, Austin, TX.

Waterhouse, J., Reilly, T., Atkinson, G., & Edwards, E. (2007). Jet lag: Trends and coping strategies. *Lancet, 369*, 1117–1129.

Watts, M. M. (2005). The place of the library versus the library as place. In M. L. Upcraft, J. N. Gardner, B. O. Barefoot, et al. (Eds.), *Challenging and supporting the first-year student* (pp. 339–355). San Francisco, CA: Jossey-Bass.

Weschsler, H., & Wuethrich, B. (2002). *Dying to drink: Confronting binge drinking on college campuses.* Emmaus, PA: Rodale.

Weinstein, C. F. (1994). Students at risk for academic failure. In K. W. Prichard & R. M. Sawyer (Eds.), *Handbook of college teaching: Theory and applications* (pp. 375–385). Westport, CT: Greenwood Press.

Weinstein, C. F., & Meyer, D. K. (1991). Cognitive learning strategies. In R. J. Menges & M. D. Svinicki (Eds.), *College teaching: From theory to practice* (New Directions for Teaching and Learning, No. 45, pp. 15–26). San Francisco, CA: Jossey-Bass.

Wesley, J. C. (1994). Effects of ability, high school achievement, and procrastinatory behavior on college performance. *Educational & Psychological Measurement, 54*, 404–408.

Wheelright, J. (2005, March). Human, study thyself. *Discover,* 39–45.

White, J. W., & Koss, M. P. (1991). Courtship violence: Incidence in a national sample of higher education students. *Violence and Victims, 6*, 247–256.

Wiederman, M. (2007). Why it's so hard to be happy. *Scientific American Mind, 18*(1), 36–43.

Wilhite, S. (1990). Self-efficacy, locus of control, self-assessment of memory ability, and student activities as predictors of college course achievement. *Journal of Educational Psychology, 82*(4), 696–700.

Wilkie, C. J., & Thompson, C. A. (1993). First-year reentry women's perceptions of their classroom experiences. *Journal of the Freshman Year Experience, 5*(2), 69–90.

Williams, J. M., Landers, D. M. and Boutcher, S. H. (1993). Arousal-performance relationships. In J. M. Williams (Ed.), *Applied psychology of sport: Personal growth to peak performance* (2nd ed., pp. 170–184). Mountain View, CA: Mayfield Publishing Co. 170-184.

Willingham, D. B. (2001). *Cognition: The thinking animal.* Upper Saddle River, NJ: Prentice Hall.

Willingham, W. W. (1985). *Success in college: The role of personal qualities and academic ability.* New York, NY: College Entrance Examination Board.

Winsor, J. L., Curtis, D. B., & Stephens, R. D. (1997, September). National preferences in business and communication education: A survey update. *JACA, 3*, 170–179.

World Health Organization. (2012). *Obesity and overweight*. Retrieved May 29, 2012, from http://www.who.int/entity/mediacentre/factsheets/fs311/en/index.html

Wright, D. J. (Ed.). (1987). *Responding to the needs of today's minority students* (New Directions for Student Services, No. 38). San Francisco, CA: Jossey-Bass.

Wyckoff, S. C. (1999). The academic advising process in higher education: History, research, and improvement. *Recruitment & Retention in Higher Education, 13*(1), 1–3.

Yerkes, R. M., & Dodson, J. D. (1908). The relationship of strength and stimulus to rapidity of habit formation. *Journal of Neurological Psychology, 184,* 59–82.

Young, K. S. (1996, August). *Pathological Internet use: The emergence of a new clinical disorder.* Paper presented at the annual meeting of the American Psychological Association, Toronto, Ontario, Canada.

Youngstedt, S. D. (2005). Effects of exercise on sleep. *Clinical Sports Medicine, 24*(2), 355–365.

Zagorsky, J. L., & Smith, P. K. (2011). The freshman 15: A critical time for obesity intervention or media myth? *Social Science Quarterly, 92,* 1389–1407.

Zeidner, M. (1995). Adaptive coping with test situations: A review of the literature. *Educational Psychologist, 30*(3), 123–133.

Zimbardo, P. G., Johnson, R. L., & Weber, A. L. (2006). *Psychology: Core concepts* (5th ed.). Boston, MA: Allyn & Bacon.

Zimmerman, B. J. (1995). Self-efficacy and educational development. In A. Bandura (Ed.), *Self-efficacy in changing societies.* New York, NY: Cambridge University Press.

Zimmerman, B. J. (2000). Self-efficacy: An essential motive to earn. *Contemporary Educational Psychology, 25,* 82–91.

Zinsser, W. (1993). *Writing to learn.* New York, NY: HarperCollins.

Zull, J. E. (2002). *The art of changing the brain: Enriching the practice of teaching by exploring the biology of learning.* Sterling, VA: Stylus.

Index

X